W9-BHO-425

SURPASSING WONDER

SURPASSING WONDER

THE INVENTION
OF THE BIBLE AND THE TALMUDS

DONALD HARMAN AKENSON

McGILL-QUEEN'S UNIVERSITY PRESS
MONTREAL & KINGSTON

Legal deposit third quarter 1998
Bibliothèque nationale du Québec

Printed in Canada on acid-free paper

Published simultaneously in the United States
by Harcourt Brace & Company

McGill-Queen's University Press acknowledges the
support of the Canada Council for the Arts for
its publishing program.

Canadian Cataloguing in Publication Data

Akenson, Donald Harman
Surpassing wonder: the invention of the Bible
and the Talmuds

Includes bibliographical references and index.
ISBN 0-7735-1781-2

1. Bible – Criticism, interpretation, etc. 2. Talmud –
Criticism, interpretation, etc. 3. Bible – Criticism,
interpretation, etc. – History. 4. Talmud – Criticism,
interpretation, etc. – History. I. Title.

BS445.A42 1998   220.6   C98-900409-0

This book was typeset by
Typo Litho Composition Inc. in 10.5/13 Times.

In memory of my parents

Contents

Figures and Tables

Acknowledgments

My debts of gratitude are as much informal as formal. Of course institutions have been helpful, and it is a pleasure to thank them, especially my friends at McGill-Queen's University Press. (And, more formally, I should acknowledge the permission of Random House to quote from Gore Vidal's *Live From Golgotha*.)

Less formally, I owe a deep debt to dozens of Swedish Baptist Sunday School teachers who put up with an excessively literal-minded child; to the patience of the Yale religion department during my undergraduate years (especially Judah Goldin and Erwin Goodenough), who allowed one to be callow without laughing out loud; to my mentor at Harvard and now long-time friend, John Kelleher. His influence has been great, not least because he has spent his life working patiently and with utmost integrity on a set of Celtic texts (pre- and early-Christian) that provide problems parallel to those we find in the three faiths the present book surveys: problems of textual evolution, context, multiple redactions, intentionally-artificial history mixed with intentionally-precise historical writing, long genealogies, law codes, all swirled together with powerful narratives. Among other things, he taught me that tough, wonderful texts are, at heart, all the same and that one approaches them with reverence.

Most important of all my informal debts are those to my parents who understood that the scriptures are a language and one either speaks it fluently or not at all: they spoke Bible every day.

For help in various ways, I am particularly grateful to: Curtis B. Akenson, Herbert W. Basser, Robert Bater, Philip Cercone, Joe Cheng, Nancy Cutway, Diane Duttle, Chris Ferrall, Roy Foster, Daniel Fraikin, the late Janice Handford, Joan Harcourt, Edward Jackman, William Leggett, Barry Levy, Susanne McAdam, Joan McGilvray, Roger Martin, Peter Mason, William S. Morrow, Jacob Neusner, Aurèle Parisien, Hannah Rapport, the late George Rawlyk, Nicholas Wheeler Robinson, Gerald Tulchinsky, David Turpin.

SURPASSING WONDER

· I ·

Introduction:
Us and the Semites

I

SOMETIME OR OTHER, EVERY UNDERGRADUATE WHO TAKES A HISTORY
course is told that modern European society (and its derivative in the Americas
and Australasia) is the joint product of Semitic and Hellenic roots. This idea is
true as far as it goes, but it is about as informative as saying that individual human beings are the conjoint product of heredity and environment: how much
of each? one immediately asks. Soon the query is lost in a squid-like cloud of
academic hedging, qualification, redefinition and virtuoso havering.

Much the same thing happens with the Semitic-Hellenic question, in the
rare moments it is engaged by modern historians. For the most part, the query
is not even raised, however, for the right answer is something that we just
seem to know, in the same way that the master of, say, a pre-war Oxbridge
college automatically knew whether one wore black tie or white tie for the
annual feast day of the college's patron saint. As Eric Christiansen has observed of one such don, "The best-selling *History of Europe*, written in the
early 1930s by H.A.L. Fisher (to alleviate the tedium of being head of an
Oxford college) began with the sentence, 'We Europeans are the children of
Hellas' – and went on through nearly two thousand years summarizing and
judging the 'trend of events' by standards of rationality and civility at that
time usually associated with the Ancient Greeks."[1]

Of course. So much nicer and classier to be descended from patrician
slaveholders and master intellectuals than from disputatious Semites, the
greatest of whose writers are not even known to us by name and the best of
whose intellectual talents were given over to social litigation rather than to
the pursuit of pure reason. Even Matthew Arnold (one of the Victorian era's
most generous students of other cultures) could not avoid being snobbish and
dismissive. In a generally subtle and generous essay, "Hebraism and Hellenism," he unselfconsciously refers to "the later, the more spiritual, the more
attractive development of Hebraism" – Christianity![2] In fact, in seeing Christianity as a branch of Semitic religion, Arnold was unusually generous for his

time. As Eric Meyers has gently noted, "Christianity throughout history has identified more with its Hellenic roots than with its Semitic ones."[3]

I do not think anything so sinister as anti-Semitism is here involved (that is a very charged word, indeed, and should be reserved for very precise, very rebarbarative phenomena). Instead, what I see among my fellow modern historians (by whom I mean anybody who makes his or her living studying the world since, roughly, the Norman conquest – which includes all historians of the Americas and of the former European colonial empires) is a certain vague and unconscious snobbishness based on the unexamined belief that we are society's vestigial gentry. A tiny vanity, a tiny snobbery.

Snobbery, however, turns the corner and becomes something more, something nastier. I recall listening to a visiting English colonel, the guest of the officer's mess at the Royal Military College in Kingston, expatiating to the bored local military about the comparative virtues of various fighting units with which he had served: Gurkhas, Sikhs, and on and on. "But," he asserted, taking a large drink of whiskey, "the Irish troops are the best." He paused. "Especially when headed by white officers."

Since I have spent most of my life as an historian, trying to sort out the viciously entwined tendrils of the several Irish forms of Christianity (with side trips in Afrikaner and Israeli sacralized culture), Irish references will appear in this book now and again. Here the case in point is a brief, relevant moment observed in the Irish countryside by the sometime English Poet Laureate, C. Day Lewis, and told in his mystery-writer persona of "Nicholas Blake." He observed an Irish politician campaigning down the country in the early 1960s. The politician gave a great stump speech: "Irish culture owes nothing to Byzantium. Irish culture owes nothing to Greece or to Rome. Irish culture owes nothing to Great Britain" (storms of applause). "Irish culture is a pure lily blooming in a bog." (Voice from audience "And that's the bugger of it, misther.")[4] We, as heirs of the Ancient Near East, are not lilies blooming alone, self-incarnated, with no historical roots.

At minimum, we have direct and continuing historical roots that run back to the Iron Age in Palestine. That can be taken as roughly the twelfth to the sixth centuries BCE, the period in which the most important material in the Hebrew scriptures settled into a more or less agreed form. In that era, dynastic Egypt was in decline, Phoenicia was becoming the first international trading power, and not-yet-classical Greece was pulling together the disparate threads that would make a major civilization. Yet, with none of those three extraordinary cultures do we have continuity, although we have enough knowledge of them to view them with appreciation. But our sense of empathy with them is synthetic, in the sense that most of the corpus of classical learning we so admire was long lost to the west and only discovered after a long break; and both Egyptian and Phoenician cultures are known to us not through a continuous line from the past to the present, but as a result of modern archaeology and epigraphy.

With the late Iron Age culture of Israel, the West has never lost touch. Indeed, we cannot even read about the ancient Hebrews in English without at once being in their debt for the very act we are performing. Many scholars believe that, by a circuitous route, our own alphabet is a descendant of ancient Hebrew. *Alef*, *bet*, in a real sense, is how everything that is us begins.

2

Anyone who studies and discusses the Bible and its character, would do well to wear as a motto on a scapular (or, more appositely, as a parchment inside a secular tefillin), the following words taken from the preface to the 1662 revision of the Book of Common Prayer:

> And having thus endeavoured to discharge our duties in this weighty affair, as in the sight of God, and to approve our sincerity therein (so far as lay in us) to the consciences of all men; although we know it impossible (in such variety of apprehensions, humours and interests, as are in the world) to please all; nor can expect that men of factious, peevish, and perverse spirits should be satisfied with any thing that can be done in this kind by any other than themselves ...

Optimists, no. But because these liturgical scholars were as good at their business as any ever had been, they inevitably were realists.

Their realism is a valuable example. Although in present-day biblical studies one has the pleasure of encountering some of the most dextrous minds of our time – and the additional pleasure of employing scholarly apparatuses, such as parallel Bibles and versions of the Talmud that are aesthetic wonders as well as scholarly monuments – one is in need of protection. Part of this necessity stems from the sheer, often oppressive weight of commentary on the Bible and its associated documents that have piled up over the centuries. The number of books, articles, treatises, and homilies that have been written has to be well over a million in number, and one becomes aware that one cannot master even a minuscule proportion of them. One is always uneasily aware that whatever idea one has, probably someone has had it before, and perhaps better.

When one immerses oneself in recent scholarship concerning the Bible (meaning work done since the end of World War II), the effect is curiously anesthetic, even depressing. Hardly anyone seems to be having any fun, and if they are, they do a good job of keeping their pleasure well hidden behind stone faces and dirge-like prose. Instead, it seems to me that biblical scholarship should be one great ode to joy. Too rarely does one encounter "abiding astonishment," a concept put forward by Martin Buber and adopted by Walter

Brueggemann as the title of his exemplary study of the Psalms.[5] The field presents to scholars some of the most fascinating puzzles that the human mind can encounter. The questions are, in sum, the issue of who we are and why. Any first-class research scientist will tell you that the real trick is to find a problem worth solving. And here, in the Bible and its associated documents, are questions that make the nature of wee things like the Big Bang relatively inconsequential. This is the big one.

Yet, in biblical scholarship and its associated disciplines one finds (with a few wonderful exceptions) little sense of excitement. On the one hand, one encounters the work of fundamentalist Protestants, orthodox Jews, and old-fashioned Catholics, each of whose work is characterized for the most part by compulsive-obsessive behaviour. Of course this is a generalization, but I have read tons of the stuff. It consists mostly of asking the same old questions, in slightly new ways, so that the answers turn out to be the good old conclusions. This scholarship, if such it is, has the virtue of keeping its engagés from thinking about big issues. Much of it reminds me of the weekend morning television cartoons for children, where one or another cartoon animal runs off the edge of a cliff and manages to keep running on thin air, always provided he does not give in to temptation and look down. There is, in the literature I am describing, a real terror: a fear of looking down, of having received views checked against external reality.

On the other hand, Christian "liberal" scholarship – for the most part done by Protestants, but increasingly by Catholics as well – often has a lost, bewildered and gloomy quality to it. Later (in Appendix D) I shall discuss the famous "Jesus Seminar" which typifies much of liberal Protestant and Catholic thought. Taken collectively, reading the publications of the Jesus Seminar is like stepping into a church basement where the pastor is conducting a support group for guys whose partners have dumped them.

In recent years, the group of biblical scholars who seem to have enjoyed themselves the most, the one that has had a genuine sense of the joy of discovery, has been comprised mostly of Jewish scholars, Reformed or non-observant for the most part, with a few Orthodox outriders. They are in the midst of mining the great lode of material from the Qumran caves. (The way certain scholars, mostly Christian, inhibited this work until the early 1990s is a well-known international scandal.) The so-called Dead Sea Scrolls have considerable interest for the understanding of early Christianity, but the real excitement has been on the Jewish side of the material. This is because the most enterprising of the recent Jewish scholars have essentially turned the methods used by Christian scholars upside down. Instead of using the Qumran material to illuminate early Christianity (it does that, but not nearly as much as had been hoped in the early years after the Scrolls' discovery), both the Qumran material and the documents of early Christianity are used to bring about an understanding of the highly volatile and transitional forms of Judaism that existed near the end of the age of the Second Temple.

The scholar who best indicates the joy that should invariably emanate from any serious encounter with the scriptures and the great historical puzzles they enhull, is not, however, one of the guild of full-time biblical scholars. It is the literary critic Harold Bloom. Though fully competent in biblical Hebrew and given to studying the scriptures with a hawklike eye, he is too frighteningly bright and too much of an incorrigible beard-puller to be welcomed by the more solemn of the guild. His *The Book of J* (1990) is a dazzling analysis of the nature of the "J" source, the most important segment of the Books of Moses. Having mastered the scholarly literature, Bloom made the mischievous, but not entirely frivolous, suggestion that the author of this, the heart of the ancient Israelite religion, was written by a woman. The biblical establishment dared not stone him to death, for as America's most powerful literary critic, he was too big a monument to be dented by flints. Instead, they just looked the other way, as if nothing had happened. That is too bad, because Bloom's book virtually bubbles with joy – joy stemming from the enveloping quality of the intellectual puzzle that he was engaging, and joy at the very quality of the texts that he was encountering.[6]

Both sorts of joy are crucial. Being cool when dealing with the scriptures does not work. Anyone who is not awe-struck by the nature of the texts, by the quality of the world-making they exhibit, is too much of a philistine to be allowed into this amazing cultural gallery.

Rarely expressed though it may be, the common goal of most modern biblical scholars is to figure out how the Bible works. To do so, one cannot approach it like some thick-fingered mechanic who is trying to figure out how a watch works. Granted, it is easy enough to take the thing apart, but then it no longer tells time. The trick is to figure out how the great device works without destroying it. If ever the whole is more than the mere sum of its parts, this is it. The necessity of combining analysis with respect was well expressed by the great scholar Frank C. Porter who, in his 1908 presidential address to the Society of Biblical Literature, envisioned a stage of enlightenment wherein "the rights and achievements of historical criticism are freely accepted," (and, in our own time, one would add philological, archaeological, and literary criticism), but, simultaneously, "the power that lives in the book is once more felt."[7]

To a remarkable degree, the scriptures tell us how to read the scriptures, although these self-contained instructions are now out of fashion among biblical scholars. For one thing, the Hebrew scriptures suggest that we approach even the most serious matters with a lightness of heart. The Hebrew Bible is a book of puns, of irony, and the occasional joke, and these, while not the heart of the text, are like a set of stage directions: read the solemn part solemnly, but know also that almost every word can have a second or third meaning and that word-play is the analgesic we have been given to keep the heavy parts of the scriptures from becoming more of a load than we can bear.

Secondly, and even more importantly, one must read the scriptures *as if* they were history. That is how the book tells us to read the book. Taken collectively, the Hebrew and Christian scriptures, the Apocrypha, the Pseudepigrapha, are a vast set of historical investigations, wonderful in their quality, surprising in their character. They cry out to be read as many things – as poetry, romance, law – but, first, they are history, because they attempt to situate sequences of events along the skein of time. Even the Mishnah and the Talmuds can be construed as commentaries upon historical texts and traditions. I will enlarge upon that point in a moment, and will return to it in later chapters. Here the issue is that we have to encounter these documents on their own grounds, the historical, before dealing with other perspectives. The sort of historical reading one hopes for will be technically sophisticated, but always within the context of Martin Buber's warning: "We shall not regain a historical nucleus of the saga by eliminating the function of enthusiasm from it. This function is an inseparable element of the fragment of history entrusted to our study."[8]

(This is not to gainsay the fact that outside seminaries and departments of religion, in the secular world, as it were, some of the greatest advances in understanding how the Bible works have been made by scholars of literature. The pioneering work of Robert Alter and of Frank Kermode immediately comes to mind. When transposed back into the biblical academy, a genre of biblical scholarship has arisen that has become virtually a discipline of its own.[9] This is all to the good, provided that the claim for the validity of the purely literary approach to the Bible and its associated texts is not consciously or unconsciously a ploy for excusing one's self the labour of learning and understanding the historical background. When dealing with an historical document, that is more than a little dangerous.)

And, thirdly, the scriptures implicitly tell us to be critical of the scriptures, and the Talmuds tell us to argue, to think critically about the issues they raise. Time and again the later books of the Bible and the associated texts cite earlier items. On the surface this is always respectfully done. But, there is often an undercurrent of subversion. One frequently finds that when the more recent quotations of earlier texts are checked against the originals, the meaning has been changed, sometimes just a touch, sometimes completely subverted. Later writers and commentators are straightening out the scriptures, correcting them for their own purposes. What this implies is that the scriptures grant the reader the licence to recognize that they are open to criticism. Indeed, there are some very dumb things in the Bible and quite a few that you would not want your children to read.

When, in this book, I treat the Bible and its ancillary volumes as a series of truly great inventions, this is largely belief-neutral. However, if you believe, as do some, that the Bible is inerrant in its every word, then this study will be of no interest to you. Anyone else, however, should be able to read onward without danger to conscience. Whether the Almighty was the author of these great inventions, or whether they are merely the greatest of human creations, or both, is a matter of your own faith. To appreciate the architectural integrity and the extraordinary creativity of these great inventions, one does not have to be a believer of any sort. One can, after all, appreciate Bach without believing in the Mass. Conversely, merely because one is a practising Jew or Christian does not mean that one necessarily appreciates the full beauty of the objects of faith: sadly, in the religious world there are fewer gourmets than gourmands.

3

My suggesting that the Hebrew scriptures and their derivatives (including the Christian scriptures) should be read in the first instance as history, is apt to bring a shudder to most members of the guild who earn their daily bread in the modern scholarly study of the Bible. One could fill a room with books and articles by twentieth-century scholars, each of whom utters the conventional wisdom that the scriptures "are not primarily works of history in the modern sense of the word."

This is a bit unsettling, because the scriptures, both Hebrew and Christian, announce themselves as being works of history. The heart of the scriptures is a covenant that God makes with the human race. This covenant is reported as an historical matter and the relationship of God to his people is charted down throughout the ages. There is very little theology in the scriptures and certainly no systematic exposition of theological doctrines (which is why there has always been a demand for theologies). Even the strange, meteoric apocalyptic books of Daniel and of Revelation are essentially historical, for they encompass references to things past and then provide predictive narratives of things to come. They are histories of the future.

If the scriptures and ancillary documents are not "history in the modern sense of the word," then, apparently, readers and writers of modern history are precluded from using their skills to deal with them. Thus, as the result of a syllogism which is more the product of industrial sociology than of logic, the subject has become the property of persons with stronger interests in theology (or, if one prefers, ideology) than in history. "Biblical scholarship is viewed by most of its practitioners, and by nearly all non-practitioners, as a theological discipline," is the observation of one of the most independent of senior biblical scholars, Philip R. Davies. "The common habitat of the subject is the seminary or the theological department of a college or university."[10] Therefore, biblical scholarship takes place in institutions that have strong ideological or theological commitments. One notes with a certain morbid fascination the conclusion in 1970 of the influential Brevard Childs, that any reconstruction of what really happened in Israelite history was theologically uninteresting.[11] Rather more encouraging in its openmindedness is the viewpoint of one of the leading anthropologists of our time, Marshall Sahlins: "Culture is precisely the organization of the current situation in terms of a past.... The categories by which objectivity is defined are themselves cosmological,"[12] and thus both what "really happened" and what any group makes of that "objective" past is part of a single process of historical analysis.

"Biblical scholarship ... functions as a pontifical discipline," is the shrewd observation of one of the leading historians of religion in North America.[13] This warns off outsiders, the Harold Blooms of the world. The historical narrative that is the Bible becomes hidden in neologisms – terms such as *Heilsgeschichte*, salvation-history, and scores of others – all of which carry the coded message that even if the scriptures are viewed as taking an historical form (being history-like), this is an arcane and hermetic sort of history that is incomprehensible to you, outsiders.

That I do not buy. While having respect for the technical virtuosity of many biblical and Talmudic scholars (respect that passes over into awe in the case of scholars such as Geza Vermes, David Flusser, and Jacob Neusner), I think that those scholars who posit a chasm between the biblical sense of history and that of our own times are dead wrong. They are correct in noting that the Bible does not read like a dissertation for a Ph.D. in history, but for that we can only be thankful. The Bible does, however, deal with cause and effect, chronological sequences and, sometimes, origins, all within the guise of being an historical narrative. Clearly, the form of the scriptures and the underlying epistemology is not that which we would find in a monograph written by a present-day historian of the modern world. But the scriptures evince an historical sense similar to that of the everyday person, as it is revealed, for example, in the daily newspaper of any major city in the English-speaking world. Take the average newspaper. It is a jumble of simultaneous stories, some of which are verifiable, others of which are not; a mélange of magical and superstitious statements that imply faith in the causal power of invisible forces (the astrology column is a staple of most newspapers, and the weekend editions usually have a homily from representatives of the major churches); there are found, often on the very same page, reports of serious scientific advances, ideas for "folk" medicine, and, at least on the sports pages, predictions of the future, expressed in terms of what teams will beat the point spread; royalty and presidents are chronicled, but so too are births and deaths of historical nobodies; "cards of thanks" to doctors, saints, and rabbis are found in the classified advertisement columns. The newspaper inevitably has an underlying ideology (which varies according to country, region, and who the owner is). Such present-day newspapers are history and consciously claim to be, but no more than the scriptures can they be said to be "history in the modern sense of the word."

You see, the concept of "history in the modern sense of the word" is bogus. It is a concept that is being employed as a glass wall, one that permits all of us to recognize the existence of a body of material that anyone with historical consciousness might well investigate, but which we are precluded from getting close to by virtue of our being "modern." It is true that the scriptures and their ancillary documents are very different in style and epistemology from modern historical monographs. But the scriptures are no more different from those same monographs than those monographs are different from the everyday newspaper. Fundamentally, there is no difference between sorting out the meanings of the item known as the Book of Revelation, and one of the publications put out by Rupert Murdoch, save that the former leaves one with an entirely cheerier notion of the future.

Within the community of biblical scholars there is a misplaced notion that historians search for objectivity. The word "scientific" still appears in historical discussions in biblical journals; it is a term that has not been used without embarrassment in secular departments of history since, roughly, the end of World War II. No one, save perhaps the odd eccentric, believes that there is such a thing as objective historical truth. Paradoxically, when done well, professional historical work is the most modest of modern disciplines. It is accessible (not easy, necessarily, but accessible) to anyone with the equivalent of a university education and the willingness to do a little homework. Only the work of the incompetent is smug, self-referential, and impenetrable. What professional historians do is three things. First we try to get a rough idea of what "really" happened, all the while recognizing that all historical writing is merely a series of heuristic fictions and that both complete adequacy of description and complete accuracy of "fact" is beyond the bounds of the possible. Second, and more important, we spend our time studying what people *think* happened. That is the heart of our job, and in essence we are engaged in documenting the development of humanity's consciousness of itself and its world. And, third, there are occasions when we can observe how certain élites, religious or secular, told people what they were supposed to think happened. Sometimes it is possible to work with all three strands at once and that is very rewarding indeed.

Modern historians have done an impressive job of studying the evolution and meaning of religion in North American society (the works of Perry Miller, Martin E. Marty, Mark Noll and George Rawlyk come to mind), and one hopes that modern scholars will be permitted to deal with earlier time periods. If the welter of sects and churches in North America, buzzing around like a cloud of gnats around a lantern, can be successfully dealt with, perhaps the same methods, when applied to the earlier period, would be productive: all the time recognizing that each era and each sect has its own integrity, its own singular context, and its own unique cosmology.

Therefore, in the present book, I am writing as much as possible with the vocabulary and outlook of a modern historian. I will try to keep the discussion as free of "biblical" jargon as possible. Most of the technical terms have serviceable English equivalents. Commonly used words such as the "Hebrew language" are perfectly sensible, even if some philologists prefer to refer to the tongue as "Old Canaanite." Certain words will be avoided. One of these is "cult." Although this term is almost universally applied by specialists to the festivals and rituals associated with the worship of the ancient Israelite deity, the term today has such opprobrious overtones as to be unusable. "Historiography" is here used only in the sense employed by modern historians. That is, whereas in the specialist literature historiography refers to all writings that recount the past, here "historical writings" will do. This has the virtue of allowing us to save "historiography" for reference to the history of history – that is, to the way various historians have looked at a particular matter.

The reader will notice that I use the terms "Old Testament" and "New Testament" only in quotation marks. Those terms, used without such qualification, are a Christian arrogance. They imply that the Christian dispensation was superior to and, indeed, replaced the "Old" one that stems from the ancient Israelites. Such usage contains at minimum an implication that the Hebrew scriptures are in some ways old, tired, worn out. Yet, there is nothing old about the "Old Testament." If ever there was a book that is alive and disturbing, this is it.

Dating of events is done according to the increasingly common practice of replacing BC (Before Christ) and AD (Anno Domini, the year of the Lord – that is, after the birth of Jesus Christ) with BCE and CE. This is a small courtesy and too much should not be made of it. Understandably, some Jewish scholars, while accepting the Christian calendar as a social convention so widespread in the modern western world as to be virtually universal, bridled at using terms that proclaimed Jesus to be "Lord" and to be the Christ. Hence, they came to use the terms "Common Era" and "Before the Common Era," implying at least an equality of status as between Judaism and Christianity. In so doing they were being remarkably generous in that they still were accepting a calendar whose fulcrum was the birth of a man whom most Christians took to be the conclusion to the history of the Chosen People. (And just to add injury to insult, the Christian calendar did not come very close to getting the date of Jesus' birth right. This occurred by dint of the early church fathers counting the period from I BC to I AD, in their system, as a single year, and by their miscalculating the reign of Herod the Great. Most scholars now place Jesus' birth sometime between the year I BCE and the year 5 BCE.)

Slightly more fraught is the question of what one calls God. "The Lord" and "Almighty" are acceptable to almost everyone. However, the Hebrew scriptures are mostly about a god who takes the name YHWH. Nobody knows for certain how this name was pronounced by the ancient Israelites, since vowels were not added to the Hebrew scriptures until well into the Common Era. Even then, the scribes refused to permit the vocalization of the holy name and whenever YHWH appeared in the text, placed the vowel letters for the word "Adonai" (meaning "Lord") underneath the consonants for yhwh. Thus, every time the word of this deity was uttered aloud, it was pronounced "Adonai." (From this arises the erroneous English language transliteration "Jehovah.") Almost universally in scholarly circles the convention is to pronounce the divine name as Yahweh and that is here followed. (And, as a consequence, later, when the "Yahwist" source in the Pentateuch is referred to, it will be in its anglicized form "Y," not the European form "J.")

Undeniably, what version, or versions, of the scriptures one employs is of some moment, but rather less so now than it was even half a century ago, when there were denominational wars about which version was theologically most pure. (This was largely a Protestant-Catholic piece of infighting.) Still, it is fairly confusing to consult standard bibliographic sources, such as the catalogue of the British Library and that of the Library of Congress and find that there are more than sixty translations in English of the Bible or of individual books of the Bible. In an era when the scholarship on the words found in biblical texts (as distinct from the theological interpretation of those words) is increasingly ecumenical, the sensible thing to do is to compare the most important versions of any passage one is reading with the other major versions and to examine the scholarly notes that are attached. This is not difficult, because of the "parallel Bibles" that conveniently place the major versions side by side. That said, when writing about the Bible, one should adopt a single text and correct it where necessary – chiefly to prevent readers from experiencing the jarring effects of having to jump from the rhythms and style of one translation to another.

Perforce, the basic text that I shall use will be one of the Christian versions, since the Hebrew scriptures do not include anything of the Jesus tradition, a fundamental matter. The Roman Catholic scriptures are trustworthy (and these days almost identical to the Protestant translations), but they include a batch of material – the so-called Apocrypha, and "Deuterocanonical Books" – that present-day Protestants and Jews occasionally read as historically interesting, but do not consider to be authoritative. This material, mostly from the two centuries before and after the birth of Jesus, is indeed historically valuable, but has to be read with a somewhat different cast of eye than the primary canonical scriptures. Fortunately, there is not much disagreement in basic matters between the Jewish and the Christian versions of the "Old Testament." Not that the two are identical: some books have different names; the versification within books, a medieval introduction into the Hebrew scriptures borrowed from Christianity, is sometimes different. None of that is insuperable.

However, there is a very important point of difference that must be respected. The Tanakh (the Hebrew scriptures) arranges the books of the Bible in a significantly different order than do the Protestant and Catholic Bibles. The Tanakh shares the five Books of Moses (the Torah)[14] as the cornerstone of the scriptures, but thereafter the arrangement into the Prophets (Nevi'im) and the Writings (Kethuvim) is markedly different from the Christian Bible. Thus, the inclination to read the collection of books that is the Hebrew scriptures as a single book – almost as if it were a novel penned by many hands – has to be resisted. One cannot do what Northrop Frye did in *The Great Code* and read the Hebrew scriptures as progressively unveiling a tightly scripted story.[15] (That Frye used the Christian order of books is hardly surprising. The story would have progressed in an entirely different way had Frye permitted the "Old Testament" to end not with Malachi, but with I and II Chronicles as occurs in the Tanakh.) Still less can one legitimately append to the Christian versions of the "Old Testament" the Christian scriptures and then read the whole thing as a unified saga. Frank Kermode's view that the Bible offers the most familiar modelling of meaningful history – that from "in the beginning" to the concluding Christian apocalypse it provides "the ideal of a wholly concordant structure"[16] – can be sustained only by a wilful refusal to acknowledge the structural tradition of the Jewish scriptures.

Among the available translations, there are some fine versions (for example, the New English Bible of the 1960s and 1970s) and some painful ones: especially the Revised Standard (RSV) Version which appeared in the 1880s and 1890s. Although it usefully corrected a large number of errors in previous English-language editions, the work was done by and for the tone deaf. One treasures the report of the American evangelical clergyman who tried to burn in his pulpit an RSV because of supposed errors in translation. He found it impossible to ignite. "Just like the devil," he observed. "Fire doesn't bother it."[17]

If one is to use an English-language Bible, we would do best to go back to that of the person who taught us English, William Tyndale. Before his martyrdom by strangulation and burning in 1536, he had managed to translate the "New Testament" directly from Greek, while on the run from the authorities. (This book, printed in 1526, has been described as "the most important printed book in the English language." The sole surviving copy was purchased in the spring of 1994 by the British Museum for more than one million pounds sterling.[18]) Thereafter, still on the run, Tyndale taught himself Hebrew and directly translated into English the Books of Moses. This was published in 1530. He kept translating from the Hebrew right up to his unfortunate end. Tyndale's translation of the Books of Moses and of the Christian scriptures were largely assimilated into the Geneva Bible of 1560, the first complete English-language Bible that was widely available in England. It was from this version that John Bunyan and William Shakespeare learned the Bible stories and acquired a sense of the possibility of the English language.

Even more importantly, in the "King James Bible" (also called the "Authorized Version") of 1611, roughly 90 percent of Tyndale's edition of the "New Testament" stands unaltered.[19] It is from this book that the English-speaking world learned to read and to think. As the novelist and critic Robert Stone has noted, "The greatest vehicle of mass literacy in the English-speaking world has been the King James Bible. It has been the great primer."[20] And that same book taught all those who would hear, how to listen to words as music.

Probably we will never recover the mixture of mission and ultimate optimism that Tyndale and his immediate successors felt concerning the scriptures. Indeed, one must lift an eyebrow when encountering the wish of Tyndale's contemporary, Desiderius Erasmus: "I wish that even the weakest woman should read the gospel – should read the Epistles of Paul."

Even more optimistically, and with the Hebrew scriptural practice of rhetorical parallelism getting the best of him, Erasmus continued. "And I wish these were translated into all languages, so that they might be read and understood, not only by Scots and Irishmen, but also by Turks and Saracens."[21]

Granted, there are things wrong with the King James Bible (hereafter KJB), mostly mistranslations that are easy enough to correct by reference to recent translations. But there are in fact points where the KJB's translations are more accurate. The notorious "thou," "thee," and "thy" are actually more accurate than recent translations in dealing with the second person singular and plural which is obscured in present-day English.[22] This is an important distinction to honour in a text wherein God is frequently directly telling someone, or several persons, to do something, or to avoid doing something else.

The real problem is that the King James Bible sometimes is too good. It transforms some parts of the Bible that are fairly pedestrian into great literature. Krister Stendahl recalls Arthur Darby Nock's suggestion that the Gospel of John did not become a beautiful piece of literature until 1611. At that time, the KJB (following Tyndale) gave it a grace far beyond what was found in the Greek.[23] The same holds for some of the minor prophets, whose scolding is transformed from high-pitched whines to Delphic arias. These are vices that we can live with.[24]

The scriptures teach us, everywhere and in all places, that gratitude for good fortune is the only appropriate posture to adopt. Ingratitude is punishable, and surely. That, I think, is what W.H. Auden had in mind, when he remarked to a friend, concerning the church's replacement of the King James version of the Bible, "Why spit on your luck?"

Inventing the Covenant

· 2 ·

Apparent Woe and Great Invention

I

SOMETIME IN THE MIDDLE OF THE SIXTH CENTURY BCE – THE YEAR 550 will do as a rough marker – the greatest religious genius whose name the world has never known, surveyed a desert. He was the son of the "diaspora," the offspring of one of the minority of Judaeans who had been forcibly removed from central Palestine by the Babylonians forty to fifty years earlier. He was of a priestly family. His father, now dead, had sired him when he was himself full of years. Trained from his earliest days to be a religious savant, the young man had become the hope not only of his own family, but of an entire phalanx of ageing priests, and, now, their children, who banded together in the city of Babylon on the river Euphrates. The older men, those who had known his father, schooled him as deeply as they could, but they recognized that even as a youth, he had an inner vision, a way of listening, and then of recasting what he heard which set him apart from the merely clever, the students who could memorize and could argue, but who rarely could understand. As he entered his twenties, increasingly the older men brought him with them, when they walked together along the banks of the Euphrates. There, alone with the grief that only those who had known the service of Yahweh in the temple of King Solomon could fully grasp, they wept, as they remembered Zion.[1]

The preceding description is an historical model, presented through the device of personification. It will become clear as the argument unfolds why this model – this bundle of hypotheses – is an appropriate one in the present state of our knowledge of biblical texts and, indeed, that it has the virtue of being parsimonious, an unusual characteristic in this particular area.

To return. The desert our young man, now thirty, surveyed was not physical. Although later chroniclers were to dramatize the physical and social dimensions of the "Babylonian captivity," it was not by standards of the Ancient Near East (or, even, the standards of the twentieth century), a particularly nasty conquest. Only a minority, at most 10 to 20 percent of the population, actually was sent into exile. The "poorest sort of the people of the

land" were left behind (II Kings 24:14) to be farmers and to tend the vineyards. Their life in a war-levelled land must have been bleak, the more so because the skilled artisans such as carpenters and blacksmiths, who could have
rebuilt the city, were taken away (Jer. 24:1). But it was moderated by the
Babylonian official who was in charge of the former kingdom of Judah giving
to the poor land and vineyards, probably an indication that some of the lands
of the exiled elite were redistributed to the poor (Jer. 39:10). No new national
or ethnic group was introduced into Judea. It was not colonized in any formal
sense, but rather was a tiny, poor satrapy.[2]

The key to understanding the Babylonian captivity is to see it from the vantage point of Babylonian *realpolitik*. The standard Babylonian practice was to
strip conquered territories of their political and religious elites. This removed
most of the potential troublemakers, the local leaders, but there was more: the
very top men in the conquered societies were brought to the capital and were
treated well, while they were indoctrinated in Babylonian learning, which in
some areas, such as astronomy, was prodigious. Thus, King Jehoiachin, who
had been on the throne of Judah in 597, was taken with his family to Babylon
and treated well. He was still alive in 562 when Nebuchadnezzar died, and
members of his family took a leading role not only in the exile community in
Babylon, but also in Judah after the exile ended.[3] Admittedly, King Jehoiachin's successor, and the last of King David's line, the puppet King Zedekiah, 597–586/7, was treated horribly. His sons were killed before his eyes
and then he was blinded and incarcerated until he died (Jer. 52:10–11). This,
however, was not routine policy. Zedekiah was punished because he had
taken an oath of loyalty to the Babylonian king and had broken it by treating
with the Egyptians. (Ezekiel 17:11–24 interprets this as Yahweh's punishment for breaking of a solemn oath.) That was unusual, however. For the
most part, the Babylonians treated the deported elites well, and probably used
many of them, those who were not artisans, as what would today be called
middle-level civil servants.

Below the level of royalty, the displaced Judaeans were not treated badly.
They were given religious toleration and were not dispersed. In addition to
those who lived in Babylon proper (located in what is today the suburbs of
Baghdad), another concentration of diaspora Judaeans lived in "Tel Aviv," an
ancient Babylonian location of some debate, and not to be confused with the
modern city of that name.[4] There they may have been engaged in reclaiming
land, a form of manual labour which must have been painful to a soft-handed
elite. The key, however, is that even there the Babylonians permitted sufficient concentrations of Judaeans to coalesce, to preserve their language, and
their literary and religious traditions.

The Babylonian exiles were very conscious that they were an elite, the
keepers of the nation's heritage. Yet, there was the constant danger that the

"remnant" in the old homeland would eventually get above itself and take over the national patrimony, or that any other section of Judaeans, now living abroad, would seize leadership of the diaspora. The "Egyptians" were a constant worry. The Babylonian exiles' concern about their own position is clearly seen in Jeremiah (24:1–10) where an unambiguous metaphor compares the exiles with the remnant left in the land of Judah. In this vision of Jeremiah, two baskets of figs are placed before Yahweh, this occurring after the exile. One basket has very good figs, ripe; the other has figs so bad as to be inedible. The good figs were the captives of Judah who were now in exile; the evil figs were the "residue of Jerusalem, that remain in this land, and them that dwell in the land of Egypt." Ultimately, Yahweh judged one set to be evil. The other was good. These were the Babylonian exiles, and they would re-inherit Jerusalem, Yahweh promised (Jer. 24:8–10).[5]

So the desert that the young man of the Babylonian exile saw was not one of physical oppression, but of spiritual apprehension. He and his fellow legatees of Judah's religious aristocracy were sick to their very marrow with fear, longing, and loss. Their fears were that neither they nor their children, nor their children's children, would again see Jerusalem. Or, worse, that when they did finally see the holy mountain it would be too late: others, the stay-behind remnant of callus-handed, thick-necked peasantry would have grabbed control of the holy sites and of the ritual offices. Or perhaps it would be the untrustworthy "Egyptians," Judaeans who lived in Upper Egypt and were now beginning to lose Hebrew as their first language, and who might arrive first in Jerusalem, and seize control of religious life. These apprehensions, while having within them certain carnal aspects (no one likes to lose power, prestige, or money), were fundamentally spiritual, as were the longings of the religious leaders of the exile. A longing for God is not like any other.

But why could not the exiled Babylonian priests get in touch with Yahweh? Was he not everywhere? Yes, but he denied them access, save through the fleeting visions of the prophets.

They could not deal with him, because, under the covenant, he could be directly approached only one way: through an idol.

And now that idol was broken, so fragmented that it floated as dust across the desert.

This fact is what the young religious genius understood, and to understand that man's genius, we must break through the subsequent belief (one that has been normative for at least the last 1,500 years) that the Chosen People had no idols. They did, but they did not denominate them as such. While denouncing the iconic idols of their neighbours, the Chosen People produced an aniconic idol whose dimensions exceeded those of almost any religious artifact in ancient history: the Temple of Solomon. Just as Yahweh could be limned only in the covenant, so the covenant could be touched only in the Temple. There, in the Holy of Holies, in the tabernacle in which the earliest Israelites had travelled with their god in the Ark of the Covenant, Yahweh was physically present (see Exodus 29:42, 33:9). There one killed all manner of beasts, their blood being a direct offering to him. By an easy act of association, one did not merely worship in the Temple. One worshipped the Temple. This form of aniconic idol is not as unusual as one might think.[6] What is unusual is the direct denial of its function. But, as we shall see, such denial of reality was one of the ways in which the ancient Hebrews and their heirs transcendent, by-passed reality.[7]

Surveying this spiritual wasteland, the young scholar – he would in later times have been called a saint, a great rabbi, a sage – made one of those leaps of faith and of human will that bend forever time's arrow in a certain direction. His decision: that he – and if they would help him, the surviving elders from pre-exile days, and their sons, his contemporaries – would gather up the most important things that could be known of the history and worship of his people and place it in one set of scrolls. Some things, such as the writings (or transcriptions) of the early prophets (the "Major Prophets"), already were in circulation in partial form. But other items, and these the most central to the nation's history, were in fragments. Several versions of some events were about while other, crucial matters were still only told in story form, passed from one bearded ancient to another.

To essay such a task was heroic, to complete it divine. The hardest thing for a present-day observer to comprehend is the level of faith required. We have the knowledge that the Temple eventually was rebuilt, the idol repaired, the sacrifices reinstituted, the covenant again physically honoured, and thereby reaffirmed. However, the young man had no such foreknowledge. He was proceeding, with the same kind of faith that is ascribed to Moses, to lead the people spiritually, yet, unlike Moses, to some destination that he knew not. In collecting the central traditions of the Chosen People, in editing them so that they fit together rather better than they otherwise would, in writing down ancient oral tales and fitting them into his text, and in adding touches of his own, the young man was inventing a great religion. This is not the same as creating one; inventions are made by the imaginative recombination of pieces that are lying around a culture's workshop, with the addition of the occasional newly-machined part. This was invention, not creation.

The only way the young man could tie everything together was by writing history. He had no choice, because that was the way his culture and his religion worked. The fragments and stories he had to work with all were historical in nature. It may sound tautological to suggest that he wrote historically, because that was the way his culture had taught him to think, but that is the case nonetheless.[8]

The history he wrote, this great invention, was intended, I think, to correct the recent past. That is, if one believes that Yahweh, the god of the covenant, works in human historical events (as clearly our young man did), then the only way to figure out where and why recent events had gone so terribly wrong, was to put them in the long perspective of the Chosen People's entire relationship with Yahweh. The first step to rehabilitating a pathological present was to lay down historical tram lines, parallel, straight, long, and true.

Beyond that, his faith, I think, held out to him two hopes. One of these was that in writing down in great detail the characteristics of the Temple (parts of the Book of Kings read like the transcription of an architectural seminar), and the ways in which ritual worship had been conducted in the past (the Book of Leviticus is almost a drill-manual for priests), he was providing the blueprint for a restoration of what he believed to be the central aspects of the religion of the Chosen People. In other words, a detailed record of the past was to serve as a detailed blueprint for the future.

If that failed – if the Temple was never rebuilt, or if the priestly caste never made it back to Jerusalem, and they were usurped either by the "Egyptians" or by the ill-educated and instinctively-apostate peasantry who had remained in the land – the young man had another hope. This was that the scrolls he put together, with their story of the nation's history and with their definitions of the true form of Temple worship, would themselves become the Temple. It is not such a great step from worshipping an aniconic idol to worshipping an invisible one. If the faithful among the Chosen People could not be a people of the Temple, they could become the people of the Temple's book.

Before his hair had turned gray or his eyes dimmed, the young man had collected, with the help of his allies, young and old, the traditions and manuscripts of his people and turned them into nine scrolls, which became the first nine books of the Hebrew Bible (the Christian "Old Testament" has things out of sequence at this point); Ruth belongs later:[9] Genesis, Exodus, Leviticus, Numbers, Deuteronomy, Joshua, Judges, Samuel (broken in early medieval times into two separate volumes) and Kings (also broken into two in the early medieval era). These nine books are a unity. They take the story of the covenant – the interaction of Yahweh and the Chosen People – from the creation of the earth down to the 560s BCE, when after thirty years as a prisoner in the equivalent of a gilded cage in Babylon, Jehoiachin, former King of Judah was set free. The Book of Kings ends with marvellous ambiguity. Jehoiachin, released, is set upon a throne by his Babylonian host, and it is a higher throne than that of the other conquered kings who are with him. And he was given a daily allowance of food for the rest of his life (II Kings 25:28–30). That is an end to an historical chronicle written by someone who had hope, but who had no idea of what the next chapter of the Chosen People's history would contain.

2

In suggesting that the first nine books of the Hebrew Bible are a unity and that they are best modelled as being the invention of a single great exilic mind, a mixture of national religious curator, seer, historian, priest (however much help he may have had from his confreres, and, however much small details of his work may have been tinkered with by later Pecksniffian minds), I am sailing broadside to several currents of scholarship. One of these is the largely unconscious but pervasive, almost instinctual, belief in modern biblical studies that authors and editors are separate categories of human beings. That is to say: the creative and the conservative do not meet in the same person. The sub-field of biblical scholarship that deals with "textual criticism," has been imprinted very strongly by people who tend to see the world as being a place where rational and non-rational forms of knowledge are sharply distinguished. In their work this has meant that hypotheses about the development of the scriptures separate very sharply writing and editing: different functions, therefore different people. This, I think, is unnecessary (and therefore by the basic test of Ockham's Razor, to be discarded) and in fact flies in the face of the single most manifest quality of the first nine books of the Hebrew scriptures: they are the work of a genius, in both the editing of old material and the inclusion of new. (Most literate North Americans will have less difficulty than the specialists in accepting this viewpoint, as they are acquainted with the career of the African-American genius, Toni Morrison. Not only did she serve for decades as one of the most active and influential of American literary editors, but for her own work received the Nobel Prize for literature in 1993.)[10] So, we use interchangeably the terms writer-editor, author-editor, and editor-writer, editor-author: it was all a single activity, both integrative and inventive.

Here, the word "invention" is used for the product of the great and nimble mind that produced the first nine books of the Hebrew Bible. Inventors do not create, for creation is to make something where there was nothing. Inventors use what is to hand, and then they add something of their own genius, whether it is new ways of recombining old elements, or tiny little improvements in existing parts so that what otherwise would not work does; or they take out their tools and make a part of new design and suddenly everything works. And the really good ones do so with marvellous efficiency and little flash. One thinks with admiration of the medieval inventor who first whittled from a piece of oak the eccentric cam, and attached it to the rim of a wagon wheel, thereby permitting the translation of rotary motion to linear force; on that elegant simplicity hangs all modern mechanical transportation.

Between the very good inventors and the few really great ones, there is a line: the truly great ones instinctively and fully collaborate with their users. There is nothing more useless than a physical invention that is ahead of its time or a cultural invention that is ahead of its audience. (The sadly risible nineteenth-century Frenchman who invented a perfectly workable facsimile machine comes to mind.) If ever there was a case of successful collaboration between inventor and audience, it is the first nine books of the Hebrew Bible. Not only were they embraced by their exilic audience, they were carried, eventually, back to the city of Jerusalem where they became the reference point for the establishment of a spiritual world. One cannot read these nine books of history without entering into their world, arguing with them, interrogating them for hidden meanings. Genesis through Kings: a truly great invention.

Another place where the idea of the first nine books of the Hebrew Bible's being a unity clashes with modern scholarship is that few of the most influential scholars see it as such – although the idea is gaining credence quite quickly – and that is no small problem. Here an aside is required. My view of Genesis through Kings as being a unified entity, seems on the surface to conflict with traditional Jewish scholarship, which emphasizes the first five books, the Books of Moses, as the primary unit, the one on which everything else is built. Here the problem is only apparent, for although traditional Judaism privileges the Pentateuch, and has done so since well before the Common Era, it has held equally firmly to the view that the Books of Moses and the first half of the Nevi'm – Joshua, Judges, Samuel, Kings ("the Former Prophets") – together form a larger unity that is the primary reference for the history of the Chosen People from Creation into the period of the Babylonian exile. It is distinct from the "Latter Prophets" consisting of Isaiah, Jeremiah and Ezekiel (the "Major Prophets") and the twelve books ascribed to the "Minor Prophets." This takes us back to my position, that Genesis through Kings form a single united entity. That leaves for later two very interesting historical questions: why, given their belief that the corpus of sacred literature we have been discussing was part of a larger entity, did the early "Orthodox" interpreters break out the first five books for special treatment? and when did they do this?

The problem with modern scholarship is greater, and more difficult to define, for the scholars fight among themselves, like an ever-shifting pack of feral canines, and it is hard to focus clearly on the myriad issues involved. Fundamentally, however, two major viewpoints among non-Orthodox scholars concerning the first nine books of the Hebrew Bible have dominated the second half of the twentieth century. The first of these stems from a brilliantly succinct essay of Gerard von Rad's *Das formgeschichtliche Problem des Hexateuchs* of 1938.[11] In it, von Rad bypassed the smaller issues of textual scholarship (although he was impressively skilled in those areas), and argued that certain books of the Hebrew Bible were a unity, and that this could be demonstrated on the basis of their ideological oneness. This unity was independent of what the original sources of the material were. He called the books so united the "Hexateuch" and they consisted of Genesis, Exodus,

Leviticus, Numbers, Deuteronomy and – this was crucial – Joshua. The unity that he perceived was a balance of centripetal and centrifugal forces. In the centre, the pivot of his interpretation, was a "creed" which comprises Chapter 26 of the Book of Deuteronomy. But it is not a creed in the modern sense of being a theological statement. Instead, it is a statement of beliefs about Israel in history: God created the world and chose the people of Israel as his own, brought them out of Egypt, led them to freedom and eventually to settlement in the promised land. Around that hub of historical belief pivots all the narrative of Genesis-through-Joshua. The basic historical creed tethers the story of the Chosen People, like the radius of a circle, and as the narrative line races around the circumference of the circle, it has redundancies and repetitions (that is what one would expect in a story that circles on a fixed radius) yet the integrity of the narrative is undivided. But none of this works if one stops at the end of the Book of Deuteronomy, for the narrative effectively concludes with the heartbreaking vision of Moses, taken to Mount Nebo, just on the east side of the Jordan River, where he looks into the promised land, and then, this vision granted, dies. If, as von Rad argues, the fundamental historical creed includes the settling of the people in the new land, then the Book of Joshua has to be part of the circle of narrative that the historical creed defined. Hence, the Hexateuch is a unity. This I find both compelling and convincing.

Equally, I find convincing (if less elegantly argued) the other dominant opinion of the second half of the twentieth century, that of Martin Noth, articulated in *Überlieferungsgeschichtiche Studien* of 1943.[12] Noth's argument runs as follows: (1) that although the sources that underlie Genesis, Exodus, Leviticus and Numbers run into the Book of Deuteronomy (2) there begins with the first verse of Deuteronomy a separate literary unit, one that continues to the end of Kings. This unit – Deuteronomy, Joshua, Judges, Samuel, and Kings – was compiled by a single writer, Noth believed, whom he called "the Deuteronomist." Later scholars have tended to see several cooperating hands, rather than a single one on the scribal scroll, but the fundamental point of Noth's argument about the unity of the "Deuteronomistic history" has carried the day. This has obvious implications for the consideration of the Books of Moses. "At the end of Numbers there is a deep incision," Noth noted. "For with Deut. 1:1 there begins the deuteronomistic historical work which fundamentally has nothing to do with the Pentateuch and became attached to it from the literary point of view only later ..."[13]

Thus, the two dominant approaches to the fundamental books of the Hebrew scriptures have only one thing in common: they reject the idea that the Pentateuch (the five Books of Moses) are the basic unit. Gerard von Rad's approach gives one a Hexateuch (Genesis through Joshua) and then the rest of the Former Prophets (Judges, Samuel and Kings) as separate entities. Martin Noth's approach provides us with a "Tetrateuch" (that is, Genesis through

Numbers) and a deuteronomistic history that runs from Deuteronomy through Kings. Clearly, the problem is with the Book of Deuteronomy, for the two leading textual scholars of their generation read it quite differently. Yet, I think each is correct.

If it is true (as von Rad argues) that the Book of Deuteronomy is demonstrably part of a unified entity that includes all of the Pentateuch and also the book of Joshua; and *if* it is also the case, as Martin Noth demonstrates, that the Book of Deuteronomy is part of a unified entity that includes the last book of the Pentateuch and all of the Former Prophets, *then* a reasonable suggestion is that, in fact, we are here dealing with a single historical narrative, the product of a single coherent viewpoint, that runs throughout the first nine books of the Hebrew Bible.

In suggesting this, I am not being opportunistic. My own views of the unity of the first nine books are developed independently of the semi-syllogism given above. Frankly, I cannot see how any other hypothesis could be the first line of investigation: one has a coherent story, from creation down almost to the time of post-exilic writing and compilation, and one has a motive for the writing and editing to be done. That may be simple to state, but in historical explanations, as in mathematics, simplicity is elegance, and elegance is strength.

Acceptance of the unity of the first nine books of the Hebrew Bible, as the invention of a single religious genius (however much he may have been helped by colleagues), is dependent upon an understanding of the wonderful flexibility of the Book of Deuteronomy. It is not one thing – either the tie-up of the pre-history of the ancient Hebrews, or the beginning of what, in the context of the times, was the nation's "modern history" – it is both. The editor-cum-author here knew exactly what he was doing. The Book of Deuteronomy is a strong spine with two mighty arms. That spine and those arms can support, on the one hand the first four Books of Moses, and on the other the four "Former Prophets" (Joshua, Judges, Samuel and Kings). There is a symmetry here that is immensely skilful. The four books on each hand balance each other; and each set of four becomes a set of five because they are thematically and historically integrated with the central volume, Deuteronomy. By using the Book of Deuteronomy in this dual role, the editor-author – the inventor – was carving in his own way two sets of five tablets. He, the most self-aware of historians, knew full well that he was invoking here the image of the two sets of five laws brought down by Moses from the mountain in the establishment of the Sinai covenant. The use of this image speaks well of the good sense of the inventor: he did not risk Yahweh's wrath for vain-glory by carving out ten scrolls, and thus making himself equal with Moses. But, his nine, presented in the manner he did, was very close, and close enough to tell us that he knew that he, like the Moses whom he depicts in his historical text, was creating a religion that was virtually new.

By his recombination of existing elements and his own creative additions, he permanently replaced the religion of ancient Israel with a new one. This, because of its conceptual locus in the southern kingdom, focusing on Jerusalem, is best called "*Judahism*," and its followers "Judahists" or "Judahites." This is not a word trick. The new system of belief and practice has to be distinguished both from what came before it (of which, note, we have no direct knowledge, only light filtered through the writings of the Judahists). And, equally, it has to be distinguished from its successor, the great invention of the second through fifth centuries of the Common Era, "*Judaism*" whose followers we know as the "Jews." The difference here is not linguistic: all variants of "Jews," "Jewish," Judaism," "Judahism," trace their origins to the Hebrew word "Yehudah," referring to the tribe of Judah. The difference is historical and one of the primary rules of historical work is not to use one term for two distinct phenomena. The religion of Judah, based on Temple sacrifice to Yahweh, up to the destruction of the Second Temple in 70 CE, is distinct historically from its descendent, the post-Temple faith, usually known as "Rabbinic Judaism."

The first legacies of Judahism's unknown genius were fourfold. The writings that he collected from a hodge-podge of manuscripts, hand-me-down folk tales, and his own controlled creativity, remain among the most compelling historical and literary documents known to humanity. The direct rules that he preserved, modified, and promulgated, including those for priestly behaviour, maintained the Judahist faith intact (albeit with some internal strife) until 70 CE. The blueprints he provided for the re-creation of his beloved idol, the Temple, permitted its rebuilding, and there, until the year 70, the covenant between Yahweh and the Chosen People was daily confirmed. And, on a tactical level, the newly-codified story of the Chosen People, with its very strong Yahwist centre, was a tool by which heresies and "syncretistic" cults were defined, and then destroyed upon the return to Jerusalem of the exiled elite.

One longs to know whether or not the great inventor ever saw Jerusalem. I think not, for he had to understand that the working of parallelism within his writings was not metaphorical only, but normative. He could not permit himself to enter the land of promise, even if he had the opportunity to do so, for what Moses, his consciously-defined predecessor had not done, he could not himself do. To be true to his god, he had to die on the far side of Jordan.

3

The great inventor was nothing if not respectful. He was as much a curator of old traditions as he was an editor, and he was more an editor than he was an author. His shaping of old stories may seem to modern eyes, almost too gentle, too respectful, for he preserves archaism and forms of words that few, if any, of his own generation fully understood. And he keeps in one long narrative duplicate versions of the same story, and these frequently do not entirely agree. (Compare, for example, Moses' extensive instructions concerning public worship in Exodus, chapters 25–31 and chapters 35–40.) But that is what historians do, even today: when their sources do not agree, they do not destroy one version and march blithely on with a false consonance. If two versions of a report are equally apposite, but incompatible with each other, the reader is not denied that knowledge. The more an historical account includes primary material, the more such dissonances are preserved.

So, he collected stories, documents, bits of poetry, hymns, mnemonic litanies of dos and don'ts, rules for priestly ritual, and architectural details of votive structures. The final version of the inventor's great work contains plenty of clues as to how he worked. For instance, in Kings he several times cuts short what otherwise would be a long and tiresome discussion of some second-line king, with the query, are not the acts of King So-and-So "written in the book of the chronicles of the kings of Israel?" (for example II Kings 1:18; 15:26; 15:31; 15:36) or written in the "book of the chronicles of the kings of Judah?" (for example II Kings 15:36; 16:19; 20:20; 21:17; 21:25). He also refers to a volume known as the "book of the acts of Solomon" (I Kings 11:41). Clearly, he is referring to historical scrolls that he has to hand, and, further, these are not rare items. They must have been widely known within the religious elite, or he could not have referred to them with the easy confidence that his colleagues would be acquainted with them. Also, the great inventor (or perhaps one of his predecessors, for he was the final curator, editor and author of a mass of material that had been piling up for centuries), refers to some books of scripture that the ancient Israelites possessed, but which are now lost, seemingly forever. Thus in Numbers (21:14) there is a tantalizing reference to the Book of the Wars of Yahweh. In this case, our editor-author gives no hint that he has actually seen the book, and it may be that his reference is second-hand, encapsulated in an earlier scroll that he is using for part of his collection of ancient Israel's central traditions. But if so, even this is revealing: he has not tinkered with the text he has received, even if it leaves him, like us, yearning to see the original Book of the Wars of Yahweh. In a more familiar way, indicating that he has seen the original, the editor-author cites in the Book of Joshua (10:13) the contents of the Book of Jashar, which deals with Joshua's making the sun and moon stand still so that the children of Israel could finish their slaughter of the Amorites unimpeded by nightfall.[14]

Part of the cultural and religious inheritance of the Chosen People was preserved orally: hymns, epic poems, short verse compositions that border on doggerel, folk tales, law cases, and, perhaps longer epics, items that came close to being sagas. The use of these items is not directly referred to in the Genesis-Kings scrolls, but it is fair to point out that transformation of oral information into written form went on well after the return to Jerusalem by the

exiles. Witness here the clearest case, that of the Book of Esther which purports to give the origins for the festival of Purim. It is set entirely in post-return
times (that is, after c.538 BCE) and is a folk tale of a fairly standard type: a vicious man is punished through the cunning of a virtuous woman. The Book of
Esther probably was the last book to be admitted to the Hebrew canon, and is a
good example of how oral material became scribally perpetuated. One could
produce dozens of similar cases, if one instanced later material in the Apocrypha and Pseudepigrapha and the Dead Sea Scrolls. That is not necessary: the
clear point is that anyone collecting and caring for the history of the Chosen
People would have been aware of oral custom, and would have weighed the
more important items for possible inclusion in the written word.

All this is so obvious – the great inventor was an historian, and how else do
historians work, but by being the magpies of the intellectual world? Yet, the
minute one mentions "sources," a great buzzing occurs, as if a nest of wasps
were about to swarm. One has to ignore part of this swarm, the group with
which there is no negotiation whatsoever: the Ultra-Orthodox Jews and their
Christian counterparts, the more extreme evangelicals and their phalanx of
Berserker Right outriders, the Christian fundamentalists, and especially the
cadre known as "Dispensationalists." If one takes the view of various Haredi
sects, the question of sources is irrelevant as they believe that the first five
books of the Bible are not merely named the Books of Moses, but were actually written by his hand. That does away with any problem of sources, although it does leave the inconvenient issue of how, at the end of the Book of
Deuteronomy, Moses was accurately able to report in the past tense the details of his own death. The other books of the Bible are held each to be a composition of a single person, their integrity being a function, in part, of each
book's being integral to itself. No source problems, therefore. When one
turns to the Christian equivalent of these beliefs, those of the keener evangelicals and fundamentalists, one finds that the source issue also disappears in
this instance because of the belief in the "verbal inerrancy" of the scriptures.
The Almighty dictated them to "holy men of old." (That this is roughly the
same method of composition postulated for the Koran is not a point the
Christian Right is disposed to dwell on.) Within the belief systems of many
Orthodox and most evangelicals (and of all of the Ultra-Orthodox and a lot of
the Christian Fundamentalists), to suggest, however tactfully one might do
so, that the scriptures are a collection of pieces that originally were not found
in their present packaging, is to invite instant denunciation. This is particularly difficult to deal with because the evangelicals, and most especially the
"Dispensationalists," rearrange the Bible pretty much according to their own
whim. The situation is well summarized by Jon Butler:

> Then came the twin disasters of fundamentalism and dispensationalism. Fundamen-
> talism heightened the developing antiintellectualism of evangelicalism by disguising

complex, crude and controversial theological statements as literal interpretations of the Scriptures, a trend capped by the influential *Scoffield Reference Bible* (1909). Dispensationalism completed this canonization of Biblical mechanics by manipulating the arbitrary versification of the scriptures completed in the sixteenth century and turning the Old and New Testament into a kind of gigantic Christian puzzle, all parts interchangeable. Now, words and sentences could be manoeuvred to create and defend simplistic interpretative schemes from any angle, brushing aside the verses' original context while also rigidly classifying modern events with a few simple-minded categories.[15]

This sort of thing cannot be fought, so it is best ignored.

Considerably more amenable to rational discourse is the world of biblical "criticism." The word "criticism" is unfortunate, as it unfairly tars a set of scholars who, at their best, are serious appreciators of the text. In the nineteenth century and the first half of the twentieth, the "higher critics" (the people who worked on the big questions) were a distinct occupational category from the "lower critics" who did all the dog work of sorting out the hundreds of thousands of variant readings of the manuscripts. In fact, these are among the most impressive scholars one can encounter.) Today, that distinction has gone away, but the word "critic" still has ugly overtones, given that we are dealing with a text many people view as in some sense sacred. "Biblical scholars" will do, as the term carries no accusation of arrogance.

4

The first scholarly problem concerning the sources of the great invention, Genesis-Kings, is that there has yet to emerge any satisfactory method of either identifying or analyzing oral material. This has two aspects. One of these is the immediate one of identifying what elements the exilic author-editor picked up by word of mouth, from his contemporaries and from elders. He does not label his oral sources. If only he had occasionally said the equivalent of "and the truth of this is vouchsafed by…" but he does not. It might be theoretically possible to sort out the oral sources by subtracting from the total text whatever he picked up in written sources, and then denominating the residual material as "oral" in source. That, however, is patently impossible in practice. It resembles the time-honoured way of defining miracles in the Jewish and Christian traditions – explain everything one can by rational means and then ascribe the remainder to "miracle" – and it is equally barren of result. Not only do we not know the full extent of the written sources which the great inventor used but, because he was also a writer, it would be impossible to determine what part of the thus-defined residual material was his own wordsmithing, and what came from oral sources.

Where the indeterminate nature of scriptures' oral sources becomes a problem, and one that cannot be dealt with satisfactorily, is at the distant end of the time line: the period before King David, especially the stories that tell about the patriarchs, the wanderings with Moses, and the supposed conquest of Canaan by Joshua. Now, it is a truism that in a society that was overwhelmingly non-literate, the most important events were talked about, and probably passed from one generation to another and to another, before they were eventually written down. But that says nothing, really. The real question is, how long was the religious memory maintained in oral form before being written down? Even if one takes a "good old-fashioned" dating of the earliest written scriptures as being about the year 1000 BCE, in the court of the United Monarchy, this means that, if the narrative of the pre-monarchical years was not entirely a fabrication of the court historians, then the religious memory, said to cover roughly 1,000 years, was enhulled in the Hebrew equivalent of sagas and epic poetry. Fair enough: where this becomes problematic is if one abandons the "good old-fashioned dating" and asks, as scholars have, how long was the ancient oral tradition kept in that form, before being written down? One could argue for the maintenance in oral form of the saga material (and all the other folklore aggregations of a developing religion) all the way down to the eve of the Exile, or even after it. But, whether one accepts either of those extreme dates – 1000 to roughly 550 BCE – or anything in between, the ultimate result is the same. One ends up dealing with *written* texts and the earliest solid version of the central text of the Hebrew Bible comes from about 550 BCE. There is no way of validating the suppositions being made concerning the pre-biblical (meaning pre-written) history of the biblical text.[16] Nor should one assume the antiquity of any supposedly "oral" portion of the written text: merely because an oral tradition refers to a distant era does not mean that the tradition itself originated long ago.

All modern speculations about the formation of the Hebrew scriptures exist in the shadow of the "Documentary Hypothesis." This is doubly unfortunate in name. The speculations involved are not "documentary," for that is a term which includes probative material of all sorts, including oral. It is about *documents* and how they relate to each other. Moreover, it is not a hypothesis in any meaningful sense. At no time has this "hypothesis" been given operational specificity. That is, never have any of its proponents spelled out the "hypothesis" in such a way as to permit testing, by observing certain characteristics that are produced independently of the hypothesis, and thus to permit assessment of whether it is confirmed or disproved. And the necessity of framing something so basic as null-hypothesis entirely escapes the notice of the practitioners. The "documentary hypothesis," then, simply does not exist. What exists in its place is really a very useful item, as long as one understands what it is. It is an heuristic fiction, and can best be labelled the "Documents Model." Heuristic fictions, unlike hypotheses, are evaluated not by whether they are proved or disproved, but by their fecundity. And, in that context, the Documents Model is very successful indeed.

The Documents Model is a fictive machine that has few basic parts, and these easily comprehensible. It began with two elements, which stemmed from the observation made as early as the eighteenth century that there were two gods – or at least two names for God – in the basic scriptures of the Hebrew Bible, most especially the Books of Moses. One of these was Yahweh. The other was Elohim, a form of the basic god-name "El" common in Palestine in the period, roughly 1000 to 600 BCE. The biblical texts that discussed Yahweh were observed to deal favourably with the interests of the southern kingdom, Judah, and those that focused on Elohim to favour the northern kingdom, Israel. There were other distinguishing points, too numerous to mention, but the key is that a list of distinguishers, broken into two distinct columns could be adduced. Therefore, it was suggested that in Genesis, Exodus (and perhaps in subsequent books), there were two basic sets of documents underlying the final texts. These were named "Y" (meaning Yahwist; it is still usually printed as "J" in the scholarly literature, but this is an affectation. The English-language "Y" will do quite nicely) and "E." This was a sensible expedient: if one found, say, the report of a Royal Commission on the theory of government, in which some of the references to the head of government were to "the King" and most of the rest were to "the President," one might reasonably conclude that the committee had split down the centre and that some hapless civil servant had been left to tape over the differences and hope that no one noticed.

The documents associated with "Y" and "E," however, were found not to cover the entire Books of Moses, so two other sources of documents were postulated (again, on the basis of painstaking examination of the original texts). These were said to be the Priestly Source – "P" whose documents are concerned more than anything else with defining and protecting the professional position of the priestly caste; and the "D" source, which in its early formulation was limited to the Book of Deuteronomy. And, because the pieces still did not quite fit, a later editorial hand – called "R" for redactor – was postulated. "R" became the equivalent of the "miscellaneous" category in a salesman's expense account: "R" was responsible for whatever could not be accounted for elsewhere.

Conceptually, this Documents Model was elegant, and its fecundity was amazing, for it, like Helen of Troy, launched a thousand battleships. Given its elegant simplicity – there were only five moving parts, Y, E, P, D, and R – one would have thought that the Documents Model could have been made to approximate one or two versions of possible historical realities. Yet, I can find only one even-moderately successful instance of an attempt at producing a version of the Books of Moses that distinguishes between the various models.

This is Paul Haupt's "Polychrome Bible" of 1891, and he accomplished this task only by leaving out the Books of Exodus and Deuteronomy![17] Search as hard as one may, nothing turns up. Perhaps I am missing some obvious item, but unless that is the case, we are here encountering something that in most fields of historical scholarship would be taken as diagnostic: a model, fundamental to a field of study, for which no one has yet found a real-world counterpart.[18]

Although the Documents Model still has its uses, the present situation reminds me of a scene I witnessed one day at my farm implement dealer's. He was short of help and had hired three city lads, each a qualified motorcar mechanic. None had any experience with farm machinery. They were set to taking from its packing case a machine they had never seen before, much less operated, and they were to assemble the machine and tune it for field work. Watching them was a treat. They were good mechanics and not stupid, but each part as it came out of its package had several possible uses: industrial parts are made to fit several different places, just as religious formularies are. They argued, and they worked hard and eventually they got the thing together. (That the other mechanics, all country boys, just happily let them work away, giving each other the occasional wink, hardly needs stating; some things are universal.) Eventually, the city lads got the machine together – it was a big self-powered haybine – without too many pieces left over. The thing started, most of the parts moved, but the cutting head, on which everything depended, was on upside down. They went back to arguing.

Now the argument level on the shop floor of biblical scholarship is prodigious. The Documents Model has moved from being an elegant five-part machine, to one with a thousand pieces, strewn all over the shop.[19] For one thing, it is now generally accepted that document source Y and document source E did not just make their impact in the early parts of the Books of Moses, but are also found in Deuteronomy and also in the Book of Joshua, and possibly in Judges. Second, and much more important, the last fifty years of biblical scholarship have multiplied the sources of documents from five, to more than a score. Each has its tiny siglum, which, like the Masonic handshake, is known only to the initiates. Baruch Halpern comments ironically on the "welter of sigla" and lists some of the more prominent of the new codes – Dtr, Dtr[1], Dtr2, Dtr[2], Dtr(hez), Dtr(jos), Dtr(x), DtrG, DtrH, DtrN, DtrP, E(Dtr)n, E(Dtr)p, E(Dtr)x, H, H(Dtr), H(Dtr)het, H(Dtr)x, JE, M+, M−, Rdtr, Rdt3, SDeb....[20] The effect of this fragmenting of the sources brings to mind Edmund Burke's denunciation of political factionalism – "this tessellated pavement without cement," he called it. Whereas, the relationship between putative documents in the classic Documents Model had been limited (by the basics of statistical theory) to about twenty-four possible patterns, now the possible relationships spin into the thousands, and all of them based on merely heuristic original sources, of whose independent existence there is no documentation. Robert Alter, one of the pioneers of the literary study of the Bible, surveyed this scene and commented that: "In many cases a literary student of the Bible has more to learn from the traditional commentaries than from modern scholarship. The difference between the two is ultimately the difference between assuming that the text is an intricately interconnected unity, as the midrashic exegetes [Jewish textual interpreters of the Common Era] did, and assuming it is a patchwork of frequently disparate documents, as modern scholars have supposed."[21] This has been very detrimental to historical understanding. "By its concentration on these smaller units, rather than the larger compositional units, form-criticism has ignored the possible significance for dating, origin and function of the biblical literature of the larger genres which constitute the shape of the biblical narrative," is the judgement of Philip R. Davies, who is hardly a romantic about ancient Israel. He continues: "Form-criticism largely and perhaps conveniently forgets that meaning, structure, and social setting are also dimensions of those larger compositions, and in its obsession with the "original" forms does not direct its methods to the elucidation of the larger (and less hypothetical) units. One of the major larger genres of the biblical literature is historiography, and yet this genre, without parallel in the "Ancient Near Eastern" literature, has hardly attracted until recently a fraction of the structural, rhetorical and comparative analysis of other smaller *Gattungen*."[22]

Clearly, if the text unambiguously implies a fragmentation of its origins, the biblical scholars must honour that. However, one can easily find instances in which a single verse of the Hebrew scriptures is allocated to as many as three different sources according to various scholarly criteria. This is the equivalent of watching someone who has never heard of the concept of statistical significance, work out the percentage of voters in a small sample to the twentieth place to the right of the decimal point. A lovely example is found in David Hackett Fischer's *Historians' Fallacies*: a sixteenth-century scholar worked out the average weight of a stone cannon ball of 10.75 inches, a highly variable object, both in density and indeed in size, to be sixty-one pounds, one ounce, two drams, one scruple and $15 \frac{685644}{1414944}$ grains.[23] That is what such tight parsing of "sources" by documents exegetes does: it violates a basic rule of all historical explanation, which is that if the potential random variation in any phenomenon is greater than the differences that one is defining and explaining, then the exercise has no probative value whatsoever and has to be abandoned. Real differences must exceed random probabilities, or one is not doing history, but necromancy. And, given that the Masoretic Text (which, for most parts of the Hebrew Bible is the text scholars employ) has shown itself to have literally hundreds of thousands of variants on the verse-by-verse level (and those are the ones we know about; how many other variants are lost?), then it follows that a single verse (and, in some cases, even a pericope) is too small a unit to split analytically into fragments.

Because the Documents Model is fundamentally right-headed – it asserts the incontrovertible argument that the Hebrew Bible which we now possess is based, at least to some extent, on earlier documents – it warrants continual employment: some day it may stimulate a big intellectual payoff. However, for the individual who is interested in considering the first one-third of the Hebrew Bible (Genesis-Kings) as an historical narrative (which is what the scriptures announce themselves to be), then, ironically, the Documentary Model in its myriad present-day guises has little to say. This is because the question of the etiology and relationship of the various document-components of the Hebrew scriptures is *completely irrelevant either to their historical accuracy or, more important, to whether or not they were believed by their audience and thus became historical realities in themselves.*

That sounds harsh, but consider: (1) The actual date of one of the documents upon which the scriptures are based, and whether or not that date is earlier or later, has no relationship whatsoever (within reasonable time limits) to whether or not the accounts are either accurate or convincing. This must be emphasized, because biblical scholars have tended to think that the earlier a document or tradition can be dated, the more historically accurate it is apt to be. They have therefore had a considerable investment in positing as early a date as possible for a given source (if the scholars are believers) or as late as possible a date (if they are skeptical of belief). The *reductio ad absurdum* of this process is the "eyewitness-syndrome," wherein the report of an event that someone claims to have seen is taken as being more accurate than an event a later person described from assembled evidence and circumstantial argument. We only need to remind ourselves that up to the sixteenth century, virtually every eyewitness to the operation of the solar system swore that the sun revolved around the earth. Indirect evidence, of course, was more closely correct. Further, in evolving documents, such as the scriptures were, the later editors could frequently improve accuracy, through the knowledge they had acquired from later sources. Newer sources, therefore, were often more accurate than older.

(2) The arrangement of the relative temporal order of the sources believed to lie behind the Hebrew Bible is extrinsic to the issue of the documents' accuracy and also to whether the final unity was a convincing entity to the religious community towards which it was directed. To take an extreme example, concerning the Y source, it is the customary wisdom among biblical scholars to hold that the Yahwist documents are the oldest in the Bible (being written either just before, during, or just after the reign of King Solomon) and that one cannot explain the evolution of the Hebrew scriptures unless one starts with "Y" as the foundation stone. Yet it has been shown that a convincing

arrangement of the sources can be postulated that makes the Y source a product of the last years of the kingdom of Judah and the *last* source to be incorporated.[24] The point is that, fascinating as all the rearranging of the mosaic tiles of the Documents Model is, the manner in which they are combined does not in any way affect either the historical accuracy or the useability of the final product. That final product was a tool for the reconquest of Jerusalem by a narrow, highly motivated, exiled religious elite.

(3) Nor does the Documents Model's suggestion that the history of the Bible before its final redaction was a very fragmented entity, cut one way or the other on the historicity issue. The first reaction to biblical "criticism" of nineteenth-century believers (and the reaction today of Christian evangelicals and of Orthodox Jews) was that if there were several early sources for the Bible, then that somehow "disproved" the Bible's historical accuracy. More importantly, the Documents Model was taken by some biblical scholars as implicitly proving the opposite possibility, that the Bible was historically accurate. This does bear notice, for it is a fallacy that appears pervasively in "New Testament" studies, albeit less so in "Old." The leap of illogic here stems from the sound historical principle that two sources are better than one, and three are even better, in confirming an event: *independent* sources. Now, when the pioneering scholars of the late nineteenth and early twentieth centuries developed their Documents Model, they were quite pleased to find that (for example, for the life of Moses), they had material from two sources. So, the more they fragmented their sources, the more attestation they thought they had to events far in the past. In "New Testament" studies, which struggle with a scarcity of independent documentation that makes the difficulties with the Hebrew Bible seem trivial, a great deal of stress is laid upon "multiple attestation" for chronicling the life of Jesus. The Quest for the Historical Jesus, like the Quest for the Historical Moses, depends upon multiple attestation. Except that is not what we have when we have multiple sources that are subsumed into a single entity either by a writer-editor or by processes of discrimination whereby religious authorities, acting collectively, include only certain items in a "canon" because they are ideologically compatible one with another, and with the viewpoint of those same authorities who control the religious system. The various heuristic items posited by the Documents Model do not constitute multiple attestation, for they are not independent witnesses.

Anyone who enjoys doing anagrams or playing with jigsaw puzzles can find a great deal of pleasure in reading biblical scholarship, for one is able to watch some first-class minds try to figure out how the Hebrew scriptures came together. However, the only intellectual constant that I have found in my reading is that through this activity runs a *single* principle of historical evidence, indeed the only one on which all the scholars would agree: that the report of a given historical event is always after the event. (There are a few religious zealots who claim otherwise, but they are not here germane, even if their view of biblical prophecy is diverting.) The trouble is, this is nothing that a beginning history graduate student would not know and act upon. Indeed, a real problem is that even this elementary principle is misread. David Noel Freedman, who in his generation was among the most powerful arbiters of what was and what was not first-line biblical scholarship, stated his version of this basic rule as follows: "In the Bible, historical narratives generally come down to the time of the author(s); therefore the latest episodes recorded are roughly contemporary with the writer(s) of the stories. Put another way, the work is composed or completed shortly after the last of the stories is finished, and the work may be dated accordingly. A significant burden of proof rests with those who wish to extend the period between the end of the narrative and the composition of the work."[25] This is indeed astounding, and I can think of no other field of history wherein anyone would dare declare a similar evidentiary principle, solely upon faith. It virtually equates what is usually termed a *terminus a quo*, the earliest point at which something could have happened, with a *terminus ad quem*, the latest date at which something could have occurred. The earliest date (the point where the last episode ends) is just that: the very first possible date of composition. Why the composition should be assumed to have occurred at the earliest date in biblical history (but not in secular history) defies explanation. Indeed, it would not be unreasonable to argue that in cultures wherein the oral memory was prized, events were not written down until a generation or two after they happened, and then only because the public memory was beginning to slip somewhat, and the historical occasion needed to be frozen in time by its being written down. Actually, the only acceptable method in historical scholarship for suggesting a probable date for an occurrence is that there be some reason for the dating which is independent of the mere possible range of dates. Thus, for example, I have suggested that the author-editor of the first nine books of the Genesis-Kings volumes worked in the mid-sixth century, not because Kings ends in the 560s, but because there was a social context in that period which made his work necessary for the maintenance of his own religious polity.

5

In the nine books of scripture that the great editor-writer produced while in Babylonian exile, there is a grammar of invention. These are the rules of what it was permissible, and not permissible, to do in the religious culture of his time, caste, and ideology. This grammar can be inferred by our first examining, at a macro-level, what the editor-writer did in his work, and then what he did not do. This inferred grammar of invention is important in itself, but, more than that, it is potentially valuable because it may be applicable to the way religious invention occurs in the two main offshoots of the Judahist religion, namely early Christianity and Rabbinic (or "Talmudic") Judaism.

What the author-editor wanted to achieve (and, I think did so with masterly success) was almost brutally simple. He wanted to win, and to do so decisively. So the heart of the Hebrew scriptures, Genesis through Kings, is a chronicle of victories. Some of these are clearly marked, but the most important ones are so pervasive, that they do not require labelling as such, for they become the structural warp upon which the weft of his verbal tapestry is articulated.

The first, and most pragmatic of the victories which the editor-writer celebrates is that of Judah over Israel. He has the good sense not to be triumphalist about this, but this only makes his message more effective. The rivalry of Judah and Israel from c.928 BCE until the destruction of Israel by the Assyrians in 722/721 is chronicled with masterly economy and restraint. What is usually read as a soporific set of succession lists, enlivened by the occasional apostasy and genocide (see Appendix B), is actually masterful propaganda. This is an anachronistic term, stemming as it does from an office of the Vatican, but appropriate nonetheless. The basic chronicle of the northern kingdom – the ten tribes – comes to an end because "the children of Israel had sinned against the Lord their God, which had brought them out of the land of Egypt, from under the hand of Pharaoh, king of Egypt, and had feared other gods" (II Kings 17:7). They had built "high places" (meaning raised altars) in all their cities, and had set up images (idols) and sacred groves on high hills, to the worship of other (undefined) gods (II Kings: 17:8–12). So, they perished.

The interesting point, though, is that the editor-writer of the scriptures is too shrewd to merely let the Israelites disappear. Granted, they disappear as a social group after many of them are taken captive by the Assyrians and never again rise as an independent political power. (This opens a question which most scholars avoid, given the problematic nature of the evidence: what are we to make of the Samaritans, a northern group that acquired both its own Pentateuch and Temple?) Still, if Judah and Benjamin, who take on the collective governmental name of the "kingdom of Judah," are the sole repositories after 722 BCE of the covenant, why does the editor-writer of the most important books of the Hebrew scriptures not excise altogether the subsequent reference to "Israel"? Why does he continue to refer to the Kingdom of Judah as in some sense being "Israel"? And why does he several times associate Judah with the sins of Israel? Biblical scholars have frequently explained these characteristics of the final text, by suggesting that priestly or scribal refugees from the old northern kingdom of Israel found their way south and brought with them not only their own national chronicles, but a degree of moral force that permitted them to assert the necessity of including their northern history in any discussion of the history of the Chosen People. This well may be correct, but, independent of that, one may suggest two further reasons. The first of these is simply that, as an historian (probably the first real historian humanity has known), the editor-writer was respectful of sources. He was predisposed to maintain largely intact (if not unedited), items that indicate, shed light on the history of Judah (as the history of Israel certainly did), as long as those inclusions were not morally objectionable. And, crucially, he was a brilliant propagandist for Judah. By assimilating into his larger invention the books of Genesis-Kings, the editor-writer achieved a smooth and irreversible feat of cultural imperialism. He subsumed into the history of Judah all the desirable aspects of the history of its ancient rival Israel and simultaneously wiped the political entity Israel from history's slate. A brilliant job, and in conceptual terms Israel became a mere colony of Judah. (If the reader is uneasy with the idea that being a great historian and a brilliant propagandist are incompatible activities, let me emphasize that the opposite is the case. The great historians – from Gibbon to Macauley to E.P. Thompson – have always been both. Disinterested objectivity and an absence of moral fervour is achieved only by truly bad historians.)

Further, in establishing the complete victory of Judah (and thus validating the creation of Judahism), the author-editor instinctively understood something about the nature of propaganda that social scientists only came to understand during the era of the Cold War. This is that propaganda that is too smooth, too seamless, that is lacking in imperfections and in occasional contradictions, is not convincing. And it is vulnerable, because the implication of perfection invites disproof through the discovery of even a single imperfection. Better, instead, to say (or imply), that the story being spun is not perfect, but that it is both as honest and accurate as possible. Therefore, imperfections become warranties of honesty and thus, instead of discrediting the tale, they validate the integrity of the teller, and thus of the tale. That is why the editor-writer is able without damage to the credibility of his historical narrative to include hundreds of "doublets" (the biblical scholars' term for duplications, repetition, redundancies, and, sometimes, thematic amplifications). The contradictions in these doublets are legion. (How could it be otherwise, when such basic things as the name of God and the names and, indeed, the naming of the twelve tribes are given in incompatible forms?) But they are also validating exercises. And almost all of them in the Genesis-Kings scriptures stem from the Judahist editor-writer having taken what the proponent of the Documents Model would call the "E" source (northern) and kept it alive, whilst subordinating it to the southern "Y" source. Judah wins.[26]

A central strand in the invention of Judahism is the capture of King David. He is the first fully-formed figure to be found in the Bible and, indeed, is probably the first human being for whom we have a biography. Without making any judgement about the historical reality of Moses and of the Patriarchs, the fact is that their presentation in the scriptures is not in the form of subjects of biography, but of saga-heroes, perhaps demi-gods. David is human: very. We follow him from childhood to youth at the royal court of King Saul, through his becoming, first, a military hero (by defeating Goliath), then as a fugitive when he was a rival for Saul's throne, then his becoming a king and a war-lord whose territory centred around Hebron. Eventually he captures Jerusalem and moves his administration there. In between all this we are permitted to glimpse a real human being: frightened, cunning, a sexual glutton and a murderer. And yet, he is the chosen servant of Yahweh, one with whom the Almighty makes a direct covenant, just as he did with Moses.

Here, as elsewhere, the editor-writer of the Judahists' key scriptures does not court scepticism by overstating his case. He is good; he never over-reaches. Instead of presenting a genealogy of David that would have tightly tied him to Judah, and therefore only to Judah, he is nicely allusive. Great historian and artist that he was, the inventor planted a lodestone in the Book of Genesis. It is found in Jacob's dying blessing of the various tribes of Israel (Gen. 49:1–27). There, Judah is promised the prime blessing of all the tribes. "Judah, thou art he whom thy brethren shall praise: thy hand shall be in the neck of thine enemies; thy father's children shall bow down before thee" (Gen. 49:8). That aligns all future genealogies. The interesting point is that when David's own birth is defined in the Genesis-Kings unity, he is described as the youngest of the sons of Jesse, of the tribe of Judah who lived in Bethlehem (I Sam. 17:12). This information is given to the reader in passing, in the middle of a description of the terror being wreaked by Goliath, the Philistine giant, and it is not something that we would think to check. There is no attempt to trace a tight line from Judah, whom Jacob blessed, to David. So the assertion of his genealogy is not open to disproof. We accept it, or not, according to our view of the verisimilitude of the battle story in which it is wrapped (and a very good story it is).[27]

That is the top end of King David's genealogy. In a culture that used genealogical descent as part of the vocabulary of authenticity, capturing King David's line of descent for Judah was the equivalent of seizing the high ground in a military contest. But, unlike a citadel on a hill, this genealogical strong point was mobile. In a bizarre way, it surrounded the opposition. Look at chronological Table 2 in Appendix B. Ignore the individual kings. What the table says, quickly, is what the genealogy says in detail: Judah was there before Israel and it was there after Israel.

Judah is victorious, again. And, again, the great inventor uses this victory not to exterminate Israel, but to colonize it, conceptually speaking. He has not done what an unthinking and vengeful warlord would have done: wipe out the succession lists of the Israelite kings which, of course, are lists of genealogical succession as well, with a few coups intermixed. He maintains those succession lists of Israel, alongside those of the Kings of Judah against whom they sometimes warred. Thus, the kingship of Israel, being assimilated to the Davidic kingship of Judah, becomes a subordinate part of the history of Judah, which is the theme of the historical narrative of Genesis through Kings.

In rhetorically capturing King David, the great inventor automatically gained control of David's city, Jerusalem. This was almost a matter of military necessity. The exiled elite had been forced out of Jerusalem, and they planned to return and to push aside the riff-raff who had remained behind, and those interlopers (including, one infers, heretics from the north) who threatened to gain permanent control of the holy city. Those of the religious elite who would return from Babylon needed an ideological justification for their resuming power, one that would be acceptable throughout the diaspora, as well as within Palestine.

This pragmatic necessity played into a more basic piece of historical organization that the editor-writer accomplished – and this is one of the times one is desperately curious as to whether he created this himself or worked from earlier editions of Judah's history – namely the mammoth dislocation of the ancient Hebrews' holy mountain. In the parts of the Genesis-Kings narrative that the reader (or listener) first encounters, the holy mountain for the Chosen People is Mount Sinai, a height in the Sinai desert whose location is forever lost (this despite modern Bedouin claims to the contrary). There, after the Exodus from Egypt, the Chosen People received the laws, through Moses, and thus entered into the covenant with Yahweh. Sinai is *the* holy place, for it is there that God reveals one of his names to his people (Exod. 3:14). Yet (employing the internal time scale of the biblical narrative) within two to four hundred years, Sinai is entirely replaced as Yahweh's dwelling place by another mountain, Zion. This was so closely associated with King David, that the "city of David" and "Zion" were synonymous (II Sam. 5:7, I Kings 8:1). (The actual location of "Zion" is probably the Temple Mount, the present-day site of the Islamic shrine, the dome of the Mosque, in Jerusalem.)[28] At no point is Mount Zion declared to have replaced Mount Sinai, it just quietly happens.[29]

In having Mount Zion occlude Mount Sinai and in having the covenant with David overlay the covenant with Moses, the writer-editor is taking enormous risks. That he is aware of this can be inferred from his not calling the two changes to our attention. Like a novelist moving imperceptibly from external dialogue to interior monologue, he takes us with him on an audacious journey, without telling us that he intends to do so. His great risk is to his own credibility. The one narrative attribute that a piece of historical writing cannot afford to lose is believability. I think the author-editor gets away with it, quite brilliantly. The millions of adherents who have followed in the various religions that use the Hebrew scriptures as part of their own beliefs have accepted the shifts. That degree of success, or any success at all, was not certain when the editor-writer put it all together, and one can only admire his courage.

Because Jerusalem and the kingdom of Judah have been mentioned so frequently, this is the appropriate point to prevent what might become a point of false emphasis. Although Judahism, as invented in the mid sixth century, had Jerusalem as its centrepoint and the kingdom of Judah as its spiritual genealogy, this does not mean that in the times prior to the Babylonian exile, a totally tight set of north-south dichotomies existed. Some scholars like to draw a set of parallel lines down the page. On one side is the north, the Mosaic covenant, Mount Sinai and, ultimately, the kingdom of Israel; on the other is the south, the Davidic covenant, Mount Zion, Jerusalem, and the kingdom of David. As Jon Levenson makes clear, first, the pre-exilic lines of demarcation were not that clear between the north and the south. There was after all a period of a united monarchy and, in any case, religious interactions continued after the split, even though differences between two high priests had been the starting point of the bifurcation. It is more accurate to think of the "spatter diagrams" so beloved by early sociologists. Certain beliefs (and practices) tended to be more common in either the north or the south, but every variety could be found throughout the cultural penumbra of the land settled by the ancient Hebrews. Secondly, as Levenson points out, some of the differences that are taken to be north-south distinctions, are actually sequential, not spatial in nature.[30]

That said, I must reiterate: however enjoyably seductive the speculations and inferences of biblical scholars are about the pre-exilic world (I will indulge in a few myself in a moment), the only direct reality that we have to deal with is the text which was invented in the form that we have it after that world had disappeared. Thus, we should adopt and expand an observation of Franz Rosenzweig which Gerhard von Rad quoted with strong disapproval. Namely that "R" who was conceived as the redactor of the "Hexateuch" should be called Rabbenu, meaning our master, "because basically we are dependent only on him, on his great work of compilation and his theology and we receive the Hexateuch at all only from his hands." Von Rad disapproved of this formulation because he believed that Christians "receive the Old Testament from the hands of Jesus Christ...."[31] With von Rad's opinion, I could scarcely agree less: we get the Hebrew scriptures from the Hebrew scriptures, not from the hand of Christianity. Rosenzweig is right and the reverence he suggests holds even more if one accepts the argument presented here, that not only do we receive the Hexateuch, but all of Genesis through Kings from a single hand, and, moreover, that hand was not merely a redactor, but a brilliant historical writer as well.[32]

From the viewpoint of modern biblical scholarship, the least controversial observation one can make about the Judahist editor-writer of Genesis-Kings is that he was very careful to protect the professional position and privileges of the religious elite, especially the priests. Of course the situation that is described in Genesis-Kings concerning the role of the priests is pre-exilic in origin, but the key is that the editor-writer is tailoring both manifest details and latent content so as to guide future behaviour of the entire religious polity. His guise is entirely that of an historian, but that mode here is one of the fundamental ways in which he is able to invent Judaism: *historical depiction is used as future prescription.*[33]

If one had a tired eye and an excess of the world's experience, one might read the Book of Leviticus and the first segment of the Book of Numbers as an early counterpart to some Trades Demarcation Agreement from the high noon of British trade unionism. One can almost hear Peter Sellers (in the shop steward persona he adopted in "I'm All Right Jack," 1959) droning out the details of which section of the Charcoal Burners and Wood Hewers local could provide fuel for which ritual sacrifices. But, petty as the details may seem to modern eyes, they were a very big deal indeed, for they provided nothing less than control of access to Yahweh. Access to him is only through ritual sacrifice, for it is in such sacrifice that the covenant is re-enacted (the covenant, remember, is a two-party bargain, and the sacrifice is part of a bargain in which the Chosen People kill something valuable and in turn their god blesses them, or at least does not punish them.) Crucially, this access to the Almighty is a monopoly that is given to the priesthood in an historical story that carries the highest possible weight: God is said to have told Moses (the ancient Hebrews' original bargainer with Yahweh in covenant-cutting) that there should be no sacrifices unto him except at "the door of the tabernacle of the congregation" (Leviticus 17:9). And there it can only be done by priests.

The actual details deal primarily with three aspects of professional priestly conduct. One of these is the way that a small ark of animals is to be killed, cut up, burned, and scattered about. The methods of slaughter are particularly nasty.[34] Second, rules for ritual cleanliness are tightly defined, and third, the nature and control of several sacred festivals is fixed. In each of these three areas, priestly control is absolute.

As already noted, the writer-editor has a shrewd ability to let sleeping dogs lie. He neither calls to the reader or listener's attention certain difficulties, nor tries to sort them out if they are noticed. It is not clear, for instance, what the relationship between the priests of Aaron's line and the priestly tribe of the Levites actually is. Aaron has priority in the historical narrative, as he is the brother of Moses, and the first priest designated as such. Yet, the Levites have a genealogy that is prior to Aaron (see Exodus 6:16–25, and Numb. 26:58–60) and this line of descent incorporates both Aaron and Moses within it. Further, there is a third priestly line, the Zadokites, who are descended from a co-chief priest, Zadok, who King David introduced into the equation (II Sam. 8:17). Any number of explanations of these matters are possible, and do not require excessive ingenuity. The signal point is that the great inventor does not bother. He focuses on what counts: that the channel to Yahweh, in the future as much as in the past, shall be controlled by the priests.

These, though, are not just anybody's priests. They are the priests of Yahweh, and that points to the biggest victory that our author-editor is determined to ensure: the victory of Yahweh over his rivals as the god of the Chosen People. So skillful is he, that in reading his text, Genesis-Kings, we forget that there were even alternatives to Yahweh in the minds of the Chosen People. There were: various forms of the Canaanite god, Baal, and a handful of "El" gods, local deities associated with specific places in Palestine. (More of this in section 6). The most salient indication of how successful the great inventor was in making Yahweh the god of the south and especially of Jerusalem, the god of the Chosen People, is the way in which subsequent readers – certainly from Talmudic times onwards – have simply forgotten that there was a major alternative deity to Yahweh and one of his or her names has not been scrubbed from the scriptures. This deity, in fact was not *a* deity, but several – Elohim – and sentences with that name mean "the gods," not "god." It is diverting to observe the ingenuity of literally centuries of biblical scholars explain this away, in our times with virtually cabalistic semiotic arguments.[35] But it need not be such a tax on the devout mind. Indeed, the plural (gods) did come to mean the singular (god), because of the narrative force of the world's first historian. He convinces us, by the strength of his narrative, that, indeed there can be only one god for the Chosen People: so that when "they" refers to the supernatural and divine forces, the word of course refers to a single god. So successful is the great inventor, that any other interpretation is unthinkable. That, indeed, is victory.[36]

There are entertaining, indeed enjoyable aspects of Yahweh (again, see section 6, below), but here the point is that he is not a monotheistic god. He is simply the toughest god on the block. He is the divinity of the Chosen People, but not of the whole world. Other peoples have their divinity and Yahweh hammers those folk, at least so long as his own people have been loyal to him and have kept the terms of his bargain with them, the covenant.

Within the context of the tapestry of interrelated victories that the writer-editor is establishing, it is significant how closely Yahweh resembles King David, touchstone of the Judaean dynasty. The one indisputable point about King David is that he is one hard case. But that is what he is supposed to be. He does what he has to do to preserve his power at all costs: just ask his seven brothers whom he jumped in the quest for his family's patrimony; King Saul whom he undercut as monarch; Abimelech the priest whom he gulled out of

Goliath's sword; Uriah, whom David arranged to have killed so that he could sleep with Uriah's wife Bathsheba; and the tens of thousands of dead he left strewn about Palestine as he conquered his various neighbours, aggressive and pacific alike. That is exactly how a monarch should act. He preserves his honour and his power; everything else is secondary.

Yahweh works similarly, but to the nth power. He maintains his power, powerfully. Take, for example, the time when, during the period of the judges, the Chosen People fell into apostasy. Then, as he frequently did, he used heathen people to punish his own people:

> And the anger of the Lord was hot against Israel, and he sold them into the hands of the Philistines, and into the hands of the children of Ammon.
> And that year they vexed and oppressed the children of Israel eighteen years.
>
> (Judg. 10:7–8).

Roughly four centuries after that event (by biblical chronology), King Manasseh, the king of Judah, began to worship idols and lead the people astray. Yahweh, through one of his prophets, sent this terrifying judgement: "Behold I am bringing such evil upon Jerusalem and Judah that whoever heareth of it, both his ears shall tingle" (II Kings 21:12). In a remarkable image, this judgement continues: "And I will wipe Jerusalem as a man wipeth a dish, wiping it, and turning it upside down" (II Kings 21:13).

Yahweh defended his honour, as well, by defending his people, when they were in virtue. Those who cursed Abraham's seed frequently were punished, severely.

Take the case of Eglon, a king of Moab who enslaved the Chosen People for eighteen years (Judg. 3:12–30). The people were delivered from his heavy hand by one of history's first recorded professional assassins. This was Ehud, a left-handed man who had a special two-edged dagger made, eighteen inches long, which could be hidden under his clothes. This he strapped along his right thigh. The assassin went to King Eglon, an immensely fat man, and presented him with a gift from the children of Israel, and, having given him the gift, added that he had a secret message to give him in private. Alone with the Moabite king, Ehud said, "I have a message from God unto thee." He rose, swept the dagger out from under his clothes, and thrust it into the king. Because of the obesity of the Moabite, Ehud could not pull the dagger out. This assassination was the signal for an Israelite rebellion and the killing of 10,000 Moabites. Thus was Moab subdued and Israel made triumphant.

Paradoxically, by making Yahweh such a triumphant god (and, particularly, triumphant in rhetoric over his rival gods in the land of Israel), the writer-editor made for himself a terrible problem. How was he to deal with the Babylonian exile? It was all very well to point out that King Zedekiah had broken an oath of fealty to the Babylonian King Nebuchadnezzar, but even if this were a sacred oath, sworn on Yahweh's name, the punishment was so obviously incommensurate with the sin as to be faith-shaking. To end the covenant with King David, through the extinction of the Davidic line, for one instance of false-swearing, to a foreign oppressor at that, was way out of scale. One possible response of the exiled religious leaders had to be the same as that an Auschwitz survivor once told me. (It is a story that I am sure many others have heard, in various forms.) As a very young boy in the camp, this lad noticed that the leading elders were being unusually secretive, and going off to meet several times a day. Finally, he learned what they were intensely discussing: had God broken the covenant? That question was anything but a query of doubt. It could only be asked by persons who took the covenant totally seriously and in its original meaning: a bargain made by two parties, which had to be honoured by each of them. So, in Babylon, it must have been asked. Had Yahweh broken the agreement? If so, where was the future?

The great inventor of Genesis-Kings dealt with this set of problems by bypassing it entirely. No lame excuse for Yahweh, no well-we-deserved-it. And, certainly, no entertaining the suggestion that Yahweh had broken the covenant. Instead, in the very heart of the Genesis-Kings history, he positioned a palliative device that made the ending of the Davidic dynasty irrelevant, and defined a new, and continuing covenant with the Chosen People. This he did by recreating the Temple, the smashed idol. Though they are presented as being historical (and perhaps they are), the long descriptions of the Temple in the Book of Kings are actually future-oriented. They are both architectural in nature and architectonic. If the Temple can be rebuilt, then these are verbal blueprints; and if it cannot be, that will not matter: it will be a mind-temple, its exact character agreed upon by its devotees, because its contours have been so precisely defined in words by the great inventor. In either case, physical or conceptual, the Temple will be controlled by the professional priesthood whose interests have been so carefully protected by the writer-editor.

The editor-writer had either seen the now-detritus Temple himself, or, at minimum, his father and grandfather had seen it, served in it, and so too had some of the old men who now hung about the young holy man, giving him advice, finding old pieces of text for him, and regaling him with memories of a time when the glorious priesthood had not yet been transformed into a memorable past, and into a hopeful future. As in the work of almost all historians, the research-path of the editor-writer and the path of his eventual narrative went in opposite directions. He worked with what he knew, using what was close to his own time as his base and he worked backwards to gain an understanding of how the holy seat of Yahweh had come to be in Jerusalem. Then, as most historians do, he told the story starting from the earliest point, building from there. The earliest material in the Genesis-Kings unity is a trifle fuzzy, and some of the transitions are difficult, but when it gets down to the era of the actual Temple, the details become precise, and, in a curious way, beautiful.

The genealogy of the Temple begins on Mount Sinai with Moses. During his first negotiation with Yahweh on the divine mountain, God, dwelling there, had given Moses the law. Now, another set of negotiations, this time covering forty days, resulted in another bargain. Yahweh, in return for ever-greater fealty from the Chosen People, agreed to the creation of a moveable home for himself, so that the people could have him with them always.[37] Therefore, he gave Moses a formula, the details of how to build an "ark" (Exodus 25:10–22). It was to be a throne where Yahweh could sit, flanked by two golden cherubim. "And there I will meet with thee, and I will commune with thee from above the mercy seat, from between the two cherubim ..." (Exodus 25:22). The great thing about the ark was that it was portable and could be taken anywhere, just like any of the idols of the nations that were the Hebrews' rivals for control of Palestine. The portability of the ark, however, was slightly dangerous. Yahweh was nothing if not a war god, so it was not unnatural that the people took the ark with them when they engaged in a war with the Philistines. Unhappily, the Philistines not only won the battle (30,000 Israelites were reported lost), but they captured the ark of Yahweh (I Sam. 4:1–22). That, one suspects, is where the original story ends, but the great inventor knows that the final Temple had an ark of some kind in it, so the ark cannot just disappear. Therefore, he explains that the possession of Yahweh's ark brought such ill luck to the Philistines that after seven months they returned it, along with golden sculptures, by way of fearful apology (I Sam. 5:1–6:13).

Thereafter, the Chosen People were more careful with the ark (or at least with the ark, Mark-2), for the ark that went into Solomon's Temple seems to have been basically a box that held the tablets of Moses (I Kings 8:9)). Moses had laid down very precise details for a movable tent – "the tabernacle" – that was to protect the ark, from both physical and spiritual profanation as the ancient Hebrews moved about the countryside (the details are found primarily in Exodus 25:23 – 27:21). This was nothing less than a movable Temple, with altars, lamps, places of ritual slaughter of animals. This tabernacle eventually was brought by King David to Jerusalem. Now, I think one can argue that the writer-editor or his father or some of his older colleagues had seen a later version of this tabernacle ("later," because the original fabric has been partly pillaged)[38] before the temple that was destroyed in 587. The elaboration of detail of lines, fittings and dimensions of cloths, bespeaks observation of a real entity. Crucially, so too does what he leaves out: he forgets to tell us how it all fits together. He takes it for granted that we know. That is the kind of unconscious omission only an eye-witness would make.

Therefore, we have a concentric architecture of holiness, one that is also a genealogy of legitimacy. First, there is the ark (which, incidentally, becomes so secondary to the tabernacle and the Temple, that the Bible never tells us when it finally disappears). It is surrounded by the tabernacle, and, finally, by the Temple of Solomon. This Temple is the dwelling house of Yahweh and that is not meant metaphorically. "I have surely built thee an house to dwell in, a settled place for thee to abide in for ever," are Solomon's words to Yahweh, when the Temple edifice is being dedicated (I Kings 8:13). This Temple, the dwelling place of Yahweh, placed upon a holy mountain, is of course an idol. When one sacrifices in it, one also sacrifices to it.

But it is not merely an idol. It is simultaneously a cosmic metaphor. It is nothing less than a physical encapsulation of how the world of the transcendent works, as far as the Chosen People are concerned. It carries in its stones, linens, carvings, altars, lamps, and holy objects a physical incarnation of an historical narrative that is considered by its worshippers to be a divine tale.

The point at which the great inventor of Genesis-Kings distinguishes his genius from that of all his predecessors and rivals throughout the Ancient Near East is that, though he accepts the fact (as do many of them) (1) that an idol can be both a physical manifestation and a non-corporeal, cosmic entity and (2) that the physical form of the idol can be destroyed (3), he does not permit himself to be trapped in the conventional belief that the two are inextricably bound together. Thus (4) he is able to escape from the conclusion that because enemies have destroyed our idol, our god, or gods, are powerless, and that the destruction of the physical manifestation proves that the cosmic analogue was not real.

He turns everything inside out. The Temple is gone physically, yet in stentorian voice he repeats the dimensions and details of the Temple that has so recently been turned to dust, along with the tabernacle and (if it still was inside), the ark of Yahweh as well. (See I Kings 6:1–38, 7:13–51). The description is so vivid that it glitters like the Temple's physical adornment which is accomplished in gilt and precious stones. Two points bear note. First, that despite the usual belief that the Chosen People totally eschewed figurative representation in their religious idols, the First Temple had carvings of lilies, palm trees, flowers, and fruits, as well as carved cherubim, representations of other-world figures. Secondly, Yahweh, seeing the Temple begun, promises that he will dwell among his people and not forsake them (I Kings 6:13). Yahweh makes this promise while the Temple is mostly only roughed out, and the details are a glint in Solomon's mind. He responds, in the great inventor's version, not to the finished Temple, but to the concept of it. That is what brings forth Yahweh's great promise.

The editor-writer of Genesis-Kings puts his work together with a similar faith: if we conceive of a temple, if we lay down the foundations for it, in terms of priestly discipline and ritual purity, if, above all, we believe that the Temple is a reality, *then* whether or not it actually is ever rebuilt, we have fair hope of Yahweh's responding to the conception, with the same response he gave to Solomon, at a time when the great Temple was mostly a matter of imagination. This was a gamble of cosmic proportions on the great inventor's part, for he was betting that, if necessary, words would turn out to be more lasting than stones. Northrop Frye once commented that "the supremacy of the verbal over the monumental has something about it of the supremacy of life over death."[39]

In the actual event, the great inventor did not have to find out if it was possible to run for long a religion of temple worship with a temple that was no longer on this earth, but in the minds of Yahweh's believers. Judahists, without the Temple, had to survive only until the Temple was rebuilt (not completely, but enough to permit worship) in about 520. And the conceptual Temple, the one that the great inventor had so lovingly preserved, along with the rules for worship, was brought down to earth, there to serve until the beginning of the eighth decade of the Common Era.

6

That is what one of the greatest writers and editors in the world's religious history did: put together a coherent religious program that was so strong, so convincing, that it replaced whatever had been there before. Judaism reigned. His direct, positive decisions are those that most affected the history of world religion. However, to understand the way he worked, and in particular, the grammar of invention that underlay his work, we must briefly note a few things that he did *not* do. This is a touch dangerous, because (in my view) entire battalions of biblical scholars have gotten lost behind the lines, as it were, trying to figure out what the "real" or "original" version of the various religions of the ancient Hebrews actually was. Speculating about the "real text" is an enticing activity, the more so because there is no way to check through third-party evidence the validity of most speculations, at least if they involve the period before the eighth century. A little of that sort of speculation is fun, perhaps even improving, but I keep in mind the statement of John V. Kelleher, Professor of Irish History at Harvard, who spent much of his scholarly life dealing with the Irish annals, a first-millennium (CE) text that, in its being a multiple rescencion of earlier sources, resembles the basic Hebrew scriptures. Reflecting on the annals and its antecedents, he concluded: "So extensive was the revision of historical evidence that we have, I should say, about as much chance of recovering the truth about early Christian Ireland as a historian five hundred years from now would have if he were trying to reconstruct the history of Russia in the twentieth century from the broken sets of different editions of the Soviet Encyclopedia."[40] Making the appropriate changes for time and location, that holds for the heart of the Hebrew scriptures, the books of Genesis-Kings.

So, in noting very briefly some things that the writer-editor of those books did not do, I am not attempting any great reconstruction of events before 550, but, rather, making a few small guesses about issues that may help us see how the highly compelling artistry of the great inventor, the world's first true historian, worked.

First, he does not ever fall out of his role as an historian. He is engaged in a massive invention – "worldmaking" it has been called – but he understands that in his culture the only form of worldmaking that will be accepted is one that uses old pieces and does so unembarrassedly. "Worldmaking as we know it, always starts from worlds already on hand; the making is the remaking," is a wise formulation.[41] So, the writer-editor includes in his texts, quite unembarrassedly, items that his readers and listeners immediately would recognize as being expressed in archaic language. This is especially the case with poetry, such as the Song of Deborah and Barak (Judges 5:2–31) and the Song at the Reed Sea (Exodus 15:1–19).[42] Instead of editing them into the contemporary language of his own time, he provides context. As to the substance of the ancient sections, he lets that speak for itself.

Second, the great inventor never for a moment admits to any creativity. To do so would be to guarantee instant disaccreditation. The rule of this form of religious invention is that the more inventive it is – the more creatively it rearranges the past – the more it has to be seen as totally reportorial. Also, the older in origin any report can be said to be, the better. This is just the opposite from the way that modern writing works: originality, creativity, inventiveness, insight, inspiration, authorial epiphany are all celebrated – and usually more by the author than by his readers, one must add. No admission of creativity here, on the part of the writer-editor, and he extends the same it's-just-the-news credentials to all the sources that he incorporates into his great work. The test case is the report of the alleged finding of "the Book of the Law" in the late seventh century by the high priest Hilkiah in the Temple (II Kings 22:8) while he was rummaging about preparatory to some repairs being done on the Temple. What this book actually was has never been adequately determined, but a fair guess is that it was one of the legal segments of what is now the Book of Deuteronomy. According to the story, when this book was read to King Josiah, he rent his clothes in grief, and decided on a religious reform that would drive out the various gods his people were worshipping and replace them with the worship of Yahweh (II Kings 22:11–23:27). Now, this finding of the "book of the law" is (in my view) the least convincing bit of business in the entire Genesis-Kings unity. It requires great credulity to accept that the religious elite who controlled the First Temple, and who prized the words of their god, beyond measure, would have simply

lost a central part of the Torah, the holy law, thrown it literally into the basement of the Temple. And, then, voila! it turns up just at the moment that the
king of Judah, a suddenly-enthusiastic Yahwist, is about to begin a purge of
those whose religious views are not his own. (And "purge," in the Stalinist
sense is the right word. The king's actions are usually called the "Josianic reforms," a gross euphemism: he is reported to have trashed all the religious
sites of his opponents and to have slain the priests of the other religions and
burned their bodies upon their very own altars. Reforms indeed.) A modern
historian would suggest two central possibilities here, each of which is considerably more likely than the finding of Yahweh's words in the disused junk-
room of the Temple. One is that Josiah determined on a set of actions –
namely destroying all places of worship outside of Jerusalem – that were both
religious (he was a keen Yahwist) and political in nature (he wished to
strengthen his political control over his kingdom and perhaps gain a bit more
influence in what had been the kingdom of Israel) and therefore caused to be
manufactured and then discovered a set of writings that gave divine assent to
his activities. Or that, writing roughly seventy-five years later, when the
memory of Josiah's "reforms" still was very much alive (killing priests was
nothing if not a memorable activity), the writer-editor creates on his own a
reason why Josiah was justified in acting the way he did. Now, both of these
two explanations – these two indications of potential originality on somebody's part – are much more plausible *even by the beliefs of the time* than is
the digging-in-the-basement tale: for who is going to buy the idea that Yahweh's priests had been that careless with the Torah? Yet, the great inventor of
Genesis-Kings sticks to his story without so much as a twitch of his eyelid.

Third, at no place in his great work does the author-editor claim authorship. Not in code, not in acrostic, not at all. This melds beautifully with the
great inventor's refusal to admit the possibility of creativity in Genesis-
Kings. Indeed, the conjoining resembles the way a well-made weld works in
the physical world: the resulting joining is physically stronger than either of
its two constituent elements. By refusing to take credit, the author-editor increases the air of authenticity of his work. Taking personal credit for one's
editing or writing was something no real religious historian would do: prophets perhaps, but not even all of them.

Fourth, as mentioned in Section Five, the editor-writer was not at all afraid
of redundancies and repetitions. If he had taken a degree course, say a Master's of Fine Writing, he would have failed it, because he absolutely refused
to clear doublets out of his text. Repetition of minor elements, however, establishes consistency and believability; and repetition of major elements is
the way in his culture that one changes the original meaning of an item. One
cannot abandon the major motifs of the scriptures, for they are historical artifacts and the author is an historian. But items such as the Exodus, the cove-

nant, the nature of kingship, the reasons for blood sacrifice, the concept of redemption, and many more, can be redefined by repetition in new contexts, and by repetition with just a slight change in their meaning each time. This is not so prevalent in the Genesis-Kings unity, but one does note such things as the changing of the meaning of the term "Israel" (from a designation of a unified nation to an appellation for the northern kingdom, to a term for the victorious kingdom of Judah which acquires cultural hegemony over the patrimony of what was once that of the kingdom of Israel). Where the trick is to become enlarged and much more important is later, in the Christian scriptures and the Rabbinic literature, where the meanings of the Judahist writings are transformed (often totally reversed) and appropriated, all under the guise of respectful repetition.

Fifth, and again as mentioned in Section Five, the editor-writer does not clear out those contradictions in his text which are merely epidermal. He is no fool. Indeed, anyone reading him has to recognize how alert and sophisticated he is. Contradictions are left in because he, as an historian, does not like destroying evidence, and, besides, multiple reports yield an aura of authenticity. This means that there are occasionally inconveniences. One can make a list of these, ranking from the three incompatible versions of the Ten Commandments (compare Exodus 20:3–17; Exod. 34:10–27; and Deut. 5:7–21), to the two Creation stories, and two different versions of the Flood, and so on and on. Almost all of these contradictions (or "doublings") occur in stories that deal with the Hebrews' equivalent of epic-history, that is before the time of King David. In the late nineteenth and early twentieth centuries, when there were great public debates between the literalist interpreters of the Hebrew scriptures and their opponents who wished to "disprove" the scriptures, these items were matters of a debate that was constituted in equal parts of vitriol and ingenuity. Both sides missed the point that the contradictions do not matter at all. If they did, the editor-writer would have removed them. In fact, the contradictions, far from being debilitating flaws, have a positive purpose. They are the equivalent of the yellow caution flag on a road-racing track. They say to the reader, slow down, things are a bit rough here and you should not proceed as you would on a smooth run.

This leads to a sixth aspect of the great inventor's approach: although he is respectful of his entire text, he does not himself place equal degrees of reliance on the historical character of each section. Here a modern comparison is in order. Assume that you are writing a biography of an individual (this is the comparison most apt, since Genesis-Kings is a biography of Yahweh drawn in the only way possible, through indirect sources).[43] And assume that you are only going to include things that you believe probably occurred (a reasonable rule, albeit an unfashionable one, given the way late twentieth-century biography, especially literary biography, is often written). However, of the events that you collect from archives, from early books, and from interviewing friends of the subject, some of these you believe certainly happened – they had a virtually 100 percent probability of having occurred – whereas others are likely, but not certain (say, a 75 percent probability), and others probably happened, but have a probability of having occurred just slightly more than their not having occurred (say, a 51 percent probability). If you are a conscientious historian, you will find an unobtrusive way of communicating to your reader the varying levels of probability behind your statements of events. That is what the great inventor does, and in three ways. One of these, as just mentioned, is to include contradictions in those reports that are less-probably accurate than those that are not. (He still only reports events as happening that he believes actually occurred; it is levels of confidence that he is marking for the reader or listener.) Further, when he is not entirely sure of the background or context of an event, he telescopes the time frame with which the event is surrounded. This mostly occurs in the pre-Davidic material, wherein at times one finds several hundred years being tossed off quickly, often by the device of suggesting that in ancient times, people lived very long lives, sometimes centuries. This contrasts sharply with the genealogical precision the editor-writer attempts in periods and on topics where he is confident. Moreover, and most importantly, he has another coded way of letting one know when he is a little uneasy about the probability-levels. This is particularly clear when he deals with the patriarchal narratives,[44] as compared to later material, and I think he is communicating his lower level of confidence quite unconsciously. To get this point, forget the fragmenting mentality of most modern biblical scholarship and assume again that you are a modern biographer, or a diplomatic historian, or a novelist, or a documentary scriptwriter. (That so few biblical historians have had these abilities is one major reason that biblical scholarship is so often out of contact with the biblical story.) In composing the historical and artistic unity that is your final product, you will, again, use only material that you think is probably correct. Now, unless you have a rare, almost unprecedented degree of self-discipline, I promise you the following will happen: the material in which you have the highest confidence – dull things, such as the date of birth of important players in your story – will be reported quickly, without much fervour, for your reader will need little convincing about them. But items that are only just-barely probable in your judgement, and are the very sort of events that your reader is most apt to question, those are the items that will draw forth your best writing. Your evocative powers will be sharpest there, and what cannot be established by mere statistical probability will be sold by rhetorical intensity. So, a handy rule-of-thumb runs through the Genesis-Kings unity, namely that a gradient prevails: the more energy and detail and artistic genius is found in a given story, the less the editor-writer had faith in it; and the more matter-of-fact, dull, the sections are, the more he trusted his source material.[45] And, I think, the editor-writer respects his audience a good deal, and assumes that they will pick this up.

Seventh, despite the high seriousness of his project, the editor-writer does not remain stolidly poe-faced, and this adds immensely to his creditability. P.J. O'Rourke, who is not well-known as a biblical scholar, noted in *Give War a Chance* (1992) that "seriousness is also the only practical tone to take when lying. The phrase 'to lie with a straight face' is prolix. All lies are told with a straight face. It's truth that's said with a dismissive giggle."[46] He has a small point there. The quite frequent use of irony, puns, and the occasional burlesque, that are the keys to the obverse side of Yahweh's personality – the heavy side is obvious enough and already has been remarked upon – are mostly lost in our own time, in the very success of the best English language translation's turning the ironic into the epic. In any case, humour changes greatly over time (tragedy is always the same; comedy never) so that even when the Hebrew puns (intentional or unintentional) are defined, they often seem to us to have little point. Here, I have no intention of explaining the nature of biblical humour (or any other humour for that matter; the one lesson that Sigmund Freud's attempt to explain jokes has left behind is that the explanation of humour is frequently the proximate cause of acute depression). Yet there are the few moments that still speak to us and indicate that there were many more jokes, ironies, sarcastic puns that the early listeners and readers understood. For instance, within the Exodus story, the figure of Pharaoh is made into a figure of farce. Imagine him on stage: one moment he refuses to let the Chosen People leave his kingdom, the next moment a load of excrement lands on his head (the scriptures may say frogs or whatever, but the howling audience knows what is meant), until he says, "yes, go ," and then he changes his mind, and then another load buries him. He is made into a figure that would have been right at home in the broader works of a Roman comic playwright, such as Plautus. The story of the Exodus is immensely serious, but Yahweh's dumping all over the ridiculous Pharaoh is part of the deliverance from slavery: freedom from Egyptian bondage is contingent not only upon getting away from Egypt physically, but from its prestige. Humour liberates. Harold Bloom argues that Yahweh in the "original" version of the Y source was a fabulous imp, given to puns (such as the Y creation story implies, with *adam*, the first man, being a play upon *adamah*, the word for mud) and also attracted to instances of deception, as was Shakespeare: Jacob and Esau come to mind immediately. And, when not infuriated about something, Yahweh is given to acting according to a wryness of vision, and with an ironic tone.[47] Most, but not all of the humour, or the dismissive giggle, in the Hebrew scriptures stems from the texts that most scholars associate with Y the Yahwist. I think Bloom (and, indeed, most biblical scholars) are correct in seeing this material as consistently the strongest, most readable in the Hebrew scriptures, and that judgement holds whether one thinks the original matter stemmed from the court of King Solomon or was put on parchment for the first time during the Babylonian exile. In either case, the great editor-writer used it well.[48] His allegiance to the kingdom of Judah and to its Yahwist convictions meant that for purely ideological reasons he would in any case have employed the Yahwist material. Our bonus is its literary quality, including its occasional light moments. (One would happily utter the solipsism, "Thank God for Yahweh," save that one recalls the public reaction to a parallel solecism: in 1932, when the World Eucharistic Congress was held in Dublin, a massive banner stretched across O'Connell Street – "God bless the Trinity.")

Eighth, although the great inventor's historical narrative can stand a goodly number of minor internal contradictions, and, indeed actually is strengthened by them, there are some things that cannot be permitted, inside the text. And yet they happened historically. In these instances, the writer-editor's strategy is (a) to deny the obvious and (b) otherwise to project it outward, onto some group other than the Chosen People. Two matters are especially fraught, namely the Chosen People's having believed for much of their history in multiple gods (that is, in gods in addition to Yahweh) and the issue of human sacrifice as part of their religion. We must always remember when reading the Genesis-Kings unity, that it is an historical narrative whose ideological cement is the belief in centralism. Judah is the politically centralized kingdom that overcomes the fragmentation of Israel; and Judah's god, Yahweh, is a centralized god: there is only one god for Judah. So successful is the writer-editor in taking us along the historical path that deals with these congruent centralisms, that we forget that history always has paths not taken. Neither Yahweh nor Judah had to become dominant. Yet, so persuasive is the historical rhetoric of the writer-editor that we easily lose sight of the possibility that Yahweh might not have ended up victorious, for there were many other gods that the Chosen People worshipped at various moments in their history. Indeed, so persuasive has the great inventor been that one finds modern scholars using the term "syncretism" to describe moments of polytheism in the Chosen People's history, a loaded term that assumes the dominance of Yahweh and the mere adulteration of the superior faith in Yahweh by incremental beliefs. Very loaded. There are endless (but quite fascinating) arguments among modern biblical scholars about whether or not Yahweh was ever a subordinate deity to El; about whether Yahweh had a consort in the person of the goddess Asherah; about Baal, whose worship was sponsored by Ahab, king of Israel and who, according to the editor-writer, went head-to-head with Yahweh in a test of strength (I Kings 18:17–40). The writer-editor knows of these and of several other gods that the Chosen People worshipped at one time or another, but he does not permit the unthinkable thought: that Yahweh and Judah could have lost and that multiple gods could have prevailed. He is not yet a monotheist, but his god, Yahweh, is regnant for the righteous and every time a god other than Yahweh is mentioned in any direct way, the other god is identified as a false god for the Chosen People, its worship defined as religious deviation, and its votaries punished; often they are put to the sword (as in the Josianic "reforms").[49]

Human sacrifice was a topic that also was too hot for the writer-editor to handle. He had to project it out of the realm of possibility as far as his readers were concerned. Here the logic of his own sacrificial system, and of the more ancient of the tales that he incorporated into his text, caused potential trouble. Specifically, the problem is that the covenant with Yahweh, as defined under the priestly system of Temple worship that the editor-writer so convincingly chronicles, requires that blood be spilled. The covenant has to be both regularly and frequently reaffirmed by the ritual slaughter of various of the higher species. It is a blood covenant. In an historiographic survey of the scholarly literature on the Hebrew scriptures, Horace D. Hummel noted in 1966 that "it is particularly striking that so little further exploration has been made into the nature and meaning of sacrifice. The relative neglect of this area is all the more surprising because of the intense interest in other areas of Israel's cult" (and that observation remains true to this day).[50] The literature remains thin, but the avoidance of the topic should not surprise anyone. The killing of live things to propitiate a deity offends modern sensibilities, and we would like to ignore the details, if possible, or at least allegorize them. The scriptures, though, will not let us blur the focus. They provide very precise instructions, filling several biblical chapters, on how to dispatch ritually and to dismember liturgically various living things. The opening of the Book of Leviticus serves as a fair example. Five species from the animal kingdom are defined as acceptable for ritual slaughter: castrated bovines (I suspect that bullocks and oxen were employed by the Israelites because bulls were votive objects in ancient Egypt), sheep, goats, turtledoves, and pigeons. This is the instruction for killing a sheep or goat:

> And if his offering be of the flocks, namely, of the sheep, or of the goats, for a burnt-sacrifice; he shall bring it a male without blemish.
>
> And he shall kill it on the side of the altar northward before the Lord: and the priests, Aaron's sons, shall sprinkle his blood round about upon the altar.
>
> And he shall cut it into his pieces, with his head and his fat: and the priest shall lay them in order on the wood that is on the fire which is upon the altar:
>
> But he shall wash the inwards and the legs with water: and the priest shall bring it all, and burn it upon the altar; it is a burnt-sacrifice, an offering made by fire, of a sweet savour unto the Lord. (Lev. 1:10–13)

One could multiply such details, but the point is clear: the children of Israel were quite serious about ritual killing of at least five species.

A natural question arises – was there a sixth sacrificial species – humankind? That making human sacrifices – albeit only partial ones – was close to the ancient Hebrews' sense of religious duty, is found in the fact that they practiced circumcision. The Abraham story makes circumcision part of the primal covenant. "This is my covenant, which ye shall keep, between me and you and thy seed after thee; Every man child among you shall be circumcised" (Gen. 17:10). "And the uncircumcised man whose flesh of his foreskin is not circumcised, that soul shall be cut off from his people; he hath broken my covenant" (Gen. 17:14). This is not ambiguous. Male genital mutilation is part of the blood-spilling required by the covenant. One does not need to reach any of the farther shores of psychoanalysis to note that it is not a finger or a toe being partially removed. This is about mutilating, and thereby endangering, and thereby sacrificing the implement that permits the perpetuation of the Chosen People. It is a symbolic death yielded up to Yahweh.

The logic here cuts uncomfortably close and the writer-editor has to deflect his immediate audience of readers and listeners from something that they know, but do not want to know, that there are tales of some of the Chosen People having sacrificed their children, indeed, their first-born males. Here, Frank Kermode's observation is germane, that, although the primary function of narrative, especially in the Bible, is explanatory and persuasive, it also has a hidden function: to generate secrecy.[51] Possibly – just possibly – one of the oldest tales in the Genesis-Kings unity, the Abraham and Isaac story, is such an instance of skilfully generated secrecy. Abraham is instructed by God.

> And he said, Take now thy son, thine only son Isaac, whom thou lovest, and get thee into the land of Moriah; and offer him there for a burnt-offering upon one of the mountains which I will tell thee of. (Gen. 22:2)

He obeys:

> And Abraham rose up early in the morning, and saddled his ass, and took two of his young men with him, and Isaac his son, and clave the wood for the burnt-offering, and rose up, and went unto the place of which God had told him. (Gen. 22:3)

Isaac, realizing that there is no lamb, asks his father about it. He is told that God will provide the lamb for the burnt offering. When they come to the holy place:

> Abraham built an altar there, and laid the wood in order, and bound Isaac his son, and laid him on the altar upon the wood.
> And Abraham stretched forth his hand, and took the knife to slay his son.
> (Gen. 22:9–10)

Only at the last moment, when Abraham is about to kill his son, does an angel of God call out and stop the proceedings. The Lord is pleased, "For now I know that thou fearest God seeing thou hast not withheld thy son, thine only son from me" (Gen. 22:12). The Lord provides a ram for the slaughter, caught by its horns in a nearby thicket.

Now, in practical terms this story sets an immensely important precedent. Higher mammals can be substituted for human beings in the blood sacrifice that is required to maintain the covenant with the Almighty. But the secrecy of this apparently open and dramatic tale is all-enshrouding. It diverts us from asking the obvious question: why was it necessary for an ovine to take the place of a human being in this precedent-setting tale? How many Isaacs had been slaughtered by how many Abrahams before the new precedent stopped the old practice? Our great inventor is good: very few ask what is the real purpose of the new practice: is it not to stop an old one?[52]

The Exodus story raises the same problem. The final breaking of the Egyptians comes with the "tenth judgement," when the first-born males of all species, including humans, were to die, unless they were of a household in which the men were circumcised and in which everyone ate unleavened bread. Thus occurred the first Passover, for the angel of death passed over the children of Israel and visited the Egyptians. A very revealing commentary on this event occurs in the midst of the text. The Lord tells Moses that when the Chosen People come to the Promised Land, they must set apart to him every first born, of lamb, ass and other beasts. These either had to be sacrificed or "redeemed" through propitiatory offerings to the Almighty. "If thou wilt not redeem it, then thou shalt break his neck" is the rule (Exodus 13:13b). Then comes the crucial part: "and all the firstborn of man among thy children shalt thou redeem" (Exod. 13:13c). Given how biblical parallelism works, there is an unstated, but clear final clause, one that balances the details of what one should do with an unredeemed beast – one should break the neck of the first-born human male, just as one would a beast, unless a sacrificial redemption has been achieved. The annual celebration of the Passover is the redemption that obviates the need for child sacrifice (Exod. 13:1–16). This is unambiguous. So too is a later explanation why child sacrifice now can be stopped: although "all the first born are mine," says the Lord (Num. 3:13), he will not insist on the sacrifice because "I have taken the Levites among the children of Israel instead of all the firstborn" (Num. 3:12). The key here is simple. In both the explanation of the meaning of the Passover and in the explanation of the special status of the Levites ("therefore the Levites shall be mine," Num. 3:12), the background presumption – the assumption without which neither the story of the Passover nor the legitimation of the Levite priesthood makes sense – is that child sacrifice is a normal procedure. Only exceptional devotion by the Chosen People renders the requirement for child sacrifice nugatory.

Most societies rely on formal laws (and no ancient society was more law-conscious than were the Chosen People). Laws, both formal and customary, dealt with things the Chosen People were worried about, and the scriptures show that the Hebrews were very frightened of the idea of child sacrifice and there are repeated prohibitions against it. This abhorred practice was associated with the gods of other nations. The king of Moab, for example, when the Israelites pressed him hard in battle, offered up his eldest son as a burnt sacrifice (II Kings 3:27). When the Bible refers to human sacrifice, it usually mentions a child as the burnt offering; these sacrifices probably involved ritual killing and burning in a manner similar to the Israelites' procedures for their five sacrificial species. The biblical descriptions of child sacrifice sometimes mention a specific alien deity to whom the offering is made: Molech (Lev. 18:21; 20:2–4) and Baal (Jer. 19:5), although the actual deity is sometimes unnamed (Deut. 12:31; Isa. 57:5). The fascinating characteristic of these denunciations of child sacrifice is that the practice is not denounced because it is intrinsically evil. There is no talk of the sanctity of human life, nor in these instances is it even implied. Child sacrifice is wrong because it is associated with the worship of false gods. Note incidentally, this particular form of idolatry wastes Abraham's seed by cutting the lines of genealogical descent. Therefore it wounds and diminishes the corporate body that is the Chosen People.

That is the inventor's genius. He has taken a practice which was very much thinkable – indeed, was part of the logic of covenantal sacrifice and was the terrifying palimpsest of the heart of the founding myth of the people, the Abraham-Isaac story – and has made it unthinkable for the Chosen People. It can only be conceived of as part of a religious system – Baal, Molech – that is external to the religion of Yahweh.[53]

Ninth, although in the history that he was establishing, the editor-writer of Genesis-Kings has an unmistakeable agenda, he nevertheless did not think of himself as writing scripture. If we miss this simple point, we miss everything. "Scripture" in the sense that the word is now used did not exist, and arguably, did not exist in the full sense of the term until well into the second century CE, either in the Jewish or the Christian traditions. Instead, in the Babylonian exile, there were a wide variety of texts, stories, and codes of conduct, each of which had some degree of authority. But "canonical" authority – the hallmark that said this is real sterling, the real god-given writings – was a concept not yet extant. And that stamp, coming much later than the creation of the actual works involved, cannot be viewed as being prior to the invention of the texts (at least not if one accepts the historian's fundamental dictum, that time's arrow flies only forward).

Thus, the summary of how people of the time must have read the Book of Samuel put forward by Baruch Halpern, one of the relatively few biblical scholars to understand how narrative history actually works, is germane. Ancient audiences, he suggests, did not read or listen confessionally: "Hearing the stories in their original settings, they sometimes recognized that the stories mixed literal with less literal claims. For the storyteller, for the historian, it probably was not relevant whether they understood just what was romance: the fiction, the narrative as a whole, communicated the author's point."[54] That the first real historian in world history later had his text turned into sacred writ – indeed, many subsequently declared it to be the word of God – is not an honour he sought. Nor, one suspects, would he have understood it. He knew that Yahweh was perfect, but that his own text was imperfect. He knew that the only inerrantly divine word was that which Yahweh gave to a special messenger, face to face, and he had himself seen such messages in old forms, in tattered papyri, but never directly. Totally beyond his conception would have been the fact that his Genesis-Kings invention was to become, several centuries later, the plinth on which two great derivative religions, Christianity and Judaism, were based. That the set of scrolls he produced became the founding documents of the Judahist faith – the celebration of the hegemony of Judah and of its holy site, Jerusalem – would have been reward enough.

7

The arguments here are extremely simple. (1) The first nine books of the Hebrew Bible (using the Jewish, not the Christian arrangement of the scriptures, and ignoring the early medieval division of both Samuel and Kings into double volumes), are a unified invention. (2) The form of the great invention was historical writing. Mostly, its formation involved using pieces that were already available, but had not previously been fully integrated into an integral unit. (3) This unified composition, in its final form, was the product of a single great mind (however much help he may have received from his colleagues), a combination of great editor and great writer. This mind has been personified in this chapter to avoid the dessication that too often drains the élan vitale from discussion of one of the world's most lively texts. Of course, the writer-editor I have posited is a model, an heuristic construction, of someone (or some group of people acting as a single mind) whom we can never know directly. However, I would argue that *if*, as I have argued, the Genesis-Kings text is a unity, indeed the primary unity of the Hebrew scriptures, and *if* one accepts that the final portions of that unity (which are stylistically integrated with what comes before, and are not just a late add-on), contain a knowledge of the destruction of Solomon's Temple and of the Babylonian exile, *then* it is clear that Genesis-Kings *in the form that we at present possess it*, must be seen as an invention – a mixture of collecting and editing old material, adding new, tossing out some items and integrating all the material that was kept – and an invention that takes place between the beginning of the

Babylonian exile and before the return to the Holy Land: in other words, the middle years of the sixth century before the Common Era. This does not mean that all the investigations and speculations about earlier sources ("Y," "E," "D" and so on) and about their possible dating and place of provenance are useless, but merely that they are irrelevant to the point at hand: the great moment when they were all put together in a single entity – the Genesis-Kings unity. It is from that moment that we begin the long cultural genealogy that continues to the present day, the moment when Judahism is formulated in a clear and permanent fashion. It is that great unitary text, Genesis-Kings, upon which both Christianity and modern Judaism eventually are built, and it is a text that, unlike those of classical Greece and Rome, was never lost, and was never separated from the cultural consciousness of western and western-derived civilization. So, what more natural – and more in tune with the primary evidence – than to suggest that it was a product of a single consciousness? Yes, an editorial committee perhaps could have done the same job, in their collective mourning near the waters of Babylon. Yet, why posit many minds-working-as-one, when a single figure is both more economical (remember Ockham's Razor) and ultimately more convincing?

Those three points can easily stand separate from the following – "4" –, and the reader may wish to accept one, two, and three, without accepting "four," for it concerns motive. Consider that this great act of historical writing (which later generations turned into a sacred text) was accomplished during the Babylonian exile, and probably completed about 550 BCE. The completion date is not so important (a decade earlier or later would not make any difference to the argument), but the stimulus-date, the moment when such an invention became necessary, is. It was 587 when the Babylonians levelled the great Temple of Solomon and forcibly removed from Jerusalem the remainder of Judah's religious elite. Point (4) is pivotal, because it allows us to escape from the one methodological folly that seems virtually to be pandemic in the forms of biblical scholarship that focus only on the text, upon philological arguments, upon literary fragments, and consequently upon the transformation and transpositions of sub-genres of biblical forms; namely that the various observed transformational processes (which, in terms of historical methodology, are effects), are seen to be autonomous, operating by their own momentum (which means that they are also a cause). That won't do. Effects have to be explained by reference to causes that are external to those effects. Cause and effect can never be the same. The strength of my suggestion of the Genesis-Kings unity having been established during the middle years of the sixth century, is that (a) there is a plausible (I would argue highly probable) cause-and-effect relationship between the effect (the invention of the text) and the cause: the destruction of the Temple and the Babylonian exile which provided the exiled religious elite with the choice of either creating a new religious system or going extinct; and (b) these items of cause-and-effect are independent of each other in terms of definition and operationality. No circularity here; and (c) unlike most apparently independent causes of biblical developments, the destruction and associated deportations are well documented in non-biblical sources. Therefore, we have that rarest of occurrences in biblical history, namely, an independently-attested cause for a biblically-evidenced effect. And the effect is consonant with the cause.

·3·

Returning with Yahweh to Jerusalem

I

IN 538 BCE A MIRACLE HAPPENED, AT LEAST FROM THE VIEWPOINT OF
the exiled Yahwist elite in Babylon. They, and all the other members of the
Judaean diaspora were permitted, indeed encouraged, to return to Jerusalem.
This followed upon the decade-long campaign of Cyrus, King of Persia,
against a series of middle eastern enemies which concluded with his conquest
of Babylon in 539/538. Thus, not only Babylon, but Palestine was within the
Persian empire and was destined to stay there for more than two centuries.
These two centuries were crucial for the establishment of Judaism as the
dominant religion of south-central Palestine and for the further evolution of
that religion and its scriptures.

The religious elite that returned from Babylon in 538 was not the same as
the one that had left in 587. A generation of leaders had died and new ones
had emerged. The new set of leaders preserved not only the historical memory of the pre-exilic past, but a shared experience of Babylonian living. Undoubtedly they picked up some attitudes and ideas from their imperial
keepers, although precisely what these may have been is a matter of such
deep scholarly dispute as to be indeterminate. Clearly, however, as an exiled
elite, they had become increasingly homogenized in viewpoint (they were all
extremely keen Yahwists), and were committed to imposing their view of the
sacred upon the holy city and its votive sites. One is not being flippant in suggesting that they hoped to be the religious equivalent of a Special Forces unit,
keenly motivated and well-prepared to seize religious power.

What did they carry in their kitbags? The key elements were the several
Hebrew religious texts that had been collected, and edited, and amplified during the Babylonian captivity. These items were not yet scripture in the modern sense of the term, but already they carried authority in two senses: in
terms of quality and comprehensiveness they were the best versions available
of the teachings that could be ascribed to the ancient founders of the Judahist
faith and, second, they were authoritative because the band of returnees from

Babylon paid them the deepest respect. They were, in effect, a flag, one behind which the Babylonian returnees could unite.

The texts which came back to Jerusalem from Babylon included, first and most importantly, the Genesis-Kings unity that the great editor-writer had invented. This was the Judahists' Magna Carta, Bill of Rights, Declaration of Independence and Constitution, all wrapped into one: a founding document against which all later documents in their tradition would be metered. (Indeed, not only would the Judahist faith measure its subsequent documents against the primary unit of Genesis-Kings, but so too would its later offshoots, Christianity and Rabbinic Judaism.) Second, and closely related to the priestly concerns of the Babylonian exiles, was a version of what is today called the Psalms. Some of these purported to be quite old (and in their archaic language and early ideology, some clearly were). Others were more recent. The necessity of a hymn book is obvious; and in ascribing as many of the songs of praise as possible, even the recent ones, to King David, the compilers of the hymnal were only following the basic rule of scriptural invention: always ascribe as much as possible to earlier figures; older is better, creativity cannot be admitted. Third, large portions of the Major Prophets were part of the kitbag of the returning exiles. The first portion of Isaiah (chapters 1–39; later, additional sections would be attached to this basic document, but that was in the future); the book of the prophet Jeremiah probably was included. The Jeremiah scroll, a vivid carousel of curses and metaphors rarely equalled in the other prophetic books, was especially useful to the Babylonian exiles because the prophet denounced the Judaeans who dwelled in Egypt and he called down upon them sword, famine and pestilence (see Jer. 44:13–14). The third major volume of prophecy, the post-exilic Book of Ezekiel, almost certainly was brought back home, though whether in its present form is debatable. Fourth, a handful of "Minor Prophets" were included. Certainly Amos, Hosea, and Micah were part of the set, as their reference point was more than 100 years before the Babylonian captivity. Others, however, are hard to guess, for some of the minor prophets – especially Jonah and Joel and Obadiah – have no external references to permit anything but the most speculative suggestions concerning dating. Perhaps the Book of Lamentations also was included.[1]

This was a big kitbag. All of the items were compatible with the program to make the worship of Yahweh the only religion in Jerusalem and the priestly heirs of the Kingdom of Judah the heads of that religion. Undoubtedly, the returning exiles also brought with them chunks of tradition and certain texts which are now lost. The items that are referred to so casually in the Genesis-Kings history, items such as the Book of Jasher, and the Chronicles of the Kings of Judah and the Chronicles of the Kings of Israel, may still have existed and have been returned to Jerusalem. There have to have been both religious writings and collections of real tales that were not included in the written scriptures. And, in proto-form, there probably were tales, and historical memoirs that later were worked into biblical form, items such as the Book of Ruth, and some of the sayings that later became the full Book of Proverbs and are used, in his own way, by the writer of the Book of Qoholeth (Ecclesiastes). But, above all, the exiles who returned from Babylon had their blueprint for the future, which was the history of the Chosen People, as found in the newly-invented great unity of Genesis through Kings.

When the returning Babylonian exiles met the future, it must have been an enormous disappointment. Jerusalem was a poor city set in a poorer periphery. Its walls were crumbling, many of the former houses still were uncleared piles of rubble, and the locals were apathetic at best, given to worshipping Yahweh in tandem with other gods, at worst. The flood of exiled Judaeans from the diaspora did not materialize. Some, yes, but not the stream of devout Yahwists that had been assumed.

This situation transformed the returned exiles from being a self-confident religious commando unit, into a bunch of stragglers who, in victory, looked as if they had been defeated. The warrant of how dispirited the returning exiles became was that the real energy for rebuilding the Temple came from the Persian King. He was no enthusiast of the Judahist religion, but Persian policy was to conciliate its conquered peoples by encouraging them to worship their local deities. So it was King Cyrus who in 538 ordered that the house of Yahweh, "in Jerusalem, which is in Judah" be rebuilt (II Chron. 36:23; also Ezra 1:2–4, and Ezra 6:3–5). Various gold and silver vessels from Solomon's Temple, which had been pillaged by the Babylonians, were to be returned to Jerusalem. Cyrus put a senior official in charge of the rebuilding and the implication was that some, perhaps most, of the expenses were to be borne by the Persian treasury. This Persian official, a Babylonian Jew, Sheshbazzar, saw to it that the foundations of the Temple were laid, but there the building stopped (Ezra 5:16).

What was missing was a great surge of enthusiasm from throughout the diaspora, and from the Judaean indigene who had not been deported. Given the chance to rebuild Solomon's Temple, the followers of Yahweh decided that they had better things to do. Only after Darius became king of the Persians in 521, did the Persian authorities turn their attention again to the Temple. This time, their interests coincided with the preachments of two prophets who scolded the Chosen People so successfully that they finally got to work. The more effective of these prophets was Haggai, who in the year 520 directed an unusually eloquent lecture to the governor of Judah (one Zerubbabel) and to the high priest, a man named Joshua. Though a drought was upon the land, and though the people of Judah said that "the time is not come, the time that the Lord's house should be built" (Hagg. 1:2), he chided the leaders into action, and both leaders and people began again to work on the Temple. Writing (or speaking) only a few months later, Haggai's contemporary, the prophet Zechariah, noted that Zerubbabel had already begun work on the Temple and prophesied that "his hands shall also finish it" (Zech. 4:9). Significantly, Zechariah prophesied within the context of an elaborate ecclesiological vision in which the house of Judah was mightily praised: "for the Lord of hosts hath visited his flock the house of Judah, and hath made them as his goodly horse in the battle" (Zech. 10:3).

Judahism prevailed, certainly, but the rebuilt Temple must have been a great disappointment. Although some of the serving vessels, made of precious metals, were recovered from Solomon's Temple, this Second Temple certainly did not have the ark of the covenant, the single most venerated artifact of pre-exilic Yahwism. Within months of Haggai's successful exhortation, the Temple was a satisfactory place of worship, but improvements undoubtedly continued, generation after generation, until this second Temple was replaced by Herod's massive Temple in the first century BCE. (Confusingly, the era of Zerubbabel's and of Herod's Temples are conventionally referred to as comprising the "Second Temple Period.") Because Herod razed most of the previous structure, we shall never directly know how Zerubbabel's Temple was constructed.[2] However, there is some chance that present-day archaeological diggings at Mount Gerizim, where the Samaritans constructed a duplicate (and rival) version of that Temple, will yield information on the configuration of the structure in Jerusalem, upon which it was modelled.[3]

However unimpressive the newly rebuilt Second Temple may have been, it was unambiguously identified as being under the control of the house of Judah. And, here, a brilliant dialectic switch was made. Because there was no longer a king of Judah, a new figure had to be interposed, a spiritual equivalent of the Davidic monarch. The office of "high priest," something totally new to the followers of Yahweh, was created. Previously, the king (David's line especially) had been a sacralized figure, for Yahweh had made a covenant directly with King David. Now, with the monarchy gone and with civic authority held by Persian conquerors, the head of the nation of Judah and the head of the Judahist religion became one and the same person, the high priest.[4] The Book of Zechariah contains a hymn of praise to the first of these high priests, Joshua – "Behold the man whose name is the Branch; and he shall grow out of his place and he shall build the temple of the Lord" (Zech. 6:12). Joshua's enthronement in the year 520 presumably marks the creation of the office that was to be pivotal in the subsequent history of Judahism, and of Christianity.[5]

So, in a general way, arrangements in Jerusalem had by, say, the year 515, taken a form the great writer-editor of Genesis-Kings would have approved:

the Temple had been rebuilt sufficiently to permit public worship, the religion of Yahweh prevailed; and the kingdom of Judah (though now only a spiritual kingdom) was recognized as the sole heir of the ancient Israelites; power over the Judahist religion was in the hands of priestly professionals, whose powers were greater than those of any previous priests, since there no longer was an intermeddling monarchy in existence. But yet, though the parts were all there, the machine was not working very well.

One finds strong suggestions of this in the short prophetic message of the Book of Malachi. The priests were lazy and unenthusiastic (Mal. 1:6–14). Their moral laxness set an example that the people were all too ready to follow (Mal. 2:8–9). Intermarriage with non-Yahwists was common among the children of Judah (Mal. 2:11). In sum, the people of Jerusalem and its environs were not ready to accept the religion of Yahweh as the only possible faith for themselves, and the priestly caste – many of whom must have come from the local survivors, rather than from the Babylonian elite – was sloppy, indifferent, and self-indulgent. What had seemed such a clear task to the Babylonian exiles of the time of the great editor-writer, was not anything near so crystalline in reality. The Chosen People were not very keen on Yahweh, alas.

What was required was another infusion of enthusiasm from the Babylonian elite, and it came in the form of two men who combined the abilities of colonial administrators and religious leaders, Ezra and Nehemiah. Although, inevitably, a certain amount of hagiographic lint clings to these two figures,[6] they were authentic persons. Their work is reported as being sequential, but it is sequential in the classic biblical form: their careers form parallels. Both Ezra and Nehemiah were keen Judahists who were descendants of the Babylonian exiles. Each of them had some entré into the Persian imperial administration and first, Ezra, and then Nehemiah, was sent to Jerusalem, there to sort out a religious situation that was sliding into chaos. Each was given official approval for his actions and a significant degree of financial resources from the imperial government. The book of Ezra-Nehemiah (written within a century of their activities being completed) is quite clear on their achievements, and the subsequent history of Judaism confirms their effectiveness.

Nehemiah rebuilt the ruined walls of Jerusalem and this in the face of considerable ridicule by some of the local inhabitants (Neh. chs 3–6). This was symbolically pivotal, for the completion of the wall around the holy city was a counterpart to the earlier rebuilding of the Temple. Built on a hill, the Temple was now ringed about by secure walls. Secondly, the priesthood was purged. Some, perhaps most, of the priests in Jerusalem "had not separated themselves from the people of the lands" (Ezra 9:1), which is to say that they had not accepted the central demand of the Judahist faith, namely that Yahweh be their only god. Instead, they mixed Yahweh-worship with that of other gods indigenous to the peoples of Palestine. This frequently (perhaps generally) had been the case from the earliest days of ancient Israel (witness the frequent pogroms reported in Genesis-Kings against backsliding Hebrews who worshipped alien gods), and it had to be stopped, once and forever. Third, the Chosen People themselves (not merely their priests) were not given to following Yahweh as their sole deity. This is reported both directly (e.g. Ezra 9:1) and indirectly, as implied by the concern of Ezra and Nehemiah that so many of the people had married "strange wives," a term for mixed marriages with non-Judahists. Even the sons of priests had taken these strange wives (Ezra 10:18). So one of Ezra's greatest achievements was to have the men who believed in Yahweh as the sole deity dismiss their wives and the children of those wives (Ezra 10:10–44). From now on, ethno-religious purity was to be maintained. To conclude his work, Nehemiah had the leaders of the priests and Levites sign a "covenant," to signify their adherence to the stringent Judahist rules (Neh. 10:1–29). The Temple was ritually cleansed (Neh. 13:4–5) and the hierarchy of the Judahist priesthood re-sacralized (Neh. 12:44–47).

Thus, by roughly the middle of the fifth century BCE, the vision that had been articulated a century earlier, by the great author-editor of the books of Genesis through Kings, became a reality.

2

But there was more, much more, in the legacy of Ezra and Nehemiah and their close associates (such as, perhaps, the author of the Book of Chronicles) than simply making effective in everyday life what the great inventor had contemplated only in imagination – great as that achievement was. I think Ezra and Nehemiah were also responsible for effecting one of the biggest shifts in the history of the Judahist faith. It is one so big that it is rarely talked about, for as we have already seen in detail, one of the crucial techniques in introducing innovations is to act as if they have always been there.

This innovation is the privileging of the Torah. The biggest mystery in the history of Judaism is when was the Torah broken out of the other books of religious learning and given a special position? When were the faithful told that the first five books of the Hebrew scriptures were the Books of Moses and were more authoritative than any other? When, why, and how was this accomplished?

Ezra-Nehemiah provides the basis for a dating that is now traditional: the mid fifth century, perhaps 458 BCE, and given circumstantial evidence that I shall mention in a moment, this is more convincing than any alternative date. (For the sake of convenience, take the date to be 450, since there is a bit of give in the chronology at this point. See Appendix B, Table 4 for a table of relevant dates.) Ezra was a scribe, expert in the law (or teaching) of Moses

(Ezra 7:6). As part of the Judahist purification of Jerusalem, he gathered the people together and, day after day, from morning to midday, he read to them from the scrolls of the teachings (or laws) of Moses (Neh. 8:1–8). This is taken in Orthodox Jewish circles to mean that he read to the people of Jerusalem the Pentateuch. This seems a reasonable interpretation, provided one notes two caveats. One of these is that the text in the Book of Ezra-Nehemiah does not state that the scrolls read by Ezra were the full five volumes that have come to be known as the Books of Moses, although that is not an outré inference. Second, even if we assume that it was the first five books of the Bible which were read out by Ezra, this does not mean that they were identical with those that we at present possess: close, perhaps, but not precisely the same (as Appendix C's discussion of the transmission of the Masoretic Text makes clear). Still, the most reasonable inference is that Ezra established the permanent dominance in Jerusalem of the Judahist religion, through his stentorian reading of a five-book text that he claimed to be by Moses.

If we take as being authentic the occasion of Ezra's reading to the people from the first five books of the Bible as a mandate for control of Jerusalem, the question that logically arises is: why was it thought necessary to break out from the existent unity of Genesis-Kings – a complete and coherent story running from creation to the Babylonian exile – the first five books and to ascribe them to Moses? What had previously been a unified composition became truncated by a great glass wall driven between the pre-Promised land sections (the Books of Moses, the Torah) and the Promised land sections (which become known as the "Former Prophets" in the final Hebrew canon, consisting of Joshua, Judges, Samuel and Kings). Once that had occurred, it would be the rare reader who would approach the basic history of the Chosen People (Genesis through Kings) as a unity. Preconceptions, based on the privileging of the so-called Books of Moses, would preclude that. Was it really necessary to destroy an organic entity, an extraordinarily sustained historical narrative?

Yes: if the Judahist religion, with Yahweh, Jerusalem, and the priesthood as its centre, was to be victorious. The slowness in rebuilding the Temple after 538, the lament of Malachi, the reports of priestly slackness and religious syncretism in Ezra-Nehemiah, and the prevalence of intermarriage with peoples who did not believe that Yahweh was the only god to be worshipped, all indicate that if something had not been done, the battle would have been lost. Judah and Yahweh would not have triumphed.

What was lacking was authority. The descendants of members of the religious elite who had been exiled to Babylon did not, on their "return" command authority. Here a little scriptural stratigraphy will indicate what the problem was and why a major invention was necessary to overcome it. Let us do some simple arithmetic. In the Book of Kings, written within easy living memory of the beginning of the Babylonian captivity, the great editor-writer gives some very realistic estimates of how many persons were taken prisoner. Almost all were males, except in the case of princely families. A total of 10,000 persons were taken to Babylon, the author-editor estimates. Of these, 7,000 were soldiers and 1,000 were craftsmen and blacksmiths. Those numbers are schematized – "rounded off" as it were – but they are not unrealistic or exaggerated. There is no wailing in this report, just a straight-faced historical tone. Using those estimates, one infers that the total of princely families and retainers and of scribes (both civil and religious) and priests was only 2,000 persons. Assuming even a moderate number of princely exiles, the number of scribes and priests deported can have been no more than 1,750 persons.[7] (See II Kings 24:14–16.) (The best modern estimates are that the world's "Jewish" population at this time was 150,000, mostly in Palestine.)[8]

Consider what this must have meant fifty years later, when the religious elite was permitted by Cyrus to return to Jerusalem: they must have been woefully short of manpower. Given that only men were deported (except for female members of the royal family), there had been in Babylon no women of the proper religious background for the Judahite devotees to marry. Either they had to intermarry with Babylonians, and thus effectively drop out of the Judahite cause, or import women from the old homeland or from Egypt: or remain without issue. Whatever the prevailing collective choice, the number of trained and enthusiastic and physically resilient Judahite religious leaders had to have been greatly reduced between 587 and 538. If there were 1,000 exiles and their sons and grandsons to straggle back to Jerusalem, it would have been surprising. And, further, we know that not all of those of Judahite conviction did return. Both Ezra and Nehemiah are testimonies to that; they, though highly trained and allegiant to Yahweh, did not return until the last moment, and then only when the Judahist attempt at securing Jerusalem had nearly failed. In sum, the number of the returning Babylonian exiles was too small – pitifully small – in comparison to the Judaean majority who had been left behind, and the Judahist leaders were too valetudinarian, too lacking in authority, to permit the carrying out of the program mooted by the editor-writer of the books of Genesis through Kings. Only by the external, and very late, intervention of Ezra and Nehemiah, the best part of a century after the Babylonian exile was over, did the Judahist religion win.

That brings us to a second set of numbers. These are found in the Books of Chronicles and in Ezra-Nehemiah. Whether or not these volumes are by a single hand is a question long debated by biblical scholars. Here it makes no difference, for they manifestly come from the same moment in history. They are each a response to the victory of Ezra and Nehemiah's form of Judaism and are written within 100 years, at most, of the events. Most importantly, they share an identical purpose on major ideological axes.

Both the Book of Ezra-Nehemiah and of Chronicles rewrite the estimate of the editor-writer of Genesis-Kings, a man who, at minimum, was in contact with many eyewitnesses to the Babylonian deportations and they replace the earlier estimates with ones that are less realistic historically and make a different story altogether. According to Ezra (2:1–65), some 4,363 priests and Levites, accompanied by 128 religious singers and 139 temple porters, led a return from Babylon after Cyrus's decree. The number of returnees was said to total 42,360 persons, plus 7,333 servants (presumably of foreign origin). This was a great band indeed, and one could plausibly claim that they were effectively the sum total of the Chosen People. Crucially, in Chronicles (the companion volume to Ezra-Nehemiah), the eyewitness-based report of the Book of Kings is rubbed off the page. Whereas the editor-writer of Kings made it clear that the lower-caste majority of the population of the former Kingdom of Judah remained in the homeland and was not exiled (see also Jer. 39:10), the author of Chronicles (II Chron. 36:20–21) introduces the new – and certainly historically inaccurate – myth that everyone in Jerusalem was either killed or carried away to Babylon and that the whole land experienced a sabbath of desolation for seventy years (that is, from 587 to the rebuilding period, 520–15).

Where the material in the Book of Kings, balefully accurate though it probably was, was faulty from an ideological point of view, was that it explained all too well the failure, for a period of nearly three generations, of the Judahite religion to win over the people of Jerusalem and of the surrounding countryside: the number of returnees was too small, their character was insufficiently authoritative, and the local majority, who had been left behind, had developed religious institutions which resisted successfully the No-Way-But-Yahweh sloganeering of the Judahite returnees. In other words, the numbers provided in the Book of Kings concerning the number deported to Babylon and the majority that had been left behind, had to be erased, because they provided too accurately, an historical explanation of why the Judahite retaking of Jerusalem for the religion of Yahweh had failed for so long.

The Books of Ezra-Nehemiah and of Chronicles replace the testament of the Book of Kings with numbers that explain success, not failure. A vigorous and numerically deep band of Judahists is presented as returning to redeem an empty land. When, eventually, in the time of Ezra and Nehemiah, they win, it is a normal organic outgrowth of that demographic situation.

Obviously, this is pretty sloppy story-telling, way below the level of sophistication of the writer-editor of the Genesis-Kings unity. It makes the success of the Judahist religion seem normal, but it leaves behind an unanswered, acrid little question: if the number of returnees was so large, and Jerusalem and its environs so desolate, why did it take so long for the Judahists to win? Question avoided.

What I think we are seeing in the effective erasing of the data on the Babylonian deportations in the Book of Kings (and also in Jeremiah) is a tiny, revealing symptom of an antipathy – or sense of rivalry – to the Genesis-Kings unity on behalf of the writer (or writers) of Ezra-Nehemiah and of Chronicles. This becomes a little more obvious when one looks at the Book of Chronicles. On the surface, it is the least necessary book in the Bible. For the most part, it is merely a precis of the Genesis-Kings unity, a fact that its author tangentially acknowledges (II Chron. 24:27). Fully 95 percent of the text is an abstract of material found in Joshua-Judges-Samuel-Kings, and, therefore, Chronicles appears to be intended to supplant these volumes. The Book of Chronicles lacks artistic charm and grace, and has no memorable phrases that are its own. Granted, its author may have had access to independent sources,[9] but he does very little with them.[10]

In fact, there are only two significant inventions in Chronicles but I think these are the reason the book came into existence. One of these, the introduction of the myth of the empty land, we have already seen. The second is that in three words, the author of Chronicles rewrites the "finding" of the book of the law in the First Temple during the rebuilding of the Temple by King Josiah. Whereas in the earlier version (II Kings 22:8), the scroll that is "discovered" is described as the book of the law, or the teachings (a book of torah), the version in Chronicles (II Chron. 34:14) changes the entire meaning by saying that "Hilkiah the priest found a book of the law of the Lord *given by Moses*" (emphasis mine). A more direct translation of the Hebrew would be "the law of Yahweh given through the hand of Moses." In either case, the key is the mention of Moses. He thereby is introduced as the hand who wrote at least part of the first five books of the scriptures.

Keep in mind that this was being written some time after the victory of the Judahite cause under Ezra and Nehemiah. When projecting into the material from the Genesis-Kings unity the idea that Moses actually wrote part of the early books by his own hand, the Chronicler is implying the superiority of those items that Moses allegedly wrote, over all other written texts. And, through a form of holy contagion, the Chronicler is making it possible to take the spiritual superiority of those items supposedly written by Moses' hand and to spread it to any item that could, by any stretch of the imagination, be associated with Moses. The reason therefore that the Book of Chronicles was necessary, ugly production though it is, is that it served as an alternative history to the historical narrative of Genesis-Kings, on two important points: it made the return from Babylon a triumph, and it gave a legitimation for breaking certain books out of the Genesis-Kings unity, and privileging them by identifying their authorship, at least in part, with Moses. When the Chronicler (II Chron. 34:30) later described what had been found in the Temple in King Josiah's time, as the book, or scroll of the covenant, he was making the expansion of the alleged scribal work of Moses easier, from comprising solely law texts to implying the entire story of the covenant.[11]

The same expansion of meaning occurred in Ezra's reading of the text publicly. What is later described in Nehemiah (8:1) as being the book of the law and teachings of Moses (the torah of Moses), easily moves through the slightest of change in emphasis, to be the Torah of Moses, something quite different.

There was, then, good reason for an ideological rivalry by the authors of Ezra-Nehemiah and Chronicles (and, probably, by Ezra and Nehemiah themselves) against the author of the early great narrative history, Genesis-Kings. In particular, the historical data at the close of the Book of Kings made it all too easy to see the subsequent return from the Babylonian exile as inglorious. Triumph had to replace sad reality. So an alternative general narrative history of Genesis-Kings was created (the Book of Chronicles), and the statements about the small number who went into exile and the majority that stayed behind was contradicted. This done (in Ezra-Nehemiah and in Chronicles), there remained a major problem, namely that anyone familiar with the Hebrew scriptures would also be familiar with the contradictions between the earlier Genesis-Kings unity and the later statements in Chronicles and in Ezra-Nehemiah.

Here, there were in theory two possible strategies of propaganda, but in reality only one. In theory, the author, or authors of Chronicles and Ezra-Nehemiah could have bad-mouthed the material in the Book of Kings, alleging that it was inaccurate. That, however, was not a real alternative, for the material in Kings was part of a larger corpus, Genesis-Kings, that was authoritative and, by its association with the fundamental material of Israel's early history, Kings would carry the day. And, the more certain this would be if the chroniclers actually called to their readers' and listeners' attention the divergences between their version and the earlier one. To do so would be first to invite comparison, and then rejection.

Instead, the shrewd path was to shove to the back of the library shelf the uncomfortable portions of history. This could be done only by separating the discomfiting material from the earlier scriptures. And, since negative criticism was not permitted (one could not impugn these texts and stay within the Yahwist camp), the trick was to so strongly praise the early portions of the Genesis-Kings work, that Joshua, Judges, Samuel, and especially, Kings, could be demoted. Thus, the invention of the concept of the Books of Moses as being of especial authority because some portions of them (and later, it comes to be believed, all of them) were taken down by Moses as a scribe for Yahweh. As a strategy, this is what we are seeing being played out in the work of Ezra and Nehemiah and later being recorded in the book that bears their names; it is a brilliant strategy and is no less than the invention of the Torah.

The only problem is that the first five books of the Bible do not entirely co-operate. At no place in the five Books of Moses is it directly averred that Moses wrote them.[12] The most that is directly claimed is that Moses wrote part of some of the five books, and even then the claims are not terribly strong.[13]

The places where Moses' authorship are specified are quite limited. One of these (Numbers 33:2) states that Moses wrote out the journeys of the people which Yahweh had directed (KJB). The Tanakh, of the Jewish Publications Society, says only that Moses recorded the starting point of the various marches; either translation fits the Hebrew and "stages of the journey" is a good indication of what Moses wrote down. The key is that however one reads the text, the only thing that Moses is said to have recorded is the journeys in the wilderness after the Israelites left Egypt. That leaves an immense amount of earlier history – from Creation to the Exodus – unaffiliated with him.

Only in the Book of Deuteronomy does the persona of Moses as a curator of ancient Israel's heritage come to the fore, and, curiously, it is not as a writer, but as a speaker that he stands on the stage. Deuteronomy is essentially a collection of long speeches: "Hear O Israel, the statutes and judgements which I speak in your ears this day" is the stage direction that holds for the whole book (Deut. 5:1). These speeches are immediate and not in indirect discourse. Nothing could be less scribal, more aural, than Moses' telling the people that they "shalt return unto the Lord thy God, and shalt obey his voice according to all that I command thee this day, thou and thy children, with all thine heart, and with all thy soul" (Deut. 30:2). If one wants to accept the rolling speeches of Deuteronomy as being the actual words of Moses (they are so splendid in form that one desperately wants them to be Moses' own words), then one has to posit that they were transcribed accurately by someone who heard them. However, the tradition that eventually gains ascendancy, probably from the time of Nehemiah and Ezra onwards, is that Moses wrote down his own words, and then subsequently wrote the section concerning his own death, just slightly before his demise.

The only place in Deuteronomy where direct claims are articulated of Moses' having acted as a scribe is in 31:24–25 where Moses is reported as writing the words of "this law" (or "this teaching" or "this torah") on a scroll, and the scroll is placed in the ark of the covenant. The definite "this" is unambiguous. It refers to the material Moses has just been giving to the Chosen People in his long speeches. Some of it is already written down (as reported in Deut. 30:10), which implies that Moses is reading from a scroll already in existence and now he writes down the rest of what he has been telling the people. Therefore, in total, all that is being suggested about Moses as author is that he recorded something about the children of Israel in the wilderness (and even then it is a stylized journey based on the magic number "40"), and that he wrote out parts of the teachings that are found in Deuteronomy. It is not a strong case for ascribing the first five books of the scriptures to Moses, and contemporaries can not have accepted it entirely without reservation.

Why did not Nehemiah and Ezra fudge the record a bit? After all, the invention of ancient traditions was the way that biblical writers worked: all new cloth had to appear old. One can make a case that the reference in Numbers 33:2 to Moses recording the stages of the journeys in the wilderness is an interpolation by Ezra (the surrounding text, which this verse awkwardly interrupts, reads smoothly without it), but we can leave this instance as moot. Why did Ezra and Nehemiah, as they brought final victory to the Judahists in Jerusalem, not simply suggest at the end of Deuteronomy that this, and all scriptural writings that preceded Deuteronomy, from the beginning of Genesis onwards, were written by Moses?

Although that is what they want their followers in Jerusalem to believe, they dared not insert it into the Pentateuch for one reason: the people, both in Jerusalem and in the diaspora, already had these books. This is implied in Nehemiah, for the Levites commented on the text and explained it to the people; clearly the religious elite already was well acquainted with it (Neh. 8:7–9). Almost certainly this text, as part of the Genesis-Kings unity, had been brought to Jerusalem in 538 at the close of the Babylonian exile. Presumably, Ezra brought with him from Babylon his own copy of the Pentateuch, but it was one in which he had virtually no room for direct invention, because there was a pre-existing text that the local religious leaders could compare to his version. Ezra and Nehemiah had ideological reasons for needing to vaunt Genesis-Deuteronomy and thereby to downplay Joshua-Kings, but they were in a very tight box.

Yet, as we know, they succeeded. Both the "Samaritan Pentateuch" (a rival northern version of the now-privileged Torah) and the library of scrolls at Qumran make it clear that by, roughly, 200 BCE the Torah, as the five Books of Moses, was considered something quite separate from the remainder of the Genesis-Kings unity. The residual was now called the "Former Prophets." However, both precisely when, and how this separation was completed, is unknown. I would suggest that a good guess-date for the general acceptance (general, but not universal) within the world of Judahist belief in the separation and privileging of the Torah was 400 BCE. That is within the period when the books of Chronicles and of Ezra-Nehemiah were written, and these are books of victory, or at least of success. Had Ezra and Nehemiah failed, Ezra-Nehemiah could not have taken the form it did, nor could Chronicles.

The real mystery, though, is *how* did Ezra and Nehemiah as inventors of tradition, succeed? I suspect that the answer is so simple that it is almost embarrassing to state: that, although the later chroniclers of the two men's actions dared not insert new claims for the special status of the first five books, as being of Moses's writing, there was no inhibition on Ezra and Nehemiah claiming this verbally. Again, and again, and again. Thus, the five books of the evolving Hebrew scriptures would change from being thought of as containing the teaching (the torah) of Moses, to being *the Torah* of Moses. One is able to view later indications of the continuation of this process – in which the definition of scripture changes without the actual character of the scriptural texts changing at all – in the last century before the Common Era and the first two centuries of that Era, when the term "the Torah" comes to mean on occasion not the Books of Moses but the entire body of sacralized religious texts; moreover, later than that the concept of "Oral Torah" was articulated which held that word-of-mouth material concerning spiritual matters, passed from Yahweh to Moses and then from him to a skein of holy men, and embodied as high a degree of accuracy and authority as did the written Torah. All this took place without the texts themselves changing.

It would be easy to underestimate the importance of the victory of Ezra and Nehemiah in their securing for the Judahite religion full, and seemingly permanent, control of Jerusalem. The great invention of the editor-writer of Genesis-Kings had not on its own been strong enough to capture Jerusalem from the local populace and their priests: multiple gods were worshipped, and Yahweh was only one of these. Yahweh, no matter how strong in the scriptural text, still needed foot soldiers on the ground. Ezra and Nehemiah were the generals in Yahweh's victory.

As discussed earlier, when their triumph was recorded in the Books of Chronicles and of Ezra-Nehemiah, it was imperative (1) to make the return from exile lead automatically to the empowerment of Ezra and Nehemiah as temporary heads of the Judahist religion and (2) that their decision to privilege "the Torah" was at least indirectly alluded to, and the implication that the first five books of scripture were written by Moses, kept alive. Neither of the two books that stem from the events of the mid fifth century, is a distinguished piece of writing. Ezra-Nehemiah lacks literary distinction and Chronicles has all the wit and power of a deputy minister's precis of a document for his cabinet minister.

But tactically, the new scriptural books were brilliant, for they laid out an alternative menu of texts:

1 The Genesis-Kings unity, which (a) did not privilege the first five books, and (b) included embarrassing material in Kings concerning the character of the Babylonian exile.

And, now

2 The Torah, whose creation is identified with Moses, and whose five books are given special status; an alternative to Joshua-Kings, namely the Book

of Chronicles; and new set texts, Chronicles and Ezra-Nehemiah, which bring the story down to the triumph of the Judahists in the mid fifth century. This triumphal conclusion was infinitely more satisfactory than the picture of a tiny minority being taken off to exile in Babylon, which is the conclusion to the Book of Kings.[14]

Thus, an alternative set of scriptures had emerged, within two centuries (probably less) of the creation of the original Genesis-Kings unity. The older text was not destroyed, but there now was a route around the portions that the religious leaders of fifth-century Judahism found uncomfortable. In the long-run, the most important result of this tactical rearrangement of the scriptures was that the first five books became the Torah and received more attention, respect and exegesis than the rest of the Hebrew scriptures combined. This had not been the case when Genesis-Kings was first invented. In ancient history, as much as modern, major changes frequently are effected for petty reasons.

3

We are now where we can pinpoint the major difficulty in reading the Hebrew scriptures: such reading almost inevitably suffers from a major parallax effect. The nature of the documents makes it easy to read them from a misleading angle. An apparent displacement of the religious history we are observing occurs because of the misaligned position we assume when we view it. Things seem to be where they aren't. The difficulty is entirely one of historical perspective.

Specifically, the problem is as follows: although the really decisive events in the creation of the Judahist religion occurred between the second Babylonian deportation of 587 BCE and the end of Persian rule over Jerusalem (330 BCE), the overwhelming majority of the religious texts – and particularly the central texts – focus on the period before, mostly long before, 587 BCE. If we wish to understand the formation of Judahism (an absolutely necessary prologue to understanding the later creation of Christianity and of Rabbinic Judaism), then our eyes should focus on events *after* the Babylonian empire razed Jerusalem. Yet, like children watching a conjuror, our attention keeps being diverted to the enticement of "ancient Israel," to events claimed to be several hundred, a thousand, even 1,500 years before the real history of the Judahist religion starts.

The real history is a set of events that (unlike events prior to 587) have multiple third-party witnesses to their context (such as archaeological and historical evidence that is found outside the Bible) within the Babylonian and Persian empires; actions carried out by religious leaders that are consonant with these contexts and, most important, the production of major religious texts that have come down intact (or almost so) from the exilic and Persian periods, to our own time. And these texts interacted with religious activities in a generative way, so that a tightly unified priestly elite, thoroughly Yahwist in allegiance, acquired control of the primary sacred site of the Chosen People, Jerusalem and its Temple. In sum (1) during the exile an authoritative set of scriptures was compiled, one that postulated the sole authority of Yahweh for the Chosen People and discipline by a priesthood that had extremely high ritual standards; (2) after the return from exile the building of the Second Temple was completed; and (3) eventually full control over Jerusalem was gained by Judahists, who enforced stringently the worship of Yahweh, and no other god. These pivotal events occurred between 587 and, roughly 450 BCE (if one takes Ezra's reforms as a terminal date) or 430 BCE (if one takes the end of Nehemiah's governorship as a terminus). The only thing not effected before 430 was the promulgation of a set of texts that memorialized the achievement of Ezra and Nehemiah, rewrote the story of the Babylonian captivity, and legitimated the privileging of the Torah. These were completed before the end of Persian rule. If 400 BCE is a reasonable guess-date, the absolute terminus for this great period of achievement in the Judahist religion is 330. So, in that sense, everything important happened between 587 and 330.

Everything? Yes, in that in this period the texts and the power-positions (in Jerusalem) that determined the major outlines of Judaism were set. Some infilling came later, but that was filigree, not structural.

What then about all the stories of "biblical times," by which most people mean pre-exile material going back to King David, Moses, and the Patriarchs, and beyond? They are not immediately relevant if one wishes to understand the creation of the Judahist religion, the faith that cleaved only to Yahweh.

Hard as it is to fight parallax, we must focus on this simple fact: the creation of the historical narrative of the Chosen People and the securing of religious power over Jerusalem are the historical events that made Judaism possible. These events occurred in the period 587–330 BCE, not before. We must keep our eyes on these events, despite the temptation to turn and stare at the pyrotechnics that occur on the distant horizon.

The text is the primary item. The primary unity, Genesis-Kings, is an historical narrative, collected, edited, and in part written, by a religious genius. He was the world's first true historian, and he remains one of the best. Consider his power: *if* he had not included, say, the heartbreaking tale of David's wayward son Absalom, *then* it would not have existed. Simple as that: because there is no third-party attestation for any specific story included in the Genesis-Kings unity (except the Babylonian deportations), and because, indeed, there is precious little confirmation of even the general context of events described in the narrative of the Chosen People, therefore there is no way for any story or belief to be included in the Judahist creed *except that the framer of the historical narrative decided to include it.* Thus, the pivotal events in the history of Judahism (and of its offspring, Christianity and Rabbinic Judaism) are in large part the decisions made by the historians who were the editor-writers of the texts. If the editor-writer of the Genesis-Kings unity (and to a much lesser extent, the writer or writers of Chronicles and Ezra-Nehemiah) say something occurred, then, for the purposes of Judahist belief, it did; if they ignore an event, person, place, or belief, that item never existed, for the only way a thing can come into existence in a system that lacks third-party verifiability, is through its inclusion in the historical memory.

Thus – *the most important events in the history of the "Old Testament" are the decisions that the writer-editors of the texts performed, day by day; without their attestation, nothing occurred.*

That is why the present book focuses on the "greatest inventions" of western history. We shall later find, when examining the "New Testament" texts, and the texts that established "Talmudic" (or "Rabbinical," or "Normative" Jewish beliefs), that in the Common Era, the situation repeats itself. In the absence of external verifiability (and on the central historical assertions there is none), the real history of the religion is what gets into the historical narrative.

Since this crucial set of decisions about the character and substance of the historical narrative of any religion is inevitably made later – usually much later – than the events which are described in the texts that embody the faith's historical memory, most of us develop a crick in the neck from trying to force ourselves to keep our eyes on the later, and duller, period, in which the historian makes the decisions that determine the future religion, while all the time wanting to gape at the technicolour stories that are shown on the silver screen of "biblical history."

Is there not something wrong with an argument that suggests the decision of the author-editor of the historical narrative about what gets into the narrative is more important than the "actual" events found in the historical narrative? On the surface, yes, but I think not at heart. My assertion is not that the historian who put together the narrative that is the core of the Hebrew Bible is more important theologically or morally or religiously than the events he records, nor that the decisions he made concerning what to include and what to exclude are more metaphysically consequential than the putative events. My assertion is solely within the context of the way that professional historians study the past, a useful, but modest discipline. Recall here the point made in Chapter One: that in recent years historians have come to view what people believed happened in the past as more causally important in determining events and of more value in explaining them, than what "really" happened, whatever that may have been. Further, the extent and manner to which people in authority (religious or civil) have controlled, or at least influenced strongly, what the demos thinks happened in the past is of more explanatory salience than the parsing of details about the actual past. It is nice if historians can get the original story straight (and pursuing the oldest versions of events usually tends to be more fun), but this usually is of secondary importance.

The editor-writer of the Genesis-Kings unity was self-consciously an historian and acted with equal parts artistry and scholarly probity. We can take it that whatever he included in his great work he believed to be true. What we cannot take as given, however, is either the sense in which he believed a given block of narrative or fact to be true, or to what extent he believed a report to be accurate (something quite different from the entire truth). As mentioned in Chapter Two, the books of Genesis-Kings contain hints about the degree of reliance the editor-writer of the final version placed on a given report. In general, when he believes something but is not convinced of its overwhelming probability, he includes doublets, thus catching in his net contradictory reports, one of which he believes is accurate, though he is not sure which. The earliest case in the text is the Creation story as found in Genesis. There he covers himself by skilfully conflating two completely independent versions (Genesis 1:1–2:3, and 2:4–3:24).

Throughout Genesis-Kings, the author-editor filled in transitions and awkward places with grace notes. He includes reports that he believes to be true, in the sense of being true to the nature both of Yahweh and of his own text, but which he also knew not to be strictly accurate. For example, there is a moment in the middle of Kings, when it would help the narrative along if the prophet Elijah would leave the stage, so that the part of the story concerning his successor, Elisha, could be taken up. A mere death for Elijah would be historically accurate, but would let the story down, just at a moment when an energetic transition is required. So, one has the dizzying rhetorical arabesque introduced wherein Elijah is in the act of passing his mantle to Elisha, and a great whirlwind, announced by a chariot of fire, takes Elijah to heaven (II Kings 2:1–11). When read aloud to groups of the faithful, they must have delighted in this confection. And they believed it, but we must credit them with believing it in a different way than they believed the story of King David. There is history and there is history. They understood. And so should we.

None of this is to gainsay the ingenuity and intellectual depth of the large number of scholars (most of them not historians, but persons who have some historical concerns) who try to assess what the situation really was in Palestine at any moment before the Babylonian deportations, and to sort out what, when and where the references to the pre-Babylonian era are accurate (and in what way) and where they are not. One could easily give several scholarly lifetimes to this activity, so one has to be grateful for their work. If an historian *pur laine* (as distinct from philologists, epigraphers and archaeologists who occupy most of the pre-exilic time zone) were to approach the topic, he or she would look at it like any other one-source question, which, in fact, is a very common approach in modern history. He or she would first assume the retroactive existence of the laws of physics (the earth is not flat and the cosmos did not appear in 168 hours), and the biological characteristics of humans and beasts (no human has ever lived more than 150 years; twenty-five years was an above-average lifespan 3,000 years ago), and so on. Second, he or she would assume the validity of deductive logic, inductive data collection, and the applicability across time of statistical theory, and the parameters of the demographically possible. Then, from that point onwards, everything would be forensic. That is, like a court case in which generalized theory is of little use: because one is making a decision not about an entire class of events, but about one single, specific event – whether or not it occurred – one uses anything and everything that might be relevant to illuminate the situation. The one rule is no cheating: every argument has to be overtly articulated, and its assumptions specified.

I hope that some professional historians, trained in the late twentieth century in the methods of post-classical history, will turn their attention to such a task. Mixed with the methods of other disciplines, they might prove to be a helpful bunch. However, for myself, I still believe that the most immediately productive way to learn some new things about the history of the Judahists who made Yahweh victorious and about their heirs, the Christians and the Rabbinical Jews, is to watch, and watch very carefully, the men who wrote texts; in how and why they shaped their texts lies the kernel of each of those faiths.

4

The narrative history of the Chosen People as it appears in the Bible ends at 430 BCE, when Nehemiah's governorship is over. And, whenever the Books of Chronicles and Ezra-Nehemiah were completed – certainly by 330, but probably sooner – marks the end of the narrative chronicling of the Chosen People in the Hebrew scriptures as an historical entity. (Thereafter, they become a literary figure – as in apocalyptic literature – but are no longer the focus of an historical narrative.)

Of course there were ancillary modes of religious text-making that developed, but because they were non-historical, they have left us with an enormous gap concerning what went on in and around Jerusalem during the successive imperia that the former political capital of Judah experienced. Jerusalem – and thus the Judahist, or Judahite, religion – was under Persian rule until the rise of the extraordinary Alexander of Macedon (Alexander the Great). In 330 BCE he ended the Persian imperial rule over Jerusalem and for the remainder of his life (until 323) Jerusalem was under his administration. Thereafter, the heirs of Alexander, less in amity than enmity with each other, ruled Jerusalem until the Maccabean Revolt of 167 BCE which resulted in the revival of a Judaean administration that was largely independent of outside rule. Until that revolt, however, Jerusalem remained the capital of a religious kingdom, not a secular one: it was a kingdom without a worldly king.

How the Judahist religion developed in the late-Persian and Greek periods is largely a mystery. The priestly arrangements for control of the religious sphere that Ezra and Nehemiah had introduced held firm, that is clear. But how far the penumbra of Yahwist worship extended outside of Jerusalem is at present unknown. Nor is it clear how tightly the Judahist priestly authorities enforced unity of discipline and belief within their own precincts. Certainly they insisted on the Yahweh-only creed and on strict forms of ritual sacrifice, but what they demanded besides that is unrecorded. That away from Jerusalem there existed numerous variant versions of Judahism, at least in the Greek period, is strongly implied by the large number of Judahist sects that are found to exist after the Maccabean Revolt, when the available records considerably improve. This suggests that although the Yahwist priesthood was completely in command of the Second Temple, there was no single normative form of the faith.

This point is well illustrated by the fact that there was no recorded attempt at regulating the scriptures. Certain parts of Hebrew religious literature were more important than others and were becoming, with each passing decade, more and more revered: the Torah, as the "Books of Moses" were particularly important. In the Nevi'im, the books of Joshua-Kings had been set since the exile and the major prophets, largely completed by the time of the return from Babylon, were also a set piece. The twelve minor prophets were recognized to be a complete group not long after the Maccabean Revolt.

That these texts, the Torah and the Prophets, which form two of the three categories of the present Hebrew Bible, were extant, and circulating in a fairly familiar form by the end of the Persian period, is slightly misleading, in that their existence and their collective form should not be taken as meaning the same thing it came to mean some hundreds of years later: there was not yet a canon of Hebrew scriptures, but merely convenient collections of scrolls. Through their use, generation after generation, the books of this great cultural archive gradually acquired both secular, and, eventually, sacred status. But their becoming solely sacred in character was far in the future. Until well past the period of Hellenic rule, the Hebrew scriptures were flexible. Many new books entered during the Persian and Greek periods. These we have: what is maddening is that we do not know what books dropped out, or why. We know from fleeting references within various biblical texts that there were many authoritative books of Hebrew writings that were lost.

The third major section of the Hebrew scriptures, the Kethuvim – the Writings – was overwhelmingly the product of the late-Persian and Greek eras, although its roots go back to pre-exilic times. The Writings are extremely varied and they remind one of the doleful motto of the New Zealand book publisher, Cape Cately Ltd., which said, with more realism than pride, "Each book good of its kind." The Writings were a very fluid category and did not settle down and become a fixed canon until well into the Common Era. However, the inventory of the Qumran library indicates that most of the Writings were in circulation by the conclusion of the Hellenic period. It is well to remember that the books of Ezra-Nehemiah and of Chronicles were part of the Writings and in the Hebrew texts they were migrating towards what eventually became fixed as their proper position in the Hebrew Bible: at the very end. Chronicles becomes the conclusion of the Scriptures. This is very significant in relation to my earlier suggestion that Ezra-Nehemiah and Chronicles had a specific ideological agenda that was incompatible with the second half of the Genesis-Kings unity. The Book of Chronicles was framed as an ideologically-acceptable substitute for Joshua-Kings. By placing Chronicles at the end of what became the Writings in the Hebrew Bible, and, therefore, the last book of the Bible, that book was being privileged in a manner similar to the way that the Pentateuch was being privileged at the other end of the Bible. The Books of Moses and of Chronicles became the parameters, the exterior borders within which the Hebrew scriptures eventually were defined. In time, they formed a spiritual envelope and to be outside of that envelope was to be outside the boundaries of acceptable Judahite thought.

Prominent in the Writings were the Psalms and the Book of Proverbs, each of which had ancient portions, but each of which was still evolving as new elements were added and old ones deleted. A simple example is Psalm 151. At present there are only 150 approved psalms, but the Greek version of the Bible preserved Psalm 151, a song ascribed to the young David after he had fought and killed Goliath in single combat.[15] Scores of other psalms of praise must have existed, though they never became canonical.

Aside from the now-familiar Psalms and Proverbs and the Books of Ezra-Nehemiah and Chronicles, what is most exciting about the Writings as they develop is the gloriously miscellaneous nature of the material. The material is new, not just in what it deals with, but new in form. The old forms – narrative history and classical prophecy – are forms that now are less employed, not because they are mendacious, but because they have told most of their truths and are now almost used up. The well has nearly run dry by the end of the Persian period. (The continued use of narrative history as an interesting, but merely peripheral, form, is discussed in chapters 5 to 7.) This is because the forms of narrative history and of classical prophecy had served a single purpose: to shore up the Judahist version of what the religion of the Chosen People should be: Yahweh-only in belief, Temple-centred in liturgy, Judah-dominated in ethnicity. With the Judahite phalanx fully in charge of the religion of Jerusalem and its environs from c.450 onwards, the prophetic voice became redundant, and the narrative voice unnecessary, for the story had ended the way it was supposed to. Yahweh had defeated polytheism.

The retirement of historical narrative as the primary religious form, and prophecy as its aide-de-camp, released an enormous amount of energy.[16] Now, sure of Judahism's control of the Temple and of the priesthood, religious writers had the confidence to turn to new forms and, simultaneously, the religious authorities had the self-assurance to allow the writers to do so, even when some of the newly-minted texts seemed to be far removed from the central spine of Judahist beliefs. Indeed, in some cases, the new writings seemed somewhat subversive of those beliefs. This era of the Writings is wonderfully rich. It begins in the later Persian period and continues through the Greek era and even into the Common Era. Wondrously varied are its products, the sweet fruit of a cultural renaissance of whose full knowledge we are deprived, for time's cruel banditry has stolen away most of its records.

The fascinating characteristics of all these varied writings is that *if* one takes as a norm Hebrew religious texts (both narrative historical and prophetic) through the creation of Ezra-Nehemiah and Chronicles, *then* these new forms seem confusingly non-scriptural, to use an anachronistic term. The most astounding of the new ways of writing is found in the Book of Ecclesiastes, or Qoheleth, its alternative title. The book, in now-familiar fashion, is ascribed to an earlier figure, in this case the "son of David" (usually identified as King Solomon), who also calls himself "the Preacher." The book is a very clever, very jaded, one-man play, cum worldly almanac. One pays it a high compliment in noting that it is exactly the kind of thing Oscar Wilde would have composed, had he been living in Jerusalem under Hellenic rule. The book's theme is "vanity of vanities; all is vanity" (Ecc. 1:2). The author-narrator parades the stage as Solomon, or, alternately, as the Preacher who was "king over Israel in Jerusalem." In Aramaicized Hebrew, the preacher flounces about the stage, first telling about his great works (as King Solomon). These he judges to be mere vanities. Next, he seems to praise the concept of spiritual wisdom. However, the form of wisdom he endorses is tantamount to a rejection of the rigorous spiritual discipline of the Judahite religion. The song of chapter three, "To every thing there is a season" which became a good song indeed in the mid-twentieth century, comes close to recommending a form of hedonism, or at least enough physical self-indulgence to make most of the 613 commandments of the Judahist faith into broken reeds.

The oratorical trick of making this book a first-person play, permits some devastating japes. "A living dog is better than a dead lion" (Ecc. 9:4) is a justification of cowardice equivalent to Percy French's nineteenth-century political dictum: "better a live coward for five minutes than a dead man all your life." Just when it seems that the strutting Preacher has gone too far, he clutches his robes in senatorial style, reminding us that he is King Solomon,

clears his throat portentously, and tells us solemnly "Curse not the king …"
That's safe, isn't it? for the king is the centre of the Judahist ideology: everything descends historically from the great monarch Solomon, whom Yahweh
used as his conduit. Indeed, and we relax – until the Preacher explains why
one should not curse the king: "no, not in thy thought; and curse not the rich
in thy bedchamber: for a bird of the air shall carry the voice, and that which
hath wings shall tell the matter" (Ecc. 10:20). And your head will be for the
chopping block, the Preacher does not need to add.

After all of this Wildean wisdom, the Preacher rings down the curtain by
doing exactly what dear Oscar would have done. He produces an unassailable
piece of Victorian-mahogany moralism, one which the entire book has been
given to undercutting:

> Let us hear the conclusion of the whole matter; Fear God, and keep his command-
> ments: for this is the whole duty of man.
> For God shall bring every work into judgement, with every secret thing, whether it
> be good or whether it be evil. (Ecc. 12:13–14)

The curtain comes down and we exit smiling, but puzzled that this entertain-
ment has made it past the religious censors.

Almost equally baffling is the Song of Songs (called "Canticles" in the
Latin tradition), for it makes no pretence of being a religious artifact. The
book is ascribed to King Solomon in its very first verse (thus, another alternative name, the Song of Solomon) but that is simply the convention of Hebrew
biblical invention, not a serious ascription. The book has been the perpetual
despair of interpreters ever since the first century of the Common Era, because it is at heart exactly what it appears to be on the surface: a very good
erotic poem, a paean of longing, both emotional and physical, of a man and a
woman for each other. The song has the head-spinning, totally over-the-top
quality of besotted love poetry:

> Sweetness drops
> From your lips, O bride;
> Honey and milk
> Are under your tongue;
> And the scent of your robes
> Is like the scent of Lebanon (Songs 4:11)[17]

The poetic dialogue between man and woman, mostly composed of an alternating series of sexual compliments, has nothing to do with the relationship
of Yahweh to his people (which, in the Bible's historical narrative, is anything but tender); nor, as Christian interpreters would have it, is this about the

love of Christ for his church. The Song concludes unambiguously, with the young woman presenting to her paramour a lovely invitation to sexual congress:

> "Hurry, my beloved
> Swift as a gazelle or a young stag,
> To the hills of spices!"
>
> (Songs 8:14, Jewish Publication Society (JPS))

Yes, hurry!

The exuberant richness of the Song of Songs and the elaborate cynicism of Ecclesiastes was only possible after the Judahite capture of post-exilic Jerusalem and the rebuilding of the Temple were absolutely secure. Arguments about the dating of such items in the so-called "wisdom" literature frequently miss the central contextual point, that one can allow the educated cultural elite to play at such games, and not be threatened by their playing, only when things are absolutely without worry. One could not tease Yahweh (as does the author of Ecclesiastes) or use the sacred tongue and its poetic forms as a sexual solicitation (as does the author of the Song of Songs) unless the Judahist religious establishment was very established indeed. That is why a Hellenic dating for the final version of these and similar non-traditional items is most reasonable.

Something of the same underlying confidence in the security of the religious culture of Judahism characterizes the Book of Tobit, which is a picaresque novella written in the half-century or so before the Maccabean Revolt. Versions of it are found in the Qumran library and the book has been included in the secondary canon of the Roman Catholic branch of the Christian tradition; Protestants accepted it until roughly the late nineteenth century. It was not included in the Jewish canon that developed in the second century of the Common Era, and after, but it was widely known. The novella is the story of six ordinary people, and is a mixture of gentle irony, optimism, and an artificially happy ending that the reader knew was coming from chapter one. Tobit is very much like the less-assiduous "historical" novelists of our own time: the volume is set in a far-off exotic period, in this case Nineva of the eighth century, and includes reference to King Shalmaneseer and other historical figures. Many of its historical references are anachronistic, in the casual way of historical novelists. Still, it is a solid Judahist story, for the main character and narrator, Tobit, though a northerner, is not like most others who live in the northern kingdom: he is a righteous man and worships in Jerusalem. The story makes no pretence to being an epic. Rather it is nice, generous and sometimes amusing. One of the amusing moments is when a woman of faith contemplates suicide because she has been married seven times, but is still a virgin because an evil demon "Asmodeus" has murdered each of her bride-grooms. Tobit's son, Tobias, overcomes this impediment by listening to the advice of a relative who tells him to arm himself with rotting fish parts. "When you enter the bridal chamber, take some of the fish's liver and heart and put them on the embers of the incense. An odour will be given off; the demon will smell it and flee, and will never be seen near her any more" (Tobit 6:17–18). A memorable bridal night: Tobit is a nice story. Everyone lives long and dies peacefully and all within the context of faithfully worshipping Yahweh.

Perhaps the most self-confident, although one of the least original in form of the "wisdom" literature is the book of Ecclesiasticus or the "Wisdom of Jesus, son of Sirach." Like Tobit, the volume stems from the fifty or sixty years before the Maccabean Revolt – the internal dating clues are quite precise in this instance – and it was widely read in Judahist circles well into the Common Era. It was, however, excluded from the final Hebrew canon. Like Tobit, it is included in the Catholic Deutero-canon and in the Protestant Apocrypha. The Wisdom of Ben-Sira (yet another title for the book) is long (fifty-one chapters in the modern edition), consistent, and totally confident in its assertion of proverbs and observations that are based as much in a general reverence for the Judahist culture as on narrowly religious faith. "All wisdom is from the Lord, and with him it remains forever," is the opening observation, and it serves as the book's summation.

If I am correct that the triumph of the Judahist religion during the Persian period led both to an end to the usefulness of the classical forms of biblical historical narrative and of prophecy, and also that the increasing confidence of the now-secure Temple-based religion of Jerusalem provided a cultural ambiance that allowed some very luxuriant, very exotic plants to bloom, especially in the Hellenic era[18] – then these observations lead us to the most exotic plant of them all: full blown apocalyptic thinking, preaching, and writing. A fine example, widely cited by contemporaries, but now undeservedly obscure, is the Book of First Enoch. A composite work, formed probably between the early third century and the beginning of the Common Era, it is ascribed – in the traditional way – to a venerable figure, the ancient Israelite Enoch, a man of exemplary holiness. He had walked with god (or with the gods; the text is polysemic) and they had taken him directly to the afterworld (Gen. 5:22–23). Only the pre-Maccabean parts of First Enoch concern us here (these being basically chapters one through sixteen). They are the first portion of a rich vision that Enoch was granted directly from heaven by the angels. He was shown "the day of tribulation" which would result in "the removal of all the ungodly ones" (I Enoch 1:a).[19] The god of the universe was to come forth from his dwelling and to march to Mount Sinai and the whole earth would be rent asunder. The righteous and the unrighteous were to be judged. The wicked would be destroyed. There is more, much more, in florid detail. The salient point is that we see here something relatively new in the history of Judahism, the idea of an end of history and the weighing of every individual on a final balance scale. This is implicitly a suggestion that Yahweh works *outside of* time and it is a virtual repudiation of the fundamental view of the divine personality present in the Genesis-Kings unity and in the prophets – namely that Yahweh works *within* time, that is, within human history. Further, the emphasis upon the individual's being judged is a very different focus from that of the central portions of the Hebrew scriptures wherein, yes, individual holiness is important, but is consequential primarily as it affects the collective holiness of the Chosen People. The rewards and punishments that are adjudicated in the Genesis-Kings narrative occur within the human time scale and the really important judgements are metered to the Chosen People as a whole. Therefore, apocalyptic writing is fundamentally an inversion – and thus a rejection – of the spiritual physics of the religion of Yahweh.

Not surprisingly, therefore, First Enoch was excluded from the eventual Hebrew canon. What is surprising is that one apocalyptic creation, the Book of Daniel, was not only as widely read as was First Enoch, but was included in the final canon, as part of the Writings. Much of the Book of Daniel in its present form is pre-Maccabean (chapters 1–6 and possibly chapter 7). From 2:4 to the end of chapter seven, the manuscript material is in Aramaic, a tongue associated with the Jewish diaspora in what was once Babylon, and with demotic usage in Palestine at the beginning of the Common Era. Most of the post-Maccabean material is in Hebrew. In addition to the two crucial ideological characteristics of First Enoch – God working outside of history, rather than within it, and an emphasis upon the judgement of each individual at the end of time – Daniel's apocalyptic sections have two additional, non-traditional characteristics: God is seen as being mysterious and as communicating in veiled visions that require extensive decoding (so unlike the 613 commandments); and the resurrection of the dead is postulated. This well may have been a common folk-belief in central Palestine, but it had formed no part of the primary vision of the religion of Yahweh as found in Genesis-Kings.

The instructive point, therefore, is how the Book of Daniel's virtual repudiation of Judahist orthodoxy came to be included in the Writings. It was because the book's author (or, more likely, authors) understood quite well the principles of biblical invention and they wrapped their new ideas in these well-tested methods. The first six chapters of Daniel are fictive history, but they are presented as a form of accreditation. The book is said to have been written by someone who lived during the reign of King Jehoiakim and who survived into the reign of Cyrus of Persia. The author(s) makes a mess of the details of this period, but to an audience of adherents in the late-Hellenic or early Maccabean world, the fictive details would have provided historical verisimilitude. Then, with the context of back-projected history, the narrator (Daniel) claims to have made some remarkably accurate dream interpretations for King Nebuchadnezzar and to have predicted a succession of four world empires, from Babylon onwards, a feat roughly equivalent to my "predicting" the American, French, and Soviet revolutions from our present vantage point in time. Therefore, by making the fictive appear historical, by claiming a considerable age for what was merely recent, and by making predictions after the events, a corrosive set of beliefs, antithetical to the fundamental precepts of Judaism, were smuggled into the Writings of the faith.

Apocalyptic literature, unlike the romances such as Tobit, or the camped-up staginess of Ecclesiastes, or the erotic poetry of the Song of Songs, or the weighty empiricisms of Proverbs and of Ben-Sira, rejects Judaism as it had worked through time and as it was recorded in the great history, Genesis-Kings. After the destruction of the Herodian Temple in Jerusalem in 70 CE, the inventors of the Christian scriptures recognized just how antithetical these apocalyptic concepts were to traditional Judaism. They employed them quite consciously and, indeed, brilliantly, in their attack upon not only the older religion of Judah, but also upon its heir, the Jewish faith that was created in the rabbinical era.

That is in the future.

For the present moment, the sense of expectation is quite different. Even given the tiny slivers that we today possess of the full range of religious productivity that was occurring in the several registers of the Judahist religion in the Hellenic period, one has to be humbled by its potential fecundity. Were this potential to be realized, were Jerusalem to be freed, even for a short time, from external imperialisms, the variety of new religious species that Judahism could produce would be breathtakingly prodigious.

History's All-Embracing Arms;
the Covenant

I

HERE, BEFORE LOOKING AT THE AMAZING INVENTIVE FECUNDITY OF the last two centuries before the Common Era and first seventy years of that era, we should consolidate our knowledge of the covenant, the single most important idea that the Hebrew scriptures articulate. This conspectus is necessary to all of our subsequent discussion, because the covenant is at the heart of the several different faiths that follow upon the religion of the ancient Israelites. Each of them re-interprets the covenant. Indeed, each re-invents the covenant for its own purposes. But in so doing, these faiths find that the covenant invents them.

That, in kernel, is the great problem when thinking about the covenant. It is something that people create (whether by divine will or by a creativity virtually divine) and, simultaneously, it is something so strong that its creators cannot control it. It masters them.

There is no word in the English language that adequately covers this phenomenon, and analogies pale. One can, for example, call the covenant a metaphor for the relationship of Yahweh and Israel, and in the technical sense it is. Indeed, all words concerning religion are metaphors, for no set of words can accurately encase the relationship religion posits between the infinite and the finite. And this holds whether or not one is a believer. Even the great nineteenth-century campaigner of atheism, Robert Green Ingersoll, could denounce religious belief only in metaphor.

When it comes to the ancient Hebrew covenant, however, "metaphor" is much too weak a term, for that covenant is not like any other metaphor we encounter in human history. It has literally controlled the thinking of those who have thought about it. Even those who consciously reject it do so through methods of thought that are taught by the ancient covenant.

The covenant in the Hebrew scriptures is a threefold phenomenon, each of the facets being historical in the following sense: (1) The covenant happened. Whatever one may feel about the accuracy of the details of transactions recorded in the Hebrew Bible, no one can fail to see that the ancient Israelites made a pretty big bargain with someone or something. (2) The ancient Hebrew polity explained to itself what had happened in language that was historical. In essence, the ancient Israelites invented historical thought to explain to themselves how they came to be wrapped in the all-encompassing embrace of Yahweh's covenant. And (3) the biblical explication of the Hebrew covenant became a model for the way future generations and, indeed, future civilizations, explained the working over time, of social cause and social effect.

Seemingly, the portions of the Hebrew scriptures that deal with the covenant, are a conundrum. The scriptures take the covenant as being outside of history, in the sense that Yahweh was eternal and thus not within time's ambit. Yet, Yahweh is seen to work only in history, only in time. So there is no independent rock, high and solid, on which to stand and observe the covenant, from outside the covenantal system. Nor would the ancient inventors of the scriptures have wished there to be. They wanted the blanket of history to surround and protect them, and the form that history assumed was the covenant with Yahweh.

Therefore, the conundrum was not for the scriptural writers a problem, but, indeed, an answer. For us, however, it can be a problem, for frequently we adopt (however unconsciously) analogies from the biological sciences, and convince ourselves that we can view human beings from outside, like a biologist viewing a specimen in a Petri dish. We cannot. No matter how far we get from the human social phenomena we are observing, we are not far enough.

To switch metaphors (and, oh, how inadequate they all are), we may be able to gain some distance on the Hebrew covenant, but we are still permanently trapped within its solar system. The only real variation is the distance around which we orbit this great, central gravitational field. This is true because the biblical writing that defines the covenant, being historical in character, has taught all of us our sense of history. (I will go into this more later; hard-shell classicists and graduates of English public schools should not yet run for the exits.) From a distance, circling the original Hebrew covenant, we can see, as if on a satellite photograph of earth, certain patterns that are not discernible up close. And we can observe how subsequent versions of the covenant have emerged from the original, white-hot mass and, thus, how the ancient Hebrew covenant determined the broad outlines of other, later iterations. Yet, all that done – and it is certainly worth doing – we shall inevitably conclude, either with sulphuric rage or with the bemused humility which is the foretaste of wisdom, that having been taught to think about history by humanity's first real historians, we are evermore viewing them from a tiny satellite that circles perpetually in their gravitational field.

2

In its fully evolved form, the covenant is conditional.[1] Thus, the statement of domestic blessings in Leviticus begins with an "if":

> If ye walk in my statutes and keep my commandments, and do them;
> Then I will give you rain in due season, and the land shall yield her increase, and the trees of the field shall yield their fruit.
> And your threshing shall reach unto the vintage, and the vintage shall reach unto the sowing time: and ye shall eat your bread to the full, and dwell in your land safely. (Lev. 26:3–5)

The earliest forms of the covenant are not explicitly conditional. After the flood, God tells Noah that he is creating the rainbow: "I do set my bow in the cloud, and it shall be for a token of a covenant between me and the earth" (Gen. 9:13). Nor is the early covenant limited to any distinct group of persons or, indeed, to the human race. It is, God says, a covenant "between me and you and every living creature of all flesh; and the waters shall no more become a flood to destroy all flesh" (Gen. 9:15).

In the biblical story that inclusive, unconditional covenant soon is displaced. God focuses his attention on Abram, a man living in Canaan with his wife, Sarai, amid his father's houses and lands. Why the Almighty chooses Abram is the sort of question that rarely arises in the scriptures, and that is a signal point: God chooses whom he will and when people, individually or as a group, are chosen, they have only two alternatives: to accept God's choice or not. Abram, chosen by God, is told to get out of his father's house, to leave his relatives behind, and to go into a land that God would show him:

> And I will make of thee a great nation, and I will bless thee, and make thy name great; and thou shalt be a blessing:
> And I will bless them that bless thee, and curse him that curseth thee: and in thee shall all the families of the earth be blessed. (Gen. 12:2–3)

In accepting this divine commission, Abram becomes a different person. He is reborn. The Almighty symbolizes this newness by changing Abram's name to Abraham, meaning the father of many nations:

> And I will make thee exceeding fruitful, and I will make nations of thee, and kings shall come out of thee.

> And I will establish my covenant between me and thee and thy seed after thee in their generations for an everlasting covenant, to be a God unto thee, and to thy seed after thee.
>
> And I will give unto thee, and to thy seed after thee, the land wherein thou art a stranger, all the land of Canaan, for an everlasting possession; and I will be their God. (Gen. 17:6–8)

Notice that the covenant has been restricted, from all living creatures to one man and his descendants. Although the covenant is not yet expressed as being fully conditional, the Almighty has something that he requires Abraham and his descendants to do as a consequence of being chosen: "Ye shall circumcise the flesh of your foreskin; and it shall be a token of the covenant betwixt me and you" (Gen. 17:11).

The next stage of the covenant's evolution occurs when God chooses (for reasons that characteristically are never explained) another particular man: He appears to Moses in a burning bush. An adiabatic fire appears and is followed by God's voice: "I am the God of thy father, the God of Abraham, the God of Isaac, and the God of Jacob" (Exod. 3:6). God proposes to send Moses to the Egyptian pharaoh who is keeping the descendants of Abraham in bondage. Moses is to lead them out of Egypt, "unto a land flowing with milk and honey" (Exod. 3:8). As a token of his confidence in Moses, God answers Moses' question, "Who shall I say sent me?" The first answer is an enigmatic, oracular, "I am that I am" (Exod. 3:14) which, in a later dialogue with Moses is expanded: "I appeared unto Abraham, unto Isaac, and unto Jacob, by the name of God Almighty [Baal Shaddai], but by my name Jehovah [Yahweh] was I not known to them" (Exod. 6:3).

There is a parallel, undoubtedly consciously drawn, between the story of the Abrahamic covenant and that of Moses. In the story of Abraham, God changed the name of humankind's representative as a part of the completion of the relationship. And here the name of the Almighty is changed. The compilers of the Pentateuch clearly expect the reader to absorb the stories of Abraham and of Moses in tandem.

That intention is the key to a way of thinking that permits the covenant to be continually re-invented by later generations. New material in the Bible, both in the Hebrew scriptures and the Christian scriptures and also in the corpus that builds on those scriptures, the Pseudepigrapha, Apocrypha, the Mishnah, and the Talmuds, is almost always added within the bounds of parallelism. Once the covenant, as articulated in the Books of Moses, has solidified, rarely is anything entirely new added. Any new item is presented as having a meaning that can only be understood if it is placed alongside the earlier text. New ideas are given legitimacy by their being burnished with the patina of history: the newer an idea or practice is, the more it is claimed to be old.

Parallels in the scriptures do not lie still. They are not immobile symmetrical comparisons, but take on the nature of a dialectic that moves the story forward. Thus, whereas the arrangement between Abraham and the Almighty has led to the introduction of one condition – circumcision – Moses now goes up to Yahweh's mountain and returns not only with the Ten Commandments but with a complex set of rules that the children of Israel must follow (see Exod. 20–24; cf. Deut. 5–25). Now, crucially, Yahweh is iffy about things: "*If* ye will obey my voice indeed, and keep my covenant, *then* ye shall be a peculiar treasure unto me above all people" (Exod. 19:5, italics mine).

The if-then mode (another form of parallelism) characterizes the covenant in its full form. It is this if-then nature of the covenant that means it is not flippant to think of the covenant as a deal between God and the Hebrews. Indeed, so clear are the details of this deal that a modern-day lawyer could write out a contract embodying precise standards of performance on each side. An idiomatic Hebrew phrase of the biblical era was "to cut a covenant" and, in truth, God and man had cut a deal.[2]

If-then. It is a more complex relationship psychologically than it is legally. On the surface, the causality flows only one way: if the Chosen People follow Yahweh's rules, he will give them virtue, peace, and prosperity. If they are his holy servants, the scriptures say, he will bless them. But psychologically the causality is easily reversed. That is, a person, or an entire nation, may observe that things are going well, that people are becoming rich and fecund, and thus will conclude: I (or we) must be righteous, for we are being blessed. Undoubtedly the reader will notice that this mechanism is part of the morphology of what Max Weber called the "Protestant ethic," a belief that success in the visible world signified righteousness in the invisible.

That kind of causal reversal is integral to if-then thinking on moral matters. It is a small and natural step in covenantal thinking to affirm that the possession of might (whether in the form of economic prosperity or military power) is evidence that one is morally right.

The if-then contract with Yahweh is a very risky arrangement, because the penalty clauses invoked for lapses by the Chosen People are extremely severe:

If thou wilt not observe to do all the words of this law that are written in this book, that thou mayest fear this glorious and fearful name, THE LORD THY GOD;

Then the Lord will make thy plagues wonderful, and the plagues of thy seed, even great plagues, and of long continuance, and sore sicknesses, and of long continuance.

Moreover he will bring upon thee all the diseases of Egypt, which thou wast afraid of; and they shall cleave unto thee.

Also every sickness, and every plague, which is not written in the book of this law; them will the Lord bring upon thee, until thou be destroyed.

And ye shall be left few in number, whereas ye were as the stars of heaven for multitude; because thou wouldest not obey the voice of the Lord thy God.

(Deut. 28:58–62)

Both directly in Yahweh's voice and indirectly through the prophets, the Chosen People are warned that Yahweh is a "jealous God" (Exod. 20:5, 34:14;
Deut. 4:24, 5:9, 6:15).

A jealous God, like a jealous lover, is capable of violence, and this holds
true even if the variant reading "zealous" instead of "jealous," put forward by
some scholars, is adopted. In the scriptures, God is very clearly credited with
physically punishing those who wander from the paths defined by the covenant. Because Yahweh controls all the earth, he is able to vent his wrath in a
variety of ways. For instance, in Moses' time, a man named Korah, a proto-
congregationalist, argued that every one of the Israelites was chosen by God
and therefore that all persons were the equivalent of priests and were able to
worship Yahweh directly. Korah and 250 of the leading men of the children
of Israel rebelled against the rule of Moses and against the way that the Levite priests monopolized the positions of religious prominence. Moses wanted
these religious democrats (to use an anachronistic but not inaccurate phrase)
killed, and in an especially memorable way as they were breaking the terms
of the covenant. Moses asks Yahweh to have the earth swallow up these dis-
senters and that is what happens. Korah, 250 princes of the people, their
houses and goods all drop into a pit and the earth closes around them (Num.
16:1–35; also 26:10).

Equally spectacular is Yahweh's displeasure when expressed in the form of
fire. In a situation in some ways similar to the Korah episode, two sons of
Aaron (Moses' brother and the head of the Levite priests) usurped the
priestly pecking order by taking "strange fire" in their censers as an offering
to Yahweh. Immediately he sent down fire, "and devoured them, and they
died before the Lord" (Lev. 10:2). On another occasion, during the forty
years of wandering in the wilderness, "the people complained, it displeased
the Lord: and the Lord heard it and his anger was kindled; and the fire of the
Lord burnt among them, and consumed them that were in the uttermost parts
of the camp" (Num. 11:1).

A little later, Miriam (Moses' sister) and Aaron questioned the religious
leadership that Yahweh had bestowed on Moses. "Hath the Lord indeed spoken only by Moses?" they ask. "Hath he not spoken also by us?" (Num.
12:2). The Lord hears this and responds by inflicting leprosy upon Miriam, a
case so severe that she becomes white as snow. Only after special intercession by Moses does Yahweh decide to heal her (Num. 12:10–16).

The if-then contract, therefore, implies a set of lessons that is anything but
valetudinarian. There is no hedging, no casuistry here, just the unmistakable

message that if you do not keep the deal with Yahweh, then he, the Lord of all the earth, is capable of turning the very earth, and all of its processes, into your scourge.

The same diamond-clear, diamond-hard morality is taught through Yahweh's sanctioning of purges and pogroms. At one point, when Moses was away conversing with Yahweh, a spontaneous apostasy spread among the people. They broke the fundamental commandment "Thou shalt have no other gods before me" and made a golden calf and danced around it naked. Moses, as Yahweh's spokesman, called together the Levites, each to bring his sword. "Thus saith the Lord God of Israel … Go in and out from gate to gate throughout the camp, and slay every man his brother, and every man his companion, and every man his neighbour" (Exod. 32:27). They did so. About 3,000 men died in this purge. Obviously, such a tale is not intended to pink the conscience delicately. It says: keep the deal or else.

3

If God is one of the names that people give to whatever they believe is the ultimate reality, then Yahweh is a remarkably understandable ultimate, and that is one of his wondrous features. Despite vast later efforts to etherealize him, the God of the Hebrew scriptures is solidly anthropomorphic. Had Yahweh been some Pythagorean abstraction, we would today not know his name – or, probably, that of Israel. But, as William Foxwell Albright argued in a classic of biblical interpretation, "It cannot be emphasized too strongly that the anthropomorphic conception of Yahweh was absolutely necessary if the God of Israel was to remain a God of the individual Israelite as well as of the people as a whole … It was precisely the anthropomorphism of Yahweh which was essential to the initial success of Israel's religion."[3]

The Hebrew God is aniconic and perfect. The first characteristic is a matter of inconvenience (one longs to see his face) and the second a matter of definition. Despite a great deal of ritual incantation about the mysteriousness of Yahweh, he is quite comprehensible. (Indeed, in biblical contexts and in later commentaries, when believers refer to Yahweh as being mysterious and beyond comprehension, they usually mean that he is disagreeable or rather frightening, but since he is by definition inerrant, his unpleasant nature must be some part of a divine perfection that we cannot understand.)

Emotionally and psychologically, Yahweh works just like a human being. Not just any human, to be sure, but he has mood swings, is frustrated, becomes angry, is generous, only on a cosmic scale. His dialogue with Job is one of the best conversations ever recorded. His words as given through the prophets are emotionally shrill, but they certainly are emotionally clear. But Yahweh is most forthright and most graphic in the Books of Moses wherein the ground rules of the covenant are worked out. Anybody who spent time on a playground as a child and survived can understand Yahweh, for his stock in trade is making deals and enforcing them.

In a beautifully crafted piece, the great essayist, Edward Hoagland mentions some of the most important characteristics of Yahweh. I quote Hoagland's lapidary phrases as instances of how, simultaneously, to be immediately right and ultimately wrong.[4]

- The Hebrew God is whimsical, jealous, inconsistent: mad, of course, very soon after that first chapter of Genesis, at Eve and Adam, with somewhat the same tone of thunderous petulance he later directs at poor Job for rather less reason.
- A bristly, lovely, although hot and fearsome recklessness invigorates God in the Old Testament when he loses patience.
- Justice is not God's department; justice is a man-made concept, except in the somewhat different sense that character is often fate.
- He seems a berserk and hideous deity in some of the more perfervid remarks that Moses and others record or attribute to him. He is an angry caliph who might better suit the Serbs or Hutus of 1994 or the Hitlerian Catholics of World War II.

Well, yes. All that is true, although Hoagland does leave out what Harold Bloom sees as the impish side of Yahweh, the slightly sadistic sense of humour, and the willingness to teach lessons to his people through the use of the ridiculous and the burlesque. Where Hoagland's essay really misses the point is that these are all presented as reasons for not liking Yahweh, to which one can only respond, "so what?" I cannot believe that any sane person has ever liked Yahweh. Feared him, yes; worshipped him, of course; made offerings, performed rituals, and engaged in obsessive acts of obeisance, naturally. Like him, no. Love him, absolutely impossible.

(Him? Certainly. The Hebrew scriptures are without ambiguity on the gender of Yahweh. He is not only male, but the most unattractive of males. In the Books of Moses he is forever an octogenarian with, alternatively, the atribilious humour of a chronic prostate sufferer or the imperious manner of a recently-retired Chief Executive Officer of a highly-profitable multi-national corporation. Him.)

But not liking Yahweh is irrelevant. The reason the god of the ancient Israelites is so convincing is that, as he is limned in the covenant, he is the perfect embodiment of what is: of reality. Whatever controls the lives of individual human beings (and there is an infinity of philosophical debate about such matters), it is not consistently nice, benevolent, predictable, or even understandable. Yahweh personifies that ultimate reality exactly. Life is bounteous, so too is Yahweh; life is unfair, so too is Yahweh (just ask Job). Yahweh is the name for reality invented by Hebrew religious geniuses who paid attention to the way the world works.

The covenant between Yahweh and Israel is the only image of Yahweh that exists. It is not a direct picture, and certainly not a graven image. Rather, the covenant is like a palimpsest which shows us in shadow what he really is. Once the covenant is extant, it is impossible to speak of God without automatically referring to the covenant. Or, to put it another way: God cannot exist outside the covenant. Hence, the ultimate ground of human experience in the scriptures is this deal, the covenant, hard, inflexible, comprehensible.

4

The covenant as the ultimate ground of experience in the scriptures encompasses not only Yahweh, but his parallel construct, the Chosen People. In 1935, in a classic essay (now back in favour among biblical scholars), Henry Wheeler Robinson suggested the usefulness of the concept of "corporate personality" in interpreting the Hebrew scriptures.[5] By this phrase Robinson meant two things. First, like a corporation in the modern legal sense, the Hebrew people were a single personality. They conceived of themselves as a single entity. And this corporate identity extended over time and included all members of the Chosen People, past, present, and future. Second, the corporate entity could be represented at special moments in its history by a single individual who could embody in his own singular personality the corporate personality of the entire nation.

The Elizabethan phrase that is used in the King James Version, by which Yahweh tells Moses that the people "shall be a peculiar treasure unto me" (Exod. 19:5), captures the essential nature of this corporate identity. The children of Israel are peculiar in the now-archaic sense of their being special, and also in the modern sense of being singular – different from every other people. What makes them both different and special is that they have been given a treasure, the covenant, for which they are now responsible. Indeed, for a long period in their early history, the children of Israel maintained a reliquary of the holiest order, the ark of the covenant, which accompanied them on their wanderings and ultimately was housed in the holy-of-holies in the Temple of Jerusalem.

The singularity and specialness of the Chosen People are bound up with the concept of "seed." God says to Abraham:

> For all the land which thou seest, to thee will I give it, and to thy seed for ever.
> And I will make thy seed as the dust of the earth; so that if a man can number the dust of the earth, then shall thy seed also be numbered. (Gen. 13:15–16)

And again:

> And I will establish my covenant between me and thee and thy seed after thee in their generations for an everlasting covenant, to be a God unto thee, and to thy seed after thee. (Gen. 17:7)

The matter of seed runs through the scriptures in a very literal and explicit fashion. It should not be turned into a pale metaphor. The references are directly biological and have to do with human reproduction. This is most clear in the story of Onan, one of the sons of Judah (Gen. 38:1–10). One of Judah's other sons, his firstborn, "was wicked in the sight of the Lord; and the Lord slew him." Judah, wishing to continue his family line, urged Onan to have sexual congress with the widow of Onan's brother and then to marry her and raise the child that would result from their physical union. Onan agreed to have sexual intercourse, but, "lest he should give seed to his brother," practised coitus interruptus: he ejaculated on the ground. Now to a modern reader this decision seems reasonable, but Yahweh saw the sperm being spilled and it "displeased" him. "Wherefore he slew him [Onan] also." Manifestly, seed refers to biological reproduction and it is through the seed in the biological sense that the corporate existence of the Chosen People is achieved generation after generation. Biology is central to the definition of the Chosen People.

That is why those long genealogies are found in the scriptures. Whether or not the genealogies are historically accurate or whether they are schematized lines of descent is of no moment. What is salient is that they purport to chronicle the way the seed of Abraham, through the mechanism of human reproduction, was carried through time, increasing in each generation the corporate host that is the Chosen People. The mentality here is significant. One is not being arch in noting that segments of the scriptures read very much like one-half of a purebred stud book, the half that contains the sire's line.[6] People keep track of blood lines only if they think such things are important, and judging by the amount of attention given to genealogies in the Hebrew scriptures, such things are very important indeed.

In this context, the practice of circumcision makes great sense. Yahweh's instructions to Abraham are within the context of maintaining the covenant: "And the uncircumcised man child whose flesh of his foreskin is not circumcised, that soul shall be cut off from his people; he hath broken my covenant" (Gen. 17:14). Circumcision is a real physical act, an intentional offering to God of a piece of flesh, similar in that regard to the several other forms of flesh sacrifice practised by the Hebrews of the time. By offering up part of the male reproductive organ of each of their offspring, the Chosen People reaffirmed in each generation that physical reproduction was part of the covenant with the Almighty.

Biology, therefore, becomes as vital as belief in determining the corporate entity, the Chosen People, so there is a strong emphasis upon keeping pure the lines of reproduction: that is, of not marrying outside the Hebrew nation or race (neither term quite fits the unique polity that evolved under the covenant). Moses, as an old man, rehearsed for the people the covenantal ordinances that bound together, and bound to Yahweh, the Chosen People. One of these is as follows:

When the Lord thy God shall bring thee unto the land whither thou goest to possess it, and hath cast out many nations before thee, the Hittites, and the Girgashites, and the Amorites, and the Canaanites, and the Perizzites, and the Hivites, and the Jebusites, seven nations greater and mightier than thou.

Neither shalt thou make marriages with them; thy daughter thou shalt not give unto his son, nor his daughter shalt thou take unto thy son.   (Deut. 7:1 and 3)

Joshua, in his last counsel to the people, gave similar advice, that they must not intermarry with the people of the nations that they conquered (Josh. 23:12).

One graphic story illustrates with particular clarity the horror with which the scriptures view intermarriage. At one time the men of Israel "began to commit whoredom with the daughters of Moab" (Num. 25:1). Since in the scriptural ideology, blood impurity always leads to sacral impurity, one is not surprised to learn that as a result of their mixed marriages, the Chosen People made sacrifices and bowed down to the gods of Moab. The Lord, angered by this development, brings a fierce plague upon Israel. While many of the people are weeping in repentance before the holy tabernacle, a manifestly unrepentant Hebrew man brings a non-Israelite woman to his tent. Phinehas, the grandson of Aaron, takes a javelin and follows the couple to their tent. There, as the couple have sexual congress, he thrusts the javelin through the man's back and all the way through the woman's belly. This priestly murder satisfied Yahweh: "So the plague was stayed from the children of Israel." Even so, the Chosen People already had lost to the plague 24,000 individuals, all as a direct result of not keeping their seed pure (Num. 25: 1–9).

The way in which the covenant implies both belief and blood purity (that is, adherence to Yahweh as their one god and the maintenance of the purity of the Abrahamic seed) puts one in mind of a certain toy popular in the nineteenth century. The "thingamatrope" consisted of a disk painted on opposite sides with two quite different images. The toy was fitted with a device that allowed the disk to be spun very quickly on its vertical axis. When it spun, the two separate images merged to form a single picture. That is what happens with belief and blood in the Pentateuch: the whirl of history makes them one.

If defence of the purity of the seed is in part a social act (such as is effected by inhibiting mixed marriages), at other times it is necessarily military. Yahweh told Abraham, "I will bless them that bless thee, and curse him that curseth thee" (Gen. 12:3). Moses, in giving his great charge to the Chosen People, indicated what this would entail:

And ye shall chase your enemies, and they shall fall before you by the sword.

And five of you shall chase an hundred, and an hundred of you shall put ten thousand to flight: and your enemies shall fall before you by the sword.

For I will have respect unto you, and make you fruitful, and multiply you, and establish my covenant with you. (Lev. 26:7–9)

The covenant is not primarily intended to bring peace, but victory.

5

From the if-then character of the covenant follow three interrelated habits of mind. Each of these is made possible because the covenant is essentially empirical in nature. In fact, the covenant could be converted into a hypothesis easily tested by a modern observer: if condition A occurs, then response B ensues. There is nothing mystical about it. It is a matter of cause and effect, stimulus and response, action and reaction.

The first mental habit that derives from the nature of the covenant is the tendency to make sharp distinctions between the sacred and the profane. Virtually all cultures make this distinction in one way or another, but in the scriptural code the line is drawn especially clearly. This clarity is perhaps best captured in the book of Leviticus, for example:

> But I have said unto you, Ye shall inherit their land, and I will give it unto you to possess it, a land that floweth with milk and honey: I am the Lord your God, which have separated you from other people.
> Ye shall therefore put difference between clean beasts and unclean, and between unclean fowls and clean: and ye shall not make your souls abominable by beast, or by fowl, or by any manner of living thing that creepeth on the ground, which I have separated from you as unclean.
> And ye shall be holy unto me: for I the Lord am holy, and have severed you from other people, that ye should be mine. (Lev. 20:24–26)

There it all is: the reference to the covenant, to the benefits derived from it (a land of milk and honey), if the Chosen People keep separate (sacred) from other peoples (the profane). Notice that all the natural world is divided just as is human society, into clean beasts and unclean (sacred and profane). Such a division of the world into easily understandable black and white categories is emotionally comforting, because it erases those ambiguous grey areas of human experience that cause so much anxiety. Thus, the Hebrew conceptual grid is very attractive. It has a major disadvantage, however: people who exist within such an ideology – whether as individuals or as a corporate group – do not have much room to manoeuvre. That is why the process of re-invention becomes so important in the history of covenantal peoples. Re-invention allows the old forms to be given new interpretations, and thus the covenantal peoples escape the moral vise that otherwise crushes in on them.

Otherwise, individuals can engage in new experiences and can encounter new persons only with great care. They must decide whether the stranger at their door is one of themselves, and act accordingly. And, as a nation, the children of Israel are given little opportunity to compromise with their enemies. Undeniably, human beings, being endlessly ingenious, can argue long about the details of the divine distinction between sacred and profane, but there is no avoiding the fact that ultimately all decisions are supposed to be made within the stark rubrics of the sacred-profane dichotomy.

The second habit of mind that follows from the covenant is functionally related to the sacred-profane distinction, namely the legal mode of thinking. It is entirely appropriate that the book of Psalms begins with a hymn to the law and to those who follow its precepts:

> Blessed is the man that walketh not in the counsel of the ungodly, nor standeth in the way of sinners, nor sitteth in the seat of the scornful.
> But his delight is in the law of the Lord; and in his law doth he meditate day and night.
> And he shall be like a tree planted by the rivers of water, that bringeth forth his fruit in his season; his leaf also shall not wither; and whatsoever he doeth shall prosper.
>
> (Ps. 1:1–3)

The law in the scriptures is of three sorts: apodictic, false-apodictic, and casuistic. Apodictic commandments consist of absolute laws in their pure form. Such laws state a rule of behaviour but give no indication of the consequences if the command is not obeyed. The so-called great commandment is the purest example:

> Hear, O Israel: The Lord our God, is one Lord:
> And thou shalt love the Lord thy God with all thine heart, and with all thy soul, and with all thy might. (Deut. 6:4–5)

The Decalogue ("Thou shalt not kill," etc.) is perhaps the best-known apodictic framing of behavioral imperatives (see Exod. 20 and Deut. 5). What I term "false-apodictic" (the term is mine, although I cannot imagine that in the vast libraries of commentary someone has not used it before) refers to laws such as "And he that smiteth his father, or his mother, shall be surely put to death" (Exod. 21:15). This is not true apodictic law; because there is an unstated if-then clause. The statute really says *if* a person strikes his father or his mother, *then* he or she shall be executed. The same holds for the famous formula "Eye for eye, tooth for tooth, hand for hand, foot for foot" (Exod. 21:24). *If* a person maims another, *then* an equivalent revenge-maiming shall be visited upon him. The third, and most common form of law in the Hebrew scriptures is casuistic. This is if-then thinking at its most explicit and precise: "If a man shall steal an ox, or a sheep, and kill it, or sell it; he shall restore five oxen for an ox, and four sheep for a sheep" (Exod. 22:1). This kind of statute gives rise very quickly to case law and to the search for precedents in the common event of cases arising that are not exactly covered by biblical statutes. What, for example, should be the punishment for a man who steals an ox but is apprehended before he either can kill it or sell it? Does he merely return the animal or must he pay the five-oxen compensation, or something in between?

The omnipresence of the Hebrew legal code is one of its crucial characteristics. It translates the sacred-profane distinctions that stem from the covenant into practical rules for everyday life. Granted, some of the requirements, particularly the food taboos, are complicated and involve some inconvenience, but the rules are specific and can be met with a reasonable amount of effort. This legalistic approach to behaviour yields a mentality that is both very exacting in its grasp of details and highly pragmatic. Yahweh's law is a practical discipline, and because the laws are so precise and so practical, it is easy for members of the group to monitor accurately who is and who is not conforming fully to Yahweh's covenant. And, simultaneously, the laws are a continuing and visible reminder to the Chosen People that they are not the same as everyone else, the profane.

The third habit of mind engendered by the if-then character of the covenant is that the Chosen People think historically. To what extent the material in the scriptures represents accurately written history is one of those questions about which holy and unholy wars have been fought, but at present that question is not germane. The intellectual grid that is formed by the scriptures is nothing if not historical. And how could it be otherwise? The covenant is presented in terms that imply sequence (if-then); the emphasis upon the Abrahamic seed results in a desire to plot the descent of the seed over time (as is evidenced in the long sequential genealogies); the legalistic cast of mind implies not only a concern with the sequence of events in individual cases, but with the aggregation of wisdom (case law) over time. History in the scriptures therefore is central. That the past can be known and recorded is an assumption that makes the existence of scriptures possible.

Within this historical mindset are four secondary characteristics. First, the scriptures teach the Chosen People to think in terms of cause and effect. That is no small thing. Also, the scriptures implicitly teach that if one is to think well in cause-effect terms, what is happening on both sides of the equation must be specified very precisely. (Modern social scientists call this "operational specificity.") So, for example, when someone sins, his transgression is specified and his punishment is precisely defined: cause-effect. A second aspect of the scriptural-taught ability to think historically is something so obvious that it is easily overlooked: the scriptures teach those who read and hear their contents to think in terms of time in general and in terms of chronology in particular. Just how seminal an intellectual influence this is becomes obvious when one contrasts the Hebrew scriptures to, for example, the holy texts of most Far Eastern religions. There all events at more than one lifespan's remove from the scribe are reported as if time occurred on some great white wall, and as if every event in the past were shown on that wall, equidistant from the present – "in the old gods' time" is one formulation. In contrast, the Hebrews meter time, and they use the same measuring system consistently, all the way back to creation. Modern scholars sometimes point amusedly to earlier attempts to date happenings in the scriptures by calculating the passage of time as shown in the Hebrew genealogies (Archbishop Ussher's classic seventeenth-century chronology that dates the creation of the world at 4004 BCE comes to mind). But one should not patronize the scribes. That they used lifespans instead of years as a way of measuring time is hardly primitive: until well into the present century, the standard agricultural lease in England, the first country to undergo the radical transformation that we call the Industrial Revolution, was in terms of "lives," not years. A third aspect of the historical mindset is that the Hebrews' discourse became numerate: accurate numerical description, or attempts at it, are part of clearly defining cause and effect. Thus, large portions of the Pentateuch are given over to early enumerations (the book of Numbers contains some of the best examples). These population censuses were an attempt to gain a definition of the Chosen People and to chart their growth. And fourth, the historical sense also produced a very precise sense of geography in the holy texts. The point I want to stress here is the prodigious topographical detail in the scriptures. Spatial description is as essential an axis of historical description as is chronology: the Chosen People move not only through time, but through specific, tightly boundaried space.

All this sounds very modern, and it is. Yet to note this fact is to fly in the face of what is virtually a small industry, the line of scholarship that emphasizes how different the biblical sense of history is from that of our own time. Of course it is different: the historical sense of each generation and each culture is different from that of every other, and the Hebrew nation had some singular mental habits of its own. But its historical sense was not all that much different from our own. Granted, the scriptures start with the Almighty as the ultimate cause of everything. Yahweh, in fact, becomes a very specific actor and, once his bargain with Abraham is sealed, he is known only through the covenant. He therefore operates in very specific ways, not unlike any great historical figure. It is easy to be misled by the later theologizations of Yahweh. As Harold Bloom has argued, "Modern scholars, Jewish and Gentile alike, cannot seem to accept the fact that there was no Jewish theology before Philo. 'Jewish theology,' despite its long history from Philo to Franz

Rosenzweig, is therefore an oxymoron, particularly when applied to biblical texts... Yahweh is an uncanny personality, and not at all a concept."[7]

It is sometimes argued that the scriptures are radically different from modern historical discourse in that they inevitably imply a lesson. History, in the scriptures, teaches, but so too does modern history. It is true that modern historians like to dissemble concerning the lessons that they draw and to disguise them behind certain tricks of professional distancing. Yet, actually, we are forever drawing lessons. Has anyone read any volume about, say, the history of the Vietnam War that did not contain an implied lesson? Even the most anodyne of modern histories – for example, the studies of the *longue durée* by the Annales school – are undertaken in order to teach the reader something about the nature of human existence, and hence they contain an implicit lesson, however subdued.

And it is sometimes suggested that the Hebrew scriptures, replete as they are with poetic expressions, are thereby rendered incompatible with our own way of thinking. "It is a language in which every other word is a concealed metaphor" was Henry Wheeler Robinson's view of the sacred tongue, expressed half a century ago.[8] Today his observation would alienate few historians, for, if there is one thing that the application of critical theory has forced professional historians to realize, it is that *all* words enhull concealed metaphors, those of the allegedly antiseptic historians of our own time as much as the Yahwist scribes of nearly three millennia ago.

That the historical sense of the Hebrew scriptures should be so similar to our own should surprise no one, for it is from those scriptures that western society learned how to think historically. What should surprise us, however, is the constant denial of this fact by people in my own trade: professional historians. Indeed, professional historians love to point to Hecataeus, to Herodotus, to Thucydides as our founding fathers. This putative descent was even more a matter of pride in an earlier generation when the classical languages and literature were dominant studies in the humanities. Nevertheless, the Hebrew scriptures, not the classics, were the medium in which, from the time of Constantine onward, most literate westerners first encountered the study of the past. These scriptures – which, unlike the classics, were not lost to western society during the alleged Dark Ages – are markedly older than those of classical antiquity. Older roots, unbroken continuity, and a vastly wider audience: that is why the scriptures, not the Greek classics, are the hammer and anvil by which our western sense of history first took shape. In our understanding of history as narrative and as process we in present-day western society are the descendants of the children of Israel, and that is no mean heritage.

*Inventive Fecundity
and Judahist Multiplicity:
the Later Second Temple Era*

· 5 ·

Siloam's Teeming Pool – I

I

TO DESCRIBE, EVEN IN TONES OF HUSHED AWE, THE HEBREW SCRIPTURES as inventions, as I have been doing – and to do so with the derivatives of those scriptures, the Christian writings and the Talmudic literature, as I will be doing – is of course patently inadequate. "Of course," because no image or figure of speech can capture the fullness of the metaphor that has itself formed western culture, the ancient Hebrew covenant with Yahweh. But "invention" has the virtue of being a belief-neutral concept and it permits persons who have no faith in any of the Yahweh-based religions nevertheless to gaze in wonder at their complexity, richness and subtle cleverness. Simultaneously, believers can see the hand of the Almighty in any (or all) of these inventions, the gentle touch of the holy spirit guiding the inventors. My goal is to serve both groups, to show how these inventions came to be, in a discussion that is belief-neutral, but which is appreciative of the surpassing wonder of it all.

But here I need help, for, usually, even the greatest inventions have a museum quality, and until very recently, with the advent of genetic engineering, they were inanimate. What we need here is an animator. No, not the chi-chi *animateur,* who has replaced the "moderator" at upscale academic colloquies, but the cybernerd who invades all our lives daily, with soup cans that talk, flashlight batteries that march, and cinematic special effects that are especially affected, but hardly specially effective. Like all God's creatures, this being has value, for he has created software packages that permit us to observe animation in almost any set of objects or artifacts.

That is germane, because in the period we are here dealing with – from the desecration of the Second Temple in 167 BCE and the subsequent Maccabean revolt, to the destruction of the Temple in 70 CE by Roman forces – the culture of Judaism was immensely rich, yet what is left to us is mostly a set of fragmented documents that are too easily misperceived as being inanimate. The closest parallel to the cultural richness of this era in the earlier history of this planet is the Cambrian Period, during which a biological plentitude reigned. In the "Cambrian explosion" of multi-celled organisms, living entities encountered each other and re-invented themselves, as separate species; thousands, probably millions, of times. A similar primal richness characterized the period between the Maccabean revolt and the razing of the Second Temple. In religious terms, this era was as animated and as inventive a period as ever existed on this planet.[1]

So diverse, so lively, so copious was the inventiveness of the late Second Temple era, that until recently the reaction of most biblical scholars and of almost all believers (both Jews and Christians) has been to hide from the implications of this era of virtually-Brownian motion in the pool of religious life. False linearities have been grasped at. This is neither surprising nor reprehensible. The whirl of the period can be unsettling. Take the Christian case. It would be very reassuring to have a nice clean backdrop against which the rise of the followers of Yeshua of Nazareth could be explained. This is especially important, because almost every Christian document in its present form was written after 70 CE. The assumption of linearity (that is, of regular, even historical progression) during the period from roughly 200 BCE to 70 CE would permit the telling of Yeshua's story with greater clarity, and therefore with more conviction, than if a constantly moving *moire* pattern must serve as backdrop. As for Talmudic Judaism (often called Rabbinic Judaism), it is a creation of the years 70 to 600 CE and most of its advocates have had an even greater investment in averting their gaze from the whirl of the last two and a half centuries of the Second Temple period. They have wished to see a clear, single line between the rabbis of the second-through-sixth centuries of the Common Era who created Rabbinic Judaism and those leaders of the fifth century before the Common Era who, following the Babylonian captivity, rebuilt the Temple. Therefore, understandably, a strong strain in both Jewish and Christian apologetics has had at its core a need to minimize both the fecundity of religious invention in later Second Temple times, and to deny the unpredictability of the outcome of that period of religious whirl.

Not that the period was one of incoherence: it is still appropriate to think of Judahism (not yet "Judaism," for that is not invented until well into the Common Era) as being a cultural spine that was shared throughout Palestine and the diaspora. It implied, still, worship of Yahweh only; the celebration of Judah as the true covenantal line with the consequent recognition of Jerusalem as the spiritual metropole; and a recognition of the importance of the priestly offices in the Temple (although, increasingly, a conviction took many of the seriously religious that some of the Temple officers were far from being persons of spiritual discipline). So, there was a central line of Judahist religious attitudes: yet, outside of those central affirmations, so divergent were the forms that the Judahist religion assumed, and so variegated the beliefs, that they cannot be harmonized. "There was no orthodoxy," is the unambiguous judgement of Jacob Neusner. "We find distinct social groups, each with its ethos and ethics, each forming its distinctive ethnos, all of them constituting different people talking about different things to different people."[2]

When historians deal with this teeming pool, they cannot approach it with the same, relatively straightforward methods as they would use when dealing with, say, the Industrial Revolution (highly complex though that was). This has nothing to do with the nature of the surviving sources. Instead, it is the case because the mindset that is employed in dealing with linear evolutions in human history (in the case of the Industrial Revolution, for example, the sequence of evolution from handloom weaving through factory-based textile production by way of tiny, incremental inventions), is not rewarding: we are here dealing with one of history's rare eras, when the production of maximal cultural disparity (within the limits of the Yahwist faith), rather than a narrowing evolution, was the heart of the historical process. Moreover, so much of the interaction of these maximally-disparate, ever-increasing religious inventions, one with another, was virtually random, so as to preclude the linear cause-and-effect explanation that historians usually employ. Earlier I used the term "Brownian motion" – the irregular, unpredictable, essentially random movement of particulates suspended in liquid – as a parallel. The nature of such chaotic event-systems (chaotic in the scientific sense of being non-linear in cause-and-effect patterns) is hard for those of us in the historical profession to cope with: we keep hoping that with just a bit more documentation everything will become clear, stable, and precise. It won't.

Third – and crucially – the way the era ended is even more difficult for professional historians to handle. That is: for the religious cultures of Judah, it concluded with the equivalent of a meteorite hitting the earth. The Roman destruction of Herod's Temple had an even greater impact than did the Babylonian destruction of Solomon's Temple. Most (but not all) of the forms of religious life that had animated Siloam's teeming pool were exterminated. In the long perspective – taking, say, the year 500 CE as a vantage point – only two major forms had survived with any vigor. They had radically modified themselves through radical re-invention and modification, and had become the Christian and the Jewish faiths.

Believers in either of those two faiths can handle that: it is simply the hand of God working in time. However, for historians (who, whatever their personal convictions, are allegiant to certain rules of evidence), the results of the great meteor strike, with its permanent destruction of the central icon around which all the various Judaisms of the later Second Temple era circulated (roughly, the two-and-a-half centuries before 70 CE), are maddeningly inexplicable. In "secular" history there is no reason that the filaments of belief which subsequently spawned the Jewish and the Christian entities should have survived the great disaster of 70 CE. Any of the dozens of related strands of belief had an equal chance of making it. What occurred was the social equivalent of a "decimation by lottery" in the world of biology. By sheer fortuitiveness – let's be honest and use the right term: by sheer good luck – these two filaments came out the far side of the engulfing disaster. It is possible to describe historically what the nature of that good luck was – it ranged from certain leaders of each group physically escaping the Jerusalem conflagration, to each religion's having more than one new inventive genius arise in the post-70 CE years – but describing such things should not give us a false sense of control.

Nor should it be the cause of our retrospectively layering the two survivors with a lacquer of hardness or of heroism. I think we should assimilate the suggestion, rich in analogy, that the human race owes its existence to mammals having been, at the moment in the Cretaceous period when so many life forms were wiped out, small beings. Sometimes a random virtue – such as smallness, or relative inconsequence – makes all the difference.

2

The political history of Judah is not a central matter in this book, but some moments of great religious consequence were defined by events that were as much political as religious. One of these is the 160s BCE when the Seleucid (that is, Syrian Hellenist) monarch King Antiochus IV, self-named "Epiphanes," came to rule Palestine. A second moment was the late 60s CE when the Roman rulers of Palestine suppressed a civil revolt. The period between these two occurrences was not an "era" in the political sense of the word, for it mixed everything from Seleucid despotism to local revolt, to "home rule" for Palestine, to various forms of Roman governance, all intermingled with a medley of local faction fights, many of them involving devotees of the Yahweh-faith fighting one another. It was a turbulent time and politically confusing. The major political boundaries are worth brief attention, however: if the culture of Palestine, centring on Jerusalem was analogous to a teeming pool in which all sorts of religious life-forms evolved, interacted, and mutated, then the boundaries of that pool were set by political forces.

At the beginning of the second century before the Common Era, a compact and homogeneous Judahist population existed only in Judea proper: the southern part of Palestine whose metropole was Jerusalem. This corresponded quite closely to the former kingdom of Judah.[3] That noted, the Judahist population of the rest of Palestine was considerable if not necessarily a majority, and the diaspora outside the holy land was of indeterminate, and probably sharply fluctuating, size.

The rule of Palestine by the Syrian Hellenists need not have been any different in character than its rule by Egyptian Hellenists, but in fact it was. In part, this stemmed from Roman imperialism pressing onto the edge of the map, compressing the possibilities open to ambitious Seleucid monarchs. Thus, in the year 167 BCE, the Seleucid monarch, having attacked Egypt, was forced by the Romans to give up that effort. In his vexation, he found a thorough conquest of Palestine an appealing and pride-salving enterprise. That monarch was Antiochus IV Epiphanes, and even making allowance for the nature of the historical sources that survive (none of which was written by his admirers), he probably was not just frustrated and pride-bound, but a seriously deranged personality.

This was not the right moment for a psychotic Syrian monarch to begin stirring in the Holy Land. Judah may have been a small principality, but it was the intersection point of several rivalries, some domestic, others international in origin. One of these was an Egyptian-Syrian rivalry, with Jerusalem the prize. To further complicate things, Rome kept a watching brief, always ready to intervene. Domestically, the high priestly families within Jerusalem were at loggerheads with one another. For several years in the 180s CE, the high priest Onias III had to fight to defend himself against deposition by rival families. Eventually, in 175 BCE he appealed for protection to Antiochus Epiphanes (who had just come to the Seleucid throne following the murder of his brother). Antiochus's response was to take the high priest captive and, in return for a bribe, to put his brother Jason in the high priesthood. Then, in 172, Antiochus dumped Jason and replaced him with Menelaus, who was a priest of a rival family. (Note for future reference the Hellenistic names, Jason and Menelaus, of the main Judahist figures in the story.) None of these appointments was in accordance with Temple law. Yet the fact that the moves were supported by a sizeable proportion of the religious elite indicates just how deeply fractured things had become in the Temple establishment. The strife between the parties has frequently been simplified as being between "Hellenizers" and a true-to-Judah party, but in fact it was as much about family greed and dynastic lust within the highest echelons of the Temple administration.[4]

So nasty were things among the Judaean religious elite, that Jason employed physical force to seize Jerusalem and to take back the high priesthood from Menelaus. Since Menelaus was now the accredited puppet of Antiochus Epiphanes (having offered him a larger bribe than had Jason, and thus having purchased Jason's earlier dismissal), the Syrian was virtually forced to intervene in protection of his own control of Palestine. Therefore in 169 BCE he attacked Jerusalem, killed many, and, almost in passing, looted the Temple. He left behind an occupying force situated in a specially-constructed military building near the Temple. Then, in 167, having been frustrated by the Romans in his attempts to conquer Egypt, Antiochus turned again on Jerusalem and this time he came as a berserker. He demolished the city walls, declared circumcision and the observation of the Sabbath to be forbidden, prohibited

Temple sacrifice and took to having one of the Baal gods worshipped in the Temple. Among the Baal icons were images of swine. Such foaming-at-the-mouth persecution was very unusual within the context of previous centuries of imperialism in the Ancient Near East. The usual practice was to allow local populations to follow their religion. This veering from usual practice is the datum line that makes one realize that Antiochus Epiphanes was not a mere run-of-the-mill monarch, but a deranged personality, and in the nature of such personalities, deeply destructive of his own interest.

The indigenous response was the Maccabean rising, led by a priestly family of "Hasmoneans" (probably a place name, whose origins are now lost), a father and five sons. One of the sons, Judas, was a military genius, and by 164 BCE Judea was liberated from the Seleucids and the Temple reconsecrated. Subsequently, large areas outside of the old kingdom of Judah were added to the new state. The campaign was an impressive piece of military strategy and it is well memorialized in 1 and 2 Maccabees, in the writing of Josephus (who relies mostly on 1 Maccabees) and, indirectly, in the Book of Daniel.[5]

From the mid-160s until the year 63 BCE, when Rome turned most of Palestine into a province under its own rule, Jerusalem was the centre of an independent state. The Maccabeans became eventually priests and kings, a conjoint eminence that not even David or Solomon had dared to assert. (In 63 BCE the high priesthood and the ruling civil power were again separated.) In their later years, before Rome intervened, the Hasmonean (or Maccabean) dynasty of high priest-kings became factionally split and venal. Still, the Maccabean achievement has to be recognized. The nation of Judah was politically independent; the Temple was in daily operation; the priestly elite and the political elite were one. Everything circled around Mount Zion.[6]

Yet the instability and corruption of the Maccabeans produced their own downfall. Some representatives of the Judaean population, preferring what they hoped would be orderly Roman governance to the violence of the Hasmoneans, approached the Roman governor Pompey and suggested that he intervene. He did so in the year 63 BCE and, thereafter, Palestine was under various forms of Roman rule. Pompey required physical force to subdue the Hasmonean factions, and he is remembered for having used a battering ram to break into the Temple. The indignant author of the Psalms of Solomon denounced Pompey and complained about Yahweh's supine fecklessness as follows:

> Arrogantly the sinner broke down the strong walls with a battering ram and you did not interfere.
> Gentile foreigners went up to your place of sacrifice: they arrogantly trampled it with sandals. (Ps. of Sol. 2:1–2)[7]

Actually, Pompey engaged in no depredations. He did not plunder the Temple and the day after his victory he gave orders for the Judahist religious rites to be resumed.[8] The Maccabeans continued for another three decades as high priests – under the title "ethnarchs" – but they no longer held political power. The brief moment in the history of Judah when the high priesthood and the kingship were united in one person had passed forever.

Frequent small-scale civil revolts characterized the 50s BCE and in the 40s instability in Rome itself further roiled the waters. Thus, it was a great simplification when, in 37 BCE, "Herod the Great" was able to conquer, under Roman seal, most of Palestine, and set aside permanently the remnants of the Maccabeans who had engaged in periodic revolts against Rome. Herod the Great had something of the mixture of abilities that characterized the Tudors, particularly Henry VIII: a powerful physical presence, considerable military ability, great cultural ambitions (mostly expressed through architecture), and a wily sense of his own self-protection (he was especially good at keeping his Roman masters sweet). His family background was Idumean (that is, from the region south of Jerusalem, running down to the Negev desert), which the Maccabeans had conquered in 129 BCE. At that time, the Hasmoneans had forcibly converted to Judahism the adult population of the region. Herod had Hasmonean blood in his family and he married a woman of the Hasmonean elite. However, after conquering Jerusalem, he was shrewd enough not to claim the high priesthood for himself, for this would have invited religious revolt. For a time, he kept Hasmonean high priests in place, but then, recognizing that they were potential rivals for political power, he had them replaced by a series of puppets of non-Hasmonean blood.[9]

Herod's sense of himself was monumental, literally. He built entire cities (Caesarea and Sebaste), pagan temples (an especially notable one to Augustus), several palaces (the ones at Masada, Caesarea, and Jerusalem being the most famous), and, indeed, virtually every town in Palestine had an aqueduct or monument or amphitheatre or temple or baths built at his behest. Jerusalem, however, was his jewel, and there he reconfigured the city with the clear ambition of making it Judea's Rome. In addition to his own palace, he constructed an amphitheatre, a hippodrome, and a theatre. Yet, even these were side-pieces.[10] His central monument was nothing less than the building of a new Temple. New? In practice, yes, because during reconstruction most of the pre-Herodian portions of the Second Temple that had been built after the Babylonian exile were razed or completely reconstructed. Herod's Temple approximately doubled the size of the previous Temple.[11] Josephus reported that Herod had the foundation stones of the previous Temple removed and new ones laid in their place.[12]

Begun in the year 20/19 BCE, this massive project had progressed sufficiently for Temple worship to recommence before a decade had passed.[13]

Details remained to be completed, however, and the Gospel of John (2:20) states that the Temple took forty-six years to build. In fact, work was still reported to be in progress in the early 60s of the Common Era, not long before the Temple was fated to be demolished.[14] This was the third Temple, succeeding that of Solomon and of Zerubbabel, but by a rhetorical convention Herod's Temple is considered part of the "Second Temple" era and the term "Third Temple" is used in the present day in the apocalyptic sense, to refer to a temple that at some future date is thought by Jewish and Christian fundamentalists to be destined to be constructed in Jerusalem where the Moslem faith's Dome of the Rock mosque now is located. Thus, although from the year 20 BCE onwards, the followers of Yahweh actually were worshipping in the Third Temple, scholars continue to refer to it as the "Second Temple" and to the period up to 70 CE as the "Second Temple period." That protocol fits well with the basic rules of innovation within the Judaeo-Christian tradition (which, as we have seen, dictates that innovations be discounted, or disguised as being ancient traditions); however, that Herod the Great had replaced Zerubbabel's Temple with a massive piece of Hellenic architecture, based on the Caesareum found in Alexandria, Egypt, was hardly a development lost on people of the time.[15]

Herod's Temple would have served equally well for the founding of a new religion or for continuing an existing one. Josephus, who knew the building in his youth, and who had seen a great deal of the Roman world, said that "it was a structure more noteworthy than any under the sun."[16] In Herod's time, a succession of tame high priests, whom he chose, continued the sacrificial tradition.

The Temple was the hub of worship in the later Second Temple era, but it was not the only place where one could worship the God of Judah. In the diaspora there were synagogues, mostly held within the house of some of the more wealthy of the faithful, and three purpose-built synagogues have been found in Palestine, dating to the pre-70 CE era: at Masada, Herodium, and Gamala. Since in Palestine, as in the diaspora, most synagogues probably were located in private homes, there clearly were more than three in existence: literary sources suggest over fifty.[17] Although the Jerusalem Temple was the only accredited place where, through ritual sacrifice, the covenant between Yahweh and Judah could be re-enacted – with the spilling of blood in return for the blessing of Yahweh – it is well to note that going back as far as King Josiah there had been rival locations for ritual sacrifice and in this period one operated at Leontopolis in Egypt.[18]

As we shall see in a moment, many individuals who were deeply committed to the religion of Yahweh were repulsed by the behaviour of the Temple priesthood, especially the high priests; they preached reform. Others went further and sought nothing less than a new Temple, but whether on heaven or earth varied. Yet, even these critics, reformers and revolutionaries, were dominated by the Temple: for the Temple was the one thing to which one had to react if one were committed to Judaism. It could be rejected, denounced, embraced, or eulogized, but it could not be ignored. Herod's Temple merely heightened this situation. It was one of the great buildings of the ancient world and in itself was a religious object. Like the first Temple of Solomon, it was aniconic as far as divine images were concerned but, like Solomon's Temple, it had carvings of decorative botanical motifs: a high cluster of grape vines was carved over the gold-covered entrance gate, and the individual bunches of grapes (which also were gold-covered) were as big as a man.[19] Also, within the sanctuary was an idiographic tapestry which gave the position of the stars and planets but which, significantly, did not include the signs of the Zodiac.[20] Like the original Temple of King Solomon, Herod's Temple functioned as an idol. Its closest analogue in our own times is the great black stone at Mecca, which is not an image of God, but is a guarantor of God's presence at a specific place on this earth, and which is worshipped as though it had been placed there by the hand of the Almighty. The foundation stones of Herod's Temple may have been laid by 10,000 of the most skilled of workmen, supervised by 1,000 priests, liveried in brand new priestly robes, as Josephus suggests;[21] more certain is Josephus's conclusion that Herod "surpassed his predecessors in spending money, so that it was thought that no one else had adorned the temple so splendidly."[22] In other words, Herod had outshone Solomon, a supernal victory indeed.

Whatever else it may have been, Herod's Temple was an indication of a culture, focused on the ancient capital of Judah, which was financially prosperous, religiously self-confident, and noticeably assertive.[23]

3

Like any life-filled pond, the teeming pool of Siloam is not easy to view from the surface. There exist, however, portholes or viewing windows, that potentially give one a clear, if limited sight-line into what was going on. These are the scores of Judahist religious texts that were produced during the years between the Maccabean revolt and the destruction of the Temple. However, before dealing with these texts, many of which are so unusual and so fantastical in their design as to leave us rubbing our eyes in amazement, we must clear away a heavy layer of condensation that blurs our vision through these portholes. This is the problematic influence of Greek culture within Palestine and within the diaspora. The basic problem is that Greek cultural influence upon the followers of Yahweh was immensely complicated. It varied greatly by geographic location, social class, and according to the cultural and religious commitments of those who encountered it. Secondly, although the impact of Greek culture on the followers of Yahweh has been discussed frequently by scholars from the late Renaissance onwards, inevitably it has been in terms of analyses that reflect as much about their own "modern" concerns as about the ancient world.

The most immediately revealing symptom of just how fraught the matter is, is found in there being no agreed scholarly vocabulary concerning even the most basic definitions of the question of the degree of Greek cultural influence on Palestine and upon diaspora followers of Yahweh. Scholars use the same words, but without shared meaning, and thus they talk past each other. The fundamental terms are "Hellenism" and "Hellenisation" (or "Hellenization"). In using either of these terms, the foundation stones of any rational discussion of the matter, one needs to know in each piece of scholarship (a) if these words are taken as having separate meanings or if they act as synonyms; (b) does either term refer to forced cultural change engendered by Greek authorities? (c) does either one refer to the assimilation of Greek ideas and institutions being enforced by the elite of the Judahist religion? and (d) does either term refer, instead, to a voluntary assumption of certain Greek-derived attitudes, beliefs and practices by the Judahist masses, occurring in roughly the way that the citizens of the former Soviet Union took up blue jeans and rock and roll?[24]

Rather than parse the arguments concerning terminology, I am here issuing a simple fiat for the purpose of the present discussion: (1) since, in the period we are here considering, Palestine was not under Greek control, nor was Egypt, home of the most important diaspora communities, the possibility of enforced Hellenization is of minor import. The one instance, associated with Antiochus Epiphanes, fairly exhausts the list of occurrences; (2) "Hellenization" therefore will be used to refer to the energetic and purposive attempts of some Judahist leaders to introduce cultural, religious, and social practices that had their origin in Greek culture, broadly defined. (3) "Hellenism" is employed to describe the osmotic process whereby, without compulsion, programmatic or moral suasion, Greek-derived beliefs and practices seeped into the Judahist culture and religion. (4) The adjective form "Hellenistic" refers to things that are in some significant way influenced by Greek substrata. I do not use the terms "Hellenistic Judahism" as an antipole to "Palestinian Judahism" for, as Shaye Cohen presciently observes, all forms of the Yahwist religion were influenced to some degree in this period by Greek cultural constructs;[25] and (5) "Hellenic" is used as an adjective referring to items directly associated with Greece.

The blurring of our understanding, which is caused by a lack of an agreed vocabulary for talking about Greek influence, points to something fundamental about the nature of the scholarly enterprise on this question: it is ensnared in non-rational, non-scholarly attitudes, and hampered by ideological and religious commitments. There is a split between classicists and Semiticists. On

the surface this looks like a simple industrial dispute, the kind that characterizes so much of academic life. However, there is much, much more to it. Until recently, classicists and "ancient historians" (usually a code name for
historians of Greece and Rome) were in charge. They held the endowed
chairs and these were among the most prestigious posts in the older universities of Europe, the British Isles and North America. Anyone who sat at the
classicists' table dined by their rules. It is only in the last decade or two, with
the rise of non-western history as a major sector of study in most universities,
that the assumptions the classicists and ancient historians introduced into historical scholarship in the nineteenth and early twentieth centuries have been
questioned and largely abandoned. Yet, "for any historian whose education
was influenced by the European classical tradition, there was an inclination to
see the spread of Greek culture as the central historical phenomenon of the
era of Alexander and his successors...."[26] So Tessa Rajak notes. Thus arose a
set of alleged polarities between Semitic and Greek cultures.[27] As recently as
the mid-1990s, one of the world's leading classical historians, Fergus Millar,
could write a history of the Roman Near East wherein the discussion took as
a fundamental assumption that "in each period it will not be inappropriate to
start from the model, or hypothesis, of a sharp contrast between Greek city
(and later Roman *colonia*) on the one hand and Jewish community on the
other."[28] Although modern scholars (such as Millar) have been innocent both
of the snobbery and of the latent anti-Semitism that such polarized thinking
engendered in early times, there is no question that such a distinction implicitly privileges the Greek.

One method of escape from the artificial polarization of Semitic and
Hellenic simply declares victory for the Greeks. The modern keystone of this
approach is the work of Martin Hengel, who in his 1966 doctorate in the Fac-
ulty of Protestant Theology in the University of Tubingen, concluded that the
Yahwist religion and its accompanying culture had become so Hellenistic by
the time of the Maccabean revolt (or perhaps even earlier) that the Semitic-
Hellenic polarity is conceptually redundant.[29] This position, though extreme,
has the appeal of making the dichotomous mindset disappear; but, like most
psychosurgery, is a cure worse than the disease it wipes out. It results in the
suppression of a whole body of historical data on Judahist practices that were
not Hellenistic and which remained clear of Hellenism and Hellenization
right up to the end of the Second Temple period. Moreover, if the traditional
Hellenic-Semitic polarity, when employed by classical historians, implicitly
makes the Hellenic the dominant form, this viewpoint goes even further and
makes it essentially the only one.[30]

Such a line of argument is especially attractive to some Christian scholars,
because it provides the ideational equivalent of a biblical slingshot, one
which allows early Christianity to shoot past the stage of being part of the

Semitic mindset of the followers of Yahweh. The (to some) embarrassing fact of Christianity's having been founded upon Judahist foundations is nicely elided by an argument that effectively removes the Semitic from the historical process at a very early stage. Christianity, which later becomes strongly influenced by classical cultural forms, is thereby perceived as having been a classical form from its very beginning. Just how strong the demand was for an argument such as Hengel's is indicated by the statements of the great Protestant theological biblicist Rudolf Bultmann, made a full two generations before Hengel's work was even begun. Bultmann contrasted Greek thinking about God with Judahist thought: "For the Greek it is in the first place axiomatic that God, like other objects of the world, can be examined by the thinking observer; that there can be a theology in the exact, immediate sense. That Judaism has no such theology is due not to any incapacity or lack of development in its thought, but to the fact that Judaism has from the beginning a different conception of God; He does not in any sense belong to the world of objects about which man orients himself through thought."[31] That is virtually a cry for help: Christianity is a Greek form – will no one rid me of its pestilent Semitic heritage? In denying, as David Flusser puts it, that "ancient Christianity is constructed primarily upon Jewish premises,"[32] the history of Christianity is damaged. Equally, the alleged Hellenic displacement of the Semitic obscures almost totally the kaleidoscopic historical development within the Judahist religion in its most fertile period, the last two and a half centuries of the Second Temple era.

One response among Semitic scholars (Jewish for the most part, but not entirely) has been to accept the idea that there was a natural and unavoidable polarity between Hellenistic and Yahwistic thought, culture, and society, but to argue that in fact the Greek cultural invasion was almost entirely unsuccessful. The clearest articulation of this view, that Greek-derived culture was almost entirely ectopic to the Judahist religion in the last two and a half centuries of the Second Temple, is that of Louis H. Feldman of Yeshiva University in New York. He argues that the Greek language was little used in Palestine, however much it may have been employed in the diaspora; that the characteristic forms of Hellenic culture (epic drama, the gymnasium, and rationalist philosophies) were resisted in Palestine and especially strongly in Jerusalem. He suggests that it was not until the middle of the second century of the Common Era that one finds evidence of a Hellenistic cultural invasion in any depth. (The evidence for it at that time is found in the letter of the Jewish rebel chief Bar Kochba, who wrote to his subordinates in Greek.) Feldman concludes: "the question is not so much how greatly Jews and Judaism of the Land of Israel were Hellenized, as how strongly they resisted Hellenization."[33]

Certainly Feldman and those who hold his viewpoint, have some striking moments to refer to, indicating that, yes, there was a war between Hellenistic and Judahistic forms, but that there is a potential case for arguing that within the Promised Land, the followers of Yahweh were the victors.[34] The showcase exhibit in their argument is the heroic and undeniably successful revolt, and revolution, of the Maccabees. According to 1 and 2 Maccabees, two forms of force or programmatic Hellenization set off the successful revolution of 167ff BCE. The first of these was persecution from outside the country, directed by one of the last outriders of the etiolated Greek empire, the Seleucid King Antiochus IV Epiphanes. The revolt thus engendered and the governmental forms that emerged out of the successful rebellion are well documented in third-party sources, ranging from artifacts (coins, etc.) to Roman governmental documents.

What is less sure is the extent of the second form of Hellenization reported in 1 and 2 Maccabees. This is the assertion that prior to the invasion by the foreigner, Antiochus, a strong Hellenizing party existed among the leaders of the Yahwist faith. According to one account, these leaders actually went to the Syrian monarch and gained permission to set up a gymnasium in Jerusalem and "to observe the ordinances of the Gentiles" (1 Macc. 1:13). They undid the process of circumcision (presumably by stretching the foreskin with weights) and, in sum, "they joined the Gentiles and sold themselves to do evil" (1 Macc. 1:15). Another report suggests that they went even further and bought from Antiochus Epiphanes the appointment to the high priesthood and that the person so appointed – Jason – oversaw a Hellenization campaign which included the establishment of a gymnasium and inducing the young members of the Jewish aristocracy to dress like Greeks. Worst of all, the report suggests, the priests under Jason neglected the conduct of Temple sacrifices and took to spending their time at the Greek arena, watching wrestling and other sports. Under the high priest Jason's direction, money was raised from Jerusalem's citizenry with the intention of providing a sacrifice to Hercules. This was frustrated only by the decision of Jason's intermediaries to use the money to construct triremes instead! (2 Macc. 4:7–20). Although neither 1 nor 2 Maccabees says so directly, the clear implication is that not only was the process of forced Hellenization promoted by the highest level of the Judahist establishment, but that this domestic treason (if such it was) led to the persecution that came from the outside. One has to worry about this chain of cause-and-effect. The books of 1 and 2 Maccabees were written thirty to seventy years after the events in question and for an audience that already was accustomed to Maccabean rule. Even granted that the two volumes were written separately, they share a common agenda: the glorification of the founders of the Hasmonean dynasty and the broadcasting of the imputation that anyone who questioned the Hasmoneans was in a direct descent from the Hellenizers who had brought disaster on Jerusalem a generation or two earlier. Lacking third party confirmation, one remains agnostic.[35]

Having noted the one exceptional and unsuccessful attempt at forced Hellenization, it seems best to focus instead on Hellenism, by which is meant the voluntary assimilation of ideas and social practice that originated in Greece, but which may have arrived in Palestine after being mediated by other cultures. This removes the cartoon-like quality of much of the debate, for one cannot set up simple dichotomies, such as domination versus resistance; imperialism vs. localism; the Greek and Roman city vs. Jerusalem. And it removes the implication that Hellenistic ideas and practices, when adopted by Judahists, were the product of some volitional, programmatic and anti-Yahwist campaign. No, they were adopted because it made sense to the people to do so.

Here, a comparison may help. (If, in dealing with the late Second Temple period, I am using a plethora of metaphors, it is because the era, the richest in world religious history, cannot be captured directly; its wondrous complexity often is beyond words that are merely denotative.) One is a comparison to "Americanization," a phenomenon that many European and Asian cultural leaders worried about in the first thirty or forty years after the Second World War. Seemingly, American culture was taking over large chunks of the earth, and many national governments reacted to protect their local cultures from this contamination. American culture was the Hellenistic culture of a later age, in the sense that it – like the Hellenistic – became ubiquitous, was seductive to most members of contact societies, while distrusted by traditionalists and some local cultural elites; and, in common with the Hellenistic, it was misnamed. "Americanization" for the most part was just something that happened to America first. It had some unique features determined by America's heritage as a republic and as a sometime New World, but mostly it was merely what happened to the USA first, a stage of modernization. Understandably, this stage of modernization was misnamed, and therefore misunderstood, as constituting Americanization. Presently, at the start of the twenty-first century, it has become clear that several other societies are farther along this path of social-cultural evolution than is America, so the optical illusion, that the world is being Americanized, has disappeared. Hellenism was like that. It had a few features that were unique to Greece, but mostly it was a stage of social-cultural development common to the ancient Near East and fast-emerging southern Europe. Hellenism was something that happened to Greece first, so we have the optical illusion that developments in ancient Greece were a mammoth causal engine, driving change throughout the then-known world.

It follows that Hellenism (defined as a stage of social-cultural development) should have become pervasive in a country like Palestine once that region had passed certain economic and social thresholds – the recovery from the depopulation of the wars of the sixth century BCE, the reforging of thick economic ties with surrounding regions, and the maintenance of a reasonable degree of civil order – and once the region engaged in frequent cultural contacts with surrounding nations. The robustness of these extra-Palestine cultural contacts was guaranteed by the nature of the Judahist diaspora, which implied a set of two-way cultural exchanges: the metropole, Jerusalem, provided religious standards and stability for the several diaspora communities, and in turn, the diaspora served as a conduit of new, foreign ideas back to Jerusalem. Therefore, "all of the Judaisms of the Hellenistic period, of both the diaspora and the land of Israel," were Hellenistic: "that is, were integral parts of the culture of the ancient world." Some were more prone to Hellenism than were others. "But none was an island unto itself."[36] How could it be any other way?

Yet, is this not to accept the argument of Martin Hengel about the domineering pervasiveness of Hellenistic culture? No: although Hellenism was pervasive, this does not mean that there necessarily was an opposition between Hellenistic culture and that of Judahism. One must honour the insight of Samuel Sandmel who held that the Yahwist faith could become Hellenistic, but without loss of its own identity and without the destruction of any of its own essential characteristics.[37] Of course Hellenistic influences affected the several variants of Judaism that were flowering in Palestine and beyond, but this was a synergistic situation. As Eric M. Meyers has observed, the Hellenism we find, for example, in Palestinian architecture, and in linguistic contacts, should not be considered "so much an invasion of indigenous culture from the outside, but rather a new means of expressing local culture in alternative and often exciting ways. The appearance of some forms of Greco-Roman culture in a Jewish context need not signify compromise or traumatic change."[38]

But the context for these synergies could vary greatly. Variations occurred according to geographic region, according to social class, and according to the particularistic belief structure of the sort of Judaism one deals with. Some effects were subterranean, others easily visible. Crucially, one must realize that even those groups that vigorously refused to accept Hellenistic influence and who viewed the impact of Hellenistic tendencies on the part of the Temple establishment as being spiritual corruptions, nevertheless had the major characteristics of their own existence influenced by Hellenism. After all, if one spends one's life fighting some evil, that evil perforce becomes one of the primary ways one defines what is good.

4

The ubiquity of Hellenistic influence, delineated as a stage of the society, economy, and culture of the entire Ancient Near East being granted, four cases of the positive interaction of Hellenism and Judaism bear note. Each of these four cases is an instance of the harnessing of Hellenistic cultural patterns for the benefit of the religion of Yahweh.

The first of these requires only brief mention, because it is discussed in Appendix C: the creation of the Septuagint, the translation of the Hebrew scriptures into Greek, which was the primary language of the Judahist diaspora. This was mostly accomplished in the Ptolemaic royal city of Alexandria. The legend of the translation is the fullest story we possess concerning the inscribing of the scriptures, for the process was detailed in the Letter of Aristeas, a Greek-language document of Jewish authorship that was later used by Josephus. (Its date is probably 150–100 BCE, but that is here immaterial; it certainly is pre-70 CE, which is what counts in the present discussion.) According to the Letter of Aristeas, Ptolemy II (285–247 BCE), an avid collector of the books of the entire world, wanted a copy of the texts of the followers of Yahweh to be translated into Greek. He wrote to the high priest in Jerusalem and suggested that seventy-two scholars, six from each tribe, be sent from Palestine to Egypt to render the translation. (That there were no longer twelve tribes, and had not been for several centuries, is irrelevant; we are dealing with legend.) The Letter of Aristeas describes in rich detail how the translators were treated (very well indeed) and celebrates the extraordinary "fact" that each translator completed his task in exactly seventy-two days.[39]

Legend-tinted as this story is, parts of it are more gimlet-eyed concerning the establishment of one form of the scriptures than anything else we find in biblical, para-biblical, or Talmudic sources. The heart of the story has little mystification. The translators are all said to come from Palestine, a fairly strong indication that (whatever the actual number of these men) a strong cadre of the religious elite was able to move back and forth between biblical Hebrew and literary Greek, and this at a time when Aramaic was the vernacular tongue of Palestine. Significantly, although it is said that all seventy-two translators completed their sections in seventy-two days, this is not transformed into a miraculous claim. There is no mountain here, no voice in the burning bush, only the subtle statement that the business of translation occurred "just *as if* such a result was achieved by some deliberate design" (L. Aristeas, v. 307, emphasis mine). The seventy-two days symphony can be taken as a figure of speech; what it really means is that in the mid-third century BCE, a group of Palestinian scholars, under Alexandrian patronage, translated significant portions of the Hebrew scriptures into Greek, probably the Pentateuch and perhaps the Former Prophets. Later, the rest of the Hebrew scriptures were added, so that by the beginning of the Common Era, a full set of the scriptures was available to those who no longer understood Hebrew.

This Greek translation was not the Hebrew original, of course, but it was given equivalent status to the original in diaspora communities. Otherwise, how could the separated brethren worship? First-line religious scholars, such as Philo Judaeus of Alexandria (of whom more in a moment) used the Septuagint as the basis of their own work. Also, the evolution of the synagogue in the diaspora was made possible by this work. The claim to authoritative status for the Septuagint was clearly articulated in the Letter of Aristeas where it is said that when the work was submitted to the priests and elders of the community, they declared that "since this version has been made rightly and reverently, and in every respect accurately, it is good that this should remain exactly so, and that there should be no revision" (L. Aristeas, v. 310). That is an assertion of the authoritative status of the Septuagint, made during the period of great religious energy, between the Maccabean revolt and the destruction of the Temple.

This point bears emphasis, because in the second and third centuries of the Common Era, when Christians began to make polemical usage of the Septuagint, the Jewish authorities backed away from it and retreated to a Hebrew-text-only policy. However, in the two and a half centuries before the destruction of the Temple, the Septuagint served as a marvellous conduit of religious energy. It allowed Greek-speakers easy access to the Hebrew scriptures in a period before the Tanakh had reached its full canonical form: the Writings still were in flux and, in any case, the final arrangement of the canon was not yet certain. What influence members of the Greek-speaking Judahist communities had upon the final shape of the Tanakh is a topic that has not, as yet, been well examined; but certainly they were involved. Reciprocally, the Septuagint permitted the penetration of Judahist ideas into non-Yahwist cultures. This could occur any place Greek was read. If, as Louis Feldman asserts, there was a large-scale Judahist "missionary movement" in the later Second Temple era, it was made possible by there being a convenient Greek translation of the Torah and the Prophets.[40]

Another, smaller, example of the positive interaction of Hellenism with the Judahist religion is found in the Treatise of Shem, an astrological table that is ascribed to Shem, eldest son of Noah and the direct progenitor of the Hebrew people. This extraordinary volume was probably written in the last one-third of the first century BCE, but certainly before the end of the Second Temple era.[41] It consists of a melding of Judahist religious beliefs with Greek astrology (that is, with the Greek notion that the planets, carefully observed, are determinative of several aspects of human life, as distinct from the tradition of Babylonian and Persian astrology which tended to employ unsystematic observation of the night skies as a basis of divination). The author probably was a resident of Alexandria, for he shows a good deal of concern about the water levels in the River Nile. The treatise operates in time-honoured if-then statements: "If the year begins in Aries ... from Passover until the New Year produce will have a blight." (Treat. Shem, 1: lines 9–10); if the year begins in Aquarius, "in the beginning of the year rain will increase. And the Nile will overflow its full rate." (Treat. Shem, 12: lines 2–6). Most of the predictions are for ill events to occur, although there is the occasional prediction of a welcome event, such as good fishing and decent grain crops.

Even this minor astrological treatise conforms to the grammar of Judahist religious invention that was defined in Chapter Two: it claims ancient authority and denies its own recent creation and its own inventiveness. If the case of the Septuagint indicates one form that the interaction of Hellenistic culture and Judahist religion could take (the faithful-as-possible direct translation), the Treatise of Shem is an exemplar of what is best described as a tangential relationship. That is, this astrological text has one point in common with the scriptures and with the extra-biblical texts that were circulating at the time of its creation: acceptance of the Jewish liturgical calendar. Other than that, it makes all of its predictions from local conditions either in Egypt, or, to a much lesser extent, Palestine, and according to Greek astrological rules. Here Judahist and Hellenistic culture barely touch.

A more complex form of interaction is found in the book of 4 Maccabees, a beautifully polished piece of expository prose, written by a Yahwist, whose first language was Greek, sometime between 63 BCE and 70 CE.[42] Whether his home was in Alexandria in Egypt or in Antioch in Syria has been a matter of scholarly debate; almost certainly it was not Jerusalem or any place in Palestine. The text is a surprising, seductive, very artful construction. It begins by announcing itself as a philosophical argument, of the graceful sort in which the author employs the word "I" without either embarrassment or being self-vaunting. Purely Greek, one might think. But, very quickly, the author breaks away: Reason is described as being the force that makes one choose a life of Wisdom, and that, the author argues, is exactly what the Law does. So, at minimum, the highest Greek virtues are equated with the highest Judahist virtues. Indeed, the rhetorical force of the early pages leaves the distinct impression that obedience to Yahweh's law is a subsuming virtue, encompassing, at least for the Chosen People, all the Greek virtues, and more.

This opening sequence established, the author steps back and, as if we were viewing a cinematic sequence shot with an ever-widening lens, we realize that his opening piece of Greek philosophy is really a plinth on which a set of compelling dramas are enacted. There are two martyrdoms. One of these is taken from 2 Maccabees and describes in gruesome detail the killing of the eighty-nine-year-old scribe Eleazar by Antiochus Epiphanes, for his refusal to eat pork. Not only does the old man refuse, but when kindly guards suggest that he fake eating pork by substituting some other meat of his own choosing, he adamantly rejects the idea. He dies horribly on the rack (2 Macc. 6:18–31). In 4 Maccabees, this account is conflated with another tale of martyrdom taken from the same historical moment and same source (2 Macc. 7:1–41), that of seven brothers and their mother (all unnamed) tortured by Antiochus.

These stories are run together in 4 Maccabees, expanded, and are outfitted with details of the tortures: they are so graphic as to pull one ineluctably forward, reading more and more, while being ashamed that one is doing so. It is a tiny masterpiece of the pornography of violence, and is the more compelling because the author creates dialogue for the martyrs and their tormentors, lines that are good enough to take from the page right into a Greek or Roman amphitheatre.

Yet, 4 Maccabees ends not with the symmetry of Greek expository prose (which, in the usual instance, would have required a return to high philosophical discussion), but rather with an invocation of a whole skein of faithful martyrs, children of Israel, who had maintained their faith in the Law of the Almighty and thus had controlled their own weaknesses and passions. The book's last word is simply "Amen."

The great achievement of 4 Maccabees as a piece of persuasion is that it turns upside-down what a Greek-influenced audience of the time (and a modern audience as well) would have expected. The path one expects is an argument that would justify following the Law of Moses because that Law was consonant with abstract Reason and Virtue in Greek philosophies. Instead, by slapping the reader violently with historical events, the point is made that actual (not abstract) good behaviour, actual control of the passions, actual rejection of the flesh's weakness, are primary, and that these are obtained by faithfulness to the Law. If the abstractions of Reason and Virtue possibly bring one to engage in the same kind of proper behaviour, then it is the Law of Moses that is accrediting the concepts of Reason and Virtue, not the other way around. Thus, the book of 4 Maccabees simultaneously implies the compatibility of the mind of Greece and the religion of Yahweh, while establishing the primacy of the latter.

Within this text – read it, it's too compelling to miss! – two ideas are taken for granted, ones that are not found in the original Genesis-Kings unity, but which in the two or three centuries before the destruction of the Second Temple were taken up by a variety of Judahist religious groups. One of these is the doctrine of the immortality of the soul. Here the concept is unfocussed (does the immortality of the soul imply the resurrection of the body?), but it unmistakeably is affirmed. (See 4 Macc. 14:5–6, 16:13, 17:13, and especially 18:23–25.) Secondly, the idea that individual blood sacrifice could act as an antidote for sin is introduced. The martyrs became "as it were, a ransom for the sin of our nation" (4 Macc. 17:21). "Through the blood of these righteous ones and through the propitiation of their death the divine providence rescued Israel, which had been shamefully treated" (4 Macc. 17:22). The martyr Eleazar, just at the point of death as his flesh is being burned from his bones, turns his eyes heavenward and cries out, "You know, O God, that though I could have saved myself I am dying in these fiery torments for the sake of the

Law. Be merciful to your people and let our punishment be a satisfaction on their behalf. Make my blood their purification and take my life as a ransom for theirs" (4 Macc. 6:27–29). This is not the same thing as the doctrine eventually created by Christianity – that of a divine man-god's blood being spilled for the salvation of individuals – but one senses what is in the air: among certain Judahists, concepts of ransoming from bondage, and of propitiation for sin through the spilling of blood, are flickering about, like St. Elmo's fire, from one religious group to another. Eventually this fire is captured, lightning in a bottle, and after the Temple's destruction in 70 CE is used with great effect by the inventors of Christianity.

This brings us to the most impressive instance of the fruitful interaction of Hellenic and Judahist thought, that of the first theologian in Jewish history: Philo Judaeus, alternatively called Philo of Alexandria.[43] Philo's position in the history of Judaism, and of its heirs, the Christian and the Jewish faiths, is paradoxical. Philo left to posterity the largest body of religious writing set down by one person that exists prior to the destruction of the Second Temple. And Philo, in so doing, gave us the largest body of religious writings in the Jewish-Christian tradition that can accurately be ascribed to a single author, before the Middle Ages. Indeed, he is one of only two religious writers in the Yahwist-derived tradition who wrote before 70 CE whose works can be identified by author. (The other is the Apostle Paul, whose authentic writings certainly were composed before the Temple's destruction.) Both the range and the extent of Philo's writing is impressive to the point of being intimidating. In its modern form his work comprises twelve volumes (in the Loeb Classical Library) and this even though probably one-quarter of his works have been lost. Despite there being problems with some of Philo's writings (he is sometimes so discursive that one forgets by the end of an argument exactly what the topic is), he provides an unrivalled opportunity to observe the workings of a highly-devout diaspora Judahist who is up-to-date on the writings of the Greek-derived philosophers of his own day. Philo's writing is a clear case of loyalty to Yahweh being prepotent over Hellenic-derived philosophy, and this even when Hellenistic forms of articulation are employed.

Yet, Philo is referred to relatively infrequently in discussions of the pre-70 CE period, and this despite his having been situated smack in the middle of the period that is the most controversial and most problematic in biblical studies. In large part, this occurs because the Dead Sea Scrolls (meaning the manuscript fragments found in the Qumran caves and elsewhere, mostly in the 1940s and '50s) have held centre stage for more than half a century and seem destined to continue there for at least another generation. In 1962, when the second edition of Erwin Goodenough's *Introduction to Philo* was published, the book jacket stated, "it is amusing to speculate on the fury which would have arisen in scholarly circles had the works of Philo been newly discovered instead of the Qumran scrolls."[44] A future generation may indeed come to the conclusion that Philo is the most articulate and best-documented interpreter of the beliefs of the Judahist diaspora, but for the moment he is cold-shouldered.

Philo's exact dates are not known, but they can be bracketed by the period 20 BCE–50 CE. He was a central pillar of the largest community of the diaspora. His family was immensely wealthy and their position has been compared to that of the Rothschilds in Europe at the end of the nineteenth century.[45] Philo's brother, Alexander, was one of the richest private citizens in the ancient world. He lent large sums to the imperial government and made massive donations to the Temple at Jerusalem. When the Alexandrian diaspora community was facing severe discrimination, Philo served as head of a delegation that presented the community's case in Rome. Inferential evidence from his writings suggests that he spent a good deal of time as a political leader, trying to stabilize the position of his co-religionists in Alexandria. So, we have in Philo a lay leader of diaspora Judahism, who wrote prodigiously about his faith and his people, and who did so at the very time that many of the people who in later times were denominated as the great religious leaders of the era – Hillel, Gamaliel, Shammai, Yeshua of Nazareth, John the Baptist, and Paul – were engaged in their missions.[46]

The writings of Philo Judaeus fall into three categories. One of these consists of his purely philosophical works. His mixture of Platonism and Stoicism is useful to the historian of philosophy who wishes to determine which philosophical notions were common currency in the great library-city of Alexandria at the beginning of the Common Era. These writings, a relatively small portion of Philo's entire output, do not directly shed light on religious matters. Secondly, and much more valuable for our present purposes, Philo wrote a small body of texts that detailed recent history. Philo's "Flaccus" concerned one Flaccus Avillius who, in 32 CE, was made prefect of Alexandria and of the area surrounding it. At first he was a moderate governor, but after five or six years he became allied with what could be called "the anti-Semitic party" in Alexandria and, among other crimes, he permitted the sacking of the Jewish quarter of the city. Synagogues, as well as houses, were burned. In very bitter, very engaged prose, Philo chronicled the full cycle of this pogrom. Although his account may not be perfectly accurate historically,[47] it fills in a period of Judahist history that we otherwise would know only sketchily.[48] Similarly, Philo's *De Legatione* (better named in English as "On the Embassy to Gaius"), is a book-length description of the anti-Semitic actions of the Emperor Gaius, and their influence not only on the Alexandrian community, but also in Jamnia and Jerusalem. It includes Philo's own participation in an embassy to Gaius in 30 or 40 CE. Philo's description of the Alexandrian pogrom of 38 CE is rendered with the horrid vividness of someone who himself saw much of what happened and who had access to direct witnesses of those atrocities that he did not himself see directly. This is important history.

Yet, most valuable is the third component of Philo's writings, and these constitute the bulk of his work: the interpretation of the Books of Moses (especially Genesis) according to the vocabulary of Alexandrian philosophical thought. Previously, in surveying the interaction of Hellenistic and Judahist ways of thought, we have seen three modes of inventing new texts: (1) by direct translation from one language into another as in the case of the Septuagint; (2) through the creation of "tangential texts," that use scriptures only as a launching point for a trip into an alien orbit (as in the astrological Treatise of Shem); (3) stacking-texts, in which the Greek ideational structure is used as a stage for a drama that is fundamentally a piece of Judahist historical prose (4 Maccabees, for example). Now, here we have a fourth kind of religious invention in Philo's major writings: the creation of a parallel-text to the scriptures, one that simultaneously honours the older writings, and re-writes them.[49] Crucially, in doing this, Philo is not acting heretically. In fact, he is a very strong adherent of the two beliefs that become central to Rabbinic Judaism as it develops after the destruction of the Second Temple: he was firmly convinced that Moses was the actual author of the Pentateuch[50] and he believed there existed in oral traditions valid knowledge of events and beliefs concerning the Chosen People that went all the way back to the times of Moses.[51] This is a large step towards the later Rabbinical doctrine of the "Dual Torah," which posits an unbroken oral tradition that is co-equal in authority to the written texts.

Philo's method of writing a parallel text was primarily through allegory, a method he sometimes took to extraordinary lengths.[52] In the typical case, he would take a relatively small portion of the Pentateuch (the creation story, the story of Cain and Abel), or a specific issue that is referred to in the Pentateuch (drunkenness and sobriety, for example) and through a form of rhetoric remarkably discursive and confusedly allusive, he would continually reinterpret the basic events of the history of the Chosen People, emphasizing that they were mostly literally true, but, crucially, always true in some eternal sense. The major figures of early Judahist history are presented simultaneously as real people and also as Platonic types of various forms of truth; the Temple is transformed in allegory from being the sometime residence of Yahweh (in Tabernacle times he dwelt therein) into a cosmic representation of the unity of the one god that is Truth.[53]

Now, the central question about Philo is whether or not he became so airborne through his allegorical method that he effectively abandoned his Judahist faith and became a follower of his own Greek "mystery religion." That view has powerful proponents,[54] but I think it misses two key aspects of the way Philo's mind worked. One of these is that, despite his use of the terminology of Plato and of the Stoics, and despite his looking for secret mysteries within the stories of his own people, he remained dominated by history. That is to say, in Nahum N. Glatzer's phrase, "his basic views are biblical and Jewish."[55] No discussion of religious truth is possible unless it begins with historical experience, and his usual texts are the Books of Moses. Secondly, and more centrally, are the criteria by which the truths of Moses and of the Greek philosophers are related. The truth of Moses has priority in time, and hence, it is implied that (all truth being One) the philosophers borrowed from Moses! This matter of temporal priority is subordinate to a hierarchy of ethical priority. Philo accepts the Platonic worldview that undergirds his allegorical method of thinking, because that method is consonant with Mosaic history, not the other way around. That is, Judaism is anterior to Platonism and Platonism is not a foundation of Judaism's truth, but a useful, but necessarily ancillary, validation of that truth. Therefore, the parallel-text method of religious invention employed by Philo, though it frequently changes the meaning of biblical passages, operates from within the assumptions of the traditional faith in Yahweh.

Within Philo's religious works, written as they are from within the Judahist faith, are five pointers to the future of the Christian and Jewish religions. First, in two books, "Questions and Answers on Genesis," and "Questions and Answers on Exodus," Philo goes halfway to the form that later becomes familiar in the Mishnah and the Talmuds. This is a question-putting form, but it is not to be confused with Socratic questions, for the sequence of questions is not programmed tightly to lead to a pre-determined conclusion. The form Philo uses must have been common in both the diaspora and the homeland. This is the clearest extant pre-Rabbinic set of examples of question-putting as a Judahist form of religious pedagogy. Second, in his allegorization of the Jerusalem Temple, Philo presages one of the possible ways for both the religion of Yahweh and for Christianity to deal with what was to become their massive common problem: how, after 70 CE, to reconstruct and perpetuate a Temple that was no longer extant physically and which, as time's passage made increasingly clear, would not be rebuilt? Philo's writing showed one way out of the problem: convert the earthly Temple into a cosmic one, and thus the Temple could continue to exist, independent of the vagaries of the physical world. Third, in employing the Greek concept of *Logos*, as Philo does in "On the Creation," he shows an awareness of the sort of thinking that was to characterize one branch of the post-70 Christian evolution, most especially the thinking that produced the Gospel of John.[56] As in the case of Philo's question-asking technique, this was not an invention of his own; rather, it is a strong confirmation that the mode of thinking was part of the common currency of Judahist culture in the diaspora. One suspects that, through the conduit of the diaspora, it was simultaneously finding its way into the Palestinian homeland. Fourth, Philo's extreme emphasis upon Moses as the central figure in the Judahist tradition means that in his interpretation of the Yahwist tradition Moses becomes a mediator between the *Logos* and the people of God.[57] This mediation is a theme picked up by Christian apologists, and in their system Jesus Christ replaces Moses as the great mediator. Fifth, in his thinking in "types," Philo presages one of the chief ways in which post-70 CE Christians invented their religion. Once the trick of thinking of individuals as embodiments of large, abstract universal categories is mastered, it is easy to turn the technique on its head. Whereas Philo presents (for example) the patriarchs as embodiments of aspects of Universal Mankind, one can, as Christians learned to do, employ the patriarchs as types of the Incarnate Deity, the one called Jesus Christ.

· 6 ·

Siloam's Teeming Pool – II

I

THE JERUSALEM TALMUD RECORDS THE COMMENT FROM THE THIRD century of the Common Era of Rabbi Johanan, that the reason the Chosen People were exiled through the destruction of the Temple, was that there had arisen twenty-four parties of heretics.[1] From the viewpoint of the third century, the religious richness and whirl of late Second Temple times must have seemed heretical, for ultimately only one main form of Jewishness evolved and Rabbi Johanan took it as natural that this form was his own. However, we can take his report as meaning, in everyday language, that there were lots and lots of Judahist religious groups flourishing in pre-70 CE times, each related to the Judahist main stream, but each different, and, increasingly, given to self-invented variations. The Rabbi's use of "twenty-four" is not a real number, but rather an expressive number: twice the number of the original twelve tribes, and it simply means that there were more forms of Judaism than could be counted. Using available contemporary sources, one can easily list two dozen religio-political parties in Palestine and in the diaspora during the period between the Maccabean revolt and the destruction of the Temple, but even this can only be a fraction of the full number of groups: many must have coalesced, met for a time, and then dissolved, leaving behind no religious writings and no notices of their brief careers in the surviving records.

Later, we will refer to the characteristics of the main religious parties, but to focus too much on the individual groups is to miss what was going on. Most of the religious parties were like fire flies, short-lived and leaving no material record. Moreover, an emphasis upon individual factions or parties too easily turns into morphological analysis, rather like that done in old-time biology, when what really counts is the process: the ideas, and the inventions. Instead of concentrating on the minimal structural details that we have for a few of the religious parties, we should concentrate on the riches that they left in the form of writings. In fact, the array of writings far exceeds the number of known Judahist sects, and that is all to the good, for it precludes our engaging in the folly of ascribing a certain text to one party, and another to another party and so on. In fact, only a tiny minority of the hundreds of religious texts from the late Second Temple period can be ascribed to any particular group, and forcing a factional label on these texts not only is misleading, but is mystifying: it obscures the fact that what we, as historians, have to work with is a little (very little) institutional information concerning the later Second Temple era, but whole libraries of wonderful texts. These texts include Judahist religious inventions of wide variety. These inventions determine the possible futures of Judahism, so we must repeat the imperative articulated in Chapter Two: read the texts, for the history of the texts is the history of the inventions that determine the nature of the religions that we are chronicling.

Lawrence H. Schiffman has observed that all Judahist groups "in the Second Temple period endeavoured to assimilate extra-biblical teachings into their way of life."[2] That is crucial. Although there was not in the year 70 CE, any more than there had been in the year 167 BCE, a "Bible," Schiffman's meaning is clear. Authoritative scripture consisted of the Pentateuch (which, if the writings of even the most Hellenized of scholars is an indication, had by the beginning of the Common Era become generally, though not universally, accepted as having been written by Moses)[3] and the Former Prophets. But the Writings were still shifting and there was an immense amount of room for inventions that might (or might not) become "scripture" in the sense of gaining and maintaining authority. Certainly Schiffman is right: every Judahist group was experimenting with inventing its own scriptures, sometimes only orally, sometimes in writing.

That, in spite of an immensely high loss-ratio of these possible-scriptures (did one-thousandth? one ten-thousandth of these inventions come down to us?) we still have several hundred "extra-biblical"[4] manuscripts or fragments of histories, hymns, apocalypses, and books of wisdom, from the Maccabean times to the end of the Second Temple, is in equal measure humbling and gratifying.

These extra-biblical texts are fascinating in themselves, and, taken together, they forcibly assert the fact that the vocabulary of scriptural invention within Judahist tradition was increasing at an exponential rate, decade after decade, in the last two and a half centuries of the Second Temple. The grammar of scriptural invention, as described in Chapter Two, remains the same, but the vocabulary becomes immensely more complicated and more creative. Of the para-biblical books of the period, two of them – the Books of Daniel and of Esther – eventually made it into the canon of the Jewish and the Christian faiths and others were admitted to the Secondary Canon of the Christian church: the most important of these being 1 and 2 Maccabees, and also the Book of Judith, which is essentially the same folk-tale as the Book of Esther, the story of a virtuous woman who outsmarts an evil, non-Judaean king.

However, the greater historical significance of the extra-biblical scriptures is that they indicate clearly the expanding diversity of religious invention that characterized Judahism on the eve of its great disaster.

James H. Charlesworth has assembled an extraordinary collection of extra-biblical writings, and he has suggested that they are defined by four major characteristics. If one remembers that such generalizations necessarily exclude out-liers in the data, and that in the historical process out-liers can undeservedly receive more attention than the norm, his observations bear attention.[5] First, Charlesworth suggests that in the religious writings of the later Second Temple period, Yahweh becomes increasingly transcendant. The personal eccentricities, the gritty anthropomorphism that characterizes Yahweh in the Genesis-Kings unity is sublimated. He becomes high spirited and often assumes a high rage (as the punisher of wrong-doers), but now in a cosmic guise. No longer is he the most irascible God in the universe. Secondly, there is a concern with the problem of evil, both its origin and also how it eventually is to be overcome. In the primary history of the Judahist faith, wrong-doing was punished, but never really explained. It was accepted for what it was – wrong – and dealt with, but its origins were never probed. Increasingly in the later Second Temple writings, evil is personified. Various versions of a proto-Satan emerge. Third, some of the groups that write religious texts engage the new concept of Messiah. This is a very vexed matter, because some of the texts seem to indicate that most Judahist factions had no concept of a Messiah whatsoever and had no interest in discussing the matter; others had ideas of a Messiah that were little more than the equivalent of the eighteenth-century rioters' slogan, involved with the calendar changed from Julian to Gregorian, "Give us back our eleven days!" That is, that the Messiah simply meant a return to a Jerusalem kingship with a good won-lost record. Still others had much more complex ideas. (The Messiah question will be discussed in detail later; it is a big question indeed.) Fourth, the idea of the resurrection of the dead became increasingly common. How long this had been a common folk-belief in Judahist circles is hard to say, but it left very few traces in the early, bedrock Hebrew scriptures. It is only in the post-Hellenic period that one finds a strong evidence for a widespread belief in the resurrection of the dead. Even then, major segments of Judahism rejected it. How new this belief actually was is impossible at present to calculate.

One can see at this point a paradox: generally speaking, Yahweh becomes more and more transcendant – more suitable to a monotheistic religion – while at the same time evil becomes more and more personified. Yahweh withdraws into a cloud, almost into a philosophic haze, while evil descends and becomes encapsulated in the form of various devils and, ultimately, in that new invention, Satan.

Behind that paradox is a final characteristic, one too vulgar for most biblical scholars to articulate: increasingly and generally (remember, this is a generalization and it has exceptions) the new religious writing turns nasty. There is not a specific text or specific historical event to which one can point and say, ah, that's the turning point: for there is no turning point, but rather a long, slow bend in the road. As the historical turn of mind increasingly transmutes itself into a mind focused on future-history, hatred becomes the dominant tone. Certainly conventional historical narrative, in the tradition of the Genesis-Kings unity, continues in, for example 1 and 2 Maccabees, and in some of the writings of Philo of Alexandria, but, more and more, historical narrative becomes the prologue to apocalyptic visions. The concept of Yahweh's justice (which dominates the Genesis-Kings unity and the major prophets) is shoved aside by the concept of Yahweh's vengeance. Justice is an historical concept; vengeance is prospective. Why the new religious writings that were read alongside the Torah and the Prophets should have taken this spiteful new tone is not easily explicable. But, undeniably they did so evolve and they forced a re-interpretation of the entire corpus of Hebrew scripture. And, by the vagaries of Judahism's grand-chance lottery – the frightening lottery of religious decimation that occurred in 70 CE – the groups, or individuals, or, perhaps simply texts, that survived, had a great deal of the vindictive in them.

2

For the past half-century, biblical scholarship that has dealt with the so-called "inter-testamental period" has been dominated by the mis-named "Dead Sea Scrolls." There is in fact only one Dead Sea Scroll: this is a copper scroll that is totally uncharacteristic of the trove, for it is an inventory of physical objects, not a religious text. The remainder are not scrolls, but fragments of what were once scrolls, written on organic material, rather than on enduring copper sheets. When one thinks of the Dead Sea Scrolls, therefore, one should wipe aside the romantic picture of great learned treatises or of rich religious texts and realize that, mostly, one is dealing with fragments, most of which are tiny and not readily identifiable, and none of which constitutes a full document. Fragments indeed.

Because most of the pieces of the fragments from the 1,000 or so Dead Sea Scrolls are from the area of the Qumran Caves, comprising eleven sites near the northeastern shore of the Dead Sea, it has been natural, if slightly misleading, to equate the Qumran finds with the entire Dead Sea miscellany. Roughly 800 of the 1,000 Dead Sea items are from near Qumran. Of the fragments from the 800 Qumran manuscripts, roughly 225 are from biblical books and another 275 to 300 consist of fragments so tiny as not to confer any coherent meaning. Two hundred or so of the remaining 300 bits of manuscript are long enough to carry independent meaning.[6] Taken together, the

Dead Sea Scrolls have overshadowed all other sources of the period between the Maccabean revolt and the destruction of the Second Temple and have absorbed much of the energy of many of the potentially most productive biblical scholars of the later Second Temple era.

That is a pity.

Geza Vermes has remarked that the situation with the Qumran fragments constitutes the greatest scholarly scandal of the twentieth century[7] and, if anything, it has turned out to be even more of a scandal than he at first realized.

Certainly the cumulative intellectual results of the study of the Dead Sea Scrolls, and especially of those from the Qumran area, have been extremely disappointing, and this despite immense amounts of money, most notably that of the Rockefellers and of the Israeli government, that have been poured into the project. Operationally, the Scrolls have been like a deep-sea trawl net, which, along with great mounds of debris, also brings to the surface a few fascinating specimens: fascinating, but not so significant as to force a basic reappraisal of how life in the sea evolved.

The chief impact of the past half-century of scrolls scholarship has simply been to confirm the conclusions towards which earlier scholars had been working independently of the Scrolls, using documents already known: Hebrew and Christian scriptural texts and the rich range of para-biblical writings that already were available.

The already-extant hypotheses, which the Dead Sea Scrolls confirmed, were that: (1) given the astronomical number of opportunities for scribal error, generation by generation, the Masoretic text of the Hebrew scriptures is remarkably accurate; (2) the Septuagint is indeed an accurate witness to the Hebrew texts from which it was taken; (3) in the Second Temple era there were a plurality of texts in circulation of the books that eventually became the Tanakh; (4) the concept of canon – of a Bible – was alien to the Second Temple period, although some items of religious literature were accepted as having more power, of being more authoritative, than were others; (5) there existed a wide variety of texts in circulation in the era between the Maccabean rising and 70 CE that easily could have become canonical – that is, biblical – had the throw of Clio's dice been slightly different; and (6) although there was a Temple establishment and a spine of beliefs that all followers of Yahweh embraced, there was such a wide variety of these beliefs that it is impossible to speak accurately of a single religious culture, and this is despite the desires of the more traditional followers of Christianity and of Rabbinic Judaism to have a nice clean line of origin to which each could tie its own invention.

The Scrolls have provided confirmation of these six basic points and thus have given courage to those who were developing these conclusions from other sources. What the Scrolls did was let scholars get behind the censorship of Christian and Rabbinic authorities of the post-70 CE period.[8] Perhaps the most important result of the Dead Sea discoveries was to confirm that much of the allegedly-Judahist material collected in the Christian deutero-canonical sources and in pseudepigraphic sources, was indeed genuinely Judahist. These were texts that had been wiped from Jewish history by the Rabbis of the second through sixth centuries, and they are absolutely fundamental to an understanding of the creation of Christianity and of Rabbinic Judaism.

These results were very expensive in terms of money and scholarly energy, but not to a degree that was scandalous. Where the scandal emerged was elsewhere, and its course is well known, for as events unravelled from 1990 onwards, they were watched with morbid fascination not only by the academic community but by readers of general news magazines, who were led to conclude that sloth and greed ran through biblical scholarship like a river in spate. A brief summation of a long and unedifying tale is this: the team which was set up in 1947 to deal with the Qumran fragments, implicitly turned itself (and those new members whom it co-opted) into a scholarly monopoly that operated like Standard Oil had done in the nineteenth century, a nice coincidence, considering that Rockefeller oil money funded much of their work. They locked out other scholars, and after roughly a decade of solid work and useful publications, settled into a pattern of making great promises and then evincing even greater indolence. Members of this holding company (and it was a holding company in the literal sense: scholars who retired passed on the manuscripts that were under their individual control to their colleagues or former graduate students) simply held on. Some had their graduate students do translations as dissertation topics. Little quality work was done during the 1980s and as the fifth decade of the monopoly began, a variety of biblical scholars began pressing hard for access to the materials. The cabal was cracked by a combination of widespread academic pressure led by Hershel Shanks, the editor of *Biblical Archaeology Review*, by the computer reconstruction from a concordance of one of the major documents that Qumran insiders were keeping to themselves, and by the Huntington Library's decision to make available a full set of negatives of the Qumran scrolls that had been made as a safety-copy in case the originals were destroyed. (This was a reasonable precaution, given the parlous state of the Middle East.) These pressures broke things and the Israel Antiquities Authority opened up the texts. (That personal lawsuits occurred between scholars on opposite sides of the controversy, amidst a cacophony of personal vilification, was unfortunate, but not unexpected.) Thus, technically adept scholars, independently of the Qumran junta, now finally can examine decent quality photographs, or, sometimes, the original fragments. Therefore, one expects a critical and controversial literature to follow, questioning what has until recently been the received wisdom concerning the Qumran fragments.

And there, in the received wisdom, is where scandal lies. I think the real scandal is this: the Qumran cabal not only controlled access to the scroll-fragments, but through this control was able to dominate the grounds of debate whereby the outside world came to think about the Dead Sea treasure. Thus, they were able to determine much of what was believed to be the historical reality of the world of Judahism in the last two and a half centuries of the Second Temple era. The exercise of this influence and the surprising degree of unanimity among Qumran insiders need not be ascribed either to cynicism or conspiracy on their part. But, when a self-coopting band of the elect talks primarily to each other over long periods of time, the elect are apt to start thinking alike and to assume intimidating and superior airs when dealing with the barbarians beyond their walls. It is this intellectual scandal, more than the scandal of their holding the Qumran fragments hostage for so long, that intersects with our present purpose, for it is hard to see how, despite their technical virtuosity, the Qumran team, over two generations, could have got things more wrong.

This occurred because (as will be detailed in Chapter Seven), the Qumranologists tried to ascribe almost everything they found to a single Judahist sect, the Essenes. Now, in fact, whether they posited the Essenes, the Pharisees, the Sadducees, the Therapeutae or any of a dozen other Judahist factions as the authors of the Dead Sea Scrolls is not the issue – that any one institutional origin should be suggested, and the texts interpreted with the prior assumption that this putative institutional affiliation was a determinant of textual interpretation is an invitation to delusion. This is all the more so because, as I will indicate in Chapter Seven, the actual knowledge extant about the institutional framework of late Second Temple Judahism hovers between the minimal and the non-existent. The only sensible course is to read the texts that were produced in the last two and a half centuries of the Temple era without interpolating historical assumptions that are at best unconfirmed, and at worst easily disprovable. To the extent that we can still our hectoring hearts, we should be quiet, and let the texts speak for themselves.

3

In approaching the mass of texts that existed simultaneously – the Dead Sea Scrolls, the evolving Tanakh, and those books of the Apocrypha and Pseudepigrapha which are soundly dated as being written between 167 BCE and 70 CE – we run the danger of creating an optical illusion. That is, when examining, as an indication of the panoply of forms of scriptural invention that were taking place in the later Second Temple era, some of the major items (and limits of time and space preclude looking at anything but the major exhibits), we have to do so sequentially. That can unintentionally produce the impression that these texts comprised a spectrum of invention and that they had natural anchor points at each end, the first and the last exhibits that we discuss. Also, it is possible to gain the misleading impression that there was a pre-ordered evolution to these forms. Both impressions are wrong. Unlike the optical spectrum, there are no anchor points on the spectrum of Judahist religious invention; one side of the spectrum bends around and joins the other, forming a circle. And these texts, so full of new inventions, did not evolve one from another in nice tidy sequence, but arose almost spontaneously. This virtual synchronicity means that the religious inventions of the period are forever spinning. One can only stand in awe, feet planted in the centre of the circle of gyring texts and marvel at the forms that revolve endlessly by.

We can take as given the character of the biblical texts, for they were ubiquitous amidst the Dead Sea Scrolls.[9] However, as modern readers, we must make one very big leap of historical empathy. We must realize that although fragments of all the books of the Hebrew Bible (save Esther) were found among the Dead Sea Scrolls, this does not mean that the people of the time viewed them as being part of the Bible. That was a later invention, one that did not occur until the second through fifth centuries, when the canon was finally set. Certain books of what later became the Bible had considerable authority, but not necessarily what they were later granted. This point can be quickly illustrated by a simple fact: that in all the Qumran scrolls, only one text refers to the first five books of the Hebrew scriptures as being the Books of Moses.[10] That title is not found in the writings of Palestinian Judahism that have thus-far been discovered. Ironically, it is found in Hellenistic writings, notably those of Philo of Alexandria.

If we can make that leap, and realize that whatever respect was granted the scriptural books in the later Second Temple era, it was different (and, usually, less) than they later received, then we can approach a second point, namely that the texts that whirled around during the later Second Temple period were themselves potential scriptures. One has to recognize that the Christian Bible and, to a much greater extent, the Hebrew Bible as it finally became canonical in the second through sixth centuries of the Common Era, were the result of several massive acts of censorship.[11] If today we know scores of items from within the Yahweh tradition that were intended to claim authority alongside the older items, such as the Genesis-Kings unity and the Prophets, there must have been hundreds that have been lost to history, each text the product of an inventor or group of inventors who believed their work merited authoritative status. The imaginative leap required here is to realize that each of the extra-biblical items that we will be discussing in a moment was potentially a piece of scripture, potentially a book of the Tanakh. If the later censors had felt slightly differently or if a different set of winners had emerged from the chaos that followed upon the destruction of the Temple – then these items would have been included in the Bible, and, possibly, some of the items at present included would have been discarded.

Two items that are included in the Christian deutero-canonical collection, but not in the Tanakh, have already been mentioned, the books of 1 and 2 Maccabees. These are straightforward works that apostrophize the Maccabees and explain the origin of Hanukkah. The books confirm that the tradition of narrative history, of the same sort found in the Genesis-Kings unity, was alive and still respected in the later Second Temple period. This is of consequence, because the absence of similar historical narratives in the Dead Sea Scrolls has led to the unfounded speculation that the historical sense of the Chosen People either had changed radically or disappeared entirely between 167 BCE and 70 CE. No, it was still there.

Another example of the continued force of historical narrative in the later Second Temple period is the brilliant historical novel, the Book of Judith. This item, found in the Christian deutero-canonical collection, was excluded from Hebrew scripture proper, but was kept alive as an extra-biblical story upon which midrashim were based. In many ways, the Book of Judith is a sister to the Book of Esther. Each is set on a fictional historical stage and each involves a beautiful and virtuous woman who saves her co-religionists by outwitting an evil man. Like Esther, the Book of Judith was written some time after the Maccabean revolt against Antiochus Epiphanes, roughly in 100 BCE. Neither of the two books is found in the Dead Sea Scrolls, but Esther became the last book to be admitted to the Hebrew canon. Why Esther was eventually included in the Tanakh and Judith was not has many explanations, none of them entirely convincing. My own view is that both of the books were repugnant to the Rabbis who set the final canon, because the stories star women as major actors and as figures whose actions redeem the Chosen People from seemingly inevitable disaster. Both, therefore, invited rejection. The Book of Esther, however, had to be kept, because it explained how the feast of Purim, a festival taken over from pagans, came into being as a festival unto Yahweh. The Book of Judith, performing no such function, was disposable.

The Book of Judith is also a distant literary cousin to the Book of Daniel, portions of which are also responses to the actions of Antiochus Epiphanes and, perhaps, to the subsequent excesses of some of the Maccabean kings. Like Daniel, Judith is set in a distant fictional historical past, the Assyrian empire in the time of Nebuchadnezzar. Like Daniel, its historical facts are a bit wonky, but in neither case is that important: history is used as a stage set for the presentation of a message.

Where the Book of Judith differs both from the Book of Daniel and the Book of Esther is in the remarkable literary skill with which its narrative unfolds. (And this holds true whether as some scholars believe, it is the product of two authors, or of one; the final product is extraordinary.) The novel begins with a straightforward stage-setting narrative, explaining that King Nebuchadnezzar was cutting a swath through the Ancient Near East. This was not long after the Chosen People had returned from the Babylonian exile. Neb-uchadnezzar placed a general named Holofernes, the Napoleon of his genera-tion, in charge of the campaign and it was his army that marched towards Jerusalem. The children of Israel prepared to resist him. That was the situa-tion. Here, very skilfully, the author introduces a new voice, a man named Achior, the leader of the Ammonites, who explains to General Holofernes the history of the Chosen People, and he tells the Assyrian that as long as the Israelites are true to their God, He will defend them. This does not please the Assyrian general.

Next, the scene shifts to a fictional town, Bethulia, and the voice again be-comes that of the narrator. Said to lie near one of the passes that guarded the entry to Jerusalem, Bethulia was the home of Judith, a young, beautiful and wealthy widow, renowned for her piety. When the leaders of her town con-templated surrendering to the Assyrians, she rallied them. She scolded them for putting the Lord Almighty to the test, and promised that she would do something – she would not tell them what it would be – "that will go down through all generations of our descendants" (Jud. 8:32).

And so she does. In a beautifully controlled narrative that intersperses Ju-dith's voice with that of the Assyrian general and his soldiers, we observe Ju-dith and her maid go out and, under the pretext that Judith is abandoning her people, have themselves captured. Before doing this, Judith has put on her most seductive garments, bedecked herself with gold and silver jewellery and covered herself in perfumed oils. Not surprisingly, General Holofernes' men turn her over to their general (soldiers always have an eye to promotion). He is greatly taken with her, but she remains demure, eating her own food (be-cause of dietary laws) and going outside the camp to pray and bathe each night. (The last act was as much a piece of seduction as of ritual purification, one surmises.) By the fourth day, Holofernes is both deeply attracted and vexed because his masculinity has been offended. He thinks, "It would be a disgrace if we let such a woman go without having intercourse with her. If we do not seduce her, she will laugh at us" (Jud. 12:10). So, Judith, in her most sexually attractive finery has dinner with him; she eats her own food, and he eats and drinks his and he becomes so drunk that he passes out. His slaves withdraw, assuming that he will regain consciousness in the bedchamber and that nature will take its course. Instead, the course is determined by Judith, who takes Holofernes' sword, and crying "Give me strength today, O Lord God of Israel!" strikes his neck twice, cutting off his head (Jud. 13:7).

It is at this point that one realizes the story is not only being told brilliantly, but that the plotting is admirably tight. Whereas in the case of a folk-tale, the story would have ended here, with a clear and simple victory over an evil en-emy, this is different, a tightly planned novel. As the story continues, Judith takes the canopy from Holofernes' bed, wraps his head in it, and then leaves his tent. She has her maid stuff the parcel into their food bag. Judith and the maid then leave the Assyrian camp; they have been going out to pray and bathe on previous nights, so this arouses no suspicion. The two women return to their home town, and, having assembled the people, Judith shows off the head of the Assyrian general and the now-bloody canopy under which the great man lay. The people bow down and worship the Lord. "Blessed are you our God, who have this day humiliated the enemies of your people" (Jud. 13:17). And the miracle is all-the-greater, because, as Judith assures them, she did not have to defile herself by having sexual relations with the Assyrian.

Then – and I suspect this more than anything else is what resulted in the book's being kept out of the Hebrew canon – Judith herself becomes the general of her people. She takes over tactical planning for the Bethulia forces. As she commands them to do, the locals sally forth, pretending to attack the Assyrians. This cheekiness at least gets the attention of the enemy sentries who inform their officers, who in turn go to wake up General Holofernes, just as Judith had foreseen. So distraught are the Assyrian officers at finding the headless Holofernes, that they panic their own men, who retreat pell-mell. The Chosen People cut them down mercilessly and chase them, it is said, past Damascus. In their victory they enjoy thirty days of plundering the Assyrian camp and then they sing and dance their way to Jerusalem, Judith making up a new psalm along the way. The final verse of her composition is:

> Woe to the nations that rise up
>   against my people!
> The Lord Almighty will take
>   vengeance on them in the
>   day of judgement;
> He will send fire and worms into
>   their flesh:
> – they shall weep in pain
>   forever.   (Jud. 16:17)

The novel ends on the satisfying note that Judith lived to be 105 years of age and that "no one ever again spread terror among the Israelites during the lifetime of Judith, or for a long time after her death" (Jud. 16:25).

This extraordinary book deserves our attention in part because it is the most compelling and developed strong-woman story in all the writings of the Judahist tradition, including its Jewish and Christian derivatives. It is also a predictor of a form which, in much less sophisticated form, becomes a part of later Rabbinic thought – Aggadah, which includes folktales and non-biblical historical stories that are told to illustrate moral and ethical points. The later Rabbis may not have approved of the picture of Judith, the fictional woman who saved Jerusalem from the Assyrians, but they would have done well to have honoured the artistry of Judith's inventor, who, whatever else he or she may have done, knew how to employ the Yahwist tradition of the historical narrative for the enspiritment of God's people in hard times.

Although the Book of Judith and also 1 and 2 Maccabees testify to a continuing employment of historical narrative (or of historicized narrative) as a major form of Judahist religious invention, this use of narrative was different from that found in the classical documents of Yahwist historical writing, those of the Genesis-Kings unity. This was not so much a matter of new beliefs being asserted in the newer literature, but of something less easily defined: the historical writings of the later Second Temple period lack the force of the earlier material. Even when dealing with horribly wrenching incidents, as in the martyrdom tales concerning the Maccabean era, one does not encounter the primeval force that distinguishes the Genesis-Kings unity. There, the editor-author was wrestling not only with how to create a viable historical narrative, but how to explain the order of the entire universe. That Genesis-Kings narrative has immense tensile strength, by virtue of the force that had to be applied to the primal material, to turn it into a single unit. No later historical narrative in the Judahist tradition, no matter how finely crafted, contains the controlled force of this original version. Everything thereafter is derivative. The historical narratives that are constructed during the period between the Maccabean revolt and the end of the Second Temple are extensions of an historical story, the main parts of which were set down centuries earlier; or they are revisionist (to use a terrible word) in that the new historical writings attempt to change the meaning of the older historical narratives, all the while using the original narratives as their own construction materials. Although none of the new histories has the force of the Genesis-Kings unity, some of the new histories are very successful.

A good example is the Book of Jubilees, which employs the "parallel texts" method of effecting a major revision of the Pentateuch, most especially Genesis and Exodus. This volume deserves to be much better known than it is, particularly because it was widely used in later Second Temple times, and because it reveals certain very important points about the history of the period. Its title refers, in the first instance, to time that is metered in "jubilees," that is, periods of forty-nine years (seven "weeks" of seven years), that are followed in the fiftieth year by a major sabbatical. It is a big book and appropriately enough, it is divided into fifty chapters.

Like other parallel-text essays in religious invention of this period, it adopts the outlines of an existing text, but Jubilees does this not so much to revise the content of the original text as to honour it. The Book of Jubilees, therefore, deals with historical material found in the Pentateuch, but begins by repairing what had long been one of the problems of the so-called Books of Moses: although from the mid-fifth century BCE onwards some (but not all) Judahists ascribed the first five books of the scriptures to Moses, references to Moses' alleged authorship were muddy at best within the text. The key invention of the Book of Jubilees takes care of that problem immediately. The author begins with Moses going up the mountain to obtain the stone tablets from Yahweh and then he has Moses spend forty days and forty nights in the presence of the Almighty. God tells him, "Set your mind on everything which I shall tell you on this mountain, and write it in a book…" (Jub. 1:5).[12] Later, the Almighty deputes an angel to write down for Moses the history of the world from creation onwards (Jub. 1:27). This is a bit confusing, but the sum is simple enough: this book, the Book of Jubilees, comes directly from Moses, for either it was dictated to him by Yahweh or it was dictated by God to an angel who then passed the book on to Moses. Therefore the credentials of the Book of Jubilees – its provenance, as it were – are much stronger than those of the Pentateuch.

Put so explicitly, this implied claim sounds shrill and slightly egomaniacal. Yet, in tone, the Book of Jubilees is remarkably matter-of-fact and almost devoid of rhetorical excesses. The new beliefs it introduces are limited. Whoever wrote it was a good tinkerer, a minor historical revisionist, but not a great inventor.[13]

The importance of Jubilees lies in the way it forces us to read other texts. The Book of Jubilees was excluded both from the Hebrew Bible and from the Christian deutero-canonical writings. It was preserved on the periphery of Christianity, the only full version being in Ethiopic, which itself was a translation of a Greek version that was taken from a Hebrew original.[14] With that skein of translation, and with the book's being preserved in full only in Christian sources, as an indicator of Judahist thought in the later Second Temple period the text might well be treated with suspicion. Yet, portions of the Hebrew original turned up in several of the caves near Qumran[15] and the Hebrew fragments correspond surprisingly closely to the Ethiopic version.[16] This suggests that the Christian curators of pre-Christian Jewish manuscripts took their responsibilities very seriously. Despite the later Rabbis' suppression of the Book of Jubilees (presumably on theological grounds), the text manifestly is an authentic pre-Common Era document. One should not overgeneralize, but this case suggests that the Dead Sea Scrolls should be read within the context of the much fuller texts which Christian sources have kept and which date in many instances from the same period as the Scrolls. And it also suggests that some of those Christian-preserved texts which at present have no cognates within the Dead Sea Scrolls, probably are authentic Judahist documents. Until the 1950s, the Book of Jubilees was considered by most Jewish scholars to be a Christian forgery. Yet, it was found in five of the eleven Qumran caves, which means that it was among the most-copied and widely-distributed of the extra-biblical manuscripts in the Qumran collections.[17] Further, the idea of the Book of Jubilees (and, therefore, one infers, some form of the text itself) was known to Paul and to the authors of Luke and Acts, James, Hebrews, and 2 Peter.[18] Indeed, outside the Pentateuch and the Prophets, Jubilees may have been among the most widely-read Judahist texts in the early years of the Common Era. Although the Book of Jubilees is cited in the Damascus Rule of the Essenes[19] this does not mean that it was a document of any specific religious party.

One resists identifying Jubilees with any specific party, because the moment one adopts such an equation, it becomes difficult to read the text with an open mind: factional writings are almost automatically taken to be touched with hysteria. This would be an exegetically misleading assumption to make about the Book of Jubilees because the leading characteristic of the text is its calmness. The author does not wallow in recriminations; his prophecies do not have the mephitic quality of the apocalypses of the disaffected; hate does not fill his bones. The author, it seems, is a learned and concerned member of the Judahist community, who is at peace with his co-religionists on most matters. So, if we juxtapose the calm and steady tone of the Book of Jubilees with the fact that the volume was very widely read, and therefore represents something more than a product of a single sect, then we have something unusual: a quietly normal piece of religious writing, produced by a well-informed, concerned, but not agitated, follower of Yahweh who lives in the home land.

Yet note what he is willing to do, and without hesitation or embarrassment: rewrite what was supposedly the most sacred, most inviolable parts of the evolving Hebrew scriptures. He does nothing less than correct the Books of Moses. Jubilees is, therefore, a Parallel-Torah, superior in authority (because it actually was transmitted, so the text says, by the hands of Moses) to the older one.

This casts a very large shadow over the traditional idea that the Hebrew scriptures (at least the Pentateuch and the Prophets) were inviolable sacred writ well before the Common Era. The Book of Jubilees (and several of the other texts I have already discussed, and others which will follow) indicate that one could be sharply critical of the Pentateuch and the Prophets and still remain within the fold. Provided – and this is the key proviso – that one respected the grammar of invention that had been worked out in the primary texts of the Judahist faith, the Genesis-Kings unity. Thus loyalty to the ancient tradition and quite-radical re-invention of that tradition existed side by side. It is as if the several re-inventors of Judahist historical traditions all subscribed to the admixture of old loyalty and new revisionisms that is asserted in the opening words of one of the great inventive documents in the English language, the Prayer Book of 1549: "there was never any thing by the wit of man so well devised, or so sure established, which in continuance of time hath not been corrupted." Since time's passage corrupted things, re-invention and revision purified.

In this re-invented Book of Moses, Jubilees, the author had two radical revisions in mind, one involving law in the narrow sense, and the other accomplishing a theodicy. The first of these, the Parallel-Torah, is intended to turn the old Torah only a few degrees and this according to a restricted priestly interest. The usual title of the book, "Jubilees," points to this material. The reference to the Jubilees year comes from a Pentateuchal text (see Lev. 25:8–10), and refers to a major sabbatical to be taken every fiftieth year (after seven x seven years). Clearly, the author is concerned with liturgical time-keeping. The *idée fixe* that runs through Jubilees is the necessity of sorting out the Judahist religious calendar so that the various major religious festivals (Passover, Atonement, Unleavened Bread, Tabernacles, and Weeks) all fall on the same date and on the same day of the week each year. The author believes that these festivals were created by the patriarchs (this is a new invention, which the Pentateuch does not contain). The author of Jubilees makes it a religious imperative to reject the lunar religious calendar (which had a 354-day year and therefore no regularity of days of the week) and replace it with a solar calendar of 364, which was divisible by seven into fifty-two weeks, and therefore was regular.[20] The author of Jubilees cares greatly about this matter, for he has Yahweh tell Moses to inform the people that unless the solar calendar is employed "…they will mix everything, a holy day as profaned and a profane one for a holy day, because they will set awry the months and sabbaths and feasts and jubilees" (Jub. 6:37). Probably to most present-day readers, the details of liturgical time-keeping seem of secondary importance, if not downright petty, but that casts into even sharper relief this fact: that it was permissible in later Second Temple Judahism to further a devotional viewpoint by revising the basic historical narrative of the Chosen People. And it is hard to think of any bigger revision within the tradition than inventing words of Yahweh to Moses.

The priestly figure behind the Book of Jubilees also rewrote the history of the Chosen People, from Creation to the Exodus, to deal with a matter that he never would have dared to formulate explicitly. It is an issue so flesh-searing that even Philo, the first person in the Judahist tradition to handle abstract ideas in a theological fashion, did not touch it. This is the issue of the origin of evil and the ineluctable question that follows from considering it: the nature of Yahweh. The problem that the inventor of Jubilees has is that he cannot believe that evil came into the world by an act of the Almighty, nor that Yahweh would be involved in specific actions that tempted the Chosen People into infidelity, or that Yahweh would act in a way that was precipitate, high-handed, and callous.

The primary Judahist texts, the Genesis-Kings unity, deal with this potential problem with straightforward ease. They report that Yahweh acts as his own agent and they show him doing all sorts of things that are unreasonable, and by any rational standard, unnecessary. The Yahwist tradition, as articulated in Genesis-Kings, does not require that one believe Yahweh is both all-powerful and all-good. He can, at times, be a very nasty piece of work indeed, but he still is our God: that is the message.

By the time the Book of Jubilees is written, this is no longer universally acceptable. Many followers of Yahweh now demand that he be both God and good. The inventor of the Book of Jubilees gets Yahweh partially off the hook by introducing a cast of characters whose existence limits the Almighty's direct agency in the world. Therefore, he no longer can be charged with acting capriciously or callously (Jubilees avoids the question of who is ultimately responsible for the action of this new cast of characters; the book's inventor is satisfied to get Him off the primary charge). The new set of intermediary figures are angels, and their opposite, demons. Angels certainly are found in the primary text of Judahism, Genesis-Kings, but there, for the most part, the Almighty runs his own errands. However, in the Book of Jubilees, angels become the agents of Yahweh's will, doing everything from bearing messages to controlling the forces of nature to interfering on earth to protect certain chosen individuals from mishaps. That is half of the equation: Newtonian moral physics dictates that if there be angels, then there must be demons. They too are found in the primary narrative of the ancient Hebrews, but there they are circumscribed in their behaviour and eccentric in characteristic.[21] By contrast, in Jubilees, the demons are a unified type and they act in the world in a manner antipathetic to the way the angels behave. This means that not God, but they, are immediately responsible for the evil that befalls mankind.

There is more. The symmetry that Jubilees creates concerning angels and demons requires playing out on a higher plane. And here the inventor of Jubilees introduces Satan, although by another name. This is "Mastema," who is chief of the evil spirits. This figure is not found in the Hebrew scriptures, at least not as a figure who heads the forces of evil in both the visible and the invisible world and is an implacable foe of Yahweh and almost his equal.[22] Jubilees is the earliest documented case of Satan becoming a specific and powerful individual, one who has an invisible army that fights against Yahweh and his invisible army.[23] Mastema (introduced in Jubilees 10:8) becomes the general of the army of evil. It is he who plots the test of Abraham, by inducing Yahweh to tell Abraham that he must offer up his son Isaac (Jub. 17:16). And it was Mastema who hardened the hearts of the Egyptians during Israel's captivity and facilitated the Egyptians' pursuit of the children of Israel as they left their place of bondage (47:9–12). Such a radical rewriting of the history of the Chosen People frees Yahweh from the responsibility of having to arrange the Egyptian bondage and similar events, as is reported in the Pentateuch. Thus, a semi-theodicy is accomplished.

It is only "semi" because Mastema and his demons engage in evil by permission of Yahweh. This is explicitly stated in Jubilees, not merely a point of inference. Mastema received his influence only by directly petitioning the Almighty. As "chief of the spirits" he was concerned by the possibility that Yahweh might bind up all the demons and dispose of them. He petitioned, "O Lord, Creator, leave some of them before me, and let them obey my voice…" (Jub. 10:7–8). The Lord replied by sending nine-tenths of the demons to "the place of judgment" and leaving the remainder to serve alongside Mastema in his work of corrupting the sons of men (Jub. 10:9). Even if this revision of the Pentateuch leaves Yahweh with clean hands, in the sense that He no longer directly inveigles the Chosen People to commit evil, He nevertheless has given licence for evil to exist.

The inventor of Jubilees is no theologian: the concept of theology as a form of thought detached from narrative was totally alien to him and to his readers. Therefore, he uses the only tool that he has in his workshop to try to fix the machinery: he continues to invent new historical narrative, and in the middle of his discussion of the life of Abraham he briefly extends his narrative into the future. He describes a future generation that will arise and states that a great judgement will follow. In the end, there will be "no Satan and no evil one" (Jub. 23:29). This is not an apocalyptic passage, but rather a projection into a narrative future of a partial solution to the problem of evil that exists, and cannot be resolved by the author of Jubilees through his use of a narrative of time past. The book, though of limited success as a theodicy, stands "at the head of a mighty tradition that was to subsist for some two thousand years, and still subsists today,"[24] an initial milestone in the introduction of the figure of the devil into Jewish and Christian cultures.

The Book of Jubilees' rewriting of crucial portions of the Pentateuch is an example of the willingness within some sectors of later Second Temple Judahism to treat the primary history of the Chosen People as something to be revered, but also something that was plastic and transformable. One could easily produce a dozen solid examples of this practice from pre-70 CE times, and there are several dozen more examples that are as yet unsubstantiated in their dating, but which are potentially within the same period of origin. The most important of the historical inventions that can firmly be attributed to the period before the destruction of the Second Temple are as follows: a reworked Pentateuch found in the Qumran caves, the Apocryphon of Joseph; the Genesis Apocryphon, a radical revision of the Creation story and the patriarchal narratives; the Book of Enoch, mentioned in Chapter Five, and discussed in Section 5 below; the Book of Giants, which deals with a period when imperfect angels mated with human beings and produced giants on the

earth; the very fragmentary Book of Noah; the Testament of the Twelve Patriarchs, said to be the last words of each of the sons of Jacob, a document
which exists in a full version containing later Christian interpolations, but
which also is found in fragments in pre-Christian versions in the Qumran
caves; four books that either purport to have been written by Moses or to capture the teachings of Moses not found elsewhere, and known as the Words of
Moses, Pseudo-Moses, the Apocryphon of Moses, and Pseudo-Moses Apocalypse;[25] the Letter of Jeremiah, an item of 100 BCE or earlier that purports to
be a missive sent by the prophet to the Babylonian exiles; Third Maccabees,
of approximately the same period, an intermingling of various biblical traditions with more recent matter concerning the diaspora people in Alexandria;[26] Pseudo-Philo, an early Common Era retelling of the primary history of
the Chosen People, from Adam to David; the Lives of the Prophets.[27]

Neither these, nor the dozens of other potential examples of inventors tinkering with texts that we nowadays think of as being scriptural, stemmed from
any one sect, or from any single sector on the circle of Judahist religious belief. These were not merely morally improving religious fables or Aggadah,
but a fundamental re-ordering of some of the central beliefs of the Judahist
religion. Seemingly, all those who had strong religious opinions re-invented a
portion of the primary history of the Chosen People in order to confirm their
own positions.

4

For purposes of discussion, it is convenient to separate from the extensive
literature that re-invents and thereby revises Judahist history, a complex of
ideas and writings that re-invents the Temple. Most of these are apocalyptic
books which make the Temple a future concept, part of a renewed kingdom
of David or a new, wider Kingdom of God, and they will bear note later. Here
I wish to focus on the most extensive, and most radical of the re-inventions of
the Temple, namely that found in the Temple Scroll of the Qumran caves.

Because the idea of the Temple as the great aniconic idol is so central to
Judaism, it is easy to confuse this central idea with a single idea. The Temple was many things. Indeed, from the period that begins with the Maccabean
revolt and ends with the destruction of the Temple in 70 CE, the concept of
the Temple was represented in four physical forms. One of these was the
Temple of Zerubbabel, built after the return from the Babylonian exile. This
is the "Second Temple," properly so-called (the Temple of Solomon having
been the First Temple). However, a completely new structure, Herod's Temple, about 20 BCE replaced Zerubbabel's structure. (It is traditionally included in the rubric "Second Temple," although it was virtually a brand new
edifice.) Co-existing in time with Zerubbabel's Temple was a Samaritan
Temple at Mount Gerizem, said to be a duplicate (or a very large-scale

model) of the Jerusalem Temple and, like Zerubbabel's Temple, it was modelled on Solomon's Temple. This centre of sacrifice was considered heretical
by the Jerusalem religious authorities. The Samaritans claimed to be the true
descendants of those members of the northern tribes of Israel who had escaped destruction by the Assyrians in the eighth century. This was a particularly vexing assertion to the Jerusalem establishment, because it made the
Samaritans the true descendants of the kingdom of Israel, the confederation
whose cultural inheritance the author-editor of the Books of Samuel and
Kings had so skilfully transferred to the southern, Judah-dominated, Jerusa-
lem-centred tribes. Therefore, when in the late second century, the aggressive
Maccabean king, John Hycranus, captured and destroyed the Samaritan temple, it was more than a simplification for the Jerusalem religious authorities;
it was the removal of a visible and viable threat to their own legitimacy.[28] In
addition to these three temples, a fourth structure existed in the diaspora, at
Leontopolis in Egypt. This was a temple, not a synagogue, and sacrifices
were conducted there. The existence of this fourth temple had its origin in the
deposition from their hereditary offices of the traditional high priests of
Judah – the "Zadokite" line that traced its putative genealogy back to the
reign of King David – by the Maccabeans. Onias IV, son of the last Zadokite
high priest (who was murdered), sought refuge in Egypt and was given permission by King Ptolemy Philometer to create a Jewish sacrificial site. This
diaspora temple, which was able to claim a purer priestly genealogy than the
temple in Jerusalem, operated until it was destroyed by Vespasian in 73 BE,
three years after the demise of the Jerusalem Temple.[29]

This pluralism of sacrificial sites would have been known to anyone who
was concerned with the nature of Judahist faith. The existence of multiple
temples encouraged the contemplation of other possible-Temples. These
would not necessarily have been new institutions, but could be cleansed or reformed iterations of the Jerusalem Temple. Moreover, alternate temples did
not even have to exist in the physical world. They could be entirely conceptual, entirely imagined, and yet, for a believer, entirely real.

Such was the case of the inventors and devotees of the Temple Scroll,
found in Cave Eleven at Qumran. The actual scroll has no name on it, but was
named, quite appropriately, the "Temple Scroll" by the scholar who acquired
the manuscript, Yigael Yadin.[30] Less appropriate was Yadin's immediately
labelling the Temple Scroll as being a product of the Essene community. This
is a claim about which we should remain agnostic.[31] Here, however, the factional provenance is not important, for what we are interested in is how a religiously acute mind of the later Second Temple era might re-invent the
concept of the Temple; in that context, the specific Judahist party to which
the author belonged – or, indeed, whether he belonged to any party at all –
does not impinge on our analysis.

The Temple Scroll is the largest set of fragments among the Dead Sea Scrolls. It runs to roughly 9,000 words, plus editorial interpolations, about the length of a longish short story. The range of dates suggested for its composition extends from as late as the reign of Herod the Great (which ended in 4 BCE) to as early as 150 BCE, for the final version, with an earlier version having been drafted around 190 BCE.[32] At any point between 150 BCE and 4 BCE, knowledge of the three sacrificial temples – Jerusalem, Mount Gerizem, and Leontopolis – would have been widespread, and, if the final draft was done during the reign of Herod the Great, his massive temple rebuilding program would have been well known indeed. Thus, in this era, temples were both a matter of constant notice, and, simultaneously, it was easily perceived that any physical temple was capable of variation.

The Temple Scroll is an extraordinarily audacious document. What seems to be its logical foundation ("seems" because we have only fragments of the original and one does not know what is missing) is a willingness to accept the Yahweh of the primary scriptural unity, Genesis-Kings, in all his atribilious power. Do not bow to another God, the reader is told, because Yahweh "is a resentful God."[33] Indeed he is, and a very demanding one, according to the Temple Scroll. In the Temple Scroll there is no sense of the need for a theodicy, quite unlike what we saw in the Book of Jubilees. There is no hint of the then-avant garde notion (as exemplified by the Book of Jubilees) that Yahweh, if he was God, also had to be good. Here, the tough old doctrine is in force: obey Yahweh because he is god; that is reason enough.

To obey God, however, one must hear His voice. It is on this point that the Temple Scroll distinguishes itself as perhaps the most outrageous, the most hubristic, of the inventions that were taking place within later Second Temple Judaism. The Scroll is nothing less than a rewriting of the Sinai covenant, but with the removal of Moses as an intermediary between the voice of Yahweh and the text of this newly-written Torah. Instead of having Yahweh speak through the spiritual genearch of the Chosen People, Moses, the Temple Scroll purports to contain the actual words of Yahweh, unmediated by a human being. In so doing, the Temple Scroll is unambiguously claiming superiority to the "Books of Moses." Granted, the matters with which the Temple Scroll is concerned (effectively those starting with Exodus, chapter 34, and running to the end of the Pentateuch), are determined by the older texts of Judahist tradition; but a superior spiritual legitimacy is assumed by the Temple Scroll.

This self-vaunted superiority is demonstrated by the Temple Scroll's employing the words of Yahweh as to what the architectural characteristics of the Temple should be. This is a brilliant pre-emptive move, because nowhere in the primary unity of the Hebrew scriptures (Genesis-Kings), does the Almighty give instructions as to how his Temple should be built. Some details of the First Temple are provided, but these are historical reports concerning how the Temple actually was built, not of Yahweh's instructions for its architecture. "Surely, if the 'books of Moses' are truly a Torah, they would include the plans for the Temple, for that is the focal point of His worship": that is the unspoken point of argument put forward by the inventor of the Temple Scroll. It is both obvious and impossible to ignore.

Thereupon, a detailed plan of the Temple is provided, ostensibly uttered by Yahweh in the desert journeying of the Chosen People (Temple Scroll, cols 3–13). As interpreted by Yigael Yadin, the Yahweh-designed Temple was to consist of three perfect squares, concentrically arranged, each focusing on the great altar. The plan was massive in its ambition. The planned outer court seems to have been about the size of the city of Jerusalem in the second century BCE, and its wall was to be three stories high. The wall of the middle courtyard was to be approximately the same height, and the central buildings (containing the altar) were to be massive, probably the equivalent of five stories in height.[34] Details were provided for golden veils, cherubim, and so on.

Crucially, unless one brings to the Temple Scroll an agenda, or set of beliefs, that are formed exterior to the text, one cannot read the document's design for Temple architecture as an apocalyptic exercise. These are plans for a real temple; not one in the heavens but in the physical world. It is not to be initiated by divine hands, but by everyday workmen. Nor can one read the Temple Scroll as some sort of pre-Messianic exercise. There is nothing in the surviving text that can be stretched to imply Messianism.[35] The text can only be read as what it says it is: a Torah. Indeed, because it is given directly by Yahweh's voice, it is *the* Torah.

Most of the book is given over to providing Torah, in the sense of rules of behaviour. These are not heretical by the standards of the time (at least not in the portions of the Scroll that have survived). For the most part, the Temple Scroll compresses and harmonizes commandments that are scattered throughout the Pentateuch. Some new ones are added (concerning, for example, how to treat birds' nests and the necessity of having parapets on roofs, so that no blood should fall from the house on anyone beneath. (Temple Scroll 15:2–6).

None of this is exegesis. This is not a commentary on the "Books of Moses." It is a straight-out replacement of them. The same motifs, and much of the same material that is found in the Pentateuch is used as the basis of the Temple Scroll, but the inventors of the Scroll take these older pieces and add two new elements: the direct voice of Yahweh, and the details of the Temple as the Almighty commanded it to be built. Unlike, for example, the Book of Daniel, the Temple Scroll does not engage in the creation of a false history, one that is easily shown to be unreliable. Instead, the Scroll simply states that it contains the word given by God, directly, at Sinai, a claim that goes beyond mere dating. Here, the author says, here is the true Torah.

In a remarkably gentle formulation, James A. Sanders has remarked, concerning the Second Temple era, "that all communities of the Book have held the concept of canon more lightly than conciliar modes of thinking admit."[36] Because we have literally no idea who wrote the Temple Scroll or what community or what type of Judahist used it as a spiritual guide, it is tempting to shove the Temple Scroll aside or – what is essentially the same thing – pigeonhole it by labelling it "Essene," and therefore as a deviant from mainline Judaism. This will not do. The Temple Scroll was a complete and authoritative text (how much more authoritative can one be than to be written in Yahweh's own words?) and it was directed to all of the Chosen People. This was done by an inventor (or inventors) who were thoroughly familiar with the existing "Books of Moses," but who had no hesitation about radically re-inventing the Torah. The Temple Scroll goes farther than any of the other "Parallel-Torahs" that we have analyzed so far, but that should not blind us to the fact that it was merely one of a wide variety of re-inventions of ancient text. Such re-inventions were continually in process in the later Second Temple period. It is of little importance what the factional affiliation (if any) of the inventor of the Temple Scroll was, for he was engaged in a practice that was so widespread in later Second Temple times as to seem, among the devout, to be ubiquitous.

It is obvious how adaptive this way of thinking – this ability to conceptualize new Temples and to create new Torahs – would be later. When, in 70 CE, the Jerusalem Temple was turned into dust, an urgent need would arise to create new Torahs and to replace the physical Temple with a conceptual entity. The propensity for re-inventing the basic constructs of Judaism – its primary history and its liturgical centre – was therefore to prove a highly adaptive habit. It permitted the survival, in a highly altered form, of the religion that had returned from Babylon, with the Chosen People, and their basic scriptures, the Genesis-Kings unity and the major prophets. We will never know exactly why or how the two truly successful heirs of this Judaism – namely Rabbinic Judaism and Christianity – survived. What is certain is that each exhibited the ingenuity and the creativity of mind that we are observing in the later Second Temple context in the proliferation of "Parallel-Torahs" and in the various conceptualizations of the Temple and, in its inevitable concomitant, the New Jerusalem.

One fragmentary item, pieces of which are found in four of the Qumran caves, has been given the name "Description of the New Jerusalem," and this document helps to illustrate another basic point: that abstract descriptions of alternative Temples and environs could easily be employed as a component of apocalyptic thinking, a way of looking at the world that became increasingly common in the later Second Temple era. These fragments on the New Jerusalem are undated, although almost certainly, in their present form, they originate between the Maccabean revolt and 70 CE. The fragments are apparently the report of a tour of the New Jerusalem, given by an angel, to the author of the text.[37] Unlike the Temple Scroll, the temple here described is not to be built until the end of time and this presumably implies that it will be a structure built not by human hands, but by the divine. This being the case, the interesting thing about the Description of the New Jerusalem, is that the divinely-made Temple is to be square (like that of the Temple Scroll and unlike the rectangular character of Solomon's Temple and of Zerubbabel's Temple, and quite unlike the Herodean temple which was a rectangle encompassed by a trapezoid). Further, there is to be a gate for each of the twelve tribes, remarkable testimony of allegiance in the abstract to a system of tribes that had not existed in concrete form for at least 500 years before this document was written.

David Flusser has presciently observed that such apocalyptic visions of a new Temple and a new Jerusalem are not necessarily hostile to the Hasmonean rulers. Nor, one might add, was it necessarily hostile to the Temple establishment. It was quite possible, as in the vision found in Ezekiel, chapters 40–48 (which clearly influenced the Description of the New Jerusalem) to believe in the eventual removal of the present Temple and its replacement with a heavenly-built structure and to do so "not in any antagonism to the actual sanctuary, but simply in the hope for a more splendid future."[38]

5

That comment by David Flusser rightly implies that there are two usages of apocalypses in the later Second Temple period, the undercutting of the existing religious order or, alternately, its affirmation. This brings our attention to three crucial apocalyptic documents: the Book of Enoch (alternatively called 1 Enoch), the War Scroll, and the Book of Daniel. The frustrating point about each of these documents is that there is no certainty concerning how their readers used them: to attack the existing Temple establishment or to indicate a pious hope for a better long-term future. That said, from a present-day point of view, each of them seems somewhat incompatible with a pious acceptance of the existing religious order as embodied in the Temple establishment in Jerusalem.

These three apocalypses (like their collateral descendant, the Book of Revelation in the "New Testament") are very difficult to come to terms with, because they are constructed on two opposing emotional planes. On the one hand, each provides a vision, delivered to humankind by supernatural beings, and there is a dazzling quality to this, like a flash of sunshine from behind a bank of heavy clouds. Yet, simultaneously, the actual religious vision that is presented has an aphotic origin. It comes not from light, but from darkness and the louring character of each apocalypse clashes with this coincident brightness. So dealing with an apocalypse is as difficult as dealing with a passive-aggressive friend: one never is permitted to settle into a comfortable attitude.[39]

As mentioned in Chapter Three, section 4, parts of the Book of Enoch were pre-Maccabean in origin (most probably Chapters 1–36), and 72–82. The rest is later second Temple, almost certainly.[40] "First Enoch" (which we shall use interchangeably with the term "Book of Enoch") is an historical treasure that the Jewish and Christian worlds long possessed, but did everything possible to lose. The book became known to European scholars only in the later eighteenth century. It had been preserved only by the Abyssinian branch of the Christian church, in Ethiopic. Hence, it was in none of the standard canons, Jewish, Roman Catholic, Protestant, Greek, or Slavonic, and not in the collections of Apocrypha or deutero-canonical items. First Enoch had been known to the early Christian church fathers, however, and they had paid it heed until the fourth century, when it fell out of favour. The volume probably had a direct influence on the Book of Jude (see especially Jude 1:14) and perhaps on other parts of the "New Testament." Significantly, the Rabbis of the second through sixth centuries rejected the book's inclusion in the Jewish canon, and suppressed entirely knowledge of the work. So, until fragments of Enoch turned up among the Dead Sea Scrolls, it could easily be ignored. But the fact that it was the second-most-widely represented of the non-biblical books found in the Qumran libraries – it was exceeded only by the Book of Jubilees, another long-suppressed volume – meant that a curiosity that had been fully available in English since the early nineteenth century, suddenly was in the van of late twentieth-century biblical scholarship.[41]

And what a sprawling marvel it is. The book manages to be simultaneously a Parallel-Pentateuch and a massive anthology of apocalyptic literature, fashioned by many hands, over centuries, and running to 108 chapters! This sounds almost impossible: but the contributions of the several authors mesh, in large part because the final author-editors had the good sense to use a stable form as a model, namely the Pentateuch. Thus, First Enoch is broken into five books:

1 The Book of the Watchers (chapters 1–36)
2 The Book of the Similitudes, alternately called the Book of Parables (chapters 37–71)
3 The Book of Astronomical Writings, sometimes called the Book of the Heavenly Luminaries (chapters 72–82)
4 The Book of the Dream Visions (chapters 83–90)
5 The Book of the Epistle of Enoch (chapters 91–108)[42]

This five-form division was well known to the readers of First Enoch and it was the most credible form such a volume could take: the "Books of Moses" had trained readers to regard a five-fold division of material as authoritative.

Moreover, when a vision is ascribed to Enoch, seventh son in line from Adam, father of Methuselah, and a man so pious that he was taken to God's bosom without experiencing death, it claims a spiritual lineage and contact-piety superior to that of Moses (who was not even permitted into the Promised Land, much less assumed into heaven directly). Therefore the Book of Enoch is yet another Parallel-Torah. However, this Torah is different, because although its form is basically that of an historical narrative, it is based not upon remembering the past, but upon remembering the future.

The surprising literary quality of First Enoch is manifest in how well its simple structure encompasses and controls a terrific mishmash of material. Earlier, I said the Book of Enoch was an anthology. True enough. But the five-book structure actually includes at least a dozen different apocalypses. Thus even if the final editor had not been so skilful, this would have been an extremely important document from an historical viewpoint. It established in the richness of style and content of its apocalypses, that apocalyptic writing was a widespread activity in Second Temple times. In including only one example of apocalyptic thought in the Writings section of the Tanakh (the Book of Daniel), the controllers of the final canon were intentionally misrepresenting the character of religious thought in the later Second Temple era. That they had ideo-religious reasons for doing this is undeniable. One notes, however, that such actions inevitably run counter to our present enterprise, which is to uncover, rather than to suppress, the prevalent tendencies of the Second Temple period.

Inevitably, an anthology such as First Enoch, which has individual components that stem from roughly 300 BCE to 70 CE, bears relationships to a wide variety of strands of Judahist devotional thinking. The most obvious is to the Book of Daniel. The pre-Maccabean parts of Enoch (the Book of the Watchers and the Book of the Heavenly Luminaries) are considerably older than the final version of the Book of Daniel. Arguably, these parts of Enoch are the first true apocalypses in the Judahist tradition.

The parts of Enoch and of Daniel that are coterminous are strangely similar in their symbolism, but not in a way that proves any direct interaction. The events to which each responds are the depredations of Antiochus Epiphanes, of the 160s BCE. As is well known, in the Book of Daniel, Antiochus is well and truly abhorred, but the interesting point is the way he is symbolically represented. He is the "little horn" which stems from a buck goat (Dan. 8:9–14; 11:21–). Significantly, the Book of Enoch includes Antiochus Epiphanes in the Dream Vision section (chapters 83–90). This section comprises a sequence of dreams that Enoch recounts to his son Methuselah. The visions deal with world history from the Great Flood to the time of Antiochus, and then go on to a time of future judgement. The vision breaks all the rules of normal literary composition, both of its own time and of our own, and is all the better for that. It takes a single metaphor – a series of white animals, but for the most part, sheep – and makes them symbolic parallels to the Chosen People. The metaphor runs so long that the reader loses the parallel and becomes engrossed in a bizarre bestiary-cum-morality play. The various white animals, harried and encompassed, are rescued by a white ram who grows a great horn (is this partially a reference to one or all of the Maccabeans? who can say for sure?). Thereupon, the white sheep safe, the Almighty punishes those shepherds who had not taken good care of the sheep and also, "a great sword was given to the sheep; and the sheep proceeded against all the beasts of the field in order to kill them; and all the beasts and birds of heaven fled from before their face" (Enoch 90:19).

This portion of First Enoch has in common with the Book of Daniel that: (1) the history of the Chosen People is divided into four distinct periods of time; (2) the magical number seventy is central, there being seventy shepherds in Enoch and seventy "weeks" of years in the time-scale of Daniel; and (3) in each case a major symbolic entity is a horned figure of the goat and sheep family; and (4) Antiochus Epiphanes is clearly an animating figure in each apocalypse.

These commonalities should not be taken to mean either that Enoch was the source of ideas that were later adapted in Daniel, or of the opposite case. Rather, a more productive inference is that we probably should perceive apocalyptic thought in the later Second Temple era as being environmentally (as distinct from directly) interactive. This is a simple point, but it is easily missed. On reflection, it seems reasonable to suggest that people who thought in the rich symbolism of the "Revealed" form that was apocalyptic literature, had to have been keenly aware of other people who thought in a similar mindset and who wrote in a similar manner. They interacted. This does not mean that the authors of a given text directly lifted things from another; it was more diffuse than that. But even when they disagreed, apocalyptic thinkers had to have been aware of each other. The apocalypses they wrote were not secret documents (even if the interpretations of the texts may have been a form of secret knowledge). Apocalypticism was environmentally interactive not only within its own genre, but it was part of the swirling ideational mix that was Judaism between the Maccabean revolt and the destruction of the Temple.[43] Therefore to limit apocalyptic thought in any historical discussion to any one sect (the Essenes are the usual candidates) or to one canonical book (the Book of Daniel) is to denature by presupposition the polychromatic ichors that were the lifeblood of the Judahist religion.

Just as it is important not to miss the contemporary intermingling of apocalyptic and "ordinary" thought among the followers of Yahweh, so it is necessary not to create a false ladder of descent, whereby the apocalyptic writings of the later Second Temple period are seen as being derivations from some of the more hyperactive of the earlier prophets. Three passages in the Prophets are sometimes pointed to as being apocalyptic in nature: Isaiah 24–27, Joel, Chapter 3; and Zechariah 9–11. This, I think, is a mistake. Despite these three passages being written in reference to an indeterminate future, and even though they include imagery that is somewhat more vivid than that found in most of the Prophets, there is such a great difference between them and the apocalypses which multiply between the Maccabean revolt and the destruction of the Second Temple, that even to call the earlier material "proto-apocalyptic" is misleading. For one thing, each of the earlier passages is embedded in a larger text that dictates the respective passages are to be read in the voice of a prophet, and the prophets always operated with a totally different base-assumption than did the apocalypticists: that the future is mendable. However in contrast, as Norman Cohn observes, "there is no suggestion in the apocalypses that human beings can, by their obedience or disobedience, affect the shape of things to come. The future is already determined, in fact its course is already inscribed in a heavenly book, and its outcome will be different from anything foretold in classical prophecy."[44] Prophecy in the Hebrew scriptures is about collective righteousness and collective guilt; apocalypse is about individual redemption and individual sin; prophecy is the hand of the Almighty writing in time, whereas apocalypse is the hand of God ending time; prophecy may introduce the idea of a collective resurrection of the dead (as in Isaiah 26:19), but apocalypse has an individual resurrection and, connected in some way to that resurrection, a judgement of each individual.

Two further characteristics make even the three passages mentioned above, of allegedly apocalyptic thought in the Prophets, exist a great distance away from the later, fully-formed apocalypses. One of these is verbal. The material in the Prophets, in comparison to the apocalypses, is virtually blank-faced. The difference between even a supposed-apocalypse and a real one is the difference between an Abyssinian iconic figure and one of Bruegel's later canvases. Compare, for example, the uses of sheep-and-shepherd images in Zechariah, chapter 11 and the Book of Enoch, chapters 83–90. No one with an eye would confuse the two. Second, and of greater diagnostic significance, is the inclusion in the apocalypses of the other-worldly figures that are pivotal to the form. Prophets speak as the voice of God; apocalypticists write down what they are told by angels. In the usual instance, the apocalyptic form asserts an angel conduit; the prophetic does not.[45] And, many of the apocalypses (at least those of which we have whole copies) introduce a devil figure or demon-emissaries from the Evil One. (The implications of the introduction of such a figure into Judaist religion was discussed in connection with the Book of Jubilees in Section 3.)

That the visionaries who wrote the apocalypses believed them to be embodiments of religious truths, I have no doubt; that they also believed them to be within the spirit of the Yahweh-faith also seems highly likely, even if they were willing to take the occasional swipe at the Temple authorities. What I doubt they perceived, however, was that their pious and intoxicated inventions were fundamentally antithetical to the basic ethos of the religion of Judah, as it had coalesced in the Babylonian Exile and in the early days of the Return.[46] Apocalypticism, when placed against the backdrop of basic Judahist beliefs – of Yahweh working through history, of judgement being collective rather than personal, of Yahweh's worship being accessible, not arcane – stands out either as being revolutionary or as profoundly abnormal in content: its form, which is narrative history projected into the future, is compatible with the dominant mode of expression of the Tanakh. Content is the problem. That point must be emphasized as a preface to our turning to the Book of Daniel. Because Daniel is included in the Tanakh, we accept it as belonging there and therefore slide over its potentially revolutionary character, considered within the Judahist context.

Here, only the post-Maccabean parts of Daniel are our focus, these being chapters eight through twelve, inclusive, and, probably, chapter seven as well.[47] Fragments of nine separate copies of the Book of Daniel were found in the Qumran caves (as compared with fragments of eleven separate versions of the Book of Enoch),[48] and it obviously was well known to several of the sects within the Judahist faith. (Had it been only an Essene document, it would not have been included in the Tanakh.)[49]

The heart of the post-Maccabean part of Daniel, which includes the most interesting of the book's apocalyptic material, is easier to date than is any other biblical book. This is because the author (or authors) follows very closely the grammar of scriptural invention that we have seen operative several times earlier. One aspect of this grammar is that anyone who engages its paradigms is forced to think historically. As credential for the sections of Daniel that deal with the future, the author places himself at a fictive date in the past and then "predicts" from that position events that already have taken place. Now, the critical point is that the grammar of biblical invention dictates that historical statements be as accurate as possible. And historical accuracy (whether presented as history in the usual narrative form or, as in the Book of Daniel, as "predictions") is most apt to be possible when the events have occurred within the writer-inventor's lifetime. Thus, the first six chapters of Daniel, which the editor-inventor takes from pre-Maccabean materials, have historical verisimilitude, but it would be excessively demanding to expect it to be fully consonant with historical accuracy.[50]

No matter. What does count is that when the inventor of the Book of Daniel comes to events that occurred within his own lifetime, he is very accurate, and this gives us a tight framework for dating of the work. (That, in so doing, one transposes his "predictions" into historical statements is here taken as given.) One needs recall here that an appalling profanation of the Temple had been accomplished by Antiochus Epiphanes in 167 BCE when it became a place of worship to Baal Shamen. A severe anti-Judahist persecution followed. This led to the Maccabean revolt and to a bloody war. Now, Antiochus Epiphanes of Syria appears in Daniel as the "little horn" (Dan. 8:9) that grows on the head of a notably vigorous and aggressive goat. The "little horn" magnifies himself and prevents the daily sacrifice from taking place in the Temple. The sanctuary is desecrated (Dan. 8:11–13). The rise of Antiochus and his bloody actions are discussed in considerable detail, in symbolic language (Dan. 11:21–35).

These "predictions" of the activity of Antiochus Epiphanes are accurate, right up to the point that they cease being historical statements and become real predictions. Then they go awry. And that is the point of deviation which permits the dating of the book. One place of error occurs with the prediction that the Temple would be defiled for 2,300 days before it would be purified (Dan. 8:14). Clearly, the editor-inventor does not know the date of the Temple's purification; it occurred in December of the year 164 BCE[51] which means that the desecration lasted three years, rather than the six to seven years that is predicted in Daniel. Therefore the prediction was written before December 164 BCE. Confirmation of this terminal-date for the composition of Daniel is found in the book's detailing future battles and activities of Antiochus Epiphanes. In fact, he died in late 164 BCE and the predictions concerning his future conquests, including his capture of Egypt (see Dan. 11:36–45) are wildly inaccurate. This means that the predictions were written while Antiochus was still alive, and threatened to become a world conqueror, at least in the view of the inventor of Daniel. Our conclusion, then, is that the post-Maccabean portions of the Book of Daniel were brought together in the years 167–164 BCE. The irony here is obvious. What is by far the most ideologically heterodox of the Hebrew scriptures is the item whose provenance can be most precisely dated. Indeed, the Book of Daniel is more tightly dated than any item in either the Jewish or the Christian scriptures and more closely dated than any of the extra-biblical texts.

The logic train that we have just employed in the dating of the Book of Daniel is not primarily of interest because we need the actual date, although it is a useful piece of information; the greater value is that this train of inference illustrates that the grammar of invention, which we first saw in the Genesis-Kings unity, still prevails in the later Second Temple era. Crucially, even though the ideological content of apocalyptic writing is very different from that of basic Judahist beliefs as defined in Genesis-Kings, the rules of religious invention are fundamentally unchanged: creativity is not acknowledged; new ideas are presented as being old ones; recent occurrences are transmuted by their being placed in environments that lend them a patina of age; and even the wildest of apocalyptic visions is presented in a form that makes them into historical narratives, and this even if the history is to occur in the future.

In connecting the immediate reference of the Book of Daniel to events of 167–164 BCE, one risks leaving a false impression, mainly that the book is "unireferential" and that its symbolism refers to one thing only, its immediate historical situation.[52] No. Daniel is a rich apocalypse and its editor-inventor has more on his mind than just his immediate world. He does, indeed, attempt to predict a future, and therein lies the continuing fascination of the book. Right to the present day, devotees spend long hours trying to crack what they believe is a God-given map to the end of human time. The famous "seventy weeks of Daniel" is a puzzle so compelling that it is addictive. Television evangelists thunder mightily about it and colporteurs go door-to-door with brightly illustrated pamphlets explaining its predictions. These present-day manifestations of the power of the Book of Daniel are warranties of a quality of strange genius among those who composed it, and especially the final author-editor. A really great apocalypse has the ability to be forever read and misread.

Still, its contemporary references are of value, because they relate directly to the bank of religious ideas and attitudes that swirled through later Second Temple Judaism. Just as a vein of haematite tinctures the way one must perceive an entire marble slab, so apocalyptic thought comes to enhue the entire Judahist enterprise, even the parts that the dark and venous vein does not directly touch. The key to Daniel's power in its contemporary setting is that it was a trope of the Book of Jeremiah immediately recognized by its readers and listeners. The theme passage is set in Jeremiah as follows:

> The word that came to Jeremiah concerning all the people of Judah in the fourth year of Jehoiakim the son of Josiah king of Judah, that was the first year of Nebuchadnezzar king of Babylon: (Jer. 25:1)

Jeremiah then prophesies and the heart of his messages is this:

> And this whole land shall be a desolation, and an astonishment; and these nations shall serve the king of Babylon seventy years.
> And it shall come to pass, when seventy years be accomplished, that I will punish the king of Babylon, and that nation, saith the Lord, for their iniquity, and the land of the Chaldeans will make it perpetual desolations. (Jer. 25:11–12)

This prophecy is amplified as follows:

> For thus saith the Lord, That after seventy years be accomplished at Babylon I will visit you, and perform my good word toward you, in causing you to return to this place. (Jer. 29:10)

Seventy years: that is not a calendarial concept, but rather a motif. It is a "wrong" number historically – the Babylonian Exile did not last seventy years and the Babylonian empire was defeated well before that period of years was ended. Yet the passage in Jeremiah had great power for the people of Daniel's time. This was because the spirit of the prophecy, if not the exact letter, was absolutely right. Yahweh had taken care of the Chosen People. Those who heard the Book of Jeremiah read knew that to take a prophetic text seriously, one must not take it literally.

This presupposition, that to take a predictive text seriously one need not – indeed should not – take it literally, is basic to all of the Book of Daniel and is particularly important to Daniel's development of Jeremiah's motif of the "seventy weeks":

> In the first year of Darius the son of Ahasuerus, of the seed of the Medes, which was made king over the realm of the Chaldeans:
> In the first year of his reign I Daniel understood by books the number of the years, whereof the word of the Lord came to Jeremiah the prophet, that he would accomplish seventy years in the desolations of Jerusalem.   (Dan. 9:1–2)

Never mind that Darius the Mede did not exist; Darius was a Persian. The editor-inventor's ancient history is wobbly, but the force of his vision slingshots not from his mention of Darius, but from his evocation of Jeremiah. This authority is doubled when, in the manner of apocalyptic writing, he invokes angelic intervention, for Gabriel comes to him. "And he informed me and talked with me, and said, O Daniel, I am now come forth to give thee skill and understanding" (Dan. 9:22). The heart of the message is resonant of Jeremiah:

> Seventy weeks are determined upon thy people and upon thy holy city, to finish the transgression, and to make an end of sins, and to make reconciliation for iniquity, and to bring in everlasting righteousness, and to seal up the vision and prophecy, and to anoint the most Holy.   (Dan. 9:24)

Daniel, however, goes farther, and ties the final victory of the Chosen People, after seventy "weeks" to a divine intervention by the Archangel Michael, who is said to be the guardian of the people (Dan. 12:1). The great victory shall take place both on earth and in the heavens.

The "weeks" of Daniel are universally taken to be weeks of years, meaning that each week signifies seven years. (This interpretation is clearly indicated by Daniel 9:2 which states that the vision is about "the number of years": some biblical translations, such as the Revised Standard Version, use phrases such as "seventy weeks of years" to translate "seventy weeks" in Daniel 9:24). Here, as an exercise, let us engage in a little misplaced literalism and say that Daniel is foretelling a victory for the Chosen People, one of both ter-restrial and cosmic significance, which will occur after a period of 490 (70 × 7) years. But at what moment does his clock start? At the time of the prophet Jeremiah, about 600 BCE? at the destruction of the Second Temple and the Babylonian captivity, 587 BCE? or at Cyrus of Persia's granting permission for the people to return from exile in 538 BCE? None of these dates works for someone who is writing about 165 BCE, because they produce predictions for the final victory (which will come 490 years after the clock starts) that are too far in the future to be meaningful from the inventor's viewpoint: from 110 BCE to 48 BCE, by which time every adult involved in the contemporary events of the Antiochus Epiphanes era will be in his grave.[53]

So the phrase "seriously but not literally" comes into play. Just as the car-toon identification of Antiochus Epiphanes is to be taken seriously but not lit-erally (the man was seriously evil, but he did not literally spring from the horn of a goat), so are the numbers to be taken. The period of "seventy weeks" is not really 490 years, but is more akin to an eon. It is not a precise measure of time any more than the description of Antiochus is a precise phys-ical description. The period of years is a passage of time which, when time is full, will bring victory over the Syrian oppressor of the Chosen People. Given the context of the compilation of the Book of Daniel, the 490 years are best thought of as an eon of time which would end sometime in the future, when Antiochus would be destroyed.

That the "seventy weeks" are not to be considered an expression of calen-dral time is confirmed by the numbers involved: forty-nine (7 × 7) is a central symbolic number in the thinking of later Second Temple writers. That it was a sacred number was clearly established in our discussion of the Book of Ju-bilees, wherein a Jubilee is declared after every forty-nine years. And in the Book of Enoch, there is a section called the "Apocalypse of Weeks" wherein seven weeks is the period by which a succession of cosmic events are delin-eated (Enoch 93:1–14). Earlier, in the pre-Maccabean sections of Enoch, sev-enty generations is the term of punishment set for certain rebellious other-world figures (Enoch 10:12). Clearly, seven and its variations, 70, 49, and 490 are magical numbers.

This pattern indicates that we must avoid the common error of reading the visual portions of the vision of the seventy weeks as something to be taken se-riously, but metaphorically, while the numbers portion is to be taken literally. No, the author-editor accepted the same grammar of invention throughout.

Part of this grammar involved a secondary rule of invention, one that runs through the entire Book of Daniel: distant history can be fairly sloppy – it is there for the purpose of mood-setting, a verbal equivalent of background mu-sic in a film – but recent historical events, especially those occurring during the lifetime of the writer(s) must be quite tight: not, emphatically, mathematically precise, but tight enough to make believable to contemporaries a prediction about the imminent and inevitable victory of Yahweh over Antiochus Epiphanes.

Thus, in three specific instances, we can observe varying degrees of precision in the use of symbolic numbers. The first of these is a number from the distant past, relating to the restoration of Jerusalem and the Temple after the return from exile: "from the going forth of the commandment to restore and to build Jerusalem unto the Anointed One comes will be seven weeks" (Dan. 9:25).[54] Actually, forty-nine years from the decree of Darius of 538 BCE is not a date of any significance, but the editor-writer of Daniel is not interested in precise time. What he means as historical fact (and presents as prophecy) is that it took a while, a big handful of years, between the time that the order to rebuild the sacred city was given and the task completed with the appointment of a legitimate anointed high priest, so that the central sacrificial acts of Yahweh-worship could be reinstituted.[55] After that point, the Second Temple operated for a long skein of years, sixty-two "weeks" according to Daniel 9:26, before the "Anointed one" was again cut off. The period of sixty-two weeks of years is another indeterminate period of time meaning, roughly, a bunch of time. However, the far end of that period, the time nearest the author, is when measures of time become more precise: not literal, but more sharply referential in their symbolic way. This is because the terminus of the period of time (the end point of the total of sixty-nine "weeks") is a precise point. It is the moment an evil prince cuts off the Anointed One, makes Temple worship impossible, destroys the city of Jerusalem and trashes the Temple sanctuary. This is a real moment in the life of the final author-editor of Daniel, the one time-point in all of the Book of Daniel that is both serious and literal. The date was 169–168 BCE when Antiochus Epiphanes threw down the walls of Jerusalem, killed thousands, and polluted the sanctuary. The editor-inventor of Daniel conflates this set of disasters with an occurrence that had happened slightly earlier, in 169 BCE, namely the killing of the legitimate high priest (the Anointed One), Onias III, by a priestly rival, Menelaus who was "pro-Hellenist," and who, according to 2 Maccabees, bought control of the high priesthood by bribing the Seleucid overlords (see 2 Macc. 4:23–38). Thus was the Anointed One, Yahweh's high priest, cut off. That occurred in real time.

This moment in real time continues. The editor-inventor "predicts" that a covenant will be confirmed between the evil prince (Antiochus) and "many" within Jerusalem. A covenant is always a deal with at least two parties; the undefined "many" are the sort of self-ambitious priestly aristocrats exemplified by (but not limited to) Menelaus and his family. This deal had already been cut by the time the ninth chapter of Daniel was written, but the arrangement between Syrian outsiders and the usurpers of Yahweh's priesthood had yet to run its course.

So, after this short period in real time, the Book of Daniel again launches itself into figurative time. Now, however, the editor-inventor is not looking backwards, but forwards; he is not making historical references, disguised as predictions, but real predictions. He predicts that the duration of the false covenant will be one "week," thus bringing the total number of weeks in the entire Danielic prophecy to seventy "weeks": a magic number, being the product of seven (the distance in a week between Shabbats) and ten (the sacred number of the Decalogue). At the end of this final, seventieth week, both the earthly victory of Israel over Antiochus was to occur and also the simultaneous cosmic victory of the archangel Michael over the other-world foes of the Chosen People. One week here could be five years, it could be seven, it could be ten. The editor-inventor means: we will be delivered, we will win, it will happen soon. This is not only a prediction, it is a Maccabean anthem.

The words of the anthem blur, however. We will win, we will be delivered, and it will happen soon – but what is soon? Daniel's prediction on the point involves two self-contradictory estimates of how long the desecration of the Temple will last: either it will be 2,300 days, counting from the cessation of the daily Temple sacrifice (Dan. 8:14), which is less than seven years and is a very messy number to find in an otherwise stylized piece of writing; or it will be one "week," that is seven years, counting from the time the legitimate Anointed One was deposed and the false-covenant introduced with Menelaus and his family (Dan. 9:27). That prediction is especially muddy because the text says that the false covenant will permit the sacrifice to continue for half a week (three and one-half years) and then will cease, until restored another half-week later.

These mutually incompatible predictions are a litmus item. I think here we are seeing the editor-inventor of Daniel, compiling material at a time of epochal national crisis, losing control, for just a moment, of the invention he is constructing. He is standing amidst a social earthquake, creating an historical narrative that pretends to be from the far past, and simultaneously he is trying to create an inspiring, convincing and, he devoutly prays, a real set of predictions concerning a future that is menacing, unsure, and confusing. In that context, his losing his compass, and spraying his prediction (nay, his desperate and fervent prayers for the future) loosely, almost uncontrollably at time's horizon, is hardly surprising.

Yet, Daniel wins. The book is a good set of prophecies, at least in its real-world aspects. At a point not far beyond the time of the final editing of Daniel, the Maccabeans triumph. The Temple is reconsecrated. Daily sacrifices begin again. That, I would speculate, is why the Book of Daniel, alone of all the apocalyptic writings produced within the Judahist community in the later Second Temple period, was included in the Tanakh. The book affirms the centrality of the Temple for Judahism and provides an electric, hyper-coloured version of how the Second Temple was rescued from desecration by divine intervention. If one assumes that the story of the Second Temple's salvation from the despoliation by Antiochus Epiphanes required preservation in the Hebrew scriptures (and it is hard to see how it could be excluded, given that this was the greatest moment of danger for the aniconic idol of Yahweh that occurred between 520 BCE and 70 CE), then there were (to our present knowledge) only two alternate versions of the story: that in Daniel and that in 1 and 2 Maccabees. The latter books, however, glorified the Maccabeans. Their later descendants had a bloody war with the Pharisees, who are generally perceived as the precursors of the Rabbis and who, in the second through sixth centuries, decided which books would be included in the canon. The Book of Daniel had the advantage of engaging the passage through the moments of greatest danger to the Temple, but without glorifying the Hasmoneans.

But there is more to the Book of Daniel than a lot of slightly inaccurate history and one very nearly accurate prediction: especially compelling is the book's concept of end times, of the resurrection of the dead, and of the judgement of individuals at the end of time. These are things that help make Daniel fascinating to generation after generation of readers, the more so when such concepts are combined with misguided attempts to read the expressive numbers in the prophecy of "weeks" as if they were a precisely encoded chart, set down by some divinely inspired cryptographer-cum-accountant. Daniel 12:2–3 is especially important because it is the only place in the Hebrew scriptures where the resurrection of the dead as individuals is mentioned. Elsewhere there are references to the resurrection of the children of Israel as a group (such as Isaiah 26:19 and Ezekiel 37:11). However, these are geopolitical references; that is, references to the restoration of Israel as a corporate group from a state of metaphorical death.[56] The idea of each individual being resurrected after death and then appearing before a divine judge is not a singular invention (it is found several places in the Book of Enoch, for example), but its inclusion in the Book of Daniel is crucial for later developments. The resurrection of the individual became a component of Phariseeism and thus of Rabbinical Judaism, and, in a much sharper, harder-edged version, it became central to Christianity. When the Book of Daniel suggests that "many of them that sleep in the dust of the earth shall awake, some to everlasting life, and some to shame and everlasting contempt" (Dan. 12:2), it is replacing the collective unity of the Chosen People, which characterizes all of the rest of the Hebrew scriptures, with a tripartite truncation: some will remain in the dust (presumably in the traditional Hebrew underworld, "Sheol"), some will be resurrected from the dead and sentenced to everlasting shame and contempt, and still others will be judged worthy of everlasting life.

That the last book to be written of what eventually forms the Hebrew canon (with the probable exception of the Book of Esther, of which there is no trace in the Dead Sea Scrolls) should imply such a radical rejection of much of the ideology, although not the liturgical forms, of the Judahist faith, requires particular notice. The replacing of the communal righteousness, or waywardness, of the Chosen People (with its associated collective punishments and rewards), with a final judgement in which everyone is on his or her own before the Almighty, opens myriad possibilities for subsequent development. It opens the door to any group that wishes to re-interpret the liturgical life of Israel (especially as it focuses upon the Temple), as being not a form of collective devotion to Yahweh, but a set of individual expiations. Once the pathway is opened to the individualization of sins, virtues, punishments, and rewards in the final judgement, the concept of collectivity becomes redundant. Such individualization implies that the Chosen People as a physical entity are no longer a corporate entity, for if they were a united entity, why should some go to Sheol, some to eternal damnation, some to eternal bliss? The Book of Daniel, then, was a solvent that weakened gravely the seams of collective identity. In certain circumstances, it would be possible for devout individuals, following the commands of Yahweh, as best their consciences dictated, to replace the Chosen People with the chosen few, an aggregate of individuals.

6

Historically pivotal as is the Book of Daniel to the development both of the Jewish and of the Christian religions, it would be a mistake to leave the discussion of signal apocalyptic writings with Daniel as the final exhibit. The Book of Daniel is the only truly apocalyptic book in the Tanakh, but we need to be reminded that apocalyptic thought was very widespread in later Second Temple times. It is only because of the exclusion from the canon of the scores of these texts, that we have been blinded to the fact that apocalyptic thinking was not singular, but common. This is one of the important facts established by the Dead Sea Scrolls. Thus, as a final exhibit, and as a reminder of the variety of apocalyptic thought, the War Scroll is appropriate.

The War Scroll was suppressed for nearly twenty centuries, but it was widely read in pre-70 CE time, if its being found in several fragmentary versions in the Qumran caves is taken as indicative.[57] The War Scroll is later than the Book of Daniel and it reads as if it is a response to Daniel 12:1, wherein the archangel Michael serves as a field general in a great victory by the Chosen People over their enemies, a victory that is both heavenly and earthly. Michael in the War Scroll has an extremely robust military program for a thirty-five-year-long war (War Scroll 2:9), plus five sabbatical years. It is this military enthusiasm that makes it inappropriate to assign the text too quickly to the Essenes: they were pacific and, in their desert form, hermetic. In fact, there is no hint anywhere in the various surviving fragments of who actually wrote the book, what the context of its creation was, or when it occurred (save that it clearly post-dates the Maccabean revolt and that it was written before the destruction of the Second Temple). That indeterminacy is fine for our purposes, however: in its abjuration of specific historical referents, the War Scroll is much more typical of the apocalyptic literature of the later Second Temple era than is the Book of Daniel, which is quite clearly referential to specific events in the recent past.

The War Scroll is as bloodthirsty as any wronged person could ask and more than a touch triumphalist:

> Get up, hero,
> take your prisoners, glorious one,
> collect your spoil, worker of heroic deeds!
> Place your hand on the neck of your foes
> and your foot on the piles of the dead!
> Strike the nations, your foes,
> and may your sword consume guilty flesh!   (War Scroll 12:10–12)

That is to be expected. The unexpected part is how ice-coldly architectonic the bulk of the manuscript is. Most of the text is given over to planning a military machine which will allow the "sons of light" to launch a pre-emptive strike against the "sons of darkness." The sons of darkness are a composite group. Its lead company is "the army of Belial," led by the arch-demon, and it includes as well an array of companies from the traditional enemies of the Children of Israel: Edom, Moab, Philistia and the like (War Scroll 1:1–2). In the simplest terms, the Chosen People, aided by angelic forces (War Scroll 12:8) will fight the various Gentile nations and their demonic allies, and win. Well over half of the surviving portions of the document describe in detail exactly how the army of virtue will be organized. It is to be ordered on a schematic principle that is chronological, rather than logical. The three-and-a-half-decades long war will have a cadre of primary warriors who are between forty and fifty years old at the start (which means that some of these soldiers would be over eighty years of age when the war was over). The military camps were to be governed by men fifty to sixty years of age. The cavalry was to consist of men thirty to forty-five, with their officers being forty to fifty-year-olds. Logistics (the carrying of supplies and related duties) were to be conducted by men aged twenty-five to thirty. No young boy (apparently meaning anyone under twenty-five) or any woman was to enter the several military camps (War Scroll: cols 6 and 7).

The clothing and armament of this eschatological army (for such it is; no real-time army would be organized on these lines) are given in precise detail. The shields, for example, are to be "surrounded by a plaited border and will have a pattern engraved, a work of art in gold, silver and copper blended together, and precious stones, many-hued decorations, work of a skilful craftsman (War Scroll 5:5–6). Every aspect is plotted out like that, including a plethora of labels that are to be inscribed upon the various pieces of military paraphernalia. For example, the trumpets used to sound assembly are to have "Rallied by God" written upon them (War Scroll 3:3). All this planning is subordinate to the overall strategic plan which involves six years of training, followed by twenty-nine years of campaigning, plus five sabbatical years. The targets of the army of light are specified decades in advance (War Scroll 2:9–15).

The calculation and coldness of all this planning is a surprisingly effective contrast to the white-hot blood lust of the battle cry: "Strike the nations, your foes, and may your sword consume guilty flesh" which is repeated antiphonally (War Scroll 12:11 and 19:4), with slight variation.

The War Scroll, in addition to providing an emotionally satisfying response to contemporary curiosity about the details of the great battle referred to so succinctly in Daniel, chapter 12, provides later scholars with an indication of the nature and pace of a crucial transition that occurs between biblical prophetic literature and later Christian documents. Whereas classical prophecy in aid of Yahweh involves the prediction of this-world armies fighting real battles, in the "New Testament," (as Norman Golb notes) the people of God, real people, have no part in determining the outcome of any battle. That takes place in the heavens and the Almighty and his angels very effectively deal with the enemy.[58] So, one might wonder, did the later, "New Testament" view evolve from within the beliefs in Second Temple Judahism, or did the Christians do something revolutionary in inventing this new belief? The War Scroll, like a great deal of the religious literature of the later Second Temple period, suggests that what later became the Christian tradition was the result of developments inherent in the trajectory of evolving Judahist beliefs, and not anything uniquely Christian.

7

Siloam's Teeming Pool – III

I

IN DISCUSSING THE CHARACTER OF APOCALYPTIC THOUGHT IN THE period between the Maccabean revolt and the destruction of the Temple, I intentionally walled off a question that now must be dealt with: the hair-trigger question of whether or not the documents we have available from late Second Temple Judahism indicate any concept of Messiah – and, if so, in what sense? The issue is particularly important with respect to the Book of Daniel, for, given that it is the Tanakh's one apocalyptic volume, it is the place we are most apt to find Messianic concepts.

It is just at this point that the glories of the King James Bible fail us, for here the translators have made an error of monumental proportions: and not an innocent one. The term *MSYH* appears thirty-eight times in the Hebrew Bible as meaning "anointed one." (The Masoretic Text indicates the word was pronounced, roughly, "Mosheeah," but there are nasty little fights about whether the proper transliteration is "Moshiah," "Moshiach," "Mashiah," "Mashiach," or some other variant. In employing "Moshiah," I am not making an indication of sectarian allegiance; anyone who is annoyed by this transliteration may supplant it with his or her own version without changing the import of my argument.) Of course there is no capitalization in the Hebrew text, but it is fair to read Moshiah as "Anointed One." Also, Moshiah usually appears without an article in front of the term. Translators from Hebrew frequently use either the general "an Anointed One" or "the Anointed One" to move the term into idiomatic English. However, in the latter case – when a definite article is employed – it most emphatically must *not* be taken as meaning "*the* Anointed One" in some transcendant sense. If "the Anointed One" is employed, it means: the one person appointed at a specific time for a specific task. The reference is to a precise situation, not to a history-transcendant typological figure.[1]

The litmus indicator here is that thirty-six of the thirty-eight times Moshiah appears in the King James translation of the Tanakh, it is used correctly, to mean "Anointed One." However, in two instances – Daniel 9:25 and 9:26 –

a new word suddenly appears: the term "Messiah." This is a bastardized form of the Greek "Messias" which was created in the late 1550s by the translators of the Geneva Bible.[2] Neither "Messias" nor "Messiah" functions as a neutral transliteration of Moshiah. "Anointed One" would have done quite adequately in the King James rendering of the Book of Daniel; here the insertion of the new term "Messiah" perforce implies the insertion of a new idea into the Hebrew text, and one alien to the original. It is nothing less than a rewriting of the Hebrew text, to insert a much later idea, a reference to Yeshua the Nazarene whom Christians define as Jesus-*the*-Messiah, or Jesus-the-Christ.

Were this not the King James Bible, one could ignore the mistranslation, or even enjoy it, for re-writing the scriptures is what the tradition of biblical invention is all about. However, before noting the marvellous creativity in the Christian invention of Yeshua as "the Messiah," we need a baseline of judgement determined by what the term Moshiah meant when it was used in pre-Christian times. Here the probative material is found in virtually every other English-language translation of the Bible. Therein, Moshiah is called "Anointed One" in most cases, although in some, "the Prince." This contradiction to the KJB translation of Daniel 9:25 and 9:26 is found in the following translations of the late nineteenth and the twentieth centuries: the New International Bible, the Living Bible, the Revised Standard Version (various editions), the Tanakh of the Jewish Publication Society, the Anchor Bible, the New English Bible, the Revised English Bible, the Modern Readers' Bible, and one could go on. The point is that the King James Bible got it very wrong, and later translations, though they get the translation right, are still overshadowed by that greatest of seventeenth-century texts.

In the Book of Daniel, the "seventy weeks" is not about the coming of a Messiah in the Christian sense, but about an Anointed One, a purely Judahist idea. It is hardly a recondite piece of exegesis to note that in Daniel's chapter nine, the Anointed One does not exist except as a conjoint entity with the Temple. This is not to make the simplistic statement that the reference is to a holder of the High Priestship, although that is part of the reference. In fact, the reference to an Anointed One works only when there is a High Priest within the context of the Temple. Moshiah in Daniel's "seventy weeks," then, personifies the situation in which a covenantal relationship between Yahweh and his people will flourish: when the liturgical-sacrificial system operates with its two major components intact, an authentic High Priest, and a purified, daily-sacrificing Temple. Moshiah here is the divinely sanctioned system whereby the Chosen People and Yahweh touch and mutually affirm their covenant.

Putting aside, then, the "Messiah" reference in the KJB version of Daniel, the question remains as to whether or not there is any reference in the Tanakh to Messiah, in the sense that Christians later use the concept, to mean a redeemer or saviour both of individual souls and of the righteous as a collective group. No. There are passages that are later re-invented (and quite brilliantly) by the creators of Christianity, but in the Tanakh they do not carry those meanings.

In those parts of the Tanakh that predate the Maccabean revolt (that is to say, almost all the Hebrew scriptures), the term Moshiah (anointed one) is used in three very tight contexts. One of these applications is to kings. For example, King Saul is referred to as Moshiah of Yahweh (I Sam. 12:3) and King David is described as Moshiah of the God of Jacob (2 Sam. 23:1).[3] In this, and other royal usages, the monarch's being anointed signifies that he is a servant of Yahweh. That this use of Moshiah has no reference either to Moshiah being a redeemer or to his being an apocalyptic leader of the Chosen People is indicated in Second Isaiah (that is, Isaiah 40–55), wherein the phrase "Moshiah of Yahweh" refers to King Cyrus of Persia who grants the children of Israel a boon (Isaiah 45:1). Secondly, Anointed One is used to refer to both the holder of priestly offices in general (Leviticus 4:3 applies the term Anointed One to the generic office of priest) and more importantly, to the High Priest (as the Book of Daniel exemplifies). Thirdly, Psalm 105:15 issues a warning:

> Do not touch My anointed ones;
> Do not harm My Prophets. (JPS)

This comes close to equating the prophets with the several Anointed Ones.

One cannot avoid the conclusion that, although the concept of Messiah is present in the Hebrew scriptures, it is there only as a limited and peripheral idea. In each of its usages Moshiah implies a person anointed either by, or on behalf of, Yahweh as a specific office holder or a person with a specific task, such as prophesying. Certainly, Messiah is not a major part of the Hebrew scriptures, much less their ideational spine. Moshiah is not at any point associated with a future redeemer or saviour.

However, because Moshiah as a concept became fairly significant in later Rabbinical Judaism, and became absolutely central to Christianity, strenuous efforts have been made to find Messianic references in places where the word "Moshiah" is not employed. (One of the most famous of these passages in the "Old Testament," where theologically-determined exegetes wish to find Messiah, even though the term is not used, is the "suffering Servant" passage in Second Isaiah; it will be discussed in Chapter Eight.) Here the central point is one of method and of logic. It hardly seems sensible to deal with Messiah in the Hebrew scriptures by refusing to accept those places where Moshiah is actually used as a term to refer to kings, priests, and prophets, and yet look for the "real" references to Messiah only in places where the scriptures do not introduce the concept. Granted, there are such things as sub-texts and arguments-from-silence, but the forcing of Moshiah into places where the writers did not use the term is surpassing strange. As William Scott Green has noted, this forced exegesis seems to "suggest that the best way to learn about the Messiah in ancient Judaism is to study texts in which there is none."[4]

Yet, if Messiah has little to do with the canonical Hebrew scriptures, conceivably the idea could be central to the later development of Judahist thought, during the years between the Maccabean revolt and the destruction of the Second Temple. And, perhaps, this could occur even in the sense that is totally absent in the "Old Testament," of Moshiah being a future redeemer. Perhaps. Let us look first at the biggest body of data, the Pseudepigrapha, the Apocrypha and the Dead Sea Scrolls.

Although the case is slightly stronger here than in the Tanakh, it still is not very powerful. For instance, if one takes as a data base all the (as yet) known extra-biblical Judahist writings composed after 167 BCE and before 70 CE, other than the Dead Sea Scrolls, only two documents refer to Messiah.[5] One of these is the portion of the Book of Enoch that is called the Book of Similitudes or the Book of Parables (chapters 37–71). This, most scholars believe, is the latest portion of the Enoch-anthology to have been written. In two places (48:10 and 52:4), the term Messiah is used, but in a strangely subordinate form: as if referring to an archangel rather than to an independent figure. In the first instance, a judgement is announced against those who "have denied the lord of the Spirits and his Messiah," and in the second, an angel explains to Enoch that at the final judgement Yahweh will cast a number of judgements, which will "happen by authority of his Messiah...." Apparently, in the latter case, Moshiah would not be an active participant in events, but rather, the guarantor of their authenticity.

In the Songs of Solomon, hymns number 17 and 18, there is found praise of "the Lord Messiah," a future super-king of the Davidic line who will destroy Judah's enemies and purge Jerusalem. Whether the voice here is closer to old-time classical prophecy or to later Second Temple apocalyptic rhetoric, is open to question. The clear point is that Messiah is a king who will reign in the manner of a powerful and righteous monarch. This is not a piacular or redemptive figure, but an Anointed One, in the same sense that King David was.

That is all. Moshiah as a proper noun does not appear elsewhere, although the verb form "to anoint" occurs on a few occasions. If Messiah as a concept was central to the thinking of the followers of Yahweh in the late Second Temple era, they found very effective ways to keep this a secret.

The Qumran Scrolls are equally revealing, and also in a negative sense. The term is clearly located in four of the Qumran fragments and ambiguous references that may be to Moshiah are found in two or three more. In the War

Scroll the term is employed in the plural. Victory over Israel's enemies will come "by the hands of your Anointed Ones" (War Scroll 11:7). In the "Damascus Document" or "Damascus Rule" (a text that will be discussed in more detail later), Moshiah is employed in the plural to refer to the prophets[6] (CD 2:12 and 5:21–6:1). Another usage in the Damascus Document is in the formula "Messiah of Aaron and Israel" (CD 12:23–13:1, 14:19, and 19:10–11). The "Messiah of Aaron and Israel" is an apocalyptic figure who ends the "time of wickedness" (CD 12:23), and he will "atone for their sins" (CD 14:19). This atonement is either for the sins of the whole Chosen People, or of the members of the religions faction that produced the document: the text is unclear. A small fragment found in Cave Four talks of a time when the entire heavens and earth shall listen to Yahweh's Moshiah and he will honour the devout individual "and call the just by name."[7] If (and it is a big "if") this fragment stems from the same belief-system as does the Damascus Document, then that text's references are to Moshiah redeeming, not the entire Chosen People, but only a fraction, comprised of those individuals who are devout and just, by factional standards.

Three characteristics of the apparently Messianic usage of the Damascus Document are noteworthy. First is the way that this Moshiah – whom one would expect to be central to the discussion – is only mentioned briefly, almost with a passing nod. The concept of Messiah is there, certainly, but the Damascus Document almost says that, really, it's no big deal. This is very curious indeed. Secondly, there is the matter of the title "Messiah of Aaron and Israel," or, more accurately, "Anointed One of Aaron and Israel." This seems to apply directly to a future High Priest, for it is to Aaron that the competing high priestly lines traced their ecclesiastical ancestry. So the future Moshiah will be a High Priest with the proper credentials. This position, that Messiah will be a proper High Priest, is buttressed by a fragment from Qumran Cave No. 11 (again *if*, and only if one accepts that this document comes from the same belief system as does the Damascus Rule). This fragment is an apocalyptic piece in which Melchizedek is presented as the active agent of God, and Moshiah as the messenger of Melchizedek. Messiah is identified as the man "anointed of the spirit about whom Daniel spoke" (11Q Melchizedek 2:18). The reference almost certainly is to the high priest who is forecast in Daniel's prophecy of the "seventy weeks." Thirdly, in what seems to be a related Qumran document, one given the name "Rule of the Community," or "the Community Rule," there is a fleeting eschatological reference to the way the religious community in question was to be run "until the prophet comes, and the Messiahs of Aaron and Israel" (Rule 9:11). Note the plural. From this many scholars have concluded that not one, but two Messiahs would appear to redeem the righteous. This belief in two Messiahs is injected thence into the Damascus Document, with the assertion that "Messiah of Aaron and

Israel" really means Messiah*s* of Aaron and Israel, and is best differentiated as meaning "Messiah of Aaron" and "Messiah of Israel."[8]

This is not bad scholarship, but it certainly is confusing eschatology. What, indeed, did the texts in the Qumran library mean when they referred to Messiah? We must remain confused, because the authors of the documents were confused. The concept of Messiah in the Qumran documents is neither central, nor is it very well thought out, and these judgements hold whether one wishes to read the Qumran manuscripts as independent and unrelated items, or as texts that dovetail into one another.

Yet, consider the context in which these Qumran documents were found: in a library that included copies of various complex texts that were basic to the Judahist tradition. These ranged from entire sets of what later became the canonical Hebrew scriptures (save for the Book of Esther) and big and complex volumes, such as the Book of Jubilees and the Book of Enoch. This means that whoever wrote the four Qumran documents I have referred to above, almost certainly knew how to frame complicated and important concepts within the tradition of Judahist religious invention. Yet, despite this knowledge, the concept of Messiah is left so vague as to be almost evanescent. (That we cannot be sure whether the belief was in one or in two Messiahs is vague indeed.)

This leads to a simple conclusion, but one that most biblical scholars – especially those whose background is the Christian tradition – being dead keen to find any Messianic reference, resist: that *the concept of Messiah was only of peripheral interest to later Second Temple Judahism.* Even if one speculates that future scholarship on the Qumran libraries may produce from the remaining fragments as many as half-a-dozen more possible references to an Anointed One, or Anointed Ones, it still would not shake the basic point.[9] As indicated by the contemporary texts – the Dead Sea Scrolls, the Apocrypha, and the Pseudepigrapha – Messiah was at most a minor notion in Judahism around the time of Yeshua of Nazareth. The Chosen People were not awaiting the Messiah.

2

Nevertheless, something was going on among some of the dozens of parties, sections, and factions within late Second Temple Judahism, and it was something potentially unsettling. We catch hints of it, like flashes of distant heat-lightning on a summer's night, in the writings of Flavius Josephus. These writings are post-70 CE, but Josephus was a direct witness of pre-destruction events and, further, he collected a good deal of historical material on events that occurred before his own lifetime, much of it extremely valuable. For instance, Josephus reports that in the middle one-third of the first century CE, there were a number of movements in Jerusalem and its environs which mixed extreme, probably apocalyptic, views of the future and radical, perhaps revolutionary, politics, with either the threat of violence or, in some cases, violent insurrections. For example, one Theudas, a prophet, persuaded his followers to take all their worldly goods and follow him to the banks of the Jordan River. There, in a trope of the Children of Israel crossing the Red Sea, he promised his followers that the Jordan would be parted for them and they would be able to cross easily, thus making an exodus from a corrupt land. The Roman procurator of Judea sent a squadron to deal with this problem, and his horsemen did so expeditiously: they killed many of the enthusiasts, and cut off the head of the prophet and brought it back to Jerusalem.[10]

Josephus himself found such charismatic movements distasteful, and he related their existence with a palpable reluctance. At mid-first century there were numerous "deceivers and impostors," in his words. "Under the pretence of divine inspiration fostering revolutionary changes, they persuaded the multitude to act like madmen, and led them out into the desert under the belief that God would there give them tokens of deliverance."[11] Instead of deliverance they found death: the procurator, as was public policy, sent heavily armed soldiers to destroy them, and a large number were put to the sword. Josephus mentioned yet another prophet of the mid-first century whom he called "The Egyptian." According to Josephus, this prophet attracted 30,000 adherents. He and his followers made a pilgrimage to the Mount of Olives, which was as much a tactical site, overlooking Jerusalem, as it was a place of religious veneration. Josephus suggests, that either The Egyptian was bent on attacking the Roman garrison or was putting his faith in a miraculous collapse of the walls of Jerusalem (both versions are found in Josephus). The Roman response was predictable: 600 of the religious enthusiasts were killed and another 200 taken prisoner; The Egyptian escaped.[12] Still another "imposter" (this time unnamed) is reported as having led his followers into the wilderness, promising them salvation. And, yet again, the Roman governors killed the prophet and many of his followers.[13]

Even in Josephus's purse-lipped accounts, one clearly learns that something different, something catalytic, had been added to Siloam's teeming pool. Josephus reports that prior to the charismatic movements mentioned above, serious insurrections, probably as much political as religious, had occurred. One set-off point was the death of Herod the Great in 4 BCE. When Herod was on his death bed, two men, Judas and Matthias, who were said to be the most learned and beloved interpreters of the Torah, learned of his terminal illness. They began preaching that Herod had done certain things that were forbidden in ancient law, the worst of which was his placing a Roman symbol, the gold eagle, over the Temple gate. These devout teachers told their disciples to pull down the Roman imperial eagle, and they did so. As punishment for this, Herod, from his deathbed, ordered the replacement of the High

Priest whom he blamed for permitting the incident (a man named Matthias who is not to be confused with the joint-instigator of the Temple incident) and the two interpreters of the Torah were put to death: Matthias was burned alive, along with some of his followers; the method of Judas's death is not recorded, but one suspects it was equally unpleasant.[14]

Then Herod died.

After these martyrdoms, and following Herod's death, young men, mourners for the teachers Judas and Matthias, used the opportunity of Passover, when worshippers from all over the diaspora flowed into Jerusalem, to demand that a new high priest replace the one appointed recently by Herod. They seized part of the Temple and were supported in their occupation of it by ordinary worshippers, who provided them with food. Eventually, Herod's eldest son, Archelaus, fearing that he would lose control over Jerusalem, sent troops into the Temple. They killed roughly 3,000 young men, Josephus reports, but many escaped into the Judaean hills.[15]

Seemingly, this religio-political rebellion was a Hydra, for the suppression of the Temple riots soon was followed by four separate religious or revolutionary movements: one in Galilee led by a bandit chief named Judas, who had monarchical pretensions; one in Transjordan headed by a certain Simon, a massive man and a former slave of King Herod, whom his followers declared to be a king – he wore a royal crown; in Judaea, an uprising was led by a man named Athronges, a shepherd known for his great size and strength: according to Josephus, Athronges also aspired to kingship and also assumed a crown and title; all this in addition to a mutiny of 2,000 of the Herodian soldiers quartered in Judaea. None of these movements was frivolous or of small moment. Large sections of the countryside came under the control of rebel forces and it eventually took four Roman legions to regain control. Pacification of the countryside involved, at one point, a mass crucifixion of 2,000 dissidents.[16]

Yes, something definitely was going on. And, it is fair to ask, were not these movements of the late Herodian era and immediately thereafter – involving kings of the Jews, as it were, and being focused on the Temple – were these not Messianic movements? And were not the prophetic movements of the mid-first-century of the Common Era, which the governments of the day treated as being fully as threatening to the political order as were the eruptions of 6–4 BCE, also Messianic?

Absolutely not: neither in the strict, textually-constrained sense of the word, nor in the general, modern sense of the term. Neither the Hebrew "Moshiah," nor the Greek equivalent, "Messias," is used in Josephus's account, nor any term that might be taken as a synonym (the word "Christos" for example). One cannot argue that this omission is a personal quirk of Josephus, for it fits perfectly with our previous survey of para-biblical literature of the period (the Apocrypha, the Pseudepigrapha, and the Dead Sea Scrolls). Namely: that the idea of Messiah, though extant, enjoyed minimal usage and exercised little force in the crucial era between the Maccabean revolt and the destruction of the Second Temple.

At this point, a skeptic of good intentions might agree concerning my argument, that, yes, Messiah indeed is virtually absent in this period – or, at minimum, agree that there is no evidence of any general expectation of Messiah – and still argue that, indeed, the kind of movement we have been discussing, involving prophets, priests, and self-anointed kings, comprised a "Messianic movement," even if people of the time did not define it as such.

Here lies trouble. The adjectival usage of Messiah is acceptable, if not always illuminating, in describing certain phenomena in the medieval and modern period of history: persons as disparate as Oliver Cromwell and Huey Long have been described as heading Messianic movements. In such instances, the Christian definition of Messiah (and to a lesser degree, the Rabbinical Jewish definition) are taken as cultural givens, and the idea of a Messianic movement becomes a giant metaphor, one that invokes the entire construct of Messiah as it evolved in the three or four centuries after the Second Temple was destroyed. It is a very different action, however, to take a metaphor based on that same construct and press it back into the pre-70 CE period. To do so is to perform a piece of historical vandalism of criminal proportions. Forcing the connotation of Moshiah and Messiah, as they evolved in the post-Second Temple era among Jews and Christians, back into the later Second Temple period, has two disastrous effects. First, it prevents our seeing the religious culture of late Second Temple Judaism, an amazingly fecund, vivid, and varied kaleidoscope of beliefs, parties, and practices, on its own terms. And, second, it makes virtually impossible any historical understanding of the development of either Christian or of Rabbinical Jewish beliefs, for, by projecting back into the Second Temple beliefs that only came to the fore after the Temple's destruction, it destroys one of the fundamental base lines from which we can meter the later development of both Christianity and Rabbinic Judaism.

Unless we are willing to accept the overwhelming evidence that Moshiah, or Messiah, does not emerge as a primary idea until *after* the Second Temple was pulverized, the nature of Second Temple Judaism, and its heirs, Christianity and Rabbinical Judaism, will forever be obscured behind an opaque pigment whose application is entirely ahistorical in character. While it is by no means certain that we can ever really grasp the vertiginously dazzling character of these historical phenomena, it is entirely certain that if we insist on focusing upon the Messianic idea, in contradiction to the available historical evidence, then we will grasp nothing; we will have taken a large brush and obscured with heavy tar one of the greatest of Old Masters.

3

Yet, even while abandoning the idea of Messiah as having been central to the followers of Yahweh in the later Second Temple era, and having given it up as an appropriate concept around which to organize our understanding of the period, we still have to recognize that many high-energy fractiles were constantly being produced. Some of these were incarnated as religio-political movements, while others were purely conceptual entities.

The most highly energized of the conceptual entities to emerge strongly during the later Second Temple era have already been discussed: the concept of the resurrection of the dead, the idea of the individual being judged by the Almighty, and the depiction of the end-times. Here we should add three more: the idea of the Kingdom of God, of the Son of God, and of the Son of Man. Each of these is a relatively new concept which blossoms fully only after the Maccabean revolt. Each of these ideas has been the subject of hundreds of books, many of them distinguished pieces of scholarship. However, the bibliodensity of the writings is apt to obscure a fundamental fact: that in *none* of the texts known at present is there indicated an identity *at the time of the later Second Temple* of the concept of Messiah and of Son of God, Son of Man, and of the coming of the Kingdom of God.[17]

Consider first the idea of the Kingdom of God, in the future and apocalyptic sense, as distinct from a triumphant nationalistic kingdom for the Chosen People that would exist in real time and on the present earth.[18] Another phrase for this concept is the "Kingdom of Heaven." There is, first of all, no mention of the Kingdom of Heaven in the Hebrew scriptures, nor, as yet, has it been found in an explicit form in the para-biblical literature of the later Second Temple era. There is, however, a concept of the "Kingdom of Yahweh" (translated as "Kingdom of the Lord" in the KJB), found twice in the Tanakh. In the first of these instances (1 Chron. 28:5) the reference is to the enthronement of Solomon, and in the second occurrence (2 Chron. 13:8) the context is historical, namely the dynastic war between Abijah and Jeroboam. The only other pre-70 CE reference to the Kingdom of God (or the Kingdom of Yahweh) is in the Psalms of Solomon which were written between 63 BCE and the Temple's destruction. There (in 17:3) it is declared that "the kingdom of our God is forever over the nations in judgement." This is an important (albeit unique) Second Temple reference, because it is found in the same psalm in which the term Moshiah is employed to describe the descendant of King David who will purify Jerusalem and will place the Gentile nations under his yoke. This future kingdom could be this-worldly, or otherworldly and occurring at the end of time (the psalm is unclear), but certainly the propinquity of the concepts of Moshiah and of the Kingdom of God is intriguing.

That, however, is all there is in terms of direct reference. Given the basic body of biblical and para-biblical writings, three direct references (only one of which appears in association with perhaps-apocalyptic visions) is a very small body of data. The natural reaction of those who are committed to the belief in the ubiquity, or at least the centrality, of the Kingdom of God as a pervasive idea in the Hebrew scriptures and in the "inter-testamental period," is to frame a litany of *inferred* references to the apocalyptic Kingdom of God. That is exactly what we saw taking place when it was pointed out how rare the concept of Messiah is: inferred evidence replaced direct, and modern interpolations were interspersed into the ancient text. The same thing happens with the apocalyptic Kingdom of God. It is said to be found in the interstices of text after text, just waiting to be liberated from the cramped confines of what the text actually says.

Normally, one would not obstruct the attempts to liberate the sub-text from the primary text; after all, close and subtle reading usually increases our understanding. But in this case one must resist, for the inferential reading is all tilted very heavily in one direction: namely to find reference to the Kingdom of God in as many places as possible and to tie these references to a future apocalyptic, end-of-time state, and, further, if at all possible, to tie all these references to the appearance of Moshiah. In other words, an entire hermeneutic industry has invested itself with the task of destroying the following historical realities: that, *in Second Temple times* (1) the concept of the Kingdom of God was not much used; (2) when it was employed, it was not clearly articulated; and (3) it was not yet bonded to the idea of Moshiah or to the genre of apocalypse.

A parallel set of conclusions holds both for the concept of Son of God and Son of Man. Take, first, Son of God. Unless one chooses to assume that every time the kingship of Judah or of Israel is mentioned, the holder of the office is "a" (or even "the") Son of God – this in the manner of many kingdoms of the Ancient Near East – then the concept is virtually absent in the Hebrew scriptures. The Book of Samuel has the prophet Nathan relating these words of the Almighty concerning King David: "I will be his father, and he shall be my son" (II Sam. 7:14). One of the Psalms has the voice of King David saying, "the Lord hath said unto me, Thou art my Son; this day have I begotten thee'" (Ps. 2:7). Another Psalm, of Ethan the Ezrahite, reports Yahweh's words that King David is the Almighty's "first-born," and "higher than the kings of the earth" (Ps. 89:27). Elsewhere, the prophet Hosea calls the Children of Israel "the sons of the living God" (Hos. 1:10). This is within the context of a prophecy concerning their future state, where these sons of God "shall be as the sand of the sea, which cannot be measured nor numbered" (Hos. 1:10). None of these references is apocalyptic and, though meaningful, the phrase "Son (or sons) of God" is not used as a focal point around which to construct a narrative, a prophecy, or a hymn. One must conclude that either the concept of Son of God is peripheral to the Hebrew scriptures, or that it is so well understood as never to require articulation, an alternative that seems unlikely indeed.

However, in the extra-biblical literature of the later Second Temple era, there is one small fragment, no more than a tiny dot on an otherwise barren landscape, which suggests how the concept was developing in at least one band of Yahweh's followers. This is an Aramaic fragment found in Qumran cave number four, which has been given the unrevealing name "Aramaic Apocalypse." It consists of little more than 200 decipherable words, but among these are reference to an eternal king who "will be great over the earth." "He will be called son of God and they will call him son of the Most High." Crucially, this kingship is welded tightly to the concept of the future apocalyptic kingdom. "His kingdom will be an eternal kingdom ... The sword will cease in the earth and all the cities will pay him homage ... His kingdom will be an eternal kingdom."[19]

Manifestly, this is a much different conception of Son of God from that found in the Hebrew scriptures: it involves a single person, a future king, who will rule a world at the end of time. Because this is one small fragment and because its social context and authorship are completely unknown, we should not overread it. However, it seems to suggest that among some groups – perhaps a small band of enthusiasts, or perhaps the idea was held more widely, as a folk-belief – the concept of Son of God had moved from being associated with a real-world monarchy to being attached to an apocalyptic imperium, a future-world kingdom. In the present state of biblical studies concerning the later Second Temple era there is no direct evidence of this God's-son construct being bonded with the idea of Moshiah, but such a union would be a natural occurrence eventually, and did in fact occur after the year 70 CE.

The information on the related construct, "Son of Man," is richer. Nevertheless, it is barely present in the Hebrew scriptures, except as a general designation for a human being. This holds with two exceptions. One of these is the Book of Ezekiel, wherein the prophet is addressed by Yahweh ninety-three times as "Son of Man." The term here is specific to the prophet Ezekiel and has no generalizable or time-transcendant quality. (In fact, the usage in Ezekiel is uncertain; "Son of Man" may not in fact refer to a singular son of a singular father, but rather to a person who is a member of a certain plural group, in this case, humankind.)

In contrast, the other important usage, in the Book of Daniel, chapter seven, is a reference to a super-human being, one who exists beyond historical time. This chapter probably (but not absolutely certainly) is part of the portion of Daniel written after the desecration of the Temple by Antiochus Epiphanes. It contains a vision of four world empires and the rise of the "little horn." These empires are destroyed, however, and thereupon appears the Ancient of Days, a figure of snow white hair, white garments, regnant on a snow-white throne. Thousands of souls stand before him for judgement. And then Daniel sees "one like the Son of Man" (Dan. 7:13, KJB) who joins the Ancient of Days and is given "dominion, and glory, and a kingdom, that all people, nations and languages should serve him: his dominion is an everlasting dominion, which shall not pass away, and his kingdom that which shall not be destroyed" (Dan. 7:14). Who is this person "like the Son of Man?" He is not the Anointed One of Daniel's chapter nine (for the Anointed One's role is specific to Jerusalem). And he is not a human being, at least if one permits the text to take itself seriously, for this figure is *like* the Son of Man (KJB). This is not a later translator's interpretation, but an accurate indication that the author-editor of the Hebrew text consciously employed a simile. Given that "Son of Man" in the Hebrew original has no article attached to it, and given that "Son of Man" in the scriptures usually simply means a human being, the Jewish Publication Society's version is a more accurate translation than is the King James Bible: "one like a human being." The logic that follows from this is that if the figure is "like" a human being, it is not one. Most probably, the text refers to an angelic messenger whose form resembles that of a human being. The Archangel Michael, who is strongly privileged in Daniel (remember, it is he who, in chapter twelve, carries the great cosmic battle to deliver the Chosen People), and if this figure is not Michael, it is an angel of similar power and prestige.

From the viewpoint of religious invention, the great virtue of the Book of Daniel is that it is capable of being endlessly reshaped. It has provided components that several varieties of Christianity and of Rabbinic Judaism later used to great effect. However, here we would like to know how Daniel's "Son of Man" vision was employed among the followers of Yahweh before the Second Temple was destroyed and consequently the meaning of all Hebrew texts was thereby irrevocably altered. There is one major opportunity to see how it was employed in the Second Temple era and this is in a portion of the Book of Enoch (var: 1 Enoch) called the Book of Similitudes or, alternately, the Book of Parables: it consists of chapters 37–71. This fascicle of Enoch is a self-conscious expansion and re-interpretation of the Son of Man segment of Daniel, and it illustrates graphically how the concept could grow and be conflated with other ideas, especially other apocalyptic ones.

But, while appreciating the possibilities of the Book of Similitudes as a laboratory case concerning the growth and transformation of certain religious constructs, we must approach it with a good deal of caution. This is because, first, we do not know who invented the Book of Similitudes, or in what environment. Given the large number of variegated forms that motilized their way around Siloam's pool, there is no way of knowing how close, or how far, the Similitudes were from other visions of the meaning of faith in Yahweh. Whether this text was the vision of one man, or the shared hope of a hundred thousand, is beyond our ken. So, as if we were examining an unidentified cell from some complex organism, we must focus on its general metabolic character, on the processes integral to that cell and reluctantly set to one side the issue of where, in the morphology of the larger organism, this individual unit fits.

Secondly, the dating of the Book of Similitudes is uncertain. Basically, biblical scholars debate two points. Is the book a Christian invention that has been stuffed into an otherwise-Judahist anthology of apocalyptic visions, the Book of Enoch? And, was the Book of Similitudes actually written before the destruction of the Second Temple?

These questions arise because the Book of Similitudes is the one part of the larger Book of Enoch that is not found in any of the fragments of the Dead Sea Scrolls. All the other major sections of Enoch are represented. Even so, the balance of scholarly opinion comes down strongly on the side of a judgement that the Book of Similitudes is not a Christian invention, that it was written before 70 CE, and was incorporated into the Enoch anthology by the end of the first century of the Common Era. The reason that the Book of Similitudes was not included in the Qumran library, it is suggested, is that, as was frequently the case with extra-biblical manuscripts, there were multiple versions of Enoch in existence, and the version that was preserved in the Ethiopic church (whence comes the fullest modern copy) was different from that preserved at Qumran.[20] Arguments from scholarly consensus are frequently the most dangerous (the thundering of learned feet in a Gadarene stampede is a frequent phenomenon), so I must emphasize that I am not here hiding behind "consensus." On the sort of probative grounds that are employed by a professional historian of the modern world (that is, without reliance on palaeography, radio-carbon dating, or similar arcana, but resting solely on direct textual evidence), Similitudes appears to me to be neither Christian nor post Second Temple. There is no reference in the Book of Similitudes that can be interpreted to be even a veiled allusion to Yeshua of Nazareth or to his later Christian incarnation as Jesus the Christ. That is the adamantine rock: this, therefore, is a purely Judahist production. As for the dating, the earliest possible date of composition is set by a reference to the Parthian invasion of 40 BCE. The latest date is 70 CE, for there is no reference, direct or indirect, to the destruction of the Second Temple, and that is an event that no writer of apocalyptic literature could have ignored.

This discussion of the origin of the Book of Similitudes, necessary though it is, is apt to take our minds off the real issue, which is our observation of a deeply mystical religious mind as it articulates answers to questions posed by the Book of Daniel. What the inventor of the Book of Similitudes does with the plastic parts that Daniel has left him to work with is quite astounding.

The premise on which the book is based is an unspoken question, a silence shared between the author and reader: both know, without having to frame it, that the question is, "What happens before, during, and after that scene in Daniel, chapter seven, where the Ancient of Days appears? – Can you not tell us more?" Indeed, the inventor of the Book of Similitudes can, and in so doing expands and blends together motifs that are found in the Book of Daniel and in three other major sources. One of these is Psalm 2, wherein Yahweh, on his heavenly throne, laughs at the world's rulers and sends his adopted son to reign on Zion, his holy hill. The Book of Isaiah (specifically, First Isaiah), chapter eleven provides another source of predictions of a future kingdom to be set up "out of the stem of Jesse" (Is. 11:1). This nationalistic prophecy puts forward the case for the primacy of Judah and of Jerusalem within the Hebrew polity after the Assyrian conquest of the tribes of Israel. It is a wonderfully rich prophecy in its visual imagery and it contains the famous image of the wolf lying down with the lamb. A third source is Second Isaiah (Isaiah 40–55), specifically chapter forty-nine, a prophecy concerning the restoration of the Chosen People after the Babylonian exile. It has a "Redeemer of Israel," a "Holy One," as the active agent of Yahweh's will. There are other sources of motifs for the Book of Similitudes (some known to us, most not yet uncovered), but these three major sources – the Psalms, and First and Second Isaiah – allow us to see how apocalyptic literature, even when it was at its most radical, still honoured the grammar of invention that runs through biblical and related para-biblical writings.

However, merely parsing its grammar of invention would obscure the explosive alchemy of the Book of Similitudes. Nothing could be more misleading than a clinical description of the work: a set of four parables each containing several visions granted to Enoch, filling in many of the lacunae left by Daniel, chapter seven. That is accurate enough, but it is akin to describing James Joyce's *Finnegans Wake* as a very long Irish short story about the history of the world from the fall of Adam to the resurrection of mankind. The Similitudes has a cast of characters that includes every higher entity, whether human being or angel or demon, who ever has existed. The human multitude alone consists of "ten million times ten million souls" (Enoch 40:1). They stand before the throne at judgement day. Historically they serve as a massive Greek chorus, as a resonating board for the pronouncement of the major players, and as a pliable medium upon which the powerful characters work their will.

The distant comparison of the Book of Similitudes and *Finnegans Wake* is apposite, not only because each starts before human time, but because each is a cyclical composition. Indeed, Joyce would argue that *Finnegans Wake* doesn't start or end; it just keeps going round and round. And that's also the way the Book of Similitudes works. Although one has to read such inventions linearly (one word follows another on the page), in fact the pictures that emerge are not like frames in a cinema film, but, instead are more like a deck of photographs that can be endlessly reshuffled to give a different story each time. In the case of the Book of Similitudes, the characters in one vision often seem to show up in another, under a different name. But it may only seem this way, because the inventor of these visions does not make equilibrations or specify identities across visions. So we are forever on tenterhooks as we see characters tumble from one gyring vision to another. Or do we? And the same holds for "plot," if that is the correct word. The several visions ascribed to Enoch in the Book of Similitudes can neither be taken as forming a sequential series of events, nor as happening coterminously; and one cannot declare them to be either mutually incompatible or to be capable of harmonization. At one moment they are one thing, then, another.

Consider the characters. They include (as noted in Chapter Six) two fairly off-hand mentions of Messiah (Enoch 48:10 and 52:4), in which Moshiah is a figure of authority, but passive. The really active figures are, first, the archangels: Michael, of course, and Raphael, Gabriel, and Phanuel (En. 54:6, 60:4, 71:8–10). Among other tasks, they are responsible for throwing evil kings and potentates into the fiery furnace at the end of time, a prototype of hell. Second, myriad good angels serve under the generalship of these archangels. Third, however, the figure of Satan is explicitly introduced as a primary figure of evil (En. 53:4). This figure, almost equal in strength to Yahweh, is a character we saw earlier in the Book of Jubilees, which almost certainly was known to the inventor of the Book of Similitudes. Satan is a relatively new invention as far as the tradition of Yahweh is concerned, for in the Hebrew scriptures he is a subordinate and biddable messenger of the Almighty. Not here. Whether or not Satan is the same entity as "the Evil One" (En. 69:15) is, in the fashion characteristic of the Book of Similitudes, left to the reader to determine. The text lets one have it either way. Fourth, no fewer than twenty-one evil angels are named. They have deliciously mephitic names, noisome of sulphur: Kokba'el, Azaz'el, Baragel, and so on. Part of their noxiousness is that their very names involve impious incorporation of the God-name "El." Fifth, each of these chiefs of the fallen angels has a phalanx of fallen angels at his command (En. 69:1–3). Added to this, sixth, is a female monster named Leviathan who lives in the ocean (En. 60:7–8) and, seventh, a male monster, called Behemoth who lives in an invisible desert located east of the Garden of Eden (En. 60:8).

Opposed to the forces of evil is an eighth set of characters (in addition to Messiah and to the angels already mentioned). These are power figures on the side of the light: "the Righteous One" (En. 38:1–2), the "Son of Man" (En. 46:3), and "the Elect One" (En. 49:2). Now, when turning from one vision to another, it is impossible to tell whether or not these are names for the same figure or for someone entirely different. The absence of verbal equilibrations as between these figures means that the names, and the association of those names, tumble from one vision to another. Momentarily, they juxtapose themselves so that, for example, "the Righteous One" and "the Son of Man" seem to be synonymous, but then the rhetorical drum turns another rotation, another vision starts, and the two names come to represent separate, entirely different entities. The same things happen with the God-figures who comprise the ninth bundle of characters. Yahweh is not present in the text under that name, which is hardly surprising, given that the text has been preserved in Ethiopic. However, there are various figures who could be the Almighty. These include the "Lord of the Spirits, who created the distinction between light and darkness" (En. 41:8); the "Antecedent of Time" (En. 47:3 and 55:1), who is directly derivative from the "Ancient of Days" of the Book of Daniel, and the similar figure, the "Before-Time," who at one point is identified with the "Lord of the Spirits" (En. 48:2). All these god-figures seem consonant with each other, if not quite congruent, in contrast to the figures of the Son of Man, the Messiah, the Chosen One, and the Elect One, which are never really joined.

The series of visions in which all these characters play their parts is cyclical, in the sense that the visions circle back, one on the other. Each vision provides its own distinct answer to the question, "what really happened in Daniel, chapter seven?" For modern readers, the most difficult aspects of the Book of Similitudes to come to terms with are (1) its assumption that one can start any place in the book and read one's way around it; or, indeed, the major items can be read in random order, an assumption, incidentally, that holds for Similitudes' cross-time counterpart, *Finnegans Wake*; (2) its assumption that even as one reads a specific vision, one has knowledge of all the others; and (3) its assumption that the cumulative effect of reading all of these visions is not hindered, but indeed augmented, by the ambiguous relationship between the varied visions and that any contradictions are not distractions, but are enrichments, for they are indications of the multiplicity of truth granted to those who experience (not read: experience) the book.

This carousel of apocalyptic tales operates on a time scale that is adapted at one end from the Book of Genesis (the tales start before human time) and at the other end from Daniel, and perhaps other apocalypses that are now lost, and these go past the end of time. What is striking, and new, is the ground-base belief that the Almighty (whatever he may be called in the specific vision in question) not only knows everything, but has known everything since before the beginning of time. (See esp. En. 39:11.) Further, the very act of knowing every occurrence from before time to past the end of time means that the Almighty is himself eternal: "There is no such thing as non-existence before him" (En. 39:11). This is very close to being a theological argument, although it is not articulated as such. It means that the Almighty is (a) omniscient, (b) the ground of existence in which all things, good and evil, exist, and (c) it implies a pre-determinism of all life, angelic, demonic, and human, from before time to the days which follow the end of time. The Book of Similitudes, in addition to being a very complex body of literature, is well in advance of most pieces of Judahist writings of the late Second Temple era in its theological sophistication.

All that recognized, forget the analysis. Pick up a copy of the text and whirl with it until it takes you into the Dervish-like state of enlightenment that it commands. Let yourself be carried off by the "wind vehicle" which takes you to the west, where you can see all the secret things of heaven. See there the great mountains of copper, of silver, of lead, and of coloured metals (En. 52:1–4). Fly across the "deep valley with a wide mouth," where all the human race brings gifts and tributes, but yet the valley does not become full (En. 53:1–2). Observe Michael, Raphael, Gabriel, and Phanuel seize the wicked rulers of the earth and throw them into the furnace of hell (En. 54:1–6). See those who were oppressors on earth drown by rising flood waters (En. 54:10). Spin around again and observe, in light so bright that it scarcely can be faced, the righteous ones passing before the Lord of the Spirits and on to eternal life (En. 58:1–4). Spin back before time and observe the storerooms where hail, mist, and wind are kept. Observe the storeroom of the sun and the moon, from which, with each cycle diurnal and monthly, they exit and then return (En. 41:1–5). Spin again and see the Son of Man who will open all the hidden storerooms, both physical and spiritual, and who will depose kings from their thrones and crush the teeth of sinners (En. 46:3–5). Spin, spin, there is so much more to experience in the cycles that flash by: Sheol being emptied with the resurrection of the dead (En. 51:1–2), angels preparing ropes that will hoist the righteous to heaven (En. 61:1–3), and the ultimate light-refracting structure, a multi-crystal structure built into the heavens, with tongues of living fire issuing forth light from the interstices, where one crystal abuts its neighbour (En. 71:5–6). Spin, spin, spin!

And then, finally, crash to earth. The apocalyptic ecstasy cannot be long sustained, even in a masterpiece such as the Book of Similitudes. The visions are too demanding, our senses too prone to overload. We have to be protected from an intoxication from which some devotees never return.

But consider what the Book of Similitudes means to the history of late Second Temple Judahism. It suggests that in at least one stratum of the Yahweh-faith, a vocabulary, a set of symbols, a proto-typology, and a set of beyond-time narratives were emerging: these were based on scriptural originals, but were much richer in their inventiveness than anything we have yet encountered in the later Second Temple era. If we can momentarily put the brakes on the carousel that is the Book of Similitudes, we can see that there are many components that will later be used by Rabbinic Judaism and by Christianity to develop their own official views of what happened before time began and what will happen when time comes to an end. The Book of Similitudes is a wonderful machine in itself and, when later disassembled and re-used by others, an apparent source for many of the ideas upon which later inventions depended.

I have said "an apparent source" because there is nothing to be gained by arguing whether the motifs found in Similitudes that are also found in later Christianity and later Rabbinic Jewish thought actually were transmitted by Similitudes, or came, instead, from the general milieu that was the ambient condition for the invention of Similitudes. I strongly suspect that there were other, parallel, now-lost apocalypses in circulation prior to the end of the Second Temple period. It is hard to see how something so evocative as the Book of Similitudes, so soundly based on a deep bank of apocalyptic motifs, could be a one-of-a-kind production. The Book of Similitudes may have been the best of its sort (we never will know, really), but it must have come from a rich tradition of para-biblical invention. To find a document such as the Book of Similitudes and to declare it to be singular, and thus interesting but of limited consequence, would be the equivalent, say, of discovering a full version of *Carmen* in a musical culture which previous scholars had believed knew only plain-song, and therefore dismissing it as anomalous. I think the Book of Similitudes testifies that there existed in the general religious environment of late Second Temple Judahism a bank of apocalyptic concepts in addition to, and different from, the rather limited range of constructs we find in the Tanakh, where the Book of Daniel is the only true apocalyptic conduit.

But what if I am wrong? Perhaps the Book of Similitudes is Jewish, from the second century CE, or Christian, from the last quarter of the first century? While it would be interesting indeed to have a set of apocalyptic visions from Christian sources that present the Son of Man in a very different light from that which prevails in the Christian canon; and while it would be equally interesting to have a set of rich Jewish apocalyptic documents dated to the same time when the Rabbis were trying to close down the more vivid and more inventive forms of religious expression, neither of these fascinating speculative occurrences would undercut our understanding of the way that biblical (and para-biblical) invention occurred. The chronology would be altered, but the substance would stay the same. The Book of Similitudes, like all good inventions created within the grammar of biblical invention, assumes the name and mantle of an ancient author; it hides its own author; it eschews any claim to originality or creativity; it takes parts of the scriptures that are accepted as being authoritative (the Psalms, Isaiah, and Daniel) and gives them new meanings; it gives – or at least starts to give – new definitions for old terms (such as the Son of Man); and it interweaves all this with new cloth that has been skilfully treated so as to appear old: a blend so skilful as to have no visible seams.

Wherever one dates the Book of Similitudes (and I stick to pre-70 CE) and whatever its provenance (I still think it is almost entirely Judahist, even in the Ethiopic form that we have), it is a masterpiece and a crucial milestone by which we trace the path of history through one of the most confusing and complex of landscapes.

4

The final matter we must deal with was touched on at the start of Chapter Five: the nature of the religious parties, factions, or (if one prefers) denominations in later Second Temple Judahism. The famous later rabbinic report that there were twenty-four parties in Judahism is not to be taken literally. The report simply multiplied the number of the original tribes by two and thus said that there were a lot of factions around, though not any specific number. Although the ideological spine of Judahism was shared by the various factions – the beliefs that there was one God and this was Yahweh, that the covenant-agreed worship of Yahweh should focus around a pure and holy Temple in Jerusalem, and that a holy priesthood should control that worship – the details of factional divergence were myriad. And, as the ancient saying avers, the devil is in the details.

I have put off discussing these factions for several reasons. The first of these is a matter of perspective. Although a survey of the religious literature of later Second Temple Judahism has revealed an extraordinary creativity and fluidity of belief within the rubrics of the grammar of Hebrew invention, it is very easy to start pigeon-holing various beliefs as belonging to this faction or that. Thereupon, the movement of ideas between religious groups becomes obscured, and we miss the obvious facts that every group must have changed its beliefs over time and that, at the margins, where one group rubbed against another, they learned from each other. Whatever the labelling of the various factions, ideas moved between groups, like fluids through a semi-permeable membrane.

This caution would hold true in the best of circumstances, but things are very far from the best: in fact, once one starts digging, the disappointing result is that the actual direct contemporary data on religious factions is found to be pitifully limited. Even if one employs post-70 CE data – much of which is strongly tainted by ideological arguments that stem from circumstances post-dating the Second Temple – the data are very weak. So, to let these very ill-documented party labels dominate our discussion would be a mistake. The worst mistake of all would be to reify the party labels – to think that they indicate parties in the sense that the names of modern religious denominations are indications of strongly institutionalized systems of belief and of ecclesiastical discipline. Instead, it is best to think of the factional labels of the later Second Temple era as flags of convenience for loose aggregates of religious enthusiasts, many of whom moved from one religious belief to another, as an attractive prophet, teacher, or nationalistic orator came along.

In contrast to this evanescent social situation, the religious documents we have surveyed are permanent (they exist, unchanged) and they are real. Whereas our knowledge of the Judahist factions is late, secondhand, and often of questionable accuracy, the texts represent direct evidence of the range of religious belief that existed between the Maccabean revolt and the destruction of the Temple. Therefore, our knowledge of the religious ideas of the period, which is based on solid (if often challenging) texts, must always take precedence over the suppositional reconstruction of Judahist factional life: never the other way around.

Most factions of the later Second Temple era we know of only from reports by persons who were not members of the group in question and who usually were hostile to the group or, at best, skeptical. Earlier (in Section 2), we encountered four separate politico-religious movements that existed around the death of Herod the Great. And we discussed the mid-first century prophetic movements of Theudas, of "The Egyptian," and of an unnamed "impostor," the cumulative result of which was several thousand dead devotees.

There were more such movements, many more, but the reports on them are like the information garnered from ancient coins found on otherwise-unrevealing archaeological sites: we know some names, we grant that some reality lies behind the labels, but what? What, for instance, does one make of the "Knockers," and their associated cohort, "the Awakeners"? Post-Second Temple rabbinical authorities identified the Knockers as a group distinguished by their smiting sacrificial animals between the horns (presumably to stun them before slitting their throats, a form of humane killing that went against the ritual code of the Temple authorities). What do we make of them? Especially when it appears that the Talmudic text got it wrong and that the real distinguishing mark of the Knockers and the Awakeners was that they were Hasmonean outriders, left over from the days prior to the Maccabean revolt, when groups associated with the Hasmoneans had no access to the Temple.[21]

And how much more mysterious are the distal groups, located far from the Temple, in the less-accessible parts of Palestine or in the several parts of the diaspora. For example, Philo of Alexandria describes a group that operated in Egypt in the early first century of the Common Era, known as the Therapeutae. Presumably this faction had a fairly long history, because the core of the group had developed a cohesive community located near the Mareotic Lake. There they lived in individual houses, studying the scriptures and other religious writings from sunrise to sunset. On Shabbat they came together for a religious service. These were real people whom Philo himself had encountered and whom he admired for their spiritual purity. We can credit his account because in another instance, that of the Essenes, a faction on which he had much less direct information, he reported accurately, as confirmed by mid-twentieth century discoveries. The most intriguing part of the religious life of this community was that, being separated by considerable physical distance from the Jerusalem Temple, it developed an annual ritual meal (either at Passover or Pentecost; the text can be read either way) which foreshadowed what both Rabbinic Jewish authority and Christian leaders did, once the Temple was no longer available as a central ritual site. Philo's report is that of a contemporary and thus both extremely rare and valuable.[22]

Closer to Jerusalem, one has the case of John the Baptist who may have been a prophet or a king-in-waiting; but certainly he was significant, for both Josephus and the "New Testament" mention him. Granted, neither of these sources is contemporary. Indeed, in the form that we have them, each report of John the Baptist was written well after the destruction of the Second Temple, and in each case strong ideological beliefs filter the data. Josephus reports that John the Baptist was a prophet who exhorted his fellow-religionists to live a righteous life and to engage in baptism as a preliminary cleansing, prior to being found acceptable to God. Herod Antipas put John to death, according to Josephus, because such an eloquent preacher well might have turned the crowds who followed him into seditious mobs.[23] The reports of John the Baptist in the Gospels and in the Book of Acts suffer from the need to subordinate John to Yeshua of Nazareth, and are characterized by a degree of contradiction. However, these sources leave no doubt that John the Baptizer was a person of considerable renown in the 20s BCE, that he was a charismatic preacher of an ascetic form of holiness, that he adapted the traditional Judahist ritual of water-cleansing to a wider meaning, and that he was executed by the authorities.[24]

Contemporary discussions of John's apparent ally, Yeshua of Nazareth, who became Jesus the Christ in later Christian tradition, are non-existent. None of the Christian documents that is available in the present day was completed before the destruction of the Second Temple, save the writings of the Apostle Paul – who directly and clearly states that he never saw Yeshua in the flesh. The character of the historical material in the Christian tradition concerning Yeshua will be considered in Chapter Eight. Here the point is that the Yeshua movement, like the movement founded by John the Baptist, though notably short of contemporary notice, nevertheless was a real phenomenon, and part of the great religious whirl of later Second Temple Judahism.[25]

Another Yeshua reported by Josephus was Yeshuah the son of Hananiah. In the early 60s CE he took to preaching against the corruption of Jerusalem and of the Temple. He did this at major festivals when thousands of pilgrims came from the diaspora and, when there was no festival, he preached his lament in the back streets and by-ways. For his troubles, he was beaten at the behest of richer citizens of Jerusalem, the cat cutting to the very bones of his body. Yet he persisted. He continued for more than seven years to cry "woe unto Jerusalem," until, finally, when the Roman siege of Jerusalem began in the later 60s, he was killed by a rock from a catapult.[26]

Now, in the case of all the various prophets, revolutionaries, and potential kings (or messiahs, in the limited monarchical sense of the word), it would be a major error to simplify the situation through the application of modern taxonomies. Horsley and Hanson,[27] among others, employ modern criteria to distinguish prophets from Moshiah, from political protestors, from revolutionaries, from bandits, and from terrorists. These, however, are modern distinctions and their employment is grossly anachronistic. To the people of the time, they all overlapped. Any prophet worth his sackcloth was automatically an enemy of the Roman state; any organizer of a tax revolt used not merely financial arguments but assertions about justice and about the rights of the Chosen People; political revolutionaries inevitably traced their right of governance back to King David; bandits talked of justice as well as pelf; and terrorists framed their blood lust in the vocabulary of enforcing truth. The persons who best understood this undifferentiated nature of the phenomenon were the successive governors of the various parts of Palestine. They treated each prophet as a potential monarch, every bandit as a potential revolutionary, and they were right: holiness and societal revolution were the opposite sides of a single coin.

Consider the instances of "social banditry." This is an interpretive concept borrowed from modern historians and probably inappropriately. The people involved in Palestine were not so much social bandits, in the sense that Eric Hobsbawm developed the term to cover rough defenders of an oppressed peasantry,[28] but rather ideologically-constrained, or religiously-determined thieves and brigands. The ideology or religious influence on their behaviour determined not what they did (they were bandits, after all) but what they would not do: support either the Hasmoneans or, later, the Romans. This is very different from Hobsbawm's social banditry. Evidence for the existence of Palestinian religio-political banditry is found both in contemporary reports – for instance, those of Strabo the geographer – and in later references in the writing of Josephus. Six major episodes of brigandage occurred in Palestine between the later first century before the Common Era and the destruction of the Second Temple: that led by one Hezekiah (late 30s and 40s BCE), that of unnamed Galilean cave brigands (30s CE), that of Eleazar ben Dinai (30s to 50s CE), that of Tholomaus (40s CE), that of Yeshua, son of Sapphias (60s CE), and that of John of Gischala (mid-60s CE).[29] That it would be a mistake to conceptually segregate banditry from prophetic or king-anointing movements is dramatically symbolized by the reports of the death of Yeshua of Nazareth: according to the report in Mark, he was crucified between two bandits, with a sign over his head sarcastically referring to him as the king of the Jews (Mark 15:26–27).

Josephus refers to a "Fourth Philosophy" – the others being those of the Pharisees, the Sadducees, and the Essenes, all of which will be discussed in a moment – that was founded by one Judas the Galilean shortly before the beginning of the Common Era. "This school agrees in all other respects with the opinions of the Pharisees, except that they have a passion for liberty that is almost unconquerable, since they are convinced that God alone is their master." Josephus adds: "They think little of submitting to death in unusual forms and permitting vengeance to fall on kinsmen and friends if only they may avoid calling any man master."[30] Although Josephus does not identify the Fourth Philosophy with the Zealots (one of the keenest of religio-political parties in the late Second Temple era), many scholars have seen the Fourth Philosophy and the Zealots as one and the same movement. Others use "Fourth Philosophy" to include not only the Zealots, but also the Sicarri, a group of urban terrorists who assassinated those they believed to be venal, whether Roman authorities or officials of the Jerusalem priesthood. Whether the Sicarri and the Zealots were actually related groups, and whether one should use the term "Fourth Philosophy" for either is still undecided by scholars.[31] However, whatever separate factions the term "Fourth Philosophy" may have covered, its use by Josephus points to one simple inference: that there was a great deal of factional activity taking place in the late Second Temple period, and most of this is either unrecorded, or only marginally recorded in the historical record. For every feisty little group that has left its mark on the pages of history, there must have been several that did not: groups headed by visionaries, prophets, thugs, mystics, assassins, tax-evaders, civil revolutionaries, all expressing themselves within one of the multiple religious idioms that proliferated within the Judahist world between the Maccabean revolt and the destruction of the Temple.

But here, just before observing the "big" groups – the Pharisees, Sadducees, and Essenes – note something unusual. Thus far, we have employed two significant bodies of data: (a) some of the several-score primary texts whose contents directly indicate the variegated religious beliefs possible in the later Second Temple period and (b) the few extant contemporary reports on the two dozen or so religious groups whose names we know. However, these reports include only the most casual of references to the actual beliefs of the individual groups. We do *not* have direct evidence, or even compelling indirect evidence, which ties any of the religious factions or parties or movements we have discussed thus far, to specific texts, or to specific portions of the great treasure-box of Judahist religious ideas that we looked at earlier: the Apocrypha, the Pseudepigrapha and the Dead Sea Scrolls.

The severe limitation imposed when we use institutions (groups, factions) as distinct from complexes of religious ideas (as found in contemporary texts) as the basis for thinking about the later Second Temple period, becomes even clearer when we turn to the major religious factions.

Consider first the Sadducees. I would be grateful to be shown any document originating in Second Temple times that is labelled by its author or by its editor as being Sadducean in origin. Failing that, I would appreciate being shown any piece of religious prose or poetry that a contemporary from the Second Temple period identifies as being by a Sadducee. And, failing that, I would greatly appreciate being shown any piece of religious exposition, prose or poetry, that modern scholars can identify with certainty as being Sadducean. These are the sort of simple desiderata a modern historian would require before beginning to run on about any major religious group; but they seem not to exist. Perhaps I have missed some obvious item that biblical scholars all hold in common, but, failing that, one really has to worry that they are not playing with the same scholarly deck that has been issued to the rest of us.

Further, I cannot find even a single individual in the late Second Temple era who stood up and said "I am a Sadducee," or even any who later in life, after the Second Temple was dust, was willing to admit "I was a Sadducee," except Flavius Josephus who claimed that he tried out the belief when he was a youth.[32] Thus, scholars of the "inter-testamental period" are in a position similar to that of, say, an historian writing an article on "British conservatism from 1688 to 1901"who cannot find a single person who said "I am a Tory," or, even, anyone who averred "I was a Tory."

This does not mean that there was not a major religious bloc in the Yahweh-faith known by contemporaries as the Sadducees; however, it dictates that every time one says anything about the group, or any time one reads a discussion by biblical scholars that refers to the beliefs or actions of the Sadducees, one must realize that the evidentiary base is so tiny as to be only slightly more useful than having no evidence at all.

Granted, Josephus, writing after the fall of the Second Temple, and from a somewhat anti-Sadducean perspective,[33] defined them as one of the three main groups of Judaism in the period between the Maccabean revolt and the Second Temple's destruction. According to him, they were very traditional in their beliefs. They believed in free will, rather than in the idea of predeterminism which underlay several of the apocalyptic pieces we discussed earlier. And they were very traditional in their emphasis upon the written scriptures and the written law of Moses. They did not accept the relatively new idea of the resurrection of the individual soul after death, nor the notion, just beginning to be mooted, that there was a second Torah, an oral one, that had as much authority as did the ancient written Torah.[34]

The Christian "New Testament" refers several times to the Sadducees, but usually in a formulaic manner – such as in the phrase "Pharisees and

Sadducees," which indicates neither much acquaintance with the group, nor much concern with them.[35]

The two Talmuds are of little use in determining the Sadducees' historical position, since they were compiled by the spiritual heir of the Sadducees' rivals and, further, are dated centuries later than the contemporary scene. The Mishnah, of the late Second Century CE, is of potentially more use, but it confines itself to questions of Halachah and avoids historical data almost phobically.[36] If it is correct that the term Sadducee comes from the word "Zadok," referring to the hereditary priestly line that was permanently displaced by events of the early Maccabean era,[37] then one would expect the Sadducees to be less than enthusiastic about the various priestly regimes that prevailed during the Maccabean era and the Roman governorships. Yet, the usual view – based largely on Josephus's statement that the Sadducees were wealthy and that one of the later high priests was a Sadducee[38] – is that the Sadducees were close to those who ran the Temple establishment after Hasmonean times. This closeness to the establishment is also implied in the Book of Acts, where they are tied in with the priests and the sergeants at arms of the Temple (Acts 4:1).

What this adds up to is very little. Granted, we can accept that a group which contemporaries called "the Sadducees" existed up to 70 CE. However, since they left no identifiable text, no contemporary avowals of membership, and only post-Temple reports of their beliefs (and these by their rivals), "Sadducee" is best taken as a flexible, umbrella term for an undefined group of religious conservatives. Whether they wore the label "Sadducee" with pride is unknowable: certainly their enemies used it as a slur term – like "Tory," meaning outlaw or bandit, was used centuries later to refer to political conservatives. So anechoic was the situation that we actually do not even know if the Sadducees knew themselves by that name.

We are in a slightly better position with the Pharisees.[39] Although there exists as yet no piece of religious writing produced between the Maccabean revolt and 70 CE that is self-declared as a Pharisaic production, at least we know of two men who admitted that they had been Pharisees: the Apostle Paul and Flavius Josephus.[40] Paul, of course, gave it up, but Josephus stayed at least a nominal Pharisee from the beginning of his adult life onwards. As is the case with so much concerning the late Second Temple period, scholars owe most of what is known about the Pharisees to him. And this is a debt that chafes upon many scholars: Josephus's writings, rich though they are, often are denigrated, even while they are relied upon.

That "the Pious," or "the Separated" (translations of the name "Pharisee" vary),[41] were a religious, and probably political, party that arose during Maccabean times is rarely gainsaid. Josephus first mentions them in a late second century BCE context and although this is not a date-of-origin, it indicates the point at which they became influential. Neither is there any significant scholarly objection to Josephus's depiction of the points of argument between the Pharisees and the Sadducees; it is also implied in the Mishnah, a much later source.[42]

The point at which matters become problematical is when one asks some simple questions. The first of these is just how flexible and innovative should we adjudge the Pharisees to have been? That they were beginning to develop the idea of the Oral Law as the Second Torah indicates great possibilities for invention and adaptation, a valuable asset in quickly-changing circumstances. The evidence is not extant, however, to suggest that in pre-70 CE times, the Oral Torah was already considered equal to the Biblical Torah.[43] However, at minimum, the Pharisees' acceptance of the relatively-new idea of the resurrection of the dead and of the judgement of the individual implies that they were able to listen to, and to adapt, their practices and beliefs to the burgeoning apocalyptic beliefs, which were the most distinctive ideological development of the late Second Temple period. This has led as sober a scholar as Martin Noth to speculate that the final form of the Book of Jubilees, which is both an apocalypse and a rewriting of the Book of Genesis, was Pharisaic in origin.[44]

This innovative stance among the Pharisees, asserted by Josephus and at least indirectly confirmed by the Mishnah[45] runs smack into the depiction of the Pharisees in the "New Testament." There they are painted as being hidebound, pettifogging legalists who opposed the new and flexible teachings of Jesus Christ. (See for example, Matthew 9:10–15, 9:34 and Mark 2:13–20.) Now it is certainly true that the Pharisees were greatly interested in Halachah, the proper interpretation of Torah. They were particularly fastidious about dietary matters: Jacob Neusner estimates that two-thirds of their legal texts must have dealt with dietary regulations.[46] Yet, a concern with what, to most modern observers, must seem like merely niggling details, should not be equated with inflexibility or fear of innovation. I suspect that the Pharisees were developing and enforcing new practices, and working out new interpretations of old ones, in a very creative attempt to get to the true spirit of Torah. It is hardly surprising that the Christian scriptures (all of which, save the Pauline letters, stem from post-70 CE, when the self-proclaimed heirs of the Pharisees and the quickly-spreading Christian faith were in sharp competition), would not include an advertisement for this process. Both the followers of Yeshua of Nazareth and the Pharisees seem to have been engaged in an attempt to discover and honour the kernel of the Law and to meld that discovery with the quickly-emerging concepts of the resurrection of the dead and of the future judgement.

The other problematical matter is the question of just how powerful politically the Pharisees actually were, and this matter seems insoluble on the basis of present-day evidence. The "New Testament" has the Pharisees acting as a very influential power-bloc, one that of course opposes Jesus the Messiah. (See, for instance, Mark 3:6; Matthew 12:14; John 7:32.) The matter is complex, because the Pharisees seem to have had a relationship with the civil and religious powers that fluctuated radically. Josephus has them pelting the fierce Maccabean King-cum-High Priest Alexander Jannaeus (103–76 BCE) with lemons and reeds at the Feast of Tabernacles when he was preparing to make sacrifice. The immediate result of this religio-political protest was that 6,000 Pharisees were killed.[47] Manifestly, Alexander Jannaeus did not see them as part of the religious establishment. However, the present-day scholarly debate focuses upon Jacob Neusner's hypothesis that in the reign of Herod the Great the Pharisees retreated from activities that could be interpreted as being political, and did not become politically active again until after the destruction of the Temple.[48] This view has its opponents, not least because it requires a suspension of the "New Testament" picture of the Pharisees. That is not unreasonable to do, however, given that the post-70 CE rivalry of embryonic Christianity and embryonic Rabbinic Judaism naturally resulted in the Christian texts demonizing the Pharisees. This was done retrospectively, of course, projecting backward into the historical accounts of the pre-70 CE era views of the Pharisees that actually developed after the destruction of the Temple, and the consequent total re-ordering of what had once been the Yahweh-faith.

Thus in the case of the Pharisees, we are only slightly better off than with the Sadducees. There are no texts that assert directly their Pharisaic origins. There are not even any texts that can with probability be said to have been written by Pharisees. Only guesswork is possible. And known to history are only two recorded individuals who claimed to have been Pharisees. Yet, clearly, the group existed and was significant indeed.

No pleasure stems from the necessity of squarely facing such negative conclusions; the study of the scriptures and the historical situations that surrounded them should bring joy, not disappointment. Nevertheless, in recognizing that, in fact, the veneer of evidence concerning the Pharisees and the Sadducees is micro-millimetre thin, there is profit. This occurs because we are necessarily reminded once again that it is the texts that count. The amazing library of biblical and para-biblical invention of the later Second Temple era should be the primary focus of our attention. An institutional (or factional) analysis of later Second Temple Judahism, in contrast, yields little trustworthy information. The texts, however, are not only contemporary, direct, and real, they are celestial smoke-markers of the criss-crossing, spiralling, diving patterns of one of the greatest intellectual air shows ever conducted.

Moreover, the inability to tie historically either the Pharisees or the Sadducees to specific texts, or to specific institutions, helps one to understand what is otherwise the most curious of scholarly phenomena in any field of twenti-eth-century intellectual endeavour: the stampede during the second half of the century of biblical scholars over the Essene precipice.

Given that frustration frequently acts as a stupefacient, this is the kindest way to understand how the Qumran monopoly, working over two genera-tions, managed to deal with small matters with amazing technical virtuosity, but to get the big picture astonishingly wrong. It is hard to think of anything more frustrating for biblical scholarship than to have studied Josephus, to have read over and over his descriptions of the three major parties (Pharisees, Sadducees, and Essenes), and yet to not have been able to identify a single text originating in any of these groups. The case of the third group, the Ess-enes, was especially frustrating, for a knowledgeable and accurate contempo-rary, Philo of Alexandria, had given detailed descriptions of that group, and they had also been mentioned, with geographical references, by Pliny the Elder.[49] The collective frustration of scholars of the later Second Temple pe-riod in, say, the 1930s and 1940s can easily be understood: frustration of such magnitude inevitably produces a diminution of sensibility.

Thus, when fragments of late Second Temple texts were discovered in 1947, it was not surprising that biblical scholars rushed to pin on these texts a label whose name they knew: the Essenes. At last! a set of texts, post-Maccabean revolt, that could be attached to a specific group, and, thus, to an institutional setting.

And at first this hypothesis made historical sense, particularly on geo-graphic grounds. Khirbet Qumran, the ruin associated with the Qumran caves from which the eleven caches of fragments emerged, is a plausible Essene site. It overlooks the Dead Sea between Jericho and En Gedi: Philo had reported that the Essenes were found in parts of Syria, and in several of the cities and villages of Judea; Pliny the Elder located them in the region of the Dead Sea between Jericho and En Gedi. The locations fit.

Both Philo and Josephus had made the Essenes appear quite attractive. The two writers agreed that the Essenes held property in common and made all important decisions for the common good. They were said to hold themselves to a high standard of behaviour. Probably, they were celibate.[50] The tone of both Philo's and Josephus's reports is admiring. One is not being facetious if one notes that in these sources the Essenes resembled an idealized version of a Christian monastic order, minus, of course, the Christian theology. Indeed, minus any theology for, like the Sadducees and Pharisees, the Essenes had left no text whose provenance could be confidently asserted.

They were, therefore, the perfect vessel into which to pour the contents of the newly-found Qumran manuscripts. This was not frivolous or lazy, for at first there were few manuscripts, and as a starting point the Essene hypothesis was promising. Geza Vermes describes how it grew: "As soon as the first

Dead-Sea Scroll extracts appeared in print, the late Professor Eleazar Lipa Sukenik suggested that the sect responsible for them was that of the Essenes, a theory subsequently argued with cogency and enthusiasm by Professor André Dupont-Summer. Other competing theses were also forcefully propounded associating the community with Pharisees, Sadducees, Zealots, Judaeo-Christians and even with medieval Karaites, but the Essene hypothesis quickly gained ground, and after the discovery and exploration of the Qumran ruins [the "monastery"] became, despite continued opposition from certain quarters, the dominant view among experts, a kind of *opinio communis*."[51] The chief failure of the Essene hypothesis was simply that it was never tested, least of all by those who were most able to assay its validity, the group that controlled the Qumran manuscripts. During the late 1940s and early 1950s, the number of Qumran caves grew to eleven, and the number of manuscripts of which there were fragments increased exponentially. By the mid 1950s there were approximately 800 identifiable individual manuscript fragments. Simultaneously, fragments found in other caches of the Dead Sea Scrolls (most notably that at Masada) were agglomerated to the Qumran collections and it was hypothesized that these other Dead Sea fragments also came from an Essene community that had been located at Khirbet Qumran.

This position was not so much proved, but approved of. It was especially congenial to Father Rolande de Vaux, the French Dominican archaeologist who was in charge of the Qumran project until his death in 1971. That the Essenes, as pictured by de Vaux's Qumran team, came to resemble a group of French monks, hard at work copying religious manuscripts in holy isolation, is hardly surprising. This romantic picture caught the attention of Edmund Wilson. Incapable of writing a dull word, Wilson's riveting endorsement of the Essene hypothesis made it part of the general culture of the chattering class the world-around.[52] The Essene hypothesis did not need testing; it just fit.

What had been a perfectly sensible initial hypothesis, developed when there were no more than half a dozen texts, would require more than mere repetition, when applied to the roughly 1,000 manuscripts that comprise the Dead Sea Scrolls. So, just for the sake of speculation, how would one do what the Qumran scholars never did: test their basic hypothesis? One would first engage in three simplifications. First, one would avoid all side issues and focus only on the texts that come from the Qumran caves. (Whether the Masada material, in particular, is from the same source as the Qumran material is significant, but is not here central.) Second, one would forget entirely the question of whether or not the texts found in the Qumran caves actually were produced at Khirbet Qumran. That is an interesting question, but can wait until later. Third, one would put aside for the moment the question of whether or not the documents were Essene (or Pharisaic, or Sadducean, or something else) as being a secondary issue.

The only question one would ask – the one that should have been asked in 1956 when Cave Eleven was found and the number of Qumran manuscripts rose to 800 (many of them duplicate copies, to be sure) is this: could the religious beliefs and practices found in these documents conceivably be encompassed within a single system of belief? Remember that all the books of what later became the Tanakh were represented (save Esther), as well as several items found in modern collections of pseudepigrapha, as well as scores and scores of items that were previously unknown. *Unless* one can fit the whole business into a coherent belief system, *then* one does not have a set of Essene manuscripts – or Pharisaic or Sadducean or anything else. Rather, what one has is the remains of a library of scrolls, *some* of which can reasonably be described as Essene and some (I think most) cannot.

In that case, the task suddenly changes, from explaining the nature of fragments that are automatically assumed to be Essene (which is what the Qumran project did for most of its years, well into the 1990s), to working out methods of sorting out which items are Essene and which are something entirely different. This is a task that biblical scholars finally began in earnest in the mid-1990s, but not without a good deal of rear-guard action by the remnant of the old Qumran monopoly and, more effectively, by their former students, now in positions of power.

Under the basic rules of experimental design, an hypothesis should be constructed so that positive proof is required in order for it to be confirmed. In a properly-defined hypothesis, lack of positive evidence constitutes disproof of the hypothesis. In this case, had the Qumran team framed their hypothesis properly – by requiring positive proof that the fragments they had could be contained within a single belief-system – they would have known by the middle 1950s that they were not dealing with a related set of Second Temple texts, each of which could be identified with a single group (their beloved Essenes) but rather with a massive and heterogenous library. This library contained some traditional texts common to all forms of Judaism, some that probably were Essene, and many that were from groups, movements, and factions for which we do not as yet even have a name. No scholar has shown (as distinct from merely asserting) that the pieces fit together. Indeed, the contradictions between items, the clashes of tone, belief, and practice, are too great to be harmonized. If actually pressed together, as one set of beliefs, they would resemble nothing so much as schizophrenic discourse.[53]

The misguided attempt at simplification, the Essene hypothesis, has robbed two generations of an appreciation of one of the great treasures of world religious literature, a virtual rainbow of religious opinion. Far from coming from a single source, the texts are indications of the enormous variety and fecundity of Judaism in the years between the Maccabean revolt and the destruction of the Temple.[54]

One must strenuously argue against the Qumran-establishment position on the Scrolls, not only because it has blocked our view of the true richness of religion in the later Second Temple period, but also because it has served as a by-pass through which biblical scholars have avoided the full implications of a basic issue of the "inter-testamental period." This is: although the early twentieth-century idea that there was such a thing as "normative Judaism" – a ruling orthodoxy in Jerusalem that enforced conformity and that served as a direct, and pure, line of descent from the time of exile to the era of Jesus (in the case of Christian scholars) and of the Rabbis (in the case of Jewish scholars) – has been abandoned by most present-day scholars (save those attached to Orthodox or to Fundamentalist institutions), the implications of that abandonment have not been faced as squarely as they might be. By unreflectively lumping together as "Essene" almost all of the Dead Sea Scrolls, the Qumran establishment has given both biblical scholars, and the larger community that is interested in these religious matters, an excuse for not facing the full messiness, heterogeneity, richness, and power of the religious minds operative in later Second Temple Judahism.

5

This does not mean that the Dead Sea Scrolls enterprise was a complete waste, although the Qumran monopoly was indeed scandalously wasteful both in financial and intellectual terms. The effort can easily be resuscitated by two simple bits of uncoupling. The first of these is to uncouple the Dead Sea Scrolls in general, and the Qumran manuscripts in particular, from their apparent geographic setting. Some of them may indeed have been written or studied near the sites they were found, some not. And even if many of the manuscripts were copied out near the caves where they were found, this does not necessarily mean that the place of intellectual origin of the ideas they contain was anywhere near the site. Ideas travel, far and quickly.

Then, uncouple the manuscripts from each other: abandon the assumption that merely because most of the manuscripts were found within a few hundred metres of each other, they are intellectual, religiously, politically, or even emotionally related one to another. One would not enter, say, the storage library of any major university and, encountering within a few metres of each other the Collected Statutes of New Zealand and the Collected Recipes of Julia Childs, conclude that they came from the same belief system – although with misplaced ingenuity a really determined scholar might join them by noting that each has an occasional concern with the integrity of lamb. Even if individual scholars continued to hold the belief that all the Dead Sea Scrolls were copied out by Essenes, they still would have to accept that not all the beliefs indicated in the manuscript can be Essene. It would be reasonable to permit such die-hards to argue that part of the collection of the Dead Sea manuscripts was kept by the Essenes on a know-thy-enemy basis, the same way that strict Yeshivas and Fundamentalist Christian colleges keep works of which they disapprove: so that advanced students can prepare themselves to meet the arguments of the enemy.

I suspect that increasingly we will find Dead Sea scholars accepting the basic point about the diversity of the Scrolls. Then they will begin to work out both the speciation involved in the Scrolls and the phylotaxy of families of manuscripts within each separate species. The precise details of this taxonomy should be the primary goal (and achievement) of the next generation that studies the Dead Sea Scrolls. That generation, one hopes, will be able to do what the previous two scholarly generations did not: distinguish between individual trees and the larger pattern of the forest. They will be doing nothing less than delineating the belief systems of the Yahweh-faith in the last 300 years before its great disaster. The flowing variety of beliefs will be both a source of frustration (where, indeed, do they all fit?) and of wonder, in the variety of relationships. Also, even within strictly biblical texts, the degree of variety should be both explored and respected. As Emanuel Tov notes, within Judaism, in this period, "the approach to the biblical text was not a unified one."[55] Geza Vermes points to the "considerable degree of freedom" given to scribes. "Copyists evidently felt free to alter the compositions they were reproducing," and this occurred even when dealing with texts from the "Books of Moses."[56]

If the key to thinking freely about the period between the Maccabean revolt and the Temple's destruction is to use texts, rather than factions within Judaism, as the key avenue of entry and the chief organizing principle for the period – thus replacing vaguely-defined social collectivities with sharply-defined complexes of ideas – this freedom allows us to go back into the period and consider the nature of religious parties, unimpaired by preconceptions. It is clear that, indeed, there was a group called the Essenes and, unlike the Pharisees and Sadducees, certain texts can with a reasonable degree of probability be attached to their institutional identity: for these texts link smoothly with the external sources concerning the Essenes (Philo, Josephus, and Pliny the Elder). That is a very big deal, for the Essenes are the only group in pre-70 CE Palestine for which this linkage of texts and beliefs can reasonably be attempted.

Biblical scholars in the generation to come, must necessarily do the resorting of all the later Second Temple texts for themselves. One would be pleased if they proceed modestly and began with a null-assumption, namely that not a single one of the Dead Sea Scrolls or other Second Temple texts is an Essene fragment. Being Essene is not a presumptive category: proof must be positive, neither assumed nor residual. Manuscripts that eventually are discerned to be Essene will have three very clear characteristics: first, they will be sufficiently complete so that modern scholarly interpolations into the manuscripts are not decisive in adjudging their overall character. The texts have to be able to speak their own message. Second, they will conform to contemporary and near-contemporary descriptions of the Essenes, always making allowances for the distances that contemporary observers were from the phenomenon. And, third, the texts that are denominated as Essene must fit with each other, both in their liturgical and related details and in their angle of vision on the world in general.

With these criteria in mind I would suggest that at present there are only four documents (plus some tiny fragments) that one can hypothesize are unambiguously and uniquely Essene.[57] The first of these is usually called the "Rule of the Community" or, alternatively, the "Community Rule" or "Manual of Discipline." It was found in twelve sets of fragments that are so incomplete and so randomized that it has been impossible to put together a single master-text. However, the total of the existing material is substantial and since, being fundamentally a manual of sect-discipline, it has no real narrative structure, one does not lose the meaning by virtue of the order of the passages being uncertain.[58] The extant fragments suggest that even if we possessed a complete version of the text, it would be wildly truncated, with abrupt and inexplicable transitions from one topic to another: this has given rise to the speculation that it went through several stages of evolution and revision before reaching its final form. The best one can do is to view the Community Rule as a set of regulations for a monastic-like community, one which viewed itself as embodying a new covenant with Yahweh. This idea of a new covenant is striking; it should not be identified with the later Christian notion of a new covenant, but it shows that the idea of God rewriting the fundamental covenant was already current in later Second Temple times. The context of this new discipline, which is the physical embodiment of a new spiritual covenant, is believed to be an eternal battle of light against darkness, a contest that finally will be settled in the end-times. The new covenant is an active agent as well in the present-day battle of the righteous against the representatives of the "dominion of Belial" on the earth.

Note these characteristics, for I think that they are the primary defining nodes of Essene literature: an intense sense of real-world community, of a new covenant on this earth; a deep sense of grievance about what is going on in the outside world, where evil empires are a-forming; and a belief in long-term cosmic battles between the forces of light and of darkness. Such characteristics all are found in the Community Rule. To these may be added a characteristic that one sees more clearly in other documents that I believe are Essene: a deep, virtually paranoid distrust of "internal" enemies, either members of the community who may prove untrue or, worse, of sometime members of the covenanted community who have in some way demonstrated disloyalty.

A second set of texts that is probably Essene in origin – but probably not Qumran Essene – is the Damascus Document (sometimes called the "Damascus Rule," and usually referenced as "CD.")[59] It was found in a trash-room of a synagogue in Cairo (the famous "Cairo Genizah") early in the twentieth century and fragments of ten manuscript versions of it have been found in the Qumran caves.[60] The religious order therein described is consonant in tone and most details with that implied by the Rule of the Community, save that whereas the latter was intended for an isolated and all-male religious order, the Damascus Document gives rules for an urban and non-celibate community. (This is not incompatible with a common Essene origin, as the contemporary external sources mention two types of Essene communities.) Crucially, like the Rule of the Community, the Damascus Document explicitly affirms a new covenantal entity. Further, the images of the Prince of Light and of his enemy Belial are similar to those occurring in the Rule of the Community. A future "Messiah of Aaron" is mentioned, but the main present-world figure is the Teacher of Righteousness who, if not the founder of this new-covenant group, is its authoritative voice of Torah. The Damascus Document presents massive problems of interpretation – such as who the Teacher of Righteousness might have been, and, not least, whether "Damascus" is to be taken as a real place or as a metaphorical location.

The third document that we may hypothesize as being Essene is usually called the "Pesher on Habakkuk," or "Habakkuk Commentary." A pesher is a form of running commentary on a biblical text. It works well within the tradition of biblical invention, for it allows the commentator to change the meaning of the original text to fit present circumstances. Under the guise of interpretation, it is revision. Hence it fits perfectly with the grammar of religious invention that we defined earlier in this book: innovations are never admitted as such, and the new is always presented as being old. In form, the pesher foreshadows the way the Talmuds of several centuries later took particular biblical texts and annotated them, sometimes in ways so innovative as to be breathtakingly original, all without admitting any originality. Pesherim were a form that could be used by any Judahist religious group, but the Habakkuk Pesher found in the Qumran caves fits nicely with the Rule of the Community and the Damascus Document, which we are hypothesizing are Essene. The Book of Habakkuk in the Tanakh is a particularly useful piece of scripture to re-write and modernize, through interpretative commentary: it is short (only three chapters), it contains few historically-fixed referents, and it is emotionally of a piece: it maintains an unremittingly scolding tone. Also, it contains a vision of God which is phrased in terms of light-imagery, an idiom to which the Essenes were particularly attached, if our previous two examples are a trustworthy guide. The bitter antagonisms within the Essenes (at least within this particular branch of the party) are indicated by a contrast drawn between the Teacher of Righteousness, who received words of truth directly from the mouth of God, and his enemy, the Man of Lies. There is also a Wicked Priest who vindictively pursues the Teacher of Righteousness.[61] Coded references to the Romans ("Kittim") abound.

Fourth, a parallel document from the Qumran caves is the pesher on the writings of the prophet Nahum, another minor prophet of choleric disposition and rich imagery.[62] And, fifth, there are tiny fragments of several pesherim that are close in character to those we have already mentioned.[63]

One of the real achievements of Dead Sea Scrolls scholars in their earlier days was that of Geza Vermes, then a doctoral student, who in 1952 put forward an interpretation that, with minor adjustments, has stood the test of time.[64] He presented a convincing *mise en scène* for the texts that are truly Essene, namely the period between the depredations of Antiochus Epiphanes (mentioned in the Nahum Pesher) and the war that resulted in the Temple's destruction. This may seem obvious now, but it was not so at the time of the early Qumran discoveries. (Notice that the time period Vermes defined for the Qumran Essene texts is congruent with the time period that I have described as being the years of Siloam's teeming pool, in Chapters Five, Six, and Seven.) In the early part of the period, the early Maccabean era, the two brothers Jonathan and Simon took over the priesthood (hence the "Wicked Priest" character in the Habakkuk Pesher) and the Teacher of Righteousness (probably a Zadokite priest of high rank) went into the wilderness. Vermes suggested that, of the two Maccabeans, Jonathan was the more likely to have been the Wicked Priest. Who the enemy, the "Man of Lies," may have been is beyond reasonable speculation. There are many alternatives to Vermes's theory of the origin of the central Essene texts, but his work has the great virtue of economy (other theories sweep all the way back to Babylon, picking up tons of historical detritus along the way) and of fitting with an historical environment on which we have solid information from sources external to these texts.[65]

Here, almost peremptorily, one leaves the Essenes.[66] They were only a small fragment within the larger Judahist community of later Second Temple times. Their inward-looking discipline and communal structure must have severely limited their influence among the general population of followers of the Yahweh-faith. Their ideas are deeply fascinating, to be sure, but it is easy to get them out of perspective, to magnify their importance, since the Essenes are the only group within later Second Temple Judahism to which one can reasonably link specific texts.

I hope that it is clear why, if we wish to appreciate the richness of religious life, the seemingly unending spirals of invention that characterized the later Second Temple era in Judahism, we must focus not upon religious factions (call them sects, denominations, parties, whatever one likes), but instead must focus on the ideas that move about so magically. They do so only in texts. Ideas (not factions), are expressed in the documents: they are the marrow of Judahist divinity.

The Pool of Siloam was a rare phenomenon, a vent in the earth's skin, where ambient conditions were just right for the multiplication of life, in this case religious life. Extant forms of religious life were forever being re-invented, and new, more exotic, more complex forms were continually appearing. Just as all carbon-based physical life forms work within a shared grammar of genetic invention, so these mutating and multiplying religious life-forms worked within a common grammar of religious invention. This grammar, however, was not "normative Judaism," in the sense the term was once used, but rather a grammar that permitted endless invention as long as its very simple rules were followed. Of the many genetic strains of Judaism that were evolving (of which, probably, those of which we are today aware, made up only a tithe of the number that actually was there), none was inherently superior to the others. Each line – from the purely apocalyptic to the obsessively ritualistic; from the hermetic to the populist and demagogic, each fit an ecological niche. That niche was in the world of the late Second Temple. None of them was designed for an unknowable future, so none of them was predestined either to survive or to be destroyed if the conditions of life in Siloam's pool suddenly changed.

The Invention of Christianity

· 8 ·

The Re-Invention of the Species

I

THE SOCIAL EQUIVALENT OF A HUGE METEOR HIT THE POOL OF SILOAM in 66–73 CE, with devastating results.

The last Temple sacrifice was conducted about the beginning of July, in the year 70.[1] That is the date on which the sacrificial worship of Yahweh, the ancient religion of Judah, ceased, apparently forever.

Immediately, the invention of its successors began.

2

The Roman-Jewish War of 66–73 is as thickly chronicled as any military campaign in the history of the Roman Empire[2] and certainly does not here require reprise. However, the background conditions deserve summation. In the first place, in the first century of the Common Era, the Judahist aristocracy, priestly and secular, was fragmented amongst itself, albeit united against the peasantry. The elite was not above the use of force, and factions frequently hired thugs to press their own viewpoints. Secondly, the imperial Roman authorities, from mid-century onwards, appointed a series of governors of the most insensitive and inflammatory sort. Thirdly, within popular Judaism, there arose a great bundle of prophets, patriots, visionaries, and crazies, enough, as it turned out, to fill the Temple courtyard. And, fourthly, in the years 68–69, dynastic instability reigned in Rome itself, so that small events in Jerusalem, which could have been dealt with early in their course, were let run and the entire empire was shaken.[3]

On the ground, the course of events can be said to have begun with the governor, Florus, being detected in stealing money from the Temple treasury. The citizens responded by publicly ridiculing him and this, in the gentle Roman way, led to several of those who protested Florus's thefts being crucified. From then onwards, events rolled out of control. The Temple was seized by protestors, Roman soldiers attacked and were defeated, a general revolution occurred, spilling from Galilee down through southern Judea; as the

Romans fought to reconquer the province, the Judahist forces split among themselves and, as would happen in later world history in revolution after revolution, the keener of the patriots took to executing those less keen; thus zealots murdered moderates; new high priests were acclaimed and then deposed; one, perhaps two, self-anointed kings of the Jews emerged. Finally, Roman troops, having conducted a five-months-long siege, rampaged out of control in their moment of victory, and burned the Temple; thereafter Jerusalem was levelled to the ground, save for three towers from Herod's great palace and one segment of the Temple wall. The population was scattered, many of the rebel leaders being used as slaves, or as the fodder for gladiatorial entertainments. The central public practice of the religion of Judah, the sacrificial worship of Yahweh, stopped.

A temple religion without a temple either had to die or re-invent itself. Recall that we have previously encountered a similar moment: the destruction of Solomon's Temple, followed by the Babylonian Exile. At that time, a furious burst of inventive genius occurred: the traditions of the Chosen People, which previously had been scattered and maintained in diverse forms, were knit into a coherent and unified religious invention, the Genesis-Kings unity. The practices of Temple worship were written down and the architecture of Solomon's Temple was memorialized, so that even if the Temple were never to be rebuilt on the surface of the earth, it could be rebuilt in the mind of Yahweh's followers. In the actual historical event, Cyrus of Persia permitted (indeed aided) the building of the Second Temple, but had that structure never been inaugurated, a spiritual Temple had been defined in the Torah and the Former Prophets.

In a strikingly parallel fashion, both the Rabbinic Jewish faith and the Christian religion, to use the names they later acquired, were to re-invent the religion of the Temple, without a physical temple being extant. This time, however, there was no Cyrus of Persia. The faithful did not rebuild the Temple on this earth, but in their hearts.

One of the paradoxes of history – and one which all our instincts lead us to resist – is that Christianity was much quicker in using the pieces of the old Judahist religion to invent a temple-religion-without-a-temple than were the founders of what became known as the Jewish faith. That the Christian construct is older than the Jewish one is so deeply counter-intuitive that we are apt to deny it strenuously and thus to miss the rich irony of the historical process, and the stunning originality of each group as it struggled to re-invent itself and hence to survive.

That Christianity and Rabbinic Judaism are the only well-documented survivors of the massive impact of the events of 66–73 CE does not mean that they were predestined to be so from the moment the Temple sacrifice was stopped. Other groups, adopting and adapting other complexes of ideas from the deep treasury of the pre-70 years, must have tried to work out modes of survival. Yet they have left behind few traces and these exceedingly faint. That there were other groups which, for a time, fought to survive in the new climate, is indicated by the mysterious rising of Jews in Egypt, in Cyprus, and in Cyrene (Libya, North Africa) in 115–117. It is also confirmed by the vigour with which, in the years 132–135, the "Bar-Kochba Revolt" was mounted in Palestine. This too is an event of mystery, even though a cache of letters by Bar-Kochba has been found: neither the Egypt-Cyprus-Cyrene rising, nor this later revolt had a Josephus to collect its historical remnants. The result of the Bar-Kochba affray was that Jews were banned by the Roman authorities from what had been the old city of Jerusalem: only non-Jews were permitted to build and reside there. The Romans, unlike the Persians, would not permit a Temple again to be raised in Zion.[4]

If Christianity, as we know it, was a product of the destruction of the Second Temple, the phrase "as we know it" must be emphasized. Time's path runs in only one direction, and there is no way of knowing what might have happened to the followers of Yeshua of Nazareth and to the complexes of ideas they espoused, had not the events of 66–73 extruded them from their former spiritual home. Previously, they had maintained their spiritual taproot in late Second Temple Judaism. Perhaps Yeshua's followers would have become a major Judahist group, as the Pharisees, Essenes, and Sadducees are said to have been; perhaps they would have faded out altogether, to become just another of those religious parties of whom we know the founder's name and little more. Possibly Yeshua's followers would have become a bridge between the Judahist world and the Gentile religions; equally, Yeshua's followers could have split violently and permanently: those who stayed within Judaism and those who left, nurturing toward each other a permanent enmity. (Recall the vitriolic splits among the Essenes between the Teacher of Righteousness and the Man of Lies.) All we can know, however, is that the destruction of the Temple changed forever the religious geography of the Holy Land and nothing was ever again the same.

In approaching these developments, the expository path we shall be following in the chapters ahead will be just the opposite of the conventional. The usual way of looking at the development of early Christianity is to start with the historian's equivalent of a zoom lens: to begin with the details of the life of Yeshua of Nazareth and to chronicle his emergence as Jesus in the Gospels; such a discussion usually involves an evaluation of the nature of the historical sources and thus, inevitably the question of the "historical Jesus"; next, conventionally, the evolution of the early church is defined, as outlined, primarily, in the writings of Paul and in the Book of Acts; and finally, the emergence of the canonical shape of the "New Testament" is either discussed or, frequently, simply taken for granted.

Here we will turn that rhetorical structure upside down. It is crucial, I think, to begin with the canon and to understand it as the product both of wonderful inventiveness of some ideas and relationships and, simultaneously, of quite ruthless suppression of others. Secondly, I think we must recognize that the nature of the one "New Testament" we possess (among the myriad possible "New Testaments" that were rejected by the church authorities) is remarkable: whatever most biblical critics may say, it is not a collection of books, but a cohesive unity, and any particular piece of the work can only be understood in relationship to the whole. Thirdly, in my view, we should next note that almost all of the components of the massively powerful invention that is the "New Testament" were the very items that we saw being constructed, but not quite integrated with each other, during the fecund period in the history of Judahism, namely the late Second Temple era. Then, fourthly, we must observe the way that these Second Temple bundles of ideas, while being integrated into a single entity, the "New Testament," were re-shaped by their author-editors, so that they acquired a resonance based on the Hebrew scriptures. In this process, the author-editors adhered to exactly the same grammar of scriptural invention that we have observed in case after case when reading the Tanakh, the Dead Sea Scrolls, the Pseudepigrapha and the Apocrypha. They followed the rules and that is why their investment of new meanings in the old texts was so successful. Whether one admires the "New Testament" or not (I view it as one of the wonders of world culture and see no reason to obscure my being awestruck by it), one has to recognize it as one of the most successful of "strong readings" of earlier texts that our culture is able to display. Fifthly – and only after the previous points concerning the nature of the "New Testament" as a great invention are assimilated – it is appropriate to discuss the questions of when specific texts were written, how the early versions were stacked together, and what their dates of origin may be, and how these matters of dating relate to early Christianity and to the questions of the "historical Jesus." In that discussion (see particularly Appendix D), I shall suggest that, from the viewpoint of a professional historian, there is a good deal in the methods and assumptions of most present-day biblical scholars that makes one not just a touch uneasy, but downright queasy. Try as I might, I cannot come even as close to believing in the soundness of their enterprise as King Agrippa did to believing in Pauline Christianity: "Almost thou persuadest me ..." (Acts 26:28).[5]

3

The "New Testament" that most branches of Christianity today accept is just one of a large number of "New Testaments" that could have become standard. The present Christian scriptures in their primary canon (that is, excluding the books of the "Deutero-canon" or "Apocrypha") contain twenty-seven "books." The term "book" is anachronistic in referring to the individual items comprising the scriptures of the early church, but it is serviceable so long as one remembers that these "books" eventually are comprehended within a single larger book, one that is not an anthology, but is a very carefully constructed literary-historical entity. The books, in their usual order of presentation are:

1–4   The Gospels: Matthew, Mark, Luke, John
5   Early church history: The Acts of the Apostles
6–19   The fourteen epistles of Paul (including those attributed to him, but of questionable authorship) named according to their recipients: Romans, 1 and 2 Corinthians, Galatians, Ephesians, Philippians, Colossians, 1 and 2 Thessalonians, 1 and 2 Timothy, Titus, Philemon, Hebrews
20–26 The "Catholic epistles," named according to their putative authors: James, 1 and 2 Peter, 1, 2 and 3 John, Jude
27   Apocalypse: The Revelation of St. John

These items are so familiar to readers of the Christian scriptures that most people who have any interest in the "New Testament" can run the list off by heart. It is automatic, a given. However, we are brought up short when we encounter a list of volumes that comes to us from the early years of the Christian church. This list consists of books that were produced by devout believers, and accepted as such by many early Christians. Yet, none of these items are part of our "New Testament." These items seem exotic to us only because we are unfamiliar with them. Actually, for the most part, their contents are no more cabalistic or bizarre than are those of the Christian scriptures we are accustomed to reading. Given below is a partial list of the various books – gospels, allegedly-apostolic letters, pastoral epistles, apocalypses – that were circulating in Christian circles in the late second century and during the second and third centuries:

Acts of John
Acts of Philip
Apocalypse of Paul
Apocalypse of Peter
1 and 2 Clement
Dialogue of the Saviour
Diatesseron of Tatian (a harmonization of the four Gospels)
The Didache (a spiritual rule book)
Epistle of the Apostles
Epistle of Barnabas

Expositions (by Papias, a church father)
Gospel of the Ebionites
Gospel of the Hebrews
Gospel of Marcion
Gospel of Mary
Gospel of the Nazoraeans
Gospel of Peter
Gospel of Thomas
Infancy Gospel of Thomas
Infancy Gospel of James
Secret Book of James
The Shepherd
Testament of Isaac
Traditions of Matthias the Apostle
Treatises of the Montanists (several)

These volumes claimed authority in the same way that the items which eventually became canonical did: by asserting direct knowledge of original Jesus-tradition, or of apostolic actions and beliefs; by claiming authorship by an early authoritative figure, such as one of the apostles; or by being pieces of advice given by major figures in the history of the church during the late-first or the second centuries. To the extent that they can be recovered (some of the books are known by name only, some only in quotation in other writings, and some in fragmentary form; while others are recoverable in full), they are the sort of items that would have been useful to members of the fledgling Christian church as they tried to define their faith in a very confusing world. Thus, these books had to have been taken seriously by any early church authority who tried to draw up a list of written items that contained the true Christian tradition.

Once that is recognized, the possibility of the "New Testament"'s having very different content and contours from the ones we at present know becomes very clear. This point is emphasized, if one adds to the previous list of biblical and para-biblical books, earlier written documents upon which the canonical Four Gospels are thought to have depended, but which are now lost: the "Q" gospel hypothesized to be one of the sources for Matthew and Luke is the best known of these earlier sources. Each of these several earlier sources, now encapsulated in the canonical scriptures, had at one time possessed the possibility of being a canonical book on its own. Had they remained distinct items, this would have changed the shape of the "New Testament." Further, one should add to the list of possible canonical scriptures the very large number of texts included in the collections of the Gnostic

Christians. The "Nag Hammadi" finds, discovered in Egypt in 1945, included more than three dozen books, or fragments of books, from the second and third century, and in the case of one prize item (the Gospel of Thomas), an item that some scholars believe is mid-first century. These books eventually were suppressed by "orthodox" church authorities, but several of these scriptures would have fit into the "New Testament" at least as well as did the Gospel of John, which several of the early church fathers objected to, because it seemed to be tainted with the sulphur of Gnosticism.[6]

If one wishes to engage in a brief, but very illuminating, exercise, take a hand-held calculator and attempt to compute the possible number of Christian canons there could have been. To do this, just note the total number of books that are mentioned above and factor in the possible variations of the total number of books in any possible collection (from one to several score) and then calculate the possible variations in the order of the books in each of those possible canons. This exercise in elementary permutations will yield a simple, graphic result: an ordinary calculator will not have enough display space to produce the total number of possible Christian canons.

Yet, we have only one "New Testament."

The train of events by which a single canon emerged is largely a mystery.[7] A few markers in the process remain visible, but how they are connected each to the other in their historical development is purely conjectural. Three points concerning what can be observed in the formation of the Christian canon are striking. First, the process seems to have been a very wobbly one in its earlier stages. That is, wide swings of inclusion and exclusion were essayed. Watching the canon emerge is similar to observing a child's top being put into motion in a slightly off-centre position: at first the device lurches about in a large arc, but eventually basic physics takes over until finally it gyrates upright, hardly moving off a single fixed point. Second, the matter of the canon's evolution is affixed to the difficult question of when the process of determining the canon was completed. One school of thought argues that it was never formally closed and that it still is an open canon. However, for practical purposes, the fifth century can be taken as marking the end of any major revisions: the Council of Chalcedon in 451 is a convenient point to declare the process finished, and it is historically defensible. Still, it is worth noting that the church in its first few centuries did not make the form and content of the canon an article of faith. Thus, within the dominant branch of Christianity, the process of canonical development was not so much formally completed as generally accepted.[8] And, third, the beginning of the process is indeterminate. It is very difficult to discern when early church authorities began to be concerned with deciding which of the myriad writings in circulation were authentic and authoritative and which were not. Clearly they began asking these questions before the term "canon" came into use for, in fact, in the technical sense the word did not find employment in Christian circles until the fourth century.[9]

It has become a commonplace to suggest that during the last two-thirds of the second century, church leaders began to worry about what the faithful should be reading and (in the usual case) what should be read to them. A major figure in this development was Justin Martyr (martyred c.165), the first figure in the "orthodox" genealogy of the Christian canon. (Orthodox in this context does not refer to the Eastern church, but rather to what eventually became the winning side in several fights with various "heretics" – "heretics" and "heresies" being the church's name for the losers in the battles about power and belief.) Justin, in an apologetic work composed about the year 150, wrote that the usual practice in Christian congregations in Rome was to read aloud some of the "memoirs of the apostles," or some writings of the prophets. He was referring, in the first instance, to what later became known as the Four Gospels, and in the latter instance, to the prophets as found in the Hebrew scriptures. Justin's writings also indicate that the congregations he dealt with had knowledge of some of Paul's letters, although exactly which ones is unclear. Also, Justin and his fellow worshippers were familiar with the Book of Revelation.[10] The list of scriptures that Justin refers to can perhaps be described as a "proto-canon," but its merely local reference has to be noted. Also, one must recognize that Justin's discussion was more reportorial than normative in nature. He was not describing what should be read in a Christian congregation, but rather what was actually done in his own locale.

That Justin reflected on such matters well may have been the result of the activities of an influential preacher active in western Asia Minor, the "heretic," Marcion, who was the first Christian of record to focus his thought directly upon the question of what should – and what should not – be read as being authoritative. Marcion, being a heretic, has frequently been marginalized in discussions of the canon, but he should not be. Not only was he the first canonical thinker of whom we have any knowledge, but he probably came much closer to winning than later church authorities liked to admit. The doctrine that Marcion espoused, and which resulted in his excommunication about the year 144, was "Docetism" (from the Greek *dokein*, to seem or to appear): the belief that Jesus' body was not real, but was either a phantom or composed of some ethereal substance. This ran against the emerging "orthodox" view that Jesus the Christ was both True God and True Man. From our point of view, the most interesting aspect of Marcion's thought was that he entirely rejected the idea that Christianity should have anything to do with the religion found in the Hebrew scriptures. Christianity, he believed, was a totally new religion. Marcion seems to have been acquainted with the Four Gospels, but, given that each of them includes numerous passages that resonate with the content of the "Old Testament," he found them unsatisfactory.

Hence, he proposed a radical canon, one that involved not only scrapping the Hebrew texts, but also rewriting the story of Jesus and the early church so as to get rid of any Judahist overtones. Thus, he produced the Gospel of Marcion. The actual text has not survived, but it is referred to in other writings of the period. Apparently it was based mostly on an expurgation of Luke. He completely distrusted the other three Gospels. Significantly, although Marcion did not trust entirely the Pauline letters, he saw Paul as the founder of true Christianity. Therefore he accepted ten of Paul's epistles: the nine letters to individual churches and the letter to Philemon. Evidently, Marcion's canon consisted of his sanitized version of Luke and the bulk of the Pauline epistles, cleansed of Hebrew overtones, such as references to Abraham and his descendants.[11]

Later movements, even ones of such magnitude as the Protestant Reformation, were mere administrative juggling acts compared with what Marcion had proposed: the self-conscious establishment of Christianity as a new religion, independent of its base in the ancient worship of Yahweh. Given that the church was just beginning to contemplate sifting the array of local writings held sacred by scattered Christian communities, sorting out what counted from what did not, Marcion's canon represented the biggest wobble the church's gyroscope ever took: Marcion, unlike every other early church figure of any consequence, refused to accept the grammar of religious invention that dominated the Hebrew scriptures and which thereby became the underlying paradigm for the later Christian texts. Marcion's canon, had it prevailed, would have produced a very different western world.

Among the "orthodox," the first considered response to the "heresies" of Marcion (and also, it appears, to the threats posed by the Gnostics) was that of Irenaeus (c.140–200), the bishop of Lyons. Clearly the Marcionites frightened Irenaeus, for in his major theological work, *Against Heretics*, written about 180, he affirmed that there was a systematic line of argument, proof, inspiration, and illumination, running between the two sets of scriptures, the Hebrew and the Christian. He did not speak in terms of "canon," but he came as close as one can to defining a "New Testament," without quite employing that term.[12] This untitled "New Testament" included the Four Gospels (in the order: Matthew, John, Luke, and Mark), the Acts of the Apostles, twelve epistles of Paul, the letter of James, 1 Peter and 1 and 2 John, the Revelation of St. John and the apocalypse of the Shepherd of Hermas.[13]

In his anti-heresy campaign, Irenaeus was fighting not only the Marcionites, but also the Gnostics. The Gnostics are a group of great inherent interest, but here we must limit ourselves to their potential impact on the Christian canon. Next to Marcion's "canon," their scriptures represented the greatest potential deviation from the tradition of biblical invention that the early Christian church inherited from Second Temple Judaism and, ultimately, from the earliest Hebrew scriptures. As mentioned earlier, more than three dozen Gnostic scriptural books, all outside the eventual Christian canon, have been disinterred by scholars, mostly since 1945. Given that Gnosticism, with its radical dualism in thought between light and darkness, and between the physical and the spiritual world, was not entirely Judahist in origin, it is hardly controversial to suggest that, had the Gnostics won the day, the Christian scriptures would have been very different from what we now have: indeed, different to the point of virtual unrecognizability.

The one Gnostic item that impinges directly upon present-day historical work is the Gospel of Thomas. This document, dated by scholars between the years 50 and 200, purports to be a genuine record of Jesus' sayings. Those scholars who accept its authenticity argue that its bundle of Jesus-sayings was collected independently of the Four Gospels that are now canonical. For the most part, the Gospel of Thomas agrees with the Four Gospels, but it was suppressed by the early church fathers, probably because it was revered by the Gnostics. The book did not become fully available until the second half of the twentieth century.[14]

The "orthodox" church was even more successful in suppressing the practices and the texts of "Montanism." This "heresy" is bracketed, roughly, by the years 150–250, and can be thought of, in modern terms, as a mixture of Pentecostalism and folk prophecy. The founder, Montanus, and two female associates in Phrygia, took to speaking in tongues and prophesying. They developed a considerable following. They were particularly fond of strong apocalyptic texts, such as the Revelation of St. John, and the Shepherd. Their "canon" must have been an extremely vivid collection, comprising not only apocalypses already extant, but also their own oracular utterances. That, however, is about all that is known, for they were excommunicated by one local Christian church after another and eventually, after Christianity became the state religion of Rome, all Montanist documents were destroyed. Bruce Metzger argues that the chief effect of the Montanists upon the eventual canon was that they caused a backlash. Any tendency toward liberality and inclusiveness was quashed. Indeed, for generations after the Montanists, the scriptures that they had most tightly embraced were either viewed with suspicion (as in the case of the Epistle to the Hebrews and the Revelation of St. John) or rejected altogether (as in the case of the Shepherd).[15]

Montanism was the last great wobble in the formation of the "New Testament." From roughly the middle of the second century onwards, the "orthodox" tradition in both the eastern and western churches was defined with increasing precision, and ultimately a unified and coherent set of Christian scriptures emerged. However, the outcome of this process should not be assumed. Even if one removes from the possible permutations of the "New Testament" all those items produced by groups that were eventually labelled as heretics, and even if one makes the arbitrary assumption that a serviceable Christian canon would have roughly twenty to thirty items in it – even so, the number of possible sequences is in the hundreds of thousands. And each of these would have been serviceable, "orthodox," and would have consisted only of documents that leading figures in the early church found authoritative and beneficial in the development of the faith.

And yet there is only one canon.

Following the suppression of the three major "heresies" – Marcionism, Gnosticism, and Montanism – one can obtain brief glimpses of what must have been an extremely complex process of canonical selection. Its visible markers are the writings of Eusebius (c.260–339); the Codex Claromontanus, an eastern document of the mid-300s; the Cheltenham Codex, a North African list of the same period; a list of authoritative scriptures by Athanasius, Bishop of Alexandria, of slightly later date in the fourth century; the decrees of the Council of Laodicea of c.360; the decisions of the Synod of Carthage of 397; the "Vulgate" Bible, the Latin translation associated with Jerome and probably completed early in the fifth century; the allegiances elicited at the Council of Chalcedon in 451.[16] So scanty and so *parti-pris* are these records, that the ideological motives and power-positions of those who gradually narrowed down the hundreds of thousands of potential canons into a single item, cannot be inferred with any accuracy whatsoever. To Christian believers this presents no problems, because they can see the hand of God working through the church's early fathers, shaping and protecting the Christian scriptures. That, however, is not an historical explanation, at least not in the sense employed by professional historians. A more intellectually presentable argument (but not one necessarily of any more value than that of the believers) is that in the canon of the "New Testament" we possess a single random permutation among hundreds of thousands that might have turned up.

It might be more helpful to take a different tack. It may be more useful to consider the evolution of the canon as having been a purposive process, albeit one wherein there were always alternative ways to achieve a satisfactory result. Like many mathematical problems, the evolution of the canon had more than one "right" answer; but all the right answers shared certain characteristics. I think that from the moment the first document of what became the "New Testament" was drafted (it probably was Paul's First Letter to the Thessalonians), one is dealing with a self-conscious literary construct; it is one whose overwhelming interest is in history (in the Jesus-story and the various responses to it), but written at a time when direct physical experience of Jesus was impossible. Thus, the writings themselves are the way that subsequent generations will encounter history.[17] It is easy to forget the simple fact that the "New Testament" was written almost entirely in Koine Greek, which was not the language of most believers before the scattering of the years 66–70, and it almost certainly was not the language of Yeshua of Nazareth. So, from its very first word, the "New Testament" was a self-conscious construction, not naive reportage. It had to be, or it would have failed, utterly.

Granted, it is possible to argue that the eventual canon was merely a ratification of what local churches found useful in their everyday religious life. That leaves untouched the question of why a given arrangement of certain local texts had power in a given situation. And it yields as an explanation for the shape and content of the final canon, the unstated hypothesis that it was formed by the bigger and more powerful of the local churches beating up on the less powerful, thereby imposing their own view of Christian reality. There is a touch of realism in such a suggestion, for there was a good deal of the bully in many of the church fathers, and the church councils of the third and fourth centuries seem to have had the tone about them of the school yard. Even so, why did these bullies care so much about certain scriptures and about maintaining a certain order among these items?

Clearly these arrangements – these canons – worked for them and worked not as scattered pieces of information, but as a comprehensive witness. I would suggest that unity, limit, and authority – in other words, canon – were implied, however subliminally, and were sought, however unconsciously, every time a new page of scripture was drafted. The seemingly astronomical number of possible canons was therefore limited. The final product would not necessarily be the present "New Testament," but it would be a unity and it would possess an immense authority.[18]

That assertion is not capable of disproof, since it is not framed as an operational hypothesis. Were it to be put into testable terms, however, it still would not be of much value in terms of strict historical logic, because the information we possess on the actual formation of the canon havers between sketchy and invisible, and is not rich enough for detailed hypothesis-testing. One way of getting behind this veil of non-information is to proceed heuristically. I would suggest that we engage in the verbal equivalent of what economists and other social scientists do when they computer-simulate a situation. They develop an heuristic device which says, in effect, "*if* we assume that 'X' operates in a given way, one that we can imagine as being possible but cannot empirically document, *then* would we gain a better understanding of phenomenon 'Y'?" The earliest successful example of this mode of proceeding actually arose long before computers: the economists' concept of "economic man," which is an entity that never on land or sea actually was seen, but whose fictive existence allows one to tie together disparate bodies of data and to define hypotheses that can indeed be either verified or falsified by empirically-derived information.

Here, our heuristic device is to pretend that the canon, in its final form, had a single editor. We will call this man (and the "New Testament" was indeed edited from a male point of view as many recent feminist biblical scholars have argued)[19] the "editor-inventor" of the "New Testament." This is not a real figure, or set of figures who worked together. He is entirely a heuristic device. We will assume that this "editor-inventor" was an "orthodox" Christian of the sort who triumphed in the church councils of the third, fourth, and fifth centuries. He probably was not a terribly nice man: persecution by the Romans, interspersed with periods of heresy-hunting when he tried to do to other Christians what the Romans had tried to do to him, and, then, his becoming a *de facto* functionary of the Roman empire, when Christianity became the official imperial religion – none of this would have produced a calm and generous demeanour. But he had read widely in the Christian and Hebrew writings and he held his own beliefs intensely.

What would the "editor-inventor" of the "New Testament" have believed? Above all else, he would have believed that Yeshua of Nazareth was an historical figure, one who in some way was touched by the divine. There were many rival theories of what that divine touch may have been, but no quibbling about the basic belief. And what is the one body of religious literature that we know with absolute certainty the "editor-inventor" would have read, indeed, have mastered? Obviously: the Hebrew scriptures both in the form found in the Septuagint and in the Tanakh (Jerome had knowledge of both, so the final "editor-inventor" would have had an equal facility). Knowledge of almost everything else is conceivable, from the texts of Greek mystery cults to the Gnostic writers, to the immense range of Judahist religious literature of the late Second Temple period, but all of these things are irrelevant to our model, because the "editor-inventor" in putting together his amazing book, the "New Testament," employed as components only texts that were written within the grammar of invention established by the Hebrew scriptures, and only those whose motifs and methods of explication found a resonance in those earlier scriptures.[20] Therefore, his final product in all its lineaments – symbols, figures of speech, narrative strategy, and in the arrangement of material – was both a replication of, and a re-invention of the Hebrew scriptures, considered as a whole. Within his religious architecture, nothing else fit.

Consider the basic structural question: where does one start to build? There is only one sane answer and the Hebrew scriptures defined it perfectly: a primary, indeed primordial, historical narrative can only begin at the beginning. There is no room for being cute, for starting in the middle or for playing about with flashbacks; that works with lighter matters, not here. Just as the Genesis-Kings unity had to come before the discursive sections of the Tanakh, so the Four Gospels and the Book of Acts had to begin the "New Testament." Matthew-Acts is to the Christian scriptures what Genesis-Kings is to the Hebrew.

In presenting his five foundation books, the "editor-inventor" of the "New Testament" shows a belief in the historical veracity of the basic narrative equal in trust to that shown by the author-editor of Genesis-Kings. Recall here that the editor-inventor of the first nine books of the Tanakh was not at all worried by apparent contradictions in the text. His faith in the underlying truth of the narrative which he unfurled was so strong that dissonances in mere details did not bother him. In fact, the Hebrew text is full of "doublets," many of which are literary tropes, salient phrases presented in parallel for heightened effect; other doublets, however, are different versions of a single narrative and frequently they do not mesh entirely with each other. In discussing this phenomenon, I suggested that these inclusions were far from accidental, but were warranties of good faith on the part of the writer-editor. Instead either of erasing from history's record one of the dissonant versions, or harmonizing the accounts (either of which course would have been easy to effect), he did what anyone who thinks historically, and does so with integrity, would have done: he preserved his primary sources.

The heuristic "editor-inventor" of the "New Testament" acts in the same way as did his real predecessor of nearly a millennium earlier. Once he has accepted an item as authoritative, he lets it be. Details were the accidence of the story; the substance was deeper. To worry about the incompatibility of details would be to mark a shallowness in his belief in the basic historical narrative. That is why the massive literature on the contradictions found within the five basic historical books of the Christian scriptures, while being useful for purposes such as dating the texts and for helping to determine the sort of person who compiled each of the books, is of no relevance whatsoever when one is considering the construction of the "New Testament" as a work of historical creation. Our "editor-inventor," hearing the tiresome list of doublings (and, sometimes, triplings) that are mentioned as flaws in his work would have shaken his head, sadly, at the lack of comprehension implied by such objections.[21]

Like the inventors of many of the para-biblical writings that had whirled around during late Second Temple times, the writers, readers, or editors of the various books of the "New Testament" lent authority to the volumes by attaching names to them of historically weighty figures. Sometimes this occurred within the book itself, and at other times external labels were added by later readers or editors and they came to be accepted as part of the text. Matthew, Mark, John, Luke, Peter, Jude, and James all had their names attached to gospels, epistles, and apocalypses which in all probability they did not themselves write. The real author of course is anonymous, for in these instances the "New Testament" writers were honouring the grammar of biblical invention. The retrospective naming of the first five books of the Tanakh as the "Books of Moses," which occurred long after the books' completion, was parallelled by the retrospective attachment to the Four Gospels of the names of four of the leading apostles.

Of course, not all works were pseudonymous. Just as some of the prophetic books of the "Old Testament" were probably attempts at setting down something akin to the actual utterances of specific prophets (one thinks of Baruch's acting as secretary and memorialist of Jeremiah), so some of the Christian scriptures were author-specific: most notably the letters written by Paul. Here, however, the interesting point is that the recognition of Paul's authorship of several letters is not appended in the present-day mode, where an author asserts ownership of a piece of intellectual property which he or she has created. The name on the Pauline letters is there because it is a warrant of authenticity, not a claim staked on a piece of property. The epistles assume their force not solely by virtue of their content, but also by virtue of their having actually been written by Paul.

Most importantly, the "editor-inventor" of the Christian scriptures adopts a set of architectural contours that are remarkably similar to those that ultimately came to characterize the Jewish version of the Hebrew scriptures: that is, the proto-Masoretic text, as distinct from the Christian arrangement found in the Septuagint. Here it is helpful to forget for a moment the present-day formal divisions of the Tanakh and to recall how the major structural members of the Hebrew scriptures locked together: a fundamental historical narrative was followed by several high-definition prophetic voices; these were succeeded by an almost-miscellaneous set of writings whose collective character was undeniably discursive; and, finally, another piece of historical narrative (the two books of Ezra-Nehemiah and of Chronicles) was used to complete the structure, being joined as if by mortise-and-tenon to the narrative histories that began the whole collection. The architecture suggests that the covenant contained within the four-sided structure was best encountered, first and last, in historical narrative.

The "New Testament" is constructed in almost exactly the same form. It begins with five books of narrative history; then come the high-definition writings of Paul, which in their intensity and specificity of vision are parallel to the "Old Testament" prophets; next the "Catholic epistles" find their place and, taken as a whole, they meander through various topics with the same discursiveness as do the Writings in the Hebrew scriptures; finally, the Apocalypse of St. John closes the Christian Bible. Recall here what we have observed several times in regard to Second Temple religious writings: that apocalypse is a form of historical narrative in which the future is chronicled as if it already had occurred. So, the Book of Revelation does for the Christian scriptures what Ezra-Nehemiah and Chronicles do for the Tanakh: make the structure four-square, by joining the initial history to a closing history. The Christian structure encompasses, defines, and protects a covenant – a "new covenant" – just as the Hebrew scriptures surround, define, and protect their covenant.

This is not to suggest that the "editor-inventor" of the "New Testament" would have directly modelled his canon on the Tanakh, although fifth-century Christian scholars did know of the arrangement of the Hebrew canon that was becoming standard, if not quite universal. No, what the "editor-inventor" did was not imitative; instead, he came to the conclusion that the best way to organize a book which articulated a covenant, and which employed for the most part inventions that had been articulated within late Second Temple Judahism, was to proceed in the same way as were the Jewish authorities of the second through sixth centuries in making final their arrangement of the Hebrew scriptures.[22]

This means that the hundreds of thousands of possible permutations of the canon were greatly reduced, because this basic four-square structure limited the room for manoeuvre (assuming, as we have been doing, that the material from the various major heresies is scrubbed from the menu of possibilities that an "orthodox" "editor-inventor" would employ). Granted, one could argue about whether or not Jude or Second Peter or the Epistle of James or the Letter to the Hebrews, or one or two of the Johanine letters should be included and, indeed, the church fathers certainly did argue about such matters. But, given that one virtually must start with the books of historical narrative, and then go on to the most authoritative and sharply-defined teacher of Christianity, Paul, it would not make much sense to end with anything but the Book of Revelation. To do otherwise would be akin to giving away the climax of a three-volume novel at the end of volume two.

Revelation – the Apocalypse of St. John – is the crucial final structural element, the one through which the lock-pin slips, tying together Jesus in the earthly past, and Jesus in the heavenly future. Revelation is not a nice book, nor in any conventional sense is it morally edifying. Understandably, many of the church fathers were wary of it, not least because various "heretics" embraced it all too fervently. Those considerations, however, should not distract us from acknowledging that the employment of the Book of Revelation at the end of the canon was an architectural master stroke. Here, yet another analogy may hold. If one has spent much time studying the history of the British isles, one comes to note a fairly frequent characteristic of country houses. This is that houses built in, say, the early eighteenth century, later were turned on their axis, seemingly by *force majeure*, so that the orientation of the house may be 90 degrees or even 180 degrees from its original attitude. When one investigates how this was done, frequently one finds that a nineteenth- or early twentieth-century architect accomplished the radical re-orientation simply by changing the design of a single term in the architectural vocabulary. One finds that a Palladian house can be turned 180 degrees just by reversing the front and back entrances; and a four-square Georgian house can be rotated ninety degrees merely by blocking up the front entrance and opening one in the centre of one of the side faces of the building. From such simple redefinitions of architectural terms, everything else in the house's reconstruction follows.

That is what the Book of Revelation does in the Christian scriptures. It takes the same structural elements that are found in the Hebrew scriptures, a four-sided structure that encompasses a covenant – and turns the Christian structure so that it points in a completely different direction than does the Hebrew. The Book of Revelation turns the whole Christian historical narrative into an apocalyptic one. The book forces one to read the entire text of the "New Testament" as an apocalypse, one which starts with the birth of Jesus and ends with Christ's kingdom in eternity. Norman Cohn notes that Revelation, though a profoundly Christian work, is a document wherein "the Jewishness of the work is everywhere apparent. Not only is it influenced by Jewish apocalypses – many passages are simply translated from the Hebrew Bible and in addition there are more than three hundred references to Daniel, Isaiah, Second Isaiah, Jeremiah, Ezekiel and Zechariah."[23]

Through the force of the Book of Revelation, the Christian scriptures must be read not only as Jewish, but Jewish with a difference. They have the same fundamental architecture as the Tanakh, but a completely different sight-line: they look out over a very different countryside than does the Tanakh. To understand the importance of the Book of Revelation in affecting this result, imagine how the reading of the Tanakh would have been altered if it, like the "New Testament," employed as a final structural member an apocalypse; specifically, how would we read the Tanakh if the Book of Daniel were given the climactic, concluding position? Alternatively, consider a parallel question concerning the Christian scriptures. How would our reading of the "New Testament" differ if it concluded with the Christian equivalent of Ezra-Nehemiah and Chronicles, namely the Book of Acts? What a difference in each case! In each instance, the final editor-inventors knew exactly what they were doing.

4

Our "editor-inventor" of the Christian scriptures is a fictionary entity, an heuristic device intended to help us recognize that, whatever the vast vagaries of the historical process may have been, the final "New Testament" is an extremely cunning invention. It is not a mere anthology; it is a single entity.

In addition to its basic architectural integrity, the "New Testament" knit together so effectively because of a mechanical principle that ran between individual books and also between segments of the individual books: interdigitation. The term comes from the combined observations of physiologists and of mechanical engineers of how the fingers of a human hand can interweave with those of another hand, or set of hands, to produce alignments that are simultaneously surprisingly strong and amazingly supple.

Not only do the Christian scriptures possess an overall architectural plan that is an extremely effective unity, but they also possess a filigree of motif and symbol that runs from book to book. Like a cohort of human hands, working together on a single task, these motifs and symbols, when they inter-digitate, gain strength and suppleness.

Of course the "editor-inventor" selected for his canon books whose reso-nant elements were compatible with those of the other books he was includ-ing in his text. We should take that as a given in the present discussion. Simultaneously, we should remember that although the canon was formed relatively late, the individual books of the "New Testament" were written comparatively early: by 150 at the latest and, for the most part, before the year 100. They were written by separate individuals who seem to have had little direct contact with each other. Yet, the authors and editors of the several books of the "New Testament" shared three characteristics. The first of these is that each of the authors (or author-editors) of the biblical books was selec-tive. The author of the Gospel of John acknowledged the reality of the pro-cess of selection (and, therefore, of suppression) in his own work when he wrote: "And there are also many other things which Jesus did, the which, if they should be written every one, I suppose that even the world itself could not contain the books that should be written" (John 21:25).

Secondly, with the exception of Paul (who is a pre-70 case and will receive attention later), each of the Christian authors, and author-editors, included in the "New Testament" agreed on one assumption. Namely: Judaism was no more. The destruction of the Temple meant that a religion demanding a visi-ble temple and a visible ritual sacrifice no longer existed. The writers of the Christian historical books, of the Catholic epistles, and of the Book of Reve-lation, all labour hard to create a Temple religion for a religion that is without a Temple.

(The manner in which Paul's writings, which alone among the Christian writings in the "New Testament" are prior to the destruction of the Temple, fit into the "New Testament's" reaction to the all-pervasive problem caused by the Temple's destruction, will be discussed later: the domestication of Paul's writings and their subordination to the larger structure of the "New Testament" is one of the most subtle aspects of the whole process of scrip-tural invention.)

And, thirdly, the "New Testament" writers (even Paul) all work within an agreed vocabulary of motif and symbol. These men did not meet in a first-century equivalent of a conference call and hammer out their common vocab-ulary. They did not need to. We have surveyed in Chapters Six and Seven the several themes, symbols, and motifs that were free-floating in later Second

Temple times and have documented their articulation in text after text. It is hardly surprising, then, that when the chroniclers and propagandists of the emerging Christian faith were confronted with the necessity of explaining the importance of Yeshua of Nazareth, they employed exactly those items that were conveniently to hand: the idea complexes of later Second Temple Judahism.

Without denying the ubiquity of Greek-derived ideas in the contemporary Near East (the importance of such ideas is fully acknowledged in Chapter Six), we must here emphasize that there is very little in the Christian scriptures that does not come directly from late Second Temple Judahism or from the Hebrew scriptures. This is crucial, because one frequently encounters a vein in the scholarship on "Christian origins" that, while not denying that Christianity is formulated in Judahist terms, does everything possible to look the other way, to discover themes from Greek mystery cults or Roman sodalities and to focus obsessively on them: anything to avoid embracing the fact that the "New Testament" is so embarrassingly non-classical, so, oh dear, Jewish. Against this grain, one does well to heed A.N. Wilson's observation that the "New Testament" writers are not even remotely interested in classical concepts of mind, of mathematics, of politics, of law. "The New Testament posits a quite different way of viewing the *kosmos*, a way which we find in the pages of the Old Testament and in the Dead Sea Scrolls, but not among the Greeks."[24] After a lifetime spent in study of the Tanakh and of later Second Temple texts, David Flusser wrote: "from ancient Jewish writings we could easily construct a whole gospel without using a single word that originated with Jesus,"[25] and Joseph Klausner, one of the pioneers among Jewish scholars in the study of texts concerning Jesus and early Christianity, concluded that "there is nothing in all the teachings of Paul, as there is nothing in the teaching of Jesus, which is not grounded in the Old Testament, or in the Apocryphal, Pseudepigraphical and Tannaitic literature of his time."[26]

With two exceptions (the Virgin Birth and the physical, as distinct from the spiritual, Resurrection of Jesus), the motifs and symbols that interdigitate throughout the "New Testament" are the common currency of religious speculation in late Second Temple Judahism. We observed these items earlier, in a context that was independent of Christianity (Chapters Five-Seven). Revolving freely through the rich milieu of Judahist thought in the years between the Maccabean revolt and the destruction of the Temple, was a set of concepts concerning a master figure. These were not yet joined together. The Son of God, the Son of Man, and the Moshiah were the most important forms of this icon. Equally common was a sector of Judahist religious writing that organized itself around light-vs-dark as its chief conceptual and rhetorical axis. Yet another set of free-floating concepts were the ideas of the Kingdom of God and the Kingdom of Heaven as future entities, as well as several versions of the idea of the end-time. In later Second Temple Judahist thought, good and evil had tended increasingly to be personified. Satan, angels, demons, arch-angels became the intermediaries of the ultimate, so that Yahweh's direct agency was moved increasingly farther away from the everyday physical earth. Simultaneously, the relatively new other-world concept of the resurrection of the individual after death was becoming increasingly popular, and in some circles, belief in an individual's being judged after death was accepted. And, finally, in some items of later Second Temple literature we observed the introduction of the ideas of a new covenant, of an invisible temple, and of a piacular figure who would give himself as a hostage or as a sacrifice to redeem the Chosen People.

These ideas had not been melded together before the great disaster of 66–73, and one can only speculate whether they would have bonded with each other had the Temple tragedy not occurred. However, if the Book of Enoch is any guide (see Chapter Seven), the motifs and concepts were drawing fairly close and one suspects that some Judahist faction would have put them all together and become a very strong contender for leadership in the crowded field of Judahist religious competition. In the actual event, however, the Christian scriptures subsumed into a single functioning entity the most important concepts of late Second Temple Judahist thought.

Even to state this fact is unintentionally to misrepresent the course of invention. We should not conceive of some external agency – called Christianity – taking over the innovative conceptual units of later Second Temple Judahism and transforming these units by dint of that external agency's power. Christianity was not an independent force: indeed, the label "Christian" makes us misperceive it as such. The Christian writers did not act independently of Judahist thought patterns, but instead were acted upon by those very patterns. Christianity, then, should not be perceived as a cause, but rather as an effect. It was a natural product of the intersection of the rich and variegated conceptual life of late Second Temple Judaism with the skein of political events that destroyed the holy city of Judah and Yahweh's Temple.

That leaves Yeshua of Nazareth out of the picture entirely. For the moment, let us continue to do so, as a means of clarifying the way the Christian scriptures came into being. What was written down by the author-editors of each of the books of the "New Testament," and was later assimilated into a single canon, has determined almost entirely what we know about the man who became Jesus Christ. Certainly, the beliefs expressed in both sayings and actions by Yeshua of Nazareth influence the content and, perhaps, the structure of the Christian scriptures. However, if one remembers that Yeshua and the scriptures are separate historical entities, one should also remember the basic power relationships: whereas Yeshua must have influenced what is in the scriptures, the text determines preemptively what we know about the deity

Christians named Jesus Christ. What was written down is the only reality we now possess. Jesus did not make the scriptures; the scriptures made Jesus.

Therefore, when we see some of the more vibrant of the ideational components of late Second Temple Judahism being pulled together in a manner that is both religiously creative and pragmatically inventive, we must accept the possibility that this great work-in-progress might well have been achieved with another religious personage as its totem. All the major components are stock items, right off the shelf of Second Temple Judahism, and they could have been made to fit a number of contemporary factional leaders. (Would a "New Testament" with John the Baptist as the central figure have been all that different?) *The specific icon given centre stage was not so important as were the motifs and symbols that were assembled around the figure.*

The narrative interdigitation of late Second Temple belief-units that the several editor-authors of the Christian scriptures employ (and this includes Paul) was masterful in its simplicity: effecting the blurring of definitions so that equations of identity and the implosion of meaning could occur. In tying together ideational units that previously had not been united in Judahist thought (for instance, Son of God, Son of Man, and Messiah) the author-editors of the various "New Testament" writings did not follow the Greek pattern of thought, requiring hard proof. The classic Greek proofs with which most modern readers are familiar are those involved in plane geometry, where things-equal-to-the-same-thing-are-equal-to-each-other is a paradigmatic way of proving identity. The Christian writers, operating by thought processes that were derived from late Second Temple thought, instead produced equations of identity not by hard proof, but by association, repetition, and by altering and alternating nomenclature. Thus the reader eventually concludes, without its having been logically demonstrated, that the entities described are one and the same. This technique, though the bane of theologians (who, quite properly, spend much of their time drawing distinctions rather than obscuring them), works nicely within each given book of the "New Testament." It works even better between books, because the fuzziness of definition and the use of multiple-nomenclature permits intertextual joinings of ideas and images. Things that are not exactly the same blur together. This technique should not be treated dismissively: blurring in the conceptual world is similar to welding in the physical world. It joins separate elements that would not otherwise lock together. And, if done properly, the strength of the weld is actually greater than that of the separate entities which it conjoins.

To return to specific details. If, as I argued earlier, the "New Testament" is a coherent narrative, a history that is transformed into an apocalypse, the narrative has a backdrop. This is a tapestry whose warp and woof incorporate three elements. Examined closely, one realizes that these three elements are distinct; however, when viewed from a few metres away, the threads blur together, providing a single coherent backscape against which to view the Christian scriptures' action. These three intertwined materials are, first, a simple vertical scale, with God being in the heavens. Up is good; down is bad. Virtue is associated with heavenly ascension, vice with descent to earth and, perhaps, to Sheol. Second, the body is corrupt; the spirit or soul is incorrupt. Paul expresses this clearly in the Epistle to the Romans:

> Therefore, brethren, we are debtors, not to the flesh, to live after the flesh.
> For if ye live after the flesh, ye shall die: but if ye through the Spirit do mortify the deeds of the body, ye shall live. (Romans 8:12–13)

The eternal life of the spirit is associated with ascension; eternal damnation, which is perpetual corruption, with descent. Third, the backdrop interweaves with these threads the contrast of light and dark. It is a simple device, very common in later Second Temple thought, but very effective. In the Gospel of John, light represents both the eternal perfection of God and also its incarnation in Jesus Christ. John reports Jesus as saying "I am the light of the world: he that followeth me shall not walk in darkness, but shall have the light of life" (John 8:12). Thus are joined the motif of light (which always radiates downward, from the heavens) and of eternal life. These three integrated scales are so simple that it is easy to miss how sophisticated they are, not in a pure intellectual sense, but artistically. The dramatic action of the Christian scriptures would not play nearly so well without this backdrop. It is, one must emphasize, a melding of ideas that were clearly articulated, albeit as discrete entities, within the Judahist religious community of later Second Temple times.[27]

Against this backdrop, the character most sharply outlined is the Son of Man, who blurs into the Son of God, who blurs into the Messiah. The attachment of each of these terms to Yeshua of Nazareth is the primary way that the "New Testament" employs to transform him into Jesus the Christ. "Son of Man," it will be recalled (see Chapter Seven, section three) was barely present in the Hebrew scriptures, except as a general term for human being: as in, "Lord, what is man, that thou takest knowledge of him or the son of man, that thou makest account of him" (Ps. 144:3). It was, however, found in the latter portions of the Book of Enoch, namely the Book of Similitudes, and there the figure is one of force and power and therefore carries quite a different meaning from that associated with the concept in the Tanakh. It is this late Second Temple "Son of Man" that Christianity takes over from Judahism. The Gospels have Jesus refer to himself as Son of Man about eighty times. The self-reference is both to himself in the immediate physical sense and to himself as an apocalyptic figure. It is somewhat disconcerting: the way the Gospels have Jesus refer to himself in the third person produces the slightly disoriented feeling one experienced when hearing a speech by Charles de Gaulle or by Richard Nixon, both of whom were comfortable discussing themselves only from a transcendent viewpoint.

The most effective use of "Son of Man" by someone other than Jesus is found in Revelation (14:14) where the apocalyptic visionary who takes the name "John" sees someone, sitting on a cloud, with a crown on his head and a sharp sickle in his hand. This figure is "like unto the Son of Man...." That is a phrase we have heard before, in the Book of Daniel (7:13) where it carried the Tanakh's meaning: it referred to a figure who resembled a human being. But now, when we read the phrase in Revelation, the meaning has changed entirely. The indeterminate usage of "Son of Man" in the Hebrew scriptures has now, by virtue of its being a self-description ascribed to Jesus, been tied to him, both in his physical and his future forms. So, one "like" the Son of Man in the Revelation of John means one like Jesus, and clearly it refers directly to him. This is as forceful an end to the narrative of Jesus as one could imagine: his coming back to earth to precipitate the end-times. It is also a re-writing of the Book of Daniel that is so strong that it precludes most Christians ever reading that portion of the Hebrew scriptures without projecting into the Tanakh the figure of Jesus Christ.

Although arguments from silence are always dicey, I think it is worth noting that in none of the letters that are uncontestably by Paul, is the concept of Son of Man employed. Given that the Pauline letters are the only Christian documents that we possess which, in their present form, certainly were written before the destruction of the Temple, this may clarify a matter of chronology. The absence of Son of Man in Paul's writing seems to confirm the inference one draws from the Book of Enoch, where the Son of Man as an ideational unit is included only in the latest portions of the volume. (It is not found in the portions of Enoch that are in the Qumran caves.) This inference is that the concept of the Son of Man as an individual, forceful figure developed extremely late in Second Temple Judaism and that it was not widely known until just before the Temple was destroyed. A reasonable suggestion is that Paul did not employ the Son of Man concept because it was not part of the vocabulary of the branches of Judahist thought with which he was familiar. In contrast, the Gospels, the Catholic epistles, and Revelation, all being completed considerably later than were Paul's letters, were formed in an era when the idea apparently had become a much more familiar and much more comfortable concept.

The construction "Son of God" in the Hebrew scriptures was not an apocalyptic notion nor one that was attached to a specific person (see Chapter Seven, section three). And even less than Son of Man was it found in an apocalyptic and personalized context in the literature of later Second Temple Judaism: it is found unambiguously only in a single text of which we are aware today (the "Aramaic Apocalypse," of which only a few more than 200 words are clearly decipherable). Nevertheless (in contrast to Son of Man), the idea of Son of God was sufficiently well known within the form, or forms, of Judahism that Paul was familiar with, to permit him to be comfortable with it as part of his religious vocabulary. Originally the Hebrew concept may have been, first, a reference to a member of the group of gods, and then, later, to "sons of God." By Paul's time it meant "son of God" and Paul employed it with great effect:

> For what the law could not do, in that it was weak through the flesh, God sending his own Son in the likeness of sinful flesh, and for sin, condemned sin in the flesh.
>
> (Romans 8:3)

The motif of Son of God runs from one book of the Christian scriptures to the next. Mark, the earliest writer of the Jesus narrative, starts with a bold assertion: "The beginning of the gospel of Jesus Christ, the Son of God" (Mark 1:1).

In the Four Gospels, Jesus is seen to be much more at ease in calling himself Son of God, than he is in using Son of Man. In part, this is a technical matter: the Gospel writers have the luxury of giving him an alternative to self-reference in the third person, for when he is discussing himself as Son of God, he can talk about "my Father," the sonship being implied and thus first person dialogue being made easier. Further, the concept of Son of God is easier for the Gospel writers to present comfortably than is Son of Man. The model of father-son relationships is simple to work with and easier for most readers and listeners to comprehend. It is a comfortable idiom, unlike Son of Man (who is the father of the Son of Man? – a natural answer is not readily to hand). The personalization – the attachment of the construct Son of God – to Jesus is entirely successful.

The way this personalized concept is employed varies from book to book, and that is no failing: blurring, not definitional sharpness, is the way the "New Testament" achieves its interdigitation of major motifs. Thus, in the Synoptic Gospels, Jesus is presented as the Son of God, but it is never stated that he *is* God.[28] In contrast, the author of the Gospel of John presents Jesus as a divine figure: see, for example, John 1:9, where Jesus is the "true Light," which, for John, is the divine principle. In the Letter to the Hebrews, Jesus, as Son of God, becomes a divine being who has existed from before the creation of the world: the reverberations of "the Before-Time" of Enoch 48:2–7 are obvious. And in Revelation, the Son of God returns to help judge the earth.

That both Son of God and Son of Man are attached to Jesus means that these concepts become, if not synonyms, names for different facets of a phenomenon that the writers of the Christian scriptures find too large to denominate by a single name, too compelling to ignore. The author of Mark comes close to making an overt equation when he has Jesus say that the Son of Man would come again to earth "in the glory of his Father with the holy angels" (Mark 8:38). Since "Father" here refers to the Almighty, the Son of Man and the Son of God are, therefore, one. Wisely, Mark leaves the reader to draw this inference, for the employment of a full-fledged Greek-style syllogism would have been intrusive and disruptive of the narrative. In a similar fashion, the author of Revelation makes the equation, but expresses it only by implication. Early in the first vision that is ascribed to John, the author presents the Son of Man as having eyes "as a flame of fire," and feet "like unto fine brass" (Rev. 1:14 and 15). In a subsequent action, the Son of God has "eyes like unto a flame of fire, and his feet are like fine brass" (Rev. 2:18). The motifs meld together.

"Messiah" is the third component of this conceptual trinity. The author of Mark lays out the matter clearly when, in his very first verse, he refers to "Jesus Christ, the Son of God." This means: Jesus, Son of God and Messiah. And in the Gospel of John, Jesus is observed in a conversation with a Samaritan woman:

> The woman saith unto him, I know that Messias cometh, which is called Christ: when he is come, he will tell us all things.
> Jesus saith unto her, I that speak unto thee am he. (John 4:25–26)

So, throughout the "New Testament," Jesus is called Messiah (that is, Jesus Christ).

The terms "Jesus," "Messiah," "Son of Man," and "Son of God," all collapse into one iconic point, the historical person who was Yeshua of Nazareth. Theologians and biblical exigetes spend a great deal of time and effort trying to distinguish the possible differences between these terms. They delineate the contexts in which each phrase is most apt to be used and they attempt to draw out sub-texts that are not found in a narrative reading of the Christian scriptures. These are legitimate exercises, but they are valid only if one honours a prior understanding: that the writers of the Christian scriptures intended to implode these meanings, rather than to differentiate them. And the canon is constructed so that these individual meanings collapse in upon each other.

The concept of Messiah is central to this conceptual amalgam – "Jesus Christ" could easily have been translated as "Jesus Messiah," with "Messiah" effectively serving as a family name, so this is another instance of the Christian text's providing a very "strong reading" of the Hebrew scriptures: that is, a radical and compelling re-invention. As I discussed in Chapter Seven, section one, "Moshiah" in the Hebrew scriptures means "Anointed

One," and was used for kings, for high priests and, perhaps, for prophets. The idea of Moshiah as saviour or redeemer is totally absent in the "Old Testament." During the later Second Temple era, the term Moshiah was used with somewhat greater freedom and frequency. This was particularly true in the Dead Sea Scrolls where there are fleeting references to Moshiah as a vaguely eschatological figure. Moshiah thus became a recognizable figure in the rich and quickly-evolving world of pre-70 Judaism, but the Chosen People were not spending their time watching and waiting for his arrival.

Once the inventors of the Christian scriptures identified Yeshua of Nazareth as Messiah, a massive retro-reading of the Hebrew scriptures occurred. To many Christians, every "Old Testament" reference to an Anointed One became a foreshadowing of Jesus, the Messiah. In the next chapter, I shall provide some examples of how a nearly total re-invention of the Hebrew scriptures was forced forward by the writers of the Christian scriptures. Here one wishes to emphasize the importance of the major Christian invention which made all of the secondary inventions possible: the historical conceit that the Chosen People were awaiting Moshiah as their only hope of salvation. This ahistorical assertion makes possible the colonization, for Christian usage, of the Hebrew scriptures.

The conversion of the historical figure of Yeshua of Nazareth into the theological figure of Jesus Christ, occurs through the attachment to him of the three motifs of Son of God, Son of Man, and Messiah. But why bother? Could these ideas not remain on their own, operating as abstract entities, as they had done in the later Second Temple texts? Perhaps: but it is clear that the religious community for which the Christian texts were prepared desperately desired personification of religious ideas. One of the commonplace, yet shrewd, observations about the development of the Yahweh-faith is that it started out with a God who was convincingly anthropomorphic in many of his postures and reactions; and that, in the centuries running up to the Common Era, Yahweh became increasingly transcendent and true monotheism emerged. That trend is undeniable (compare the God of Genesis with that of the Wisdom literature) but as Yahweh came more and more to resemble an overarching and abstract principle, he simultaneously became much less satisfying to many (probably most) of the faithful. Thus, we observe in the parabiblical literature of the later Second Temple period, the invention of numerous active figures – angels, demons, and so on – who do many of the things that Yahweh used to do, including dealing with humankind. Collectively, they personify an otherwise abstract God. Jesus, in the Christian scriptures, is the counterpart of Yahweh in the Genesis-Kings portion of the Hebrew scriptures. He is a figure around whom one can build a great historical narrative. The justification for such historical (and perforce anthropomorphic) narratives, is that their inventors believe that any reader, any listener, will be able to understand that the light of something divine shines in the story, usually gently suffusing, sometimes intensely irradiating, it.

5

Given that the force of virtue is personified in Jesus Christ, it is natural that the side of evil should be personified, and also that the secondary agents of hope should also be personified. In this regard, the "New Testament" at times seems to be an aviary filled with spirit-creatures who have fluttered into its precincts from their original niches in Judahist writings from the pre-70 era. The angels and demons of the Books of Jubilee and of Enoch, and of the Dead Sea Scrolls, are found in abundance. The angels are the emissaries of the Almighty, the demons the servants of Satan.

This master-figure, Satan, whom we encountered emerging in later Second Temple writings, is crucial. The "New Testament" really depends on him as much as it depends on Jesus. The author-editor(s) of Mark, for example, begins with the baptism of Jesus by John the Baptist. This is concluded by a dove descending from heaven, "And there came a voice from heaven saying, Thou art my beloved son, in whom I am well pleased" (Mark 1:11). Immediately thereafter, the Son of God goes into the wilderness where he is tempted by Satan for forty days and forty nights (Mark 1:13) – a period of time that harkens to the forty years the children of Israel spent wandering in the wilderness. That set of personifications – Jesus versus Satan – runs through the entire Christian corpus. "Satan, although he seldom appears on stage in these gospel accounts, nevertheless plays a central role in the divine drama," Elaine Pagels notes, "for the gospel writers realize that the story they have to tell would make little sense without Satan."[29] Or, to put it less gently: no Satan, no Jesus.

Satan and Jesus battle in dozens of different arenas in biblical book after book. Sometimes the battle is on this earth; at other times, as in the apocalyptic segments of the gospels and in Revelation, it is cosmic. Norman Cohn summarizes these battles with lapidary brevity. "In the Synoptic gospels, Jesus fights Satan by reducing his servants, the demons, to impotence. In Revelation, he fights Satan by destroying his creation, the Roman empire."[30]

Three supernatural characteristics are attributed to Jesus by the "New Testament" writers. One of these – his reported resurrection from the dead, in a transcendent, not physical, sense – is a logical outgrowth of the ideas which the writers took from the shelf of Second Temple Judaism. The other two, the Virgin Birth (which is not accepted or attested by most of the "New Testament" documents) and the physical resurrection, are the only important motifs attached to Yeshua of Nazareth whose provenance is not situated in the Judaism of the late Second Temple era. Let us reserve for Chapter Nine the matter of the Virgin Birth and the corporeal resurrection, and here look at the spiritual resurrection with a view to seeing why it merges so well into the fabric of symbol and image that loops from one segment of the Christian scripture into another.

The spiritual, transcendent resurrection of Jesus makes sense from a narrative viewpoint, because it was the last domino in a sequence. The sequence began with the picking up, and complete re-invention, of an idea that had been little used in either the ancient Yahweh-faith or in late Second Temple Judahism: the concept of the Kingdom of God, sometimes referred to as the Kingdom of Heaven. As we saw in Chapter Seven (section three), the concept is present only in two instances in the Tanakh. Further, in the para-biblical religious inventions of late Second Temple times, it was little used, and then muddily, and it was not yet bonded to the idea of Messiah or to the genre of apocalypse. One of the indications of the inventive genius of the strands of Judahism that eventually became Christianity is that the potential of this ideational unit was recognized first by the Apostle Paul, then by the Four Evangelists, and, finally, by the author of the Book of Revelation.[31] E.P. Sanders points out that the Gospels ascribe to Jesus' usage six different meanings of "Kingdom of Heaven": the Kingdom is the transcendent realm of heaven; it is the transcendent realm of heaven which will in future come to earth; the Kingdom is a future realm that will be introduced by a cosmic event; it is a vague future kingdom of virtually no specificity; the Kingdom is a special realm on earth; it is a kingdom that is present immediately on earth in Jesus' own ministry.[32] Which one (or more) of these versions is the proper one is one of the liveliest areas of Christological debate; and which one (or more, if any) represents Jesus' own views is the fountainhead of a massive amount of historical-critical writing by "New Testament" scholars. However, both of these major controversies are here moot: from the viewpoint of how the Christian scriptures interdigitate, as an historical narrative that climaxes in an apocalypse, there is only one form that really counts. This is the Kingdom of God as the Kingdom-to-come, brought in as an apocalyptic event at the end of time. From the viewpoint of historical story-telling, it makes no sense to have a Kingdom of God concept, if it is to be surpassed by something that comes later.

So, as part of the interdigitation of motifs that link the books of the Christian scripture, the Kingdom of God is (a) tied to the concept of Messiah, which automatically means it is melded to the concept of Son of God and Son of Man and to the personification of these ideas in Jesus; then (b), the Kingdom of God is blurred together with a motif that had been highly developed in later Second Temple times, namely the apocalyptic depictions of the endtimes. The richness of apocalyptic thought that runs through the Books of Daniel, Jubilees, and Enoch, and through scores of documents that we know only in fragments, packs a kinetic energy of seismic proportion when it is conjoined to Jesus, Messiah, Son of God, and Son of Man. This occurs, for example, in Matthew (chapter 24), Mark (chapter 13), Luke (chapter 21) and in the Apocalypse of St. John, to name only the main instances.

That is the first step to the transcendent resurrection. The second involves joining to it an idea that was increasingly common (though far from universal) in Second Temple para-biblical writings, the idea that the Almighty would judge not only nations, but also would judge individuals, once their lives' course was run. In the para-biblical literature we find individuals being raised after their physical deaths to stand before the Ancient of Days, or the Before-Time, or a similar figure, and there they were sorted out for all eternity, the righteous from the unrighteous. Jesus (the Son of God, the Son of Man, the Messiah) becomes in the Christian scripture a figure who, by his return to earth, begins the end-times; and he also becomes both the principle and the judge by which the resurrected souls are adjudicated.

Now, the third step is an obvious one, but like a small detail in the plot of a mystery novel, it is one that cannot be funked – and the Christian writers were too shrewd to do so. If Jesus, in his several guises, is to be the agent who brings on the end-times and is also the principle by which the souls of the dead are adjudged, he must himself not be subject to the dominion of death. Nothing works if he is. For reasons of what could vulgarly be called "plotting" or, more accurately, for reasons of narrative coherence, Jesus had to overcome death. Without the resurrection, the "New Testament" would not hold together.

To note this is not to indicate in any way whether the resurrection of Yeshua of Nazareth occurred or even whether the disciples actually thought he rose physically from the dead. My observation is belief-neutral. The point here is that the way the re-invention of late Second Temple Judahist material is accomplished in the Christian scriptures forces the inclusion of the transcendent, spiritual resurrection of Jesus, whether or not it actually occurred.

Similarly, in my earlier discussion of the way in which Son of God, Son of Man, Messiah were merged into a personification, I was not making any judgement concerning whether or not Yeshua of Nazareth considered himself to be any, or all of these things; or whether his disciples believed such things about him. That is a separate matter from our present task, which is to gain an understanding of how, as an historical narrative, the Christian scriptures, composed for the most part after the destruction of the Jerusalem Temple, presented the life of a Judahist religious leader who had lived at a time when the disappearance of Yahweh's Temple was a possibility very difficult to conceive.

6

The Temple, indeed, is a (perhaps *the*) central motif of the "New Testament," but unlike all the other major elements, it is conspicuous by its

absence. It is comparable to Banquo's ghost in *Macbeth*, the driving force
that is mostly unseen. When glimpsed, it is slightly beyond the ghostly
Pale. The void left by the Temple is the reason there had to be a "New
Testament."

Re-inventing the Temple was nothing new in the later Second Temple era
(see Chapter Six, section four). There had been four distinct physical temples
in the years between the Maccabean revolt and 70 CE (two of them heterodox, admittedly). Moreover, as the Temple Scroll of the Qumran caves
proves, and as the smaller document, the Description of the New Jerusalem,
confirms, it was perfectly natural to think in terms of new Temples, ones that
could replace the present one, either in this world or at the end of time. Therefore, when the writers of the Christian scriptures re-invented the Temple, they
were working within pre-existing Judahist thought patterns. Crucially, however, whereas the Temple proposed in the Temple Scroll actually could have
been built on this earth (the architectural contours were within human possibilities), the Temple that the Christian scriptures proposes could not be. This
had immense implications for the later development of Christianity, for that
faith was never limited to a Promised Land found on this earth. This freedom
from the geographic specificity which the planning and building of an earthly
Temple would have entailed, made it possible for Christianity to circumnavi-
gate the globe in a way that the site-anchored descendants of Judahism never
possessed. By moving Jerusalem and the Temple from real-time and from the
physical world, to the end-times and to the spiritual world, Christianity
simultaneously re-invented and rejected the spatial and temporal coordinates
of the ancient Yahwist faith.

Crucially, the writers of the three Synoptic Gospels each showed an awareness of the fact that the Jerusalem Temple had been destroyed. Each has Jesus
"predict" that the Temple will be destroyed. "There shall not be left here one
stone upon another, that shall not be thrown down," is Matthew's formulation
(Matt. 24:2). The author of Mark has Jesus saying, "Seest thou these great
buildings? there shall not be left one stone upon another, that shall not be
thrown down" (Mark 13:2). And the author of Luke formulates Jesus' "prediction" slightly more fully:

> And as some spake of the temple, how it was adorned with goodly stones and gifts,
> he said
> As for these things which ye behold, the days will come, in which there shall not
> be left one stone upon another, that shall not be thrown down.   (Luke 21:6)

Obviously these three passages depend upon a common source, one which
was framed by someone who was all too aware that the Temple had been destroyed.[33] Crucially each author-editor chose to endorse the interpretive

framework that they had inherited from later Second Temple Judahism, namely an apocalyptic schema. In each case, the "prediction" by Jesus is enclosed in a pericope that is clearly apocalyptic; these are the "little apocalypses" of Matthew 24, Mark 13, and Luke 21, each of which resonates very strongly with the Apocalypse of St. John.

The full logic for replacing the Jerusalem Temple with one that cannot be destroyed is worked out in the Book of Revelation. There, a new heaven and a new earth finally replace this present, corrupt world; a New Jerusalem descends from heaven, "prepared as a bride adorned for her husband" (Rev. 21:2). The New Jerusalem is described in loving, but humanly unrealizable detail. It is a four-square city (is there an influence here from the Temple Scroll?) with walls of jasper; the city proper is made of pure gold. Yet "John," who recounts this vision, notes an amazing omission. "I saw no temple therein" (Rev. 21:22a).[34]

Keep that phrase in mind for just a moment, for the author of Revelation is on the verge of articulating Christianity's resolution of the fundamental problem faced by all branches of Judaism after the events of 70 CE: how to have a Temple religion without a Temple.

He does this by throwing out a new character, yet one that is not at all new: "the Lamb" or "the Lamb of God." This icon springs from two sources, one within the "New Testament" narrative and one exterior to it. The immediate origin is the Gospel of John, where Jesus' encounter with John the Baptist begins as follows:

> The next day John seeth Jesus coming unto him, and saith, Behold the Lamb of God, which taketh away the sin of the world. (John 1:29)

That is a fairly passive presentation of the Lamb: he is announced by the Baptist and does not engage in self-assertion. The second, more distant course includes a more aggressive element. This is the vision of sheep and lambs as forceful actors found in late Second Temple Judahist apocalyptic imagery. There they are capable of wielding swords and of using them murderously. This idea, which we discussed in Chapter Seven, is found in the Dream Vision portion of the Book of Enoch (Chapters 83–90) and, since Enoch was a widely disseminated volume, it probably was known to the author-editor of Revelation. The Lamb appears twenty-nine times in the Book of Revelation, mostly as a very tough, apocalyptically active figure.

Near the end of the Apocalypse of John – in the last two chapters – the Lamb becomes the answer to the problem raised when, in surveying the New Jerusalem, the author reported "I saw no temple therein."

> *"For the Lord God Almighty and the Lamb are the temple of it"* (Rev. 21:22b).

Yahweh and the Lamb of God (a synonym for Son of God, for Son of Man, for Messiah and for Jesus) are the Temple. The visible and terminable Temple has been replaced by the invisible, cosmic, and eternal Jesus and his father. The Temple is no longer of this world, but transcends it.

The Temple had been a place of sacrifice, of ritual slaughter for holy purposes, so now Jesus becomes the one-time, for-all-of-time sacrificial victim, the Lamb that takes away the sins of the whole world. The idea of Jesus as the ultimate Temple sacrifice emerged within Christianity prior to the destruction of the Jerusalem Temple. (See, for example, Paul's stating that the faithful were "justified by his blood," in Romans 5:9.) However, that it would have become the dominant theme of the "New Testament" is not clear. The Temple's destruction forced the idea forward, urgently, and made possible the idea's being taken to its logical extreme: the idea that Yahweh and Jesus together are the Temple.

Now, by the standards of the philosophical tradition that has its roots in Greek thought, none of this makes any sense. One needs only recall how, for example, Aristotle worked so patiently at disentangling meanings, at developing categories of description that do not overlap and do not blur meaning. Recall how his successors, the first real logicians, worked at rooting out contradictions of meaning. The "New Testament" is a self-confident thumb in the eye of that tradition, a thoroughly Judahist rejection of such modes of thought. The contradiction between Jesus' being both a victim, sacrificed, and also the Son of God who shares the omnipotence of the Almighty, is obvious. The incompatibility of his being both the sacrifice on the altar and, with his Father, the Temple itself is clear. The declarations that he is both dead and alive are difficult to reconcile.

The authors and editors of the "New Testament" would not care a fig for such pettifogging. Nor should we, for such objections ignore the way the Christian scriptures work. As I indicated earlier in discussing the multiple identities of Jesus – Jesus, Messiah, Son of God, Son of Man – crucial concepts blur into each other. Implosion of meaning, not particulation of belief is intended. Similarly, the logical contradictions in the Christian scriptures' "soteriology" (the doctrine of salvation) are irrelevant, for the text forces us to embrace both sides of the bilateral meanings: Jesus as sacrificial victim and as Son of the Omnipotent God. The collapse of nomenclature and the union of contradictions is similar in effect to the implosion of a supernova. As it pulls meanings into itself, it acquires nearly infinite density and immense energy.

Some of the most effective usage of apparent dissonance of meaning occurs when the "New Testament" writers invent analogies to events in the "Old Testament" which are just slightly off-target. The most important of these is an analogy that is so strong as to go mostly unspoken: that Yahweh is to Jesus as Abraham was to Isaac. In each case, the relationship is of father and son, and in each instance the father is asked to shed his son's blood; and in each case the son is willing to be the sacrificial victim. The difference, though, is crucial. Isaac's blood was not spilled on the altar; Jesus' was. This looks at first, then, to be an imperfect analogy, and it is: but it is a perfect carrier of meaning, for it provides an implicit foundation for the concept of a new and better Covenant. The Covenant with the Chosen People is implicitly devalued and that with Christians is privileged, because Abraham's beloved son was not actually sacrificed, but Yahweh's beloved son actually was.

Similarly, when Jesus is identified as being the Passover Lamb (as in 1 Cor. 5:7–8, where "Christ our passover is sacrificed for us"), the analogy seems slightly skewed. One can readily see how the Passover celebration of the exodus from Egypt by the children of Israel and the escape from sin and bondage by Jesus' followers are conceptually parallel. But it is hard to forget that Passover in part celebrates an event that did *not* happen – the slaying of the first-born of every Israelite household – while the Christian scriptures (and, later, the Christian liturgy in its Eucharist) celebrates a slaying that did happen: the death of Jesus who is identified as God's only son. The covert meaning, therefore, is clear: our Christian Passover is superior, because it is based on real sacrifice, not sacrifice averted.

The articulation of a "New Covenant" was the product of the intricately interdigitated symbols and motifs that tumble from one book of the "New Testament" to another. The New Covenant, which replaces the ancient Hebrew covenant and its variations in the several Judaisms of the late Second Temple era, is a truly great invention, the more so because it employed almost entirely as structural elements items that were already part of the conceptual world of Second Temple Judaism. Some of these components were obscure, to be sure, but they were there, ready to be used.

The New Covenant constructed by the people who became known as "Christians," differed from the ancient covenant between Yahweh and the Chosen People in signal ways. The Christian covenant was centred on an invisible and eternal Temple, rather than a visible and temporal one; its sacrificial system as defined in the "New Testament" was not daily or on-going, but a one-time event.[35]

· 9 ·

From Yeshua of Nazareth to Jesus the Christ

I

THE "NEW TESTAMENT" IS A WONDERFULLY SUCCESSFUL UNITY ON three separate levels. Two of these we have already observed: the fundamental architecture of the canon and the body of motifs and symbols, mostly taken from late Second Temple Judaism, that interdigitate between the several books of the Christian scriptures. The third plane of artistic and conceptual unity of the Christian history is a matter of harmonics. The Christian scriptures continually re-invent the Tanakh. This is a matter not only of obvious referrals to major "Old Testament" texts, but also of thousands of little details, of seemingly throw-away references that are not as casual as they appear. They refer the reader (or listener) to passages in the Hebrew scriptures, and in almost every case, a Christian re-invention of the original meaning occurs. Some of the inventions are big, involving the reshaping, through textual torsion, of a major Tanakh text so that it obtains a new meaning. Only a few of the more important of these Christian re-inventions of ancient texts will be discussed here. One prefatory point should be clear, however: that the re-invention of ancient Hebrew texts by the author-editors of the "New Testament" was in no way heretical within Judaism. It was not an original exercise. The Christian authors proceeded according to the grammar of biblical invention which we have been observing throughout this book.

The most recent catechism of the Roman Catholic church (1992) states that Christians should:

> read the Old Testament in the light of Christ crucified and risen. Such typological reading discloses the inexhaustible content of the Old Testament; but it must not make us forget that the Old Testament retains its own intrinsic values as Revelation reaffirmed by our Lord himself. Besides, the New Testament has to be read in the light of the Old. Early Christian catechesis made constant use of the Old Testament. *As an old saying put it, the New Testament lies hidden in the Old and the Old Testament is unveiled in the New.* [emphasis added][1]

That is a modern statement of how the Catholic church wishes the Tanakh and the Christian scriptures to be read; however, with a small leap of the imagination, it could be turned into a placard that every "New Testament" author or editor had hanging over his bench, for it is nothing less than the basic instructions on how to re-invent the Hebrew scriptures so that they become Christian documents. On that placard, the phrase that I have emphasized would have been carefully highlighted, the lettering of the directive illuminated with the tones of some vivid pigment: *the New Testament lies hidden in the Old and the Old Testament is unveiled in the New.*

How that principle of composition operated is nicely illustrated in the way the "Suffering Servant" of Second Isaiah (that is, of Isaiah 40–55) was transmuted into Jesus Christ. In the English language alone, literally hundreds of books have been written on the Suffering Servant, and not surprisingly: for the Suffering Servant passages are examples of those instances of high ambiguity, so frequent in the Hebrew prophets, in which over-heated orators are prone to scatter solipsisms like sprays of saliva, and thus it is a perfect opening for Christian re-invention. On the surface, Second Isaiah is a fairly simple attempt to encourage those reluctant exiles who still remained in Babylon in the later sixth (and perhaps fifth) century BCE to come home to Jerusalem. Its final editing took place after 538 BCE, for King Cyrus of Persia, who encouraged the return to Jerusalem and who aided the building of the Second Temple is mentioned: indeed, Yahweh says, "He is my shepherd, and shall perform all my pleasure" (Is. 44:28). Strikingly, King Cyrus is called "Yahweh's Moshiah" (Is. 45:1, Hebrew text). The Suffering Servant is not given this title. Thus, the fact that "Moshiah" is employed here in relation to a pagan king reminds us that "Messiah" in the Hebrew scriptures referred to kings, prophets, and high priests, but never to a Messiah in the sense of a redemptive figure. In the original text, the Suffering Servant and Messiah are in no way related concepts.

Had Second Isaiah been solely an hortatory exercise, encouraging the reluctant Judahites to return home from the security of the "Babylonian Exile," to the dust and poverty of Jerusalem, the text would be mostly of historical interest, and Christian writers probably would not have made much use of it. However, Second Isaiah provided a splendid opportunity for Christian re-invention, because its scolding prose is interrupted by four songs, or poems, or psalms, that stand out sharply from the rest of the book. These are the Servant Songs – Isaiah 42:1–4; 49:1–6; 50:4–9; and 52:13 to 53:12).[2] Whether they are by a different author than is the rest of Second Isaiah or whether they fit so awkwardly with their surrounding texts simply because the song-genre is not skilfully melded with the prose segments, is a matter of continuing debate among biblical scholars. For our purposes, this does not matter, for each of the four Servant Songs are closely related to each other and can be read contiguously. They were very easy to yank out of context and to make into a Christian text.

The Christian re-inventors here faced two difficulties. The first is that Moshiah does not appear in any of the Servant Songs. Thus, in claiming that the Suffering Servant was not just a Messiah-figure, but a precise pre-figuring of Jesus, they have to adopt what becomes standard procedure in Christian re-inventions of the Hebrew scriptures, namely to ignore the usage of Moshiah that the Tanakh employs (to refer to anointed prophets, kings, high priests and, in Second Isaiah, even to King Cyrus of Persia) and to declare passages to be "Messianic" wherein the word itself is not used, and where, therefore, there is no context to limit what inventive writers can declare Moshiah to be. And, secondly, the Christian re-inventors encounter the elaborate personification of the Servant Songs which, despite its rhetorical richness, is highly ambiguous. The songs leave the reader with no conclusive idea of who the Suffering Servant is meant to be – a point readily confirmed by even a glance at the acrimonious modern scholarly literature on this matter. This ambiguity required that the inventors of the Christian texts should proceed with an apparent confidence that far exceeds their knowledge, the way a parent sometimes confidently explains a phenomenon to one of his or her children, despite not being any too sure of the strength of the case.

Observe how the Christian re-invention turns the Servant into a foreshadowment of Jesus Christ, as Messiah and as Lamb of God. Take the first of the Servant Songs, Isaiah 42:1–4, and compare it to its primary (although not exclusive) re-invention in the Gospel of Matthew, 12:14–21:

Yahweh says in Isaiah:	It is reported of Jesus:
	Then the Pharisees went out, and held a council against him, how they might destroy him.
	But when Jesus knew it, he withdrew himself from thence: and great multitudes followed him, and he healed them all;
	And charged them that they should not make him known:
	That it might be fulfilled which was spoken by Esaias [Isaiah] the prophet, saying,
Behold my servant, whom I uphold: mine elect, in whom my soul delighteth; I have put my spirit upon him: he shall bring forth judgment to the Gentiles.	Behold my servant, whom I have chosen; my beloved, in whom my soul is well pleased: I will put my spirit upon him, and he shall shew judgment to the Gentiles.

He shall not cry, nor lift up, nor cause his voice to be heard in the street.	He shall not strive, nor cry; neither shall any man hear his voice in the streets.
A bruised reed shall he not break, and the smoking flax shall he not quench: he shall bring forth judgment unto truth.	A bruised reed shall he not break, and smoking flax shall he not quench, till he send forth judgment unto victory.
He shall not fail nor be discouraged, till he have set judgment in the earth: and the isles shall wait for his law.	And in his name shall the Gentiles trust.

The Second Servant Song (Isaiah 49:1–6) is much less promising for Christian writers because it contains within it two identifications of the Suffering Servant, one of which definitely cannot be applied to Jesus. This is Yahweh's statement that "thou art my servant, o Israel, in whom I will be glorified" (Is. 49:3). Vexingly, the identification of Israel as the Servant is then quickly contradicted and seemingly another personification of the Servant appears. This one is exterior to Israel, for Yahweh says, "It is a light thing that thou shouldest be my servant to raise up the tribes of Jacob and to restore the preserved of Israel" (Is. 49:6a). Faced with such an unpromising text – one of the two identifications of the Suffering Servant clearly is the Chosen People as a corporate entity – Christian authors avoided using the passage as a whole. However, one of the gentlest of phrases in the song – "I will also give thee for a light to the Gentiles, that thou mayest be my salvation unto the end of the earth" (Is. 49:6b) – is placed by the author-editor of Luke in the mouth of Simeon, a devout Jew who, at the time of Jesus' birth and circumcision was "waiting for the consolation of Israel" (Luke 2:25). Simeon is told by the Holy Ghost that he will live to see Yahweh's Moshiah. The Holy Spirit leads him to the Temple where Jesus is being brought by Joseph and Mary after his circumcision. Simeon takes Jesus in his arms and then filled with emotion, praises Yahweh:

> Lord, now lettest thou thy servant depart in peace, according to thy word:
> For mine eyes have seen thy salvation,
> Which thou hast prepared before the face of all people;
> A light to lighten the Gentiles, and the glory of thy people Israel.   (Luke 2:29–32)

That becomes one of Christianity's great shared prayers, the *Nunc Dimittis*. By placing the words of Second Isaiah in the mouth of a gentle old man who is holding the infant Jesus in his arms, the possibility indicated in the original song, that the Servant might not be an individual but might be the nation of Israel, disappears. The stagecraft is just too strong.

The third Servant Song (Is. 50:4–9) is the least fruitful for the Christian re-inventors of the Hebrew scriptures, not because of its ambiguity of personification (the Servant here could be either Israel or could be a specific individual; that problem was overcome readily enough in the song just discussed), but rather because it is weak pictorially. It does contain one vivid verse, however:

> I gave my back to the smiters, and my cheeks to them that plucked off the hair:
> I hid not my face from shame and spitting.   (Is. 50:6)

And that verse is assimilated to the description of Jesus before the high priest:

> Then did they spit in his face, and buffeted him; and others smote him with the
> palms of their hands.   (Matt. 26:67)

It is the fourth Servant Song (Is. 52:13–53:12) that is the treasure trove for the "New Testament" authors. There the Servant is a redemptive figure – "he bare the sins of many and made intercession for the transgressors" (Is. 53:12). The Servant is an innocent sacrificial victim, "brought as a lamb to the slaughter" (Is. 53:7). This entire song is highly quotable and it is a restatement of the basic liturgical act and expiatory doctrine of the Yahweh-faith: that the sacrifice of an innocent animal life, if conducted in the proper ritual setting, leads to the expiation of sins.

The context within which this fourth Servant Song is set is a paean to Zion, and especially to Jerusalem, so if one reads the poem in that context, the meaning is that Israel, through its sufferings, will redeem the world. This is a doctrine that comes to the fore in later Jewish history (the Holocaust is sometimes theologized in this manner), and such a reading is not outré. On the other hand, it must be pointed out that all four of the Servant Songs seem to float free of their immediate prose context and, further, despite this context of Jerusalem and Zion, within the fourth song itself there is no clear indication as to whom the Suffering Servant personifies.

The Christian writers betray no doubts on this matter. Their apparent certainty is reflected in a story in the Book of Acts that is almost cinematic in the way it imparts information within the context of the action: the story of the Ethiopian eunuch. This eunuch was a major court official, the nation's treasurer, and was returning from worshipping at the Jerusalem Temple when he encountered the apostle Philip. This was after the death of Jesus. The treasurer rode along in his chariot, his driver keeping the pace slow so that the official could read. Philip ran up to the slow-moving chariot and asked the eunuch if he understood what he was reading? No, he did not, and he asked Philip to take a seat beside him, so that they could talk as the chariot slowly bumped along the dusty road. The portion of scripture that particularly perplexed the Ethiopian treasurer was Isaiah 53:7 and 8:

The place of the scripture which he read was this. He was led as a sheep to the slaughter; and like a lamb dumb before his shearer, so opened he not his mouth:
In his humiliation his judgment was taken away; and who shall declare his generation? for his life is taken from the earth.
And the eunuch answered Philip, and said, I pray thee of whom speaketh the prophet this, of himself, or of some other man? (Acts 8:32–34)

The answer is quick and unambiguous:

Then Philip opened his mouth, and began at the same scripture and preached unto him Jesus. (Acts 8:35)

Notice how successfully this transaction obviates two interpretive problems with the verses in question. First, by having the eunuch frame the question of the identity of the Suffering Servant in a false dichotomy – is it the Servant Isaiah or is it another individual? – the narrative is already past the point of difficulty, the possibility that the Suffering Servant is a collective reference to the Chosen People. This is a subtle stroke, the sign of a really gifted writer, for the stickiest point of the whole question, the bump where the chariot could have overturned, is passed before Philip gives his answer: Jesus. And, secondly, the Christian re-invention of Isaiah's text gets rid of a potentially awkward plural. In the Hebrew scriptures, the concluding phrase of Isaiah 53:8 employs what may (or may not be) an ambiguous plural. That is, it is possible to read the concluding phrase as saying "for the transgression of my people *was he* stricken" or, with equal grammatical probability, that "for the transgression of my people *were they* stricken" (emphasis mine). This issue is by-passed entirely in the dialogue of Philip and the Ethiopian eunuch. In all the influential modern Christian translations of Isaiah, the issue is settled by rendering the ambiguous plural in the singular.[3]

These tiny textual problems, however, are lost, like whirls of dust behind the Ethiopian chariot, as Philip's answer triumphs: Jesus. Once again, the stagecraft of the Christian re-inventors of the Hebrew text is too powerful to be resisted.

The fourth Servant Song is woven in and out of the "New Testament." A single example will suffice. Note the portions of Isaiah 53 and its usage in First Peter:

Isaiah 53:	1 Peter 2:
He is despised and rejected of men. (v.3)	Who, when he was reviled, reviled not again. (v.23)
With his stripes we are healed (v.5)	By whose stripes ye were healed. (v.24)

All we like sheep have gone astray. (v.6)	For ye were as sheep going astray; but are now returned unto the Shepherd and Bishop of your souls. (v.25)
He had done no violence, neither was any deceit in his mouth. (v.9)	Who did no sin, neither was guilt found in his mouth. (v.22)
He bare the sin of many, and made intercession for the transgressors. (v.12)	Who his own self bare our sins in his body on the tree. (v.24)

Save for the Psalms, the Book of Isaiah is the most frequently quoted Hebrew source in the "New Testament," and that is because so much of Isaiah, and especially the Suffering Servant figure, can be re-oriented so as to point to the Christian Messiah. In the case of the Servant Songs, the cumulative and direct effect of their employment is as important as is the aggregate of their direct references. The Suffering Servant comes to suffuse the entire "New Testament": Christian writers (and Christian readers and listeners) approached Yeshua of Nazareth with a set of background assumptions in which the Suffering Servant set many of the most important parameters. The Suffering Servant was, therefore, both a source for the Christian re-invention of the Hebrew scriptures and a set of limitations on that re-invention. One could not attach to Yeshua of Nazareth any behaviours or utterances that would be dissonant with the character of the Suffering Servant, the Lamb of Second Isaiah.

Crucially, the Suffering Servant passage serves as fulcrum for the most fundamental part of the Christian retro-reading of the Hebrew scripture: it permits a massive re-interpretation of the mechanics of sacrifice of the Yahweh faith. By the time the Yahweh-belief assumed written form, there were in its rubrics only vestigial indications of human sacrifice possibly having once been part of the faith (see Chapter Two); the Christian faith re-introduces it, on a once-for-all basis. The Suffering Servant is taken to be an innocent martyr, a sacrificial lamb led to the slaughter, the perpetual propitiation for human sins. This is possible for, as the catechism says, the "New Testament" is found hidden in the "Old," and the "Old" is unveiled in the "New."

Coincidentally – but not accidentally – employment of the Servant icon from Isaiah permitted first-century Christians to turn a cultural corner and to do so with ease. The words "servant" and "child" are distinct in Hebrew, but in Greek they are the same. So, when someone, such as Paul, who did much of his preaching in Greek, spoke of Jesus as being the servant of God, and, being male, a son of God, a natural conjoining of meaning – bringing together the servant of God and the son of God – creates what has been called "the magnifying effect of early Christology."[4]

This allowed Christianity in the years prior to the destruction of the Temple when there was a strong Jewish-Christian community, to effect the cultural equivalent of a two-horse parlay: being one thing to the Judahists and another to the pagans. The mordant skeptic and corrosive satirist Gore Vidal, who, whatever his own beliefs may be, is very well read in biblical scholarship, has the Apostle Paul, as observed by his acolyte Timothy, explaining such matters to James, brother of Jesus: "It's a matter of translation, really. In Greek, the language I use when I speak to the goyim, *pais* means servant. *Pais* also means child. When I say that Jesus was the servant of God, as He most definitely was, I am also saying that He is the *son* of God. Greek-speakers work out my meaning."[5] Timothy continues: "James was thoroughly tied in knots. But of course, he was right. Saint [Paul] had been changing the whole show. By always using "pais" he was actually telling the Greek-speaking-goyim that Jesus was the Son of God, but then, when accused of blasphemy by the Jews, he'd bat his eyes and say that he was only using the word "pais" for servant."[6]

The way the Suffering Servant of the Hebrew scriptures is re-invented in the "New Testament" is worth close attention, because it shows how finite texts can be borrowed, re-interpreted, and expanded. Other parts of the Tanakh are re-invented by Christians in the same way, although none of these is so important in terms of substantive beliefs as are the Servant Songs of Isaiah. Most of the hundreds and hundreds of "New Testament" borrowings and re-writings of Hebrew texts are tiny re-jiggings of old components to make them perform new functions. Equally important, however, is the cumulative effect of each little detail: scarcely a verse of the "New Testament" lacks a precursor in the Hebrew scriptures. The Tanakh was the lexicon of "New Testament" religious invention, and even when expressing ideas that were alien to the Hebrew scriptures, the "New Testament" writers employed the vocabulary, the iconography, and the rhythms of ancient writers. Strikingly, this held true both for writers who were Judahist in their upbringing (such as the Apostle Paul) and those who, according to most indications, were Gentile (such as the author of the Gospel of Luke). The result of the thousands of tiny resonances between the "Old Testament" and the "New" is that the two entities become part of one vast harmonic instrument. When either one is energized, row after row of tiny tuning forks vibrate and set off sympathetic vibrations across the river of time, in the other canon, Hebrew or Christian, as the case may be.

2

Except for two matters.

One of these is the *physical* resurrection of Jesus and his appearance in bodily form to some of his disciples, after his death.

This is a very awkward matter for the several author-editors of the "New Testament," for the idea has no resonance either in the Hebrew scriptures or in the para-biblical writings of the later Second Temple period. In none of the

thirty-eight references in the Hebrew scriptures to Moshiah is there any suggestion of Moshiah's dying and then coming back from the dead to the physical
world. Neither is there any such reference in the para-biblical texts of the later
Second Temple days. Geza Vermes summarizes the situation clearly: "The notion of a risen Messiah seems to be unknown in extant ancient Jewish literature.
Hence there can be no question of the fulfilment of a traditional expectation."[7]

Yet, as I argued in Chapter Eight, the logic of the historical narrative of the
"New Testament" requires that Jesus overcome death in some sense: given
that the Christian scriptures adopt the late Second Temple Judahist idea of a
general resurrection, and given that Jesus is defined as the sacrifice for sin,
and also as the ultimately-victorious Son of God, he had to be presented as
overcoming death. Belief in Jesus' victory over death presented no problems
either of personal belief or of narrative logic for the "New Testament" writers. The problems it presented were technical: (1) in what sense, the author-
editors had to ask themselves, did Jesus overcome death? and (2) since there
are no true harmonics between the idea of a resurrected Moshiah and the Hebrew scriptures, or in the para-biblical writings of the Second Temple era,
then how were they to obscure this anechoic moment, in what is otherwise a
sonorous and richly resonant religious invention?

These difficult technical issues explain the equivocal nature of the descriptions and interpretations of the resurrection of Jesus that characterize the
Christian scriptures. Unlike so many other matters in the "New Testament"
the indecision on the resurrection is not an instance of an intentional blurring
of meaning (whereby the item gains force, through implosion of connotation), but of outright fumbling.

The first known Christian writer to put down in writing the belief that Jesus
rose from the dead was the Apostle Paul, all of whose authentic epistles (as
distinct from the letters to Timothy, Titus, and perhaps Ephesians, Colossians, and Thessalonians which may be pseudepigraphic) were formulated before the destruction of the Second Temple. Paul is absolutely unequivocal
that the resurrection of Jesus is the central event of the Christian story. In
First Corinthians, chapter fifteen, Paul provides what is probably his (and,
therefore, Christianity's) earliest account of the resurrection. This account affirms that Jesus died for "our sins," that he was buried and rose again on the
third day.[8] He was seen by Cephas (one of the twelve apostles) and after that
by 500 of his followers simultaneously. After that Jesus was seen by James
(his brother) and then by all of the apostles. "and last of all he was seen of me
also, as one born out of due time" (1 Cor. 15:8).

Paul's story in 1 Corinthians 15:1–8 is remarkable in many ways. Its matter-of-fact tone is singular. There are none of the histrionics that characterize
the Gospels' reports of the resurrection. It happened, Paul says, and then he
builds thereupon an entire theological system. The spiritual implication, not

the details of the resurrection, is where Paul wants to focus his readers' attention. And, secondly, note what is not included in Paul's account: any indication of the nature of the resurrection, physical, or in some sense, spiritual. All
of those people Paul refers to saw something, but was it Jesus in the flesh or a
vision of Jesus as a risen spirit? Paul does not say.

But remember that Paul had been a serious enemy of Christianity and, further, at the time of the death of Yeshua of Nazareth, Paul was not one of the
company of believers. Yet, Paul draws no distinction between his seeing
Jesus and the experience of the others. All the believing witnesses (and, according to Paul's account, it is only believers who see the risen Jesus) had
seen the same figure. Paul, in his own writings, does not provide any direct
information about his own experience of encountering the resurrected
Moshiah. However, the author of the Book of Acts narrates that, within a year
or two of Jesus' death, when Paul, as part of his anti-Christian crusade, is on
a journey to Damascus, he has a vision of Jesus, sheathed in light from
heaven. Paul and the risen Jesus converse briefly, and thereafter Paul becomes a Christian and an enthusiastic proselytizer (Acts 9:1–11). The textual
bridging here is obvious enough: Paul's own account in First Corinthians
makes no distinction between his own experience of the resurrected Jesus and
that of the other disciples, and in Acts it is clear that he encounters a visual
embodiment of the spiritually resurrected Jesus, but not a physically resurrected human being. If one accepts this textual bridge, then it implies that
Paul's own view was that he and the other disciples had encountered a spiri-
tually-raised Christ, but not a physically resurrected Yeshua.

If that bridging between biblical books makes one nervous, it can be laid to
the side: for even without using the material from Acts, a minimal point of interpretative certitude emerges: nowhere in his writings does Paul indicate a
belief in the physical resurrection of Jesus. That is beyond argument. Moreover, within Paul's writings, there is a distinct implication that he accepted
the resurrection only as a spiritual event. For example, when he writes on the
general resurrection of the body, he says that "It is sown a natural body; it is
raised a spiritual body. There is a natural body, and there is a spiritual body"
(1 Cor. 15:44). If this holds for all the righteous, so much more does it hold
for Jesus. "And so it is written, the first man Adam was made a living soul;
the last Adam [Jesus Christ] was made a quickening spirit" (1 Cor. 15:45).
And, "the first man is of the earth, earthy: the second man is the Lord from
heaven" (1 Cor. 15:47). He concludes his argument by asserting the incompatibility of a physical resurrection with the triumph of righteousness. "Now
this I say, brethren, that flesh and blood cannot inherit the kingdom of God;
neither does corruption inherit incorruption" (1 Cor. 15:50).

This latter dictum is Paul's conclusion of a discussion of the difference between the natural body and the spiritual body. It says that flesh and blood, as

in a physical resurrection of anyone, Jesus included, cannot be part of the Almighty's heavenly kingdom. Therefore, since, in Paul's view, Christ certainly is part of God's heavenly kingdom, and since present-world corporeality is incompatible with the sublime post-death heavenly state, it follows that Paul viewed the resurrection as a cosmic, not a corporeal event.[9]

One of the most attractive aspects of Paul's interpretation of the resurrection of Jesus is that it – in contrast to the Four Gospels and the Book of Acts, with their introduction of the new idea of the physical resurrection of the Messiah – resonates nicely with ancient Hebrew texts: in other words, it fits within the grammar of biblical invention. There are primary figures in the Tanakh who pass from the corruptibility of the physical body to the incorruptibility of the spiritual body. "Enoch walked with God; then he was no more, for God took him" (Gen. 5:24, JPS). And the prophet Elijah was taken up into heaven, by combined forces of a chariot and horses of fire, and of a great whirlwind (2 Kings 2:1–11). Both of these accounts resonate clearly with Paul's version of the resurrection of Jesus. The Elijah story is especially nice because Elijah's mantle is left behind after his ascent to heaven, just as Jesus' cloak is left at his crucifixion. As for the story of Enoch's rising from earthly and bodily imperfection to a heavenly and spiritual state, it invokes an entire orchestra of meaning, since the Book of Enoch was one of the richest of late Second Temple religious writings. The tale of Enoch in the Book of Genesis from the ancient writings, the Book of Enoch from the late Second Temple era, and the story of the spiritually-resurrected Jesus found in Paul's writings all work together. Paul's writing on the resurrection is biblical orchestration at its fullest.

This richness is lost, however, in those parts of the "New Testament" that assumed their final form only after the destruction of the Second Temple, and this is most especially true of the Four Gospels and of the Book of Acts. The author-editors of the Gospels show some difficulty in making up their minds about what form Jesus' resurrection actually assumed. The Gospel of John, for example, within a single chapter has the resurrected Jesus being a phantasm who can pass through locked doors (John 20:19) and yet who also has corporeal solidity: the doubts of Thomas are stilled when Jesus has him put his fingers in the nailholes in Jesus' hands and into the spearhole in his side (John 20:27). Similarly, in Luke, the resurrected Jesus is described as an otherworldly figure who is able to move about invisibly (Luke 24:15–16, and 31), but just a few sentences later, Jesus is reported to show himself to the disciples in the body of an ordinary mortal: "handle me, and see; for a spirit hath not flesh and bones, as ye see me have" (Luke 24:39). The Book of Acts, too, has it both ways. Jesus shows himself alive, giving his disciples "infallible proofs" of his bodily resurrection (Acts 1:3). Yet at the end of forty days, Jesus rises in the air, "and a cloud received him out of their sight" (Acts 1:9).

The author-editor of Mark also attempts a similar straddle. The sepulchre is empty (Mark 16:8) and this implies a physical resurrection but, on the other hand, the resurrected Jesus is able to assume multiple forms and to materialize at will among his disciples (Mark 16:12), neither of which is characteristic of the human body, nor, *mutatis mutandis*, characteristic of a physical resurrection.[10] The most straightforward Gospel version of events is found in Matthew, where Jesus' adoring worshippers are able to detain the resurrected Christ by grabbing his feet (Matt. 28:9). Matthew has no phantasmagoric episodes directly ascribed to Jesus, although the resurrection itself is said to be caused by an angel from heaven rolling back the stone of his tomb; that angel, who had a face like lightning and clothes as white as snow, showed himself to two female disciples and to the functionaries who kept the tomb, and the keepers were terrified and became as dead men (Matt. 28:2–5). Otherwise, however, the narrative's straightforward character is maintained by the author-editor's refusal to indicate what finally happened to the risen Jesus. In Matthew, Jesus gives his disciples the Great Commission, and there the story ends (Matt. 28:16–20).

The insistence in the Gospels and in Acts of adding to Paul's conception of the spiritual resurrection of Jesus two more ideas – Jesus as phantasm (except in Matthew) and Jesus as a physically resurrected body – is to lose all the advantages that biblical invention has when it is done well: the acquisition of authority through apparent antiquity and the maintenance of the grounds of presumption, by virtue of new ideas being written in the vocabulary of old. Since there is no biblical or para-biblical tradition of a Messiah who dies for his people and is physically resurrected, the writers and editors of the Gospels and of Acts are stretched to find biblical pretexts for their new invention. The Book of Acts tries to tie Jesus' bodily resurrection to King David by pointing out that the sepulchre of David "is with us unto this day" (Acts 2:29), but that Jesus was resurrected and "neither did his flesh see corruption" (Acts 2:31). This, which is intended to tie David and Jesus, has exactly the opposite effect: it succinctly highlights the discontinuity between the two figures.

Failing to obtain any significant resonance with the Hebrew scriptures on the matter of the physical resurrection, the writers of the Christian documents had to make do with self-referential harmonics. The flesh-and-bone resurrection of Jesus, for example, is pre-figured within the Christian texts by Jesus' miraculous victories over death in his healing ministry: he raised from the dead the twelve-year-old daughter of Jairus (Mark 5:38–43; Luke 8:49–56; Matt. 9:18–25); also the adult son of the widow of the town of Nain (Luke 7:12–15); and, most importantly, Lazarus of the town of Bethany. Lazarus, the brother of Mary and Martha, was himself a loyal disciple of Jesus, so his death was a direct loss to the band of disciples. By the time Jesus resurrected him, he had been dead for four days and smelled foully. So this was no case of hysteria, or coma, the author of John makes clear (John 11:1–44). Jesus' ability to give this particular disciple a new physical life is used as an analogy to his ability to give each of his followers new life spiritually. Moreover, positioned as it is in John's narrative, immediately before the Pharisees are said to plot to put Jesus to death, its latent content is clear: Jesus can overcome physical death, whenever he wants to. These instances of Jesus raising the dead are the closest that the tradition of his own physical resurrection comes to striking a resonant chord in ancient Hebrew scriptures: in raising these people, Jesus is acting in parallel to Elijah and Elisha, each of whom, in his time, did the same thing (1 Kings 17:21–22 and 2 Kings 4:32–37).

Still, for the most part, the timbre is thin and reedy. The same holds for the "predictive" words concerning his own death and resurrection that are ascribed to Jesus.[11] These occur in the Gospel of Mark, for instance, wherein Jesus predicts his own death and resurrection three days later (Mark 8:31; 9:31; 10:32–34), and even then it is not clear whether he is supposed to be predicting a spiritual or a physical resurrection. (The context makes the latter seem the more likely.) Plangency is lacking, in any case. The only exterior reference that can possibly be brought to resonate with this set of "predictions" is that of Job, who affirmed that, "though after my skin worms destroy this body, yet in flesh shall I see God" (Job 19:26). It is not apposite.

Why, then, if the resonance of Jesus as suffering and dying (as in the Suffering Servant references) is so great; and why, if it was possible to be a good Christian and believe, as the Apostle Paul did, that Christ's resurrection was not physical, but spiritual; and why, given that the real sympathetic reverberations of the resurrection come in the rich sonorities of late Second Temple Judaism, wherein Son of God, Son of Man, Lamb of God, and Moshiah all implode into a spectacle of cascading celestial thunderheads – why, why indeed, did the editor-authors of the Gospels and of Acts diminish these glorious assets and park the story of Jesus' resurrection in the thud of damp earth: the physical resurrection. Why?

The query, of course, is beyond full answer. It is a truism, but relevant nonetheless, to observe that the author-editors of these five basic books of Christian narrative believed in the physical resurrection of Jesus, and did so despite the fact that their emphasis upon this belief reduced greatly the effectiveness of their narrative: they were too good writers not to understand the narrative penalties it imposed. Yet, on this issue they abandoned the basic principle of biblical invention. They cut themselves off almost entirely from the Hebrew scriptures and from the conceptual keyboard of late Second Temple Judaism. They believed.

The perplexing contrast, therefore, is between the earliest Christian writings (those of Paul), wherein the resurrection is not physical, and the later writings where, to its spiritual character has been added a stubbornly physical element: Jesus resurrected as a corporeal entity. If the reasons for this change are forever beyond recovery, that wonderfully simple tool of historians, chronology, has relevance.

The one thing that we know with complete certainty that had changed within the environment of the Jesus-faith between the time the Pauline letters were scribed and the time those of the Gospel writers were given their final form, is that the locale and the system of physical sacrifice to Yahweh, that all forms of Judahism had taken for granted, were demolished. Paul could afford to preach the non-corporeal resurrection of Jesus as part of a system of spiritual sacrifice that was in binary opposition to the corporeality, and thus the corruption, of Temple sacrifice. The Gospels' writer-editors had no such luxury. The "other" by which Paul was able to define his faith – the bodily, the corporeal, the corrupt rituals of the Temple – was no more. The Gospel writers, therefore, had to keep alive both halves of the Temple's sacrificial system – not just the spiritual, or if one prefers, the cosmic, but also the physical. They had lost the freedom of articulation Paul had possessed.

3

The other matter on which the inventors of the "New Testament" lose touch with the Hebrew scriptures and with the grammar of biblical invention, is the Virgin Birth; but here they control the damage much more successfully than in the case of the physical resurrection.

The requirement of a Virgin Birth (or some equivalent) for Jesus the Christ is what mathematicians would call "intuitively obvious": the sums don't add up without it. The series of motifs that transform Yeshua of Nazareth into Jesus the Christ – those of Moshiah, Son of Man, Son of God, Lamb of God, the sacrifice and the judge of humanity for all eternity – all these make him into a figure who, in the context of his times, was not just god-like but, in some sense was part of God. One might deal with the inevitable question, "How did Jesus become part of God?" by philosophic means; various modes of allegory were conveniently to hand in the Greek-derived philosophy of the time. But in any successful historical narrative, one needs a story, not a set of syllogisms or a piece of allegory, and it was natural that a narrative answer to the question would be propounded; and what more appropriate than to provide the biography of Jesus with a birth tale, one that explained his deity?

Unfortunately, logical as it was and appropriate as it was to the historical narrative mode, the Virgin Birth concept ran into one doleful reality: there was in later Second Temple Judahism no tradition of divine births, nor was there anything similar in the Hebrew scriptures. It would have been possible, as Geza Vermes argues, for the writer-editors of the Christian scriptures to have stayed within the tradition of biblical invention by their adopting the pattern of legendary births set down for Isaac, Jacob, and Samuel: in each case their fathers were credited with initiating their conception by natural means, but only after divine intervention by Yahweh had healed an incapacity in their wives.[12] Instead, "primitive Christianity turned from this alternative of faith in divine mediation to the totally novel belief in an act of divine impregnation…."[13]

Such a belief would have raised no difficulties with most pagan cultures, but for persons trained in later Second Temple Judahism, it was a big bolus to swallow. For instance, one can point to the Egyptian construct of the goddess Isis and her son Horus; and the Greek myth that the virgin Danae, impregnated by Zeus, gave birth to Perseus; and there are several others. Perhaps some day in the future, when the Christian equivalent of the Dead Sea Scrolls is uncovered, it will be possible to pinpoint from which pagan religion the Virgin Birth was borrowed. That, though, will not make the fundamental textual problem go away: unlike almost every other motif in the "New Testament," this one is not a re-invention of the Hebrew scriptures or of the diverse religious literature of the several Judahisms of the later Second Temple period. Moreover, as Ulrich Luz points out, the Torah implies that the idea "that God and human beings can sexually interact is the pinnacle of sacrilege."[14] The case he points to is the scene in the book of Genesis where, after the flood, the "sons of God" (KJB) or "divine beings" (JPS) had sexual relations with human women, producing thereby a race of giants. Yahweh, seeing this wickedness, decided to destroy humankind. Eventually, he changed his mind, and let Noah survive (Gen. 6:1–9).

The idea of a Virgin Birth, produced by some form of insemination by Yahweh (or by his Holy Spirit) of the mother of Yeshua was either so repugnant to most of the editors and authors of the "New Testament," or so surprising to them, that most of them avoided the topic as they would a suppurating sore. For example, the Gospel of Mark (which is usually taken as being the earliest of the Four Gospels) has no notion of the Virgin Birth. This leads one to infer that either the idea developed after the editor-author of Mark had completed his work, or that he knew of the concept but found it an unworkable invention. Similarly, the Gospel of John, which usually is dated a generation after Mark, will have nothing to do with the Virgin Birth. If, as most scholars suggest, John was written after the three Synoptic Gospels were composed, then the unavoidable inference is that the author-editor of John knew of the idea of the Virgin Birth and rejected it. The one unambiguous reference to Jesus' birth in John is a direct contravention of the idea of divine impregnation:

> Philip findeth Nathanael, and saith unto him, we have found him, of whom Moses in the law and the prophets did write, Jesus of Nazareth, the son of Joseph.
>
> (John 1:45)

Scant wonder: given how alien the idea was to the religious traditions that stemmed from the Yahweh-faith.

Most tellingly, Paul produces two statements that are directly opposed to the invention of the Virgin Birth. In his Letter to the Galatians, he says, "but when the fulness of the time was come, God sent forth his Son, made of a woman, made under the law" (Gal. 4:4). Given that Paul habitually uses "the law" in association with the corruptibility of the flesh, he is clearly saying that Jesus was conceived in the normal fleshly fashion. (That, in his misogynistic way, he says "made of a woman," is a double indication that in his view there was nothing special about Jesus' birth.) That this is Paul's view is confirmed in his Epistle to the Romans, where he writes:

> Concerning his Son Jesus Christ our Lord, which was made of the seed of David according to the flesh;
> And declared to be the Son of God with power, according to the spirit of holiness, by the resurrection from the dead. (Rom. 1:3–4)

Jesus, Paul declares, was born of the flesh, not by divine impregnation; he was made the Son of God by the Almighty's gift of holiness. This, Paul says, is warranted by Jesus' resurrection, which (as we have just observed) Paul interpreted in a spiritual, not in a physical sense. Hence, it follows that in Paul's view there was nothing special about the physical birth of Yeshua of Nazareth. One might suggest (at least as a logical possibility, if an unlikely one) that Paul was simply not aware of the notion of the Virgin Birth, but here the text funnels down this possibility to the point that it is a considerable improbability. Paul's phrasing is just too pointed to be random. He has, I think, picked something up in the air: not yet a fully-fledged, completely articulated version of the Virgin Birth, but something that is running through the margins of Christianity in the late 50s and early 60s; it is not yet important enough or sufficiently widespread to demand a full refutation. Paul, in passing, flicks it away, like an impatient high court judge dismissing a solipsistic argument by junior counsel.

This leaves the author-editors of the Books of Matthew and of Luke as the proponents of the notion of the Virgin Birth of the Messiah. How do they make their case palatable? They begin, quite unpromisingly, by Hellenising the name of the main human being involved, Miriam, mother of Yeshua. When "Miriam" became "Mary" a great opportunity for establishing a resonance with the Hebrew scriptures was lost: Miriam, the sister of Moses and of Aaron may have had her faults (she joined Aaron in organizing a rebellion against Moses), but she is the strongest female religious figure in the books of Genesis-Kings, for she is neither a prophetess nor the consort of a powerful male. She is a religious leader in her own right. Further, a chance for contemporary reference was lost. Miriam was also the name of the favourite wife of the cruel Herod the Great, who is portrayed as a persecutor of the infant Jesus, and who, incidentally, had his own beloved Miriam executed.[15]

Nevertheless, the author-editors of Matthew and Luke try to create a biblical spillway that will relieve the pressure of skepticism that their introduction of a new idea, one that violated the rules of biblical invention, engendered. Matthew's chief implement is an "Old Testament" proof text. He describes Mary's having been "found with child of the Holy Ghost" (Matt. 1:18) and then explains:

> Now all this was done, that it might be fulfilled, which was spoken of the Lord by the prophet, saying,
> Behold, a virgin shall be with child, and shall bring forth a son, and they shall call his name Emmanual, which being interpreted is, God with us.   (Matt. 1:22–23)

This is a reasonably accurate version of Isaiah 7:13 and 7:14, which states:

> And he [Isaiah] said, Hear ye now, O house of David; Is it a small thing for you to weary men, but will ye weary my God also?
> Therefore, the Lord himself shall give you a sign; Behold, a virgin shall conceive and bear a son, and shall call his name Immanuel.   (KJB)

Except that: in the Hebrew text the word is *ALMH*, meaning "young girl." In Matthew's Greek this term becomes *parthenos*, something quite different. In the Tanakh, "young girl" does not carry any connotation of virginity in the medical sense, and almost all of the recent translations of the Hebrew scriptures, Christian and Jewish alike, have abandoned the concept of virgin in the sense of one who has never had sexual intercourse with a male.[16] A form of courtesy in scholarly circles dictates that the actions of the author-editor of Matthew are here said to be a "mistranslation" of the text, but that *politesse* obscures what was occurring. This is not a mistranslation: the author-editor of Matthew was an individual, or set of individuals, who knew their Hebrew. Although the editor-author of Matthew was working from the Septuagint, he also had access to the original Hebrew text, and was a competent scholar in Judahist texts, as the rest of Matthew attests. (This holds true whatever side one takes on the question of whether "Matthew" was a Hellenised Jew or a Gentile who was deeply knowledgeable about the Judahist faith.) The author-editor of Matthew had to be aware that the word *ALMH* did not carry the freight: virgin. His alteration of Isaiah's meaning is intentional, but it is not done within the rules of biblical re-invention, for anyone with access to the Hebrew scriptures would see the change as a dissonant one.[17]

More nuanced is a reference found in Matthew that ties the birth of Jesus to other ancient Hebrew texts. The Wise Men, or Magi (usually taken to be astrologers) who appear from the east and who ask in Jerusalem where is the King of the Jews, whose star we have seen? are well founded on the Tanakh's story of the magus Balaam. In Matthew (2:1–12) the Magi pay their obeisance to the holy infant and then depart for their home country without obeying the instruction of King Herod, namely to report to him when they found the child. In the Hebrew scriptures, the foundation for this scene involves Balaam, an Israelite astrologer, who is summoned by the king of Moab to produce a vision that would bode ill for Israel and thus, effectively, be a curse upon the Chosen People. Instead, Balaam blesses the people (an equivalent of the gifts given the infant Jesus by the Magi) and then goes off home (see Numbers, chapters 22–24). Yet, even here, the fit is a bit loose. The Matthean story suffers from the narrative equivalent of blow-back: a later reference to Balaam in the Tanakh has him being slaughtered for heresy along with a group of impious Gentile rulers (Num. 31:8 and 31:16).

Much more successful is the account in Matthew of the "descent into Egypt" by Mary, Joseph and the infant (Matt. 2:13–23). This sets off several resonant notes. The Holy Family flees to Egypt when Joseph is told in a dream that King Herod will seek to kill the child. Thereupon follows the "slaughter of the innocents" wherein Herod is said to have killed all the children in Bethlehem and its surrounding region.[18] This harkens to the story of the infant Moses, whose life was threatened when Pharaoh of Egypt ordered that all Hebrew infant boys be killed immediately after their birth (Exod. 1:16). Thus, the early childhood of the man to whom Yahweh first entrusted the Torah is linked in tight parallel to the man whom Christians believe brought a new Torah. The life of Moses was saved through the combined intervention of his own sister (whom, we assume from later texts, was *Miriam*, or, in Hellenised form, Mary), and by one of the daughters of the Pharaoh (Exod. 2:3–10) who raised him. Moses' surrogate mothers, then, are merged into a figure whose salient combined attributes are (a) the name Mary and (b) royal status. These transfer smoothly to Mary, the mother of Jesus. Simultaneously, this makes possible a parallel between the royal upbringing of Moses, of the first Torah, and the claim made in several places (such as Matt. 1:1–17; Luke 1:32, 3:23–38) that Jesus, of the new Torah, has a royal genealogy.

Equally strong is the correspondence between the return of the Holy Family from their forced stay in Egypt (Matt. 2:19–21) and the exodus of the Chosen People from their Egyptian bondage. Text and unspoken subtext (the latter was too well known to require articulation by Matthew) integrate perfectly with one another.

Similarly, the annunciation of Jesus' birth by an angel (Matt. 1:18–25; Luke 1:26–38) harkens to similar angelic annunciations: the birth of Ishmael (Gen. 16:11) and of Samson (Judges 13:3–5) and, most importantly, to Yahweh's message to Abraham, that his wife Sarah would bear a child to be called Isaac, with whom Yahweh would establish an everlasting covenant (Gen. 17:15–21).

Without forcing the reading, one can find a score of additional secondary references to the Hebrew scriptures in Luke and Matthew's account of the birth of Jesus. The situation is clear: the authors of Matthew and Luke have little difficulty in establishing an intricate pattern of sonorities between the Tanakh and their own historical narratives on the matter of Jesus' birth: except when the Virgin Birth of Jesus is postulated, and then they lose touch entirely both with the ancient scriptures and with the traditions of Judahism that existed during the late Second Temple era. In the contemporary traditions that were derived from the ancient Yahweh-faith, human births were sometimes announced and perceived as instances of divine providence. The births, however, were the results of the usual modes of human reproduction, they never were the product of Yahweh interposing himself so as to abrogate the normal procreative process.[19]

4

I have been highlighting the two places where the Christian scriptures depart from the grammar of biblical invention, and thus lose true resonance with the Hebrew scriptures, not to impugn the narrative integrity of the "New Testament," but for just the opposite reason: if the concepts of the physical resurrection of Jesus and of his Virgin Birth are the farthest off-key that the Christian texts get, then, as a whole, they have not wandered very far off-line. Even in these two instances, half resonances and false sonorities cover up with partial success the fact that these two ideas come from outside of the Judahist religious traditions.

Admittedly, the Virgin Birth and the physical resurrection are big theological issues, debated today within every Christian denomination, but from the viewpoint of the Bible as historical narrative (which is what both halves of the Bible declare themselves to be), they are the least fundamental parts of the story. They lie at the two boundaries of the life of Yeshua of Nazareth, the Virgin Birth focusing on events before he was born, and the physical resurrection on events after he died. They are the most expendable of components. Were they to be expunged, the story would hardly be changed at all: it would begin with a wondrous birth, announced by angels (as in the tradition of Isaac's birth to Sarah and Abraham) and would conclude with Jesus' spiritual resurrection, his revelation of this event to his disciples, his ascension to heaven and, ultimately, his coming again in glory as described in the apocalyptic sections of the Synoptic Gospels and in the Revelation of St. John. The only differences would be that the wonderful birth would not be the result of Mary's impregnation by a divinity, and that Jesus would not have a flesh-and-bone resurrection, but solely a cosmic one. These differences would not change either the fundamental architecture of the "New Testament" or any part of the story that occurs between Jesus' conception in Mary's womb and his resurrection as a cosmic force. Except for these two components, every place else, in their search for resonance in the Hebrew scriptures, the Christian writers are right on key. They successfully re-invent all that has come before.

Take for example the crucifixion. Each of the Gospels' accounts (and the ancillary references in Acts and in the Pauline letters) uses the Hebrew scriptures as a massive echo chamber.[20] The way this chamber works is illustrated by a seemingly tiny incident that takes place when Jesus is being prepared for crucifixion: the soldiers offer him wine mixed with gall as a pain killer (Matt. 27:34; Mark 15:23 where the analgesic is wine and myrrh; Luke 23:36 where it is vinegar, mockingly offered while he is on the cross; and John 19:29, where the pain killer is vinegar and hyssop, administered while he is on the cross). This is a very small detail when viewed against the enormity of the crucifixion, but it is the pitch-note for an extended choral threnody: for the student of the scriptures (and early Christians were nothing if not serious about the study of the Tanakh) at once hears the tones of one of the greatest of the despair-psalms, Psalm 69, which begins with the soul-wrenching cry "Save me, O God; for the waters are come into my soul" (Ps. 69:1). This cry is audible because of a tiny detail in the psalmist's lament: "They gave me also gall for my meat; and in my thirst they gave me vinegar to drink" (Ps. 69:21). Simultaneously, one hears the story of Jesus' crucifixion and an immensely painful despair-psalm as its doubling.

The Gospels provide another detail, which is that the soldiers cast lots for Jesus' cloak (Matt. 27:35; Mark 15:24; Luke 23:34; John 19:23–24). This invokes the voice, well-known to any contemporary student of the scriptures, of another wrenching psalm of despair, wherein the suffering victim laments that "they part my garments among them, and cast lots upon my vesture" (Ps. 22:18). Thus, the doubling becomes a tripling, a virtual choir of lament.[21]

The introduction of Psalm 22 into the story does more. Well before the reader or listener hears Jesus' penultimate words, he has heard them at the beginning of Psalm 22, and heard them as an experience of pre-cognition.

> My God, my God, why hast thou forsaken me? why art thou so far from helping
> me, and from the words of my roaring? (Ps. 22:1)

Words-of-roaring indeed: those are the subliminal stage directions for Jesus' terrifying howl from the cross: "My God, my God, why hast thou forsaken me?" (Matt. 27:46; Mark 15:34). Even in Luke and John, which do not permit these words to be rendered aloud, they are mouthed silently, for the previous reference each has to a middle verse in Psalm 22 forces cognition of that psalm's soul-torturing first words. The cumulative effect is to use the Hebrew scriptures as a massive chorus, one which exponentially amplifies the seemingly spare narrative of Jesus' death.

The question of whether or not Yeshua of Nazareth ever said any of the words that are put in the mouth of Jesus the Christ by the Gospel writers is not in any way adjudged by our observation of the mechanism of amplification in the Christian scriptures or by our admiration of its virtuosity. The operational point is that writers of the "New Testament" employ a vocabulary, and a set of stage directions, and provide Yeshua with a script that is compelling to first-century audiences, because the audiences are already familiar with most of the stage directions, the business, and the dialogue. These items are all changed in meaning – that is how biblical invention works, as we have seen over and over – but the undeniable point is that *a goodly portion of the life of Jesus was written well before he was born.*

So, in scanning the Christian reports of the life of Jesus, one frequently runs into events, words, postures, and behaviours, that already are familiar. A few of these will suffice as illustration. Some of them are minor. For example, given that the twelve tribes of Israel are such a major element in the Tanakh (which continues to refer to them as "twelve," long after most of them have disappeared), it is hardly surprising that Jesus is presented in the central "New Testament" texts as having twelve disciples. Paul calls them simply "the twelve" (1 Cor. 15:5). Matthew has Jesus promising the disciples that when the Son of Man returns in glory, there will be twelve thrones, one for each of them, and they would be the judges over the twelve tribes of Israel (Matt. 19:28).

Notice the paradox here. The Christian text implies its own superiority over its Hebrew predecessor – thus will the personnel of the New Covenant govern those of the Old, it effectively says – while it subliminally demonstrates the dependency of the Christian narrative upon precedents that are ultimately Yahwist in origin. Jesus was not free to have ten disciples or twenty. Yeshua of Nazareth could have as few or as many as he wished, but when it came time to transmute Yeshua into Jesus, the historical narrative was subservient to the earlier texts. Twelve. This illustrates in microcosm the trade-off – one might call it a deal, or even a covenant – that the "New Testament" writers make with their primary lodes of source materials, which are the then-living traditions concerning what Yeshua of Nazareth actually did, and the great body of Judahist literature and most especially the Tanakh. In return for gaining the amplifying resonance of the Hebrew texts, the Christian scriptures are distinctly limited in what they can report concerning the words and actions of Jesus the Christ. Twelve disciples.

Other amplifications illustrate the same point. Each of the Synoptic Gospels has Jesus being tempted in the wilderness by the devil (Matt. 4:1–11;

Mark 1:12–13; Luke 4:1–13). This is, first, a rewriting of the temptation story from the primary history of the Yahwist faith (Gen. 3:1–7) and the failure of the First Adam to resist temptation contrasts to the success of the second. More importantly, Jesus' period in the wilderness is a trope of the wilderness wandering of the Chosen People – Jesus for forty days and nights in the barrens, they for forty years. And, most tellingly, Jesus is implicitly contrasted to Moses: the great leader of the ancient Israelites, because he has not followed perfectly the will of God, does not gain the Promised Land, whereas Jesus successfully resists temptation, ends his time in the wilderness, and continues on his own mission in the Promised Land. It works, brilliantly. But conjecture how ineffective the story would have been if Jesus had been depicted as taking his spiritual retreat in a village, or if he were reported as going into the desert for, say, a fortnight. Clearly, the price of resonance and of amplification is dependency.

That example of the necessity of Jesus' temptation being of forty days duration and of its occurring in the wilderness, is relatively trivial, but its being a minor case makes the fundamental point easier to assimilate. For a similar trade-off, between resonance and dependency, occurs in very big matters. One of the biggest is the Last Supper, which, in the form of the Eucharist, eventually becomes the central liturgical act in the Christian church. The writers of the "New Testament" had no choice: they had to report that the Last Supper occurred at the time of Passover,[22] rather than in the season of any other Judahist holy feast.[23]

Why? Because the minor festivals[24] were not sufficiently consequential to bear the weight of a world-tilting occurrence, and of the two major festivals – Atonement and Passover – only Passover possessed the harmonics that fit with the other aspects of the "New Testament's" translation of Yeshua into Jesus.

If the Temple Scroll's interpretation of Leviticus Chapter 16 is a guide, the liturgy associated with the Day of Atonement in later Second Temple times involved as its central act the choosing of two goats as piacular victims. (This is the origin of "scapegoating," an English-language term invented by the great Tyndale to cover an otherwise untranslatable Hebrew term.) This ritual involved features that were, from the Christian viewpoint, insurmountable. Two sacrificial victims, not one, were involved. Moreover, it would have been very difficult for the Christian writers to equate a lamb (an icon for Jesus, Lamb of God) with a kid; to distinguish sheep from goats was one of the things everyone knew how to do. And, further, in the Atonement ritual, one of the two goats was not put to death. While one of them was killed as a sin-offering, the other had the sins of the children of Israel symbolically placed on its head, and then was driven into the wilderness. It was that goat which bore all the iniquities of the people.[25] All this clashes terribly with the "New

Testament" story of Jesus: not only is the iconic species wrong but, crucially, whereas in the Atonement ritual, the animal that carries the sins of Israel lives and dwells in the wilderness, the Christian story says that Jesus returned from the wilderness and that he died.

Alone of all the Judahist festivals, Passover (Pessah) marries with the Christian story. Although, as Gillian Feeley-Harnik notes, "there is no detailed evidence for the organization of the Passover in Jesus's time,"[26] it is highly probable that the week of Pessah was a collapsing together of two separate feasts, that of Unleavened Bread, and Passover proper. The combined feasts commemorated Israel's time of wilderness wandering, the Exodus from Egypt, and Yahweh's sparing of the first-born (the passing-over of the angel of death) just before the Exodus. The rituals of the time involved the breaking of bread, the sacrifice of a lamb as an expiatory exercise, the sprinkling of blood, the solemn sharing of wine, but in precisely what context and in what order of events is unknown. Nor is it clear, in Jesus' time, the degree to which the rituals were conducted as collective and public events (we know from Josephus' reports of Jerusalem at the time of Pessah, when thousands of pilgrims converged on the Temple, that there certainly was a public aspect) and to what degree the rituals were based in the individual home (as indicated in Passover's origins as described in Exodus chapters 12 and 13). The practices of public and private liturgy of course were not incompatible with each other: the unknown element is the balance between the two.

In any case, Passover was the one Yahwist-derived festival that melded with the motifs and beliefs adopted by the writers of the "New Testament." Only it, of the several holy celebrations declared in the Tanakh, permitted a deep resonance to occur between the Hebrew scriptures and the Christian narrative. If the Christian writers were to be successful in transforming Yeshua of Nazareth into Jesus the Christ, then it was irrelevant when Yeshua died. Jesus, however, had to have shed his blood at a moment in the liturgical calendar determined by the day of Passover. In the Synoptic Gospels the crucifixion takes place on the first day of Pessah; in John it occurs on the eve of Passover.[27] The Last Supper becomes a superior version of the Passover meal, and this holds whether it was what a century-and-a-half later the Mishnah defines as a seder (the Synoptic pattern) or whether it took place in a casual setting on Passover eve (the Gospel of John's view). In either case, the meaning is that all subsequent Passovers are redundant.[28]

Here, the trade-off is clear: in return for the resonance and the amplification which the Christian writers achieve by their appropriation of the Hebrew texts, they surrender their right to be independent chroniclers. If Yeshua is indeed to be identified as Jesus Christ, he has to die at Passover. So: he did. And, as twenty centuries of the celebration of the Christian eucharist indicate, this re-invention of the Passover meal was indeed wondrously successful.

5

In discussing the Yahweh-faith and its derivatives – the various Judahisms of the late Second Temple period and the two variants of those Judahisms, the Christian and the Rabbinic Jewish faiths – we have been sharing meta-language: the discussion of one symbolic system through the employment of another. It cannot be any other way.

The form of meta-language I have been employing throughout this book owes more to literature than to linguistics. We are sharing a series of metaphors that, I hope, illuminates some of the ways that the greatest cultural artifacts of our civilization are related to each other. These metaphors, while employed as literary devices, are more than that: each of the central devices is a behavioural model which explains how thousands and thousands of tiny datum points are encompassed within a single system – and, if successful, does so with a good deal more efficiency of explanation and of communication than would a page full of algorithms. The central piece of meta-language which runs through our examination of the Hebrew scriptures, of the wildly varied texts of later Second Temple Judahism, of the Christian scriptures and (as we shall see in Chapters Ten through Thirteen) also runs through the sacred texts of Rabbinic Judaism, is that they share a grammar of religious invention. This is a set of rules that are clearly observable in the earliest Hebrew scriptures – the Genesis-Kings unity – and once these rules were set down, anyone who was to invent, write, preach, heal, in that tradition had to honour them, or be thuddingly unsuccessful.

The Christian scriptures, I have argued, are an impressively coherent, wondrously successful entity, because the "New Testament" honours the ancient Hebrew grammar of religious invention, and does so at three levels, each of which is best approached by its own metaphor. (Anyone who has been trained to believe that multiple metaphors inevitably are solipsistic had best shield his eyes; or adopt the view, long accepted by physical and social scientists, that individual sub-systems often require their own individual modelling methods.) Specifically, at the level of macro-structure, I suggested that the "New Testament" canon was organized like a successful piece of architecture. This structure takes its overall form from the general outlines of the Hebrew scriptures, but through a series of clever architectural inventions, it re-orientates the Hebrew scriptures. The structure is similar in design to the Tanakh, but it looks out over entirely different countryside. Second, I argued that the "New Testament" achieved another level of unity between the various books through the "interdigitation" of motifs, symbols, and icons. The structural members joined together through a process of definitional blurring, the ideational equivalent of welding. And, third, at a verse-by-verse level, the author-editors of the "New Testament" achieved yet-another form of unity, by shaping their individual phrases so that they resonated with those of the

Hebrew scriptures. With a few infelicitous exceptions, the phrases of the "New Testament," like reeds in a vast harmonic device, vibrate at sympathetic frequencies with those texts from the "Old Testament," upon which they are based.

The "New Testament" is an amazingly successful invention, and one of immense power. Both its coherence and its force are historical realities which exist independently of why one believes these characteristics are achieved. Recognition of them is belief-neutral: one can ascribe them either to God or to humankind, or to any mix one prefers.

Further, a recognition of the coherence and force of the "New Testament" is entirely independent of what one's view is of the question, "Did the events narrated in the 'New Testament' actually occur?" In the Appendix D we look at what is usually termed "the quest for the historical Jesus," but it really is a secondary issue, for the "New Testament," in itself, is the primary historical reality of the Christian religion. The fulcrum of the "New Testament'"s power is its unity, articulated on the various levels that we have discussed in this and in the preceding chapter.

So that we do not lose awareness of our long-range perspective, we should remind ourselves: the line or orientation that we are following is a very long one. It runs, in the Christian case, from the ancient Hebrew scriptures, through later Second Temple Judahist texts and, following the destruction of the Temple, through the "New Testament." Simultaneously, we are following an even longer trail. It runs, in the Jewish case, from the ancient Hebrew scriptures, through the texts of later Second Temple Judahism and, following the destruction of the Temple, through the Mishnah and to the Talmuds.

Each of these two lines purports to be what astronomers call a syzygy, the alignment of three celestial bodies on a straight line. Here, however, neither line is quite straight, and that is what the continual process of biblical re-invention is all about. In each case, it permits a small bending of the line, a bit of deviation from the truly-straight, but by such tiny increments that one can perceive the variance only from a fair distance away.

Given the optics of this situation, our fundamental point of method has been (and will continue to be), that the basic documents of the Yahweh-faith, and its myriad derivatives in later Second Temple times, including Christianity and, still later, Rabbinic Judaism, can be understood only in relation to each other. We are here analysing the historical development of sets of the texts that comprise four distinct entities – the Tanakh; the literature of Second Temple Judahism, as found in the Dead Sea Scrolls, Pseudepigrapha and in the deutero-canonical works; the Christian scriptures; and the foundation texts of Rabbinic Judaism, especially the Mishnah and the Talmuds. None of these four sets can be defined, much less intelligently comprehended on its own, however desperately devotees and scholarly specialists would like to do so. They are four intimately related points of observation and to understand any one of the sets, it is necessary to map it in relation to the other three. Taken together, the four sets of texts define two ever-so-slightly different lines of historical development: one results in Christianity, the other in the modern Jewish faith. Each line of development is a false syzygy, a path of development that looks to anyone close to it, as if it is a straight line. Each, in fact, is an extremely subtle curve. Recognition of this fundamental fact becomes possible only when the two historical paths are viewed simultaneously, from a distance, and with a perspective that is kindly provided to us by time's metered passage.

The Invention of the Jewish Faith

Don't Stare at the Neighbours

I

THE TWO DIRECT HEIRS OF THE YAHWEH-FAITH, CHRISTIANITY AND the Jewish faith (frequently called "Rabbinic Judaism" by scholars), are sisters: their roots in shared historical narratives take believers back before time. Their immediate common heritage was the plenteous religious culture of late Second Temple Judahism and its sudden dispersal and apparent decimation following the destruction of Jerusalem in 70 CE. Like children of the same household, these two entities are tied together: eternally joined by their common heritage and the shared moment whereby each became an independent being, the catastrophe of the Temple's destruction. Rivals for the same hereditary crown, seemingly they remain forever at war.

Other fragments of late Second Temple Judahism also survived, relatively briefly, but Rabbinic Judaism and Christianity were the ones that count. These two exhibited a mixture of great inventiveness, aggressiveness, and durability. These characteristics assured their survival, when all around them the multiple Judahisms of the Second Temple desiccated and died.

Notice here a matter of terminology that is much more than a matter of mere words. After the destruction of the Temple, the Yahweh-faiths, the multiple Judahisms disappear: not overnight, of course, but the process begins immediately. As discussed in Chapters Two through Four, the historical narratives that were the story of the "children of Israel" comprised a brilliant legitimation of the religion of Judah. The epicentre of that religion was the Temple, the heart of Judah's capital, which, from the time of King David onward, was Jerusalem. The faith was "Judahism," literally, and if it had many variants, they had at their heart the triumphalism of Judah and, as their liturgical and mythological pivot, the Temple. After the destruction of Judah's capital and of the Temple, the Judahist faith (in its many variants) had to be re-invented or die. The late Second Temple era had permitted the luxury of multiple Judahisms, a panoply of rival variants on the same theme. In the desert-times that followed Jerusalem's catastrophe, something new was needed. A faith that was based chiefly on the triumphalism of Judah no longer was possible, for Judah was anything but triumphant. Nor was a temple religion that required a physical temple possible, for the Temple was now dust, save for a few remaining stones, megaliths of a by-gone age.

The triumph of the five centuries after the Temple was destroyed was conceptual, not physical. *Judahism* was replaced by *Judaism*; the Jewish faith came into being. This change is recognized by our change in terminology from "Judahism" to "Judaism," and the introduction of the term "Jewish" as a religious denominator. To make this change at 70 CE is arbitrary (the transformation did not take place at a single time or place), but it is appropriate that we alert ourselves that something very big is going on, and that, like the invention of Christianity, the invention of the Rabbinic Jewish faith has direct ties to the world of our own time. If the invention of the Jewish faith took somewhat longer than Christianity, that should not obscure the fact that this re-invention of older concepts, symbols and beliefs, and its combination with a small number of very powerful new ideas, was a process that was every bit as dramatic, radical, and successful, as was the invention of Christianity.

At the level of everyday physical survival (no small matter) both the Christian and Jewish faiths were lucky: key inventors and key leaders survived the turmoil of the later 60s CE. Granted, both the Christians and the Pharisees (the two factions of Second Temple Judahism that eventually became dominant) had been scattered around the diaspora (albeit focused on Jerusalem) and this facilitated the survival and ultimate success of each. However, on a more limited level, each seems to have had further good fortune. Many of the Christian community in Jerusalem, being persecuted by the Zealots during the Roman-Jewish war, left Jerusalem and (according to creditable tradition), went to Pella on the far side of the Jordan River. Therefore, they were spared the worst effects of the destruction of Jerusalem. Similarly, many of the leading Pharisees escaped and regrouped, traditionally at Yavneh (var: Jabneh, Jamnia), probably located southwest of Jerusalem, although the exact site is unconfirmed.[1] Thus, some of the greatest inventive geniuses of the quickly-emerging Christian and Jewish faiths not only survived, but obtained magnified influence in the period that, in retrospect, can be seen as the crucial formative years of both religions: the two generations after the end of the Jerusalem Temple.

2

During the second half of the twentieth century, an understandable, but misleading asymmetry developed among scholars of religion, and among historians generally, about the relationship of the Jewish and the Christian faiths: namely, that from its earliest moments, Christianity was antisemitic and that the Jewish faith responded to Christian developments by ignoring them whenever possible, and surviving them whenever necessary. Considering the horrors inflicted upon the Jewish people during World War II by citizens of countries that, only decades earlier, had been officially Christian, and which, even in the 1930s and 1940s comprised populations whose majorities were at least nominally Christian, this Manichaean set of distinctions is immediately compelling. However, I fear that the use of the term "antisemitism" in dealing with the fecund era of Christian and Jewish invention – the sixty years or so after 70 CE, when the great texts of each religion take shape – one distorts by gross anachronism the character of the Christian attitudes and beliefs and thus, as if by the workings of classical physics, equally distorts the attitudes and beliefs of emergent Rabbinic Judaism.

This is a particularly emotion-charged issue but we must have the courage to deal with it directly. Initially, one must make absolutely clear certain basic historical matters. That the history of the behaviour and belief of generation after generation of Christians has been either explicitly or implicitly antisemitic is not a matter of debate: it is an historical fact, and can be observed in action from the persecutions of 1096 that followed the First Crusade to the expulsion of the Jews from England in 1290, to the genocide in Franconia (Germany) in 1298, to the persecutions by the Inquisition and the expulsion of the Jews from Spain in 1492, to the virtually-universal penal laws against Jews in thirteenth- through nineteenth-century Europe. That these actions were based in part on Christian religious teachings is sometimes ascribed to "theological antisemitism," which is often distinguished from the "racial antisemitism" that became the dominant form in the twentieth century, reaching its hideous apogee in the Holocaust. However, it is well to remember that theological antisemitism remained strong even in the era of racial antisemitism: the Roman Catholic church did not absolve the Jewish people of collective guilt for being "Christ killers" until 1965.[2]

Nor is it deniable that the "church fathers" of the second century onwards frequently were anti-Jewish in their doctrinal positions, sometimes virulently so. Marcion of the mid-second century had attempted to create a set of Christian scriptures with all references to the religion of Judah expunged. (See Chapter Eight.) That he failed and was declared a heretic obscures the fact that his viewpoint manifestly had an appeal to many members of the Christian faith.

Melito the Eunuch, the late second-century bishop of Sardis, was the first Christian writer in whose work we have a clear record of the Jews being accused of deicide. Origen, the great exegete of the first half of the third century, charged that the Jews had committed the most abominable of crimes in their conspiracy against Jesus Christ, the saviour of the human race. Gregory, Bishop of Nyssa in the latter half of the fourth century, defined the Jews as murderers of the Lord, killers of the prophet, and enemies and slanderers of God. One could go on and on. Manifestly, many of the church fathers had abandoned the views of Paul, that those who rejected Jesus were wrong-headed, and adopted a harsher view, that they were of the wrong sort, and irredeemably so, literally and permanently.[3]

Given that these theological condemnations of the Jewish faith as issued by the church fathers were directly contributory to the long skein of antisemit-ism that runs from early medieval times down to the present day, why, in the present historical discussion, is it useful to distinguish the extreme anti-Judaism of the second-through-fourth centuries from the antisemitism that clearly exists thereafter?[4] Because if we lump this particular pathology of the church fathers with the larger, later phenomenon, we obscure some historical realities we dare not miss. *This occurs because "antisemitism" as a concept implies a power-relationship* that comes into existence only in the mid-fourth century. The fulcrum of this development is the period (symbolized by the conversion of Constantine the Great in the fourth century) when the Roman empire becomes Christian. Thereafter, however privileged individual Jews may have been, the power of the state as a collective force was arrayed against the Jews as a collective group. If we subsume everything anti-Jewish into the category of antisemitism, we thereby unthinkingly apply the power-relationship of the last centuries of antiquity to earlier periods, when it did not apply.

This leads us astray in two ways. First, because it makes the eventual polit-ical and social prepotency of Christianity appear to be a natural, organic, vir-tually inevitable historical development. And, since by the ferocious calculus of our own times, wherein winners are thought to be superior, it implies a jus-tified subordination of the Jewish to the Christian. In fact, despite the inven-tive genius of its early proponents, Christianity's survival, let alone its eventual political-social hegemony, was not something a prudent investor would have put his money on in, say, 75 CE. The hideous persecutions the Christians experienced several times under the Roman authorities easily could have broken the faith. And Christianity's political triumph – signposted by the traditional date that is given to the conversion of Constantine, 312 – was in the nature of a grand-lottery win, not the product of brilliant strategy or shrewd tactics.[5] Even though Constantine signalled that Christianity was the unofficial religion of the empire (by declaring that Sunday was a public holiday, in 321), the full triumph of Christianity was hardly inevitable: the emperor Julian (who comes down to history as Julian the Apostate) in the early 360s not only turned against Christianity, but actively re-introduced "pagan" religion in the institutions of the empire. Julian was a learned despot, and, in fact, produced a number of treatises on civil and religious topics. He gave promise of being the sort of figure of intellectual, administrative, and military prowess that one sees rarely: as in the young Henry VIII of England. Moreover, in 362 CE, after meeting with Jewish leaders in Antioch, he announced that he would rebuild the Jerusalem Temple and that he would allow the traditional temple sacrificial rites to resume.[6] Had Julian not been struck by a stray arrow in June, 363, during his Mesopotamian campaign, the allegedly-ineluctable rise of Christianity might have been a brief historical vapour. In the actual event, Christianity won. Although scholars vary in their interpretations, sometime between the imposition of the death penalty for celebrating Easter on the wrong day (382 CE) and the decree in the western portion of the empire in 407 CE that ordered the destruction of all "pagan" temples, shrines and idols, the victory was effectively completed.[7] The irony is that just when Christianity was becoming the official religion of the empire, the empire itself was crumbling. Thus, what had been the Roman empire was, in its final days, transmuted into the Christian empire.[8]

Second, not only does the inappropriate application of the concept of antisemitism to the first through the fourth or fifth centuries obscure our vision – by making Christianity's capture of the once-Roman empire seem an automatic, inevitable occurrence – but, more importantly, it inhibits our appreciating the extraordinary resilience, creativity, strength, social appeal, and energy which characterized the re-grouping of Pharisees after 70 CE and their spiritual legatees, the Rabbinic Jews. They were not a band of demoralized losers. Moreover, the broad-brush employment of "antisemitism" obscures the high degree of tolerance (by the standards of the times) that the post-70 Jews received from the Roman authorities until the time of Constantine. Granted, there were special taxes on the Jews, but under most Roman administrations they were able to hold some public offices and were exempted from performing non-Jewish civic rituals that offended their religious sensibilities. It is clear that the Jews of several diaspora cities suffered because of the revolts of 115–117 CE and, following the ill-fated Bar Kokhba revolt in Palestine in 132–135 CE, Jerusalem was plowed under and the Jews banned. Harsh as these occurrences were, they were part of the maintenance of civil order (as perceived by the Roman authorities) and were not religiously motivated. They were not part of any plan to exterminate the Jews. This situation stands in sharp contrast to the various persecutions of Christians in the first three centuries of their existence, the goal of which seems to have been their extirpation as a religious group. As late as 303 CE, Diocletian instituted a war of annihilation against the Christians.[9] Until the fourth century, it appears that the Christians did not have the resources to attack the Jews physically, whatever the inclination of some of the church fathers may have been: this in contrast to the chief physical battle between Jews and Christians, which occurred during the Bar Kokhba revolt, when it appears that significant numbers of Christians who lived in the region of Jerusalem refused to join the revolt (wherein Bar Kokhba was declared to be the Messiah) and were tortured and probably put to death.[10]

It was only in the fourth century, with the Christianizing of the Roman state, that the Christians and Jews ran into each other institutionally. From then onwards, the conditions of antisemitism, as distinct from anti-Judaism applied: a virulent anti-Jewish ideology conjoined with a social and institutional structure that made the Jews a distinct and vulnerable minority.[11] Even then, however, we must guard against an historian's equivalent of Newtonian bookkeeping: one should not assume that simply because Christian institutional power in the fourth and fifth centuries was increasingly rapidly, the ideological and inventive force of the Jewish faith was declining correspondingly. In fact, as will become clear, quite the opposite was true and the Jewish faith evinced one of its greater periods of inventive genius in those very same years.

In the period from the destruction of the Temple to the conversion of Constantine the Great, the Jewish and Christian versions of the former religion of Judah were rivals within a context (the Roman empire) that kept them apart politically. But as packages of ideas, beliefs, faith, motifs and icon, they were direct rivals. (As were the dozens of other Judahist factions that had existed in late Second Temple Judaism, but of whom we know little, save their demise.) We have already seen (in Chapters Eight and Nine) how the Christian branch of Judahism invented a brilliantly successful new religion from the scattered pieces of the Judahist heritage, and in a moment we will begin to discuss how the "Jewish" leaders (for such they soon become) performed a comparable work of astonishing creativity. However, here an historical point has to be established independently of any discussion of the qualitative character of their great invention: that the destruction of the Temple, traumatic though it was to all forms of Second Temple Judaism, and terminal though it was for most, neither immobilized nor reduced the attractiveness of the branch of Judahism that became Rabbinic Judaism.

In an influential study of "pagan antisemitism," Jan N. Sevenster remarked that "to concentrate only on the anti-Semitic words and deeds of ancient times would be to form a completely distorted picture of the place of Judaism in the ancient world." He referred to several ancient non-Jewish authors who had commented favourably on Judaism and then added: "More significant in this respect are the numerous statements about the strong attraction which Judaism exercised on many pagans."[12] This has been amply confirmed by later works of John Gager,[13] Shaye Cohen,[14] and Louis Feldman.[15] Collectively, their scholarship makes three compelling observations: that by virtue of Jewish learning, public morality, courage under duress and, especially, because of the attractiveness of the Jewish scriptures, large numbers of non-Jews found the form of religion that developed after 70 CE very attractive. Further, in the late-second through fifth centuries, the emerging Rabbinic Jewish faith evolved a number of ways of gracefully accepting the varying degrees of affiliations of those non-Jews who admired the Jewish faith and wished in some way to be associated with it. The matter of conversion in this period of someone not born a Jew is a matter that is at present indeterminate (did the convert become totally equal to previous adherents, or was he or she merely "like an Israelite"?). Nor is the historical evidence clear about the exact position of what we might today call "associate members": Gentile "god-fearers," persons who followed Jewish customs but did not undergo ritual conversion. What is clear is that from the later part of the first century CE through the fifth century there existed a good deal of what could well be denominated "missionary activity." Louis Feldman argues that "paradoxically, the loss of the Temple in 70 CE may have strengthened the proselytizing movement, because it opened the way for conversion even of those who did not seek to identify themselves with a Jewish state."[16] It is possible to read the several fourth-century Roman statutes against Jewish proselytizing as an indication not only of official intolerance by the state as it came increasingly under Christian influence but, equally, as an indication that Jewish missionary activity was indeed being successful in attracting Gentiles, mostly "pagans," but undoubtedly some Gentile Christians as well. Louis Feldman concludes his study of Jewish missionary activity as follows: "In sum, Judaism in the third, fourth, and fifth centuries not only showed its vigour through the debates constituting its greatest work since the [Hebrew] Bible, namely the Talmud, but also met the twin challenges of paganism and Christianity by continuing to win converts and 'sympathizers.' "[17]

If the clarity of our vision concerning the vitality of emergent Rabbinic Judaism is improved by our distinguishing between the era of Christian anti-Judaism as articulated by the church fathers from the middle of the second century onwards, and the era of full-scale antisemitism that arose with the Christian acquisition of state power in the mid-fourth century and thereafter, we can further clear our sight-line on the creation of Rabbinic Judaism if we go one step further: and distinguish between the anti-Jewish views of the church fathers and the attitudes expressed in the "New Testament." In putting this viewpoint, I am raising a very tense issue among post-World War II historians of Christianity. And in arguing against the post-Holocaust consensus among "liberal" (for want of a better term) Christian historians, that the Christian scriptures are indeed antisemitic, I run the risk of being misunderstood.[18] The point here will, I hope, be unambiguous: that the Christian scriptures ultimately contributed to antisemitism, but to perceive them as being themselves antisemitic in nature is historically misleading. And characterizing them in such a fashion destroys one of their greatest values to the historian: as photographic plates that picked up the flares and white-hot fractals that momentarily illuminated the sky during the long dark night during which the Rabbinic Jewish faith was a-borning.

3

The Christian scriptures have a developmental relationship with the Yahweh-faith and with the various Judahisms of the later Second Temple era, and therefore their relationship with the Rabbinic Jewish faith that emerges from the destruction of the Temple through the fifth- and sixth-century compilation of the Talmuds is inevitably tense. How could it be otherwise? The "New Testament" is based largely upon the Hebrew texts that became the Tanakh and the Christian texts use the same motifs and concepts that circulated in late Second Temple Judaism. Yet, the Christian scriptures claimed both uniqueness and authority. So, while the "New Testament" affirms its dependence upon its Judahist heritage, it simultaneously tries to limit that dependence, by substituting for dependence master-status: it claims to be the one "New Covenant."

Thus, unavoidably, the "New Testament" is anti-Judahist. In the simplest terms, this occurs in three ways. First, and most fundamental, is the structural character of the Christian scriptures. As discussed in Chapters Eight and Nine, they took the entire heritage of later Second Temple Judahism and re-orientated it, creating an integrated and remarkably strong alternative to all the other Judahisms of the period. Secondly, there is a general condemnation of all the other Judahisms of the late Second Temple era. This takes place without the author-editors of the "New Testament" ever defining exactly towards whom their discountenance was directed. Instead, one encounters a heavy musk of disapproval, one which continually lets the Roman government off the hook and casts other Judahists as the conduits of ill events. As Elaine Pagels notes, "it is probably fair to say that in every case the decision to place the story of Jesus within the context of God's struggle against Satan tends to minimize the role of the Romans and to place increasing blame instead upon Jesus' *Jewish* [Pagels's term and emphasis] enemies."[19] And, thirdly – and most useful for our purposes, several of the author-editors of the "New Testament" focus special dislike upon one group: the Pharisees. Other Judahist factions – Levites and Sadducees, for example – are bad-mouthed in a formulaic way, but the Pharisees come in for a slating that, while it is unfair and offensive, is very useful as historical documentation of the rise and contemporary importance of that pivotal, but ill-documented group.[20]

The chronicling of the triumphant emergence of Rabbinic Judaism out of the myriad Judahisms of the Second Temple era depends upon knowledge of the Pharisees. This is where the "New Testament" becomes invaluable. The Christian scriptures' observations concerning the Pharisees, biased and clearly anti-Pharisaic as they frequently are, nevertheless are one of the few markers available. The Pharisees left behind not a single document that states their program (or, indeed, any contemporary documentary material whatsoever). Later texts, the Mishnah and the Talmuds, contain traditions concerning the Pharisees which were set down two to four centuries after pivotal events occurred, and these present difficulties that are always considerable, often insurmountable. Indeed, we know of only two individuals – Paul the Apostle and Flavius Josephus – who have left affirmations that they were themselves Pharisees: everyone else who is identified as a Pharisee is thus-labelled by some other person, most often in a text composed long after that individual's death. Therefore, the "New Testament," most of which was written before the end of the first century of the Common Era, becomes an irreplaceable source of information on the founders of what we today call the Jewish faith. Of course the Christian scriptures have to be read obliquely in this matter, not as straightforward statements of historical reality.

In particular, one must realize that the "New Testament" shares in a rhetorical tradition that is common to all the heirs of the Yahweh-faith, namely a remarkable ability to employ Billingsgate and to demonize one's rivals, enemies, and, especially, former friends. Slagging, indeed, is raised from the gutter and the gutturals to a literary genre, virtually an art form. This is true not only of the ancient prophets, but even of the psalmists, whose sometimes-eirenic work is equally-often blood-curdling. For example, even with melodic presentation and rhythmic articulation, one cannot slide meditatively by the psalmist's description of his rival or enemies (who, in both cases, are defined as being evil) in Psalm 140: "they have sharpened their tongues like a serpent; adders' poison is under their lips" (v.3). Forgiveness is not considered: "Let burning coals fall upon them: let them be cast into the fire; into deep pits, that they rise not up again" (v.10). The same juxtaposition – of rivals and enemies ("the wicked") being compared to poisonous snakes, and their destruction projected as a judgement-fantasy – is found in Psalm 58, where the righteous person is promised the tactile satisfaction of washing his feet in the blood of the wicked (v.10). Similar invective abounds (Psalms 35 and 109 are particularly vigorous maledictions), and, when chanted liturgically, such psalms make "Onward Christian Soldiers" seem pallid. The vilification of enemies and rivals as virtually a literary genre continued strong in later Second Temple times. Witness: the bile directed at the Man of Lies in the Dead Sea Scrolls;[21] the adumbration of the vices of the rich in the Book of Enoch, chapter 98 (an almost Marxian detailing of a rival social class); the depiction in 1 Maccabees, especially Chapter One, of the pro-Greek party amongst the religious elite as renegades who abandoned the holy covenant with Yahweh. In emergent Rabbinic Judaism, after 70 CE, the genre continued strong. The key exhibit is the Eighteen Benedictions against heretics which, more aptly, could be termed the "eighteen curses." They became part of the daily prayer ritual and continued to be so in some Sephardic rites well into the twentieth century. They are directed against everyone save the one branch of the Yahweh-faith which emerged out of Pharisaism; most interesting was Benediction Twelve which, after denouncing the Christians, called for their instant and eternal death.[22] The point is clear: in dealing with the rivals of Christianity – especially the Pharisees – the Christian scriptures are not uttering a singular and hateful banshee-like wail, but instead are lashing their rivals in a fashion long-operative within the tradition of religious invention of the Yahwist-descended faiths, and one which continues, painfully luxuriant, for centuries thereafter. David Flusser aptly summarizes this fact when, reflecting on Matthew chapter 23 (wherein a long diatribe against the Pharisees is ascribed to Jesus), he notes, "all the motifs of Jesus' famous invective against the Pharisees in Matthew 23 are also found in rabbinical literature."[23]

So, we read the "New Testament" comments on the Pharisees within the context of the conventions of the religious literature in which the observations were set down. Of course they have to be read at an oblique angle, for they hardly constitute objective reportage, but undeniably they relate to a real phenomenon: the Pharisees, an extremely important cohort within Second Temple Judahism, one which gave birth to the Jewish faith we know today. The Christian scriptures as they relate to the Pharisees break into two portions: those written before the destruction of the Second Temple (which means only the authentic letters of Paul), and the great bulk of the "New Testament," which was framed after the Temple was destroyed. Paul's letters, because they are the only extant primary sources that deal with the Pharisees and which are not tainted by the retrospective knowledge of the Temple's destruction, are unique. No history of Rabbinic Judaism can be written without them.

Paul's letters document several facts about the Pharisees and these are basic in the same sense that a plinth is basic to any monument: fundamental. First, Paul makes it clear that the Pharisees indeed were a distinct and identifiable faction within the Judahist community in the first century CE and, by implication, that their history went back at least into the previous century. Secondly, this group had outreach into diaspora Jewry. Paul himself is a document in that dispersal of Pharisaism, for, a diaspora Jew, he was raised a Pharisee (Phil. 3:5) and, if one accepts the reports of the Book of Acts as accurate, he was second-generation: the son of a Pharisee (Acts 23:6). Thirdly, Paul implicitly affirms that the Pharisees were not some tiny Judahist sect, a mountaintop or desert community of ascetics, but were influential in Jerusalem. Fourthly, the clearest religious characteristic that Paul ascribes to the Pharisees is a strong halachic commitment. That he does not entirely approve of it makes his recognition of its rigour all the more valuable. Fifthly, he presents the Pharisees as being aggressive, particularly toward the Jesus-followers. There is no reason to doubt Paul's confession that, when a Pharisee, he persecuted the followers of Jesus, probably as a leader of religious hate-mobs. (See Galatians 1:13–14; 1 Cor. 15:9; Phil. 3:6). The continuity between this behaviour and Benedictions is obvious. And, sixthly, therefore, one reasonably infers that well before the destruction of the Second Temple, two forms of the Judahist faith, the Pharisaic and the Christian, were sharply at odds with each other. This should not be over-interpreted to imply that they were everywhere, in Jerusalem and in the diaspora, at daggers drawn, but rather to suggest that in specific local situations they were intense rivals. Nor, indeed, should Paul's information be interpreted to imply that the rivalry between these two Judahist groups was unique. (It certainly was not, as the Dead Sea Scrolls amply demonstrate.) However, at minimum, Paul's testimony implies that the Pharisee/Jesus-follower rivalry had a piquancy that hints not at a great distance in their origins, but at how close they once had been. Paul had himself been a Pharisee and (even if one does not correct for the anti-Pharisee bias of the Gospels), Jesus reasons and argues Torah like a Pharisee, albeit a Pharisee with a difference. If one concludes that the Pharisees and the Jesus-followers once had been very close neighbours, then the intensity of their later territorial rivalry makes sense. Thus, in propinquity originated what George Steiner has termed the "tragic, possibly mutually destructive bonds" that have tied together their descendants, the Jewish and the Christian faiths.[24]

Less valuable, but still consequential, are the historical inferences concerning the Pharisees one can draw from the post-70 CE Christian sources. These are much trickier to evaluate because, unlike the Pauline letters, one is dealing with anonymous, multi-authored documents, and because the destruction of the Temple changed radically the vision of the world held by all Judahists, not least the Christian writers. The four Gospels and the Acts of the Apostles agree with the presentation of the Pharisees found in Paul's letters – with the addition of the note that they believed in the resurrection of the dead (Acts 23:8) and that the Pharisees were represented in the Sanhedrin (John 11:47; Acts 5:34) – but that is not their greatest value. Their primary evidentiary use is in the heightened degree of animus that they show towards the Pharisees. Unlike Paul, who exhibits a good deal of respect for his religious roots and does not directly blackguard the Pharisees,[25] the Gospels are frequently direct and disapproving, although not universally so. Here remember that the Gospels are compositions brought together in the swirling aftermath of the near-levelling of Jerusalem and of its sacred Temple. So, even though the author-editors of these Christian books are, on the surface, providing information that relates to the first three or four decades of the first century, the final product they left to us includes hundreds of data-points concerning developments in the time that they were writing, which is to say, after 70 CE. This observation holds whether one believes that the material in the Gospels and Acts which concerns the Pharisees is solely a product of the post-70 era which has been retrospectively positioned in the third decade of the Common Era, or whether one sees the material as being basically historically accurate, but having been selected (as all historical writing must be) from a much larger range of material: that in either case an act of selectivity occurred, and this after the Second Temple's destruction, is undeniable. Thus, as historical evidence, the basic "New Testament" narrative, composed after 70 CE, indirectly informs the reader of the responses of the Jesus-followers to the Temple crisis. The anti-Pharisaic allusions of most parts of the Gospels (particularly anti-Pharisaic as compared to Paul's letters) provide us with a set of metering points that help to chart the emergence of the Rabbinic Jewish faith in those years when its own historical documents are the least substantial. That the Gospels reflect the situation and attitudes of the post-70 CE Christian communities – and are not strictly reporting on the situation in the 20s and 30s of the first century – is indicated by their single most obvious (and thus most easily overlooked) characteristics: the author-editors of the Four Gospels and Jesus never disagree.[26]

Undeniably, the attitudes toward the Pharisees contained in the "New Testament" of course are complex, but, like a classic spatter-diagram, show a clear pattern: the later a book of Christian scriptures comes in the ordinal (that is, sequential) list of date-of-composition, the more it contains anti-Pharisaic material and the more it transforms the tension between Jesus and his followers from a general problem into a set of bi-modal tensions between Christians and Pharisees. Colloquially: later, hater.[27]

Thus, the Gospel of Mark is least hard on the Pharisees. Jesus and the Pharisees argue points of Halachah, such as dietary rules (2:16–20), table-cleanliness and cooking rules (7:1–23), matters that enhull big spiritual principles in small, everyday practices, as both sides acknowledge. The argument is presented as being generally respectful on each side, if spirited. Only rarely does Mark permit Jesus to say something nasty about the Pharisees – as, "beware of the leaven of the Pharisees, and of the leaven of Herod" (8:15). And, on the rigour-of-the-law question, Mark does not permit a simple dichotomy to emerge, with Jesus embracing the spirit of the law, the Pharisees the letter: when the matter of divorce comes up (10:1–12), Jesus asserts a position more rule-bound, less-flexible, less forgiving, than do the Pharisees. Most significantly, the author-editor(s) of the Gospel of Mark present the story of the crucifixion of Jesus in a remarkable way: although the Pharisees are mentioned early in Mark as plotting with the "Herodians" to destroy Jesus (3:6) and, later, as trying to catch him in seditious speech (12:13), when one comes to the passion story, they are absent. One has the elders, the high priest, the chief priests, the scribes, all mentioned as participants, but no Pharisees. Perhaps this is sloppy narration on the author-editor(s)' part, but I strongly doubt it: the Gospel of Mark is too tight a composition, too spare in its words, too far from being frivolous in execution to carelessly drop a major set of characters. The exclusion of the Pharisees from the passion story – and thus from direct blame for the death of Jesus – should be taken as a conscious decision. That said, the Gospel of Mark indicates that, at the time of the Temple's destruction or shortly thereafter: (a) the Pharisees were established as major rivals of the Christians, but that they were not a polar antithesis of Christianity, for in Mark's account, Jesus debates with them in a common vocabulary and is on occasion more Pharisaic than they are; and (b) that the Pharisees were neither to be declared the sole Judahist faction that opposed Christianity, nor to be demonized as the killers of the Christ.

These two characteristics are taken from Mark and are assimilated into Luke and Matthew, but, successively, the books become sharper, and often nastier in ancillary details concerning the Pharisees. Take Luke: while a bit harsher on the Pharisees, it is far from denunciatory. Jesus is reported three times to have had a meal in the home of a Pharisee (7:36–50, 11:37–54 and 14:1–35). On the first occasion, he gently explains to his host, Simon, the nature of the forgiveness of sins. In the second instance, he has an argument with the Pharisee about ritual cleanliness before meals and calls the Pharisees, "fools," and "hypocrites" for being so shallow in their devotional life. And in the third case, he visits the house of "one of the chief Pharisees" (14:1) on Shabbat and there has a debate about what it is lawful to do on the Sabbath. Not surprisingly, Jesus wins the debate. In these stories there is clearly a disapproval of the Pharisees and, in the second instance (11:54), the story concludes with the Pharisees committing themselves to catching Jesus out in some grievous error, so that they can bring him before the authorities. However, the tone of the three tales is not acrid, and, Jesus' having a meal with various Pharisees is an indication that the Pharisees and Jesus-followers were not – in the view of the author-editor(s) of Luke – beyond the civilities of being able to break bread together.

The Gospel of Matthew permits each of these three meetings to take place, but for the author-editor(s) of that book, they are not occasions of comity, but of tense incivility. The meal in the house of Simon the Pharisee (Luke 7:36–50) becomes in Matthew a visit to the home (but not a bread-breaking) of "Simon the Leper"! (Matt. 26:6–13). The third meal (Luke 14:1–35), the Shabbat meal and discussion with one of the chief Pharisees, has portions retold in Matthew (Matt. 22:1–14 and 10:37–39), but in completely different contexts and with no reference to any Pharisee, let alone any indication that Jesus shared Shabbat with one of their leaders. These two instances are revealing, but the discussion in the Gospel of Matthew at the second meal (cf. Luke 11:37–54) is the most revealing. Whereas Luke had gentled Jesus' indictment of the Pharisees' alleged vanity, pettifogging, and spiritual barrenness, by setting it within the confines of a Pharisaic house, wherein Jesus accepts food and hospitality, Matthew (23:1–39) transforms it into a long public address. The "scribes and Pharisees" (but primarily the Pharisees) are denounced for mere show-acting in wearing tefillin and prayer shawls. They grab the best rooms at feasts and the best seats in houses of worship; they make long public prayers, yet toss destitute widows out of their lodgings. And on and on: the Pharisees are called a generation of vipers and, in a rabid pericope that borders on blood-libel (23:34–35, and 37), Matthew has Jesus state that the Pharisees and scribes will either scourge or kill the prophets and wise men who will be sent to enlighten them, and thus will become responsible for "all the righteous blood shed upon the earth, from the blood of righteous Abel unto the blood of Zacharias son of Barachias, whom ye slew between the temple [sanctuary] and the altar" (23:35). That is formidable guilt indeed, running from the first human murder (Gen. 4:8–10), to the murder of a priestly reformer in the reign of King Joash, whose death by stoning (2 Chron. 24:20–22) Matthew turns into a parallel to the sacrifice of a lamb, a strong Christian motif.[28] All this guilt, Jesus is supposed to have said, will fall to the present generation of Pharisees and their accomplices, functionaries of Jerusalem's religious establishment. In the Gospel of Matthew, the allegation of blood guilt on the Pharisees' part, stops just short of its logical conclusion: that the Pharisees were largely responsible for deicide, the killing of Jesus the Christ, for Matthew follows Mark in omitting the Pharisees from the short litany of villains who are central to the crucifixion.[29]

The Gospel of John, however, transverses that line, and with a vengeance, literally. For John, the vices of all forms of Judaism are summed up in the Pharisees, and there is almost no civil interaction with them. Instead, there is demonization. In contrast to the Synoptic Gospels, the Gospel of John has the Pharisees occupying in the Judahist religious polity a position which was only obtained by their Rabbinic descendants in the years after the Temple's destruction: they are presented as part of the religious and civil establishment and as the spearhead of enforced religious conformity. The only Pharisee to receive a good press in John is Nicodemus, "a ruler of the Jews," (that is, probably, a member of the Sanhedrin) who comes to Jesus by night and asks for spiritual advice. He addresses Jesus as "Rabbi" and treats him with respect (3:1–21). Later, when the Pharisees and the chief priests resolve to seize Jesus (note the alliance), Nicodemus argues that it was a violation of Torah to seize anyone before his words were heard and his actions observed. For his courage, Nicodemus was accused of being a crypto-Galilean, that is, a follower of Jesus (7:32–53). Nicodemus is last heard of bringing a hundred weight of spices (a fortune) to the secret place where Jesus' body was taken immediately after his crucifixion (19:38–39). Nicodemus stands out, because the Pharisees as a group are painted as powerful, malicious, oppressive, and almost unrelievedly evil: in John's narrative, the figure of Nicodemus is brilliantly drawn, so as to make an ideological point: that the Pharisees' practice of evil was a matter of their own choice (they all could have acted like Nicodemus), and because their actions were volitional, they were fully responsible for them. The gravamen of the charge against them in the Gospel of John is that the Pharisees are the chief instigators of deicide. They watch Jesus carefully and are the instigating element against Jesus. (In John, unlike the Synoptics, there is only one reference to "the scribes"; it is the Pharisees whom John sees as the active agent.) After a good deal of intelligence-gathering by the Pharisees, they and the chief priests convene a council, to discuss the danger Jesus presents for all of them: if he is allowed to teach, soon we will have no followers and the Romans will see this and take away the privileged position that they permit us to occupy. So, the Pharisees and the chief priests resolve to have him killed (11:47–53). Crucially, when Judas Iscariot strikes a deal to identify Jesus to his enemies, it is a malign covenant among Judas, the high priest, and the Pharisees (18:2–3). It is hard to conceive of a more bitter hate-cocktail than that: the Pharisees, the leaders of the Jerusalem Temple, and Judah generally ("Judas" being the perfect stage name for all the Judahisms of Jesus' time) are Christ-killers: the instigators, the primary agents are the Pharisees, the touchstones of the tradition of Rabbinic Judaism.

4

If this Christian material is so morally spavined, why must anyone who is seriously interested in the invention of Rabbinic Judaism study it seriously? Because in the slope of the anti-Pharisaic gradient that runs through the historical sections of the "New Testament," one has an indirect, but clear, indication of some of the basic facts about the evolution of the Rabbinic Jewish faith, confirmation of fundamental matters that otherwise would be conjectural or, at best, positioned on a wobbly evidentiary base.

Recall how infrequently during our examination of the Tanakh and of the Christian scriptures it has been possible to cite useful third-party evidence of a given occurrence, belief, or historical development. Only rarely has there been information about the early Yahweh-faith or about the Judahisms of the later Second Temple era that is genuinely independent, in the sense of being produced in, or near, the same time period as the document we are dealing with, but by someone outside the circle of belief of whomever wrote the biblical or parabiblical text. Here the value of the Christian scriptures is that they provide a set of texts that were set down centuries before the Talmuds and a century or more before the Mishnah. If read through the appropriate corrective lens, they (a) provide independent confirmation of many of the statements made in those later Jewish texts; (b) they yield amplification or *mise en scène* on many matters and (c) they give information concerning the emergence of Rabbinic Judaism that is not included in the Mishnah or the Talmuds.

The time-gradient that I have proposed as central to the Pauline letters and to the historical narratives of the Christian scriptures[30] can be interpreted not only as indicative of Christianity's emerging anti-Pharisaic attitudes but, equally important, as confirmation by non-Rabbinic sources of the fact that in the second half of the first century of the Common Era, Pharisaism was metamorphosing into Rabbinic Judaism. This has usually been taken as a given within the Jewish faith, but for that reason external verification is all the more valuable.

The really valuable probative point, however, appears concerning the relationship of the two emerging faiths. The Christian scriptures are increasingly harsh in their depictions of Pharisaism at the time of Jesus because, in the post-70 CE period, the Jesus-followers were increasingly frightened. The time-gradient I have been employing is also a gradient-of-fear, and the fear is of the growing ideological attractiveness and of the surprisingly-resilient social force of embryonic Rabbinism as it rumbles forth after the destruction of the Temple. To the Jesus-followers, the rise of Rabbinic Judaism must have been akin to feeling the seismic shifts of a nascent volcano. Granted, in the writings of Flavius Josephus and in the Talmuds, one receives the basic factual information about the Pharisees and their evolution into Rabbinic Jews, but only in the emotional response implied in the Christian scriptures – the fear, and its false analgesic, hate – do we encounter a contemporary perception and, indeed, an informed independent one: something big was happening in the wake of the Temple's destruction. The same thing was happening among the Pharisees as among the Jesus-followers: time was compressed, immense energy was expended, great religious inventiveness exhibited. The emotional response to the fearsome venting and eventual rise of this force which is found in the Christian scriptures is a necessary antidote to the cool, carefully metered picture of evolution that the Mishnah and the Talmuds later impress upon the past. For catching the fearsome eruption of the last thirty years of the first century, the "New Testament" is unsurpassed.

More than only two of the many Judahisms of the later Second Temple times survived into the post-Temple era, but the Christian scriptures are right: the two that counted were the Jesus-followers (who become the Christian church) and the Pharisees (who become the Rabbinic Jews).[31] This means that just as it is impossible to understand the evolution of the Jesus-followers into the Christian church during the last thirty years of the first century unless one takes into account their fraught relationship with Pharisaism and embryonic Rabbinism – so too is it impossible to comprehend the history of Rabbinic Judaism without accepting, analysing and incorporating into that story Rabbinism's relationship with the early Christian church. Neither history makes sense without the other. This seemingly obvious point requires emphasis because it runs counter to the dominant tradition of Jewish scholarship, from Rabbinic times to the present day. Jacob Neusner, in discussing the development of Rabbinic Judaism in the time of the Christianized emperor Constantine the Great, summarizes the scholarly situation as follows:

> The thesis argued here contradicts the theory that Judaism ignored its competition and went its way in splendid isolation. Historians of Judaism take as dogma the view that Christianity never made any difference to Judaism. Faith of a "people that dwells apart," Judaism explored paths untouched by Christians. Christianity – people hold – was born in the matrix of Judaism, but Judaism, from the beginning until now, ignored the new "daughter" religion and followed its majestic course in lonely dignity. Since (the argument is implicitly made) Judaism is supposed always to have ignored, and never to have been affected by Christianity in any form, the future security of the faith of Judaism requires the continuation of this same policy, pretending that Christianity never made, and does not make, any difference at all to Israel, the Jewish people. This dogma of scholarship carries with it an imperative for contemporary policy. I argue here that quite to the contrary, the Judaism expressed by the writings of the sages of the Land of Israel in the fourth century – the age of Constantine – not only responded to issues raised for Israel by the political triumph of Christianity but did so in a way that, intellectually at least, made possible the entire future history of Judaism in Europe and beyond.[32]

The only amendment one could make to Neusner's statement is to add that, although the Jewish response to Christianity's political triumph in the fourth century was a central event in Jewish history (for it marks the response to a new phenomenon, antisemitism engendered by the melding of anti-Jewish attitudes with the apparatus of state power), one should accept the probability that the foundation for the vigorous fourth-through-sixth-century response by Rabbinic leaders, was laid soon after the destruction of the Second Temple. It was at that point that percipient observers could see that the multi-factional rivalry of the Second Temple era was being replaced by a bi-modal rivalry between two of the pre-70 CE Judahisms: the Jesus-faith and the Pharisaic-Rabbinic beliefs.

The rivalry, the dialectic, and the inevitable ideational interdependence between the two former-Judahisms, have not been matters that either Jews or Christians have been inclined to view squarely. From the last three decades of the first century onwards, the relationship in those developmentally-crucial years has been approached only with squinted eyes: for to look at the formative relationship directly precluded (and still precludes) either group's claiming superiority to the other based on religious genealogy. As David Flusser, the Israeli scholar and specialist in the later Second Temple era, noted: "Judaism and Christianity are not mother and daughter, but they are in reality sisters, because the mother of both is ancient Judaism."[33]

5

Like the inventors of Christianity, the inventors of the Rabbinic Jewish faith
not only accepted the paradigms of the grammar of religious invention that
were laid down in the primary section of the Tanakh – the Genesis-Kings
unity – but they worked with the various metaphors, images, and belief units
that were easily accessible to anyone familiar with the wide variety of sects
and factions that made up later Second Temple Judahism. That the Rabbis put
the pieces together differently than did the Christian writers is hardly surprising. Yet, in noting that fact, one must simultaneously recognize that they, like
the inventors of the "New Testament," made their new religion mostly
(although not entirely) from standard-issue parts.

Significantly, in their massive re-invention of the Yahweh-religion, the
Rabbis added three new paradigms to the grammar of religious invention that
had been operative since the first compilation of Genesis-Kings. The first of
these unique Rabbinic rules was: refer to the followers of Jesus (and, later, to
the Christian church) as little as possible. For Christians this is deeply frustrating, but it is a sound principle: don't advertise the opposition.[34] The lofty
dismissal of Christianity through silence was a very effective device. At this
point – on the question of how to deal with their primary rivals that emerged
after 70 CE – the inventors of the new Jewish and the new Christian texts
made radically different decisions. The author-editors of the "New Testament" referred quite frequently, and increasingly unpleasantly, to the Pharisees. On the other hand, the Rabbis for the most part treated the followers of
Jesus with contemptuous silence.

Paradoxically, a second rule of Rabbinic religious invention ran counter to
the first. It was an entirely unspoken rubric, namely: always be aware of what
the Christians are up to; don't pay them direct attention; don't dignify them
by direct debate in sacred writings; but keep them always in the corner of
your eye. On the surface that seems to contradict the first rule of Rabbinic invention, but it too was a primary historical reality. Merely because in the
Mishnah and the Talmuds the Rabbis implicitly deny that they are paying any
real mind to the Christians does not mean that we should take this at face
value. Their behaviour in the invention of a whole new range of religious
texts (from the Mishnah onwards) makes sense only if one recognizes that
one of the determinants of the ambient conditions under which they worked
was Christianity, and thus Christianity in part influenced the nature of their
religious beliefs, practices, and actions, usually in a negative way. To use an
analogy from the physical world: observing the evolutionary path of Rabbinic Judaism is like tracking a particle through a finite space. We notice that
it does not follow a straight trajectory, but yet the particle itself yields no information on what is influencing its path. We therefore hypothesize that some
force – say, in this instance, a forceful, but not overpowering, negative
magnetic pole – is influencing its trajectory. If we do our calculations and our

subsequent observations correctly, we can calibrate the interaction of the fast-moving particle and the unseen field that is affecting it, either by attraction or repulsion.

A third new addition to the grammar of religious invention follows from the first two: the Rabbis avoid as much as possible forms of discourse, motifs, and units of belief that the Christian scriptures employ. As we will note in detail in subsequent chapters, the two related rhetorical forms that the Christian scriptures employed most effectively – historical narrative and its continuation as detailed apocalyptic literature – find scant place in the Rabbinic texts, even though the forms were the best known and most frequently employed in Second Temple texts. Further, although the Rabbis do indeed indicate a belief in some of the same late Second Temple ideas that the "New Testament" adopts, they are careful to vary the context, connotations, and ideational content. The concepts of Moshiah and of the resurrection of the dead are key exhibits: don't duplicate the Christians.

These three Rabbinical additions to the ancient grammar of religious invention were necessary because of the historical position of the leaders of Rabbinic Judaism in the first half-millennium of the Common Era: they had to deny and, nevertheless, always be conscious of a gravelly fact: Christianity had got there first. The inventors of the "New Testament" had assimilated to the Jesus-faith many of the most effective modes of argument and many of the most attractive ideas and symbols from the wide array available in later Second Temple times. And (as I argued in Chapters Eight and Nine), the Christian writers put them together to form a new and highly compelling invention, a religious system that works quite brilliantly. So the challenge facing the Rabbis was to invent an alternate system (all the time, like all inventors within the Yahweh-tradition, asserting that no new invention was involved, just the recovery of true traditions), and to do so without duplicating the "New Testament's" methods or material. Their task was markedly more difficult than that of the author-editors of the Christian texts.

Throughout this book, I have argued in scores of instances against the belief that older is better. The overlapping of the concepts of antiquity, authenticity, and authority has been consistently rejected as magical, muzzy, and mystifying. That Christianity was the first faith to crystallize out of Second Temple Judaism after 70 CE and the Rabbinic Jewish faith the second, is merely a statement of historical sequence. To deny that sequence, and to minimize the difficulties it implied, is to denigrate the Rabbis' genius.

The problem facing the Rabbis was the same one that had been encountered by the ancient Judahist writers after the destruction of Solomon's Temple, and the same one that later faced "New Testament" writers: how to perpetuate a temple-based religion after the Temple was razed. As in those other two cases, dazzlingly brilliant inventiveness characterized the response, and world-forming texts were the concrete embodiment of that inventiveness.

6

Although Pharisaic-Rabbinic Jewish emergence is (along with Christianity) the most important development from out of the multiple Judahisms of the late Second Temple age, the other forms did not die out immediately. Some lasted for a generation or two, tiny runnels that eventually ran bone dry and disappeared. A few texts survive from these non-Rabbinic, non-Christian factions from the Second Temple, and they are particularly helpful in documenting the trauma that the events of 66–73 CE inflicted upon all Judahist groups. We possess four primary documents from the period 70–132 CE that, although distinct from both Pharisaic-Rabbinic and Christian belief systems, are written entirely within the grammar of biblical invention, the product of various Judahist factions trying to make sense out of a world that had lost its centre. The documents are: the Apocalypse of Abraham,[35] the Book of Fourth Ezra (usually called Second Esdras in the English-language apocrypha),[36] the Book of Second Baruch,[37] and the Book of Fourth Baruch.[38] True to the tradition of parabiblical invention, each of these books is ascribed to an early figure: the patriarch Abraham, the prophet Ezra, the prophet Jeremiah and his secretary Baruch (2 Baruch), or to Baruch alone (4 Baruch). Each is in the form that we saw becoming common in later Second Temple Judaism, the apocalyptic vision. Each of these four visions is set in a spurious past. This is a standard declension in the grammar of scriptural invention. The apocalypse of Abraham places its interpretation of the destruction of the Second Temple in the oldest possible stratum of Israel's history, the life of the man with whom Yahweh made the original covenant. The other three apocalypses deal with the destruction of the Second Temple by adopting a fictional premise: that the new text they are creating is an ancient document and that they are talking about the destruction of Solomon's Temple. The post-70 CE writing of each is betrayed in the respective texts and, in fact, the historical anachronisms that indicate the post-70 invention of these texts should not be considered a flaw: the purpose of the documents is to act as an analgesic for the trauma of 70 CE, and because the main message is "this is not an unknown horror nor an insurmountable one," the wee clues are a source of reassurance to the reader or listener that, yes, this applies to us and applies now. The trauma is deep, however, as the cry of pain in 2 Esdras (10:21–23, RSV) makes achingly clear.

For you see how our sanctuary has been laid waste, our altar thrown down, our temple destroyed; our harp has been laid low, our song has been silenced, and our rejoicing has been ended; the light of our lampstand has been put out, the ark of our covenant has been plundered, our holy things have been polluted, and the name by which we are called has been almost profaned; our children have suffered abuse, our priests have been burned to death, our Levites have gone into exile, our virgins have been defiled, and our wives have been ravished; our righteous men have been carried off, our little ones have been cast out, our young men have been enslaved and our strong men made powerless. And, worst of all, the seal of Zion has been deprived of its glory, and given over into the hands of those that hate us.

In these four texts one observes many of the methods and motifs that were found in the wide range of texts in late Second Temple Judaism and several of which were bound together in the "New Testament." For example, in the Apocalypse of Abraham, the "Eternal, Mighty One" shows Abraham the destruction of the Temple from a stance that is before time begins (chapter 27), which means that the Temple's creation and destruction was predestined in the creation itself. Second Baruch promises that Jerusalem will be "restored forever" (6:9), but only after predestined disaster. Second Esdras provides a vision of a heavenly Jerusalem (10:25–28) (bringing to mind both the Book of Enoch and the Book of Revelation), and Fourth Baruch has the sacred vessels of the Temple preserved until the future coming of "the beloved one" (3:11). As that verse implies, Moshiah, or at least, Moshiah-like figures are part of the analgesic, not only in Fourth Baruch, but also in Second Baruch (especially chapters 30, 39–40, and 72–73). Through all four apocalypses the figures of angels and heavenly messengers, familiar from Second Temple texts (some, indeed, we already know by name, so familiar are they), enter and exit frequently.[39]

These four texts, with their hopes for restoration of former Temple glories, either by a Messiah or by another form of divine force, mesh with the hopes and faith of a distinctly this-worldly event: the Bar Kokhba revolt of 132–135 CE.[40] This is one of the most mysterious events in Jewish history, for, though it was a major guerrilla war in Judea – roughly 600,000 Jews were killed, according to Cassius Dio's perhaps-exaggerated account[41] – little can be said about it with certainty. What caused the revolt is unclear (the best-argued cases are for a Roman ban on circumcision and for a Roman plan to turn the still-derelict Jerusalem into an entirely new Gentile city). What social group raised the revolt is unclear: most accounts emphasize the peasant background, but the leaders were literate and received some support from the religious elite. Most importantly, it is not clear if the revolutionaries ever gained control of Jerusalem and, if they did, whether they re-instituted ritual sacrifice and began to rebuild the Temple.

Yet, for all that uncertainty, the Bar Kokhba episode brought together in one person two of the potential methods of filling the aching void left with the Temple's ruin: either take matters in one's own hands and re-establish a Judean state and rebuild the Temple, or await the Moshiah and flock to his banner. Simon Bar Koziva, the leader of the revolt, was certainly a palpable figure, for it took the Romans four years to suppress him: a military genius, certainly. However, the interesting part is the way that he was also a religious construct, and this in his own lifetime. His *nom de guerre* comes from the Tanakh (Numbers 24:17): Baalam (that most ambiguous figure) prophesies that a star (Kokhba) would come out of Jacob and would smite Moab and Sheth. This name was applied to Simon – he became Simon Bar Kokhba – by one of the great Rabbis of his time, Akiba (var: Aqiva) who declared him to be the Messiah.[42] This opinion was not endorsed by most other contemporary Rabbis, as far as the Talmuds inform us, but the fact that Akiba's opinion was not simply deleted from later records indicates that the belief in Bar Kokhba's being Moshiah was too widespread to be completely suppressed; so Bar Kokhba, having failed, was declared a false Moshiah. The ironic twist on the name of this warrior was that his enemies – and when he failed, he naturally had many – denominated him Simon Bar Kosiva, meaning Son of the Lie.[43] So, the greatest Jewish military leader of late antiquity was both a real person and a persona created strictly according to the rules of biblical invention: rather than creating a new identity, he assumed an authoritative one from the ancient past; and by the ironic double-meanings and puns used so often in the Hebrew scriptures, his own surname was transformed, first, into an heroic epithet and then into a scurrilous judgement upon him.

Where the Pharisaic-Rabbinical line of evolution intersected with the causes of Bar Kokhba's military and messianic movement is impossible to determine. It is hard to believe, however, that only Akiba was an advocate of Bar Kokhba. But if it is so difficult to define causes, the effects are obvious. The Rabbinical literature recognized Bar Kokhba's military genius but, equally, the hideous cost of life during the Roman suppression and, most important, the danger of following a false Moshiah.[44]

Thus, the final impact of the Bar Kokhba revolt upon evolving Rabbinic Judaism was to confirm the virtue of concentrating on the codification of proper religious and social behaviour. The chief alternatives were for the Rabbis to write their own primary narrative of events affecting their faith from, say, 66 CE through 135, or to project history into the future, as is done in apocalyptic writing. However, first, Christianity had appropriated these forms in the "New Testament" and, now, the lessons of Bar Kokhba seemed to be that history did not work very well, that Messianic faith was a dangerous, potentially self-immolating device, and that apocalyptic moments were less sure than were the benisons of a deeply disciplined daily devotional life. As we shall see in Chapters Eleven through Thirteen, the Rabbis moved the Temple into every home. And, in the Mishnah and the Talmuds, they invented new forms of sacred text, ones that were intellectually rigorous, devotionally demanding, respectful of tradition, adaptive to new situations, enduring.

· I I ·

The Hermetic, Perfect Mishnah

I

NOW, BRIEFLY, CONTINUE TO DO WHAT THE LEADERS OF THE TWO sister-faiths have hated to do: consider Christianity and Rabbinic Judaism in tandem, for that is how they grew. Like all the Judahisms that flourished in the first century of the Common Era, the adherents of what became Christianity and Rabbinic Judaism faced the common problem of being believers in a temple religion that no longer had a temple. Strikingly, they solved the problem in ways that were at heart very similar, albeit quite divergent in matters of detail. They did this by creating, in each case, a new Temple, one that existed not on this earth but in their head and hearts. And they used the same method to articulate this wonderful other-world invention: both the Jesus-faith and the Pharisees-Rabbis embraced the Tanakh – the "Old Testament" – and then added to it a completely new set of sacred texts, ones that were compatible with the Tanakh and which, simultaneously, radically re-invented its meaning in the light of more recent circumstances. The Christians got this job done quickly. The base-texts of their "New Testament" were available in polished form well before the end of the first century, and by roughly 150, their "New Covenant" was complete. Unlike the Christians, the Rabbis[1] never called their new texts "scriptures," nor did they label the completed product a "New Covenant," or a "New Testament." Yet they would have been justified in doing so, for their collective enterprise was every bit as radical, and successful a set of inventions and re-inventions of the old Yahweh-faith as was that achieved by the followers of their sister religion, the Jesus-faith. The Rabbinical corpus took much longer to shape than did the Christian – the year 600 is a reasonable completion date – and was exponentially larger (see Appendix E); but the fundamental activity was the same, and the respect for the grammar of invention developed in the texts of the Yahweh-faith and the various Judahisms that spun off from it was maintained. Given this basic point of Jewish and Christian inventiveness being fundamentally similar in the years immediately following the destruction of the Second Temple, the Jewish response should now be looked at on its own.

2

The heart of Rabbinic Judaism is a text that is one of the most mysterious one can encounter, for it hides its secrets in plain sight, the most cunning form of camouflage. This is the "Mishnah," a term that comes from the verb *shanah*, meaning to repeat, to learn, to teach, to study, and to heed oral instruction.[2] The book in its English language version is dense and large (between eight and nine hundred pages in Herbert Danby's translation)[3] and over eleven hundred in Jacob Neusner's.[4] The bilingual edition of Philip Blackman runs to six volumes of text and one of technical apparatus.[5] The Mishnah consists of six "Seder," (a term that literally meant "recitation," but which has come in English-language scholarship to mean Orders, or Divisions), and within each are several tractates, each of which bears a name that is used in reference systems – as is done with the "books" of the Tanakh and the "New Testament." In its present-day form, the Mishnah has sixty-three tractates. However, one of these (Aboth) is stapled on, a later addition to the Mishnah that provides a spiritual genealogy for the other tractates. (This will be discussed in Chapter Twelve.) Also, part of another tractate (Sotah) almost certainly is a later addition, for it mentions events and individuals from a time after the Mishnah's closure.[6] Still, even with those items excised, one is encountering a massive polished megalith, a huge, square-cut foundation stone not just for a single building, but for an entire city, the heavenly city of the classical Rabbis.

Encountering a phenomenon such as this, a normal, and normally curious, human being would walk around it a few times, stopping occasionally to stare intently and to blink in continuing surprise; and would look for a maker's-mark, an indication of origin. There is none. No designer's-mark (though one can speculate productively about that matter). This is not too troubling, for most of the works in the Tanakh and in the Apocrypha and Pseudepigrapha are either anonymous or are effectively so, being ascribed to authoritative figures who could not have written them. Disconcertingly, however, there is no indication of how this huge item came to be delivered to our world. That is, unlike the great majority of items in the scriptures, the Dead Sea Scrolls, and the pseudepigraphic religious texts from the later Second Temple period, the Mishnah, the founding invention of Rabbinic Judaism, has no manuscript tradition that lets us get much closer than a millennium after its creation: the earliest full and independent manuscript is from the very end of the fourteenth century. (See Appendix E.) In this world, it is a very strange parcel whose delivery-slip seems to arrive more than a millennium late. Especially such a big item.

Because I will later indicate an economical, and real-world-orientated explanation of how this monument came into being, I should here emphasize the indeterminacy that surrounds the historical situation. In the first place, there is no absolute proof that within the first seven or eight centuries after its completion this composition, the Mishnah, actually existed as a book: meaning, as a composition placed on vellum or parchment, and which was recognized as an object in itself. One traditional school of thought has posited that the Mishnah was, in fact, a living book, maintained orally by cadres of trained memorizers: that it was not taken down as a unified written composition, although large portions are included in the two Talmuds. A commentary on the Mishnah as a separate document is believed to have been made by Saadya Gaon (882–941), so a complete text of the Mishnah as an independent document probably existed in the tenth century, although not necessarily the version we at present possess. Only in the twelfth century, with the work of the great Maimonides (1138–1204) was the text standardized in its present order. Even so, the earliest complete manuscript of the Mishnah as a separate entity, a book, is dated 1399–1401.[7] The present text of the Mishnah is a conflation of various sources and should be considered open to further revision: we are a generation away from a true critical edition being completed.[8] So, at present, we work with the text that will probably be revised in the future, and which has a provenance and a history that is at best speculative.

But what a text it is!

Forbidding, enticing, obvious, impenetrable, seductive, vexing, and all at once.

What is one to make of a document that seems to be an assortment of legal arguments, many of them unsettled? To take only three examples at random:

6:8 A. He who takes a vow not to eat dates is permitted to have date honey.

B. [He who takes a vow not to eat] winter grapes is permitted to have the vinegar made from winter grapes.

C. R. Judah b. Beterah says, "Anything which is called after the name of that which is made from it, and one takes a vow not to have it – he is prohibited also from eating that which comes from it."

D. But sages permit.   (Nedarim 6:8, Neusner ed.)

....

I.   A. Two brothers –

B. one deaf-mute and the other of sound senses –

C. married to two sisters of sound senses –

D. the deaf-mute, husband of a sister of sound senses, died –

E. what should the husband of sound senses who is married to the sister of sound senses do?

F. She [the deceased childless brother's widow] should go forth on the grounds of being the sister of his wife.

II.   G. [If] the husband of sound senses of a sister of sound senses died,

H. what should the deaf-mute who is husband of the sister of sound senses do?

I. He should put away his wife with a writ of divorce, and the wife of his brother is prohibited [for marriage to anybody at all] for all time.

(Yebamoth 14:4. Neusner ed.)

....

6. A gutter-spout cannot give title by usucaption, but title by usucaption can be claimed to the place [on which it discharges]. A gutter can give title by usucaption. An Egyptian ladder cannot secure title by usucaption, but a Tyrian ladder can do so. An Egyptian window cannot secure title by usucaption, but a Tyrian window can do so. What is an "Egyptian window"? Any through which a man's head cannot enter. R. Judah says: If it has a frame, even though a man's head cannot enter through it, it can secure title by usucaption. A projection, if it extends a hand-breadth [or more] can secure title by usucaption, and the other [into whose premises it projects] can protest against it; but if it is less than a handbreadth it cannot secure title by usucaption, and the other cannot protest against it.

(Baba Bathra 3:6. Danby ed.)

A dozen more examples, or a dozen-dozen, would produce the same result: the puzzled, and increasingly bewildered query, what is going on here? One feels as if one has stumbled upon the social, business, and building code of some great metropolis, and that one is reading the précis of the intra-office memos of the by-laws enforcement branch of the government. One is. The metropolis is the heavenly city and there is no civil government, however, only divine.

One way to understand the Mishnah is to view it as the fine print, the clarifying sub-clauses, on the forever contract with Yahweh. It is a re-invention of the legal portions of the Pentateuch. The Mishnah simultaneously raises (and sometimes settles) many of the issues of everyday life on earth, but, taken as a unity, it defines a Utopia, a heaven. The text has multiple meanings and some very unusual features, but it sits comfortably within the grammar of religious invention that we have already seen in operation several times, because it takes the original covenant as its starting point, honours that covenant both implicitly and directly and re-invents the covenant, without ever admitting that it is doing so.

3

Yet, this massive religious invention possesses some characteristics so unusual that one can approach it most realistically by defining what it is *not*.

It is not narrative.

The Mishnah's inventors adopt a change in rhetorical strategy (though not in underlying ideology) that is so startling that one blinks, as if sun-struck. Previously, the overwhelming bulk of the texts that articulate the religious visions in, and stemming from, the Yahweh-faith, were narratives: the Genesis-Kings unity that forms and dominates the Tanakh; the biographical accounts of Yeshua-of-Nazareth, which, when re-invented by the author-editors of the "New Testament," create Jesus-the-Christ; the apocalyptic literature of the Tanakh (the Book of Daniel), of the "inter-testamental" apocalyptic writings, such as the Books of Jubilees and of Enoch and the later Book of Revelation in the "New Testament" all were future-narratives, and very powerful ones. Narrative is the most effective way that any society, any religion, any human being, explains to themselves who they are. It is the mode of thought through which the ancient Hebrews taught us to think about ourselves. Their narratives, unlike those of classical Greece and Rome never lost adhesion: we had to rediscover classical civilization. That of the ancient Semites was always with us, and, indeed, is the core of western identity, a spine around which are arranged other, more visible, less central cultural attributes.

So, it is stunning, literally, to find that the Mishnah, the foundation of Judaism as it evolved from the destruction of the Second Temple to the present day, abandoned narrative. This is all the more astonishing, because the form of narrative that was perfected within the Yahweh-Judahist-Christian rubrics of religious invention – the *historical* narrative – was, and is, the most compelling ever created: compelling, not merely in the literary sense, but compelling of the people whom it inspirited, to behave in certain ways, ranging from deepest saintliness to God-driven barbarism. Not always a nice narrative tradition, but as powerful as ever built: why give that up and instead produce a document that seems at first encounter to be a set of municipal by-laws, even if they are for a heavenly city? All-the-more are we puzzled for the two elements that are traditionally denominated as the components of the Yahweh-faith and of its descendants – "Halachach" (law) and "Aggadah" (narrative) – had a comfortable and effective fit. The narrative carried the legal components. (Does anyone think that the 613 commandments of the "Old Testament" would have been palatable without the Moses-narrative?) The Mishnah has very few bits of narrative: they are tiny tales only, tucked into the interstices of the by-laws, and no sustained story whatsoever.

History, in the long-narrative mode that is so familiar in the scriptures, disappears in the Mishnah and, indeed, in all of the later classical Rabbinic literature most of which is, primarily, a commentary on the Mishnah. In later expounding the Mishnah, the Rabbis sometimes introduce anecdotes and, in the early middle ages a genre of religious folk-tale emerges in the Jewish faith, but from the invention of the Mishnah onwards, the ability to articulate the big-story, the extended historical narrative, disappears for centuries. In the Mishnah, the historical writings of the Tanakh are cited only three dozen times, in the several thousand legal arguments that are put forward.[9] As Yosef H. Yerushalmi notes concerning the Mishnah and the later commentaries upon it, "where historical specificity is a hallmark of the biblical narratives, here that acute biblical sense of time and place often gives way to rampant and seemingly unselfconscious anachronism."[10] In fact, Yerushalmi argues that the ability and will to write sustained narrative history did not reappear amidst the Jewish intellectual elite until the resurgence of Jewish historical writing in the sixteenth century and, even then, it sputtered until, finally, with the Jewish Enlightenment it was fully rekindled.[11] This is not to say that time (and, therefore, history) is completely absent from the Mishnah and its commentaries, but time and history become intellectual categories, frozen series of events, resembling, as Jacob Neusner notes, a set of Platonic categories, rather than a story-line.[12] One of the few things we can infer with certainty about the author-editors of the Mishnah is that they were individuals who were heartily sick of history as a contingent narrative, a sequence of events that could end unhappily.

And so heart-scalded were they with their own recent history that they could not embrace with any enthusiasm the concept of future-history, or entertain a narrative that might come out the right way. This is indicated in three ways. In the first place, there is (in my reading) no sequence in the Mishnah that could be described as being "apocalyptic" in any meaningful sense of that word. One could stretch a point and argue that the Mishnah's description of the Temple is apocalyptic, because there certainly was no Temple on this earth when the Mishnah was being compiled. However, as I will discuss later, even this is too much of a reach, for the invisible Temple that the Mishnah defines was omnipresent: it existed at the moment of its description, not as the architectural climax to some eschatological vision, as in, for example, the Book of Revelation in the Christian scriptures. Secondly, the Mishnah is feather-light on the concept of the resurrection of the body – a concept that is often tied in with apocalyptic beliefs – and almost to the point of non-contact. I can discover only two unambiguous references to the resurrection of the body. One of these is at the very end of the tractate Sotah (9:15) and it declares that the resurrection of the dead shall come "through Elijah." This is the section of Sotah that appears to be a later add-on to the Mishnah, for it contains references to the death of the man who is usually taken to be the final redactor of the Mishnah. Therefore, the reference is suspect. The only other clear annunciation of a belief in the resurrection of the body is in Sanhedrin (10:1) where it is declared that all Israelites have a share in the world to come, save certain heretics, persons who say that the teaching of the resurrection of the dead does not come from the Torah, medical sorcerers, and those who pronounce "YHWH" as "Yahweh" rather than pronouncing it in the Rabbinic way as "Adonai" when it is encountered in a sacred text. Even here, the concept is a long step away from the doctrine of individual resurrection and individual judgement in the end-times that had grown up among several of the Judahist groups in later Second Temple times and here the physical body is not specified: the proof texts employed (Exodus 15:26 and Isaiah 60:21) each refer to collective matters involving all of the nation of Israel, not individuals.[13] And, thirdly, there is remarkably little adherence shown to the concept of Messiah, at least not as evidenced directly. The direct references are in the probably-exogenous portion of Sotah (9:15) which also contains one of the two references to the resurrection of the dead. The other reference is near the beginning of the Mishnah (Berakoth 1:5) where it is ruled that a devout man must recite his evening prayers all the days of his life, even unto the days of Moshiah. Here the signal point is that the interest is in a category of time – the Messianic age – and no mention is made of the actual Moshiah.[14] Now, one may entertain a variety of explanations as to why the editor-authors of the Mishnah did not dwell upon narratives, either in time-past or in time-future, but one has to grant that they did not, and this is one of the several unusual characteristics of this most singular composition.[15]

Given the Mishnah's abandonment of narrative, it is not surprising that it does not adopt any of the devices which would have made it sound like scripture. But that fact is striking, for, as we have seen over and over again, most compositions created within the grammar of religious invention that was determined by the early Yahweh-faith sounded biblical, at least vaguely, and this by authorial intention. The use of biblical language, icons, and devices, gave the various inventions authority, or at least an authoritative tone. The Mishnah, in contrast, sounds like itself and nothing else.

Indeed, the Mishnah's attitude to holy scripture is ambiguous and often distant. Even though the Mishnah is clearly based on the Books of Moses, among the "Halakhot" – sets of legal arguments and judgements contained in the Mishnah – the overwhelming majority do not cite scripture; nor do they contain tropes or rewrites of the scriptures without citation as, for example, the "New Testament" so frequently does. Modern scholars note that there are three forms of rulings, in relation to the scriptures: those that derive from the Tanakh directly; those that are completely independent of the Tanakh; and those which arose independently of holy scripture but which later had Bible verses attached to them or inserted into the course of the dialectic.[16] The first category predominates and the second is small indeed. Some later Rabbis would argue that the Mishnah was entirely based upon scripture, the premises of which were so deeply embedded in the Mishnah that they did not have to be articulated; others, the majority, would argue that the Mishnah was, in considerable part, an independent revelation, albeit one compatible with scripture. Each of these is an argument of apology, based on extra-textual considerations. The observable phenomenon is that in most of their discussions the author-editors of the Mishnah were able to get along without reference to the Torah, to the other scriptures, or to the panoply of religious texts of the later Second Temple period.

Nor, on the surface, do they show much concern with what could be labelled theology, or philosophy. The Mishnah may have a philosophical and theological base, and may even make philosophical and theological statements through its structure and sub-text, but the author-editors do not speak aloud about these matters. Instead, they focus on behaviour. If people act correctly, they seem to say, everything else will follow, including correct belief and a proper relationship with the Almighty. In that regard the Mishnah operates in a manner directly opposite to most modern schools of psychological therapy: with very few exceptions, therapists operate on the premise that behaviour will not straighten out until the patient gets his or her head right. In direct contrast, the Mishnah says, implicitly: behave rightly, and your heart and mind will follow, righteously.

And, finally, the Mishnah is reticent to the point of silence about the very fundamentals of its own existence. It does not specify the audience for which it is intended. It does not indicate its own authorship: numerous authorities are cited, but the compilation and editing of the text itself is not attributed. And, nowhere does it indicate the basis of its own authority, and some authority it is. In tone the Mishnah reminds one of the concept of *magisterium* in the Roman Catholic church in not-so-long-past days; the unquestioned right of the church to determine and teach religious and moral truth.

Upon hearing this, anyone who is familiar with the concept of the Oral, or Dual, Torah, might well ask, "does not the Mishnah state that its authority descends from Mount Sinai and from Moses' encounter with Yahweh at the mount's summit?" No, indeed, the Mishnah does not, although later Rabbinical figures claimed that for the document. This is a crucial point: although the authority of the Mishnah is later ascribed to its being part of a collective oral genealogy that extends all the way back to Moses, the Mishnah itself makes very little of this genealogy and does not in any way rest its authority, as a binding set of sub-clauses in the covenant with Yahweh, on that genealogy. In my reading of the document, I find only five references to Moses or to Mount Sinai, the declared site of the original theophany of the Yahweh-faith, which relate to the Mishnah's authority. And these are noteworthy for how uninterested the participants in the discussions are in the genealogical descent from Sinai on which oral authority is supposed to rest and, presumably this reflects the attitude of the compilers of the Mishnah: five mentions in well over one thousand pages of tight text. (One excludes here the supernumerary tractate Aboth, which was added after the Mishnah was completed; it is discussed in Chapter Twelve.) One of these five mentions (Rosh Hashanah 2:9), a discussion of the proper date of the Day of Atonement, comes close to being a rejection of ancient lineage, rather than a reliance on it for authority. The discussion centres on Rabbi Joshua's feeling ill at ease with Rabban Gamaliel's fixing of the celebration-time of the Day of Atonement. Rabbi Joshua checks with other Sages concerning the proper date. They confirm Rabban Gamaliel's opinion, and Rabbi Dosa ben Harkinas points out that if one were to question the rulings of the court of Rabban Gamaliel, it would be necessary to question the validity of every single court that has existed since Moses' day. Rabbi Dosa ben Harkinas further declares that any time three elders (or more) of the house of Israel called a court into existence, it was equivalent to the court of Moses himself. That is: the cascade of rulings that began in Moses' time have authority not because of Moses or of Sinai, but because the courts themselves have a legitimacy of their own and that as great as Moses. This episode ends with Rabban Gamaliel embracing Rabbi Dosa ben Harkinas and praising him for being a loyal disciple and for accepting all of his rulings.

Another complex case (Yadayim 4:3) involved whether or not diaspora Jews in certain countries had to pay a certain tax – the "poorman's tithe" – every seventh year, or whether they were exempt. The assembled Rabbis voted and later, Rabbi Eliezer, hearing of the decision wept with joy and sent word to the still-assembled Sages: you voted correctly, for I heard a similar ruling from Rabban Yohanan ben Zakkai, who heard it from his mentor, and his teacher from his teacher, that such indeed was the law of Moses. The interesting point here is that the tradition said to stem from Moses does not carry any weight in the discussions. Fortuitously, it coincided with the decisions made totally independently of the Mosaic oral tradition by the assembled Rabbis. It was the collective vote that carried power, and had the vote gone the other way, it would have been equally authoritative. In that case, one presumes that Rabbi Eliezer would have cried just as many tears, but bitter ones, for the authority of the Rabbinical court would have been sufficient to overthrow the remembered whisper of the voice of Moses.

In two other instances (Eduyyoth 8:7 and Pe'ah 2:6) juridical genealogies similar to that of Rabbi Eliezer which I have just cited, were brought forward, but this was done almost in passing, as if the opinions that go back to Moses were of no more (and no less) consequence than those of any Sage. In neither instance did the case in question end with a gavel-thumping indication that the authority of Moses carries the day. *Nor is the authority of the presumed oral link to Moses and to Sinai transferred from the specific case to the Mishnah itself.*

The only instance I can discover where one might plausibly make the case for Moses and Sinai being the source of the Mishnah's authority is a single, almost throwaway line in Hullin (7:6), a tractate that deals with the purity of animals killed for food. There (7:1), a principle called "the sinew of the hip" is articulated, under which the hollow of the thigh bone of domestic and wild animals was not to be consumed. This harkened to Jacob's wrestling with the "angel," an event that resulted in his thigh sinew's atrophying (Genesis 32:32). When the question arose of whether or not this prohibition applied to "unclean" animals, Rabbi Judah pointed out that in ancient times (all the way back to the "children of Jacob") it was all right to eat the sinews of an unclean beast. The assembled Rabbis, however, replied that this argument did

not carry weight. They told him that the rule applied to both clean and unclean animals and that this was a law that came down from Sinai but was only
written down presently. Apparently that assertion won the argument and, with
a very large exegetical lever, one might claim that this was the source of the
Mishnah's authority: that it consisted of laws of the covenant that had come
down from Sinai, had been preserved, and only now were put into writing.
Except, first, that the Mishnah itself makes no such argument, just this off-
hand reference, and, second, this transaction in Hullin leaves the Rabbinical
court in an uncomfortable straddle concerning the law of Moses: the ruling
suggests that the required rules, as found in the Pentateuch (which the Rabbis
believed was written by Moses himself) were in conflict with the required
rules as passed on from Moses by word of mouth. In this case they decided
that the ancient written Torah was superseded by a bit of oral Torah that has
only recently been put into writing. (Presumably, they were referring to an
early version of the Mishnah.) Obviously, however, when Moses crashes into
Moses, the interpreters have a problem, and not surprisingly, they walk away
from the issue as quickly as possible.[17]

Whether or not the authoritative (and at times authoritarian) tone of the
Mishnah was a deviation from, or a confirmation of, the trend of developments
within the Judahisms of the Second Temple is a matter of debate. Martin Noth
argued that well before the canon of the Tanakh was closed, law had become
"an *absolute entity*, valid without respect to precedent, time, or history; based
on itself, binding simply because it existed as law, because it was of divine origin and authority."[18] From that perspective, the Mishnah was a logical continuation of Second Temple developments. In contrast, David Halivni has
suggested that in its unyieldingly apodictic quality, the Mishnah is a deviation
(not an heretical deviant, just a deviation) from the overall trend in Judahist
and later Jewish legal thought. To validate this position he points to a later historical situation which we will ourselves see (in Chapters Twelve and Thirteen) is pertinent: that the emerging Rabbinic community could not long live
with the unyielding tone of the Mishnah, and that within a century, to a century-and-a-half of its closure, strenuous efforts were made to tame the Mishnah, through commentaries upon it and, ultimately, through the Talmuds.[19]
This disagreement between Noth and Halivni is on a fundamental matter that
cannot be simply papered over. In my judgement, Halivni sweeps the day, because his viewpoint can be framed as an historical "prediction" of later behaviour which, when tested against later developments, jibes smoothly with them.
In plain words, Halivni is right: the Mishnah really is something special.

4

But what is it? In modern scholarship, the question has been the cause of a
contest that just-barely is within the Marquis of Queensberry rules, between

the two leading scholars in the field, E.P. Sanders and Jacob Neusner. This contest is all the more thunderous because each of them represents in present-day guise conflicting viewpoints that have several generations of force behind them. Sanders's view is the more worldly, and is presented in an urbane literary style that Neusner never essays. Sanders believes that over-reading the Mishnah is the easiest way to distort it: that one should take the document at its literal word and see it as a law code. He argues that one should read the Mishnah not in terms of its subtexts and not in terms of what is not in it. His explanation of why there is no real historical narrative, no eschatological conclusions, and no prophecy is elegantly simple: one doesn't find those things in a law code, because the genre precludes it. Sanders uses a rhetorically brilliant analogy. He compares the Mishnah to sections of the British Highway Code which, like the Mishnah, is in the present tense (as one had better be, on British motorways) and according to Sanders, the Mishnah just gives the rules of the road, not metaphysics and not theology: do not interpret the Mishnah as being more profound than it actually is, he warns.[20]

Against the languid, genteel, common sense interpretation (in the English sense of that term), are Jacob Neusner's views. Neusner keeps hammering out his opinions in book after book, abrupt, jagged, repetitive pieces of argument. His belief is that *prima facie* "the Mishnah is to be read as a philosophical writing ..."[21] philosophy in this case being an envelope that encompasses both metaphysics and theology. He explains: "By philosophy I mean not what is generically philosophical, but, rather, specifically, the philosophical tradition of the Greco-Roman world, in particular, as I explain in [*Judaism as Philosophy*, Columbia SC: University of South Carolina Press, 1981], the method of Aristotle and the propositions important to Middle Platonism. While given in the form of a law code, the Mishnah sets forth a Judaic system of social order that employs (1) a method that in its context was distinctly philosophical to reach (2) a conclusion that in its time was philosophical."[22]

Watching Neusner and Sanders slug it out is not an entirely edifying spectacle, but it has the high theatrical value that one would have if the dream heavyweight fight of all time had ever been possible: Muhammed Ali versus Rocky Marciano. Other opinions exist of course, such as the view that the Mishnah was neither a law code nor a meta-treatise, but was a teaching manual[23] – but they really are shouts from ringside. (If the Mishnah is a teaching manual, one still has the basic question, what is it teaching: law or metaphysics and theology?)

I think that one can scarcely deny Sanders's primary point, that the Mishnah takes the *form* of a law code (or, more accurately, a case-book, since many of the disputed issues are not resolved) and, therefore, one should not expect to find sustained narrative history or clearly-articulated discussion of metaphysical questions. However, it seems to me a mistake to imply that the genre of the work is an autonomous variable that determines the nature of its own content. The Mishnah was invented by human beings, who constructed it in a specific way, by considered and volitional choice. It is the product of a massive amount of energy: hundreds and hundreds of cases not only had to be defined, along with the main arguments on both sides, but they had to be arranged in a systematic order – and, most importantly, in their early form, they had to be memorized, for the primary mode of early transmission and preservation was word of mouth. Now, if a group of people choose to concentrate their efforts on this activity, they perforce could not work intensively in other areas. The Mishnah was the result, the effect, of their having chosen to concentrate on this legal genre. And it was an effect caused by specific historical circumstances.

One indication that the Mishnah was a carefully crafted invention, the result of a series of precisely defined structural decisions, is that the document as a whole is a lovely mixture of architectural form and function. (My comments here are of course limited to the version of the Mishnah we at present possess; I am not asserting that what we have is the original Mishnah, but it is the only Mishnah we have, whatever its provenance, and we have to take it as being the real thing until something earlier is discovered.) The chief *desideratum* of the text was that it had to be memorable, in the most literal sense: easy to memorize. The Mishnah can be considered as comprising a set of cue-cards for memorization. Even if (as I think, and will discuss later) the main cues first came to be written down between 135 and 150 CE, long thereafter most students acquired the text not by reading, but by hearing; they demonstrated their mastery not by writing but by oral repetition and, then, if they were gifted, debate. One of the great virtues of Jacob Neusner's translation of the Mishnah (1988) is that its staccato, bumpy character is closer to the original text than is Herbert Danby's polished version (1933), and in that closeness one can see that the text was easier to memorize than at first seems to be the case. Almost every case starts with a topic sentence and then, in most instances, there is a balanced sequence of either two or four opinions. Hence, most units of discussion consist of units of three or five bursts of argument: a theme and then a balanced dialectic of two or four phrases or sentences around the theme. (A statistical sample shows that 78 percent of the units of argument are in this pattern of threes or fives.)[24] Manifestly, this mnemonic pattern makes memorization much easier than if a random pattern prevailed. Further, a section consisting of several related cases usually has a single method of declaring the main topic of each case and of arranging the answers: when a theme shifts, the pattern, the mnemonic formula, shifts. Thus, cases that are supposed to be of a single sort can be remembered in a single pattern.[25]

In its large components, in the arrangements of its Seder (Divisions or Orders) and tractates, the document makes sense, both functionally and aesthetically. If it were a building, it would be described, in its front elevation, as a symmetrical, almost square structure, whose structural weight is supported by two great load-bearing pillars, each about one-third in from the end. The two extremes – the beginning and the end of the Mishnah – are balanced: the document begins with a discussion of prayer (Berakoth) and concludes with a blessing (Ukzin 3:12). The first major division (Zera'im) deals primarily with agriculture and with the making of the land, God's land. The final division (Tohoroth) focuses upon the rules for cleanliness, which make the civil community God's community. Those are the symmetrical exterior portions. In the centre are two matched divisions: Nashim, which deals with matters of family intimacy and Nezikin which focuses upon civil order and comity as between individuals and families. These are matters of great practical consequence, but in their banausic details they are derivative ideologically and theologically from the second and the fifth divisions, which articulate the bedrock covenantal rituals of Israel. The two great load-bearing pillars that stand equidistant on each side from the centre and the ends are, in my view, the most important parts of the Mishnah, for, though these massive and broad-shouldered columns could, if necessary, stand on their own, the other divisions of the Mishnah could not: without them, the Mishnah would collapse. Seder Mo'ed (the second division) deals with the religious calendar and is nothing less than a definition of all human time as part of a divine calendar. And Seder Kodashim (the fifth division) provides Temple rules. Although the Temple was long-destroyed before the Mishnah was completed, the re-invention of the Temple as a mental construct meant that the achievement of holiness was just as possible after the destruction of the physical Temple, as it was previously. And, hence, the working out of patterns of proper behaviour that is the task of most of the Mishnah, was made into as holy, serious, and fruitful a quest as it had been in the days of Herod's great Temple.

Biblical Hebrew is notorious for its fluid patterns of tense; it is often difficult to know if a given verb operates in the past, present, or future, unless one knows the context of the action, and a good deal of textual scholarship on the Tanakh involves complicated grammatical arguments. The Middle Hebrew of the Mishnah has a clearer set of temporal distinctions, but even so the Mishnah is often muddy, and the past tense flows insensibly into the present in many pericopae. This uncertainty is not a flaw, I would argue and, indeed, seems to serve the intention of the author-editors of the text. This is particularly salient in the sections that discuss the now-destroyed Temple, for the direct witnesses to past practices slide into prescriptions for continuing action.

So, although the Mishnah contains nothing that can be denominated narrative history on anything larger than an anecdotal scale, it includes very tight historical descriptions of the way things were done in the Second Temple in, roughly, the last century of its existence. The entire tractate Middoth (meaning "measurements") is given over to a very precise verbal equivalent of a draughtsman's diagram of the structure. This has none of the architectonic quality one finds in the imagined temples of, for example, the Temple Scroll or the Book of Revelation. It is a very human record of what had been observed by the fathers and grandfathers of the Rabbis who, in the mid second century, began compiling in orderly fashion the collective halachic memory.

It is the obviously-human quality of the description that makes the memories believable. Thus, of Rabbi Eliezer ben Jacob (whose utterances are usually dated to the period 80–120 CE and who could have known the Temple in his youth) it is recalled that he twice had to be reminded what the purpose of specific rooms was (once it was the high priest's office [Middoth 5:4] and once it was a small store room where oil and wine were kept [2:5]). And, when it was noted that the priest who kept the night watch had the power to deal with anyone he found sleeping within the precincts of the Temple Mount – he could have his officers beat the offender and light his clothes on fire – Rabbi Eliezer recalled that his uncle had once been found sleeping and had his garments burned (Middoth 1:2). One can hear Eliezer chuckle. Remembering and, later, recording the Second Temple's physical characteristics of course was not an exercise in nostalgia: controlled recall, however, is one of the chief analgesics for extreme grief. But more: as we saw when we encountered a similar situation earlier, after the destruction of Solomon's Temple – parts of the Book of Kings read like the transcription of an architectural seminar – recording the physical details of the structure was one of the pre-requisites for its rebuilding. Memorizing, passing on, writing down these details was in itself a holy piece of work, a first step towards reconstruction. I think that is why there is so little high-register, clothes-rending, hysterical grief in the Mishnah. The task at hand is too important for histrionics. Instead, one has the laconic catalogue of bad things that had happened in Israel's history:

> Five things befell our fathers on the 17th of Tammuz and five on the 9th of Ab. On the 17th of Tammuz the Tables [of the Ten Commandments] were broken, and the Daily Whole-offering ceased, and the City was breached, and Apostomus burnt the [Scrolls of the] Law, and an idol was set up in the Sanctuary. On the 9th of Ab it was decreed against our fathers that they should not enter into the Land [of Israel], and the Temple was destroyed the first and the second time, and Beth-Tor was captured and the City was ploughed up. (Ta'anith 4:6, Danby ed.)

The conclusion of the passage is the polar opposite of self-pitying immobilization: "When Ab comes in, gladness must be diminished." That is the observation of serious men, who work their way through grief.

An equally important part of this holy work was the maintenance in detail of the memory of how worship was conducted within the Temple precincts, and of what the rules were for each ritual. In the level of detail the Mishnah provides, it is more dense than is the Book of Leviticus. Most of the rituals detailed in the Mishnah are based on ancient Hebrew practices as found in the Tanakh, but the wealth of new details means that the Mishnah asserts an authority of its own.[26]

The description of the Second Temple, loving, humane and meticulous though it is, is a site-plan for a now-empty site. But, in dealing with the rituals that were carried on in the Temple and with the liturgical calendar that located those rituals in time, the inventors of the Mishnah make a transition that blurs the past and the present. Brilliantly, they employ for the most part a normative form that says, in effect: this is how it was long ago, this is how it was recently, this is how it is, this is how it shall be. Jacob Neusner's translation of the Mishnah catches this deftly. Here is a description of one of the minor duties of what a priest on night watch was required to do:

> He took the key and opened the door and entered *via* the room of the hearth into the Temple courtyard.
> B. And they entered after him with two lighted torches in their hands.
> C. And they divided into two parties.
> D. These go along the colonnade eastward, and those go along the colonnade westward.
> E. They would go along and inspect [to make sure everything was in order], until they reach the place where they make the baked cakes.
> F. These met up with those.
> G. They said, "Is it in order?"
> H. "All is in order."
> I. They had those who make the baked cakes begin to make baked cakes.
>
> (Tamid 1:3, Neusner ed.)

That covers everything: the past (both the ancient past, beyond memory, and the more-recently-remembered Second Temple) and, simultaneously sounds as if it could have happened the previous evening; the report of a repetitive act ("they would go along") is the same grammatical construction that one would use of a continuing act, one that took place not just last night, but will take place tomorrow night as well. And the conclusion, that the priestly bakers begin to bake cakes, is a present act that is phrased in the same form in which one would articulate an act that is to continue in the future, provided the antecedent conditions are met, and continue without limit of time: when things are in order, perform the ritual, bake the cakes, do so forever.

Several thousand details of Temple ritual are included in the Mishnah, many of which a modern reader should not read on a full stomach: there are clinical instructions on how to kill large mammals, dismember small birds, and upsettingly clear indicators of how to tell that a circumcision has gone wrong. But, to decry ritual waste and liturgical killing of living things, or to be repulsed by the quease-inducing details, is to blanch and thereby to miss the point: these descriptions were immensely comforting to those who remembered them, put them in a coherent order, repeated them, and eventually wrote them down. The manner in which they were remembered was as important as the actual memory. The act of remembering and, most important, of remembering in such a way as to blur the lines between the past, present, and future, guaranteed that the Temple continued to exist and would have an existence in the future: an heuristic existence, a conceptual one, a virtual-reality, perhaps, but certainly an existence. This makes possible the determination that eventually becomes one of the definitive rules of Rabbinic Judaism: that studying of the laws of the Temple service is the equivalent of actually performing those acts of divine service. Thus, in the Babylonian Talmud, Rabbi Giddal states that an altar is built in heaven where the Archangel Michael presides, and Rabbi Johanan adds that those scholars who occupy their time studying the rules of Temple service are doing so as effectively as if "the Temple were built in their days" (Bavli. Menahoth, 110a). This the Mishnah makes possible.

That the Temple and its ritual calendar served as the two sets of coordinates – location and time – that specify the precise point around which the world of the early Rabbis revolved, and that these were the same set of coordinates that their predecessors, the first-century Pharisees had honoured, is nothing short of amazing when one realizes that the fundamentals of Mishnah were first drawn together by people who had witnessed the destruction of the Temple. "It is one thing, when the Temple is standing to pretend to be priests and to eat like the priests....," Jacob Neusner has observed. "It is quite another to do so amid the Temple's rubble and ruins, and in the certainty that those who did the work would not live to see the temple they were planning and to celebrate the perfection of creation at the altar."[27]

One of the subtlest ways in which the early Rabbis effected the re-invention of a temple religion that lacked a temple was in their use of the liturgical calendar to highlight the domestic aspects (the only ones possible after 70 CE) of rituals that still gained their shine from being Temple rituals. The tractate Pesahim, for instance, gains its authority from its being centred upon sacrifices conducted in the Temple; yet, as one reads the tractate, it becomes clear that the real directions are intended for individuals who will be conducting Passover at home or in a domestic gathering. The details are those of the kitchen and the yard, as much as of the high altar and the Temple courtyard. The same holds for most of the other great feasts (especially Pentecost and Tabernacles) and the lesser ones as well. (It does not, however, hold true for the directions for the Day of Atonement, the tractate Yoma being almost entirely Temple-based.) Indeed, most of the order Mo'ed (which begins with the most domestic of all the liturgical tractates, Shabbath) can be read as a set of liturgical directions for turning the individual home into a Temple, even while maintaining the central authority of the Jerusalem Temple as a conceptual entity.

In a few places, the Rabbis make explicit a fact that is implicit throughout: that they are engaged in a set of equilibrations, making up for the Temple's physical destruction by inventing new ways of worship. For example, whereas before the destruction, if the festival day of New Year fell on Shabbat, the blowing of the *shofar* was limited to the Temple precincts. After the Temple was destroyed Rabban Yohanan ben Zakkai ruled it could be sounded any place there was a religious court, and this was accepted in most jurisdictions (Rosh Hashanah 4:1–2). Further, he decided that, although it had been the previous custom during the Feast of Tabernacles to have palm branches carried in liturgical procession for seven days in the Temple and only one day in the provinces, now they were to be carried for seven days everywhere. This was in remembrance of the Temple (Rosh Hashanah 4:3). Also, rules for when it was permissible to examine witnesses in law cases were changed and this ascribed to the Temple's destruction (Rosh Hashanah 4:4). In slightly changing the rules, in subtly shifting focus, the Rabbis were creating something new, without abandoning the old.

The Rabbis' miracle – to keep the Temple in existence as a focal concept, while moving the actual centre of religious praxis elsewhere – into the Rabbinical courts and academies and into each home – was the precondition for the flourishing of synagogues. These are not to be confused with Temples. They were something very different, private homes that grew into places of communal worship and finally into formally-designated houses of worship.[28] After 70 CE, the Temple remained the spiritual pivot of worship, but Rabbinical Judaism of necessity shifted its praxis to the several homes which the synagogues occupied.[29] If the synagogue is a community house that becomes a surrogate Temple, the Mishnah effects an even more forceful transformation: the sections on domestic life (mostly the order Tohoroth and the order Nashim) turn the home of each devout person into a tiny Temple, each male head into a priest, and each member of the family into an acolyte.

The detailed requirements of how to maintain the cleanness (in the religious sense of the term), and thus the temple-like purity, of each home and how to maintain the priestly-level purity of each individual are extremely complex and involved literally thousands of individual decision-points: what was allowed and what was not. The key discriminators, however, operated along two clearly defined axes. One of these was the axis of contagion. Uncleanness could pass by contact with, or propinquity to, an unclean object, person, or household to another, and thence onward. To prevent uncleanness, the devout person had to sever the line of transmission. The other axis was a gradient of uncleanness: degrees of uncleanness existed (ten degrees in men, in one formulation [Kelim 1:5]) and, of course, the definition of degrees of uncleanness presupposed a continuation of the axis in the opposite direction: there were degrees of holiness.

The sources of uncleanness about which the author-editors of the Mishnah worry most are dead bodies, lepers, running sores, semen, and menstruating women. Food-monitions and food-prescriptions are immensely complex and detailed, for the ubiquity of food makes it an ever present, potential reservoir of uncleanness. Thus, each potential container of foodstuffs is either clean or unclean, depending on whether or not it is constructed so that it could trap a residual substance that might in some circumstances itself be unclean. The principle of cleanness here is that if something is to be ritually clean (and remember, every item in a home has to be clean), it must meet certain design codes: glass plates have to be flat so that they will not hold moisture, and the cover of a stewpan has to have a hole in it, so that it will not keep vegetable juices when it is held upside down (Kelim 2:1 and 2:5). One can proceed through the whole house and then the community; there are precise directions for everything. No priest ever lived a purer life than a devout follower of the Mishnah's religion.

Two particular sets of rules on uncleanness run very much counter to most present-day sensibilities, but there is no value in trying to talk them out of existence. One of these is found in most concentrated form in the tractate Abodah Zarah and it concerns how to deal with non-Jews. For instance, if one is travelling and puts up at an inn, any cattle that one is droving are not to be left in the charge of a Gentile, since they are inclined to have sexual relations with beasts (Abodah Zarah 2:1). Any item used for food production purchased from a Gentile must be ritually cleaned for, by definition, Gentiles are unclean (Abodah Zarah 5:11–12). One does not, of course, participate in any way in a Gentile religious practice. Certain semi-domestic relationships are to be permitted; but only under conditions of complete asymmetry. For example, a Gentile woman could be used as a wet-nurse for a Jewish child, but a Jewish woman was forbidden to be a wet-nurse for a Gentile. The reasoning here is made clear in the rules concerning midwifery: it was all right for a Gentile midwife to assist at the birth of a Jewish child, but it was forbidden for a Jewish woman to help a Gentile in childbirth, for by so doing, the Jewish woman would be assisting to bring forth a child who would be an idolater (Abodah Zarah 2:1). These, and scores of related rulings concerning non-Jews, make sense within the classification of clean-unclean which the Mishnah defines. Indeed, given this dichotomous mode of thought, it is hard to see how anything more than distaste and distrust for any non-Jewish group could have been possible.

A great deal of ingenuity was spent in the second half of the twentieth century in trying to explain away the Mishnah's views on women. More forthright is the recognition: "The law of this Judaism, set forth in the Mishnah…is masculine, reflecting a male perspective, treating women as abnormal, men as normal."[30] Almost an entire tractate (Niddah) is given over to discussing women when they are at their most abnormal – which, in the Mishnah's scheme, is when they are most apt to be sources of uncleanness – when they are menstruating. Menstruating women rival corpses as sources of uncleanness and the rules for determining when a female is a source of uncleanness are presented with not a trace of prurience, but instead with the explicitness of a clinical manual of gynaecology. Women, even when ritually purified, have virtually no place in the public worship in the Mishnah's re-defined Temple religion.

However, since, in a sense, the Mishnah moved the Temple into each home, the maintenance of purity that previously had been required of Temple priests now devolved on women. Food, in particular, was their domain and hundreds and hundreds of complex rules had to be honoured. In that way, women became a functioning religious caste: not capable of responsibility for conducting public worship, but the vergers of the altar that was the home hearth. Naturally, the transfer of women from one hearth to another – through marriage, divorce, widowhood – was to be done with great care: five tractates are given over to these matters. Still, though women are thus treated seriously, they are given highly asymmetrical rights. The metonym for this is the matter of divorce. A woman has no right, no matter what the circumstances, to compel a dissolution of marriage. On the other hand, under the Mishnah's rules, a man can divorce a woman without much difficulty, the only argument among the Sages being if there are any inhibitions at all on male-initiated divorce. In a remarkable argument (Gittin 9:10), the School of Shammai held that a man could not divorce his wife except for adultery. The School of Hillel, whom the compilers of the Mishnah favour, said no, he could divorce her for any reason, even if she spoiled a dish for him – burned his dinner, in other words. And Rabbi Akiba, one of the most influential of the scholars who constructed the Mishnah, added that a divorce was justified if a man found a prettier woman.[31]

Actually, the materials on how to treat women and how to treat Gentiles are very useful, because they make clear in memorable fashion the way the thought patterns of the Mishnah's author-editors operate, and they are very simple patterns, despite the complexity of the topics that they engage. Recall here the basic principle of the ancient covenant with Yahweh: every human action was either sacred or profane. And, now, note what we saw earlier: that in the usual instance, the Rabbis define a case and then give opinions on both sides of the argument. Despite some remarkably dextrous hermeneutics by later Rabbis, we can see that the actual decision process is extremely simple: (a) do we make a decision or do we not? and (b) if we decide to make a decision, is it yes or no? This kind of binary decision-making can make extremely subtle distinctions and for behavioural and ritual rulings it is just as useful as is analogical thinking. (An everyday comparison: a digital watch, which works by binary logic, tells time for most purposes every bit as accurately as does a timepiece that discriminates analogically, as does a quartz watch with constantly moving hands.) There is no lack of fineness of distinction in the Mishnah's mode of thought: it can slice very thin indeed.

However, binary programming in juridical thought, when combined with the sacred-profane distinction that is at the heart of the covenant with the Almighty, leads insensibly and automatically to an intellectual equivalent of hydraulic build-up. That is, the binary mode continually produces distinctions as between two situations, and the covenant demands sacred-profane decisions as moral imperatives. So pressure builds in the system, and inevitably distinct situations are taken as being morally different. Although many (probably most) things in life are neither black, nor white, but gray, the pressure builds: distinguish, differentiate, decide if you can, but don't generalize, distinguish, differentiate, decide, the framers of the Mishnah seem to chant. So distinctions in social or physical attributes usually become differences in moral status. In the case of women, for instance, once it was articulated that women were different from men, it was inevitable that they would be placed on a different rung of the moral hierarchy.

The Mishnah, then, is many things, all in the form of a massive set of legal case files: most importantly, it is a re-invention of the Temple faith by one of the surviving branches of multiple Judaisms of the Second Temple era. And it is a logic machine, one with its own mode of cutting and chopping.[32] It is predictable, in the best sense: trustworthy, for once one understands how its operational paradigms are arranged, it permits of few surprises.

5

Where this amazing invention came from God only knows, literally. There exist traditional histories of its appearance, but these have the beguiling vice of all folklore – a memorability and precision that characterizes the imaginative – and the less attractive vice of not taking seriously what the Mishnah says about its own origins: and, crucially, what it refuses to say.

The first "historian" of the Talmudic corpus (the foundation stone of which, of course, is the Mishnah) was the tenth-century scholar Sherira Gaon, who composed a history that, among other things, traced the Mishnah from Moses, all in oral transmission until, finally, a perfect copy was written out by Judah the Patriarch in the early second century. This was a useful argument in the tenth century, for the Karaite movement – which rejected the Talmuds and associated Rabbinical traditions, and depended instead upon the Tanakh – threatened to undercut the power of the medieval Rabbis. Sherira's allegedly historical argument is a useful document if one is engaged in studying medieval Jewish schisms, but it speaks to the middle ages, not to the first or second centuries.[33] Similarly, there exist Rabbinical discussions of the origins of the Mishnah that date from the third through the seventh centuries (and these will be treated in Chapters Twelve and Thirteen). They are not here germane, however, because those discussions are not in any meaningful sense historical: they are pieces of theological argument whose purpose is to establish the spiritual genealogy of the Mishnah and this is an other-worldly descent, not a this-worldly genealogy. The invention of a pedigree for the Mishnah that was convincing to the faithful was one of the great achievements of post-Mishnah Rabbinical thought, for it made possible the doctrine of the Dual Torah. That, though, comes later.

If we are not to become lost in the thick overlayering of later Rabbinical inventions, the Mishnah's origins can best be approached by employing three instruments (all the while acknowledging that the most we can know is only a tithe of what we would like to know). First, what the Mishnah says about its own origins, either directly or indirectly is central. As I indicated earlier (section 3), the Mishnah's few references to Moses and Sinai are not intended to establish a genealogy for the composition itself. (To repeat an earlier note: the tractate Aboth, which includes a self-conscious origin-myth, was a later add-on to the Mishnah and is here excluded; it is discussed in the next chapter.) What we should keep alert for is not consciously-stated origin myths, but indications of how the memory system of the Mishnah worked, and how far back it ran. Secondly, any model for the evolution of the Mishnah has to take into account real-world events that directly affected all forms of the Yahweh-derived faiths and, perforce, entered the consciousness of the inventors of the Mishnah. This point may seem otiose, but it must be articulated clearly: because the cast of mind of the classical rabbinical community was hermetic, refusing to identify directly, and thus to dignify, what was going on in the world outside their academies. Moreover, this inward-looking set of mind has inexorably imprinted itself upon most historians of Rabbinical Judaism (who tend, in any case, to be trained primarily in either Rabbinics or philology), so that, for example, the influence of Akiba is acknowledged as a causal determinant of the Mishnah's content, but the almost apocalyptic event which he encouraged (the Bar Kokhba revolt and the subsequent levelling of Jerusalem and the banning of Jews from within its rubbled boundaries) rates at most a passing mention. That the Mishnah's inventors rejected narrative history is hardly surprising, given how it had evolved during their collective lifetimes, but one of the few cultural lessons that the late twentieth-century popular consciousness has assimilated is here relevant: denial of an event does not erase its impact, any more than denial of a disease eliminates its pathology. The real world influenced the author-editors of the Mishnah: a lot. And, thirdly, one employs, to the extent one can, the textual stratigraphies of the Mishnah that technically adept scholars have developed. The only two such exercises that seem to have been conducted within the spirit of the evidentiary requirements of the modern academy are those of Jacob Neusner and of Jacob N. Epstein.[34] These are complex studies and, unfortunately, they often conflict with each other, without quite joining battle. (And, I must immediately add, that I have by no means mastered these works, much less gained the ability to judge between them on points of conflict.) Still, at certain moments they point to evolutionary turnings that coincide with the other two sources of evidence which drive our discussion. If we are successful in putting together these three sources, the result will be an evolutionary model (a model, for there are others that could cover the same body of data), and the reader's response will be the usual one when a model operates successfully: "Well, that makes sense, but of course we have guessed it already."[35]

So, a simple historical question: were the authors and editors of the Mishnah good at remembering things? Why ask such a question? – everyone knows that the Rabbinical academies produced some of the most prodigious professional memorizers in western history. Let us take for granted that this is true (though keeping in the back of our heads the niggling observation that no custodians of any culture's memory have ever boasted about how lousy their memories are; and suppressing also the fact that there is not within the Rabbinic corpus any way to test whether the Mishnah was the product of accurate remembering or just the result of one set of many conflicting oral texts becoming dominant.) Our query changes then, to this: what do the author-editors of the Mishnah tell us they remember about their own origins? Very little. Their memory-lines seem to be either short or truncated. Usefully, traditional Rabbinical reckonings divide the period which includes almost all of the distantly-remembered material in the Mishnah into five generations, running from the Schools of Shammai and of Hillel to Judah the Patriarch. Sometimes the division is into six generations, but the time period covered is the same: namely from roughly 10–20 CE to 200 CE.[36] Before that time, there are roughly a dozen-and-a-half additional spiritual leaders mentioned, and reference to them usually is blurred. The farthest one can argue for a self-conscious sense of religious pedigree is late in the reign of Herod the Great. Now, even if one takes the year 200 CE as one's assessment point, one is dealing with a self-defined spiritual genealogy (and historical memory) in the Mishnah that runs back at most seven generations and barely over 200 years. That is just the opposite of remarkable. To take only one cross-cultural comparison point: in our own time, the Maori *whakapapa*, clan and tribal genealogical trees are found to run for nearly thirty generations, and frequently to have external validation from other, independent genealogies.[37] The Mishnah's memory-line is surprisingly short. To make the point even clearer, if one moves one's assessment-point to 70 CE, which is when the Pharisees-cum-Rabbis moved to Yavneh and when, according to the stratigraphy of the text (and also to later Rabbinic tradition) the Sages began the concentrated effort of compilation and composition which eventually became our Mishnah, then the brevity of the remembered-pedigree of the Rabbis becomes even more remarkable: five generations.

Consider this in terms of a specific personality, Yohanan ben Zakkai. He performed the salvic task of creating a new centre for Torah study in Yavneh in 70 CE, and in his own youth must have had direct contact with scholars who themselves had been taught either by Shammai or by Hillel. (The legend that Yohanan was actually a student of Hillel implies a lifespan beyond credence.) Yet, in the Mishnah's thousands of citations of Sages, Hillel as a distinct individual appears in only 89 pericopae.[38] Instead, one has several times more references to the schools, or "Houses" of Hillel and of his rival Shammai. This material takes the form of "the School of Shammai say," or "the School of Hillel say," a muddy reference that can refer to students of Hillel and of Shammai, but which can also be a pseudepigraphic repository of later traditions that are retrospected into pre-Temple times. Indeed, Jacob Neusner has demonstrated that most of the material attributed to the Houses of Hillel and of Shammai is questionable, for later Sages used the two Houses to articulate points of view that had relevance to arguments going on within the Rabbinical Judaism in the mid-second century, but not in the pre-70 era.[39] If this characterizes the Houses material, which at least has some later cross-referencing within the Mishnah, how much more must one worry about the earlier authorities, whose light flashes forth once and, then, they are gone, not to be seen again?

Where this leads is unavoidable. The compilers of the Mishnah were unable to remember their spiritual pedigree and its substance more than a brief time, *or* this genealogy and the bulk of the body of pre-70 traditions were of minor interest to them; *or* the pedigree did not run very far because it was a relatively new one and the substantive material preserved from before 70 CE was thin because it always had been. As a young scholar, Jacob Neusner, with excessive politesse, opted for the memory-loss theory: "It will therefore seem that the war of 66–73 and destruction of Jerusalem led to a radical break in whatever process of transmission of traditions had flourished beforehand.... Nearly all pericopae before us [which hark back to the Pharisees] derive in their present form from the years after 70, a great many from those after 140 or even later."[40] In fact, it matters not a bit which of the three alternatives one chooses, or what permutations and combinations one may wish to derive from them. What counts is that the author-editors of the Mishnah tell us quite clearly that they have little sense of their own history. They do not believe that they possess a long and distinguished spiritual genealogy. And they do not believe that they have a body of received tradition that has been received inviolate from the years before 70 CE, and has to be maintained pristine forever. These things they tell us by their actions: what they remember. Here, once again, the unpleasant scrape of the parallel with the development of the Jesus-faith is necessary: the inventors of the Mishnah and the inventors of the "New Testament," each had a very short memory-line, ones that ran back to the beginning of the Common Era and little farther; and, in any event their memory-lines were blurry, thin, and indistinct; and, after the destruction of the Temple in 70 CE, each group invested massive energy in inventing traditions, and a new and heavenly kingdom.

Still, it helps our view of the sharply discontinuous evolution of Pharisaism into Rabbinism if we ask another simple question: if, in, say, 65 CE, there had been a "Mishnah of the Pharisees" (either in oral or written form), what would it have contained? Although the question is phrased in the conditional mode, it may refer to an historical reality. Five times occur mysterious references to the "First Mishnah" (Kethuboth 5:3; Nazir 6:1; Gittin 5:6; Sanhedrin 3:4; Eduyyoth 7:2). Jacob Epstein, who spent a lifetime working on a stratigraphy of the Mishnah, was convinced that an actual proto-Mishnah had existed and that it and subsequent "Mishnahs" lay inside the text of the final version. There are probative problems with Epstein's idea, but it deserves further investigation.[41] In opposition to Epstein are the views of Jacob Neusner:

> The laws [in the Mishnah] that may reliably be assigned to the generation or two before the destruction of the Second Temple deal specifically with the special laws of marriage (in Yebamoth), distinctive rules on when sexual relations may and may not take place (in Niddah), and the laws covering the definition of sources of uncleanness and the attainment of cleanness, with specific reference to domestic meals (in certain parts of Hallah, Zabim, Kelim, and Mikwaoth). *For the conduct of the cult and the sacrificial system, about which the group may have had its own doctrines but over which it neither exercised control nor even aspired to exercise control, there appears to be no systematic content or development whatsoever.*[42]
>
> (italics mine)

Thus Jacob Neusner: a minimalist proto-Mishnah would have been all that would have been possible, say, one-twentieth or so of our Mishnah.

And thus Jacob Neusner: "When the Temple was destroyed, it is clear the foundations of the country's religious-cultural life were destroyed.... On the Temple the lines of structure – both cosmic and social – converged."[43] And "the beginnings of the Rabbinic structure are to be located in the aftermath of the Second Temple in 70 CE. At that time, remnants of various groups in the

Judaism of the period before 70 gathered at Yavneh, and, under the leadership of Yohanan ben Zakkai began to construct the ruins of the old age into a new synthesis."[44] That Rabbinical synthesis was led by the Pharisees, but in its emphasis upon devotion to learning can be discerned remnants of the previous scribal caste, and in its knowledge of priestly details, probably the subsumption of some of the formal Temple professionals. A crucial element in the new synthesis – which eventually becomes the religion we know as the modern Jewish faith – was the strong commitment to maintaining an accurate memory of the customary laws, of new rulings, of the dialectics of debate. The luxury of forgetting was no longer affordable, for to forget would be self-extirpation. The Temple that the Rabbis invented was a mental construct, dependent upon human memory for its continued existence: unlike the physical Temple, which could be forgotten for a time and still be there, the new Temple had to be perpetually remembered, or it was forever lost. Thus, a keen cultivation of memory began, but it was not used for remembering the past as a set of narrative events – but for remembering laws, rituals, religious time-tables, all the subclauses that are now appended to the covenant with Yahweh. These clauses, like those in any contract, could be revised and rewritten (as subsequent generations of Rabbis certainly did), but they had to be remembered.

Immediately following the Temple's destruction, the Pharisaic leaders (and, probably persons from other of the many Judahist sects), made their way to Yavneh. Post-Mishnah traditions have it that Rabbi Yohanan ben Zakkai, a leader of the Pharisees, was smuggled out of Jerusalem in a coffin shortly before its fall. He somehow finds himself in the presence of Vespasian: the parallels between the tale of Yohanan's transition from an environment of death to the ambiance of imperial authority, and the "New Testament'"'s version of the last chapter of the biography of Yeshua of Nazareth are too obvious to require comment. And, like Yeshua, Yohanan saves his people, in this case the Pharisees, through his garnering Vespasian's favour by means of flattering prophecies. In return, Vespasian grants him a wish and Yohanan asks that he and his disciples may be given Yavneh, there to study and worship.[45] Behind this standard folktale probably lie two historical facts, in addition to the real person of Rabbi Yohanan: that the Roman government, even while continuing with the war (Masada still was in the future), granted a safe-area to some of those Jews it felt least dangerous; and that the leading Pharisees had been against the revolt (as Josephus tells us)[46] and, once it started, were not among its enthusiasts. So, Yavneh was granted and the first great burst of Rabbinic genius took place under Roman toleration, of sorts. The "Yavneh-period" lasted until 132, when the implicit concordat between the imperial authorities and the Yavneh leadership was destroyed by the three-year Bar Kokhba war. The end of the Yavneh era is associated with a figure even more dramatic (and certainly a more creative scholar) than Yohanan ben Zakkai, namely Rabbi Akiba, who joined the rebellion, declared Bar Kokhba to be the Messiah, and, according to post-Mishnah tradition eventually was raked to death in 135 by the long, steel-toothed combs used to card wool, all the while praising God and Torah.[47]

The fecundity of this first period of emerging Rabbinic Judaism – the Yohanan-Akiba era – is obscured because it came abruptly to an end with the revolt, the subsequent demolition of Jerusalem and the banning of Jews from its precincts. The Yavneh Sages left no written records, and to delineate their achievement we must stare blinkingly into a thick brume, and try to distinguish their phantoms. Despite the difficulty of vision, three constellations of fact are discernible. The first is that the Rabbis were energized by an antinomic cocktail of direct and recent pain in the past and of false hope for the future. The portions of the Mishnah put together in the Yavneh era share the fundamental (but, ultimately unfulfilled) belief that the Second Temple would be replaced, and that reciting carefully details of its rituals would keep them alive until the edifice could be resurrected. Secondly, on a more prosaic level, we can observe in the Yavneh era the victory of the intellectual descendants of Hillel over those of Shammai. And, thirdly, at the end of the era, the actions and figure of Akiba stand out. He provided a summary of the achievement of the Yavneh period and made possible the Mishnah as we know it.

Jacob Neusner has worked out a definition of what was accomplished at Yavneh. It is easily summarized, but one must recognize that Neusner's quite-economical inferences are based on a monumental set of form-critical-cum-historical studies[48] of the Mishnah: his history of the laws of purity (twenty volumes, 1974); of holy things (six volumes, 1979); of women (four volumes, 1979–80); of appointed times (five volumes, 1981–83); and of damages (four volumes, 1982–85). If one asks what the differences were between our hypothetical Mishnah of 65 CE and the state of a similar hypothetical composition in 135, which we may call the "Mishnah of Akiba," the answer is, of course, that the later one is much larger, enhulling the earlier material (the most important section of which was the laws of purity, the heart of Pharisaism) and adding a great deal more. Without guying Neusner's analysis, all of these additions can be lodged in one of two pigeon-holes: those that grow organically out of the pre-70 material and are easily predictable, and those that surprise us, at least a little. In the first category is an exponential expansion, based upon the pre-70 Pharisaic code of the laws and related discussions on the following topics: liturgy (the discussion of the *Shema'*, the fundamental prayer of Judaism, which begins our present Mishnah, dates from the Yavneh era); women (among other things, formal marriage contracts are stabilized); very complicated agricultural rules are laid down (concerning what crops could be planted near to each other, and also how the land is to be used, year after year); uncleanness of all sorts. Those areas are the areas that we would have expected to expand (although not so swiftly) if the Temple tragedy had not occurred and if Pharisaism had grown gradually.

In contrast, certain topics would never have been included. One of these concerned the taxes owed to the Temple priests (who are in the process of being supplanted in this era by the Rabbis) in the form of heave-offerings. Another innovation concerned the dues required for poor relief. This had been a matter of customary law and now had to be defined to fit the new circumstances. The most important new addition was some material on how animal sacrifices were to be carried out. The blood of sacrifice being the incarnadine ink with which the covenant with Yahweh was written (this from the time of Abraham onwards), it is noteworthy that portions of the sacrificial code had to be spelled out at Yavneh. Despite the hope that the Temple would be rebuilt, the Rabbis of this period began to assuage their fear that it might not be. It was a first step, but only one of many, to the creation of a Mishnah that is structurally dependent upon a Temple cast in words, not stone, and a liturgical calendar which, though it revolved around the Temple, could never be fully honoured in real time. The implicit optimism, or at least the predominance of hope over terror, in the Yavneh period is indicated by what was *not* introduced into the evolving Mishnah at this time. The descriptions of the Temple building, its dimensions and maintenance, most of the details of Temple sacrifice, and the more arcane and liturgical parts of the calendar (as distinct from Shabbat and domestic events) were not yet included.[49] In comparison with the post-135 developments, Jacob Neusner is not greatly impressed with what was achieved between 70 and 132 CE. In his view, though the Rabbis of the Yavneh era laid the groundwork for the world-embracing total social vision that emerged after 135, they were themselves merely continuing the development of a "sectarian fantasy."[50]

I wonder. Although one disagrees with Neusner only with the greatest hesitation (his scholarly distinction is unquestioned; and he has the habit of reacting to most criticism with the sort of sanguinary enthusiasm one encounters in those Saturday-morning cartoons that most of us try to stop our kids from watching), but the Yavneh era seems to me to be a period of immense achievement. The problem is, the achievement is not easily visible. Even if we could see for a moment through the haze of battle that stands between us and Yavneh, and even if we could recapture the original Yavnehian formulations that later Rabbis erased or rewrote, still we would underestimate the Sages of that era. This is because the historical growth of the period occurred the way growth takes place in complex multi-cellular organisms. In mammals, for instance, the first two or three months of life involve very little visible growth, but it is in that period that, starting from one or two cells, the most rapid rate of growth takes place and the most fundamental. So too in Mishnah-history.

The first achievement of the Yavnehian sages which, if it were their only success, still would be a monument, was that they guaranteed the survival of Rabbinic Judaism at its most vulnerable moment, that of its inception. By one of those accidents of history which we can only pretend to explain, the Pharisees before 70 had developed a set of religious beliefs and practices that were *pre*-adapted to a set of historical conditions that they had no inkling ever would occur. The Pharisees had begun to articulate a cognate for the Temple religion, one in which (while still honouring the physical Temple) each hearth became an altar, each householder a priest (provided ritual cleanliness was observed) and this at a degree of rigour nearly as demanding as the rules of the professional priesthood. The Pharisees, therefore, were perfectly positioned to become one of the two dominant survivors of the many Judahisms that were placed in mortal jeopardy by the cataclysm of 70 CE (the other was the Jesus-faith, which had its own form of good luck). Still, this pre-adaptation would have been for naught had not the Yavneh sages protected the Pharisaic inheritance physically (they could all have been dead, after all) and had they not asserted themselves as the reborn leaders of a new synthesis. Rabbi Yohanan's rising from his coffin is, in fact, an apt symbol.

The most easily visible indication of the achievement of the Yavneh Sages is the centrality of Akiba in the final version of the Mishnah. He is the one personality who, if not present, would be missed as a human being: both as an intellectual animator and something more, a man whose passion, energy, and contradictory humanity come through all the Halakhot, all the arguments. The reference in our Mishnah to "the Mishnah of Rabbi Akiba" (Sanhedrin 3:4, Danby ed.), may be an overstatement (Neusner, in his translation of the Mishnah prefers the word "version," although Epstein opted for "Mishnah," in the sense of a corpus of material), but Epstein argues plausibly that Akiba was responsible for the structural arrangement of the material of his time: into large bundles based on analytic categories.[51] This is the arrangement that separates the Mishnah from most other collections of wise sayings in several world religions: most compilations give us the sayings, arranged according to the sage who uttered them, not according to category.[52]

Once this invention was effected, the evolving Mishnah became easily expandable. New arguments, by new Rabbis, could be easily fitted in. This very arrangement, however, made the recognition of the work of the inventor of the categorical system (and, if not Akiba, who? his pupil Meir is sometimes mentioned) hard to recognize: since later work melded in so easily. And, this structural principle made it very easy to erase the actual opinions of its creator(s), for the organizational principle still could operate even if the inventor's identification and, indeed, many of his own opinions, were deleted. In relation to Rabbi Akiba this is germane, because, though he is widely represented in the final Mishnah, his presence is partial, and he comes through as the most forceful of figures, but still somehow amputated. This relates, I think, to his having backed a false Moshiah.

Of all the Sages mentioned in the Mishnah, Akiba is the one that I would most like to meet. His eclectic, wildly inventive way of dealing with both Halachah and with Scripture is indicated in a story (call it a legend, if you will) told in the Babylonian Talmud. Moses, in heaven, observes that the Almighty is delaying putting the final touches on the heavenly copy of the Torah and Moses asks why? Because in the future, Yahweh replies, a man will arise who will expound and parse the Law to a tittle. Naturally Moses wishes to observe this future genius, and the Almighty permits him to attend one of Akiba's classes. There he sits in the eighth row, behind all of Akiba's disciples and listens. He is not able to follow Akiba's arguments! At one point, however, he nerves himself and asks Akiba about one matter, "how do you know that?" Akiba replies, that it was a law given to Moses at Sinai. Moses, thereupon much comforted and now more informed, accepts this and goes back to heaven where he expresses wonder to Yahweh that, having such a great man to hand, you have trusted me, Moses, to transmit Torah! (Bavli: Menahoth 29b).

That is a legend and it is recorded four centuries or so after Akiba's time. However, the contemporary verification of the influence of Akiba and the ratification of the authority of most of his teachings is found in the simple fact that the overwhelming majority of the Sages cited in the Mishnah are either Akiba's disciples or the disciples of his disciples. The most frequently mentioned Sage in the Mishnah is Rabbi Judah ben Ilai, who is cited approximately 650 times. Another of Akiba's pupils, Rabbi Meir, the teacher whose work has the most force in the post-135 arguments, is referred to about 350 times.[53] When combined with references to Akiba's views (just short of 300 instances), these give us the heart of the Mishnah. Harold Bloom, who makes a habit of reading well, once noted that Akiba was surely the grandest of the Rabbis and that Rabbinical Judaism (which is the Jewish faith of our own times) is the religion of Akiba.[54] That means the Yavneh era was no mere sectarian fantasy.

The Bar Kokhba debacle killed any hopes of the Temple's being rebuilt. The Holy City was wrecked, and significant population loss probably occurred. Akiba was martyred. The Sages, collectively, are said to have moved, to have scattered, then when the persecution stopped after roughly five years, to have settled at Usha (in the lower Galilee region), and, perhaps, to have wandered elsewhere for a time. Usha, however, was their locus and thus, in the usual terminology, the "Usha period" followed the "Yavnehian." It is at this point that, in developing a model of the course of invention of the Mishnah, we should interject a topic almost universally avoided in historical discussions of the Rabbinical texts in general, and, especially the Mishnah: when did holy men start to write down portions of the Mishnah?

This is not a question that can be answered directly (the first full manuscript of the Mishnah as an independent document is late fourteenth-century, Talmudic lore is resistant to interrogation on this point, and the Mishnah itself gives no hint, save an ambiguous reference (in Hullin 7:6) to written material). So manifestly any suggestion has to be framed not as a testable hypothesis but as a modelling exercise which either fits comfortably with related data or does not, but which is only one of several speculations that cover the same body of data. With that as a given, I would suggest: that it was in the early post-Yavneh years, roughly 135–150 CE that the Mishnah began to be recorded. Why? Because of real-world issues, which, though the Rabbis consistently refuse to recognize them directly, inevitably affected their behaviour. In this case, the persecutions that followed the Bar Kokhba revolt (Akiba was certainly not the only martyr) and the severe dislocation of society in Palestine almost certainly had one common effect: to endanger the memory-maintaining mechanisms of the Rabbis. One can easily accept the traditional speculation (also untestable, but reasonable) that the early stages of the Mishnah, including the full Yavneh period, was an era in which memory was entirely oral. The "book" really was a chorus: a cadre of trained rememberers, who not only kept the rulings and discussions in their minds, but who could be used to edit the composition (by replacing old memory-units with new ones) or to rearrange the way large sectors cohered and the sequence in which they were remembered. All that was dependent upon the bodies being in place. Once they are scattered and, worse, once war and want reduced their numbers – as certainly occurred at the end of Yavneh – once the vulnerability of the oral method of composition and preservation became manifest and undeniably so, then, anyone seriously concerned with the preservation of a holy tradition had to look for safety systems. And a simple system of *aides-memoires* seems the most obvious answer. Thus, from early Usha times, I suggest that a habit developed of leading masters keeping the equivalent of the heads-of-acts that one finds in the records of the early parliamentary system: not the full text of debates of rulings, but a list of the topics dealt with, and maybe a phrase or two about the direction of the discussion or decision. Hence, if the Romans continued oppressive, if the line of reciters grew dangerously thin, there remained memory-prods that would reactivate the memories of the remaining rememberers. Once the practice of writing began, I suspect it became habitual (even after the major dangers receded) and that, like most human habits, it grew.[55]

The problem with that idea is not so much intellectual, but emotional. Within one branch of the Rabbinic tradition there exists an almost-magical attachment to the concept of oral transmission: oral good, written not-so-good, save for the scriptures. The classical tenth-century history of Sherira Gaon, referred to earlier, held that the Mishnah was preserved entirely orally until

Judah the Patriarch suddenly decided to write everything down and did so about the year 200. Other, related, traditions hold that the Mishnah never existed as an independent written document and that its material was entirely orally preserved until it was recorded in the two Talmuds.

One parts company with these excessive enthusiasms for orality because they implicitly devalue a primary characteristic of Second Temple Judahisms and of their descendants: the appreciation of written records as a means of preserving traditions and beliefs. Why else was the massive literature of the Dead Sea Scrolls, of the Apocrypha and the Pseudepigrapha called into being? Why else was the matter of scribal accuracy such a concern of the preservers of the Tanakh? Why else did the high priests permit the translation of the scriptures into Greek, the Septuagint, at a time when most of the faithful no longer knew Hebrew? Whatever risks there were in terms of loss of meaning by writing the sacred texts in a new language obviously were outweighed by the fact that the religious culture relied on the written word, and trusted it. So, I think that emotional responses that deny, on grounds extrinsic to the historical context of mid-second century Palestine, that the preservers of the traditions that became our Mishnah would react to extreme threats to that tradition by the use of writing, are totally out of sync with the values of Rabbinic culture.[56]

Whatever the relationship between oral and written modes of preserving the ever-growing Mishnah material (and, I am not suggesting that oral modes were not dominant, for certainly they were, then and for centuries later), the Usha period saw the expansion of material in almost all of its six sectors. The rate of adding new material was no greater than it had been earlier but the amount added was immensely larger: imagine a doubling of material between 70 CE and Akiba's time and another doubling during Akiba's years. The doubling-yet-again that occurs during the first twenty-five years after the disasters of 135, however, added an unprecedented mass of new material simply because the multiplier was operating on a much larger base. And the integration of this material was made relatively easy because of the macro-structural innovations that either Akiba or his disciple Meir had accomplished.[57] Everything grew, but in the civil area the big changes were new pericopae dealing with real estate and commercial law, with property transfers, and with what we would call civil disputes: although, in the society that the quickly-expanding Mishnah was defining, there was no such thing as a civil sphere, only a Utopian vision of a nation consecrated.[58]

What changed most, however, was the structure of the rhetorical building, the Mishnah itself. Earlier (in section 4) I argued that the reason the Mishnah succeeds as a piece of architecture (a masterpiece, really) is that the weight of the tens of thousands of precedents, arguments, and decisions it contains is shouldered by two load-bearing columns, namely the second and the fifth of the Orders: Seder Mo'ed and Seder Kodashim, respectively, the Division of Calendral Feasts and Festivals, and of Holy Things. Now, what happens at Usha – and I think happens quickly since within the history of the Yahwist-derived tradition incredible inventiveness follows real-world disaster – is that the greatest minds of the Rabbinical world were able to build swiftly in the space which the macro-categorical arrangements effected by Akiba (or Meir) provided. They were able to insert symmetrically into the structure two architectonic, unbending, beautifully decorated iron columns. Thereafter, everything previously built, and everything later added, was stabilized. And the joy of these two columns is that they are the aesthetic jewels of the whole Mishnah.

Specifically, Jacob Neusner's study of the sequence in which the work of building the Mishnah was conducted indicates unambiguously that most of the material in Seder Mo'ed and Seder Kodashim was post-135. Most importantly, to take Kodashim first, the description of the Temple, lovingly detailed (in tractate Middoth), is now inserted. Thus, the altar and all its precincts reappear. And most of the rest of the Division or Order is new as well, fully articulating the details of all the Temple-based rituals, which had only been lightly sketched by the Yavnehian Sages. The other iron column, the Division of Calendral Feasts and Festivals, which had only been half-built previously, now is completed.[59] Thus, logic, rhetoric, theology, and social geography all coincide. The rules for all life have as their reference point the Temple's altar, and both time and human relations revolve around that single point. "The underlying and generative theory of the system is that the village is the mirror image of the Temple."[60] The ritual calendar includes numerous hearth-based festivals; yet they do not replace the Temple rituals, but are congruent with them, since each annual circle of holy rites – Temple and hearth – circles around the same point, the eternal altar. By denying that the Temple had disappeared – one of the most prodigious and successful instances of denial in human history – the work done at Usha, under great stress, made possible the continuance of Rabbinic Judaism: nobody would have embraced all those rules, certainly not for very long, had not the social and civil system they enforced been based upon a transcendant, holy, and, apparently, eternal principle: the Temple, the locus of the forever covenant with Yahweh.

In Sherira Goan's traditional story, the Mishnah was completed when it was written down in its entirety by its final editor, Judah the Patriarch (also known as Judah ha-Nasi, Judah the Prince, or simply as "Rabbi"), and, from roughly 200, a perfect and complete Mishnah existed. Taking Rabbi as the final editor makes sense, so long as one does not assume that the whole Mishnah was actually written down in his time in a scribally-rigorous script, or that it was akin to holy writ: later reciters certainly changed some of its segments (sometimes intentionally, other times by memory fault) as the divergent versions in the two Talmuds make amply clear. Whatever his personal saintliness and political power,[61] the strength of Rabbi's editing was that he seems not to have edited very much. Of course one can never know what he threw away, but he clearly made a conscious effort to include divergent, often contradictory opinions: a good editor, in the tradition of those who brought together the often-contradictory material in the primary history of Israel, Genesis-Kings, and who did so without giving in to the temptation to harmonize out of existence everything that made them uncomfortable.

Does it matter much if we have a reasonably accurate model of how the Mishnah evolved (not the only possible one, certainly, but one that fits the available data comfortably)? No, and yes. No, because how the pieces came together does not affect the way one is confronted by the text as a whole. Sooner or later, one has to read this compelling document on its own terms. Yet, yes, because the process of invention that we have here modelled, appears at the start of the Rabbinic Jewish faith and more, related inventions soon follow, most of them dependent in some way upon the Mishnah. The Mishnah has been here described as an edifice of its own and it certainly is. Yet, in the march of invention, it becomes part of a larger structure, and thus is transformed into a cornerstone of the new (but ever-old) faith. As such, it requires some shifting, polishing, measuring, and aligning, before the later Rabbis are able to include it comfortably in their constantly-enlarging spiritual complex.

Taming the Mishnah: Tractate Aboth, the Tosefta, Sifra, and the Yerushalmi

I

WHEN A PEOPLE ACCEPT A NEW REVELATION, THAT DOES NOT MEAN that they give up the old: in their inherent (and inherited) wisdom the Yahweh-derived faiths not only recognized this fundamental character of all human culture, but built upon it artfully, securely. The Mishnah, whether in its oral or written form, was a new revelation, a new invention. It was the mode whereby the beliefs of one group, among the dozens of Judaisms that existed in the later Second Temple era, survived, expanded, and eventually became the wonder that is Rabbinic Judaism. But the Mishnah was a fearsome document, not an endearing one. Its force is palpable, its tone unremittingly authoritative, its self-confidence nearly hubristic. So great is the incandescent power of the Mishnah, that it threatens to blind-out everything else around it.

To be livable, the Mishnah needed taming. And its provenance needed an explanation, one that would leave the faithful comfortable in granting to it authority.

Here we must momentarily return again to the widely-resisted necessity of viewing Rabbinic Judaism and Christianity in tandem, for the Mishnah posed for the quickly-evolving Jewish faith the same problem that the letters of the Apostle Paul did for the Jesus-faith. First, Paul: his writings, it must be remembered, were the first textual productions of the Jesus-faith. There are all sorts of speculations concerning possible documents as early as Paul's writings, or even earlier, and various heuristic reconstructions of them (see Appendix D), but what Christianity possessed as its first completed writings was Paul. This has always been hard for modern scholars to accept, and particularly strenuous efforts are made at escaping from the big historical certainty: that of the texts we actually possess today, not only are Paul's epistles the earliest completed documents (forget hypothetical proto-texts; real, completed documents), but they are also the only texts that undeniably were completed before the disasters of the Jewish-Roman War. Now, the Mishnah: its relationship to all the other texts of Rabbinic Judaism is analogous to the relationship of Paul's letters to the rest of the "New Testament": it is clearly the earliest of the Rabbinic texts and it is the one that most assuredly bears pre-70 material (even if in less than pristine form).

This analogy has its rough edges, but it is serviceable and productive. Paul, again: in my discussion of the architecture of the "New Testament" (see Chapter Eight), I intentionally postponed mention of one of the Christian scripture's most impressive characteristics. Not only is the "New Testament" built with grace and structural integrity, but it is a piece of architecture that successfully disguises one of its main functions: to control, constrict, and re-direct the energy contained in the Pauline epistles. Paul's words had to be tamed. Their being the product of the earliest Christian writer (and the only one who had the authority not to write pseudoepigraphically) gave them enormous power. And yet, as I discussed earlier, Paul's beliefs and focus were very different from the way the inventors of the Jesus-faith for the most part wanted to go: he was very little interested in the earthly Jesus, but in-stead in the cosmic Christ; he indicated no faith in the physical resurrection of Jesus (as distinct from its being a spiritual event); his writings evidenced no belief in the Virgin Birth, either directly or by implication; and he felt quite free to correct Jesus on certain matters (notably divorce). The achieve-ment of the author-editors of the "New Testament" (specifically of the Four Gospels) was to erect a force-containment area around Paul's writings, al-most seamlessly integrating them into the architecture of the Christian scrip-tures, and all without seeming to do so. Paul is surrounded and domesticated so subtly that it is easy to miss how successfully the cosmological, non-corporeal interpretation of Yeshua of Nazareth was subordinated to the phys-ical and historical emphasis of the Synoptic Gospels.

The Mishnah posed the same threat to emergent Rabbinic Judaism that Paul's letters did to early Christianity. It was an extremely forceful body of thought, authoritative in tone and possessing priority-of-origin over post-70 developments, and one that, at first glance, apparently did not honour the grammar of invention of the Genesis-Kings unity, for it refused to use narra-tive sequences to cushion the hard edges of Halachah. Eventually, the monu-mental structure which is the corpus of Rabbinic literature achieved the domestication of the Mishnah. Of course this observation is made retrospec-tively; I doubt very much if many Sages thought, "We have to bring the Mishnah into line," but over four centuries that is what they did.[1]

Like almost all human activities, the domestication of the Mishnah in-volves not merely a straightforward line of development, but a series of loops, in which human intention is directed one way, but the effects are only partially as intended and, sometimes, manifest intention and latent results rush past each other, like vehicles in opposite lanes of a superhighway. That is the case with Aboth, a tractate that was added to the Mishnah after the time of Judah the Patriarch. It is an enthusiastic endorsement of the Mishnah – an "apologetic" in theological language – yet, as we shall see, in its assertion of a new reason for the Mishnah's possessing authority, Aboth actually begins the process of channelling and confining the Mishnah's enormous energies.

Aboth – "the Fathers" – is the most popular portion of what is conventionally defined as the Mishnah. By the end of the nineteenth century it had been translated seventy-eight times into modern languages[2] and this at a time when the bulk of the great Rabbinic corpus was not available in any modern language and even the Mishnah itself was translated in complete form only into German and Latin.[3] This phenomenon hints at two important aspects of Aboth that I think characterized its reception from the time of its invention onwards: it is sharply different from the rest of the Mishnah, for it is an attractive and unforbidding outline of a narrative, packaged as a spiritual genealogy. And, in relation to the Mishnah, tractate Aboth fills a deep need which many people who encounter the Mishnah as a spiritual text feel: namely, a need to be reassured that the immense power the Mishnah exercises is legitimate.[4]

Since what I am suggesting makes sense only if Aboth is indeed a later apologetic for Rabbi's Mishnah, we should understand why it must indeed be seen as a later add-on to the Mishnah and, simultaneously, recognize that there is nothing meretricious in this being the case. Textual re-invention (which Aboth does for the Mishnah) is the chief function of the grammar of religious invention derived from the Yahweh-faith, and Aboth works within the basic rules. Why does one infer that Aboth is later than the Mishnah of Judah the Patriarch? First (and least importantly), because it mentions individuals who lived after Rabbi. For example, the sixth, and final chapter of Aboth cites the words of Rabbi Joshua ben Levi, who belongs to the middle of the third century. The quickest response to this is simply to snip chapter six out of Aboth, as being a late addition.[5] To do so is not special pleading, for indeed, most scholars agree that it does not fit with the rest of the tractate. However, references that are integral to the remainder of Aboth cannot simply be pruned away. Specifically, chapter two of Aboth clearly cites the words of a son of Judah the Patriarch, Gamaliel (2:2–4). Given that Gamaliel was a successor to his father (as Rabban Gamaliel III), this indicates that the composition of tractate Aboth occurred at least a generation after the work of Judah the Patriarch, which is to say, at least thirty to fifty years after the Mishnah was compiled. Only by special pleading – by suggesting that the material in chapter 2 of Aboth is an interpolation[6] – can this inference be obviated. No, the material is integral and one cannot avoid its implications. Secondly, and somewhat more importantly, Aboth cannot be considered part of the Mishnah of Judah the Patriarch because it comes from an entirely different stylistic register. The Mishnah is almost entirely Halachah; Aboth is entirely Aggadah.[7] The Mishnah has a limited set of mnemonic patterns. In contrast, Aboth contains an almost playful engagement in number games – the numbers 10, 7, 4, and 3 are juggled in virtuoso fashion: the effect is memorable, but not easy to memorize. Further, Aboth is stylistically distinct from Rabbi's Mishnah by virtue of its self-consciously introducing theological concepts, instead of leaving them to be inferred. "By ten acts of speech was the world made," Aboth declares (5:1A; Neusner ed.) in a formulation remarkably compatible with the beginning of the Gospel of John. ("In the beginning was the Word.") Thirdly, and most importantly, Aboth has to be recognized as a later apologetic for Rabbi's Mishnah because it is *about* that Mishnah! This is the irreducible fact that special pleading and technical tergiversation cannot wish away. Aboth's purpose is to explain and thereby legitimate the authority of the Mishnah and its system of memory. This became a relevant exercise only after the Mishnah itself was completed. How much later than the compilation of Judah the Patriarch is impossible to know, but given its being a totally different genre than the Mishnah and given its integral references to Rabbi's son, Rabban Gamaliel III, 250 CE or later is a reasonable speculation.

The mission of Aboth is so tightly defined that one could draw up for it an action-agenda of the kind so beloved by the sort of executive who is proud of having a large desk that is ostentatiously clear of paper. It would read:

Major goal: legitimate the Mishnah
Intermediate mode: emphasize the integrity of our memory paths
Rhetorical attack points: (a) educational methods   and
                               (b) spiritual pedigrees.

The first of these rhetorical matters, educational methods, was developed only enough to make it clear that formal patterns of instruction had evolved sufficiently to maintain the integrity of the tradition. Rabbi Judah ben Tema, a late second-century scholar, decreed that at five a child was ready to study (meaning, memorize) scripture, at ten the Mishnah, and at fifteen the Talmud (5:21).[8] Reference is also made to a House of Study, which apparently was intended for adults (5:14). All this is tantalizing, for we want to know more about early forms of Rabbinic education (what one wouldn't give to know how Rabban Gamaliel II used the drawings of the shapes of the moon that he had on a tablet and on the wall of his upper chamber, which he employed to discuss the liturgical calendar with ordinary people! (See Mishnah, Rosh Hoshanah 2:8). Further, as Judah Goldin observes, we are only given in contemporary documents sidelights on the day-to-day nature of Torah education, the training that preserved the Mishnah.[9] However, the author-editors of Aboth are not concerned with those pedagogical details, for presumably their contemporary audience was familiar with them already. What counted was the principle of the education. The dictum of Rabbi Eleazar ben Shammua went to the heart of the matter: "the reverence owing to your master should be like the awe owing to Heaven" (Aboth 4:12, Neusner ed.). Thus would the integrity of memory be preserved.

That counted, but the heart of Aboth was the invention and introduction of a pedigree for the Mishnah, one that Rabbi's Mishnah had not claimed for itself. Textually, it is based on off-hand references to spiritual pedigrees found in the Mishnah proper, which we discussed in Chapter Eleven (Pe'ah 2:6, Yadayim 4:3, and perhaps Eduyyoth 8:7). The crucial point is that the sequence by which this genealogy was invented and the manner in which it was presented were, of course, diametrically opposed. In the conventional mode of genealogy, one reads from the farthest point to the nearest generation. But that is not how the pedigree actually was built. In common with almost all genealogies – spiritual, social, political, familial – that are constructed to legitimate a point of view (whether the right of an individual to inherit land, a king to rule, or a priest to be the sacral leader), this pedigree actually starts not with the distant ancestor, the progenitor but with *ego*, the self of the present. The initial reference point is not Yahweh and Moses, long ago, but the Mishnah as it existed after the reign of Rabban Gamaliel III. In this genealogical exercise, the Mishnah is authenticated by reference to a sequence of Sages who were alleged to have been successive custodians of Torah.

With that as background, here are the successive stages in the linkage, beginning at the point where the construction originated:

1 Rabban Gamaliel III, son of Judah the Patriarch (Aboth 2:1–4).
2 Judah the Patriarch, "Rabbi," the "editor" of the Mishnah (2:1).
3 Next occurs a period characterized by thick description (2:15–4:22). Twenty-two Sages from the later Yavneh period to Judah the Patriarch's time (roughly, 125–200 CE) who are known to us from the Mishnah-proper, are mentioned by name: Sages such as Akiba, Meir, Simeon ben Yohai (one of Rabbi's teachers), and Judah bar Ilai, another of Rabbi's mentors. No statement of spiritual or scholastic descent is made in this material, for all these Sages were recorded in the Mishnah as being active. The pedigree is for the group as a whole, as is clearly implied by the inclusion of Rabbi himself as one of the set, without special comment (4:20).[10]
4 Next are placed five disciples of Rabban Yohanan ben Zakkai, three of whose opinions are well represented in the Mishnah-proper: Eliezer ben Hyrcanus, Joshua ben Hananiah, and Jose the Priest. In addition, two names appear that are not found elsewhere in the Mishnah, and whose authority therefore is external to the Mishnah-proper: Simeon ben Nathaniel

and Eleazar ben Arak (2:8–14). These five cover roughly the period from the early 70s to Usha, to which many Sages fled following the Bar Kokhba rising of 132–135.

5 Although the join between groups #3 and #4 is smooth enough, the material for the Yavnehian years is obscured by the inclusion, at seemingly random intervals, of seven Sages, whose opinions are cited in the Mishnah, but who are not given the same pedigree through which the five students of Yohanan ben Zakkai are accredited.[11]

6 Preceding the Yavnehian Sages, as a genealogical bridge to the Second Temple era, Yohanan ben Zakkai is placed (2:8). Not only is he crucial as a tie to the pre-destruction years, but he is tightly linked as a teacher to the five students mentioned above (#4).

7 And, the pedigree specifically states that Rabban Yohanan ben Zakkai received Torah from Hillel and from Shammai (2:8), the fountainheads of Pharisaic-Rabbinic tradition.

8 Simultaneously, a genealogical-doubling is inserted. After mention of Hillel and Shammai, the words of Rabban Gamaliel I (probably a grandson of Hillel) are cited (1:16) and then those of his son Rabban Simeon ben Gamaliel (1:17–18), apparently the father of Rabban Gamaliel II of the Yavneh era.[12]

9 This brings the inventors of the genealogy to their big problem. They must now move back through what Emero Stiegman has called the "vast blank spaces of post-exilic history ..."[13] Initially, they do so with considerable éclat, through the introduction of "the Pairs": (or "Zugoth"). These are Sages who, according to the Mishnah-proper (Hagigah 2:2), held some kind of authority in the Second Temple period: patriarchs and heads of the court (Neusner ed.), or president and vice-president of the Sanhedrin (Danby ed.), or some roles that we cannot at present define. The pedigree is very specific (1:4–12):

Hillel and Shammai

received Torah from:

Shemaiah and Abtalion

who had received Torah from:

Judah ben Tabbai and Simeon ben Shetah

who had received Torah from:

Joshua ben Perahyah and Nittai of Arbela

who had received Torah from:

Yose ben Yoezer and Yose ben Yohanan.

It is possible that, as some scholars argue, the Pairs were entirely creations of the post-70 Rabbis. This is not a mean-spirited suggestion, considering that there is no creditable contemporary confirmation of the existence of the pairs,[14] but the Pairs scheme has one strong attribute:

each of the Sages in the pedigree is found at least once in the Mishnah-proper. Admittedly, when mentioned, they are not granted any special authority because of their imputed antiquity, but at least they are there. So, if they are a pure fabrication (which I doubt), they were first created by the framers of Rabbi's Mishnah. I think the real inventiveness here is not in creating entirely new characters, but in the author-editors of Aboth reconfiguring extant minor actors into major links in the genealogy that they are creating. Arguably, this clarification of a memory-line that in the Mishnah-proper is very blurry takes the pedigree back to some time near the beginning of the Maccabean regime, or at least to the mid-second century before the Common Era.

10 Then after the Pairs, the pedigree loses verisimilitude. The author-editors of Aboth cannot find a way to get back convincingly beyond the Pairs. The first of the Pairs, Yose ben Yoezer and Yose ben Yohanan, are said to have received Torah from Antigonus of Soko (1:3). He is unknown to the Mishnah and his name has no resonance in contemporary religious documents.

11 The genealogy-building continues back in time: Antigonus of Soko was given Torah by Simeon the Just (or the Righteous; 1:2). Unlike Antigonus, Simeon at least is known to the Mishnah-proper: he is bracketed with one "Yohanan the High Priest" as a participant in a purification ceremony conducted in the Second Temple (Parah 3:5). This reference in Rabbi's Mishnah provides a potential opening for the inventors of Aboth to take their genealogy back to the early years after the return of Judah from the Babylonian exile, since one of the first high priests was named Johanan (see Nehemiah 12:22–23). The resonance is nice, but it cannot be used as anything but background harmonics: for, as Aboth's author-editors clearly realize, the lifespan of Simeon the Just would have had to have been roughly two centuries.

12 So, instead, another genealogical link is inserted. Simeon the Just is said to have been one of the last remnants of the "Great Assembly," sometimes misleadingly called the "Great Synagogue" (1:2). That, in purely chronological terms, makes Simeon the Just a plausible figure. However, the Great Assembly as a body is unknown to the Mishnah-proper and, indeed, is unknown in contemporary documents.[15] The history of this fictional institution begins with Aboth and is then fleshed out in later Rabbinical writings.

13 The men of the Great Assembly received Torah from "the Prophets," a real enough group, certainly, but not one which Aboth anchors with any specificity. No names, no specific linkages: just "the Prophets" (1:1).

14 The Prophets are said to have received Torah from "the Elders" (1:1), meaning the leaders who had overseen the conquest of the land of Canaan, and, presumably, their successors (see Joshua 24:31).

15 The first set of these Elders had received Torah from Joshua (1:1).

16 Joshua had received Torah from Moses (1:1).

17 And, Moses had received it directly from Yahweh at Sinai (1:1).

There it is. The pedigree of the Mishnah of Judah the Patriarch as later defined by the author-editors of tractate Aboth. When examined from the vantage point of how it was constructed – from the immediate present to the distant past – it is not a particularly impressive invention. It appears clumsy. Inconsistent methods of describing spiritual descent are employed – ranging from thick description, to scholar-teacher descent, to the Pairs, to palpably fictional entities, and to vague pre-Exilic figures, such as the Elders. Moreover, the nearer-to-the-present part of the pedigree is bespeckled with Sages who do not occur in the Mishnah and with others that do appear, but who are not placed clearly in the genealogical pattern.

This, the very first effort at spiritual genealogy assayed by the Rabbis, is very much like that composed roughly two centuries earlier by the post-70 followers of the Jesus-faith who were trying to find a way to express the authority they ascribed to Yeshua of Nazareth. In technical terms, the genealogy of Jesus-the-Christ does not work as a genealogy any more than does Aboth for the Mishnah, for each is full of mutual incompatibilities and unexplained jumps. However, the constructive point is that the pedigree employed to legitimate the Jesus-faith and that used to legitimate the Mishnah, came out of similar circumstances: post-destruction groups, whose reference points were in Pharisaism (overwhelmingly so in the case of Rabbinic Judaism, somewhat less so for the Jesus-faith), and whose assertions of belief required a metaphor to make their authority understandable and a pedigree to make them more authoritative. In both cases, the invention of a genealogy was the response to an imperative built into the Yahweh-faith and all of its descendants: the need for an acceptable pedigree, as a guarantor of authenticity.

And, crucially and paradoxically, despite their technical failings, both the genealogy of Jesus and the pedigree of Aboth are extremely successful as religious rhetoric. Considered as a whole, each carries a message that comes across clearly despite problems in the details. Consider here only Aboth, and permit yet-another architectural metaphor (we are, after all, dealing with constructions). When I indicated how the pedigree for the Mishnah was constructed by the author-editors of Aboth, I was doing the equivalent of taking us up into the attic of a traditionally-constructed English house. There, one looks up and sees, secured on ranks of bare, uninsulated rafters, row upon row of slates or tiles. From the underside, one can see the imperfections of individual pieces, how one row of slates is thicker than another, where they wobble a bit off-true. But a slate roof is based on the principle of imbrication, that is, of the overlapping of tiles, and that overlap is designed to be effective from the outside, not from within. Despite the imperfections, a good slate roof keeps the water out.

And Aboth, despite its imperfections, protects the Mishnah of Judah the Patriarch. It is very important that we be aware how it was invented, but that knowledge should not stand in the way of appreciating it from the outside. Read innocently – as most of its adherents always have – Aboth provides a set of overlapping slates, and therefore, a narrative line and a spiritual pedigree which flow securely. Of course the pedigree is meant to be read from the top, from Yahweh downwards. At the top, the most important point, the flow is channelled by a series of triads, the triangle being both the simplest and the most stable of all structural forms. In the first verse of Aboth, three terms are joined: Moses, Torah, and Sinai (the mountain being a surrogate for Yahweh himself). Immediately, the same verse asserts that Torah was passed on to three successive groups: Joshua, the Elders, and the Prophets. That is crisp and impressive. Where the pedigree becomes supernal is that it immediately (in the second half of verse one) begins to specify aspects of Torah. These preachments, which are associated with successive generations in the spiritual pedigree, become a growing spiral of theological precepts that weave in and out of the pedigree-of-names, like the double helix in the human genetic code. The prophets said to the men of the Great Assembly.

1 "Be prudent in judgment.
2 "Raise up many disciples.
3 "Make a fence for the Torah."   (1:1, Neusner ed.)

Notice how different those dicta are from those of the Mishnah-proper. Instead of complex behavioural prescriptions, or arguments about such matters, one has maxims that are legitimately termed theological. They concern how to protect Torah, rather a bigger subject than the arguments in the Mishnah-proper about whether or not a gutter spout creates a right of usucaption. Similarly, the next stage, the words of Simeon the Just, putatively one of the last survivors of the "Great Assembly," are beyond merely Olympian:

He would say: on three things does the world stand:
(1) "On the Torah,
(2) "and on the Temple service,
(3) "and on deeds of loving kindness."   (1:2, Neusner ed.)

This pattern continues down the genealogy, each successive Sage providing a triad of advice that is theologically complex or ethically erudite and, simultaneously, practical. This mixture is found, for example, in the triad ascribed to one set of the Pairs, Joshua ben Perahyah and Nittai of Arbela:

(1) "Set up [that is, find] a master for yourself.
(2) "And get yourself a fellow disciple.
(3) "And give everybody the benefit of the doubt." (1:6, Neusner ed.)

A fine blend of practical advice and high ethics. With one minor and, I think, calculated deviation (Hillel is given extra space), the triad pattern continues to the end of chapter one, where Rabban Simeon ben Gamaliel I (the father of Rabban Gamaliel II of Yavneh) makes as resounding an announcement of theological-ethical principles as one can find. He says the world stands on three things:

(1) "on justice,
(2) "on truth,
(3) "and on peace." (1:18, Neusner ed.)

Scholars could, and have, spent lifetimes on less. The cumulative impact of chapter one of tractate Aboth is to take the reader from Sinai to the end of the Second Temple era, a time when the links with the post-70 Rabbis are certain and can be taken as a given. The chapter is a magnificent – and literally, monumental – success because its helix of theological-ethical-practical triads is so profound and genuine that one forgets that much of the actual spiritual pedigree is synthetic. Thus, the sequence-of-triads becomes the rhetorical accreditation of the spiritual genealogy with which it is intertwined. And, in turn, this spiritual pedigree is the mode by which Aboth accredits the Mishnah. We are viewing religious invention at its most skilful, and we should be the more appreciative of its brilliance because we have viewed it not just from above, but from beneath, and we know how it was done. Genius.

The remaining genealogical portions of Aboth (chapters two to four, inclusive) never approach the opening chapter in style and skill, but they do not need to: these chapters deal mostly with names familiar in the Mishnah-proper, which do not demand a special justification. Useful material is associated with each name, but nothing as crystalline as the triads of chapter one. The most important statement is Rabbi Akiba's assertion that "tradition is a fence for the Torah" (3:13 Neusner ed.; 3:14 Danby ed.). Aboth closes (if one accepts the scholarly consensus that chapter six was not an original part of the tractate) with a fifth chapter that, by juggling almost playfully with numbers, provides a balancing segment to the first chapter's variations on the number three. Here the numbers are ten (ten acts of speech made the world;

ten generations stretched from Adam to Noah; ten trials were inflicted upon Abraham; ten wonders were done in the Temple, and so on); the number seven (seven traits of a Sage and seven of a boor; seven kinds of transgression and seven punishments, etc.); and the number four (four sorts of people, four types of disciples, four kinds of personality, and so on). The tractate closes with these words: "In accord with the effort (or suffering) so is the reward" (5:23). That stands as a summary both of the nature of studying Torah, and as a summation of the moral calculus by which the eternal if-then – the covenant with Yahweh – operates.

Thus, in the words of Judah Goldin, Aboth provides "the credentials" of the Sages cited in the Mishnah of Rabbi and "it declares that in these teachers will be found the unbroken and authoritative instruction which began at Sinai."[16] In so doing, tractate Aboth establishes the nature of the authority of the Mishnah-proper. Yet, something of a trade is involved. The reason the Mishnah is to be considered authoritative (its Sinaitic pedigree) now is defined and, on that axis, certainly its authority is increased. But, in another way, the Mishnah is reduced. Considered solely on its own terms, the Mishnah is irreducibly, indeed fearsomely, autochthonous. Its force is self-generated. It is what it is by virtue of what it says, and it offers little in the way of explanation of the authoritative stance it assumes. Aboth, as an apologetic, makes the Mishnah more livable and, for most adherents, probably more believable, but this is the first step in the control, the domestication, of the perfect, hermetic Mishnah.

Aboth begins a process that continues throughout the classical Rabbinic era: the Mishnah's encasement in successive layers of amber. Eventually, the Mishnah becomes the central icon in a beautifully textured translucent vessel, an item whose original character is intentionally altered by the prismatic qualities of subsequent layers of commentary and expansion. And it becomes much smoother to the touch. Aboth's introduction of the construct of the Sinai descent of the Mishnah is fundamental to the invention of the myth of memory, the first of the translucent layers that eventually encase the Mishnah. This myth is specific to the Mishnah: the Tanakh does not need such an invention, for it was entrusted to written form from very early times.

This myth is a bespoke item, especially invented for the Mishnah. The Mishnah directly tells us that the Rabbis and their predecessors, the Pharisees, used mnemonic processes to transmit memory. And, it is undeniable that the various Judahisms of the later Second Temple period possessed traditions that were external to the scriptures: we know of dozens of examples of extra-biblical Aggadah and apocalypse, so the grounds of presumption have to be that extra-biblical Halachah also was extant. However, it is one thing to note those facts and quite another to claim a perfect memory-system for the Mishnah, one that says that the extra-scriptural halakhot of the Pharisee-

Rabbis was laid down in mythic times by Moses himself and that the mnemonic system used in the later days of the Second Temple was the memory-
mode whereby words from Sinai (a mountain whose location we do not even
know, and apparently, neither did the Rabbis) were perfectly preserved.
Bluntly, the Pharisees "had a tradition, but this was not the law of Moses; it
was additional to it."[17] Yet, so powerful is this invention of the myth of memory concerning the Mishnah, that it is not an end, but a beginning. It is the
first step in the invention of the myth of the Oral Torah and leads ultimately
to the crowning theological construction of Rabbinic Judaism: the conception
of the Dual Torah.

2

The Mishnah did not exhaust the fund of wisdom attributed to the Sages.
Other sayings – *beraitot* (pl.), *baraita* (sin.) – were in circulation, most probably by word-of-mouth, but, possibly in written form, in the third and fourth
centuries. There is no way to determine whether these beraitot were accurately attributed to the Sages in question, or whether they were pseudepigraphic creations that projected in the past concerns that prevailed among
third- and fourth-century Rabbis. That hole in our knowledge does not preclude our dealing with them as a reality in themselves, for such they became
in the invention of the Rabbinic Jewish faith, being woven into expansions of
the Mishnah, into commentaries on it, and especially, into the two Talmuds.

The most important single collection of beraitot is the Tosefta, which is
certainly the least-read, and least-readable of the items in the core Rabbinic
literature.[18] Least-read and least-readable: yet curiously powerful and an absolutely indispensable step in the sequence of Rabbinic inventions. It is an
homage to the Mishnah of Judah the Patriarch and, like all such exercises, it
exerts a control over the original.

The Tosefta is a huge enterprise. It is approximately twice the size of the
Mishnah[19] and the Mishnah, one recalls, runs to more than 1,100 pages in its
most recent English-language translation. The Tosefta takes the Mishnah as a
given, and proceeds to add to it, interweaving new attributions, providing explanations, occasionally introducing new precedents, all very respectfully. No
satisfactory answer has yet been found as to who compiled and edited this
massive document, what form it assumed (oral or written?) or exactly when it
was accomplished. The best scholarly opinion at present suggests that it was
composed in Palestine, with 250–350 CE being bracketing dates.[20] The
vagueness of the absolute dating, however, is not disabling, for the issue central to the history of the world's greatest inventions is absolutely clearly decided: the Tosefta follows chronologically (and morphologically) upon the
Mishnah, and is in turn assimilated by (and therefore prior to) both the Jerusalem Talmud and the Babylonian Talmud.[21] Indeed, if one takes "a talmud"

to mean a sustained and integrated commentary upon the Mishnah – which is what the Jerusalem and Babylonian Talmuds each is – then the Tosefta should be termed the "First Talmud." Yet, few scholars pay any attention to it,[22] and thus the mode of Rabbinic invention in the two later Talmuds appears to materialize out of thin air when, in fact, it is part of a continuing tradition of invention, whose stages we can observe.

The relationship between the Mishnah and the new material interwoven with it in the Tosefta is complicated and varies from tractate to tractate. Nevertheless, one central, global pattern embraces all the variations: namely that throughout their document, the author-editors of the Tosefta take for granted the Mishnah. Very, very few of the Tosefta's original passages make any sense unless they are read as an overlay of a specific portion of the Mishnah. And, crucially, the framers of the Tosefta affirm this fact in the most visible way possible, by accepting the architecture of Rabbi's Mishnah as a given. Despite the rearrangement of some of the tractates within a given Order (or Division), the six Orders are arranged as in the Mishnah. The beautifully symmetrical front-elevation of the Mishnah is honoured and, indeed, reinforced. The second and fifth Orders (Mo'ed and Kodashim), which define Rabbinic Judaism as a religion of a now-invisible Temple, one that exists in heart, mind, and hearth, but not on this earth, stand in the Tosefta, as in the Mishnah, as the load-bearing iron pillars on which everything else depends.

How, at the level of individual pericopae, does the Tosefta work? The range of action is straightforward: some of the passages directly quote the Mishnah and then add commentary on the quotation; others, while not directly quoting the words of the Mishnah, are clearly intended as explication of a specific Mishnaic passage; and some sections stand wholly on their own, a commentary on the general topic to hand in the specific tractate, but freestanding. A very rough estimate is that approaching 40 percent of the commentary falls in the first category, less than 20 percent into the final category, and roughly 40 percent in the second.[23] As examples, we can observe the Tosefta's acting upon passages in the Mishnah which we have encountered in earlier chapters. For instance, recall the case of the man who had taken a vow not to eat certain foodstuffs. Questions arose, which are, perhaps, redefined as follows:

C. *R. Judah b. Betera says, "Anything which is called after the name of that which is made from it, and one takes a vow not to have it – he is prohibited also from eating that which comes from it"* [Mishnah, Nedarim, 6:8C, Neusner ed.)
D. R. Simeon b. Eleazar says, "If something is usually eaten and what exudes from it is usually eaten, and one has vowed not to eat it, he is prohibited also from eating what exudes from it.

E. "If he takes a vow not to eat what exudes from it, he is prohibited from eating it as well.

F. "What is usually eaten, but that which exudes from it is not usually eaten, and one has taken a vow not to eat it – he is permitted to eat what exudes from it.

G. "[If he took a vow not to eat] what exudes from it, he is permitted to eat it."

(Tosefta, Nedarim, 3:3C-G, Neusner ed.)

Or, recall the Mishnah's advice that no Israelite should leave his cattle in Gentiles' inns, because of the bestial proclivities of the heathen:

3.2 A. *They [Israelites] do not leave cattle in gentiles' inns*

[Mishnah, Abodah Zarah, 2:1A, Neusner ed.]

B. even male cattle with men, and female cattle with women,

C. because a male may bring a male [beast] over him, and a female may do the same with a female beast,

D. and it goes without saying, males with women, and females with men.

E. And they do not hand over cattle to their shepherds.

F. And they do not hand a child over to him [a Gentile] to teach him [the child] reading, to teach him a craft, or to be alone with him.

(Tosefta, Abodah Zarah, 3:2, Neusner ed.)

Those are amplifications of a specifically-cited Mishnah text. Equally dependent upon the Mishnah, although less precise in citation, are instances such as the following. It is a reference to that vexed question, referred to in Chapter Eleven, of whether or not a gutter-spout or other architectural appurtenances imparted title through usucaption. In the Mishnah, it is established that an Egyptian-style window does not impart title through usucaption, but that a Tyrian-style window does (Mishnah, Baba Bathra, 3:6D, Neusner ed.). Without directly quoting or citing this passage, the Tosefta explains it.

2.14 A. What is a Tyrian window?

B. "Any through which a man's head may squeeze," the words of R. Meir,

C. and this is on condition that it has a frame or the shape of a doorway.

D. And so did R. Meir say, "A person should not open [meaning: construct] a door on top of the door of his fellow,

E. "or a window on top of the window of his fellow,

F. "a door on top of the window of his fellow,

G. "or a window on top of the door of his fellow."

H. And sages permit,

I. so long as he set it four cubits away [from the window or door of his fellow].

(Tosefta, Baba Bathra, 2:14, Neusner ed.)

Examples of the third type of Tosefta material, free-standing items, are easily found, but one example will suffice since, by their very nature, these are not items tightly dependent upon context for their meaning. From the commentary on Mishnah tractate Abodah Zarah, which mostly deals with avoiding the uncleanness of association with Gentiles, this interjection occurs:

> 1:19 A. R. Simeon b. Eleazar says, "If youth tells you, 'Build the Temple!' do not listen to them.
>
> B. "And if old men say to you, 'Destroy the Temple!' listen to them.
>
> C. "For the building of youths is destruction, and the destruction of old men is building.
>
> D. "Proof of the matter is Rehoboam, son of Solomon."
>
> (Tosefta, Abodah Zarah, 1:19, Neusner ed.)

This is a sensible (albeit paradoxical) apothegm and a deft and efficient explication by reference to scriptural figures: it refers to Rehoboam's preferring the advice of young, uncompromising counsellors who led to the kingdom's being split. But it could be moved almost anyplace else in the Tosefta and still be effective. Obviously, a significant minority of the Tosefta is independent of the Mishnah, and these portions (unlike the rest of the Tosefta) are not necessarily younger than the Mishnah. Possibly, they may represent independent traditions of an age equal to those in the Mishnah.

Neither in the free-standing sections, nor in the roughly four-fifths of the text which is dependent on the Mishnah, do the author-editors of the Tosefta wander far from tramlines laid down by the Mishnah. Thus, the concept of Messiah, which the Mishnah almost completely avoids, is not taken up in the Tosefta.[24] Nor is the idea of the resurrection of the dead.[25] The chief differences between the emphasis of the Mishnah and of the Tosefta is one of slight degree: although neither text shows much concern with historical matters, the Tosefta evinces a somewhat greater interest. The Mishnah cites historical material only three dozen times, the Tosefta nearly two hundred:[26] not a great number of instances, given the dimensions of the Tosefta, but still, an increase. Mostly these are biblical references, but one of the Tosefta citations tells us details we have not previously known about the destruction of the Second Temple.[27] Significantly, the author-editors of the Tosefta do not expand much upon the Mishnah's very rudimentary and indirect references to the origin of the Mishnah in the ancient days.[28] However, in two instances, new sentences occur in the Tosefta concerning the origin of Oral Torah. One of these is curious, the other historically significant. The peculiar item is the Tosefta's expansion of Hullin 7:6, a passage that deals with the prohibition on consuming the thigh bone of domestic and wild animals (see Chapter Eleven). Here the Tosefta expands the Mishnah:

7:8 A. *[The prohibition of the sinew of the hip] applies to a clean beast but it does not apply to an unclean beast.*

B. *R. Judah says, "It also [applies to] an unclean beast*

[Mishnah, Hullin 7:6A-B]

C. "because the prohibition thereof came before the giving of the Torah."

D. They said to R. Judah, "It does not say, 'Therefore the children of Jacob, Reuben and Simeon,' will not eat the sinew of the thigh, but, 'The children of Israel' – those who were present before Mount Sinai."

(Tosefta, Shehitat Hullin, 7:8A-D, Neusner ed.)

That is a claim of provenance that borders on being theologically self-destructive. It asserts an origin as ancient as one can imagine; but in its very claim of ancient lineage it is asserting a superiority over the Torah of Moses since, in the mode of genealogical thinking, the more ancient the spiritual pedigree, the more authoritative the item or person in question. Given the comparative and competitive character of all genealogical thinking within the faiths that derived from the ancient worship of Yahweh (that is: older is better, purer, more authentic, more authoritative), this inevitably diminishes the lustre of the Oral Torah's having descended from Sinai with Moses. Here is a tradition of Law more ancient than that of Moses. This idea in our own time would be the equivalent of a live hand grenade and, wisely, later commentators stayed far away from it.

Much more in line with the later articulation of the Myth of Memory and the concept of the Oral Torah is the Tosefta's introduction at a single point of a version of the full descent of Oral Law from Sinai. This occurs in its explication of a complex tax case concerning the "poorman's tithe" that we noted earlier (in Chapter Eleven). Whereas the Mishnah gives the following in the voice of Rabbi Eliezer:

Go and tell them, "Do not be anxious about your vote. I have received a tradition from Rabban Yohanan ben Zakkai, who heard it from his teacher, and his teacher from his teacher, a law given to Moses at Sinai ..."

(Yadayim, 4:3Q, Neusner ed.)

This sequence is amended in the Tosefta to read as follows (the significant changes are italicized):

Go and say to them, "Do not be anxious about your vote. I have a tradition from Rabban Yohanan ben Zakkai, which he received *from the pairs, and the pairs from the prophets, and the prophets from Moses*, a law [revealed] to Moses at Sinai ..."

(Tosefta, Yadayim 2:16H, Neusner ed.)

This unique reference in the Tosefta is not a summary of the spiritual pedigree found in tractate Aboth as it would appear on the surface to be – but is moved from Pe'ah 2:6 in the Mishnah-proper, which is itself unique. It is not an indication of a very strong belief in the Myth of Memory, since the author-editors of the Tosefta passed up their other opportunities to expand relevant Mishnaic references into assertions of a long-range spiritual genealogy. So here we should pay attention to something that the Tosefta does not do – yet another case defined by the Sherlock Holmesian practice of listening for the-dog-that-didn't-bark. The most revealing silence in the Tosefta is that there is no tractate Aboth. There are no citations of tractate Aboth's definition of the spiritual pedigree of the Mishnah. Only once in the Tosefta does a sentence so closely resemble one in tractate Aboth that it could be taken to be a quotation: and this is the statement that "A boor does not fear sin," which could have originated in a common source or, indeed, the later redactors of Aboth could have taken it from the Tosefta.[29] This is fairly heavy confirmation of the argument, put earlier, that Aboth, with its spiritual pedigree, was not part of Rabbi's Mishnah, but a later supernumerary addition. That is the minimum. Further, however, one can infer from the absence of Aboth, that one of two situations held: (1) either that the tractate Aboth did not exist at the time the Tosefta was formed, or (2) Aboth was in existence, but the author-editors of this, the "First Talmud," either rejected its having any authority, or, at minimum, denied its being an appropriate incorporation into Rabbi's Mishnah.[30]

Less conclusively, the Tosefta casts some indirect light on the difficult question of when the Oral Torah began to be written down. Earlier (in Chapter Eleven), I suggested that written notes, something like the medieval parliament's heads-of-bills, probably had become necessary consequent upon the religious persecutions that followed the Bar Kochba disaster, and that 135–150 CE is a reasonable period to assign to the most rudimentary forms of a written Mishnah. That is necessarily speculative. The Tosefta is intriguing, in part because, in contrast to the Mishnah, it is difficult to memorize. In the examples which I gave earlier, the lack of clear mnemonic patterns is apparent. Sometimes just a single attribution is fixed to a previously-anonymous statement; sometimes a single, or double, or triple amplification of a point in the Mishnah is made, and at other times a whole skein of material tumbles forth. This is very different from the Mishnah's mnemonic pattern of (most commonly) threes and fives. The cues that tell somebody that they should be remembering something are, for the most part, absent. At the phrase-by-phrase level, the Tosefta reads like a collection of slips of paper stuck into a well-read book; or, like marginalia written around the edges of a great text. So, even if one grants (which I do) that the Mishnah was for a long time preserved primarily (but, I suggest, not solely) in oral form, it is hard to believe that the Tosefta was. It is too big, too messy, too forgettable. At minimum, I think we have to see the Tosefta, when considered in its entirety, as a written event.

To state that point is to bring us close to the as-yet-unknown Instant of Paradox in Rabbinic history, when the fundamental material of the Oral Torah as it existed in late antiquity became a written text, and therefore came to be confined by the perduring character of the written form. As Judah Goldin observed, "eventually, obviously, the Oral Torah was put into written form. But just as obviously, for a long, long time there was a powerful reluctance to do so (again, despite the fact that individuals kept private notes for their own use). And to a considerable degree this reluctance was due to a realization that there was something inflexible about the written word."[31] As far as the Rabbis were concerned, that makes perfect sense, but it should not engender, as it seems to, a predilection among present-day scholars either to ignore the issue, or to post-date as far as is possible the probable existence of a written form. At the very least, the Tosefta seems to imply that in the period 250–350 CE part of the Oral Torah was set into written form. Moreover, if I am correct in suggesting that the Tosefta in its full form could only be preserved scribally, then this has implications concerning the Mishnah. It is very difficult to conceive of a circumstance when a massive collection of marginal notes on the Mishnah would be put together without the existence in a written form of the text of the Mishnah to which the marginalia refer. That seeming intuitively obvious, the next inference is that when the full Tosefta comes into being, it automatically means that, at *that* moment the Mishnah existed as a complete written form: not an immutable form, not exactly the Mishnah that we at present possess, but a full document reasonably close to the Mishnah we know today. And, unless one wishes to speculate that the first written form of Rabbi's Mishnah was found inside the Tosefta, one has to postulate the existence of a written version of the Mishnah of Judah the Patriarch as a prior requirement for the invention of the Tosefta. Which, in terms of chronology, dictates that the Mishnah had assumed a full written form at the earliest by 250 (to take the earliest date scholars suggest with credibility for the Tosefta's composition) or, at the very latest, sometime before the Tosefta was completed in the mid-fourth century. We can still grant that the primary mode of communicating Mishnah, and commenting upon it, was oral, from Rabbi to pupil, but communication and preservation were no longer identical acts. Invention of new ideas, meanings and traditions, and their communication, continued in oral form but, ultimately, the written form became the guarantor of integrity.[32]

In the long arc of Rabbinical tradition, the usually-neglected Tosefta has the pivotal position of teaching Torah scholars in the land of Israel and in the diaspora how to write a talmud. The author-editors of the Jerusalem Talmud and of the Babylonian Talmud not only read the Mishnah within the rubrics of the Tosefta, they followed the Tosefta's basic design, adding more creative flourishes, more narrative passages and (in the case of the Babylonian Talmud) virtuoso stylistic effects. The Tosefta, therefore, was no petty invention.

3

"Mishnah (with Tosefta) is one-half of the constitution of Judaism. The other half is scripture" Thus, Jacob Neusner; and I can imagine no sane argument against that position.[33] Thus far in the discussion of the invention of Rabbinic Judaism, I have been dealing primarily with law in the everyday behavioural sense, and, especially Halachah as it cascades downward in time from the Mishnah. The reason for this emphasis (which will continue) is twofold. First, because the truly unique characteristics of Rabbinic Judaism have as their foundation stone the Mishnah. The Hebrew scriptures not only are shared over time with the ancient Yahweh faith, but are shared contemporaneously with Judaism's sister faith, Christianity. However, the Mishnah, and its linear descendants, the Tosefta, and the two Talmuds, are unique to the Jewish faith and thus are the primary determinants of what is singular in the Judaism that developed after the destruction of the Second Temple in 70 CE. And, secondly, it is important to emphasize Halachah, as mediated by the Mishnah, the Tosefta, and the Talmuds, because doing so runs against a relatively modern historical trend, which obscures our view of Jewish history. One of the many trends set in train by the "Jewish Enlightenment" of the eighteenth century, and thereafter, was a tendency within large sectors of the faith increasingly to read Law as metaphor, as an analogical articulation of theology, or as a statement of principles applicable in ancient historical circumstances, sensible at the time, but no longer a set of literal behavioural imperatives. Coincident with this was a greater emphasis upon scripture and a corresponding reduction in time and respect given to legal interpretations. Whatever one may think of the Jewish Enlightenment (from my viewpoint, it is one of the great pieces of good fortune western culture has had in the last three centuries, for it brought into the general cultural mix a new and powerful reagent), it is a tinted lens when held between Rabbinic Judaism and our wish for historical understanding: it renders less visible the historical fact that Law – in the grand sense of Torah and also in detail-by-detail, case-by-case specificity – was the most distinct characteristic of the constantly-evolving Rabbinic faith.

But one can go too far, and that is why Sifra is valuable, and should be considered one of the core texts of the Rabbinic tradition. It is the voice of the loyal opposition to the Mishnah, a call to remember that scripture is, indeed, one half of the constitution. Sifra is one of several volumes known as *Midreshei Halachach*, meaning exegetical studies of scriptural law, as found in the Pentateuch. Sifra is a commentary on the Book of Leviticus and, like all commentaries formed within the grammar of biblical invention, its purpose is to re-invent the old text, to introduce new ideas, all the while denying that it is doing so.[34] Sifra is the most important of all classical Rabbinical midrashim, for three reasons. First, because it has an unusually strong and coherent thematic structure. As we shall see in a moment, it defines clearly and argues for its one central point with skill and determination, and with a concern that this argument be persuasive to the listener or reader at an emotional as well as a logical level. This apparent concern with being convincing is in especially sharp contrast to the Mishnah, which is more apt to carry its point by overpowering its audience. Second, Sifra, alone among the items of Midrash[35] is a core item in the formation of classical Rabbinic Judaism because it provides an alternative model of how to build a talmud, one quite different from that put forward by the Tosefta. And, thirdly, Sifra fits uniquely into the textual lines that run from the Mishnah to the Babylonian Talmud. This relationship is slightly complicated, but is at heart easy to understand and to demonstrate by information found in the primary documents. That Sifra, like all the documents of the core Rabbinic tradition, refuses to tell us directly who its author is, in what social context it was written, or when it was composed, should not be in any way unsettling: by now, we are accustomed to that.[36]

The spine of Sifra, its organizational principle, is directly borrowed from the Book of Leviticus, the most priestly of biblical documents.[37] That this fits well with the Pharisaic-Rabbinic tradition of making each household as ritually-pure as was the Temple, is obvious. Not only is Sifra a commentary on a book, but it is a book itself, and a fairly large one, a bit over 1,100 pages in its modern English translation. It was not designed to be memorized, although some of its arguments are memorable. It is a written commentary, intended to be read alongside pivotal portions of the Written Torah. For the most part, commentary consists of series of sentences, or short phrases, that relate to a specific small portion of scripture. In the usual instance, these phrases are not given any provenance. Either they are taken as being the collective wisdom of the author-editors of Sifra or, in other instances, they clearly are citations of the opinions of a specific Sage ("it is said that …") whose name is not given: all quite straightforward.

Where Sifra becomes intriguing, and exhibits a power that is disguised by its suppleness, is in relation to the Mishnah. This occurs in two ways. The first is that Sifra includes, at irregular intervals, opinions concerning the Book of Leviticus, which it ascribes either to specific Sages or to the Houses of Hillel or Shammai. This is material that is not found in either the Mishnah or the Tosefta. Therefore, it is material that rivals that of those documents, albeit in a muted fashion. Clearly, the author-editors of Sifra are asserting that they have knowledge of Oral Torah that is independent of Mishnah-Tosefta. Secondly, and much more importantly, they employ in their discussions of most passages of Leviticus, direct and clearly identifiable quotations from either the Mishnah or Tosefta and, occasionally, from both. By my own very conservative count, this occurs in 332 separate patches of argument within

Sifra.[38] Now, by this principle of arrangement – using material from the Sages in general, and the Mishnah and the Tosefta in particular, as implements to aid our understanding of the Written Torah – Sifra is (according to the lights of its author-editors) literally putting the Mishnah in its proper place. And that place is subordinate to scripture.

This view is expressed not only in the fundamental structure of Sifra, but time and time again in the clear articulation of a very abrasive pair of ideas: that the Mishnah is based upon a false premise, and that its methods of logic are flawed. The false premise in the view of Sifra's author-editors is that the framers of the Mishnah and the Tosefta manifestly believe that Torah can be understood through logical statements and arguments that are independent in their formulation from scripture. So, each chapter or sector of argument in Sifra is studded with phrases such as "scripture says," or "this verse teaches." Such phrases occur literally thousands of times and are in very sharp contrast to the Mishnah's quite sparing citation of scriptures. In Sifra, authority is granted to scripture as the premise upon which all Halachach must ultimately rest. Further, frequently, the opinion of the Sages is corrected by reference to the written scriptures.[39] Moreover, when the Mishnah or Tosefta is quoted, the only time it is allowed to have the last word in a discussion is if it clearly illustrates and confirms a view that already has been decided by scripture.[40] And, the author-editors of Sifra have no hesitation in quoting scriptures to correct the views of the Mishnah or to give scriptural backing to an argument which, manifestly, is not accepted as being sufficiently strong solely on the basis of Mishnaic reasoning.[41]

Moreover, as Jacob Neusner persuasively argues, the author-editors of Sifra were not entirely convinced by the mode of logical thought that underlies the Mishnah and the Tosefta.[42] Fundamentally, the Mishnah's logic-system is a simple Aristotelian machine. It works by making lists of items that have at least one thing (and, frequently only that single thing) in common. From that point of tangency, two expository paths were open. Items that had something in common were taken (by the *analogical principle*) to be governed by the same set of rules; and, when two things were unlike, it was assumed (by the *contrastive principle*) that they were governed by diametrically opposed sets of rules. The trouble is, just because two human actions or two physical situations each have a point in common, this does not automatically make them part of a single, larger, governing category. "Not everything that quacks is a duck," is the colloquial recognition of this fact. Sifra not only directly points out the logical flaws in the Mishnah, but it begins with a prefatory chapter on hermeneutics. This contains the "thirteen methods of Rabbi Ishmael" by which Torah is to be interpreted. It is a mini-text on logic, and a sophisticated one.[43]

Within the long train of Rabbinic invention, Sifra should be labelled as a "Prototype for an Alternative Talmud." It does what a talmud does: explains and expands the Mishnah. Yet it does so in a radically different way than does the Tosefta (our "First Talmud"), or the Jerusalem or Babylonian Talmuds. It rejects the Mishnah's architecture as its own organizational pattern, and mimics scriptural patterns instead. And the Mishnah (which is Oral Torah), is completely subordinated to scripture (Written Torah). If the same author-editors who composed Sifra had applied their methods to the entire Pentateuch – or, more radically, to the entire Genesis-Kings unity – not only the halachic material of the Mishnah, but the aggadic material that is found in the two Talmuds, could have been encompassed. In the actual event, Sifra was a prototype for a talmud that was never built: one in which the Written Torah clearly reigned over the Oral; or, in documentary terms, one in which the Tanakh controlled the Mishnah.

Yet, Sifra is not a mere curiosity, but a core item of the Rabbinic tradition, one that has to be included in any discussion of the sequence-of-invention that eventually results in that triumphant document, the Bavli. (That the framers of the Babylonian Talmud were aware of Sifra will be discussed in Chapter Thirteen). Here three sets of facts will help us to put together the sequence-of-invention. The first of these is that the author-editors of Sifra were acutely conscious not only of the Mishnah, but of the Tosefta as well. By my count (and again, it is conservative, and is more likely to err on the side of under- rather than over-counting), Sifra directly quotes the Tosefta in eighty-four distinct passages. This dictates that the Sifra was composed after the Tosefta. Whatever date in the period 250–350 CE one chooses for the completion of the Tosefta automatically becomes the earliest possible date for the drafting of Sifra. And the latest possible date is fixed by Sifra's first clear citation in a later document, in this case the Babylonian Talmud. So Sifra's latest possible date of composition is slightly prior to whatever moment (the end of the sixth century being a widely accepted suggestion) one sets for the Bavli's being finished. Given that Sifra is a Palestinian production (scholars at least agree on that), the most likely period of composition was the fourth century, prior to the disasters which began with the Roman persecution of the Jews of Lydda, Tiberias, and Sepphoris (the seats of three of the leading academies) and which led up to the quashing of the Palestine Patriarchate in 421 CE. The last Patriarch was Rabban Gamaliel VI who died in 425 CE. These disasters brought to a halt the higher Rabbinical scholarship in the Land of Israel and shifted the centre of scholarship to Babylon. Probably, Sifra was aborning either just before, or at the same time that the Jerusalem Talmud was being compiled (see below, section 4).

A second point relates to textual evolution: the author-editors of Sifra apparently were acquainted with the supernumerary tractate Aboth. The words of Joshua ben Perahiah that, when one is judging, one should give everyone the benefit of the doubt (Abot 1:6) are quoted in Sifra, albeit without citation.[44] (Granted, this could be a case of Sifra's author-editors latching on to the same piece of oral tradition that the framers of Aboth employed.) If this is indeed a citation of Aboth,[45] then two inferences follow: that Aboth was composed before Sifra; and that Aboth was not taken as being very important. It is granted no special authority in Sifra and its central point – the descent of Oral Law from Sinai to the Rabbis – is ignored. So, these alternatives reign: either Aboth was unknown at the time Sifra was put together, the fourth century most likely; or it was known but granted no authority. In neither case is Aboth assimilated into Sifra's conception of the pedigree of the Oral Law. Instead, Sifra has its own version of the descent of oral tradition. For instance, in a discussion of the sabbatical year, the question arises, "What has the topic of the sabbatical year of the land to do in particular with Mount Sinai?" The answer: "Is it not the fact that all religious duties were announced at Sinai?" Sifra continues, "The point is that just as in the case of the sabbatical year, both the governing principles and the details were announced from Sinai."[46] But, if the entire revelation of Torah – "governing principles and the details" – comes down from the summit of Sinai with Moses, one still wishes to know what form those items might take and how those forms would be transmitted. The most articulate response in Sifra is as follows, and very subtle it is:

12. A. "[Yet for all that, when they are in the land of their enemies,] I will not spurn them, neither will I abhor them so as to destroy them utterly":

B. Now what is left for them, but that they not be spurned nor abhorred? For is it not the fact that all the good gifts that had been given to them were now taken away from them?

C. And were it not for the Scroll of the Torah that was left for them, they were in no way be different from the nations of the world!

D. But "I will not spurn them": – in the time of Vespasian.

E. "… neither will I abhor them": – in the time of Greece.

F. "… so as to destroy them utterly and break my covenant with them": – in the time of Haman.

G. "… for I am the Lord their God": – in the time of Gog.

13. A. And how do we know that the covenant is made with the tribal fathers?

B. As it is said, "but I will for their sake remember the covenant with their forefathers whom I brought forth out of the land of Egypt":

C. This teaches that the covenant is made with the tribal fathers.

14. A. "These are the statutes and ordinances and Torahs":

B. "… the statutes": this refers to the exegeses of Scripture.

C. "… and ordinances": this refers to the laws.

D. "and Torahs": this teaches that two Torahs were given to Israel, one in writing, the other oral.

    E. Said R. Aqiba, "Now did Israel have only two Torahs? And did they not have many Torahs given to them? 'This is the Torah of burnt-offering' (Lev. 6:2), 'This is the Torah of the meal-offering' (Lev. 6:27), 'This is the Torah of the guilt-offering' (Lev. 7:1), 'This is the Torah of the sacrifice of peace-offerings' (Lev. 7:11), 'This is the Torah: when a man dies in a tent' (Num. 19:1)."

15. A. "... which the Lord made between him and the people of Israel [on Mount Sinai by Moses]":

    B. Moses had the merit of being made the intermediary between Israel and their father in heaven.

    C. "... on Mount Sinai by Moses":

    D. This teaches that the Torah was given, encompassing all its laws, all its details, and all their amplifications, through Moses at Sinai.[47]

The central topic is the continuing covenant with Yahweh, clearly, but if one reads the argument from the top to its conclusion, its meaning scatters, seed-grains in a sharp wind, and the pattern is lost. I would suggest that this crucial segment of Sifra was made to be read backwards. Like the basic sentence of classical oratory, that which was most important was placed last. And this is the assertion that the Torah, in all its laws and details and all its amplifications came from Yahweh, at Sinai, through Moses (15:D). And was there a single Torah? No, there were many Torahs, according to words ascribed to Rabbi Akiba (and found here, but not in the Mishnah or the Tosefta) (14:E). Five Torahs are mentioned, and these are distinguished not only by their mode of transmission from Sinai (written or oral) but according to the topics with which they deal. Presumably, these were examples of a much larger number of Torahs, for there are many more categories of legal topics, and this exercise says, in essence: when one thinks about the whole Torah of Moses, it is sensible first to try to comprehend it by looking at it according to the particular aspect of life one is trying to live in covenant with Yahweh. Less practical in orientation is the Rabbinical distinction between the two Torahs that were given to Israel, "one in writing, the other oral" (14:D). That is quite a different way of conceptualizing Torah, not according to the sort of issue it deals with, but according to how it came to be transmitted from Sinai to the present moment. And, of these two modes of transmission that form the united Torah, which is the more important? The answer is clear: it is the written version, for, were it not for the Scroll of Torah, the children of Israel "were in no way" different from the other nations of the world (12:C). So, Sifra knows Sinai, Moses, and the Oral Law, but it knows that law in a sharply different way than proposed by tractate Aboth, with which it is totally incompatible. Manifestly, in the Land of Israel in the fourth century, more than one theory of Oral Torah was evolving.

Finally, a seemingly trivial observation that actually has major implications in defining the sequence of Rabbinic inventions: when Sifra is citing the Mishnah or the Tosefta, notice where the references congregate: almost two-thirds of the passages that embody Mishnah-Tosefta material come from Seder Kodashim and Seder Tohoroth, the fifth and sixth divisions of the Mishnah.[48] Which is to say, Sifra, as a Prototype for an Alternative Talmud, is not a general exercise. It is a prototype that concentrates most of its considerable force on clarifying issues that are found mostly in the last one-third of the Mishnah. Now, be clear: this observation is not complex. I am not invoking any substantive or stylistic subtleties here: Sifra performs its analytic work on the portions of the Mishnah that (in the only form we know the Mishnah) come at its end. Just accept this observation, without speculating as to why it is the case; take it as an empirical given, nothing more.

4

This almost idiotically simple observation is salient because it brings us to the Jerusalem Talmud and casts a torchlight upon its otherwise-puzzling structure. Without knowledge of Sifra, that Talmud makes no sense, at least not if one is considering it as a whole.

The Jerusalem Talmud has many names: Yerushalmi; the Talmud of Eretz Israel; the Talmud of the Land of Israel; the Palestinian Talmud; the Talmud of the West.[49] This talmud[50] consists of swatches of commentary (*gemara*)[51] on the Mishnah and, sometimes on the Mishnah as clarified by the Tosefta. The commentary in the Jerusalem Talmud covers thirty-nine of the sixty-two tractates of the Mishnah-proper, although in some tractates the gemara is not complete. Of all the core documents in the Rabbinic tradition, the Yerushalmi is the most problematical, and that not in any deep theological sense, but in the craftsman-level details of its text. There is no critical edition – and probably never will be – for the manuscript tradition is simply too complicated in its corruptions. In its base text, the Yerushalmi wobbles back and forth between the Palestinian and the Babylonian forms of the Mishnah. This testifies to a textual history that is beyond the power of modern scholars to disentangle.[52] And, in many ways the Yerushalmi is the least impressive of the core documents in the classical Rabbinic tradition. It lacks polish. As one studies it, one becomes conscious of dealing with a not-quite-final draft. Whole sections of commentary in one tractate are duplicated in others,[53] something that a final editor would have cleaned up. And many passages are so badly configured that they make little sense. As Robert Goldenberg notes, the content of the Babylonian Talmud frequently is difficult, "but the Jerusalem Talmud is often just obscure."[54] This is not to deny that the Yerushalmi frequently has powerful moments, but these occur within the context of a document that (in the form we at present possess it) is damaged goods.[55]

Most obviously, even this perhaps-penultimate draft of the Jerusalem Talmud is either incomplete or cruelly amputated, and this despite its considerable dimensions (thirty-four volumes in its English translation). Five sets of material are missing. First, and most importantly, the fifth and sixth Orders of the Mishnah, Seder Kodashim and Seder Tohoroth, are absent (except for the first three chapters of tractate Niddah concerning menstruating women). Secondly, passages are missing from tractate Makkoth (chapter three, the concluding chapter, has only Mishnah and no commentary attached). Thirdly, tractate Shabbath, which runs to twenty-four chapters in the Mishnah, has no gemara in the Yerushalmi on the last three. Fourthly, all of tractate Eduyyoth, in the fourth Order, is missing. And, fifthly, tractate Aboth is not included. Now, in considering these missing portions, we should not so much mourn their absences but, rather, use the phenomenon as an opportunity to learn something about the details of the grammar of religious invention as it was being applied in the Land of Israel near the very end of classical antiquity. And in so doing, we shall guard against making a very elementary error: we shall not embrace the fallacy of assuming that a similar effect (absences of a portion or particular portions of the Yerushalmi that we would reasonably expect to exist), necessarily has an identical, or even a related cause.[56]

One of the suggestions concerning the missing material is that some of it was simply lost, and given the severe pressures that the Jews of Palestine came under in the early middle ages, this is a reasonable idea: provided it is not converted into a blanket explanation. If it is correct that fragments of the missing Yerushalmi commentary on the third chapter of Makkoth were found in the famous Cairo Genizah (a treasure trove of ancient manuscript fragments), then for that tractate the lost-text theory fits.[57] And one can speculate that the last three chapters of commentary on tractate Shabbath were victims of a similar misadventure: concluding chapters of a scroll or codex being lost.

However, the case of entirely-missing tractates is not affected by this supposition: for the Geniza fragments contain nothing of the entirely-missing tractates and supposed references to major lacunae, the fifth and sixth Orders, in later medieval texts are of virtually no probative value.[58]

In the case of tractate Eduyyoth, one can plausibly argue that its absence in the Yerushalmi is not an absence at all, but is part of a normative pattern. Eduyyoth is not found in the Babylonian Talmud, so its absence in the Jerusalem Talmud is not a deviation from the norm. Within the context of the Mishnah, tractate Eduyyoth is eccentric. Alone of the Mishnah's tractates, it is organized neither around a theme nor a topic, but according to what a given Sage said, whatsoever the topic. It really does not fit.[59] One could reasonably infer that, in their shared shunning of Eduyyoth, the author-editors of both the Palestinian and the Babylonian Talmuds were making a stylistic and substantive judgement: it did not belong.

And, the similar, apparently-shared understanding between the framers of the two Talmuds concerning tractate Aboth may stem from a similar shared critical opinion. Neither one of the Talmuds contains commentary on Aboth, although (as I will discuss), each was quite aware of that supernumerary tractate. But, as I have argued, Aboth was not a part of the Mishnah-proper, but a later add-on. So a refusal to grant it the same respect that the tractates of Rabbi's Mishnah received was the product of what would today be considered a higher-critical judgement on the text's provenance.

In my judgement, both Eduyyoth and Aboth were excluded from the Yerushalmi and the Bavli for reasons of, respectively, stylistic judgement, and questionable provenance.

That still leaves the massive block of missing material in the Yerushalmi: why, with the exception of three chapters from tractate Niddah, are the huge blocks, Seder Kodashim (the fifth Order) and Seder Tohoroth (the sixth), absent in the Jerusalem Talmud, though found in the later Babylonian? This raises the slight possibility that we are here dealing with the textual equivalent of the Lost Continent: that the Yerushalmi's commentary on the last one-third of the Mishnah actually was written, but was forever lost. This is plausible, but just barely. My skepticism of the idea is based on the observation that the big-blocks of missing commentary on the Mishnah have (according to the most recent scholarship), left no convincing trace. Portions of this huge mass of "missing" material (two of the six Orders) have yet to be found in the Cairo Geniza. And later medieval references to them are too wobbly to bear any weight.[60]

A much more economical, albeit less sensational speculation (it cannot be expressed as a completely-testable hypothesis, because of the thinness of the evidence at present available) is that the Jerusalem Talmud assumes its strangely-truncated shape because there never was in the Land of Israel any satisfactory commentary on the last one-third of the Mishnah: not even gemara that proceeded as far as the penultimate-draft stage that characterizes the rest of the Yerushalmi. The cleanest explanation of something being non-existent is that it never existed.

The easiest (but I think least likely) explanation for the commentary on the last one-third of the Mishnah being left out of the Jerusalem Talmud is that the job was underway, but circumstances (such as the suppression of the Patriarchate in 421 CE) prevented it from being completed. In other words, the men-at-work sign was just being put out, the commentary on the last two Orders of the Mishnah just begun (tractate Niddah's three chapters might be taken as indicating work-in-progress) and then the project was abandoned. This response has the virtue of fitting at least vaguely into the real-world situation of the Jews of late fourth- and fifth-century Palestine, for their difficulties are well documented in third-party (mostly Roman) sources.

But this explanation is satisfactory only if we unthinkingly buy an unstated assumption: that the sequence-of-work for the Jerusalem Talmud could only proceed in the same order in which the Mishnah (as we know it) presented its tractates. Yet, even the briefest acquaintance with the Mishnah makes it obvious to the reader that the Mishnah is not a sequential argument. The individual tractates do not depend for their logical force upon their being read one after another. Undeniably, as a piece of literary architecture, the final version of the Mishnah is elegant, symmetrical, and structurally very strong. But, assuming that they intended eventually to complete a full commentary upon the Mishnah, a set of Sages could have started with any tractate, and could have moved around, going one from one Order, another from another. That this is the case is proved by reference to the Babylonian Talmud, which left the first Order (Seder Zera'im) until late, and then completed only a single tractate. Therefore, one has to conclude that the framers of the Yerushalmi were not compelled by the intrinsic force of the Mishnah to proceed in any specific order-of-work. From this it follows that the order-of-working was a matter of considered and volitional choice by the author-editors of the Yerushalmi. This being the case, the real question becomes: "why did they put off until late (and then, in the circumstances, never complete) dealing with the fifth and sixth Orders, the last one-third of the Mishnah?"

Here, we are interrupted by the idea that, in reality, the Sages of the Land of Israel put off dealing with the fifth and sixth Orders because they had no intention of doing so, for they had lost their faith in the Temple as the pivot of their religion. This could be inferred by an overreading of some observations found in the volume of explanation that accompanies one of Jacob Neusner's massive projects, the English-language translation of the Talmud of the Land of Israel:

> So, the *persona* of the Mishnah may be described as a priest, facing the destroyed Temple and the now-forbidden city of Jerusalem. The system of the Yerushalmi, ca. A.D. 400, to emerge within two centuries after the closure of the Mishnah in A.D. 200, addressed the everyday life of Israel in the towns and villages of the Holy Land. Its *persona* is a rabbi, walking with his disciples through the streets and marketplaces of the country and abroad as well.[61]

He continues by pointing to "the contrast between the Mishnah's priestly system of an Israelite world laid out in lines of structure focused upon and emanating from the Temple, and the [Jerusalem] Talmud's striking reshaping of that system through the grafting on of a separate value system."[62] And he concludes that:

> From the perspective of the third and fourth centuries, the Mishnah speaks about the wrong things, in behalf of the wrong group of people, turning toward the wrong

time and the wrong place: sanctification, Temple, and cult, for the priests in the ever more distant past, of the forbidden city of Jerusalem.[63]

Jacob Neusner is too fine a scholar to ride these observations over the brink, but an overenthusiastic student might read his aperçu in the context of the truncated structure of the Yerushalmi and conclude that the last one-third of the Mishnah is not granted any commentary because it is mostly priest-and-Temple material and that such matters were left out because, in the context of Rabbinic Judaism in the fourth century and thereafter, they were of no great interest.

This possibiiity has to be rejected, and the reasons for that rejection clearly understood, because its acceptance would irreparably distort our reading of all the core Rabbinic literature. That the Temple and the protection of priestly holiness continues to be the centre point of Rabbinic thought (even if now possible only at a conceptual level) is indicated decisively by the other, later, Talmud of Babylon, which contains both the fifth and sixth Orders and commentary thereon. And, further, the Bavli defines study of the Temple Service as equivalent to performing it, which is to say, the fulfilment of the highest of all religious duties (Bavli, Menahoth 110a). Moreover, even if one limits points of evidence concerning the value-centre of Rabbinic Judaism to the Yerushalmi, the case is conclusive. The Yerushalmi includes commentary on all of Seder Mo'ed, the second Order, and it spends most of its efforts in defining and justifying religious rituals, sacrifices, purity practices, which revolve around the Temple like satellites around a large sun. Without the Temple as the gravitational centre for that system, the entire second Order of the Yerushalmi would destruct into a thousand incoherent details, flying ever-farther apart and becoming ever more irrelevant to the life of the people of the Land of Israel. And, even in the first Order, Seder Zera'im, one finds substantial commentary on tractate Terumoth, which deals with taxes to be paid to priests (it deals with "heave-offerings," which originally meant items saved, or heaved out of the thrashing floor as priests' dues). I think Roger Brooks is right when, in the preface to his translation of Pe'ah in the Yerushalmi, he states of the Rabbis in the era the Jerusalem Talmud was written: "These Jews created the social institutions – the rabbinate and the academy – that sustained their nation then and now. In place of the Temple as the locus of worldly power and authority, they created a religion of the mind, in which the paramount virtue was found in study of the Mishnah's various rules regarding the Temple cult and proper maintenance of its purity – in short, through study of the Torah they reconstructed the world taken away from them."[64] Therefore, the inventors of the Yerushalmi did not leave out commentary on the last two Orders of the Mishnah because they had decided that the concepts of Temple, holy ritual, and purity were antiquated.

Nevertheless, I think the basic suggestion that the framers of the Yerushalmi did not intend to complete their task by commenting fully on the last two Orders of the Mishnah is probably correct, but for quite a different reason. I would speculate that, not only did they not intend to finish the job, but that they recognized that the task was beyond their abilities. This is where we return to that diamond-sharp exercise in scripture-and-Mishnah exegesis, Sifra.

Sifra is the most logically rigorous of any of the Rabbinic documents produced up to the end of the Palestinian Patriarchate. Not only did it directly criticize the logic of the Mishnah, but it articulated a very sophisticated hermeneutic of its own. Further, it undercut the primary assumption of the Mishnah – that it was an autochthonous statement – and subordinated its content to that of scripture. Sifra was a prospectus for a radically different, much more rigorous method of thinking about Torah than was found in the Tosefta; or in any portion of the Yerushalmi which, though more articulate than the Tosefta, does not exhibit prodigious hermeneutical force. And, particularly pertinent to our present discussion, Sifra dealt with matters that in the Mishnah were confined largely to Seder Kodashim and Seder Tohoroth.

Here, it matters not whether we suppose that Sifra was completed before the Talmud of the Land of Israel was compiled, or whether, in the Land of Israel certain Sages were as-yet only discussing and drafting their scripturally-based, exegetically-determinative, Prototype for an Alternative Talmud. In either case, Sifra's methods were beyond the skills of the inventors of the Yerushalmi. So the author-editors of the Jerusalem Talmud did what the Rabbis usually did when faced with unpalatable realities: they adjusted their behaviour, but they did so while staring past the problem, refusing to indicate its existence directly. (It is no accident that Sifra is not referred to in the Jerusalem Talmud, while, in the Babylonian Talmud, which successfully meets Sifra's challenge, it is directly acknowledged.) Sifra, however, was the equivalent of a force-field in physics: it affected the rhetorical trajectory of the Jerusalem Talmud, without ever having to touch it directly. The Sages who created the Talmud of the Land of Israel were able to deal with Sifra easily enough in their gemara upon the first four Orders of the Mishnah: they ignored it, completely, which they could do, since Sifra's direct focus was on the fifth and sixth Orders. But then they had to stop work altogether. Had they continued, they either would have had to assent to the methods and conclusions of Sifra, which would have forced them to revise totally all their previous work and, if they were honest, to renounce or abandon the document that we, at present, know as the Yerushalmi; or they would have had to disprove Sifra's methods and conclusions concerning the fifth and sixth Orders of the Mishnah, something that was manifestly beyond their powers.

So, the existence of Sifra – either in finished form or as a set of corrosive, ultimately explosive, ideas – is the most likely reason the Jerusalem Talmud could not be completed.

5

Since that suggestion will strike many Rabbinical scholars as being border-line-impious, one may as well go the rest of the way: not only does the Yerushalmi strike me as being intellectually deformed (by virtue of its failed-interaction with Sifra) but its text does not contain the ideational development with which it is often credited. Specifically, I cannot find that the Jerusalem Talmud has a clear sense of the linkages in its own pedigree; or that it has a single, clearly articulated conception of Oral Torah, but merely undefined and unreflective references and, consequently, it cannot be accurately described as presenting a convincing, or even coherent, conception of the Dual Torah.[65] The virtues which the Yerushalmi does not possess are those that the Bavli actually does, and the projection backwards in time into the Jerusalem Talmud of the astounding achievements of the Babylonian Talmud is bad history and, one suspects, weak religion.

The master-scholar Louis Ginzberg once stated: "The Palestinian Talmud maintains complete silence about its history. No editor is mentioned, no time of compilation is indicated, no editorial principle is given which would enable us to tell the process of elimination and selection of the vast body of material available."[66] This refusal of the Yerushalmi to explain its own history is only broached indirectly, and then as much by observing what is not said, as what is. Obviously, the most important of these diagnostic omissions is that the Sages refuse to legitimize tractate Aboth as a complete document by including it in the Yerushalmi.

Yet, they were well aware of it. One can easily find instances of the author-editors of the Jerusalem Talmud inserting into the mélange of texts on which they are commenting, aphorisms from tractate Aboth. On most of these occasions, however, they take Aboth's bits of wisdom – phrases such as Simon the Righteous's saying that the world stands on three things, Torah, Temple service, and deeds of loving kindness (Aboth 1:2) – and break them away from the context in which they originally appear: Aboth's spiritual pedigree of the Mishnah in particular and that of the Oral Torah in general. The phrases are treated simply as decontextualized voices.[67]

Yet, at a very few (but clearly expressed) moments, the inventors of the Yerushalmi seem to endorse tractate Aboth's proposed pedigree. Thus, in one instance, Aboth's opening verse is quoted: "so did Moses receive Torah from Sinai and hand it on to Joshua, Joshua to elders, elders to prophets, and prophets handed it on to the men of the Great Assembly."[68] The quotation is very much in-passing (the context is a discussion of the reading of heretical books), but it is unambiguous: Aboth's spiritual pedigree is taken seriously.[69] However, the most direct reference to a descent of the Oral Law from Sinai does not involve the genealogical chain defined in Aboth, and is very confusing indeed.[70] The following points are made in a single discussion in Hagigah: (1) that "many laws were stated to Moses at Sinai, and all of them have been imbedded in the Mishnah."[71] This is the first unambiguous claim that the Mishnah contains a large number of direct quotations of Law, given by Yahweh to Moses. That certainly is Oral Torah. (2) Paradoxically, this assertion of Oral Torah is also a guillotine that crashes down on its future development: if (as is clearly stated) all of the oral laws given by Yahweh to Moses are embedded in the Mishnah, then any other source of Oral Law is illegitimate, including new Rabbinic dicta. (3) It is held that law that is preserved orally was more precious than that which was preserved in writing.[72] This was tantamount to saying that the Mishnah is more important than the scriptures. And then (4) the entire discussion is thrown on its head by the discussants referring judgement to another authority. They ask, "What is the scriptural basis for this view?"[73] and proceed to quote scripture. Therefore, the whole argument becomes a contradiction-in-terms, for the highest authority on the assertion that Oral Law is superior to Written Law, is Written Law![74]

What the Sages may have intended becomes even more unclear when one realizes that this, and parallel discussions in other tractates, are such a minor portion of the Jerusalem Talmud, a few hundred words in a document that runs to almost one million words. And these references, and other references that plausibly could be stretched to imply Oral Torah, are never placed in a privileged position or made part of the grounds of presumption of the entire text. One can justifiably wonder what the author-editors of the Yerushalmi actually believed, and what they believed was important.

This confusion becomes downright vexing when one discovers that these same author-editors put forward alternative versions of their own spiritual pedigree, versions which are compatible neither with that found in tractate Aboth nor, actually, with each other. For example, at one point it is claimed that a bundle of genealogies had been found in Jerusalem. (The parallel to Hilkiah, the high priest's, finding the scroll of the law in the Temple is skilfully implied.) This is what the newly discovered genealogies indicated:

Hillel derived from David; Ben Jesep from Assaf; Ben Sisit Hakkeset from Abner; Ben Qobisin from Ahab; Ben Kalba Sabua from Caleb;

R. Yannai from Eli; Ben Yehud from Sepphoris; R. Hiyya the Elder from the children of Shephatiah son of Abital [2 Sam. 3:4]; R. Yosé b. R. Halapta from the children of Jonadab b. Rechab; R. Nehemiah from Nehemiah the Tirshathite.

(Yerushalmi, Ta'anith, 4:2, XI, B–C)

This is a statement of physical ancestry, not of mentor-to-student, and yet it is clearly intended to legitimize the position of each of the Sages as transmitters of the Oral Torah. Hillel – like his contemporary in Christian tradition, Yeshua of Nazareth – is given an ancestry in the royal Davidic line and for the same reason: spiritual authority is believed to stem in part from monarchical ancestry. That is a powerful argument in the various religions of late antiquity, but it is a very different one than the sequence-of-oral transmission put forward in tractate Aboth.

And, one moves from being vexed to being completely throughothered when one encounters another justification of the legitimacy of the Oral Law that is incompatible both with the one just cited and with the spiritual pedigree that tractate Aboth endorses. This opinion (which has been alluded to in a rudimentary form in Chapter Eleven) is a response to a query put by Rabbi Joshua ben Hananiah:

> *Then up went Moses, and Aaron, Nadab, and Abihu, and seventy of the elders of Israel* (Exodus 24:9). And why were the names of the elders not specified? In order to teach you that every threesome that was constituted as a Bet Din over Israel, behold they are like the Bet Din of Moses. He took his staff and his money in his hand, and he went to Rabban Gamaliel at Yavneh on the day that worked out to be the Day of Atonement according to his calculation. Rabban Gamaliel arose and kissed him on his head and said to him: come in peace, my teacher and my disciple. My teacher in wisdom, and my disciple because you accepted my words.
>
> (Yerushalmi, Rosh Hashanah, Chapter Two, Prolegomenon, v.12)

Here one has nothing less than a repudiation of the idea that a perfectly-preserved tradition (that is, one coming down with Moses from Sinai) is spiritually prepotent. The names of the Elders (as found in tractate Aboth's spiritual genealogy) are declared irrelevant, and, by implication, so too is the long cascade of oral transmission of Law. Instead, every court comprised of three Sages is allowed to make its own rulings. These decisions are Torah, just as much as those made by Moses and his holy associates. Although dextrous exegetes can harmonize virtually any set of dissonant texts, a direct reading of the Yerushalmi leaves one convinced that, literally, its framers did not know where they were coming from.

This did not preclude their doing a serviceable job of improving upon the first two-thirds of the "First Talmud," the Tosefta. About five-sixths of the Jerusalem Talmud is halachic, commentary upon law and legal cases. The rest is scriptural exegesis, historical material and tales about specific Rabbis and their disciples, often quite charming stories.[75] Of the pericopae that deal with legal matters, roughly one-third are done at a fairly low level, adding a phrase or two of explanation, or fitting together two or three related cases in a

fairly obvious way. However, approximately one-third of the legal cases involve some form of sophisticated exegesis, sometimes of the Mishnah-
Tosefta text alone, other times of the Mishnah-Tosefta in the context of the
scriptures.[76] The Jerusalem Talmud quotes the scriptures much more readily
than does the Mishnah or the Tosefta. Although the query "what is the scriptural proof?" or "what is the scriptural basis for that statement?" is frequently
heard, scripture is not the all-powerful arbiter of cases, as it is in Sifra. This is
because law cases are matters both of fact and of principle and, though scripture may supply the principles realized in a specific law, it provides decidedly
few of the facts of an individual case.[77]

The frequent introduction of scripture as a source of legal principle means
that the Jerusalem Talmud both contains and re-invents the Mishnah. Whereas
the Mishnah and its immediate progeny, the Tosefta, employ scriptures for illustration but not for justification, the Jerusalem Talmud tames the Mishnah,
by making it co-dependent for its authority upon scripture. David Halivni has
called this "abandoning the Mishnah," and though the phrase may seem a bit
strong, it points to a fundamental reality: the Mishnah is no longer permitted
to develop on its own terms.[78] The Yerushalmi operates precisely according to
the grammar of religious invention that governed the Yahweh faith and its descendants: under the guise of trying to find true meaning of earlier texts – the
scriptures and the Mishnah – it creates an entirely new text of its own. It is
a new invention, covered, as is always the case, with a veneer that makes it
look old.

The flexibility that is inherent in the grammar of biblically-derived religious invention was absolutely necessary to the Jewish faith, because the
Jerusalem Talmud was framed in an era when the world once again was being
turned upside down. This time it was by the Christianization of the Roman
Empire. Before the early fourth century (312 is the schoolboy date, the conversion of Constantine), Judaism's sister religion, the Jesus faith, was either
persecuted or treated as a non-religion and, in contrast, the Jewish faith was
tolerated throughout the empire and privileged in the Land of Israel, which
was the Roman jurisdiction, Palestine. During the fourth century all that
changed, the contrasting fortunes of the sister-faiths forming an "X", the
Jesus-faith in the ascendant, the Jewish faith losing position, governmental
leverage, then toleration, and finally its position in the Holy Land. Jacob
Neusner has persuasively argued that the context for the composition of the
Jerusalem Talmud was these revolutionary changes and, more importantly,
that the Yerushalmi is in part a response to the challenge of Christianity: this
despite the refusal of the Rabbis to even utter the dread word, much less dignify its tenets by direct counter-argumentation.[79] However, it is undeniable
that whereas the author-editors of the Mishnah worked in an environment in
which the Jesus-faith had no governmental force whatsoever behind it, the

Jerusalem Talmud was written (and at least semi-edited) in an environment wherein the Roman state and Christianity were ever-looming. This explains two signal characteristics of the Jerusalem Talmud: its introduction of Rome as an autonomous actor in certain historical tableaux[80] and the general tone of the document: "the relationship of subordinated, patient Judaism and world-possessing Christianity."[81]

This is not context in the sense of being a mere backdrop. The relationship of the late Roman state and of Christianity was a direct causal influence on the Yerushalmi. So too was the Christianization of the bulk of the population of Palestine. Yet, we must keep these things in perspective. The Yerushalmi, though in part an encoded response to the ascendancy of Christianity, is mostly a response to the tensions inherent in the basic Jewish texts themselves: old inventions (the scriptures) and new ones (the Mishnah-Tosefta) had to be joined and this the author-editors of the Jerusalem Talmud attempted, albeit with less than complete success.[82] So, the influences of the Christian revolution as it affected the Roman state can best be understood as nudging the author-editors of the Yerushalmi into certain limited responses, but not into reshaping their efforts so as to directly counter the threat from the Jesus-faith.[83]

This reluctance to move more than was absolutely necessary is found in the fundamental refusal of classical Rabbinic Judaism in general and the Yerushalmi in particular: refusal to reshape the literature of the Sages so as to compete with the most compelling aspect of the Jesus-faith, its embedding of the story of Jesus-the-Christ in a "New Testament" that was apocalyptic. As Moshe D. Herr notes, in their Aggadah the Sages of the Land of Israel resolutely ignored the concept of the apocalypse,[84] and there was even less room for it in the halachic discussions.

The refusal to compete with the Christians in the production of an apocalyptic vision had secondary implications. Take, as illustration, the resurrection of the dead. If the Rabbis who framed the Jerusalem Talmud had intended to counter fully the arguments of the Church Fathers, as based on the "New Testament" and upon the Christian reading of the Hebrew scriptures, they would have sharply delineated a view of the life-after-death. The early framers of the Jesus-faith had adroitly used the resurrection of the individual body-and-soul as the bridge between adherence to their "New Covenant," as embodied in Jesus, and the world of eternity which was to follow the great Apocalypse. That is a very compelling doctrine, the more so because it is presented in a series of easy-to-follow, highly evocative, sometimes spine-chilling, swatches of narrative.

The Rabbis of the fourth- and early fifth-century Palestine might have been expected to articulate a competing doctrine, which they easily could have done, and without compromising their integrity, since they shared the Pharisaic premise of the resurrection of the dead with their Christian rivals. Yet, only one of the Mishnah's two clear references to the resurrection of the dead (Sotah 9:15 and Sanhedrin 10:1) is commented upon in the Jerusalem Talmud. Tractate Sanhedrin's listing of those who will not share in the "world to come" (which already had been expanded in the Tosefta) was augmented to include a man who extended his foreskin to hide the fact that he was circumcised (a serious temptation in times of reduced religious tolerance, the more so because most branches of Christianity had abandoned circumcision). And, in a reference that on the surface seems irrelevant, is added, as an example of someone who "violates the rules of Torah in public" and therefore will not share in the world-to-come, "Jehoiakim, son of Josiah, King of Judah, and his followers."[85] The reference is very relevant, however: Jehoiakim was the name given by the Pharoah to Eliakim, the son of King Josiah (his slave-name, one could say), whom he put on the throne of Judah in the place of his slain father, Josiah (II Kings 23:28–37). The coded analogy would not have been lost on any student of Torah in the late fourth or early fifth centuries:

Egypt: Rome = Pharaoh: the Emperor = Jehoiakim: Christianity

That is a nicely revealing indication of the Rabbis' awareness of the new realities of the fourth and fifth centuries, and an index of their determination to out-last that doleful world patiently (Jehoiakim's reign came to an end after eleven years). This is an encoded prophecy, perhaps, but it is not an apocalyptic elaboration of the idea of the resurrection of the dead.

The concept that the author-editors of the Yerushalmi do expand somewhat is that of Moshiah, but this should not be exaggerated. Despite Christianity's mobilizing its mythology so successfully around the concept of Messiah (the Christian canon was by now complete, although there were still questions about one or two minor epistles), the author-editors of the Jerusalem Talmud were reluctant to embrace the concept fully. If they were to do so, they had to get as far away as possible from Moshiah's being an actual personage (either past or future), for the memory of Bar Kokhba, the false Messiah of the mid-second century of the Common Era was all too fresh.[86] Thus, when they are given the opportunity to comment on the two references in the Mishnah that are unambiguously to Moshiah or to the age of Moshiah, the author-editors of the Jerusalem Talmud abstain: no comment.[87] Yet, if the concept of Messiah glows too hot for the framers of the Jerusalem Talmud to touch directly, they are willing to engage it indirectly and by the mode of synonym. Thus, Rabbi Aha quotes his mentor as having said, "If Israel repent for one day, forthwith the son of David will come," and Rabbi Levi adds, "If Israel would keep a single Sabbath in the proper way, forthwith the son of David will come."[88] This is a brief message, but manifestly a very different idea of salvation from the Christian one is here present: the Messiah of the Jesus-faith has salvic power for individuals: the Moshiah of the Jerusalem Talmud will appear when the people of Israel have collectively performed an act of self-redemption. The use of King David as an anchor for the idea of Moshiah is found elsewhere in the Yerushalmi, as follows: "The rabbis said, 'If the Messiah-King comes from among the living, David will be his name; if he comes from among the dead, it will be David himself.' "[89]

Yet, the Sages in the Jerusalem Talmud cannot even agree on the code-name for Moshiah. In one instance, an argument ensues: one side holds that the Messiah's name is "Semah" (perhaps meaning "supported by Yahweh"), and another that it is "Menahem" (or "Comforter"). The discussion continues, and is resolved by a curious tale, set at the time the Temple was destroyed. An Arab approaches a Jew who is ploughing with an ox and says, "Jew, Jew, Loosen your ox and loosen your plow, for today your Temple was destroyed!" He adds, "Today the Messiah-King was born."

"What is his name?" the Jew asks, and the Arab replies, "Menahem."

"And what is his father's name?"

"Hezekiah."

The Jew has another question. "Where is he from?"

The answer is, "From the royal capital of Bethlehem in Judea."[90]

This curious passage (is the Arab being sarcastic, goading the Jew, or is he carrying a holy message?) is curiously revealing. It is obvious that the Rabbis are here investing this variously-named Moshiah with the same credential that the Christian scriptures uses to accredit Yeshua of Nazareth as Jesus-the-Christ: he comes from Royal David's City. (See Matthew 2:6, which is based on Micah 5:2.) And, strikingly, Rabbi Bun concludes this passage by bringing scripture to bear on the background of Moshiah, and, again, he uses a text from the Tanakh that the "New Testament" writers already have appropriated to the Christ-story: "There shall come forth a shoot from the stump of Jesse" (Isaiah 11:1, which is the "Old Testament" foundation for the genealogy of Jesus that is presented in the first chapter of the Book of Matthew).

Mention of the name Hezekiah is also revealing. The Sages had perhaps lost themselves in the thicket of early royal genealogies, for King Menahem of Israel actually had preceded the great reforming King Hezekiah of Judah. (And they were not father-and-son.) No matter: what counts is Joseph Klausner's observation that the name Hezekiah in the post-70 era was considered "almost identical with the Messiah."[91] That is, it is a code-name for Moshiah. That may explain why Rabban Yohanan ben Zakkai was said to have directed, as he lay dying, "prepare a throne for Hezekiah, king of Judah."[92]

The Yerushalmi, in the form that we at present possess it, is very much a work-in-progress that has suffered interruption. It contains graceful sections and worthy exegesis, but it does not quite come together. The matter of Moshiah illustrates this. The concept of Moshiah creeps into the text in a very limited number of places and it would be wildly inaccurate to call the

Jerusalem Talmud "Messianic," especially because the concept is accorded no agreed definition – even the Moshiah's name is a point of dispute. It is therefore not surprising that when the Mishnah and Tosefta's lists of matters that keep one from having a share in the world-to-come is expanded in the Jerusalem Talmud, denial of the coming of the Messiah is not included.[93] It is not yet a core belief.

The author-editors of the Yerushalmi were conscious that their job was not complete, but they made a virtue of it: "If the Torah were handed down cut-and-dried, the world would not have a leg to stand on."[94]

· 13 ·

The Bounteous Bavli and the Invention of the Dual Torah

I

IF ONE HAD TO SPECIFY A SINGLE DOCUMENT THAT DISTINGUISHES Rabbinic Judaism from all other faiths, it would not be the Mishnah, basilisk-like and formidable as it is. Rather it would be the Babylonian Talmud – alternatively called the Bavli, the Talmud of Babylon, the Talmud of the East.[1] It not only cushions the hard edges of the Mishnah, but does so with a mixture of bursts of charm (it has hundreds of diverting, usually enlightening anecdotes) and moments of high intellectual polish: unlike the Jerusalem Talmud, it is a completed (if not quite uniform) composition. Despite its immense size – about two-and-half million words, running to thirty-five volumes in one English-language translation and seventy-five in another – it is a surprisingly comfortable creation.[2] It is livable, something one can consult every day with profit. If one can conceive of a book as being fatherly in the old-fashioned sense of the word – of being approachable, possessing wisdom, being firm, yet very protective – the Bavli is a fatherly book. At an empirical level, one has to say that the Jewish faith preserved the Babylonian Talmud; in fact, I think that the Bavli preserved the Jewish people.[3]

The benevolent strength of the Babylonian Talmud cannot be reduced to any specific element. It is, after all, a talmud, a form that is by-now familiar: a portion of the Mishnah is presented, it is commented upon (the "gemara" in this case is in Eastern Aramaic, rather than Western) and in that commentary scripture, diverse rabbinical opinions, and the occasional fable or theological reflection ("Aggadah") are interspersed with legal reflections.

The Babylonian Talmud arises out of a markedly different social and political context than does the Palestinian Talmud. The Bavli well might be termed the "Talmud of the Diaspora ." The roots of the Jewish community in Babylonia ran uninterruptedly back to the Exile which followed the destruction of Solomon's Temple. (The heartwrenching threnody of psalm 137 – "By the rivers of Babylon ..." springs immediately to mind.) The community in Babylon, though in frequent contact with the homeland, had its own traditions, its own problems, and its own political self-interests. At the beginning of the Common Era it had been ruled by the Arsacid dynasty, an Iranian house, for more than two centuries. These "Parthians" successful resisted Roman conquest and, although the combat-zone between them and the Romans constantly shifted, for the most part Babylonian Jews were beyond Roman rule. In 226 CE the Parthians were overthrown by another Persian-based regime, the "Sasanians" (named after the eponymous early second-century founder of the line), and they survived, with intermittent difficulties, until the Islamic conquest of the seventh century. Politically, the key instrument for the Babylonian Jews was the establishment of a quasi-feudal regime, perhaps as early as the '60s or '70s of the Common Era, under which they received a good deal of self-government under a state-approved "exilarch," in return for their civil loyalty and social comity. Whatever its exact date of foundation, by the middle of the second century, the Babylonian form of ethno-religious feudalism was flourishing, and life under, successively, Parthians and the Sasanids was very different than life for their co-religionists under the Romans in the homeland. In part, that is why the people of the diaspora sat out the Jewish-Roman wars of 66–73 CE.[4]

Yet, individuals and ideas travelled back and forth between Babylon and the Land of Israel. The great Hillel was from Babylon, and in the era before Judah the Patriarch apparently brought the Mishnah to closure, some of the best minds of the diaspora studied in Eretz Israel. The most important of these was "Rav," (the Babylonian form of "Rabbi" and the honorific title of Rav Abba, founder of the academy of Sura). He had studied with Judah the Patriarch and in roughly the year 220 CE set up his own academy in Babylon. Rav was a formidable figure (he is reported to have dealt with an especially awkward questioner by fixing him with the evil eye, whereupon the man died).[5] His successors were forceful men. The Babylonian academies were, therefore, strong rivals of those in the homeland. One finds the sets of Sages needling each other, rather like aging graduates of Harvard and Yale during football season.[6] The rivalry was friendly, Babylonian Sages being cited in the Jerusalem Talmud and Palestinian Rabbis in the Bavli. In the actual event, the Babylonian academies served as a fail-safe system for Rabbinic Judaism. When the development of Rabbinical institutions in the Holy Land was, first, impeded by the Roman state's becoming officially Christian during the fourth century, and then, halted by the suppression of the Palestine Patriarchate in the 420s, the Babylonian Sages and their academies provided an intellectual and spiritual escape route. The Babylonian scholars had time to perfect their commentaries on the portions of the Mishnah they chose to deal with. And, collectively, the diaspora tradition had the luxury of longevity. The Babylonian academies (mostly centred in Baghdad) continued into the high middle ages. Their adherents successfully pressed for the "Talmud of the Diaspora" to be recognized as the primary voice of Rabbinic Judaism. They had a long time to do so: the exilarchate was extinguished only in 1401 by Tamerlane. The political context, then, was permissive, allowing the exfoliated transplant from the Holy Land to flower luxuriously in a seemingly-alien environment.[7]

Running as a vapour trail in and around many of the tractates of the Bavli is an indication of two other contextual realities: the inventors of the Babylonian Talmud were aware of both the Talmud of the Land of Israel (a friendly rivalry) and of Christianity (a bitter one.) These sensitivities are occasionally indicated by specific references in the Bavli, but they are more a matter of atmospherics. Concerning Christianity: whereas with the Mishnah, the Tosefta, and the Yerushalmi one can almost see the respective author-editors become tense, necks held rigid, veins sharply accentuated, as they stare fixedly past ideas and instances that relate to the Jesus-faith, the author-editors of the Bavli have a quiet confidence. They know who they are and, when appropriate, deal with some of the same inventions that the Christians had assimilated from late Second Temple thought, and they do so without stridency and without apology. This will be seen most clearly when, later, we deal with the issues of Moshiah, of the world-to-come, and of the resurrection of the dead.[8]

That the Yerushalmi (which originated before the disaster of 421) was created prior to the Bavli is so obvious as to be almost otiose: the earliest traditional date for the completion of the composition of the Babylonian Talmud is 427 CE, when Rav Ashi died. Even most tradition-bound scholars see the process as going forward considerably later. (The closing of the Ravina academy in 499 is another traditional date), and modern scholars tend to see work on the Bavli lasting, at minimum, up to 520 CE, and others, to roughly the year 600.[9] As far as documentary succession is concerned, it is virtually certain, therefore, that the author-editors of the final version of the Babylonian Talmud (and the final version is the only one that we possess) were familiar with the early product of the Palestinian academies, the Yerushalmi.

That knowledge, however, is more maddening than comforting as far as our ascertaining the course of invention that finally produced the Bavli. The problem here is that multiple potential relationships exist and, in the textual equation, more unknowns than knowns occur, so tight deductions are impossible. The basic facts are these: first, as already mentioned, the author-editors of the final version of the Bavli were almost certainly familiar with the Yerushalmi and, second, the Bavli and the Yerushalmi strongly resemble each other. Yet, third, that is what one would expect even if the two texts had been kept sealed from each other. Each is a commentary on the Mishnah (slightly different versions, to be sure, but close). And, fourth, the author-editors of the Babylonian Talmud freely and frequently quoted Sages from the Land of Israel, so, again this would have led to similar final talmuds, even if the author-editors of the Bavli had never seen a jot of the Yerushalmi. That is: *if* the

Babylonian academies had preserved, independently of the text of the Jerusalem Talmud, traditions concerning the Palestinian Rabbis. And the fact that they indeed had independent traditions is indicated by the Babylonian Talmud's frequently quoting Palestinian sources that clash with those in the Yerushalmi.[10] These points leave us at an unavoidable point of irresolution: it is impossible to sort out how, and how much, the text of the Yerushalmi influenced the text of the Bavli: somewhat, doubtlessly, but not in a clearly demonstrable way. That is why I use the phrase "vapour trail" to indicate the indeterminate, floating, atmospheric, omnipresent, but not necessarily precise or determinative, way the Jerusalem Talmud serves as context for the invention of the Babylonian.[11]

2

The Bavli has its own character. It comprises commentary on 36½ of the tractates of the Mishnah. (The Yerushalmi has gemara on 39 but the Bavli's is much fuller, so that the Bavli is considerably denser in its argument as well as larger overall.) The structural key to the Bavli is that, unlike the Yerushalmi, it maintains the symmetrical principle by which the Mishnah was constructed. Crucially, it keeps in place the two iron columns of the Mishnah, Seder Mo'ed and Seder Kodashim (Orders Two and Five), the load-bearing pillars of the Mishnah and, now, of the Bavli. Despite being a less-than-complete commentary on the Mishnah, the Babylonian Talmud has maintained both the symmetry and the structural strength of the Mishnah by shedding the peripheral elements: there is no commentary on most of the first Order (Seder Zera'im) or on most of the last (Seder Tohoroth).Thus, the edifice is pared down, but its essential architecture remains intact.

In the Bavli, Seder Kodashim consists of lovingly detailed descriptions and discussions of Temple service. The commentary on tractate Menahoth propounds two important statements of faith: that to those scholars who devote themselves to the study of Torah, the Almighty credits them as though they had burned and presented a sacrificial offering in His Name and, that to scholars who devote themselves to the unstinting study of Torah ("at nights"), is imputed righteousness as though they were occupied in actual Temple service.[12] Thus, study of Torah (both Written and Oral) serves the Temple, which in turn honours and confirms the covenant with Yahweh. Similarly, in Seder Mo'ed, which explicates the liturgical calendar that revolves around the now-invisible Temple, one encounters a wonderful story wherein Abraham is talking to the Master of the Universe.

"Master, were Israel to sin against Thee, what would Thou do unto them? Punish them as was done to the generation of the Great Flood?"

God replies, no, that a sacrifice of a three-year old heifer, of a three-year old she-goat and other animals (as detailed in Genesis 15:9) would expiate the sin.

"But Master," Abraham continues with unselfconscious anachronism (the First Temple had yet to be built, of course). "That holds while there is a Temple. But what about the time when there is no longer a Temple?"

The Almighty's answer is that he has already provided in advance for that time. The order of sacrifice is already set out in the Torah and whenever devoted scholars study it, it will be as if they had offered up the sacrifices physically and they will be granted pardon for all their sins.[13]

The question of why the Bavli leaves out certain tractates has bothered commentators since the middle ages. There are no definitive answers, but the traditional suggestions (articulated in the late middle-ages) make good sense. It is probable that the first Order, Seder Zera'im, is not found in the Bavli (save for commentary on tractate Berakoth which deals with the crucial and universal issue of required prayers) because Seder Zera'im in the Mishnah is concerned mostly with agricultural rules for the Land of Israel. The Mishnah details crop rotations, planting patterns and the like, matters that probably were of no application in Babylon even in the third and fourth centuries, much less matters for study in the fifth and sixth centuries, after the Holy Land was Christianized and dominated both politically and demographically by Gentiles. Similarly, tractate Shekalim, the only Mishnah tractate in the Second Order (Mo'ed) not to have any gemara, is the one part of Mo'ed that does not have deep ritual implications. It concerns a head-tax for supporting the Temple. Still, one would have thought that simply for the sake of completeness, it would have been granted some commentary. The third Order (Nashim) is complete and the fourth (Nezikin) lacks gemara on two tractates, exactly the ones we would expect: Eduyyuot and Aboth. Neither of these is covered in the Yerushalmi or in the Tosefta, and presumably they are excluded from the Bavli's commentary for the same reason. Eduyyuot, it will be recalled, is stylistically out of character with the rest of the Mishnah, and Aboth is a later add-on and, therefore, neither was granted the same authority as were the tractates in the Mishnah-proper.

When one looks at the fifth Order (Kodashim), one finds it to be complete and, indeed expansive, dealing with Temple regulations in great detail. Except: the two smallest tractates, Middoth and Kinnim, dealing, respectively with the measurements of the Temple and with bird offerings. Since, in the scheme of the Babylonian Talmud, the tractates within each Order were arranged according to size, these two small items at the end of the Order may merely have been lost. One doubts that, however, because of a relevant fact: there is no Tosefta on either of those tractates (nor, of course, any gemara in the Yerushalmi). I suspect that early-on (by the time the Tosefta was formed), these two tractates were seen as beyond commentary: Middoth, because its details on the measurements of the Temple are definitive in themselves. One does not parse a blueprint. And Kinnim, on bird-offerings, is simply impossible. It deals with birds to be killed as various sorts of offerings, and whether singly, in pairs, and, if in pairs, of mixed birds or of one species and by sex. The categories cross-hatch with each other, forming dozens of cells, each of which has a potentially-different halachic implication. "The tractate Kinnim gives only the bare answers to some of these problems and does not provide the arguments leading to their solution," the great Herbert Danby noted in his translation of the Mishnah. And he strongly implied that the author-editors of the Bavli were well-advised to let the tractate go without gemara, for "the attempts of the [later] commentators to expound the text of the Mishnah, particularly chapter 3, are lengthy, labourious, and sometimes tentative and uncertain."[14] And, with melancholy candour, Rabbi S.M. Lehrman, who translated Kinnim for the Soncino edition of the Bavli, noted that "the concluding three sections have evoked the despair of all the commentators, all agreeing unanimously that they are the most difficult in the whole Talmud."[15] Kinnim may have been a small tractate in size, but it was a messy intellectual snarl, one that was perhaps wiser to ignore than to confront. As for the final Order (Tohoroth), only tractate Niddah bears any Rabbinic commentary. (Concerning menstruating women as a source of spiritual uncleanness, this tractate was also the only one in Tohoroth that the Yerushalmi dealt with: menstruation was a matter of obsessive concern for the Sages.) Unlike the case of the Yerushalmi, I can find no compelling textual or redactional reason in the Bavli why the rest of Tohoroth, which deals mostly with ritual cleanness, has no gemara, which is to say, why the rest of Tohoroth is missing. Potential reasons are easily put forward (it was lost, the material was no longer relevant, and so on), but none that I have encountered has any probative force.

Nevertheless, what one is left with structurally is unambiguous. The Babylonian Talmud (unlike the Yerushalmi) is a symmetrical structure that honours the architectural fundamentals of the Mishnah. The two iron columns, Orders Mo'ed and Kodashim, which in the Mishnah were placed as interior load-bearing pillars (as Orders two and five) are still in position, but, because Seder Zera'im and Seder Tohoroth (Orders one and six) are each reduced to a single, virtually ornamental, tractate, they now are corner-columns. They still bear the entire weight – the Temple, its ritual, its calendar are still the guarantors of the integrity of Rabbinic Judaism – but now they enclose the faith. Between these two great pillars are situated, in Seder Nashim and Seder Nezikiñ, everything necessary for the day-to-day life of Judaism in diaspora: methods of settling civil disputes, rules for marriage and divorce, virtually every detail is commented upon, explained, and the principles for further development are implicitly set down. Thus, for whatever reason the Babylonian Talmud assumed the form it did, that form was perfect for the "Talmud of the Diaspora."

3

The Babylonian Talmud is a text one either loves or slams shut with a vow to take up something useful instead, such as fly-tying or marathon running.

Since, obviously, I find it to be one of the marvels of western civilization, let me suggest how not to encounter it: do not wrestle with it like Jacob did with the Angel. If one possesses the hubris to try to solve the Bavli, as one would do with a phenomenon that is merely intellectual, one is not only bound to fail, but is apt to wind up, like Jacob, painfully out of joint.

Instead, move according to the physics of the text. A very apt medieval phrase concerning the Bavli referred to "the sea of the Talmud,"[16] and, superficially that can be taken as referring to the sheer size of the document. However, more is implied: the Bavli has a buoyant quality, which bears upon its surface the fragile coracle of the human mind. So long as one does not fight against its prodigious force, this sea is benevolent. The Babylonian Talmud can be intimidating, not least because it "was the traditional earmark of Rabbinic elitist thought and ideality," and was kept, as elite arcana, from the demos. The result is that the Bavli "is currently the least known of all Jewish subjects."[17] So wrote Rabbi José Faur in 1986, and though accurate at the time, this situation is rapidly changing: today an international program of reading circles undertakes a seven-year cycle of daily reading which brings the student through the entire text. And that is as it should be, for the Bavli is accessible to all levels of interest, from first-encounters in an English-language translation, to interrogation by philologists, theologians, and moral philosophers who spend their entire lives in its study. To its students, the Bavli is a sea that seems to possess a miraculous quality: to be continually in flood. And a rising tide lifts all boats, no matter how grand, how humble.

Roughly one-third of the Babylonian Talmud is Aggadah (meaning theology, homily, and story), as compared to one-sixth in the Jerusalem Talmud.[18] This makes the text much friendlier to modern readers than any of its predecessors – Mishnah, Tosefta, Yerushalmi, Sifra. It contains some wonderful stories that can be interpreted as self-contained moral fables, and this fits with the modern taste for short bursts of narrative. However, we should not lose sight of the basic reality: the spine of the Bavli is Halachah, and its organizing model was laid down by that most uncompromising collection of halachic statements, the Mishnah.

This is doubly important, because not only is the modern tendency in Jewish studies to underplay the halachic aspects of the Bavli, but, since the Jewish Enlightenment, the Talmud has incrementally, but markedly, been moved aside and the Hebrew scriptures given ever-more pride of place. Only a tiny proportion of the world's Jewish population has read – let alone studied – this huge document in its entirety. There may be sound votive and practical reasons for this being so, but to an historian the danger is that one of the wonders of the Bavli will be obscured: that in its long run of continuous intellectual development, without irreparable internal schisms, from the days of Rav until the late eighteenth century,[19] the tradition of the Babylonian Talmud is unrivalled in western religious thought. So, just as one has to attempt to get one's mind back past the Protestant Reformation if one is to deal with the undivided Catholic Church of the high middle ages, so one has to somehow slip behind the Jewish Enlightenment if one is to enter the world defined by the Bavli. (And, even while attempting to do so, we have to admit that we cannot have more than token success, such is the impress of our own times.)

Still, the Bavli is accessible in its own way. In fact, the rules of argument employed are similar to those that a good college debate coach teaches to his or her charges.[20] However, one of the reasons that the Bavli is a pleasure to encounter is that its author-editors are sometimes willing to end an otherwise tedious argument with a summary so crisp that it rattles your teeth. Take, for example, one of the textual examples that we have been using since our first discussion of the Mishnah: the vexed matters of whether or not particular architectural features in vernacular buildings give the right of usucaption (Mishnah, Baba Bathra 3:6). It is a messy question, especially the issue of whether or not the owner or occupier of a building in a communal set of buildings (most urban domestic structures of the time shared a common wall or a courtyard with those of other structures) had the right to open a window in a wall. Here the author-editors of the Babylonian Talmud close the interminable debate with a principle that is so simple as to be imperial: if the window is necessary to let in light, it is permitted, and, no matter how small it is, it gives title by usucaption. Case closed: sunlight has decided.[21]

In general, however, the author-editors of the Bavli are much more willing to question received logic than were the framers of the Yerushalmi, and in the usual instance they conduct considerably longer, much richer, debates than do the Jerusalem Talmudists.[22] Admittedly, there are moments in these long, usually carefully orchestrated discussions when one encounters echoes of the too-smart, too-playful, too-bored lad from the religious instruction class of one's own youth. (In my case, the pilpulistic moments in the Bavli bring back the Joycean question on Christian baptism: if it counted, if it were done with soda water.)[23] And, despite (or perhaps because of) their pleasure in presenting as many logical alternatives and reasonable permutations of argumentative interventions, the author-editors of the Bavli are even less inclined than were those of the Yerushalmi to make firm decisions.[24] This has the long-run result of yielding a continuing discussion of the case in question that reverberates from generation to generation of subsequent Talmudic scholars.[25] In this regard, Jacob Neusner has suggested that the Bavli is an exercise in continuing dialectic, in a "sustained conflict of intellect," that operates according to three principles: (1) each dispute is conducted on a rational basis, meaning that each party has a good-faith rational principle in mind as a beginning point for its argument; (2) that, ultimately, disputes will indeed be resolved (even if long after the discussion is first formulated), for the dialectic of argument is not a Sisyphean process. And (3) it is truth that eventually wins out in the individual case.[26] David Kraemer has counted 2,449 full-length argumentative sequences in the Bavli.[27] And, ultimately, when the Bavli is considered as a whole, the cumulative victory of truth in individual cases reveals a pattern of Law that lies behind the myriad individual cases.

Paradoxically, despite its willingness to lead its students into prolonged, and frequently unresolved, dialectical argumentation, the Babylonian Talmud is actually a "strong text," in the sense that it asserts its own power over its progenitors. It is very consciously a religious invention, one that remakes both the Mishnah and the Tanakh. In neither case does it falsify the original text. Indeed, on the surface it is quite respectful of them. To take the Mishnah first: what can appear more respectful than to organize a commentary around that earlier document? An estimated 90 percent of the Babylonian Talmud's commentary (including a good deal of Aggadah) is keyed to passages in the Mishnah.[28] Yet, because the author-editors of the Bavli are free to choose which portions of the Mishnah they comment on, which they do not, and to which of the Mishnah's rules they give extended attention and which ones they pass with only side-comments, they effectively rewrite the Mishnah (and a bit of Sifra as well).[29]

Thus, they maintain its elegant, symmetrical and strong structural elements, while changing the way that the motifs and the internal filigree relate to each other. On occasion, the "interpretation" of the Mishnah by the author-editors of the Bavli is nothing less than a reversal of the Mishnah's meaning. This may occur, in Eliezer Berkovits's formulation, "by limiting the general principle which it [the Mishnah] teaches to a special and exceptional case."[30] Thus, for example, in responding to two situations that are covered by a general law concerning the responsibilities of males to their dependents – in this case the instances are the dicta that a man must support his wife even if he does not want to do so, but if he does not wish to maintain his slave, he is not required to do so – the author-editors of the Bavli introduce the gently arch phrase, "perhaps the two cases are not on all fours." The general principle – that one sort of dependent is to be treated markedly worse than another, clearly makes the Sages uneasy, so, in this case, they turn the slaves into a special case. Slaves, they say, do not require obligatory maintenance, because a slave-owner can tell the slaves to keep for their own maintenance the fruits of their own labour, while this could not be done (according to the rules of Jewish society) in the case of a woman. Thus, the awkward general principle of differential entitlements does not have to be reckoned with, since one of its two defining points is shown to be a special case and therefore not of validity in defining the gradient of application in this instance.[31]

The Bavli's inventors employ a wide array of other techniques to vitiate those portions of the Mishnah that they do not accept – such as playing one set of answers ascribed to various Sages against another, or pointing out that something is obviously missing in the Mishnah and should therefore be interpolated, and so on[32] – yet they always proceed by the grammar of religious invention that descended from the Yahweh-faith. They show great public fealty to the text even as they are re-inventing it. They never admit originality; usually, they articulate their own ideas in the voices of earlier figures of authority; and everything new is made to look old.

Significantly, the framers of the Bavli have the self-confidence to correct the scriptures. According to David Kraemer, on more than 200 occasions (some minor, others not), the author-editors of the Bavli permit the Sages to suggest what the scriptures "should" have said on a given subject, rather than what it did.[33]

Sometimes this retro-writing of the Hebrew Bible was done to fill in silences in the holy text. For example, at one point a question arises concerning the Mishnah's requirement that a man who has eaten or has drunk a ritually-proscribed substance is required to bring only one sin offering as expiation, whereas someone who has both ingested an unclean substance and performed labour in a ritually impure state, must bring two sin-offerings. The discussion of this ruling begins with Resh Lakish asking querulously why is there no explicit warning about this in scripture? Thereafter one of the respondents suggests, in the subjunctive, what the Divine Law might have said, and then, several Sages make specific suggestions as to what scripture should have said. "Let the Divine Law write …" is their magisterial command.[34] Elsewhere, with even more self-assurance, the Sages are made actually to correct the Tanakh, by saying what scripture really meant, though it actually says the opposite. For example, Leviticus 6:19 [=KJB, Lev. 6:26] requires that the priest who offers a sin-offering should himself eat it. However the Rabbis do not accept this ruling from the Pentateuch, as they wish the offering to be shared out, so they give the following interpretation: the command to eat the sin-offering really means to share it! "That you may infer: he who is fit to eat shares; he who is not fit to eat does not share [in it]."[35]

Now, if one adds to these tendencies the fact that the cited portions of the scriptures are virtually never given in their biblical context – they are presented as phrases, or single verses, and in the context of the Mishnah – then it becomes clear that the author-editors of the Bavli, writing in the name of the Sages, have done nothing less than become the inventors of the scriptures. They explicitly claim this right in an assertion attributed to Rabbi Abdimi of Haifa: "Since the day the Temple was destroyed, prophecy has been taken from the prophets and given to the Sages."[36]

Given the extraordinary confidence and consequent power of the Bavli, a fundamental issue of interpretation arises, and it is not one that can be danced away from by a clever academic minuet. The question is: is the Babylonian

Talmud a unified entity, or is it "less a thematically closed book than a national library of Babylonian Judaism whose structure emulates the Mishnah."[37] This is an issue that is not soluble by the usual scholarly methods, even though the question can be posed in traditional academic terms. At heart, it is a question of individual sensibility, and here I must declare my own: I cannot comprehend how anyone who spends any time with the Bavli can come away unimpressed, indeed, virtually overawed by it as an artistic entity that works as a single, efficient, yet immensely subtle, religious invention. One has to be culturally tone-deaf not to hear the Talmud's celestial music.

Yet, why are a number of extremely competent scholars, individuals who for the most part are respectful of the text, unable to apperceive the Bavli's quality (in Louis Jacobs's words) "of having dropped from Heaven complete, as it were?"[38] It is not merely tone deafness, for that does not afflict them all. Rather, it stems from two additional sources. One of these is the necessity of any scholar of the text and its history who is true to the evidentiary canons of the modern academy, distancing him- or herself from the theological dogma that we may call the "Principle of Textual Synchronicity." That is, medieval Rabbinics and its modern derivatives run on the presupposition that all Torah was uttered in a single statement, meaning that whatever scriptural verses one collates, whatever utterances of the Sages one finds, they are all part of a single divine utterance. As a statement of faith this is unobjectionable – faith, ultimately, is beyond rational interrogation. But as an hypothesis as to how any document or set of documents came into being it is valueless to anyone who accepts the concept of cause-and-effect as it has developed in western thought since the late sixteenth century. I think it is understandable that scholars who have accepted the evidence of "secular" history – that is, that the texts of the Bible and of the Rabbinic writings indeed emerged in fits and starts, not as a seamless revelation – have found it difficult not to take that point too far. They therefore miss the artistic (or literary or ideational, or ideological) unity, possessed by many of the individual texts in the tradition. One can understand how emotionally-difficult it is to edge back towards a position that rejects the synchronicity of the totality of texts, but which recognizes those items which are unified inventions and celebrates them as such. It is difficult, but necessary.

Secondly, I think much of the failure to see the Babylonian Talmud as the soaring masterpiece that it is, is the unintentional product of bad historical method. Specifically, a basic fallacy runs deeply, albeit unconsciously, through much of modern "secular" scholarship on the Babylonian Talmud, namely the confusion of process with product. This fallacy is widespread in the historical profession, and certainly is not limited to individuals who are studying Rabbinic literature. What occurs is a form of reductionism, in which historians (of texts, of events, of economies, of societies, it matters not) become so intent on analysing the evolution and the details of the subject of their attention that they disassemble everything and seem forever unable to put it back together. The intellectual result is the equivalent of a scientifically-trained art historian analysing one of Giotto's frescoes and then describing the final result in terms of clusters of small dots over a charcoal outline. As with the texts in the Yahweh-tradition – the Tanakh, the "New Testament" and the products of the classical Rabbinic age – the layers of invention show the process, but the knowledge of that process should not blind the scholar to the glory of the final product.

In arguing that the Babylonian Talmud is a unified artistic (or literary) entity, I am not suggesting that it is some kind of intellectual purée. It is not entirely homogenized. A few segments are rougher than others, as if not-quite-revised. And in any case, the author-editors permit, within their own rules of modulation, differences in tone and articulation. Judah Goldin once remarked that "in the Talmud, you hear voices."[39]

But these voices, whether they come from the immemorial past, from Moses, from the early Pharisees or, in the usual case, from the Rabbis of the third through fifth centuries, are controlled by the inventors of the Bavli in the same way that the seemingly-authentic voices in Shakespeare's historical plays are controlled: they are not employed so much for their being historically true (though, sometimes their words may be historically accurate), but as the actors' voices in a literary project. In the Babylonian Talmud, the drama these editorially-controlled voices presents works not by emotional escalation but by a dialectic of ideas which builds up step-by-step, until either a climax is reached, or the audience is told, in effect, "Now, go, reflect on these things for yourself."[40]

4

A distinguishing characteristic of a truly great invention is that it keeps on developing long after its inventors have declared it completed. In the case of a text such as the Babylonian Talmud (as with the Tanakh and the "New Testament"), it has continued to evolve, through later generations of study, commentary, argument that are based upon it. Phenomena of this sort are the focus of an imposing literature in present-day critical-theory, and portions of this material can be read with profit. However, eventually one must face the fact that all our efforts are merely superficial and descriptive, however much our own egos wish to think they are deeply explanatory. So, one can point to platform-characteristics of the Bavli, structural features that serve as the bases for century-after-century of secondary elaboration by devotees of the text, but one must not mistake these observations as having some form of ultimate explanatory force.

Obviously, the dialectic form for halachic discussion is a primary characteristic. It provides points of engagement where serious minds can argue, if
not for ever, at least for several human lifetimes. However, three less-noticed
features of the Bavli seem to me to be significant: the visual form that
the Bavli assumed; the short-story format that characterizes much of the
Aggadah; and the willingness of the author-editors of the Bavli to introduce a
muted set of apocalyptic themes. Taken together, these last two characteristics re-introduce a concept of implied narrative back into a set of Rabbinical
documents that had been almost totally stripped of narrative force. The Bavli
remains an halachic work, but the inclusion of historical anecdotes and apocalyptic speculations permits the readers to anchor the discussion of Law in
the psychological bedrock of narrative. Thus, if the Bavli still is primarily a
set of legal arguments, the reader can scarcely be unaware that they are presented as part of the big story, the history of the big deal, the covenant between Yahweh and the children of Israel.

Paradoxically, I think that optics – in the literal sense of how the Bavli has
looked down through the ages – have played a part in keeping the Bavli alive
as an invention that is forever being re-invented. Let us grant that one of the
most tantalizing aspects of the history of Rabbinic Judaism is the question of
what the Bavli looked like when it was first written down. (And, however
much of it may have been memorized by its students, this always was a written document, not an oral one.)[41]

What wouldn't we give to see the manuscript of the first complete version? Given the nature of the text, it almost certainly was a codex – that is,
the first Bavli must have been shaped like a book. Why? Because the text
consists of a series of marginalia, and marginal notes, arranged around a
central text and this process works on a series of individual sheets of paper,
but not on a scroll. Individual sheets have borders and the edges of the paper, like a border collie with a potentially unruly mob of sheep, keep the
main text and the commentary upon it together. On a scroll, everything gets
out of hand, and pretty soon commentary on one passage runs over into that
of its successor and eventually everything is entangled to the point of utter
confusion.[42]

If we assume that the earliest versions of the Babylonian Talmud were
bare-bones models – the Mishnah's text well inside the individual page and
the commentary ascribed to the various Sages all around it – even in that form
it must have been a visually seductive artifact. This by virtue of two vital
characteristics: first, because this mode of presentation – central text and
marginalia – visually represents with great efficiency the basic fact of the Talmud's nature, that it is a multi-voiced colloquy of voices from different eras,
brought together in a single historical instant, that instant being the moment
that one studies all their opinions concerning the central text. Visually, each

page of the Talmud is a calligraphic solar system, idea-units circulating like moons around a major planet.

And, secondly, this form invites continuing in-filling. On each page, the cislunar distance between the central planet and its satellites leaves plenty of space for new commentary to be inserted by later readers. (This of course is said metaphorically; new commentary doubtless required constant revising of the physical details of each page, but in terms of space-for-ideas, there was always a lot of room.) Thus, the Talmud was an "interactive" text centuries before a word was invented to describe the phenomenon. By virtue of the comments that each successive generation of students added to the marginalia, each copy of the Bavli was unique in its details, even while the basic text remained nearly constant. This situation is clearly indicated by eleventh-century authorities having to warn copyists about the prevalence of marginal notes that were not part of the original text: "It is common that a reference, explanation, or variant is written in the margin or between the lines. A copyist thinks it is part of the text and writes it all together. He thus leads astray, for [his copy] will fall into the hands of a Sage who will treat the matter as a unit and render decisions according to the addition."[43] Had not the Christian church in the thirteenth through sixteenth centuries undertaken a massive campaign of destruction of Jewish texts of all sorts, we would doubtless possess hundreds of medieval manuscript copies of the Babylonian Talmud – not just the single fourteenth-century copy that remains – and each copy would have its own unique super-comments, the product of the interaction of the earliest commentators on the Mishnah, with Sages of the seventh century and onwards. As it is, the version we possess is quite wonderful in its multi-voiced character. Fortunately, it became standard practice with the invention of printing to present not only the Mishnah and the gemara thereon but, on a single page, to add the commentary of Rashi (the extraordinary French scholar of the late tenth and early eleventh centuries, Rabbi Solomon ben Isaac) and, further "Tosafot," which are supplements by German and French Rabbis of the twelfth to fourteenth centuries that either comment on the Mishnah, or act as meta-commentary on the gemera and, sometimes on the commentary of Rashi! A very lively page indeed. An example of a typical printed page is found in Figure I, which is taken from the recognized-standard version of the Bavli, the Wilna (Vilna) edition of 1886. So, the Bavli lives in part because it is an interactive text, with a very unusual visual format that draws each generation of students into its orbit. Of equal importance, the Babylonian Talmud includes a good deal of Aggadah, more than any previous commentary on the Mishnah. Some of this is scriptural exegesis, but the materials that enliven the Bavli and make the text crackle are a widely heterogenous blend of legends, folk tales, allegedly-historical occurrences that are crisp, relatively brief, and often highly memorable. Most of these items have

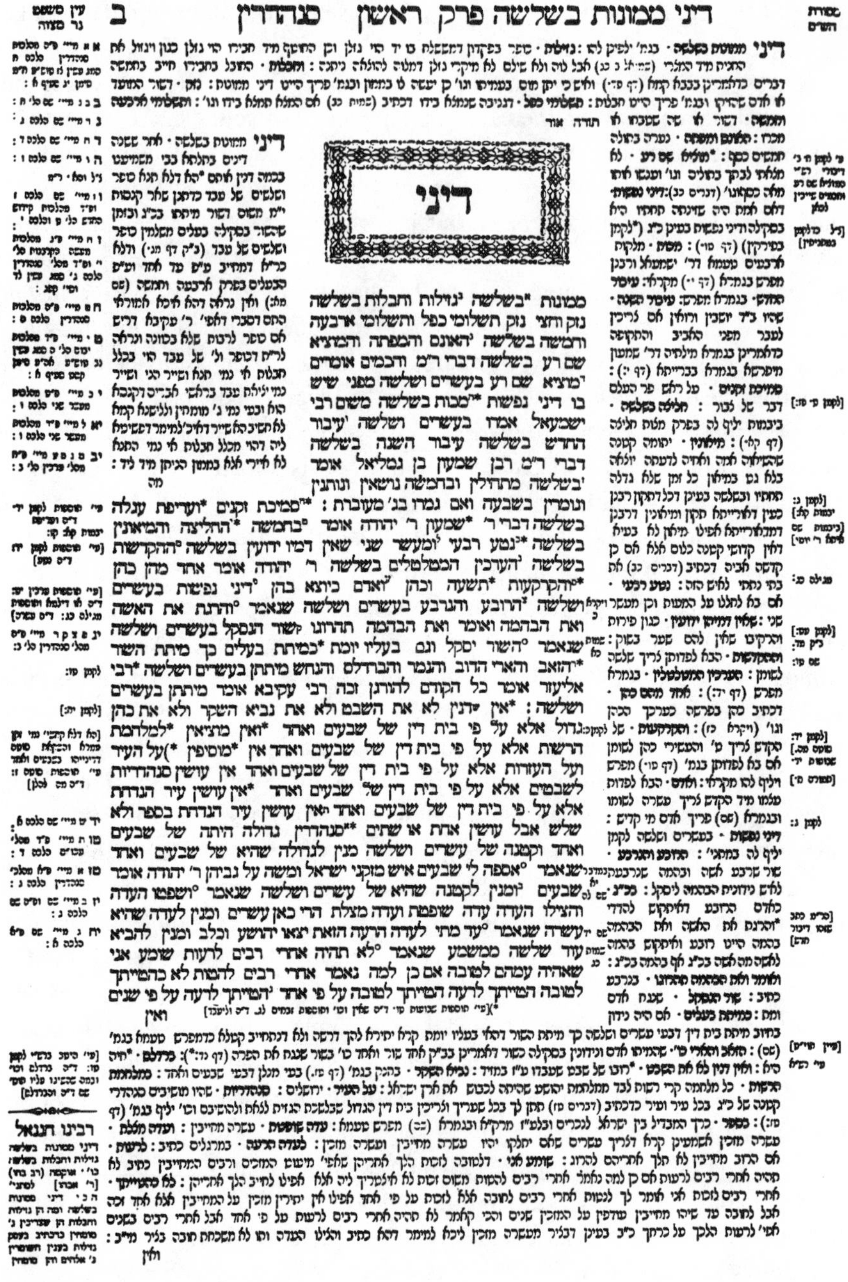

דיני ממונות בשלשה פרק ראשון סנהדרין ב

מסורת הש"ס — עין משפט נר מצוה

דיני

ממונות בשלשה גזילות וחבלות בשלשה
נזק וחצי נזק תשלומי כפל ותשלומי ארבעה
וחמשה בשלשה האונס והמפתה והמוציא
שם רע בשלשה דברי ר"מ וחכמים אומרים
מוציא שם רע בעשרים ושלשה מפני שיש
בו דיני נפשות מכות בשלשה משום רבי
ישמעאל אמרו בעשרים ושלשה עיבור
החדש בשלשה עיבור השנה בשלשה
דברי ר"מ רבן שמעון בן גמליאל אומר
בשלשה מתחילין ובחמשה נושאין ונותנין
ונומרין בשבעה ואם גמרו בג' מעוברת: סמיכת זקנים ועריפת עגלה
בשלשה דברי ר' שמעון ר' יהודה אומר בחמשה החליצה והמיאונין
בשלשה נטע רבעי ומעשר שני שאין דמיו ידועין בשלשה ההקדשות
בשלשה הערכין המטלטלים בשלשה ר' יהודה אומר אחד מהן כהן
הקרקעות תשעה וכהן ואדם כיוצא בהן דיני נפשות בעשרים
ושלשה הרובע והנרבע בעשרים ושלשה שנאמר והרגת את האשה
ואת הבהמה ואומר ואת הבהמה תהרוגו שור הנסקל בעשרים ושלשה
שנאמר השור יסקל וגם בעליו יומת כמיתת בעלים כך מיתת השור
הזאב והארי הדוב והנמר והברדלס והנחש מיתתן בעשרים ושלשה רבי
אליעזר אומר כל הקודם להורגן זכה רבי עקיבא אומר מיתתן בעשרים
ושלשה: אין דנין לא את השבט ולא את נביא השקר ולא את כהן
גדול אלא על פי בית דין של שבעים ואחד ואין מוציאין למלחמת
הרשות אלא על פי בית דין של שבעים ואחד אין מוסיפין על העיר
ועל העזרות אלא על פי בית דין של שבעים ואחד אין עושין סנהדריות
לשבטים אלא על פי בית דין של שבעים ואחד אין עושין עיר הנדחת
אלא על פי בית דין של שבעים ואחד ואין עושין עיר הנדחת בספר ולא
שלש אבל עושין אחת או שתים סנהדרין גדולה היתה של שבעים
ואחד וקטנה של עשרים ושלשה מנין לגדולה שהיא של שבעים ואחד
שנאמר אספה לי שבעים איש מזקני ישראל ומשה על גביהן ר' יהודה אומר
שבעים ומנין לקטנה שהיא של עשרים ושלשה שנאמר ושפטו העדה
והצילו העדה עדה שופטת ועדה מצלת הרי כאן עשרים ומנין לעדה שהיא
עשרה שנאמר עד מתי לעדה הרעה הזאת יצאו יהושע וכלב ומנין להביא
עוד שלשה ממשמע שנאמר לא תהיה אחרי רבים לרעות שומע אני
שאהיה עמהם לטובה אם כן למה נאמר אחרי רבים להטות לא כהטייתך
לטובה הטייתך לרעה הטייתך לטובה על פי אחד הטייתך לרעה על פי שנים
ואין

Figure 1
The first page of the Bavli, tractate Sanhedrin, from the standard modern edition, printed in Vilna, Lithuania in 1886.

their origin in the Land of Israel, as is only natural, given that Eretz Israel was the locus of Jewish activity until the 420s CE. However, in the form that we know it, the material is "Babylonian" in the sense that the Babylonian Sages preserved the material and integrated it into the Bavli.

It is from these brief narratives – "short, short-stories" would be a fair description – that most of today's homilies from the Bavli are drawn, and most of the epigrams and bits of wisdom that are usually introduced in a sermon or after-dinner speech by a phrase such as "according to the Talmud." Good stories: here one can only indicate the range and flavour of the enterprise. One sort of anecdote is the pen-picture of one or another of the holy men. For example, of Rabbi Yohanan ben Zakkai, it was said that never during his entire life did he utter a frivolous word ("profane talk") nor walk more than four cubits (roughly two metres) without studying Torah. He was the first into the academy each day, he studied all day, never dozing, and was the last out at night. And "he never in his life said anything which he had not heard from his teacher."[44] Hundreds of these sketches of one Sage or another flavour the Bavli, and they make good starting points for Sabbath-school lessons. They should not, however, be taken as being the constituent elements of anything we would recognize as biography. They are invariably presented as part of a dialectical discussion, not as items having historical value in themselves, and their historicity is epiphenomenal at best. In the usual case, their closest equivalents are the fractured stories of early Christian saints that one finds stitched together in early "Lives of the Saints."

Secondly, and of more interest to historians are passages that are placed in a semi-historical context, such as the set of tales in tractate Gittin that have as their backdrop a real event, the Roman-Jewish War of 66–73 CE. Some of these tales may have real historical referents. However, one is clearly in the realm of folk-fable when one reads that during that war, "the Emperor sent Nero against the Jews." (Not only did Nero himself never come to Palestine, but he had committed suicide in 68 CE, before the siege of Jerusalem began.) Yet more fabulously, upon approaching Jerusalem, Nero is said to have shot four arrows into the air, one towards each of the major points of the compass and each time the arrow he shot fell in Jerusalem. Nero took this as a sign and asked "a certain boy" (unidentified, but a figure of the Jewish wise-child, familiar in the "New Testament"), to repeat to him the most recent verse of scripture he has learned, and this turns out to be Ezekiel 25:14 in which Yahweh says "I will lay my vengeance upon Edom by the hand of my people Israel." Whereupon, in the story, Nero reverses the meaning of the text and concludes that Yahweh had decided "to lay waste his House and to lay the blame on me." And then, Nero runs away and becomes a proselyte and, amazingly, the story concludes that the great "Rabbi Meir was descended from him."[45] Even making allowance for the fact that this fable may enhull the contemporary legend that Nero, though he had committed suicide, was believed by some to be still alive and that he would return to reign,[46] this story opens a huge mirrors-facing-mirrors iteration. What is real, it asks: could the will of the Almighty be expressed in so complex, so veiled a fashion, that Nero becomes a Messiah figure (returning from the dead to reign), and that he could be the progenitor of one of the most influential contributors to the Mishnah, Rabbi Meir? By God's inscrutable divine will, are our enemies our friends? – for they work His will – and, therefore, are we, the Chosen People, actually our own enemies? What a complex little composition, a one-paragraph challenge to every assumption of the Talmud. And, to complete the paradox, it is found within the Bavli's own pages.

Considerably less challenging are minor stories of secondary historical figures, which are memorable chiefly because detail is done so well. An instance is the tale from the same Jewish-Roman War, concerning Martha, the daughter of Boethius, one of the richest women in Jerusalem. She sent her servant out into the strife-torn streets to find some fine-ground flour. It is all sold, her butler discovers, but he reports there is some regular white flour left. Go, she tells him, and buy some white flour. But he is too late, it is all gone. But there is some dark flour left, he reports. So go and bring me some dark flour, she scowls, and he tries: no dark flour, but there is barley flour. Get it, she orders. It too is gone. Finally, vexed, this wealthy woman decides to go out herself and see if she can find anything to eat. She goes barefoot, something she never would have done in less desperate times.

When on the street, some animal dung sticks to her foot and this most delicate and pampered of women dies from the shock.[47] An entire novel's worth of characterization is found in these few details. Indeed, the story reads as if Jane Austen's social percipience has been articulated by Philip Roth's scatological sense of humour.

At the other end of the spectrum from this essentially universal folk tale (almost all cultures agree that it's nice to see the proud laid low, and with the less dignity the better), is the Babylonian Talmud's presentation of moral fables whose theological point is impossible to miss. Take the story ascribed to Rava, concerning Rabbi Tabyomi who, even if he were given all the treasures of the earth to misrepresent truth, would not stoop to lie. Tabyomi, travelling the world, once came to a place called "Kushta" (meaning Truth), a land in which no one ever told lies and where no man ever died before his time. (The parallel to the later legend of Shangri La is obvious). There Tabyomi married and had two sons. One day his wife was washing her hair when a neighbour knocked at the door. Because it would not be good etiquette to say that his wife was washing her hair (such domestic details being for family members only), Tabyomi told the neighbour,"She is not here."

Consequently, Tabyomi's two sons died. The people of the town, holy innocents, questioned Tabyomi about this and when he explained the sequence of events, they told him, "Quit this town, and do not incite Death against us."[48] A strong statement, indeed, of the absolute demands of Truth.

One could go on and on, and that is the point. The Aggadah in the Babylonian Talmud is seductive, diverting, informative, demanding, paradoxical, and more. The conversation with the Bavli goes on and on, because one ponders, expands, produces alternative endings to the tales. Whereas one argues with the legal material, in a dialectic rhythm set by the interaction of legal principles and individual cases, one converses with the aggadic material as with an old, avuncular friend, musing, rather than arguing, and always the conversations revolve around the unspoken question, "what can we learn from this?" And that serious, but comfortable conversation, soft-voiced, punctuated by reflective silences, has gone on, generation after generation.

Earlier, I suggested that one of the reasons that the Babylonian Talmud was a great invention – one that kept on growing long after its inventors were figures of the past – is that it interwove into its largely-legal discussions a muted apocalyptic theme. Emphatically, the Bavli is not an apocalyptic document. It is nothing like the "New Testament" in its eschatology; much less does it resemble those point-platoons of the army of the apocalypse, the Book of Daniel in the Hebrew scriptures and the Book of Revelation in the Christian. No word exists that precisely fits the Talmud's tone so, with the proviso that I am not here employing a term of diminution, let me suggest that the Bavli is not apocalyptic, but is "apocalyptish." That is, its inventors incorporate, as an accent-motif, concepts that relate to apocalyptic matters, but they do not permit the motifs to become dominant, or even to be more than flavouring matter. But they are there.

Within the religious traditions that stem from the Yahweh-faith, the anteroom to the world of eschatology is reached through the affirmation of the concept of the perhaps-both physical and spiritual, and perhaps-only spiritual resurrection of the dead. Of whatever sort, the idea of the personal resurrection (as distinct from the collective resurrection of the nation of Israel) was not articulated clearly (if at all) in the "Old Testament," save in the Book of Daniel. However, some of the several Judahist parties in the later Second Temple period developed the idea and tied it to individual eternal judgement, and to apocalyptic concepts of the World-to-Come. The Jesus-faith had melded these ideas together very effectively, and I think that is one reason that in the earlier documents of the core Rabbinic tradition, the basic Pharisaic doctrine of the resurrection of the dead is touched upon so very lightly. Now, in the Bavli – the most self-confident and polished item in the Rabbinic tradition – the physical resurrection is referred to openly and, if not frequently, at least much more often than in earlier texts.[49]

Undeniably, the Babylonian Talmud contains divergent views of the after-death state and of the nature of the resurrection. One of these variants in the mythology was the singular privilege granted to the great Rabbi (that is, to Judah the Patriarch) to return after death to his previous home. According to the Bavli, he would come home again at twilight on every Sabbath eve (whether as a phantasm or as a corporeal entity is unrecorded). Eventually, with consummate modesty, he gave this up because it reflected badly on earlier saints, who were not granted this privilege.[50] That was singular.

More in line with the usual human condition were the assertions by some of the Sages that the physical body actually was to be resurrected at some time in the future, not merely the soul. This belief is reflected in the Rabbinical prescription that when a man enters a privy he should say a prayer. And, when he comes out he should say another one, as follows:

> Blessed is He who has formed man in wisdom and created in him many orifices and many cavities. It is fully known before the throne of Thy glory that if one of them should be [improperly] opened or one of them closed it would be impossible for a man to stand before Thee."[51]

Indeed. This belief that the resurrection of the individual was to occur bodily is confirmed by a parable which concludes that the Almighty, on judgement day, will join the human body and the soul together and judge them as one.[52] And this prospect is further, if indirectly, validated by the Rabbinic belief that those who perished during the Great Flood of Noah's time ("the generation of the flood") should be neither resurrected nor judged.[53] This will be the case because their bodies were destroyed and, according to one view of the resurrection, corporeal remains are a requisite for an appearance before God's judgment seat. Belief in the literal bodily resurrection also is indicated in the following Rabbinical admonition. "On seeing Israelitish graves, one should say, 'Blessed is He who fashioned you in judgement, who fed you in judgement and maintained you in judgement, and in judgement gathered you in, and who will one day raise you up again in judgement.'"[54] More graphic is Rabbi Hiyya ben Joseph's statement that the dead will rise "in their own clothes."[55]

Other pronouncements, however, raise questions. A different view was that only the soul was involved in the resurrection. Thus, after the general resurrection, the "souls of the righteous" were to be gathered together with all the "spirits and the souls which are yet to be born..." and taken before the Almighty.[56] No bodies were to be involved, just souls.

Yet another Rabbinical view was that the body existed for twelve months after death. During that year-long period the soul ascended heavenward and descended back to earth, as it wished. After twelve months, according to this opinion, the body ceased to exist and the soul ascended to the heavens there to remain permanently.[57] (Presumably, this was in the case of a righteous person, who deserved a heavenly reward.) A related view, still using a twelve-month period, was that in the case of the truly evil their bodies would be resurrected. Then, the wicked were to be sent down to Gehinnom (a hellish place, modelled on the real-life Valley of Hinnom, southwest of Jerusalem). There the resurrected physical bodies would be punished for twelve months and then both the bodies and the souls of the wicked would be totally consumed by fire and the wind would scatter both body and soul "under the soles of the feet of the righteous."[58]

Because the author-editors of the Babylonian Talmud did not systematize or harmonize the various viewpoints of the Sages, it was (and is) possible to interpret the Sages as believing that there was to be a literal bodily resurrection of each individual who has died (the position of most variants of present-day Orthodox Judaism) or that it was (and still is) equally reasonable to read the classic Rabbinic texts as involving not a bodily resurrection, but a spiritual immortality afer death (the prevailing view in present day Reform Judaism). Two points are indisputable, however. The first of these is that in the Bavli the discussions of the resurrection (in whatever form one interprets it) are sufficiently pervasive to enable us to conclude that it was a core belief of Rabbinic Judaism, the dominant religious form which by now had subsumed most of the dozens of Judahisms of the later Second Temple era. Although the belief may long have been part of the concepts inherited from Pharisaism, this is the first text in the core documents of the Rabbinic tradition which make adherence to this belief absolutely clear. (That is, unless one chooses to read the documents of the Jesus-faith as a variant of Pharisaism, an emotionally-charged, and therefore, distracting procedure.) A second point follows from the resurrection of the individual being locked into Rabbinic Judaism, namely that this concept is almost inevitably bonded to some sort of eschatology and, in its turn, eschatology leads naturally to "apocalyptish" thought.

A nice join between resurrection and eschatology appears in the most fully articulated version of the judgement found in the Bavli. According to Rabbi Kruspedai, speaking in the name of Rabbi Johanan, at the start of each New Year, three books are opened. In one of these, the "Book of Life," are inscribed the names of the righteous; in another, "the Book of Death," are inscribed the names of the thoroughly wicked; and there is a book for the intermediate sort of person, those neither thoroughly righteous nor thoroughly wicked. In this last case, judgement is suspended from New Year until the Day of Atonement and, in that period, they can earn either promotion or demotion in the eternal ledgers. (That this writing of names in eternal account-books bears a resemblance to the material in the Book of Revelation – especially

20:12 – should surprise no one: Rabbinical and Christian writers relied upon the same basic inventory of apocalyptic motifs from the later Second Temple era.) Eventually the Day of Judgement will come and there the three groups are to be dealt with as follows. The thoroughly righteous, whose names are in the Book of Life will receive everlasting life in heaven (or, at least in some heavenward location; the text is unclear).[59] The intermediate group will go down to Gehinnom "and squeal" because of the pain of fire, but shall "rise again," purified by their ordeal. The thoroughly wicked wrongdoers are to be punished as follows: some of them – the lucky ones as it turns out – have their bodies and souls burned and scattered. The really evil, the "minim" (a term which most often refers to followers of the Jesus-faith) and "the informers and the scoffers" who have rejected Torah, laughed at the idea of the resurrection of the dead, and have not lived according to Jewish social rules, "those will go down to Gehinnom and be punished there for all generations."[60]

The Bavli is never quite clear as to what will trigger the resurrection of the dead and the subsequent judgement of each individual. However, it is clear that something big must happen in future-time to provide a corridor for the final judgement. Here, one encounters nebulous concepts, somehow related to each other and to the final judgement, such as the "Time to Come" and the "Days of the Messiah." These references all are to master-events set in future time, but whether or not they are to occur in the physical world as we know it, or in a world of miracle, of suspended natural laws, varies according to the scene the author-editors of the Bavli chose to include. To allow us keep the hallucinogenic richness of these future-visions in some kind of order, it helps to think of them as being of three sorts which overlap each other, like the blades of an old-fashioned ladies' card-fan, joined at the base, but spreading out in an overlaying arrangement. The individual cards are: the World to Come as a general concept; the Future-World as a time of triumph for the Chosen People; and the Time of the Messiah.

The World to Come of the Babylonian Talmud as a general construct can be illustrated by two exhibits. One of these is summarized in a waterfall of images. According to the authority of Rabbi Johanan, when the Time to Come occurs, the Almighty will make a tabernacle for each righteous man from a portion of the skin of Leviathan. Less worthy individuals will have a body covering made for them, and those still less worthy a necklace, and the least worthy, an amulet, all made from the skin of the great sea monster.[61] All this presumes that one considers it an honour to be cloaked in the scaly covering of an ill-smelling sea monster. Rather more antiseptic is the dictum of Rav Kattina, that from creation the world was to last 6,000 years and, thereafter, a millennium of desolation was to follow.[62]

Overlapping these general formulations are visions of the Future-Time as being especially beneficent to Israel. Indeed, under this mode of thought, history will be properly sifted by the triumph of a restored nation of Israel, a prelude to the reign of God and to the Judgement Day that follows. Here is one version of that course of events. Joseph, the son of Rabbi Joshua fell into a trance and had a vision. "What did you see?" his father asked him when he had come out of the trance.

The son replied "I saw a world upside down." This, of course could only be a good thing, since in the present physical world, the Romans ruled and the Righteous suffered. It was a well regulated world, he added.

"In what condition did you see us?" his father asked, referring to those of us who are the students of Torah.

"As our esteem is here, so it is there."[63] In other words, when the world is finally set aright, the Rabbis will still be spiritually revered.

In the world to come, Jerusalem was to be transformed. Anyone can go up to the Jerusalem of the present world, but according to Rabbi Johanan, in the World to Come, only those who are invited will be welcome.[64] The New Jerusalem is an apocalyptic symbol that goes back to the several Judahisms that precede the Common Era. Notice here how gently the concept is employed, in sharp contrast to its use as an apocalyptic behemoth in Christian eschatology (especially in Revelation). In the same relatively peaceful tone, the Land of Israel in the World to Come will be remarkably fecund: silk garments, rich grain fields, baked cakes of highest quality will fill the land and the juice of a single grape will fill an entire wine cask.[65]

The third concept of a future world, overlapping with the two preceding constructs, is the Time of the Messiah. In its fulness (after some nasty moments on the way to its fruition) the Messianic Age will be a time of peace so profound that it can only be expressed indirectly. The simplest icon of peace is that in the days of Moshiah, lances shall exist merely as ornaments, for they will have no use.[66] More profound, less easy to picture, is the belief that the Messianic era will be a return to primal innocence: there will be neither merit nor guilt.[67] Under Moshiah's rule, whatever will be, will be right. The return to aspects of the Garden of Eden is clear. In the Messianic age, all animals will assemble and come to the serpent and say to him, "The lion claws [his victim] and devours him; the wolf tears his and devours him. But as for you, what advantage do you have over your prey?" And the serpent, the Tempter, will have to reply, "The man of tongue hath no advantage," by which is meant: the temptation of the human soul, by the wiles of the serpent, is no longer possible.[68] Finally, the days of the Moshiah will culminate in the Almighty sitting in the midst of his people in the Garden of Eden and every one of them will point toward him and repeat the words of Isaiah: "this is the Lord for whom we waited, we will be glad and rejoice in His salvation."[69]

In contrast to the almost inexpressible peace that will characterize the age of Moshiah, the path up to that time will be rocky and beset with violence.

The Messiah's arrival will bring back the dynasty of King David and then the "wicked kingdom" will end,[70] but only after what the Rabbis call "the pangs of Messiah,"[71] meaning an era of suffering and confusion before Moshiah appears. Rabbinical scholars will be persecuted and the land will suffer plunderers and, indeed, plunderers of plunderers: anarchy.[72] The Rabbis teach that, in the seven years before the son of David comes, the following will occur: local droughts, "arrows of hunger," a great famine, partial plenty, then great plenty, followed by a year of messages from heaven announcing the Moshiah and, finally, war.[73] And, the author-editors of the Babylonian Talmud pick up and use the same references in Ezekiel (chapters 38 and 39) to wars with Gog, ruler of the land of Magog, that the Christian apocalyptic writers employ.[74] And, like the Christian apocalypticists, the author-editors of the Bavli view "the wicked kingdom" of Rome as the immediate embodiment of evil and they make arcane coded predictions concerning the time of its downfall.[75] However, there was a signal difference in the Jewish and the Christian prophecies about Rome: whereas the Christians looked for Rome's destruction because it was a pagan state that persecuted the Jesus-faith, the Rabbis, writing later, look for the end of Rome because it is a state that privileges Christianity and persecutes the Jews.

Without pressing the issue very hard, I have frequently mentioned in the preceding discussion the relationship between the apocalyptic form articulated in the Bavli and that adopted in the scriptures of the Jesus-faith. Many of the elements are the same, icons are shared, resonances from the Hebrew scriptures are used in common, and broadly similar future-scenes are depicted: the ending of conventional history, the trials before the age of Moshiah, the coming of the Messiah, the resurrection of the dead, the judgement of the individual soul, and the existence of a new Jerusalem, a new Eden, and of an eternal Hell. These commonalities are extremely important but, most emphatically, they should not be interpreted as an indication that the Christian scriptures were copied, three or four hundred years after their invention, by the author-editors of the Bavli: or even that the success of the Christian apocalyptic style prodded the Bavli's inventors to incorporate similar, but rival apocalyptic motifs.

What I think is happening here is something very different. By the mid-fifth century, the authorities of Rabbinic Judaism in the diaspora had overcome the trauma of Bar Kokhba's messianic debacle in the Land of Israel, and, further, they had overcome their reluctance to embrace anything that the Jesus-faith had endorsed. Unlike all the other core documents in the Rabbinic tradition, the Bavli has the confidence to go back beyond Christianity and to pick up the filaments of apocalyptic thought that we observed (in Chapters Six and Seven) circulating in the rich waters of the Pool of Siloam: that is, among the culturally-fecund, extremely diverse, multiple-Judahisms of the later Second Temple era. I do not think that the Babylonian Rabbis were imitating Christianity; instead, they were finally confident enough to seize as their own aspects of pre-70 thought that were helpful, that served as a healing unguent in troubled times. Never mind, they seem to say, that the Christians used these thought-patterns; they are ours. So, in the great *summa* of Rabbinic Judaism, the Bavli, apocalyptic thought re-emerges. This re-emergence propels the impressive, but static, system of thought found in the Mishnah, into an active future.

The differences between the Jesus-faith's use of this material and Rabbinic Judaism's employment of it are considerable of course. Whereas the Christians systematize most (albeit not all) of their eschatological material, the Rabbis do not. The entire "New Testament" is (as I argued in Chapter Eight) an apocalyptic document by virtue of its overall structure, as well as its author-editors having run apocalyptic threads from one book to another, until they are joined together in the fluorescent tapestry of the Book of Revelation. In contrast, the Rabbis do not systematize their thoughts, and the author-editors of the Bavli do not force a framework upon the diverse matter. Apocalyptic items are found here and there in "the sea of the Talmud." They are widely separated, and their impact is diluted. That is why it is not a mere word game to describe the "New Testament" as "apocalyptic," but the Babylonian Talmud as "apocalyptish." In fact, one finds in the Bavli side-arguments that one never encounters in the "New Testament": that the whole idea of Moshiah and the Age of the Messiah is a mistake.[76]

Those basic points – that the two sister faiths share an ideational tradition in matters of eschatology that runs back prior to the creation of either one, but that there is a substantial difference in the articulation of that common inheritance – are made prior to (and independent of), any consideration of the person of the Messiah. This sequence of argument is absolutely necessary because the idea of Moshiah as an active figure on the stage of future-history has frequently rendered good scholars incapable of sensible comment. It is a hot zone. Literally hundreds of scholars (one suspects, thousands) have spent goodly portions of their lives explaining the difference between the Moshiah of Rabbinic Judaism and of Christianity, and have concluded that, because of their divergent views of the Messiah, the Jesus-faith and the Jewish faith have different eschatological visions. That puts matters backwards. As I have demonstrated, the two sister faiths have different styles of belief and discussion, markedly different temperatures of enthusiasm, sharply contrasted levels of emphasis and varying degrees of systematization. It is from these differences in eschatological "styles" that the contrasting visions of Moshiah are derived; not the other way around.[77]

From the Babylonian Talmud's unique eschatological style is derived the singular characteristic of its Messiah: that, as a personification, Moshiah is not there. What (or who) is there is best indicated by contrasting the sharp-definition of Moshiah of the Jesus-faith to what the Rabbis believed Moshiah would be. As articulated in the Christian scriptures, the Messiah (1) was highly personalized, being identified as one man, Yeshua of Nazareth. (2) That man was an actual historical figure. Granted, the Messiah would in the future return to earth, but the key point was that he already had been manifest in the guise of a human being. (3) The Christian Messiah, though presented to the world in human form, simultaneously was a supernatural being. In contrast, the low-definition style of the Bavli produces a figure so vague that we cannot even know his name; he has not yet appeared in any form and he is totally a future-figure. When Moshiah appears, he will be merely human, albeit a very special human being.

The closest that the Bavli comes to defining Moshiah as a divine entity is to state that his name has existed before the sun itself existed, and would endure for ever.[78] His name may last forever, but what the name really is, the Rabbis cannot agree on, and this has the effect of avoiding personalization of the concept of Moshiah. "Son of David" is the most commonly found term, but note the following snarl that emerges from a Rabbinic colloquy discussing the question, "What is the Moshiah's name?"

> The School of R. Shila said, "His name is Shiloh ..." The School of R. Yannai said "His name is Yinnon ..." The School of R. Haninah maintained, "His name is Haninah ..." Others say, "His name is Menahem the son of Hezekiah ..." The Rabbis said, "His name is 'the leper scholar.' "[79]

Whatever that nomenclature may be, it is not tight personification. And the vision becomes even more blurred with the introduction of the Rabbinical vision of the "time to come" – in which "the slaying of Moshiah, the son of Joseph" will occur.[80] And this becomes even more mysterious when, slightly later, the same Rabbis propound a future sequence in which there will be two Moshiahs: "Messiah, the son of David," who will become active when "the Moshiah, the son of Joseph is slain."[81]

If pressed, one can only find two characteristics of the Messiah that the inventors of the Babylonian Talmud agree on. The first is that he will be a descendant of King David. And the second is that, despite this descent, he will not be a fearsome figure, and definitely not the sort of warrior who holds aloft the severed head of an enemy and emits a victory cry. The Messiah whom the author-editors of the Bavli permit into their pages restores to the core Jewish texts the myth of Moshiah which had been virtually excised in the Mishnah and its immediate successors. But, as Jacob Neusner perceptively notes, Moshiah is let into the Talmud "only on the Rabbis' terms."[82] The Messiah, as found in the Bavli is almost totally resistant to depiction. Although not a supernatural figure, neither is Moshiah personalized (as in the case of Jesus or of Bar Kokhba). Were we each to be given the service of a police-artist and asked to come up with a physical description of Moshiah, our associates' pads would remain blank. And were we to ask what the Messiah actually will do, the answer would be "usher in the Messianic Age." But it is the Messianic Age which possesses certain forceful characteristics, not the Messiah himself. What Moshiah will do is to bring to an end a time of which the Rabbis disapprove and introduce one which, when the dust settles, they will find admirable. In other words, in the mega-invention that is the Bavli, the Messiah is a construct that serves the future-world wishes of the Sages. Moshiah may have the Davidic right to be a monarch, but he will exercise that right as would the wisest of Rabbis. The Bavli, thus, converts the Messiah into the King-Rabbi.[83]

The Rabbis, then, have travelled a long path in roughly 400 years between the composition of the Mishnah and the closure of the Babylonian Talmud: they have gone from treating the concept of Moshiah as something so dangerous as to be virtually ignored, to inventing a Moshiah who, though legitimated by references both to Written and Oral Torah, is created in their own image. In so doing, they have re-activated the narrative line that seemingly had gone stone-cold with the appearance of the Mishnah. History, the Bavli clearly tells us, will continue; the story of Israel and the story of the covenant will unfold further, and God's-time and Man's-time will once again intersect, as it had done with Moses on Mount Sinai.

5

One can hardly hold against the classical Rabbis that, as they worshipped God, they created a set of religious texts in which the clearest and largest image was of themselves. How else can human beings understand the infinite but in terms of the finite; or eternity except as an extension of the foreseeable future; or universal moral behaviour except in terms of what they believe to be right for their own small world? Thus, in the Babylonian Talmud, "the study of Torah…was held to be equivalent of making a Temple sacrifice; the Messiah was represented as a learned Rabbi; the Torah was no longer a single, written Scripture, but encompassed all of the writings of the Sages themselves, beginning with the Mishnah."[84]

For the writings of the Sages to be commingled with the holy scriptures as the final source of authority, a clear articulation of the theory of Oral Torah had to be affirmed. As we have seen in examining earlier documents, particularly the Jerusalem Talmud, a vague idea of Oral Torah had arisen, but it was too vaporous to be taken as a solid statement. The Bavli in four places clearly asserts the existence of Oral Torah and lays the groundwork for what becomes the crowning synthesis of Rabbinic Judaism, the concept of the Dual

Torah.[85] The most important of these Talmudic discussions is a strangely doubled-edged story. In it, a Gentile came to a Rabbi Shammai and asked, "How many Torahs do you Jews have?"

"Two," the great Rabbi replied. "The Written Torah and the Oral Torah."

That was a big assertion for it really meant that there were two sources of authority, apparently equal. The enquirer (in the story he voices the doubts of the sceptical reader or listener whom the text is trying to convince), replies that he has no difficulty with respect to the Written Torah but has severe doubts about the Oral one, and he tells Shammai that he will become a convert on condition that Shammai teaches him only the Written Torah. Thereupon, Shammai, who, in any case, was known for his short temper, yelled at him and sent him away.

So the Gentile went to Rabbi Hillel who accepted him as a candidate for conversion. On the first day of instruction, Hillel had the proselyte memorize the first four letters of the Hebrew alphabet: *Alef, bet, gimmel, dalet*. Then, the second day he taught the man that the order of the letters was *dalet, gimmel, bet, alef*. Not surprisingly, the proselyte protested. Hillel's reply was calm, and self-assured beyond the possibility of arrogance. "Have you not [necessarily] depended upon me? With respect to the Oral Torah also depend upon me."[86]

This is a double message, depending upon whether it is heard from within Rabbinic tradition or from outside. Within the context of a religious world governed by the Rabbis it says, first, that we, the Rabbis, are the earthly source of Oral Torah and, secondly, that our being the conduit of Oral Torah gives us a power to rewrite Written Torah (just as the great Hillel had reversed the alphabet, the medium upon which the Written Torah depended). Read by someone outside the tight Rabbinical tradition (by, say, an eleventh-century Karaite, or a nineteenth-century Reformed scholar), the story is dangerously self-destructive. To them it says: if the Rabbis could not even be trusted to get the alphabet right, how can we trust them as custodians of the Written Torah and, if that is the case, how can we possibly accept the Oral Torah that they propound, as co-equal with the Written? Of course, the anecdote was constructed to be convincing to those within the Rabbinic fold, so the first interpretation prevails.

The second statement of the Oral Torah in the Babylonian Talmud is a simple couplet of diametrically-opposed statements put forward by Rabbi Eleazaar and Rabbi Johanan. The former says that "the greater portion of the Torah is contained in the written Law and only the smaller proportion was transmitted orally." The latter, on the other hand, says "that the greater part was transmitted orally and only the smaller part is contained in the written law."[87] The subsequent discussion is a toss-up. Either of the two contradictory positions could be correct. Indeterminate as the argument is, it leaves one point clear: both sides take for granted in their vocabulary that "Torah" does not mean solely the five books of the Pentateuch, nor does it mean merely the Hebrew scriptures taken as a whole. Torah, both sides grant, is of two sorts, Written and Oral, and the only question concerns which form is prepotent.

The third reference to the Oral Torah in the Babylonian Talmud is a very short piece of occupational-defence. It occurs in a tale wherein King Jannai is advised by a malicious counsellor to "trample down" the Sages of Israel who were being disrespectful to him. "But what will happen to the Torah?" the king asked, meaning the Written Torah.

"It is rolled up and lying in the corner; whosoever wishes to study, let him go and study!" was the wicked advisor's reply. And there, according to the Rabbinic commentators, is where the heresy lay, for the proper answer to the suggestion would have been: "That is well for the Written Law, but what of the Oral Law?"[88]

And, fourth, a final mention of the Oral Torah was Rabbi Judah ben Nahman's suggestion that oral traditions were not to be written down and, conversely, written things (meaning scriptural texts) were not to be recited from memory.[89] His fellow Rabbis did not buy this view, which is just as well, considering that the Jewish liturgy of the period required the recitation of Psalms.[90]

These four direct mentions of Oral Law do not add up either to a theory or to a theology of Oral revelation. What they do indicate is an attitude and a faith. It is taken for granted that Oral Torah exists and that it is not sacrilegious or impious to mention it in the same breath as the Written Torah. Yet, while one can easily find dozens or references to Moses' visit to the summit of Mount Sinai, and his encounter there with Yahweh as being the source of Oral Law, curiously – and this point will become important momentarily – there is no attempt to spell out in detail the spiritual ladder whereby Oral Torah descends from Sinai to the contemporary Rabbis. This, in spite of the author-editors of the Bavli making passing reference to the spiritual genealogy that was invented in tractate Aboth.[91] Actually, this seemingly-peculiar failure to back up the Bavli's acceptance of the reality of Oral Torah with a genealogy is a key to the recognition of the way that the core corpus of Rabbinic literature is topped off: not with a heavy structural element, but with an ornament. That matter in a moment.

The immediate question is, does the Bavli successfully unite the Oral and the Written Torah? Not directly, but, yes. Its author-editors, by virtue of their engaging in a discussion of the Oral Torah only in the four instances I have just mentioned, do not provide enough purchase for their "actors" – the Rabbis whose words and thoughts they present – to engage the harmonics of Oral and Written Torah. No theoretical or theological resolution of the issue is directly articulated. However, by their own actions, these same author-editors meld the two halves of their heritage into the Dual Torah. "Action" is the key concept. The author-editors of the Babylonian Talmud arrange their material (that is, they act upon it), in a specific way, one that forces any serious student of the text to marry the Oral and Written Torahs. The really brilliant aspect of their invention is that the *process* of studying any portion of the Bavli simultaneously leads one to act upon the material (by studying it and arguing about it), in a way that replicates the inventive activities of the author-editors: they acted upon the material to create a pattern that implies a unity of the two Torahs and, in studying that material, each student brings the Dual Torah into existence. So, the Bavli teaches by example, rather than by theological or philosophical specification, that the Oral and Written Torah are part of a single entity. In effect, the author-editors of the Babylonian Talmud are teaching successive generations of students a very simple lesson: replicate the pattern of thought that we have here placed before you and you will in your own thought, unite, enact, and embrace the Dual Torah. This is teaching at its best.

So, it is profitless for modern scholars to argue whether in the Dual Torah, the Oral or the Written element predominates. Undeniably, the structural principle of the Babylonian Talmud is based on the Oral Torah (the Bavli is a commentary on the Mishnah), but in the actual arguments scripture enters freely and often (but not always) is given determinative power. In fact, neither element would work without the other.

Had the term not already been taken, one could justifiably call the Bavli, the "New Testament." Because it discusses only the portions of the Mishnah that it wishes to deal with and because it brings to bear only those parts of the scriptures that it feels are useful, it is a new invention, a meta-entity that is superordinate to all preceding documents in the Rabbinic tradition. "Stated very simply, the Talmud of Babylonia is the single most important document of Rabbinic literature – and as a matter of fact, of Judaism."[92] The Bavli is an invention that is wondrous because it is selective. As Judah Goldin, one of the wisest Rabbinical scholars of the twentieth century noted, "I should like to say that although we must not underestimate the contributions made to Judaism by good memories, we should not therewith underestimate the contributions made by forgetting. For not everything was remembered and fortunately a good deal was forgotten."[93] That, gently said, is how the Dual Torah came into being.

6

Yet, one thing still was missing: a believable genealogy for the Oral Torah. The pedigree of the Written Torah was secure – in traditional belief the Pentateuch was written by Moses, but until the Oral Torah had an equally secure genealogy, the Dual Torah would be in an unequal and, therefore, uneasy alliance. Curiously, although the Oral Torah therefore had to have a pedigree equal in authority to that of the scriptures, the author-editors of the Bavli did not provide it. This omission brings us to a document that is not only significant, but is genuinely charming. It is an ornament, beautifully written, full of nice tight little stories and, though it lacks the furrow-browed character of the core Rabbinic literature, it provides a gilding for the Bavli that makes that Talmud's embodiment of the Dual Torah understandable and thus much more credible. This text is "The Fathers According to Rabbi Nathan" (most often referred to by its Hebrew name "Aboth de Rabbi Nathan").

The Fathers According to Rabbi Nathan fits nicely into the pattern of successive Rabbinical inventions that we have been describing for the past three chapters. Recall here the position of tractate Aboth ("The Fathers"), as described in Chapter Eleven. It is an addition to the Mishnah that was added sometime after the Mishnah-proper was completed, perhaps fifty years later. Within the context of the Mishnah-proper it is anomalous, because it consists entirely of Aggadah, while the Mishnah is virtually entirely Halachah. Yet, despite its stylistic and substantive divergence from the Mishnah, tractate Aboth filled a vital emotional need for the adherents of the Mishnah: it provided the credentials for the authority that the Mishnah asserted, by sketching a spiritual pedigree for the Mishnah that ran back all the way to Moses and his encounter with Yahweh on Mount Sinai. This legitimation of the Mishnah was ultimately to become the legitimation for the entire Oral Torah, which came to include not merely the Mishnah but other rulings of the Sages that later were collected and placed alongside the Mishnah.

One of the big mysteries in the evolution of Rabbinic Judaism is when tractate Aboth came to be included with the Mishnah-proper and to be accepted by the pious as an integral part of the Mishnah (and, indeed, to be used liturgically as a standard part of the yearly prayer cycle). I think that the most likely point for this integration to have occurred was after both the Jerusalem and Babylonian Talmuds were brought to the state that we at present know them. The reason for this supposition is that neither of the two Talmuds has any commentary on Aboth, although both show an awareness of it. One plausible suggestion (we cannot here deal in documentary proof, given the decimation of Rabbinic records during centuries of persecution), is that tractate Aboth was recognized by the inventors of both the Yerushalmi and the Bavli as being a significant document *about* the Mishnah, but not *of* it. Eventually, with the development of printing, the usual practice came to be to have tractate Aboth printed in standard editions of the Mishnah without any indication of its being a later addition to that text; and it became standard to print tractate Aboth in editions of the Jerusalem and the Babylonian Talmuds, but without any Rabbinical commentary upon it. It is found at the end of Seder

Nezikin (the fourth Order). That practice (based on late-medieval manuscript traditions) cannot be taken as an indication that Aboth was considered a part of the Mishnah at the time of the creation of either the Yerushalmi or the Bavli.

Here "The Fathers According to Rabbi Nathan" becomes highly relevant. It is written in Mishnaic Hebrew, which suggests that it was begun not long after tractate Aboth itself was completed. Indeed, because a few items in it are independent of tractate Aboth, some scholars believe that it includes fragments of tradition concerning Oral Torah that antedate the final version of tractate Aboth which now exist. However, the dominant scholarly view at present is that the version of Aboth de Rabbi Nathan that is now standard – standard because it came to be printed in many editions of the Babylonian Talmud from 1550 onwards – was mostly developed in Babylon; that, in the tradition of Jewish religious invention, it is pseudepigraphic; and that it did not reach its final form until 600–800 CE. Probably, it circulated in an evolving form considerably earlier.[94]

Now, if one accepts the probability that at least one (and, most scholars suggest, probably two) early versions of "The Fathers According to Rabbi Nathan" were in existence at the time the author-editors of the Yerushalmi and the Bavli were at work, it becomes doubly clear why there is no commentary in those works on tractate Aboth: not only was Aboth recognized as being external to the Mishnah, it was also seen as being served by the development of its own talmud, for that is what "The Fathers According to Rabbi Nathan" is: a talmud upon tractate Aboth. It is an expansion, an infilling, of the details, an underlining of the signal points of the credentials of the Sages who brought down the Oral Torah. Therefore, for either the Jerusalem or the Babylonian Talmud to include a commentary on Aboth would have been inappropriate: (1) by virtue of provenance, namely, tractate Aboth's not being part of the Mishnah-proper; (2) by virtue of stylistical criteria, for it would have been editorially solipsistic to include gemara on a piece that was entirely aggadic in any Talmud that was a commentary on the almost-entirely halachic Mishnah; and (3) it would have been a redundant exercise, for tractate Aboth already had its own talmud in progress.

One can here play word-games and argue that a talmud has to be a commentary organized according to a legal code. That is pettifogging. As we have seen earlier, in the case of Sifra, it would have been possible to organize an entire talmud around scripture. And "The Fathers According to Rabbi Nathan" shows us that one could also be organized along narrative lines. If we recognize that the author-editors of the Babylonian Talmud had a spectrum of possibilities to choose from, it makes us recognize once again that they were self-conscious controllers of their material, selecting and mixing pre-existent elements, and adding their own material, as all great inventors do.

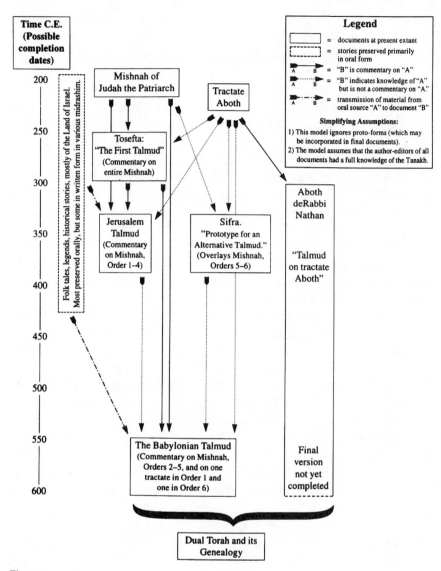

Time C.E.
(Possible
completion
dates)

Legend

☐ = documents at present extant

┄ = stories preserved primarily
    in oral form

A ▶ B = "B" is commentary on "A"

A ▶ B = "B" indicates knowledge of "A"
        but is not a commentary on "A."

A ▶ B = transmission of material from
        oral source "A" to document "B"

Simplifying Assumptions:

1) This model ignores proto-forms (which may
   be incorporated in final documents).
2) The model assumes that the author-editors of all
   documents had a full knowledge of the Tanakh.

200

Mishnah of
Judah the Patriarch

Tractate
Aboth

250

Tosefta:
"The First Talmud"
(Commentary on
entire Mishnah)

Folk tales, legends, historical stories, mostly of the Land of Israel.
Most preserved orally, but some in written form in various midrashim.

300

Aboth
deRabbi
Nathan

Jerusalem
Talmud
(Commentary
on Mishnah,
Order 1–4)

Sifra.
"Prototype for an
Alternative Talmud."
(Overlays Mishnah,
Orders 5–6)

350

"Talmud
on tractate
Aboth"

400

450

500

550

The Babylonian Talmud
(Commentary on Mishnah,
Orders 2–5, and on one
tractate in Order 1 and
one in Order 6)

Final
version
not yet
completed

600

Dual Torah and its
Genealogy

Figure 2
The Core of the Rabbinic Tradition

So, in Figure 2, I am visually presenting the pattern of religious invention that we have been dealing with in this and in the preceding three chapters. What I hope this indicates clearly is that the huge mass of material that is the core Rabbinic tradition (roughly ten million words) did not grow up haphazardly. For spiritual guidance, believers usually engage the corpus all at once, taking the material in, say, the Tosefta and mixing it with Sifra, and with the Bavli, and with "The Fathers According to Rabbi Nathan," and that is fair enough for devotional purposes. For historically-oriented individuals, however (whether believers or merely admirers of high cultural achievements), an approach by way of the sequence-of-invention not only aids our understanding of individual segments of the huge body of Rabbinic literature, but it increases our admiration for the genius of successive author-editors of the texts. To analyse and gain a partial understanding (alas, it can never be more than partial) of the ways in which persons of great talent and of equally great faith employ a grammar of invention that had been set down in the Yahweh-tradition hundreds of years earlier, and see them react to ever-changing and ever-more difficult real-world contexts – all that evokes awe.

I think that by, roughly 600 (that is, before the conquest of the Middle East by Islam), the theory of the Dual Torah was fully articulated. This articulation was accomplished not solely by the Babylonian Talmud, but rather, by the Bavli in tandem with a not-quite-final draft of "The Fathers According to Rabbi Nathan." Just as tractate Aboth gives the credentials of the Mishnah, "The Fathers According to Rabbi Nathan" provides the legitimation for the Babylonian Talmud. The Bavli, of course, is the main embodiment of the Dual Torah, demonstrating in practice, in one discussion after another, how the two parts of the Torah of Moses, integrate, operate, and therefore, dominate. However, without the extended spiritual pedigree provided by "The Fathers According to Rabbi Nathan," the Bavli's practice of Dual Torah is too abstract, too intellectually demanding for most of us to grasp fully. We need the comfort of narrative that the "Rabbi Nathan" text provides.[95]

I think that the story of the core Rabbinic inventions ends sometime in the high middle ages. Tractate Aboth is removed from its splendid isolation and is integrated into the standard copies of the Mishnah. And, eventually, "The Fathers According to Rabbi Nathan" comes to be copied into many versions of the Babylonian Talmud.

Like all the most skilled moves in the great train of invention that began millennia earlier, these developments seem perfectly natural.

· 14 ·

Conclusion:
Surpassing Wonder

I

AN OLD NEWSPAPER REPORTER, WHO WAS PROUD OF HAVING SURVIVED as a correspondent during World War II by never going within a howitzer-distance of actual combat, once told me of having covered a news conference conducted by, and in honour of, Field Marshal Montgomery. The Field Marshall knew full well that, as saviour of his people, he must maintain a proper relationship with the Almighty. "As God once said," Montgomery began, "and I think rightly ..."

The attitude that underpins the present study is just the opposite of Field Marshall Montgomery's in virtually every way. I have presented an argument that, as its basic precept, relies on the principle: Listen to the Primary Text. Do that without engaging any prior theological or ideological commitments. Of course, no human being is ever dead-pure neutral about anything – that's just not the nature of the human beast – but listening before talking is within the capability of all of us.

Further, one utterly rejects the scarcely-disguised contempt that Montgomery held for the common soldier. (Producers of World War II propaganda news reels that featured Monty found that he tolerated the average infantry-man in the same frame as himself with about the same degree of enthusiasm that the Pharaoh showed for social intercourse with the ancient Israelites.) Here, the common solder is us, that is, everyone of good spirit who is willing to deal with the Tanakh, the "New Testament," and the Rabbinic literature with an open mind and a desire to learn. Frequently, these texts raise problems that are tough puzzles of detail or are big – metaphysically big – matters of meaning. Inevitably, therefore, at points this volume has been a hard book, in the sense of dealing directly with complicated issues, but it is written for my fellow foot-soldiers and without condescension. The book is based on a firm commitment to the belief that ordinary people are much smarter than the field-marshals of our present day, dumbed-down culture assume.

This faith leaves us in an uneasy relationship with the officer-class: the priests, pastors, rabbis, and the academic specialists in Eastern Aramaic, paleography, Middle Greek philology and Semitic prosopography, to name just of a few of the specialists who make their living analysing parts of the texts that we are here approaching. They have a great deal to teach us and the reader probably has noticed that I have treated the ablest of these scholars with a respect that borders on awe. Their best work is called to the readers' attention without my cluttering the book with a welter of references to second-line studies. Learned and technically subtle as are many members of the officer-class, I hope that they will be both appreciated for their achievements and ignored when they indulge in their vices, the chief of these being what José Ortega y Gasset called the specialists' "state of not listening." He observed of the specialist that "he even proclaims it as a virtue that he takes no cognisance of what lies outside the narrow territory specially cultivated by himself, and gives the name 'dilettantism' to any curiosity for the general scheme of knowledge."[1]

The nature of our present collective enterprise has been, first, to listen, and, secondly, to reflect on large patterns, ones that lie outside of any single speciality. This is a job for the infantry. Ultimately, I believe the real victories are won not by the officer-class, and certainly not by field marshals, but by the foot-soldiers.

2

If, working together, we can here achieve some real, if limited, victory, one of its fruits will be to encourage a form of Jewish-Christian ecumenism. Indeed, an unstated but pervasive goal of this book is to effect positively that end. But any real foot-soldier will recognize that "ecumenical" is such a butt-ugly word that it has to be disinfected, cleaned, and polished before it can be paraded in public. The trouble with "oecumenical" – to use the old, most rebarbarative form – is that it referred to "oecumenical assemblies" of the bishops and other authorities of the Christian world, as convened by the Pope. If sanctioned by His Holiness, the decrees of the oecumenical councils were infallible, and among the decrees made by such councils were those that declared the Jews to be Christ-killers, hardly a constructive note in the present context. Moreover, the oecumenical councils were divisive even within Christianity. The eastern church accepted only those occurring through the eighth century (the Second Council of Nicaea of 787 being the last) and the Protestant denominations rejected those of the late fifteenth century and after, not least the oecumenical council of 1869–70 which articulated the doctrine of Papal Infallibility.

In the twentieth century, "ecumenical" took on two meanings. One of these referred to the attempt to bring together all Christian denominations and, ultimately, to achieve the re-union of the multifarious fragments of the Christian church. In practice, this chiefly involved Protestants and resulted in the creation of the World Council of Churches in 1948. The other use of the word related to a proposed rapprochement between the Roman Catholic church and certain denominations of the Protestant faith, most notably the Anglican church and some of the branches of the Eastern Orthodox tradition. This was largely a post-World War II phenomenon. It has come nearly to a dead halt, while the World Council of Churches has had a difficult time keeping its membership intact and has been unable to strike an alliance with the one form of Christianity that at present is growing: the several evangelical, fundamentalist, and Pentecostal denominations. So, today "ecumenical" behaviour is largely reduced to a vague, slightly-smarmy form of feel-goodism, which occurs, for example, when a local council of churches sponsors a food bank or a kids' athletic league. No bonus points are awarded for guessing what group was not originally intended to have membership even in this mild form of cross-faith bonding.

However, in the United States, a concept developed during the 1950s and '60s that included Jews. This was the neologism "Judaeo-Christian heritage or Judaeo-Christian tradition," and the concept was the product of a set of political circumstances unique to the United States. (Until recently, if one used the term elsewhere in the English-speaking world, one was often met with incomprehension or more frequently with the puzzled smile usually reserved for people who are making an ironic reference that no one quite understands, but is too polite to question.) The circumstances were that in the years immediately after World War II the American Jewish community required all the political allies it could muster in its efforts to maximize United States governmental support for the recently founded state of Israel; and, simultaneously, those in the evangelical-fundamentalist wing of the Christian church perceived the migration of large numbers of diaspora-Jews to Israel as preparation for the Second Coming of Jesus, as decreed in their decodings of apocalyptic texts. For them, this was an astounding sea-change in their attitudes towards Jews. Preachers who, in the 1930s had been virulently anti-Semitic, denouncing the incongruous combined evils of Jewish-promoted Communism and Jewish finance-capital, now expounded upon the doctrine that those who blessed Israel would themselves be blessed, and those who cursed Israel, would themselves be cursed. The alliance of Jewish supporters of Zionism in the United States (most of whom were liberals in politics and resident in the eastern U.S. and the northern tier of states), and the evangelicals and fundamentalists (most of whom were politically conservative and lived in the south and the Middle West) was very effective politically and there is nothing inherently wrong with that: democracy has made far stranger bed-fellows.

However, the associated concept that was intended to paper over the inevitable cracks in this alliance –"Judaeo-Christian tradition" or "heritage" – was false-ecumenical. It was based not on mutual understanding but on a mutual agreement not to understand. The American Zionists wore the label and accepted Christian support for Israel because they wanted the state not only to survive, but to prosper, grow and to forever exist in Eretz Israel. The evangelical and fundamentalist Christians adopted the Judaeo-Christian label and supported Israel because they wanted the new state to survive for a time, to indraw the world's Jewish population and to go supernaturally extinct, replaced by the Messianic kingdom of Jesus Christ. The bonding concept – Judaeo-Christian tradition – remained useful only so long as both sides maintained their own definitions and did not encourage their allies to consider the unbridgeable divergences in meaning. To the evangelical and fundamentalist Christians, Judaeo-Christian tradition was a sequential statement, one that implied that first there was Judaism and then it was replaced by Christianity. And to the Jewish groups that accepted the concept (the Orthodox were not very keen on its usage, but for the most part they were not keen Zionists) the term also was a linear statement. But in this case it referred to Judaism's being the bedrock original and Christianity a subsequent departure from that template. So, "Judaeo-Christian" was, and still is, a false-ecumenical term and it is not used in this book. Indeed, it is a label that should be consigned to the scrapheap of political doublethink.

Yet, I believe one can be genuinely ecumenical, in the sense of bringing present-day Christians and Jews into a more intelligent and more sympathetic relationship with each other. This will not occur by propagating bogus umbrella-terms, or by minimizing the differences between the two sister-faiths. Instead, one simple set of parallel cognitions must be encouraged: the recognition that Christians will not understand their own faith (in its many variants) until they are at least modestly familiar with the basic texts that form the modern Jewish faith, not just the Tanakh, but the great Rabbinic texts and especially the massive, glorious Bavli; similarly, adherents of modern Judaism (in its wide array of forms) should recognize that they cannot understand their own faith unless they are conversant with the Christian scriptures and are sharply aware of the breathtakingly successful way the "New Testament" uses motifs and beliefs that were available to several forms of Judaism in the first century of the Common Era.

From mutual knowledge and respect everything good follows. Otherwise, there can be only the dankness and half-light of self-ignorance within, and incomprehension and ultimately hatred, directed without.

3

The acquisition of knowledge in our own time generally is understood as being a purely intellectual exercise. In that, I think we fool ourselves. The acquisition of significant bodies of knowledge in adult life is usually the result of discipline, of the volitional application of the mind over a long period of time, of plain hard work. It is, therefore, as much a moral or ethical discipline as an intellectual one: for one consciously decides to invest part of one's life-time doing something more difficult and, in the short-run, less pleasant than popping one of the hundreds of brands of mind-candy that daily surround us. This is germane, because it is hard work for persons of Jewish and of Christian backgrounds to learn honestly and rigorously about each other's basic texts. (And, one should add that it is doubly difficult for persons of outside traditions, or of none, to take in the mass of data that is encountered when dealing with these two faiths; the higher seats in heaven may be reserved for agnostics who take the trouble.) The task, I think, can be most successfully assayed if one treats it not just as an intellectual quest, but as a pilgrimage.

On this journey, the two greatest obstacles are ones that have nothing to do with the actual texts that are studied – the texts are in fact fascinating, almost addictive, and they draw one along on a wave of their own energy. The difficulties are internal to each traveller. As in the case of the *voyageurs* who opened up North America in the seventeenth century, the greatest danger comes from ourselves, from overbalancing and upsetting our own vessel. The two most difficult skills to obtain are, first, simultaneously to comprehend in historical terms both the similarities and the divergences of the faiths that became, in modern usage, Judaism and Christianity. And, secondly, we must balance the concepts of process and of product. It is not easy to recognize that nearly identical historical processes can produce sharply different historical products, or that divergent histories (processes) sometimes yield very similar results. If we focus too much upon the one or the other, the process or the product, the balance of the historical evolution of the two faiths is lost. Both count.

In theoretical physics, one of the goals of the second half of the twentieth century has been to develop a Grand Unified Theory, which would integrate into a single system not everything (as the label might imply) but at least some of the most important phenomena that occur at the sub-atomic level and others that occur on a universe-wide scale. Now, the last thing I would do is to propound even a limited Grand Unified Theory for the spiritual world we have here been studying. Yet, as non-specialists we have the liberty to do what specialists are virtually prohibited by the monitions of their disciplines from doing: engage in reflection on how the bigger picture may be constructed.

In this book, I have presented three elements of that larger picture, each defined tightly according to the evidence of their own primary texts: (1) the modern Jewish faith, frequently called "Rabbinic" or "Talmudic" Judaism; (2) the Christian faith, sometimes referred to in its early forms as the Jesus-faith; and (3) the ancient Yahweh-faith, the worship of Yahweh as chief (and for most of its adherents, sole) God of the kingdom of Judah, which centred on Jerusalem and subsumed almost all of the earlier confederation known as "Israel." Since the Yahweh-faith, the Christian faith, and the Jewish faith all were religions of the book (or the scroll or codex, it amounts to the same thing), it would be false to distinguish between the invention of each of their sacred texts and the invention of the specific religions. The acts of invention are one. Therefore, I have dealt directly with the texts, not with historical speculations: the big texts that were the mode of the vivification of Yahwehism, Christianity, and Judaism.

Because one of the easiest ways for an historian to go astray is to place a single label on two or more fundamentally distinct phenomena, the reader has had to adjust to my insistence on a set of distinctions between the religion (and its several variants) that arose after the triumph of Judah over Israel – the religion of *Judahism* – and the modern Jewish faith: *Judaism* which evolved after the destruction of Herod's Temple in 70 CE and which was articulated in its essentials by the great Rabbis in the succeeding five centuries. This distinction may offend some believers, for it implies (based on detailed arguments that I have presented in the text) that the line of evolution between ancient Yahwehism and the Rabbinic Jewish faith is not a linear one and that it is inappropriate to apply the label "Jewish" to both cases: indeed, they are related, but are also very significantly different. In pleading for a touch of open-mindedness on this matter, I can make only two arguments (besides the obvious one: read carefully what I have said in earlier chapters). First, this distinction is not a disrespectful one, but quite the opposite: I celebrate the manner in which the Rabbis overcame the shattering historical discontinuity produced by the destruction of old Jerusalem and the way they constructed from the fragments of pre-70 Judahisms a new faith that honoured the spirit and lineaments of the old, but which invented radically new precepts and new holy texts to meet an unprecedented set of challenges. The Rabbis' re-invention of the old faith has lasted, brilliantly and successfully for 1,500 years. Secondly, my documentation of the discontinuities that occurred in the second half of the first century of the Common Era holds not only for the relationship between the several Judahisms of the Yahweh faith and later Rabbinic Judaism, but also for those between the Yahweh-faith and the most aggressively-assertive claimant to be the heir of that faith: Christianity. In my view (again, read the earlier chapters' argument in detail), neither the Jesus-faith nor Rabbinism falls in a line of smooth historical continuity with the older religion of Yahweh. Each went through massive disorientation in the post-70 CE years, and each was such a radical re-invention of older ideas that neither one can legitimately share a single label with its ancient predecessor.

So, we have three separate religious phenomena – the Yahweh-faith, Christianity, and Rabbinic Judaism. And we have three separate texts: the Tanakh (the "Old Testament," the heart of which is the Genesis-Kings unity, the "New Testament," and the core texts of Rabbinic Judaism). Time and time again, I have emphasized the quite-astounding vacuum in our historical knowledge of the three religions in each of their formative years. We possess only a thimbleful of information on each that is independent of its own story, as told in the primary texts. This is why, even if these texts were not the most powerful that human culture has ever produced, we still would focus most of our energy upon them. The story of these religions is mostly the story of their texts. And this is where things become so wonderfully intricate. The texts of the three faiths intertwine with each other. Sometimes this interweaving is direct and obvious (both the Christian writers and the Rabbis use material taken straight from the Tanakh) but at other times it is complex and convoluted. For example, the character of the Christian scriptures closed off certain options for the Rabbis; and the Christian scriptures clearly were influenced by the beliefs of the progenitors of the Rabbis, the Pharisees.

Now, if one were toying with the equivalent of a Grand Unified Theory, one would begin with a simple observation: the invention of the texts of each of the three faiths was occasioned by a virtually-identical real-world event, the physical destruction of their chief idol. That observation is apt to make traditionalists shudder. Anyone who has been to Sabbath or Sunday school or has taken an introductory undergraduate religion course knows that idol-worship was one of the most punishable acts in ancient Israel. And Rabbinic Judaism, no less than Christianity, formally rejected idol worship. So, idols can play no part in the story of the invention of these three religions, much less a causally central one. Wrong: that position is made plausible only by the conjunction of two major forms of special-pleading-by-definition. All three major religions defined an idol as being, literally, a god, or an image of a god, that was worshipped by someone other than "us" – meaning heretics, and unrighteous strangers. In our own time this form of special-pleading-through-special-definition has been maintained easily because it is part of our general cultural inheritance from the imperialist days of nineteenth-century Christian missionaries who efficiently propagated the belief that idols were physical objects that were worshipped as gods by groups that were primitive, morally loose, and, well, just not like us.

But consider that an idol does not literally have to be perceived as a god to be an idol, but that it can be the equivalent of a word, a phrase, a prayer: a pale representation in the physical world of an ultimate reality that is impossible ever to capture fully with human resources. Where belief in the literalness of an idol ends and where its metaphorical properties begin is impossible to know in any given case but, undeniably, the Yahweh-faith was centred physically upon such an idol. Take Solomon's Temple. It was the dwelling house of Yahweh and that was not solely a metaphorical formulation. "I have surely built thee an house to dwell in, a settled place for thee to abide in for ever," were the words ascribed to King Solomon (I Kings 8:13), and certainly some of those who heard that text (most contemporaries, I suspect) accepted it as indicating a physical as well as a spiritual god-house. The Temple, the dwelling place of Yahweh, constructed upon a holy mountain, was an idol.

If we can lose for a moment our fright of the concept of idol, we can begin to understand how fine an idol each of the successive Temples was. Within the Yahweh faith, the Almighty was captured most clearly in the covenant with his people. That covenant tied his character to certain specific practices, among them an elaborate tapestry of ritual that focussed on the killing of several species of living things. The Temple, Yahweh's home, was where one sacrificed: *in his house*. Since Yahweh's holiness was contagious, worshippers sacrificed not only in the Temple, but to it. That was a physical reality, the Temple an architectural anchor for the faith. Simultaneously, the Temple was a cosmic metaphor, a representation of how the transcendent covenant with the Chosen People worked. It was a specific place where the covenant was acted out, and as sacred drama the message was clear: keep the deal with Yahweh and he will keep the faith with you.

What held for Solomon's Temple held even more for Herod's, for it was one of the most overpowering buildings of the ancient world and was itself an object of religious adoration. (Even the Gentiles paid it respect and, in fact, one courtyard was set aside to provide them limited access.) Herod's Temple dominated all the various Judahisms of the "later Second Temple era," for this Temple was the one thing to which one had to react if one were committed to any of the several variants of the Yahweh-faith. Like the original Temple of King Solomon, Herod's Temple functioned as an idol, that is, as a physical guarantor of God's presence at a specific place on this earth and the Temple was treated by its devotees as if it had been placed there by the hand of the Almighty. Its very existence was interpreted as an indication of the hand of God, exercising power in the physical world. Yet, like its predecessors (the Temples of Solomon and of Zerubbabel), it was simultaneously interpreted as being a non-corporeal, cosmic entity, a metaphor for the Kingdom of God whose ultimate details exceed all human imagining.

So, when the Temple of Solomon and the Temple of Herod each was destroyed (in 587/6 BCE and 70 CE, respectively), the event was not architectural, but apocalyptic. In each instance, an entire grid of belief – the location of the god-house, the place of sacrifice to Him, the ritual embodiment of the covenant between Yahweh and his people and, simultaneously, all the metaphorical aspects of the Temple as an architectonic symbol of ultimate reality – all that suddenly vanished. To use the word "trauma" to describe what occurred in each instance would be to trivialize the events. Both times, a Krakatoa-magnitude eruption blasted stone from stone, and darkness covered the Land.

The twice-done destruction of the Jerusalem Temple is one of the very few sets of events in the world of ancient Judahism of which we have ample third-party documentation. Presumptively, these two events must have had a direct influence on the three interrelated religious faiths with which we are dealing. This point is so obvious that it bears reiteration, for sometimes biblical scholars become so good at attending to subtle matters that they miss the big, rough events. Put simply, if one is trying to understand the invention and the character of the texts of the Yahweh-faith, of Christianity, and of Rabbinic Judaism, it requires an act-of-the-will sufficient to move mountains to ignore, as potentially-determinative elements in the story, the two best-documented moments in the history of the three faiths.

Unlike virtually every other event that we "know" happened during the formative years of the three religions, not only is the double-destruction of the Temple attested independently of the texts of the three faiths, but in each case the Temple's destruction can be placed in a tight historical explanation that recognizes the catastrophes as directly causal (not the sole causes, but the best-documented and the most direct) in the invention of the three sets of sacred texts: the Genesis-Kings unity, the post-Pauline documents of the "New Testament," and the fundamental documents of Rabbinic Judaism. Therefore, we have in these instances a conjunction rare in biblical studies, namely, a set of independently-attested primary causes that can be tightly related to biblically-evidenced effects.

Of course there are differences in each of the three cases of cause-and-effect, and these have received a good deal of attention in my argument. However, we must not fall into the nihilism of pointing-out-differences to the extent that we lose our ability to note similarities and thus to generalize. I am here strongly keying the reader against such reality-denial, for I believe that the over-arching purpose of encouraging Jewish-Christian ecumenism is served by our recognizing that not only do the two religions share a common historical background (which includes the Yahweh-faith) but that each went through the identical intense formative fire, the volcanic eruptions of 70 CE.

Christianity and Rabbinic Judaism (to use anachronistic but recognizable labels) shared a common bank of reflexes in dealing with the catastrophes of 70 CE. They both had seen it happen before: each embryonic faith embraced the Tanakh and there, in the Genesis-Kings unity, was a template for dealing with the destruction of the house where Yahweh lived, one that was clear, aesthetically admirable and transferable across time. The author-editor of Genesis-Kings showed by his own example what the most effective response was, as follows: (1) The details of the now-dust Temple are set down so that they can serve as a guide to the human-rebuilders of the Temple, should Yahweh in his mercy permit that reconstruction of his house to occur. (2) The author-editor of Genesis-Kings does not permit himself to be trapped in the belief that the physical manifestation of the Almighty was the sole and complete meaning of the Temple. He affirms the non-corporeal, ideational aspect of the Temple as the arrangement of a set of ideas that tells something about ultimate reality, namely how God and his universe are related. Thus it becomes possible to affirm faith in the religion of the Temple, independently of whether or not the Temple ever was rebuilt on this earth. And (3) in responding to the crisis engendered by the Temple's destruction, the author-editor of Genesis-Kings brought together for the first time the previously-disparate portions of the great narrative theodicy, which articulates the ways of Yahweh with his Chosen People from the time of creation until the Babylonian Exile. We call them scriptures. This was the moment of great invention on which the subsequent survival of the Judahist faith (the religion of Yahweh as it pivoted around Jerusalem) and its heirs, the Jesus-faith and the Rabbinic Jewish faith, ultimately depended. Previously, scattered "books" of tradition had existed and the folk-memory had preserved other beliefs. That was sufficient as long as the spiritual fulcrum held and as long as the Chosen People were collectively centred around Jerusalem. Once the Temple was destroyed and the civil and religious leadership were shipped away from the Land of Israel, the preservation of the Yahweh-faith depended upon the creation of texts that would exist independently of geography and on constructs that would perdure independently of mere architecture. From his melancholy vantage point in Babylonia, the author-editor of the Genesis-Kings unity not only collected the heterogeneous variants of the earlier, pre-disaster religion, but he invented a new form, one that captured in narrative (with swatches of poetry and legal details sewn neatly in), the history of the world, its divinely decreed rules, and, most importantly, the everlasting bargain between Yahweh and his people, the covenant. No author or editor has ever faced a bigger challenge. None has ever succeeded so spectacularly and yet so sublimely.

In the actual event, another Temple – usually known as "Zerubbabel's Temple" – began to be rebuilt about the year 520 BCE and eventually it was virtually obliterated and replaced by the glittering and massive monument of Herod the Great. This was begun in roughly 20 BCE and it never was completely finished: usually, slightly misleadingly, it is termed the "Second Temple." Herod's great idol, one of the most impressive the world had ever seen, an object of veneration even by pagans, was devastated in the war of 66–73 CE. The last Temple sacrifice was conducted in the year 70 CE. That is the date on which the sacrificial worship of Yahweh and the ancient religion of Judah ceased, apparently forever. Immediately the invention of its successors began.

Strikingly, the Jewish religion and the Christian (to use the names they later acquired), each reacted in exactly the way one would have predicted, given a knowledge of the earlier pattern of response to the destruction of Solomon's Temple. Separately, but in a strikingly parallel fashion, the leaders of the Jesus-faith and of embryonic Rabbinic Judaism re-invented the religion of the Temple, but without a physical Temple being required. The faithful did not re-establish a Temple on this earth, but in their hearts, in the heavens, and in each home. Each embryonic-faith affirmed its adherence to the sacred writings found in the "Old Testament" and then proceeded quickly to create its own additional scriptures. In the case of the Jesus-faith, this became the "New Testament." Rabbinic Jews did not use the word "scripture," but the corpus of material that begins with the Mishnah and ends with the Babylonian Talmud is nothing if not the definition of a "new covenant," every bit as radical – and, paradoxically, every bit as self-consciously respectful of the original covenant with Yahweh – as is the Christian "New Testament."

Although the author-editors of each of these compelling sets of invention did everything possible to emphasize their own continuity with ancient beliefs and practices, each set of "scriptures" is a product of the post-70 era, and in two senses. Each was made necessary by the leveling of the great Temple; and each was defined in its overall structure after the Temple was gone. These two obvious points bear heavy underscoring because they run headlong into strong resistance in Christian circles, both conservative and liberal. As I have discussed in Appendix D, despite the strenuous and heart-wrenching efforts of Christian scholars to push the historical sources of the Christian religion back into the pre-destruction period, there are no Christian documents that predate the catastrophe, save the authentic letters of Paul (Romans, Galatians, Corinthians, I Thessalonians, Philemon, and Philippians), and these are notoriously frustrating as far as historical information is concerned. The "New Testament," *as we possess it* is a response to the extrusion of the followers of Yeshua of Nazareth from their former spiritual home. Previously to 70 CE they had maintained their spiritual taproot in late Second Temple Judaism. The destruction of the Temple changed forever the geography of the Holy Land and the "New Testament" was their response, at once palliative and aggressive, a masterful narrative which, for many readers, becomes their master. The inventors of the "New Testament" in the post-70 years were very similar in their approach to that of the author-editor of the Genesis-Kings unity: they included all manner of older historical traditions and re-arranged and re-interpreted them to form what we now call a scripture. Crucially, the modern reader must recognize that the question of the historical accuracy of any specific portion of the "New Testament" is independent of the single prepotent fact of that scripture's creation: that the "New Testament" was a response to the cataclysmic humiliation of the faith of Judah and the vaporization of the edifice that had been the physical embodiment of the covenant between God and those of humankind to whom he granted favour.

As I have discussed in detail, both the "New Testament" and the Rabbinic writings are ingenious in making possible the maintenance of a Temple faith without requiring the existence of a physical temple. Each works within a grammar of religious invention that honours the precepts of the earlier Yahweh-faith. However, on two points of historical moment, the two traditions, Christian and Jewish, diverged. One of the paradoxes of history – and one which all our instincts lead us to resist – is that the Jesus-faith was much quicker to use the pieces of the old pre-70 Judahist factions to invent a temple-religion-without-a-temple than were the founders of what became known as the Jewish faith. That the Christian construct is older than the Jewish one is demonstrable at a high level of evidentiary probability, but it is so deeply counter-intuitive that we are apt to deny it strenuously. If we do so, we miss the rich irony of the historical process and also the stunning originality of each of the two groups as they struggled to reinvent themselves after the Temple's destruction, and hence to survive. The second major difference is related. I think that Rabbinic Judaism took much longer than did Christianity to invent fully a temple-religion-without-a-temple because the Rabbis held on longer and tighter than did the Christians to the hope that a physical temple again would be built. (Indeed, under Julian "the Apostate," in the mid-fourth century, they came close to having their hope fulfilled.)

This observation is confirmed by a salient difference between the "New Testament" and the Mishnah, documents that were in formulation at roughly the same time. Whereas the "New Testament" only provides details (and then just sparse ones) of the physical aspects of Herod's Temple, the Mishnah records with loving precision the plan of the Temple, room by room, courtyard, wall, ramp, and rampart. The end result of this set of differences within the shared pattern is a fundamentally divergent theological outcome. Whereas, for Christians, the eventual creation of a new temple in future-time will be a by-product of the reign of the Messiah, for Rabbinic Judaism, the appearance of Moshiah will be a step on the road to future history, whose final destination will be the new, restored, and forever-Temple.

Manifestly, in the responses of, first, the Yahweh-faith and later, of the Jesus-faith and of embryonic Rabbinic Judaism to the destruction of the Temple, we have a pattern that is not random and is not inconsequential. In each of the three cases, the response relates to the invention of the texts that for our purposes *are* the religions in question: even the most devout of present-day believers do not have any idea of what Hillel, or Jesus, or Samuel said, independent of the texts whose creation was stimulated by the Temple disasters. Emphatically, I am not suggesting that this pattern of events – the same sequence in three separate instances – had to happen. My point is not metaphysical or theological, but merely historical. The pattern is what did happen. It is a modest, but reasonable, historical practice to consider the relationship of verifiable, causally-robust occurrences to the febrile and inventive way in which the human mind responds to challenges. In our three cases we observe one of the wonders of humanity: the way that humankind articulates systems of belief so that we can manage to survive the rawness of a world that is so harsh as to be almost beyond belief.

4

None of this should make most readers uncomfortable. For most, the arguments that I have presented throughout this book should be belief-neutral. They can be entertained and subsequently evaluated on their merits and on the degree of their consonance with the primary evidence. My hope is that agnostics, atheists, and the amiably indifferent, all will appreciate the beauty and integrity of the process of invention and the character of the final texts, even if they are unable to grant to these processes and documents any degree of spiritual authority. And I hope that believers (using that term in the most inclusive sense) will see in the complex filigree of invention of the Bible and of the Rabbinic texts, the hand of their god.

Throughout this book, I have used the concept of invention both as an accurately descriptive term and as a light slap on the reader's face. It is a wake-up word, and it is intended to make us stop taking the scriptures and the Rabbinic texts for granted and to recognize that they came into being through human genius. Earlier chapters explained in detail how these major texts are a conscious invention of people of immense ability. Thus, depending upon one's own theological or ideological commitments, one can think of the whole business either as being the work of remarkable humans, but nothing more, or of the hand of God working by way of humankind. And whether one believes that the historical narratives and the historically-defined legal codes are "real" or fictive, one still has to understand them as having been consciously invented: very subtle, very skilful, very successful products of human mental activity.

Most present-day Jewish and Christian believers hold in common two theological positions: that the Almighty is indeed all-mighty, and, further, that no human being can fully comprehend the mysterious ways of the Lord. This is here relevant because there are splinters within each of the major religious groups – especially ultra-Orthodox Jews, fundamentalist Protestants and Tridentine Catholics – who, with remarkable self-confidence, reject those two positions. They propound a limit on the Almighty's freedom of action, and most particularly upon the divine freedom of expression. They decree that the scriptures were literally dictated by God, employing a series of human beings as passive conduits. This Parrot-on-the-Shoulder School of Biblical Literalism is incompatible with my own argument and, indeed, I cannot imagine anyone who hews to that school making it as far as this concluding chapter.[2] One hopes, however, that most believers will be generous in pondering an issue that relates so directly to the core of all religious reflection:

discerning "the manner in which individual human events are jointly caused by both God and Man."[3]

Invention, far from being a diminuent, is one of highest respect. Never is a great invention – whether it be a poem, a mechanical device, or an historical narrative – created from emptiness. Always, pre-existing items, plus ingenuity, are intermingled to yield a new entity. In that sense, all invention is re-invention. Invention is not creation, for creation involves making something from nothing, and this is why the scriptures and the Rabbinical writings are not creations, but are inventions. The Genesis-Kings unity, for example, depended in large part upon the folk-memory of the children of Israel, and the Talmuds have as their basis the memory of legal arguments laid down by previous generations.

The series of inventions that we have in the Jewish and Christian scriptures and in the core Rabbinical literature stack together and it is possible to figure out how they work as conscious pieces of textual invention. There are rules. I have argued in detail that a *grammar of biblical invention* runs through the scriptures and, in slightly altered form, through the classical Rabbinical texts as well. Nine basic paradigms of biblical invention were discussed in Chapter Two, these being inferred from the practice of the author-editor of Genesis-Kings. Those rules held for any subsequent invention that built successfully upon the primary sector of the Hebrew scriptures, the first nine books of the Tanakh. Ones sees this grammar operative in portions of the Pseudepigrapha and the Apocrypha, and fully realized in the "New Testament" and (making appropriate equilibrations for the halachic emphasis) in the core Rabbinic literature, especially the Babylonian Talmud. New texts that honoured the normative patterns acquired stature in part by their fitting atop the original plinth, the Genesis-Kings unity. New items that violated the rules (such as some items among the Pseudepigrapha) bent dangerously off-true and crashed to the ground. Modern Judaism and modern Christianity are sister religions because they share a common sacred text (the Tanakh, or "Old Testament"); they originated in the same rich pool of religious innovation (Jerusalem and its environs in the later Second Temple era); and each honoured the biblical paradigms of religious invention.

Crucially, the grammar of biblical invention was not simply a passive set of rules. Just as in linguistics "each language is not merely a reproducing system for voicing ideas, but rather is itself a shaper of ideas."[4] So the grammar we have been discussing not only expressed ideas, but shaped them. Hence, the differences between the central texts of Christianity and of Rabbinic Judaism, while inevitably significant, are much less forceful than are the similarities. Compare Rabbinic Judaism or Christianity to any religion other than its sister-faith and this immediately becomes clear. The deep-structure is shared: the Ur-concept of the covenant and the grammar of biblical invention whereby the covenant is articulated in text. They thus share a cosmology, a definition of how the world works, as an altar to the Almighty. The two religions have been so long at daggers-drawn, not because they are so different, but because they are so close.

The texts these three faiths created – the Tanakh, the "New Testament," and, among the Rabbinic documents, the Babylonian Talmud – are probably the strongest literary texts ever invented. What the secret of that power is can be indirectly analysed but never really explained. This, because the very power of the texts is so strong that we can never step outside of them to acquire the triangulate vision necessary to assay their qualities. One of the great vanities of human beings is that they have ideas. Little ideas maybe, but when it comes to big ideas, it is the ideas that have people. So, we can note that some of the power of the Genesis-Kings unity and of the Four Gospels occurs because their inventors have taken care to arrange their words so that they will appeal as much to our ears as to our judgement. And, with equal accuracy, we can point to the synergetic congruence between the manner in which the most important of the texts were formed – in literary-historical response to the destruction of either the first Temple or the Second – and the dominant motifs of the Yahweh-history, the life of Jesus the Christ, and the requirements of the Mishnah and the Talmuds: the congruent, continually re-occurrent, themes of enslavement and Exodus, exile and return, sin and redemption, destruction and regeneration.

One could go on, but ultimately words fail, and never are they less adequate than in the service of an explanation of the very words that create us.

Us? Yes. By "us" I mean every one who lives under the rules of the now-much-maligned western culture, which today includes almost everyone in Europe, North and South America and, increasingly, parts of Asia and of the Third World. These are the societies that have embraced the if-then notion of the social contract, directly traceable to the ancient Hebrews, and a conviction that all present-day actions have future consequences. What we picked up from ancient Greece, Rome, Persia and a score of peripheral sources was culture. From the ancient Semites we acquired something broader, the prerequisites for civilization.

For me, the texts that created us surpass mere wonder and this holds whether one sees them as being human or divine in origin, or some combination. Thus, this book has been a long love-letter to the Tanakh, the "New Testament," and the great Rabbinic writings in the same way that many of the Psalms are love-letters to God. Like the psalmists, I am constantly of mixed emotion, heart-filling admiration one moment, frighted-awe the next. In his "Holy Sonnets," John Donne expressed precisely such feelings:

> Like a fantastic ague: save that here
> Those are my best days, when I shake with fear.[5]

Notes

NOTES TO CHAPTER ONE

1 Eric Christiansen, "How Europe became Europe," *New York Review of Books* (21 Oct. 1993), 83.

2 Matthew Arnold, "Hebraism and Hellenism," in *Culture and Anarchy* (originally pub., 1869; new ed., Cambridge: Cambridge University Press, 1932), 136.

3 Eric M. Meyers, "The Challenge of Hellenism for Early Judaism," *Biblical Archaeologist*, 55 (June 1992), 91.

This refers to the popular viewpoint. There is among scholars a long-running and quite important argument about how much the Hellenic influences permeated Judaism and Christianity in the century immediately before and immediately after the birth of Jesus. See, for example, Philip S. Alexander, "Quid Athens et Hierosolymis? Rabbinic Midrash and Hermeneutics in the Graeco-Roman World," in Philip R. Davis and Richard T. White (eds.), *A Tribute to Geza Vermes. Essays on Jewish and Christian Literature and History* (Sheffield: Journal for the Study of the Old Testament, supplement series, 1990), 101–24.

4 Nicholas Blake, *The Private Wound* (London: Crime Club, 1968), 66.

5 Walter Brueggemann, *Abiding Astonishment. Psalms, Modernity, and the Making of History* (Louisville: Westminster Press, 1991).

6 Bloom cannot have been unaware of Samuel Butler's 1897 work, *The Authoress of the Odyssey* which suggested that since that work featured so many interesting women, it had to have been written by a female hand.

7 Elisabeth Schussler Fiorenza, "The Ethics of Biblical Interpretation: Decentering Biblical Scholarship," *Journal of Biblical Literature*, 107 (March 1988), 3.

8 Martin Buber, *Moses. The Revelation and the Covenant* (New York: Harper and Brothers, edition, 1958; originally pub. 1946), 16.

9 That is the position that Paul R. House has set out to demonstrate in his edited volume, *Beyond Form Criticism. Essays in Old Testament Criticism* (Winona Lake, Indiana: Eisenbrauns, 1992).

10 Philip R. Davies, *In Search of "Ancient Israel"* (Sheffield: Journal for the Study of the Old Testament, supplement series, 1992), 46.

11 Mark G. Brett, *Biblical Criticism in Crisis? The Impact of the canonical approach on Old Testament Studies* (Cambridge: Cambridge University Press, 1991), 2ff. Brett's entire volume repays study.

12 Marshall Sahlins, *Islands of History* (Chicago: University of Chicago Press, 1985), 155.

13 Mark A. Noll, "Review Essay: The Bible in America," *Journal of Biblical Literature*, 106 (Sept. 1987), 504.

14 The reader will note that when referring to the first five books of the Bible, I try as much as possible to use the terms "Books of Moses," and "Pentateuch." These books are also frequently called "the Torah" (note the definite article). However, in English-language usage, a set of ambiguities has crept in that sometimes can be a touch misleading, especially to non-Jews. There are four basic usages of the term. (1) As mentioned above, "the Torah" usually refers to the first five books of the Bible. However (2), it is sometimes, although not frequently, used with the definite article to refer to the entire corpus of the Hebrew scriptures. (3) "Torah" (without either a definite or an indefinite article preceding it) usually refers to the revelation of law and covenant that is believed to underlie the entire Hebrew scriptures. And (4) "Torah" (again without articles) sometimes refers not only to the conceptual base of the Hebrew scriptures, but is taken to include the "oral Torah," the teaching of rabbinical figures from the Common Era, who claimed continuity with ancient teachers from the First Temple era.

15 See the extraordinary diagram of biblical progress in Northrop Frye, *The Great Code. The Bible and Literature* (Toronto: Academic Press, 1982), 171.

16 Frank Kermode, *The Sense of an Ending: Studies in the Theory of Fiction* (New York: Oxford University Press, 1967), 6ff.

17 Noll, 503.

18 Robertson Cochrane, "The Patron Saint of English," *Globe and Mail* (Toronto) (8 October 1994).

19 Donald Coggan, *The English Bible* (London: Longmans, Green and Co., 1963), 18–19.

20 Robert Stone, "The Reason for Stories: Toward a Moral Fiction," *Harper's Magazine* (June 1988), 72.

21 Coggan, 18.

22 This point is well made by Frederick C. Prussner, in his translator's note to Hans Walter Wolff, "The Kerygma of the Deuteronomic Historical Work," in Walter Brueggemann and Hans Walter Wolff, *The Vitality of Old Testament Traditions* (Atlanta: John Knox Press, second ed., 1982), 158n26.

23 Krister Stendahl, "The Bible as Classic and the Bible as Holy Scripture," in House, 42.

24 It is the sheer literary brilliance of the King James Bible that precludes one's doing a mix-and-match of an English-language version of the Tanakh (for example,

the Jewish Publication Society's 1985 translation) with the Christian scriptures as found in the KJB. As Harold Bloom notes (p. 50), "unfortunately, the American Jewish versions, despite their scholarly accuracy, compare poorly with the King James Bible in literary value."

The reader should be aware of the recent translation (1995) of the Pentateuch by Everett Fox as the first portion of Shocken Books projected translation of the Tanakh. Entitled *The Five Books of Moses*, it is a fascinating attempt at rendering the Hebrew text in an aural-English version. Its literalness is striking and readers either love or hate it. Those who dislike it are repelled by a form of literary literalism that has its philosophical basis in German Romanticism. Those who admire it find the work to be moving, original and frequently unnerving.

NOTES TO CHAPTER TWO

1 The notes in this study are limited to (1) quotations, (2) specific factual matters not generally known and therefore requiring documentation, and (3) items in the secondary literature that I have found useful, either as direct sources of information or as examples of ways of thinking that may be valuable if the reader wishes to follow up on any of the matters discussed. I realize that this parsimony of bibliographic referencing may prick the vanity of some scholars, at least if they are the sort who judge a work on whether or not they, or their mentor, are referred to. However, I think that my gratitude to the many truly first-rate scholars who work in biblical and talmudic studies will be clear in the citations.

Wherever possible in this study, rather than refer to secondary sources, I refer directly to the primary text. These references for the most part are placed within the argument, rather than in notes. These references are in unambiguous form and refer to standard editions. Therefore the reader can easily check what I am saying by going directly to the scriptural or extra-biblical document that I cite. Every primary text that is referred to is available at any good library.

2 There is a contradictory tradition about the Babylonian exile in Chronicles, which holds that (a) everyone who was not killed by the Babylonians was deported, and (b) that the land lay desolate for seventy years (see II Chron. 36: 20–21). This material is highly stylized, being tailored to fit a prophecy, namely, "to fulfill the word of the Lord by the mouth of Jeremiah" (II Chron. 36:21). It was written considerably later than the material in Kings and in Jeremiah, the fifth century at the earliest. The Hebrew Bible, in contrast to the Christian versions, appropriately places the Chronicles, a very late addition, at the very end of the scriptures.

3 Niels Peter Lemche, *Ancient Israel. A New History of Israelite Society* (Sheffield: JSOT Press, 1988), 179. For general background see D.J. Wiseman, *Nebuchadnezzar and Babylon* (London: Oxford University Press, 1985).

4 Ezekiel 3:15 speaks of one group of captives "at Tel-abib, that dwelt by the river of Chebar" The juxtaposition of water – as in Waters of Babylon – and the place of exile is significant.

5 The "Egyptians," of whom both the author of Kings and of Jeremiah strongly disapproved, present a problem. On the basis of the primary texts it is not easy to reconcile three assertions found therein: (1) that the elite were exiled to Babylon; (2) that the rural peasantry were left in the land; and (3) that, thereafter, "all the people, both small and great, and the captains of the armies arose and came to Egypt ..." (II Kings 25:26, cf Jeremiah 43:4 and 7). This is particularly difficult, because, if assertion "3"held true, the bulk of the people were not in exile in Babylon, but in Egypt.

I think the situation is best interpreted as an instance of a very common feature of the Hebrew scriptures: despite their dealing in theory with the entire nation, they are actually sharply focused on urban life and, most especially, that of Jerusalem, the spiritual capital of Judah. We rarely gain a clear notion of what the situation was out in the sticks in, say, Nazareth or in the Galilean countryside.

Given that strong anti-rural bias in the scriptures, the easiest way to reconcile the three seemingly-contradictory observations in the texts, and to do so in a way consonant with the obvious fears of being usurped on the part of the elite exiled to Babylon (who feared both the "Egyptians" and the locals who remained in Palestine) is as follows: (1) a minority, the elite of various occupational groups, were exiled to Babylon; (2) most of the rest of the urban population (meaning, effectively, the remaining population of Jerusalem) took themselves to Egypt; and (3) the bulk of the population, the rural proletariat and small-town shopkeepers, stayed behind.

6 Fergus Millar, *The Roman Near East, 31 B.C. – A.D. 337* (Cambridge: Harvard University Press, 1993), 11–15.

7 For a qualification of the view that the worshippers of Yahweh were completely aniconic in their tradition, see two articles in *The Triumph of Elohim. From Yahwisms to Judaisms* (ed.) Diana V. Edelman (Grand Rapids: Eerdmans Publishing, 1996): Brian B. Schmidt, "The Aniconic Tradition: On Reading Images and Viewing Texts" (75–105), and Diana V. Edelman, "Tracking Observance of the Aniconic Tradition through Numismatics," (185–225). Particularly arresting is Edelman's discussion of two coins from the province of Judea in the Persian period which depict Yahweh as an enthroned male deity.

8 For a compelling discussion about the nature of the biblical historians, see Baruch Halpern, *The First Historians. The Hebrew Bible and History* (San Francisco: Harper and Row, 1989). The entire volume demands study. See also David Damrosch's discussion of Bible history as a far-reaching transformation of earlier genres in his *The Narrative Covenant. Transformations of Genre in the Growth of Biblical Literature* (San Francisco: Harper and Row, 1987) esp. 9–57. Jacob Licht's "Biblical Historicism" is a spirited defence of "Old Testament" historical writers as just that: writers of history, people who did what historians do today: find out as much as possible about events that happened in the past and then try to make sense out of the emergent pattern. Jacob Licht in H. Tadmor and

M. Weinfeld, *History, Historiography and Interpretation. Studies in Biblical and Cuneiform Literatures* (Jerusalem: Magnes Press, 1983), 107–20. Curiously, the most resistance to the fairly-new willingness to treat the central Hebrew texts as historical in their intention, and achievement, is found among the most sceptical of scholars, Niels Peter Lemche. (One says curious, because the new historicism is an attack on exactly the fuzzy "epic" and "saga" approach to the Hebrew scriptures that Lemche himself dislikes.) In *The Canaanites and Their Land. The Tradition of the Canaanites* (Sheffield: JSOT Press, 1991, 152n1) he states that "in spite of Baruch Halpern's good intentions and well-written defence of the Old Testament historians as being actually *historians* who tried to write history and not novels…it must be maintained that these historians – irrespective of their intentions – did not possess the necessary methodological tools to write history which can be compared to the work of the historians of our age, except remotely." One wonders what historians of our age Lemche is familiar with. Try spending a few evenings with, for example, the work of Michel Foucault, and the admirable rigour and self-discipline of the author of, say, the Book of Kings will become apparent. Unless biblical historians become competent in some field of modern history, generalization of Lemche's sort are not within their brief: and, frankly, are dead wrong.

9 Ruth presented a difficult problem to the authorities who later arranged the canon, and Ruth was placed in several different locations. See James A. Sanders, "Canon, Hebrew Bible," in *The Anchor Bible Dictionary* [hereafter *ABD*] (New York: Doubleday, 1992), 1: 839–43.

10 Richard Elliott Friedman uses the term tradent to "denote one who is both editor and writer, one whose handling of received texts involves both arrangement and elaboration." It is a useful term, in my view, but unfamiliar to most readers, so it will not be used in the present text. See Richard Elliott Friedman, "Sacred History and Theology: the Redaction of Torah," in Richard Elliott Friedman (ed.), *The Creation of Sacred Literature. Composition and Redaction of the Biblical Text* (Berkeley: University of California), 25–34.

11 Gerhard von Rad's 1938 essay (originally published as a small book) was translated as "The Form-Critical Problem of the Hexateuch" and found in Gerhard von Rad, *The Problem of the Hexateuch and other essays*, translated by E.W. Trueman Dicken (Edinburgh: Oliver and Boyd, 1966), 1–78. See also von Rad's *Deuteronomy. A Commentary* (Philadelphia: Westminster Press, 1966; original German ed., 1964). A valuable comment by Rolf Rendtorff, one of von Rad's students and later professor of Old Testament at the University of Heidelberg, is "The Yahwist' as Theologian? The Dilemma of Pentateuchal Criticism," *Journal for the Study of the Old Testament*, 3 (1976), 2–10.

12 The second German edition of Martin Noth's 1943 work, published in 1957, is available in translation as *The Deuteronomistic History* (Sheffield: JSOT, 1981).

13 Martin Noth, *Numbers. A Commentary* (London: SCM Press, 1968, translated from the German original of 1966), 9.

For an elaboration of the idea that a scribal circle, rather than a single author, was responsible for the deuteronomistic history, see Moshe Weinfeld, *Deuteronomy and the Deuteronomic School* (Oxford: Clarendon Press, 1972).

For the idea that a single editorial hand was involved, see Richard Elliot Friedman, *Who Wrote the Bible?* (Englewood Cliffs, New Jersey: Doubleday, 1987), esp. 146ff.

14 In Chronicles (which, like compilers of the Hebrew Bible, I take to be later than the primary story of Genesis-Kings), one finds reference to three more lost books – the Book of Samuel the Seer, the Book of Nathan the prophet, and the Book of Gad the Seer (I Chron. 29:29). Since these items still were in circulation after the return from the Babylonian Exile, there is a good possibility that they had been earlier available to the inventor of the primary history of Israel. (The books were still extant at the time of Chronicles being written.) A reasonable interpretation of I Samuel 10:25 is that an earlier version of a Book of Samuel was available to the final editor-author of the present Books of Samuel.

15 John Butler, "Evangelical Astrology," *Evangelical Studies Bulletin*, 12 (Spring 1995), 3. The comments are part of a review of Mark Noll's *The Scandal of the Evangelical Mind* (Grand Rapids: Erdmans Publishing, 1994) which is arguably the most important analysis of the evangelical mind, and especially its use of the Bible, to be written in the twentieth century.

16 For a devastating critique of the way that "saga" is misused in some biblical scholarship, see John Van Seters, *Abraham in History and Tradition* (New Haven: Yale University Press, 1975), 131–38. This is not to gainsay that valuable comparative models for ancient Hebrew oral history may not be found in cultures that possess an ancient oral history that was not trampled on by Greek or Roman invasions. The two most accessible are those of pre-Christian Ireland and of Scandinavia. However, if my mild acquaintance with the Irish material is at all indicative, the intermingling of epic and annals, genealogy and mythology in these materials does not provide an easily transportable model, especially because some of the main pieces of the puzzle are missing.

17 Paul Haupt, *The Sacred Books of the Old Testament. A Critical Edition of the Hebrew Text, printed in Colours with notes* (Leipzig: n.p., 1893).

18 That I am not missing any major achievement concerning the relationship of Y, E, P, R, and D, is indicated by the comment in the *ABD* (1992), 6:1014, praising Martin Noth for being "one of the rare exegetes to propose a complete enumeration of the texts he considered as belonging to J." (The reference is to Martin Noth, *A History of Pentateuchal Traditions*, translated from the 1948 German edition by Bernhard W. Anderson [Englewood Cliffs, NJ: Prentice-Hall Inc., 1992], esp. 28–32.) The only other scholar instanced as trying to define all the "Y" sources was Otto Eissfeldt. Since "Y," the most important of the documents, is not as yet defined, the other sources remain the scholarly equivalent of projective tests.

19 The most artistically successful attempt at showing what the Yahwist source might have looked like is the translation and reconstruction done by David Rosenberg in Harold Bloom, *The Book of J* (New York: Vintage Books, 1991), 57–172. This reconstruction (in part intuitive, in part scholarly) of what the Yahwist document may originally have looked like should not be confused with a simple marking of the Yahwist passages in the existing Masoretic Text. It is an attempt to get to the artistic triumph that the book probably was.

20 Baruch Halpern, *The First Historians. The Hebrew Bible and History* (San Francisco: Harper and Row, 1989), 115–16, and xi-xv.

One of the few top-line scholars to resist the descent into sigla is Richard Elliott Friedman who, though adept at conventional Documents Model textual analysis, makes a strong case for simplification: namely that P and the final editor of at least the first four Books of Moses, and perhaps all five – R – is the same person. See Richard Elliott Friedman, *The Exile and Biblical Narrative* (Chico, California: Harvard Semitic Monographs, 1981).

Incidentally, the writings of Baruch Halpern and Richard Elliott Friedman are well worth reading in full. Each argues with deep scholarship and (what is more rare), wit.

21 Robert Alter, *The Art of Biblical Narrative* (New York: Basic Books, 1981), 11.

22 Philip R. Davies, *In Search of 'Ancient Israel'* (Sheffield: JSOT, 1992), 39.

23 David Hackett Fischer, *Historians' Fallacies. Toward a Logic of Historical Thought* (London: Routledge and Kegan Paul, 1971), 61–62.

24 See John Van Seters (1975), 148–312. The argument, while nimble, has not had much influence. I would speculate, however, that Van Seters' more recent book will have a much greater impact. It argues robustly that "Y" is actually a post-Exilic source. See John Van Seters, *The Life of Moses. The Yahwist as Historian in Exodus-Numbers* (Louisville: Westminster John Knox Press, 1994).

25 David Noel Freedman, *The Unity of the Hebrew Bible* (Ann Arbor: University of Michigan Press, 1991), vi.

26 The unmistakable meaning of the text, that Judah is superordinate spiritually over Israel, is so obvious that one puzzles over the fact that so much biblical scholarship has taken the opposite view. I think Jon D. Levenson has brilliantly summarized the situation and the reason for it: "The curious tendency of scholars to invert the canonical judgment by treating Israel as normative and Judah as deviant owes much to an unreflective identification of Israel with Protestantism, and Judah, with its inviolable monarchy, centralized authority, and high liturgy, with Roman Catholicism." Jon D. Levenson, *Sinai and Zion. An Entry into the Jewish Bible* (San Francisco: Harper and Row, 1985), 203–204*n*21. Implicit in this comment of Levenson is the accurate observation that the overwhelming majority of non-Orthodox scholars of the Hebrew Bible have been Protestant. This is changing rapidly at present, more from the accession of non-Orthodox Jews to the ranks, however, than from the addition of Catholics.

27 This is not to gainsay that there are other (later) definitions of David's genealogy that are much more precise. See I Chronicles 2:1–16, and Ruth 4:18–22. These, in contrast to the skilled reticence of the writer-editor of Genesis-Kings, are obviously synthetic and virtually challenge the reader to disprove them, which is just the opposite of what one wishes in a text that is supposed to inspire belief. (There are also genealogies of David in the Christian scriptures.)

David also acquires a contact-genealogy through his marriages, and this helped his ascent over the kingdom of Israel. See Jon D. Levenson and Baruch Halpern, "The Political Import of David's Marriages," *Journal of Biblical Literature*, 99 (1980), 507–78.

28 Levenson, 92. His entire book, *Sinai and Zion* (see above) is an extraordinary piece of historical scholarship.

29 My describing the editor-writer (or a predecessor whose work he approved) as having moved the holy mountain from Sinai to Zion, and the covenant from that of Moses to that of David, is not meant to imply that one source is necessarily older than the other. The change is rhetorical, in the narrative line of the history being presented. The historical priority of Sinai is argued by George E. Mendenhall, *The Tenth Generation. The Origins of the Biblical Tradition* (Baltimore: Johns Hopkins University Press, 1973), esp. 64–66. The priority of Zion is put forward by Van Seters (1994), 289.

30 Levenson, passim.

31 See Gerhard von Rad, *Genesis. A Commentary*, translated by John H. Marks (London: SCM Press, 1961, from the German original edition of 1956), 41.

32 For a sensitive response to Rosenzweig's work, see Barbara Ellen Galli, *Franz Rosenzweig and Jehuda Halevi*, (Montreal and Kingston: McGill-Queen's University Press, 1995), 52.

33 The pattern of historical depiction being conflated with future prescription runs throughout the Hebrew scriptures, the "New Testament," and the Rabbinic writings. The habit is continued in classical "Old Testament" form in the chronology of James Ussher, Protestant Archbishop of Armagh who, in the early seventeenth century, worked out a dating of world chronology, from the day of creation onwards. (The present-day Jewish liturgical calendar is based upon similar calculations, 1997, for example, being 5757, and so on.) The interesting point about Ussher's chronology is that it still is printed in versions of the Bible used by Protestant Fundamentalists and thus retains authority; and that it included not just a backward-looking calculation, but a forward projection to the end of the world. This part is left out of the Fundamentalist publications that honour his historical calculations and that is just as well, since he concluded that the world would last 6,000 years and would end on the twenty-second of October, 1996, at 1800 hours, presumably on the seventeenth-century equivalent of Greenwich Mean Time.

34 The process is particularly brutal because the equivalent of what would today be called "humane killers" is banned. The animal goes through a period of heightened terror, before having its throat slit.

35 There are many "solutions" to the "Elohim" problem such as pointing to Genesis 1:1, where a singular verb is attached to a plural noun, but one has to be struck with the completely hermetic (and therefore not disprovable) way that U. Cassuto dealt with it: "Elohim" meant the One God when it was applied to Israel and the gods when applied to any other group! U. Cassuto, *The Documentary Hypothesis and the Composition of the Pentateuch*, translated by Israel Abrahams (Jerusalem: Magnes Press, orig. ed. 1941, English ed., 1961), 18.

36 The victory, of course, is achieved through the invention of the Genesis-Kings text. However, that final victory of Yahweh over all other gods came after the destruction of the First Temple. If the text itself can be taken as having any glimmer of historical accuracy (and I certainly think it can), then one thing that it does not veil is that large numbers of the Chosen People frequently embraced cults that were, first, denounced, and then suppressed. If one takes the reasonable view that these cults were not new creations, but most often were the old gods that Yahweh supplants, then one has a significant historical question. With what did the old cults supply the people, especially the country people who were not overawed by the cultural imperialism of Jerusalem? Clearly the Temple and the 613 commandments were not enough and it took centuries of battle before the supporters of Yahweh achieved complete dominance.

37 That Moses had already built some form of a proto-temple, on a hillside, containing an altar, ringed by twelve pillars, is suggested in Exodus 24:4. There he conducted sacrifices of the sort later done in Solomon's Temple.

38 See II Kings, 12:18, 14:14, 22:5.

39 Northrop Frye, *The Great Code. The Bible and Literature* (Toronto: Academic Press, 1982), 200.

40 John V. Kelleher, "Early Irish history and pseudo-history," *Studia Hibernica*, 3 (1963), 113–27.

41 N. Goodman, *Ways of Worldmaking* (Indianapolis: Hackett, 1978), 4, quoted in Ronald S. Hendel, "Worldmaking in Ancient Israel," *Journal for the Study of the Old Testament*, 56 (1993), 4.

42 See Judah Goldin, *The Song at the Sea, being a Commentary on a Commentary in Two Parts* (New Haven: Yale University Press, 1971).

43 Readers interested in this idea will enjoy Jack Miles, *God. A Biography* (New York: Knopf, 1995). It is sensible, good-humoured, and respectful of the primary text, without being bullied by it. It is not quite a biography of Yahweh in the sense indicated in my text above, but rather an indication of the changing nature of the Hebrew God as a literary construct: in other words, a chronicle of how the picture of God changes as one reads the Hebrew scriptures (and reads them in the order that they assume in the present-day Tanakh).

44 I use the term with some fear of being denounced for a thought crime. As Walter Brueggemann has decreed, "the conventional term patriarchal' is increasingly objectional for its exclusive character. It is likely a preferable practice to refer to the narratives of Genesis 12–50 as 'ancestral narratives' " (Walter Brueggemann and

Hans Walter Wolff, *The Vitality of Old Testament Traditions* (Atlanta: John Knox Press, second ed., 1982), 171*n*1. On the other hand, one might accurately suggest that it is indeed appropriate to denominate as "patriarchal" a group of stories in which the primary figure in almost every tale is male. With rare exceptions, women enter the various dramas chiefly as the bronze age equivalent of the butler-with-a-telegram or, more often, as bits of stage furniture.

45 The one exception to this generalization is the biography of King David. It is quite unlike anything else in the Hebrew scriptures. It has drama, density of detail, and apparent facticity. There is none of the voice-from-a-clouded-mountain aspect which is found (with great success) in the patriarchal stories and the stories associated with Moses. Nor, on the other hand, does it have the narrative flatness one gets with most of the other kings, even, for example, the blood-soaked Josiah.

I think that King David is the one figure whom the editor-writer believes is 100 percent historically real and also completely compelling from a storyteller's viewpoint. King David lives.

46 P.J. O'Rourke, *Give War a Chance. Eyewitness Accounts of Mankind's Struggle against Tyranny, Injustice and Alcohol-Free Beer* (New Atlantic Monthly Press, 1992), 88.

47 It does not in any way undercut the salience of Harold Bloom's observations about the "Book of J" to note that the author he posits for the book has a sense of irony, wryness, and humour that is uncannily like that of Harold Bloom. And Yahweh is not altogether unrelated. " 'J' 's Yahweh is ... an imp who behaves sometimes as though he is rebelling against his Jewish mother, 'J' " (15).

48 Incidentally, Bloom's shrewd literary observation that the Y source material in Genesis, Exodus and Numbers is a companion piece to Second Samuel, does not require, as he suggests, two separate authors, known to each other and trading concepts and images as they go along (Bloom, 41). All it requires is that the final writer-editor drew together parallel traditions, or that, given his knowledge of the Yahwist documents, he wrote Samuel in a parallel mode.

49 The literature on the gods other than Yahweh is very extensive, and some of it pretty crazy. The items that I have found both useful and sensible (if not always convincing) are: W.F. Albright, *Yahweh and the Gods of Canaan. An Historical Analysis of Two Conflicting Faiths* (Garden City: Doubleday, 1968); Frank M. Cross, *Canaanite Myth and Hebrew Epic: Essays in the History of the Religion of Israel* (Cambridge: Harvard University Press, 1973); John Day, *God's Conflict with the Dragon and the Sea: Echoes of a Canaanite Myth in the Old Testament* (Cambridge: Cambridge University Press, 1985); John Day, "Asherah in the Hebrew Bible and Northwest Semitic Literature," *Journal of Biblical Literature*, 105 (1986), 385–408; Mark S. Smith, *The Early History of God. Yahweh and the Other Deities in Ancient Israel* (San Francisco: Harper and Row, 1990); Irving M. Zeiltin, *Ancient Judaism. Biblical Criticism from Max Weber to the present* (Cambridge, England: Polity Press, 1984), 1–106.

The following items, although not focusing directly on the issues of polytheism, are useful background: George W. Coats, *Moses. Heroic Man, Man of God* (Sheffield: JSOT, 1988); Gordon F. Davies, *Israel in Egypt. Reading Exodus 1–2* (Sheffield: JSOT, 1992); Cyrus H. Gordon, *Before the Bible. The Common Background of Greek and Hebrew Civilizations* (New York: Harper and Row, 1962); Niels Peter Lemche, *Early Israel. Anthropological and Historical Studies on the Israelite Society before the Monarchy* (Leiden: E.J. Brill, 1985); D.J. Wiseman (ed.), *Peoples of Old Testament Times* (Oxford: Clarendon Press, 1973).

50 Horace D. Hummel, "Survey of Recent Literature," in Herbert F. Hahan, *The Old Testament in Modern Research* (Philadelphia: Fortress Press, 1966), 272.

51 Frank Kermode, "New Ways with Bible Stories," in Clemens Thomas and Michael Wyschogrod (eds.), *Parable and Story in Judaism and Christianity* (New York: Paulist Press, 1989), 122.

52 The most direct indication (although somewhat disguised) of the practice of child-sacrifice sometime in the collective history of the Chosen People is the story of Jepthah's daughter (Judges 11:30–40). At war with the Ammonites, Jepthah promised Yahweh that if he were granted victory, in return he would offer up as a burnt-offering whatever first came out of his house to meet him as he returned home victorious. That turns out to be his daughter. She respects her father's vow and after two months in the mountains to prepare her soul, returns home and permits Jepthah to kill and burn her as an offering to Yahweh.

The story in the written text makes Jepthah's daughter the hero, for she made sure that her father honoured his strange covenant with the Almighty. However, anyone hearing or reading the story, and believing that Yahweh was indeed almighty, was apt to suggest that Yahweh saw to it that the girl would be the first to greet Jepthah. The Almighty thereby displays the sort of humour characterized in our own century by Joseph Stalin.

Why would the author-editor of the Genesis-Kings unity not totally destroy this disturbing tale? Because he habitually acted as an historian, and had the historian's horror of destroying evidence, even of child sacrifice as part of the early worship of Yahweh. The most he would do is round off the rough edges and change the focus of the story, so that we keep our eyes on the virtuous daughter.

53 Much of the discussion of child sacrifice gets sidetracked in the fascinating question of the nature of the cult of Molek, to which some apostate Israelites either did (or did not) adhere. See George C. Heider, *The Cult of Molek. A Reassessment* (Sheffield: JSOT, 1985). The point in the text is that whether or not MLK was a separate cult (or, as some hold, a verb signifying child sacrifice), the issue of human sacrifice runs deeper in the Hebrew scriptures than solely that matter, and indeed, is in large part independent of it. For a recent, highly controversial psychoanalytic interpretation, see Martin S. Bergmann, *In the Shadow of Moloch. The Sacrifice of Children and its Impact on Western Religions* (New York: Columbia University Press, 1993).

54 Halpern, 275. Another shrewd reader of historical narrative is Marc Zvi Brettler. See his *The Creation of History in Ancient Israel* (London: Routledge, 1995).

1 The Book of Lamentations is a set of five poems bewailing the fall of Jerusalem. The subject is most easily put in the period 587–38, but this makes one just a touch uneasy. The reasons for this are (a) there is nothing within the text that refers to dateable external contexts related to its composition. It is singularly self-contained, and (b) and more important, the book is an extremely self-conscious artistic creation. It is composed of couplets and triplet lines whose first letters comprise a set of acrostics of the Hebrew alphabet. It is quite an amazing piece of art, and that is the problem. It is so accomplished a piece of work, that it is artificial in tone, rather as if a later court poet had been assigned to write a great poem in the voice of a Babylonian exile from Jerusalem, say in the 570s.

2 See "The Temple Mount from Zerubbabel to Herod," in Benjamin Mazar, *Biblical Israel. State and People* (Jerusalem: Magnes Press, 1992), 109–15, reprinted from J. Amitai (ed.), *Biblical Archaeology Today* (1985), 463–68.

3 The Samaritans are a group that has been habitually bad-mouthed, first by the Judahists, then by the Jews, from the eighth century BCE right down to the present day. The Samaritans claim to represent the tribes of Ephraim and part of Manasseh, and to have survived the trashing of the kingdom of Israel in 722 by the Assyrians. Since most of the Israelites of those times were not deported, there is every reason to believe that some survived. The Samaritans preferred to take for themselves the name Israelites, although their rivals in ever-prospering Judah appropriated the name and the history of "Israel" for their own kingdom. Today, the Samaritans number a few hundred adherents in and around Nablus, and they are neither well off nor influential. They are easy people to patronize.

   The interesting things about these people, who claim to be the true heirs of the northern kingdom of Israel, are, first, that they have their own version of the Pentateuch – the so-called Samaritan Pentateuch – which is not much different from the Judahist version; second, and more intriguing, they possess their own holy mountain, Mount Gerizim, overlooking Nablus. Third, and most interesting of all, in Maccabean times (see II Macc. 6:2, probably written in the second century BCE), it was recorded that there was a temple on Mount Gerizim. This temple, which was destroyed by the Hasmonean ruler of Judea, John Hyrcanus in 113 BCE, or thereabouts, is now slowly being uncovered, and among the central points, will, of course, be the date of its construction, if that can be determined. Crucially, the Gerizim temple was said to be a large-scale model (or, perhaps a full-size duplicate) of the Jerusalem temple. This opens a tantalizing set of possibilities. If the replica, which is now being uncovered beneath the ruins of the fifth century CE church of St. Mary Theozakos, is a duplicate of the Second Temple that was recreated in the late sixth century in Jerusalem – and which, given its position under the Dome of the Rock, is not apt to be the focus of any digging in our lifetime – then we have a chance to see what the Second Temple was like, before it was remodelled out of all recognition by King Herod. Moreover, if it is true that Zerubbabel's Temple was built as accurately on the model of Solomon's Temple as could be done (given available funds, given human memory and, especially, the verbal blueprints left by the editor-writer of Genesis-Kings), then this is as close as we will come to visually experiencing the outlines of the First Temple. To call the Samaritan Temple a "model" is to slightly misconstrue it. It was a working temple – bones from sacrificed mammals are found in its middens – and it may have been as large as the Jerusalem original. It was destroyed in the late second century.

The Mount Gerizim temple not only may be a successful test-drilling into the very archaeological core of Judaism, but it opens a parallel case to the creation of Judaism. A group that is loyal to Yahweh, responds to the destruction of Solomon's Temple (and, perhaps their being banned from using the Second Temple) by two distinct actions: (a) by defining its own Yahwist-dominated scriptures (but with the Judahist triumphalism left out) and (b) by building a temple, based on the ancient Temple of Solomon, where they can regularly affirm their covenant with Yahweh by the spilling of blood.

These religious reactions to events in the physical world are remarkably similar to those of the Judahists. Or so it seems now. Although the Samaritans have been read out of modern Jewish history, they are a significant part of the history of the Chosen People.

4 The title "high priest" had occasionally been used earlier (for example, II Kings 22:4), but this was always at a time in the history of Judah, or Israel, or of the United Monarchy, when a sacralized kingship still existed and therefore was, in the usual instance, superordinate to the "high priesthood."

5 Martin Noth, *The History of Israel* (New York: Harper and Row; second ed., 1960), 316.

6 The matter of Ezra-Nehemiah and the Book of Chronicles is a vexed one for two basic reasons. First, it is not clear if they should be considered a unity. Ezra and Nehemiah were one book in the oldest traditions. They were split into two by early Christian canonists, but not divided in the Hebrew canon until the 1400s. Further, it was commonplace for biblical scholars, until roughly, the 1980s, to present Chronicles, Ezra and Nehemiah as being by the same hand, a conjectural "Chronicler." On the surface this seems strange, for the style of Chronicles is very different from Ezra-Nehemiah, but ideologically the works served the same primary purpose, as will be discussed in the text. The plausibility of separate authorship of Chronicles and Ezra-Nehemiah is presented by Baruch Halpern in "A Historiographic Commentary on Ezra 1–6: Achronological Narrative and Dual Chronology in Israelite Historiography," in William H. Propp, Baruch Halpern,

and David Noel Freedman, *The Hebrew Bible and Its Interpreters* (Winona Lake: Eisenbrauns, 1990), 81–142. My own view is that, given their common ideology, as will be explained in the text, it is not important whether or not one author or two produced them.

When Chronicles and Ezra-Nehemiah were written is uncertain, for the internal clues are ambiguous. Certainly it was within 100 years of, roughly 430 BCE. Nothing in any of the text suggests a knowledge of the actual end of Persian rule and its replacement by Greek.

It should be noted that the Book of 1 Esdras in the Apocrypha of the Greek and Russian Orthodox Churches was written considerably later, and is derivative from non-canonical texts, and has nothing directly to do with Ezra-Nehemiah.

7 I am here using the figures from Kings. However, there is in Jeremiah (52:28–30) an alternative set of estimates which total the exile at an even lower figure, namely 4,600. If one employs that figure, it merely reinforces my basic observations about the nature of the exile and return.

8 Louis H. Feldman, *Jew and Gentile in the Ancient World. Attitudes and Interactions from Alexander to Justinian* (Princeton: Princeton University Press, 1993), 293, 435.

9 The author of Chronicles refers to the Book of Samuel the Seer, the Book of Nathan the Prophet, and the Book of Gad the Seer (I Chron. 29:29), the Book of Shemaiah the Prophet (II Chron. 12:15), the History of the Prophet Iddo (II Chron. 12:15 and 13:22), and the Book of Jehu the son of Hanani (II Chron. 20:34).

10 One does not count as consequential, or indeed, even as intentional the change in I Chron. 21:12 from seven years of famine (as specified in II Sam. 24:13) to three years, the menu of punishments offered to King David after his unauthorized enumeration of the children of Israel.

11 This transposition was made easier because II Chron. 6:11 has King Solomon referring to an undefined "covenant of the Lord" in the ark.

12 I should emphasize that the present discussion is situated within the mind frame of the adherent of Judahism during the period of the Persian empire. The scholarship of the last two centuries of our own time is absolutely convincing on the fact that the Pentateuch is formed from the work of many hands (plus a very skillful editor). This is totally irrelevant, however, to what was going on at the time, namely a cultural *putsch* which shoved aside the editor-writer of Genesis-Kings, and placed the first five books of the writings under the putative pen of Moses, the most authoritative figure in Judahist tradition. So, we concentrate on how the claim for Moses must have looked at the time.

13 This discussion concentrates on the Pentateuch, because that is the form the "Books of Moses" actually took, and we have no direct evidence (or anything except very pale indirect evidence) that this might not always have been the case. The reader should be aware, however, that there is a responsible school of thought

that suggests the Pentateuch was originally a Tetrateuch (that is, Genesis-Numbers). According to this view, the story of Moses' death (chapter 34 of Deuteronomy) was originally the conclusion (or near to it) of the Book of Numbers. This is not as outré a suggestion as it appears on the surface, for in fact Deuteronomy 34 works well as a narrative historical conclusion to Numbers.

However, given that there is no textual evidence of this (we do not possess an early version of the Pentateuch), the suggestion is best left aside, chiefly on the cutting of Ockham's Razor. The theory raises a complication, without evidence, when simplicity and the available evidence fit quite nicely. Specifically, the theory requires that in the period between, roughly, 520 BCE and 458, a set of four books (the "Tetrateuch") was amalgamated with the Book of Deuteronomy, which previously (according to the most common version of this theory) had been part of a set of books that ran from Deuteronomy through Kings.

14 These effects hold whether one places Ezra-Nehemiah and Chronicles at the end of the Tanakh (as do the Hebrew scriptures) or immediately after Kings (as in the Christian version).

15 Psalm 151 in *The Apocryphal-Deuterocanonical Books of the Old Testament. New Revised Standard Version* (1989).

16 The operative word here is "primary." As ancillary forms, narrative history continues as part of the Judahist tradition: witness the books of 1 and 2 Maccabees, the historical writings among the works of Philo, and the extensive historical narratives of Josephus. (These are discussed in later chapters.) However, none of these items of historical narratives, or other less important items, were embraced as part of the primary tradition, the one that became canonical.

17 Jewish Publication Society version (1985). The word "bride" is not used in the legal sense, but is prospective, indicative of the physical drive to possess the beloved.

18 The reader will have noticed that in this chapter I have avoided entirely the question of the cultural impact of "Hellenization" upon the intellectual elite of Judahism. This will be discussed, albeit far from conclusively (the topic is an immense one) in Chapter Five.

19 First Enoch is found in translation from Ethiopic by E. Isaac in James H. Charlesworth (ed.), *The Old Testament Pseudepigrapha* (New York: Doubleday, 1983), 1:5–89.

NOTES TO CHAPTER FOUR

1 Because I wish to keep with us in the argument the equivalent in Biblical scholarship of "strict constructionists" in constitutional historiography, this chapter's discussion of the Hebrew covenant is limited mostly to its evocation in the first five books of the Bible, the "Books of Moses," often called the "Pentateuch." Discussion here focuses on the fully articulated covenant. Of course, in the texts, there

are hints of what the earlier, emergent idea of the covenant may have been, but those proto-forms are not here adduced in argument.

2 T. Daniel J. Harrington, *Interpreting the Old Testament: A Practical Guide* (Wilmington, Del.: Michael Glazier, 1982), 56. I am of course being willfully anachronistic in my comparison of ancient and modern idioms, but the resonance of the phrases is undeniable.

3 William Foxwell Albright, *From the Stone Age to Christianity: Monotheism and the Historical Process*, 2d ed. (Garden City, N.Y.: Doubleday Anchor Books, 1957), 165.

4 Edward Hoagland, "Brightness Visible. On learning to see the gravity of bears and the wonder of beetles," *Harper's* (January 1995), 53–59.

5 Henry Wheeler Robinson's 1935 essay and a companion piece from 1937 have been conveniently reprinted as *Corporate Personality in Ancient Israel* (Philadelphia: Fortress Press, 1964).

6 The difference between the ancient Israelite practice of tracing membership in the People by the male line, and the practice of modern Judaism, wherein membership comes through the female line is noteworthy. The change has yet to receive adequate explanation. The Mishnah (c. 200) articulates the principle that the offspring follow the status of the male in situations in which there is no "transgression," but that they follow the situation of the inferior party in the case of a marriage in which there is a "transgression" (Mishnah, Kiddushin 3:12, I and II [Neusner edition]). This would seem to imply that in any mixed marriage, the offspring would not be Jewish. However, in the Babylonian Talmud's later commentary on this question, it is suggested that if a Jewess cohabits with a non-Jewish slave, the offspring is not a bastard (and thus non-Jewish) but is merely stigmatised as unfit to ever marry a priest (Bavli, Kiddushin, 68b-69a). The entire discussion is cross-hatched with concern for social and caste status, so that the issue is never really resolved, concerning whether being Jewish follows the male or female line.

7 Harold Bloom, "Introduction," in Harold Bloom, ed., *Genesis* (New York: Chelsea House, 1986), 5.

8 Henry Wheeler Robinson, *The Old Testament: Its Making and Meaning* (London: University of London Press, 1937), 2.

NOTES TO CHAPTER FIVE

1 In the conceptualization and construction of the argument that follows, the reader should be aware of my debt to Stephen Jay Gould's fine study, *Wonderful Life. The Burgess Shale and the Nature of History* (New York: W.W. Norton, 1989). Also helpful has been another fine piece of popular scientific writing, James Gleick, *Chaos. Making a New Science* (New York: Viking, 1987).

2 Jacob Neusner, "Judaism and Christianity in the First Century: How shall we perceive their relationship?" in Philip R. Davies and Richard T. White, *A Tribute to*

Geza Vermes. Essays on Jewish and Christian Literature and History (Sheffield: JSOT, 1990), 256 and 257.

3 Emil Schurer, *The History of the Jewish People in the Age of Jesus Christ (175 BC – AD 135)* (Edinburgh: T. and T. Clark, 2 vols. New ed. 1973; first German ed. 1885), 1:140–41. Despite its seemingly vintage publication date, this volume is extremely useful, and of the many general studies of the period, one of the most rewarding to use. That is because the English edition was updated and modern references added by Geza Vermes and by Fergus Millar, then, respectively, fellow of Wolfson College and reader in Jewish studies, and fellow and tutor in ancient history at Queen's College, Oxford. Thus, one has the pleasure of reading a revision of one of the great works of nineteenth-century scholarship, updated by two young scholars who later became the major figures in their own fields. The result is a very informative dialogue between some of the best minds of the nineteenth century and of the twentieth.

4 Martin Noth, *The History of Israel* (New York: Harper and Row, second ed., 1960), 362–65.

5 Here, the characteristics of the historical sources for the period require comment, particularly the books of 1 and 2 Maccabees: these two volumes (by separate authors) were preserved by Christians. They are part of the secondary canon of the Roman Catholic church and the Apocrypha of the Protestant. They form no part of the Tanakh or of the other collections of writing that came to have spiritual authority in the Jewish faith. That is not to say that they at present are, or in the past were, unknown to Jewish worshippers, merely that they lacked authority. This is a peculiar situation, for the books have virtually nothing to do with Christianity (there are no metaphors that are easily translatable into the Christian idiom) and everything to do with the genealogy of Judaism.

Both volumes were written within approximately fifty years of the events they chronicle, which is much closer than almost anything in the history of ancient Judah, save the few verses in Jeremiah and Kings that were written immediately after the Exile. Of course there is some exaggeration and some propagandizing in each volume, but they are more straight historical narrative than anything in the Tanakh. 1 Maccabees glorifies the early Hasmoneans, and 2 Maccabees is, among other things, a tract for the creation of a new feast – the Feast of Dedication, celebrating the purification of the Temple – which is usually called Hanukkah.

I suspect that one reason for these books not becoming authoritative (and, ultimately canonical) is that late Hasmoneans had a frightful civil war with the Pharisees. Several thousand Pharisees were murdered. Given that the spiritual descendants of the Pharisees dominated post-70 CE Jewish life – the period when the canon was finally being set – it is understandable that 1 and 2 Maccabees were excluded. They remain, however, the best witness we have to the creation of the independent Judaean state.

6 Another observation concerning the characteristics of the primary sources and their usage is required. This concerns the writings of "Josephus" (Joseph ben Mattathias was his Hebrew name and Flavius Josephus his Roman name, but "Josephus" is the general and unambiguous usage.) Josephus, of a Hasmonean family, was well educated in both Judaism and in Graeco-Roman culture. As a young man in his late twenties, he served as a general on the northern front in the 66–70 war against the Romans. Then, by a passage of diplomacy not well revealed in his writings, he found favour in the Roman imperial court and spent the rest of his life on a Roman pension, writing three significant books plus his own *Life*: (1) his history of the war that resulted in the crushing of the Second Temple religion, (2) his *Jewish Antiquities* which is a reprise of Jewish history from the Creation onwards, and (3) a strong reply against *Apion*, an anti-Semitic tract of his time. The key to understanding Josephus is that his works were written after 70 CE and therefore they have the knowledge that defeat was the seemingly-last page of Jewish history. Yet, Josephus is spiritedly pro-Yahweh and believes there is something beyond defeat.

Josephus's writings are important in both Jewish and Christian history. In Jewish history they are the only continuous source running from the beginning of Greek rule until early Rabbinic times. They fill a crucial gap. Similarly, Josephus's writings provide a view of life in the period just before and after the birth of Jesus that is unrivalled. It is not perfect, but nothing approaches it in density and texture. Yet, Josephus received very little attention from Jewish scholars until the later nineteenth and the twentieth centuries. For the most part, he was preserved through Christian scholarship. Why the Rabbis of the second through sixth centuries should have been so repelled by him is difficult to see. (Having said that, it is true that as a retired Jewish general, living on a Roman pension, he was not above reproach personally, nor, in his explication of controversial events was he apt to blame Rome directly: he usually found a convenient third party, neither main-line Jewish, nor Roman, to blame.)

In the present era we are blessed. The Loeb Library edition of his writings is conveniently available. The depth of twentieth-century scholarship on Josephus is extraordinary. Louis H. Feldman's volume of 1,055 pages, *Josephus and Modern Scholarship (1937–1980)* (Berlin: Walter de Gruyter, 1984) is not only comprehensive in its listings, but provides thumbnail sketches of most of the important scholarly articles.

That scholarly richness recognized, the curious thing about the majority of Josephus scholarship as practised by individuals who read him for religious information (as distinct from classicists who are using him as a secular source) is its overwhelmingly whiny tone. Josephus is constantly being treated as if he wrote an awkward midrash, or some primitive prolegomena to the rabbinical era, when, in fact, he was an historian, and one of a type with whom we are well acquainted: the retired general, well educated, who spends his retirement years trying to explain to himself why his own life, and the life of his own people, developed the way they did. His most obvious counterpart in our own century is Winston Churchill, whose five-volume history of World War II is very similar to Josephus's *The Jewish War*. Like Churchill, Josephus writes well, using borrowed documents and research assistants extensively. Generally, though, his standard of accuracy is higher than Churchill's, for Josephus, being on the losing side of his war, got the big picture with a sharper, if crueller, accuracy than did Churchill, whose vision was obscured by the cigar clouds of victory. Further, in his *Jewish Antiquities* Josephus tells us certain things with a richness of detail that is unprecedented: we know more about the court and doings of Herod the Great (hardly a minor figure for either Jews or Christians) than we do about any comparable Greek or Roman figure of antiquity; and through Josephus we know more about Palestine than about any other Roman province.

As long as we remember that Josephus was primarily an historian and judge him that way – instead of demanding that he be a theologian, exegete, or Jewish apologist – then he is of immense value. His work requires the same kind of fine-tuning any historian's work demands: he was, after all, in secure retirement, writing an average of ten or eleven lines of Greek prose a day, and enjoying life. Factual errors of course demand correction, and unconscious attitudes require delineation, but always with the knowledge that in Josephus's writings we have a tiny miracle. Without them most of what we see stretching from the conquest of Palestine by Alexander of Macedon to the levelling of Jerusalem would be unconnected swirls of dust, interrupted by mounds of out-of-context texts – the Qumran library, the Book of Daniel, the Synoptic Gospels – which are difficult enough of comprehension without their being relieved of context. (For a sensible appreciation of Josephus, see P. Bilde, "The Causes of the Jewish War according to Josephus," *Journal for the Study of Judaism*, 10 (Dec. 1979), 179–202.)

7 Translation by R.B. Wright in James H. Charlesworth (ed.), *The Old Testament Pseudepigrapha* (New York: Doubleday, 1985), 2:651–52.

8 Noth, *Israel*, 404.

9 The political backdrop against which Herod the Great and his successors operated was, inevitably, Roman. For an excellent discussion, see Fergus Millar, *The Roman Near East, 31 BC – AD 337* (Cambridge: Harvard University Press, 1993). For a courageous and engaging effort to deal with Herod's personality in its political context, see Peter Richardson, *Herod. King of the Jews and Friend of the Romans* (Columbia: University of South Carolina Press, 1996).

10 For a still-useful bibliography of the construction program of Herod the Great, see vol. 8 of the Loeb edition of Josephus's *Jewish Antiquities*, 579–89.

11 Benjamin Mazar, "The Temple Mount," reprinted from *Biblical Archaeology Today* (1985), 463–68, in Benjamin Mazar, *Biblical Israel. State and People* (Jerusalem: Magnes Press, 1992), 115.

12 Josephus, *Antiquities* 15:391.

13 Because of ambiguities in Josephus's reporting, it is unclear whether the basic work was done within eight years or in nine and one-half years. (See Vermes and Millar in Schurer, 1:292n12.

14 Schurer, 1:308.

15 Mazar, 115.

16 Josephus, *Antiquities* 15:412.

17 Eric M. Meyers, "Synagogue," *ABD*, 6:253–55.

18 The Leontopolis Temple had been founded by Onias IV, whose father Onias III was the last high priest to have a legitimate claim to hereditary possession of the office. A double irony here reigned: the high priests of this Temple, established roughly 145 BCE, had a higher genealogical legitimacy than did those in Jerusalem, and, this Temple lasted longer than did that in Jerusalem, being closed by Vespasian in 73 CE. (*Encyclopaedia Judaica*, 12:1402–04).

One should also note that there had been a Temple, complete with sacrificial ritual at Elephantine, in Egypt, where there was a large Yahwist population. It was built pre-525 BCE (which is to say that it predated the Second Temple) and was destroyed in approximately 410 BCE (*Encyclopaedia Judaica*, 14: 606). And one should recall that the Samaritans had possessed their own temple on Mount Gerizim which operated from the early fourth century until it was destroyed in the late second century before the Common Era.

19 Josephus, *Jewish War* 5:209–10.

20 Ibid. 5:213.

21 Josephus, *Antiquities* 15:390.

22 Ibid. 15:395.

23 One should call to the reader's attention the important work of Louis H. Feldman, *Jew and Gentile in the Ancient World: Attitudes and Interactions from Alexander to Justinian* (Princeton: Princeton University Press, 1993). Feldman makes two fascinating suggestions regarding this period: first, that the "Jewish" population of the world had grown immensely since the destruction of the First Temple, from roughly 150,000 to between four and eight million persons (293). Second, this growth, he believes, can be explained only by the existence of a large-scale and highly successful proselytizing program, a virtual missionary movement to the Gentiles. This deserves consideration. Although one can be skeptical of the population estimates (real demographic evidence for the period is virtually non-existent), the argument that the Judahist religion was very attractive to many pagans is reasonable. Feldman's assertion fits with Josephus's reports that the Temple was made semi-accessible to Gentiles. For instance, they were permitted to give gifts to the Temple. Roman rulers (following the tradition of keeping local religious groups happy) gave money to the Temple for its adornment (*Jewish War* 5:562–63). Josephus speaks of the high altar as being "universally venerated by Greeks and barbarians" (*Jewish War* 5:18), and this, though obviously chauvinistic, probably has some truth to it, and is related to the

Temple authorities allowing Gentiles to purchase sacrifices to be offered up in the Temple. Also, it is worth noting that, in a clear case of religious syncretism, sacrifices for the Roman emperor were offered daily, in the form of two lambs and a bull, from the year 6 CE (and perhaps from Herod's time) onwards. This was a votive act which pagans could support with little hesitation. (See notes by E. Mary Smallwood to the Penguin edition of *The Jewish War* [London, revised ed., 1981], 429*n*35.

24 For examples of the conflicting definition of terms relating to the extent of Greek influence, see Shaye J.D. Cohen, *From the Maccabees to the Mishnah* (Philadelphia: Westminster Press, 1987), 35–38; G.W. Bowersock, *Hellenism in Late Antiquity* (Ann Arbor: University of Michigan Press, 1990), xi-xii; Louis H. Feldman, "How much Hellenism in Jewish Palestine?" *Hebrew Union College Annual*, 57 (1986), 83–111; Martin Hengel, *Judaism and Hellenism. Studies in their Encounter in Palestine during the Early Hellenistic Period* (London: SCM Press, second ed. 1974, orig. pub. as *Judentum and Hellenismus* 1968), 2:1–5; Tessa Rajak, "The Hasmoneans and the Uses of Hellenism," in Philip R. Davies and Richard T. White (eds.), *A Tribute to Geza Vermes. Essays on Jewish and Christian Literature and History* (Sheffield: JSOT, 1990), 262–65.

   A standard, if already quite dated, discussion of the entire phenomenon is in W.D. Davies and Louis Finkelstein, *The Cambridge History of Judaism*, vol. II, *The Hellenistic Age* (Cambridge: Cambridge University Press, 1990).

25 Shaye Cohen, 36.

26 Rajak, 262.

27 Of course this was not universally the case. Among the most notable exceptions was Cyrus Gordon of Brandeis University whose work emphasized the commonality and interpenetration of Semitic and Hellenic cultures. See for example his *Before the Bible. The Common Background of the Greek and Hebrew Civilisations* (New York: Harper & Row, 1962).

28 Millar, 352.

29 See Hengel, *Judaism and Hellenism* above, note 24, and also Martin Hengel, *The "Hellenization" of Judaea in the First Century after Christ* (London: SCM Press, 1989, original pub., 1989 as *Zum Problem der "Hellenisierung" Judaas im I. Jahrhundert nach Christus*). In this volume, Hengel backs off considerably from the more extreme position he took in his 1966 doctoral thesis.

30 It should be emphasized that Hengel is not patronizing or dismissive of non-Hellenic thought. He argues that "we must stop attaching either negative or positive connotations to the question of Hellenistic' influence" (1989:53). His point is simply that it was dominant.

   For useful commentaries, see Eric M. Meyers, "The Challenge of Hellenism for Early Judaism and Christianity," *Biblical Archaeologist*, 55 (June 1992), 84–91 and Robert Harrison, "Hellenization in Syria-Palestine: The case of Judea in the third century BCE," *Biblical Archaeologist*, 57 (June 1994), 98–108.

31 Rudolf Bultmann, *Jesus and the Word* (New York: Charles Scribner's Sons, 1954, orig. German ed., 1926), 133.

32 David Flusser, *Judaism and the Origins of Christianity* (Jerusalem: Magnes Press, 1988), xvi.

33 Feldman (1986), 111.

34 One thing that the traditional classicists hold in common with scholars such as Feldman is that both groups unconsciously equate everything non-Jewish with the Hellenic. This leaves out the undeniable influence of Persian thought and, possibly, the influence of Zoroastrian notions. See Norman Cohn, *Cosmos, Chaos and the World to Come. The Ancient Roots of Apocalyptic Faith* (New Haven: Yale University Press, 1993).

35 Josephus, a potential third-party witness, on this simply follows the account of 1 Maccabees. The Book of Daniel, portions of which were written in response to Antiochus's actions, is too luridly metaphorical to be used as a source of precise historical information on this issue.

36 Shaye Cohen, 37.

37 Samuel Sandmel, *Judaism and Christian Beginnings* (New York: Oxford University Press, 1978), 258.

38 Eric M. Meyers, "Galilee in the Time of Jesus," *Biblical Archaeologist* (Nov-Dec 1994), 41.

39 The translation and introduction to the Letter of Aristeas by R.J.H. Shutt is found in Charlesworth, 2:7–34.

40 See note 23.

41 See the translation and introduction by J.H. Charlesworth in Charlesworth, 1:473–86.

42 See the introduction and translation by Hugh Anderson in Charlesworth, 2:531–64.

43 The scholarly literature on Philo can be divided into two eras: that which precedes the work of Erwin Goodenough in the 1930s, and everything thereafter. Especially important among Goodenough's works were *The Politics of Philo Judaeus* (New Haven: Yale University Press, 1938) and *An Introduction to Philo Judaeus* (New Haven: Yale University Press, 1940). For a bibliography of the work done since Goodenough's era, see R. Radice and D.T. Runia, *Philo of Alexandria: An Annotated Bibliography, 1937–1986* (Leiden: Brill, 1988).

44 Quoted in Abraham Terian, "Had the works of Philo Been Newly Discovered," *Biblical Archaeologist*, 57 (June 1994), 86. Terian shrewdly suggests the possibility that Goodenough himself wrote the flap-note. Terian's entire article (86–97) warrants close attention.

45 Erwin Goodenough, *An Introduction to Philo Judaeus* (Oxford: Basil Blackwell, second edition, 1962), 2. For details on Philo's background and life, see Goodenough and also Ronald Williamson, *Jews in the Hellenistic World: Philo* (Cambridge: Cambridge University Press, 1989).

46 None of these religious leaders is referred to in Philo's works, and this despite his having good communications links with Palestine. (His brother had gold- and silver-plated the doors of the Temple.) That none of these figures had any resonance in Alexandria, the largest diaspora community, is a fairly good indication that, amidst the religious swirl of their own time, they were minor figures at best. They are turned into figures of mythic proportions only after the Temple's destruction.

47 In the tradition of Greek historians, Philo creates dialogue to suit the situation. That is not really mendacious, but rather a mode of argument acceptable at the time. Philo's statement that there were at least a million Jews resident in Alexandria and in the surrounding countryside (Flaccus, 43) is undoubtedly high, but hardly discrediting in itself to his pogrom narrative.

48 There is one passage in "Flaccus" which is very interesting, particularly if one realizes that Philo's writings were known quite early to the Christian community. This is the story ("Flaccus" 36ff) of a lunatic named "Carabas" (note the name's similarity to "Barabas" of the Christian passion story). He was a harmless lunatic, whom the anti-Semitic rioters took to tormenting. They put a false crown upon his head and gave him a sceptre made of papyrus and a rug for a royal robe. Some of the young men carried rods on their shoulders to form an imitation bodyguard and others mockingly consulted him on state affairs and on matters of justice. This occurred in a gymnasium, and there a crowd took to saluting him with the name "Lord" and using the Messianic term "maranatha," "our Lord cometh." One does not need to question the historicity of Philo's description of this event to see how easily it could have broken free of its historical setting and later been attached to the tradition of Yeshua of Nazareth, as he was being converted by Christian writers into Jesus Christ.

49 The model of text-invention that we see among "Hellenized" writers was not limited to the "pro-Hellenists." In fact, these, and other forms of invention that we will discuss later, were practised in the period between the Maccabean revolt and the destruction of the Second Temple by even the keenest anti-Hellenists among the Judahists. These are transportable types of invention, and they are here delineated by reference to the case of Hellenistic writers because this is a convenient vantage point to isolate what is actually a widely-used menu of techniques of religious invention.

50 This could be documented with literally hundreds of citations. It is here sufficient to point to the English-language title with which the Loeb Library edition of his works begins, "On the Account of the World's Creation given by Moses."

51 For instance, in his story of Moses, he tells the story "as I have learned it, both from the sacred books, the wonderful monuments of wisdom which he has left behind him, and from some of the elders of the nation; for I always interwove what I was told with what I read, and thus believed myself to have a closer knowledge than others of his life's history." ("On the Life of Moses," Book 1, 1:4).

52 A comparison of Flavius Josephus, the post-70 historian, with Philo is instructive, for despite obvious differences (not least Josephus's Palestinian origins), they had

some characteristics in common: (1) each wrote in Greek, (2) each gave us historical chronicles of the period between the Maccabees and the destruction of the Temple which are largely comprised of information we otherwise would not have, and (3) each rewrote the history of the Chosen People, starting at the very beginning, using the parallel-text method. Josephus, as an historian, did not employ allegory, but retold the story in such a way as to smoothe out difficulties, and in several cases to change the meaning of old texts; Philo did the same through allegory.

53 See Yehoshua Amir, "The Transference of Greek Allegories to Biblical Motifs in Philo," in Frederick E. Greenspahn, Earle Hilgert, and Burton L. Mack (eds.), *Nourished with Peace. Studies in Hellenistic Judaism in Memory of Samuel Sandmel* (Chico, Cal.: Scholars Press, 1984), 20–24.

54 The most famous exponent of this view, of course, being Erwin R. Goodenough, one of the twentieth century's major scholars of religion. I had the privilege of studying with Goodenough for a bit near the end of his academic career, and only with the greatest hesitation does one disagree with his views. However, I think Goodenough projected onto Philo his own religious journey away from mainline Christianity. He interprets Philo, his alter ego, as having made a journey from mainline Judahist beliefs to mystical pagan-derived beliefs, wherein Plato and Moses became one and the same.

I am heartened in my view that Philo remained at heart a thorough-going Yahwist by the opinion of the late Samuel Sandmel, a doctoral student of Goodenough's, and subsequently a leading scholar of Hellenistic Judaism. He, like Goodenough, quite properly saw the Hellenistic in Philo, but, unlike Goodenough, he did not accept that the Judahistic elements in Philo were pushed into a shadowy background. See Samuel Sandmel, *Philo of Alexandria. An Introduction* (New York: Oxford University Press, 1979), especially the chapter "Goodenough on Philo" (140–47).

55 Nahum N. Glatzer, *The Essential Philo* (New York: Schocken Books, 1971), viii.

56 See Birger A. Pearson, "Philo and the Gnostics on Man and Salvation," *Colloquy* (The Center of Hermeneutical Studies in Hellenistic and Modern Culture, Berkeley, California), 29 (1977), 1–19.

57 Peder Borgen, "Philo of Alexandria," *ABD*, 5:340.

NOTES TO CHAPTER SIX

1 Jer. Tal. *Sanhedrin* 10.6.29c. I am convinced by the argument of Louis H. Feldman that Rabbi Johanan's third-century statement had reference to the pre-70 CE situation, as well as, perhaps, relevance to his own day. Louis H. Feldman, "How Much Hellenism in Jewish Palestine?" *Hebrew Union College Annual*, 57 (1986), 105n72.

2 Lawrence H. Schiffman, "Qumran and Rabbinic Halakhah," in Shemaryahu Talmon (ed.), *Jewish Civilization in the Hellenistic-Roman Period* (Philadelphia: Trinity Press International, 1991), 143.

3 For example, Philo, in his re-writing of the Pentateuch from a Hellenized perspective, quotes the Book of Genesis on Creation and writes "Therefore, Moses says, 'God completed his works on the sixth day,' " thus making Moses the author of the first five books of the Bible. (See "The First Book of the Treatise on the Allegories of the Sacred Laws, after the work of the six days of creation," in Nahum N. Glatzer (ed.), *Philo Judaeus. The Essential Philo* (New York: Schocken Books, 1971), 43.) Philo is consistent in this usage. This can be taken as an indication that this aspect of the privileging of the Torah as Mosaic had, by the turn of the Common Era, won out.

Josephus Flavius, writing in his *Jewish Antiquities* in the twenty years after the destruction of the Temple in 70 CE, provides a reprise of the narrative history of the Chosen People in which he specifically denominates Moses not only as "our lawgiver" but credits him with writing the Pentateuch, beginning with the story of creation. Josephus, *Jewish Antiquities*, I:18.

4 Here, I think the suggestion of the general editors of the *Cambridge Bible Commentary* series should be adopted: that instead of using only the term "pseudepigrapha" as a collective term for all the literature that did not make it into the eventual primary or secondary canon (the Apocrypha) of the Christian Bible, one should also use the term "extra-biblical or para-biblical." See "General Editors' Preface to Ronald Williamson, *Jews in the Hellenistic World: Philo* (Cambridge: Cambridge University Press, 1989), vii. This has the virtue of accuracy (many of the so-called pseudepigrapha were not, strictly speaking, such) and also has the virtue of implying that any of the extra-biblical or para-biblical items could have become part of the final canon of either the Christian or the Hebrew scriptures, had the throw of the historical dice come up just slightly differently in 70 CE. That said, "Pseudepigrapha" is a useful term for the specific material in James H. Charlesworth's collection (see note 5, below).

5 James H. Charlesworth (ed.), *The Old Testament Pseudepigrapha* (New York: Doubleday, 1985), 1:xxi-xxxiv and 2:xxi-xxxiv. (The introductory text is the same in both volumes.) This is the appropriate point to pay homage – and it can scarcely be less – to Charlesworth's presentation of this vast array of para-biblical material.

6 Florentino Garcia Martinez, *The Dead Sea Scrolls Translated* (Leiden: Brill, 1994). This is a 1994 English language translation and up-dating of a 1992 Spanish original.

7 Norman Golb, *Who Wrote the Dead Sea Scrolls? The Search for the Secret of Qumran* (New York: Scribners and London: Michael O'Mara Books, 1995), 217.

8 Geza Vermes, *The Dead Sea Scrolls* (Sheffield: JSOT third ed., 1987), xiv-xv.

9 For a list of what fragments, both biblical and non-biblical, were found at each Qumran site, see Martinez, 466–513.

10 Golb, 198.

11 Paradoxically, the Christian Bible, through its inclusion of several Judahist texts from the later Second Temple era as "deutero-canonical" or "apocryphal," preserves more material from that period than does the Hebrew Bible. The authenticity of these items as truly Jewish has been confirmed by the Qumran finds.

12 The Book of Jubilees, translated from Ethiopic by O.S. Wintermute, is found in Charlesworth, 2:35–142. Both the introduction and the text are models of scholarship. The text is especially useful because it is marginally annotated with references to the biblical texts the author of Jubilees employed, as well as cognate references to the Dead Sea Scrolls.

13 Norman Cohn sees the Book of Jubilees as "a true apocalypse." (Norman Cohn, *Cosmos, Chaos and the World to Come: The Ancient Roots of Apocalyptic Faith*, New Haven: Yale University Press, 1993, 177). This seems to me to expand beyond usefulness the term "apocalypse." Granted, there are prophetic elements in the work as there are in many parts of scripture. The overwhelming body of the text is a retelling (and a correction, from the author's viewpoint), of errors in the existing "Books of Moses."

14 J.C. Vanderkam, *Textual and Historical Studies in the Book of Jubilees*, vi, cited in Wintermute in Charlesworth, 2:41.

15 Martinez, 468, 471, 472, 488–89, and 512.

16 Compare the fragments in Martinez, 238–45 with the full text in Charlesworth, 2:52–141.

17 See the listing of the contents of each cave in Martinez, 467–513.

18 R.H. Charles, *The Book of Jubilees*, lxxiii–lxxv, quoted by Wintermute in Charlesworth, 2:49.

19 Wintermute in Charlesworth, 2:43.

20 For a succinct summary of the mechanics of these two calendar systems, see John C. Kirby, *Ephesians. Baptism and Pentecost* (Montreal: McGill University Press, 1968), 66–67.

21 For a discussion of the scattered type of demons, and scripture references thereto, see Joanne Kuemmerlin-McLean, "Demons: Old Testament," *ABD* 2:138–40.

22 Despite later efforts to retro-edit the third chapter of Genesis to turn the "serpent" into "Satan," this is unsuccessful. "Satan" in the primary unity, Genesis-Kings, is used as a term of insult to persons on earth, or as a verb indicating the leading of someone astray, or as a reference to a celestial being who, as Elaine Pagels notes, "appears in the Book of Numbers and in Job as one of God's obedient servants." Elaine Pagels, *The Origin of Satan* (New York: Random House, 1995), 39.

23 One assumes that, like any good inventor, the author of the Book of Jubilees here was using something that was conveniently to hand, a concept that must have been developing in Judahist culture since the return from the Babylonian exile. For

differing views of whence this idea arose in post-exilic Judahism, compare Pagels, 35–62 and Cohn, 129–93.

24 Cohn, 182.

25 The items listed to this point are found in the Qumran caves, in fragmentary form, and are published in English translation in Martinez, 218–81.

26 The Letter of Jeremiah was a separate book in the Septuagint, but in the Apocrypha and deutero-canonical versions was a chapter of the Book of Baruch. The book of 3 Maccabees is found in the Slavonic and Greek Bibles, but not in the Roman Catholic or Protestant scriptures.

27 The preceding two items are found in Charlesworth's two-volume collection of the Old Testament Pseudepigrapha, and in the Testament of the Twelve Patriarchs, mentioned earlier.

28 Josephus (*Antiquities*, 113:255–256) reports that the Samaritan temple was modelled on the sanctuary at Jerusalem and that it had existed for 200 years before its destruction. The most widely employed date for its destruction is 113 BCE. Given that it was destroyed by John Hycranus, 104 BCE is the latest possible date.

29 Vermes (1987), 21–22; *Encyclopaedia Judaica*, 12:1404–1405.

30 The path by which the document came to Yigael Yadin's hands will probably never be known in full. Part of the story is told in Yadin's *The Temple Scroll. The Hidden Law of the Dead Sea Sect* (London: Weidenfeld and Nicolson, 1985), 8–55. See also Hershel Shanks, "Intrigue and the Scroll: Behind the Scenes of Israel's Acquisition of the Temple Scroll," *Biblical Archaeology Review*, 13 (1987), 23–27. Parts of the early story, however, still are obscure.

Yadin (1917–1984) was one of the more fascinating figures among the Dead Sea scholars, and was, some hold, an unparalleled intuitive scholar, while others suggest, an intellectual cowboy. Perhaps both. He was the son of Professor Eliezer L. Sukenik (1889–1953) of the Hebrew University, who was one of the first scholars to view the Qumran finds in the late 1940s and who, in the early 1950s, managed the purchase of some new items as they became known. Thus Yigael Yadin had something approaching hereditary access to some of the scrolls. He was Chief of Operations in the 1948–49 Arab-Israeli war, and later became Chief of the General Staff of the Israel Defence Force. This gave him privileged access both to politicians and to archaeological sites otherwise off-limits to most scholars. Yadin entered the Knesset and was Deputy Prime Minister of Israel during the 1970s. He also taught at the Hebrew University, and led several archaeological digs.

31 The reasons for my skepticism about whether or not the Temple Scroll is an Essene production are indicated in Chapter Seven. Indeed, I am skeptical of the Essene-provenance that has been attached to most of the Dead Sea Scrolls. In the specific case of the Temple Scroll, my doubts run considerably deeper, since the Temple Scroll is incompatible with those of the Dead Sea Scrolls that are most likely to actually be of Essene origin.

32 This dating seems to me most convincing. See Michael O. Wise, *A Critical Study of the Temple Scroll from Qumran Cave 11* (Chicago: Oriental Institute of the University of Chicago, 1990), esp. 98–99.

33 Temple Scroll, col. 11:12. The text here employed is found in Martinez, 154–84.

34 See the isometric drawing done by L. Ritmeyer in Yadin, 141–44.

35 It is possible to misread Temple Scroll 29:2–10 as implying a pre-Messianic viewpoint, for it has Yahweh making the future Temple part of a future covenant "until the day of creation," meaning forever, "in accordance with the covenant which I made with Jacob at Bethel." In context, however, this is not Messianic, but a caesura that is an integral part of a set of very practical building instructions, all of which are set out as future imperatives.

36 James A. Sanders, *Canon and Community. A Guide to Canonical Criticism* (Philadelphia: Fortress Press, 1984), 14.

37 The fragments are found in Martinez, 129–35.

38 Flusser (1988), 89. Flusser's statement is in the context of a reference to the Book of Enoch, but the point holds for the Description of the New Jerusalem as well.

39 I am avoiding here as elsewhere giving a prescriptive definition of what an apocalypse is. This is in large part because an apocalypse is potentially both a genre of its own and a form that can operate within another genre. Here the analogous case of satire is helpful. Satire can be a form on its own, occupying an entire text (such as, for example, Jonathan Swift's *A Modest Proposal*, 1729). But it is a form that works very well within larger works (there are wonderful moments of satire in, for example, David Lodge's academic novels, yet the form of the novels is not that of a satire). The same thing holds of apocalypse. If one limits the definition of apocalypse to free-standing productions that are entirely apocalyptic, one misses the use of the form in other books (for example, the Book of Jubilees is not a full apocalypse, but it contains passages that employ the form). On the other hand, if one over-defines "apocalypse" to encompass every text that has apocalyptic motifs, then the category becomes so ill-defined as to be useless.

   Given that one of the few things on which one could obtain the agreement of biblical scholars is that 1 Enoch, Daniel, and the War Scroll are apocalypses, it seems most profitable to use them as ideal-types and to learn from them how the genre works.

   If the reader wishes normative definitions, a sensible discussion is found in the "excursus" in John J. Collins, *Daniel, First Maccabees, Second Maccabees with an Excursus on the Apocalyptic Genre* (Washington, Del: Michael Glazier Inc., 1981), 130–45.

40 Whether or not the segment, the "Book of the Similitudes" (alternately called the "Book of Parables") is so post-Maccabean as to be Christian is a question that vexes scholars. This is discussed in the text, in Chapter Seven, section three, below.

41 My understanding of the circumstances and structure of First Enoch has been dependent in large part on the work of George W.E. Nickelsburg. Especially pre-

scient, and admirably compressed are his "Salvation without and with a Messiah: Developing Beliefs in Writings ascribed to Enoch," in Jacob Neusner, William S. Green, and Ernest S. Frerichs, *Judaisms and Their Messiahs at the Turn of the Christian Era* (Cambridge: Cambridge University Press, 1987), 49–68; and "The Qumran Fragments of *1 Enoch* and other Apocryphal Works: Implications for the Understanding of early Judaism and Christian origins," in Shemaryahu Talmon (ed.), *Jewish Civilization in the Hellenistic-Roman Period* (Philadelphia: Trinity Press International, 1991), 181–95.

42 This scheme was put forward by the Qumran scholar J.T. Milik in the early 1970s. See E. Isaacs' introduction to his translation of First Enoch, in Charlesworth, 1:7.

43 In this context, the relationship of the Book of Enoch and the Book of Jubilees becomes less problematic than suggestive of the richness of the relationship. As O.S. Wintermute observes: "It is generally agreed that Jubilees is dependent on parts of Enoch. At the same time, it seems likely that the later portions of Enoch may be based on Jubilees." Wintermute in Charlesworth, 2:49.

44 Cohn, 165.

45 Ibid.

46 See Chapter Three, Section Four, for more on this point.

47 The problem here is that chapters 1–6, and chapters 8–12 are distinct literary units. Chapter seven is much closer to the second set in content than to the first. However, uniquely among biblical books, Daniel was bilingual. From chapter 2:4b through the end of chapter seven, the text was Aramaic, while the remainder was Hebrew. Thus, in the case of chapter seven, the literary structure and the linguistic medium are at odds. Although most recent scholars see chapter seven as being written subsequent to the Maccabean revolt, I shall in this section exclude it from discussion, as the points being made are not dependent upon anything unique to that chapter.

John J. Collins, in *The Apocalyptic Vision of the Book of Daniel* (Missoula: Scholars Press, for the Harvard Semitic Museum, 1977), xvi-xvii and in his *Daniel...* (1981), 14–19, argues that 1–6 are pre-Maccabean and 7–12 post-, and that in the final version of the bilingual book, chapter one was put into Hebrew so that the whole book would be framed in Hebrew, and that chapter seven was written in Aramaic as a bridging device tying together the pre-Maccabean to the post-Maccabean material. This view at present seems to hold sway, but fashions change quickly in biblical scholarship, and Daniel is the most volatile of "Old Testament" texts.

48 See the listings of cave contents in Martinez, 467–513.

49 The Book of Daniel is the most problematical of "Old Testament" books as far as its form in the various final canons is concerned, and here, as in the case of Chapter Seven of Daniel, I am employing the least-speculative, most-conservative approach to the book, as the basis of my arguments. The problem is that the Septuagint, upon which the Roman Catholic canon is based, included four items

that are not found in the Masoretic text. These are (a) the "Prayer of Azariah" and (b) the "Song of the Three Jews," which are inserted between 3:23 and 3:24, and (c) the "Story of Susanna," which becomes a new chapter, number thirteen, and (d) the story of "Bel and the Dragon" which becomes chapter fourteen. These four items are not found in the Protestant canon of the "Old Testament" but are preserved in the Protestant Apocrypha. The most conservative procedure is to use for the present argument only those parts of the Book of Daniel upon which all three canons agree. That is to say, the version found in the Tanakh, and in the Protestant canon, *sans* the Apocrypha.

50 Belshazzar was not the son of Nebuchadnezzar, nor was he actually ever king of Babylon; Darius the Mede is either fictional or a confusion with Darius I of Persia; Medea was never a world-power in the sense the Book of Daniel uses the term. (See John J. Collins in *ABD*, 2:35–36.) A very compelling discussion of the origin and character of the four-kingdoms schema employed in the Book of Daniel is David Flusser's "The Four Empires in the Fourth Sibyl and in the Book of Daniel," in Flusser (1988), 317–44.

51 Noth, *Israel*, 371.

52 On this, see Collins (1977), xix.

53 This point holds (and all the subsequent inferences about the passage of time), whether the editor-inventor is using the lunar calendar or the solar calendar. The majority of Judahists of his time used a 354-day lunar year, into which an extra month was interpolated every three years. Others (as represented in the Book of Enoch and in the Book of Jubilees) used a solar calendar of 364 days, to which a correction was made at rather longer intervals. In each case, over any significant period of time, the result was that both the lunar year and the solar year had very close to the same length as our present astronomically-determined year.

54 In the next chapter, I will explain why the term "Messiah" in Daniel 29:25 and 26 is an inaccurate translation of the Hebrew. The Jewish Publication Society's translation, employing "Anointed One" is much more accurate.

55 One could argue that from 587 BCE to 538 is a significant period, almost exactly forty-nine years. Therefore, from this one could argue that the "Weeks of Years" usage in Daniel was supposed to be precise, not roughly symbolic. This would involve accepting 587 BCE as the base date for all the subsequent precise calculations. However, in such a reckoning, the three dates that follow in the prophecy (sixty-nine weeks and seventy weeks, counting from Day One, are specified as nodal moments), lead to inconsequential datings, namely 104 BCE and 97 BCE. Further, as made clear in Chapter Three, although in 538 BCE there was a decree given for the re-construction of the Temple, little immediately happened, and it was another half-generation before the Temple can be said to have had an Anointed One in charge of ritual sacrifices. This fact, which would have been clear to any student of Hebrew scriptures in Daniel's time, further invalidates any attempts at forcing precision-dating upon the Book of Daniel's symbolic numerology.

56 Charlesworth, "Introduction" in Charlesworth, 1:xxxiii; Collins (1981), 10–11; Noth, *Israel*, 308.

57 The version of the War Scroll I have used is found in Martinez, 95–115.

58 Golb, 378.

NOTES TO CHAPTER SEVEN

1 For an admirable survey of the Tanakh's usage of Moshiah, see Franz Hesse, "Chrio etc.," in Geoffrey W. Bromley (ed. and trans.), *Theological Dictionary of the New Testament*, 9 (1974), 497–509.

2 See the *Oxford English Dictionary*.

3 Richard A. Horsley, in "Popular Prophetic Movements at the Time of Jesus. Their Principal Features and Social Origins," *Journal for the Study of the New Testament*, 26 (Feb. 1986), 3–27, and in "Messianic Movements in Judaism," in *ABD* 4:791–97 argues that the term "Messianic," insofar as it is attached to a social movement, should refer only to those headed by a popularly-declared king, or "Messiah." This seems to me to run sharply counter to the usage of the term Moshiah in the Tanakh where it also refers to priests and prophets.

4 William Scott Green, "Messiah in Judaism: Rethinking the Question," in Neusner, Green, and Frerichs (eds.), *Judaism and Their Messiahs at the Turn of the Christian Era* (Cambridge: Cambridge University Press, 1987), 6. The article (1–13) is a major *tour de force*.

5 I am here following James H. Charlesworth, "Introduction," James H. Charlesworth, *The Old Testament Pseudepigrapha* (New York: Doubleday, 1985), 2:xxxii-xxxiii.

   In addition to the items here mentioned in the period between the Maccabean revolt and the destruction of the Temple, one should add the pre-Maccabean text, the Wisdom of Ben Sira, which, in 45:15, 46:13, and 48:8, speaks of anointing. In the first case it deals with Moses anointing Aaron, in the second of the anointing by the prophet Samuel of various princes, and in the third, the prophet Elijah is said to anoint prophets and kings. None of these is a Messianic reference.

6 The standard abbreviation for this text – CD – stems from its having been found in Cairo, and to the document's making reference to Damascus.

7 "Messianic Apocalypse," (4Q521) in Florentino Garcia Martinez (ed.), *The Dead Sea Scrolls Translated* (Leiden: E.J. Brill, 1994), 394. Unless otherwise noted, all subsequent Qumran quotations are from this edition.

8 A clear and brief statement of this interpretation is found in James C. Vanderkam, *The Dead Sea Scrolls Today* (Grand Rapids: William B. Eerdmans, 1994), 117–18.

9 Marinus de Jonge provides two further potential (albeit ambiguous) references to a Messiah in the Dead Sea fragments. ("Messiah," *ABD*, 4:783). For his earlier thinking on this matter, see his article, in Bromley, 9:517–21.

10 Josephus, *Antiquities* 20:97–99. This probably is the same Theudas who is mentioned as a boastful prophet in Acts 5:36. There it is reported that 400 of his followers were killed. The only difficulty is that Josephus's report is set in the mid-40s CE and in Acts in the first decade of the Common Era.

11 Josephus, *Jewish War* 2:258–60.

12 Josephus, *Antiquities* 20:169–72; *Jewish War* 2:261–63. In Acts 21:38, The Egyptian is reported to have led 4,000 men into the wilderness. It is this prophet with whom the Apostle Paul was confused by a Roman "chief captain" in Jerusalem (Acts 21:37–38).

13 Josephus, *Antiquities* 20:188.

14 Ibid., 17:149–67.

15 Josephus, *Antiquities* 17:213–18; *Jewish War* 2:2–13. The reader will by now be aware that Josephus used numbers not in their denotative sense, but as adjectives. "Three thousand" young men killed really should be interpreted as "many," or "a lot of young men."

16 Josephus, *Antiquities* 17:269–98; *Jewish War* 2:55–79. All these self-crowned kings help one to understand that "I.N.R.I.," reportedly placed on the cross of Yeshua of Nazareth, fit the situation. It was Roman barracks humour meaning, roughly, "Another tin-pot king of the Jews."

17 The one possible exception is the "Aramaic Apocalypse" (4Q246) which talks of one who "will be called son of God, and they will call him son of the Most High" (col. 2:1, found in Martinez, 138). Some scholars believe that the lost fragments of the text contain the designation "Messiah." (Norman Golb, *Who Wrote the Dead Sea Scrolls? The Search for the Secret of Qumran*, London: Michael O'Mara Books, 1995, 379). This would mean that the equation of Son of God and of Messiah occurred, in at least one Judahist text, before the Christian scriptures merged the concepts. However, one must point out that until there is actual evidence for this imaginative interpolation into the Qumran fragment, one would do well to stay aloof: it would not take great imagination to claim that Messiah was missing from most of the Qumran fragments and could plausibly be added. Strange, though, that the references biblical scholars most wish to find are those that are least apt to be found, and thus must be interpolated.

18 In this discussion I am led by the excellent article, "Kingdom of God, Kingdom of Heaven," by Dennis C. Duling, *ABD*, 4:49–57.

19 Martinez (ed.), 138. Its numbering in the Qumran sequence is 4Q246. This is the same fragment into which some scholars interpolate the idea of Messiah. See note 17 above.

20 The dating is summarized in James H. Charlesworth, "The Concept of the Messiah in the Pseudepigrapha," in *Aufstieg und Niedergang der Romischen Welt* (1979), II Principat 19.1, 206–207, and in E. Isaac's introduction to his translation of 1 Enoch, in Charlesworth (ed.), 1:6–7.

21 Michael Owen Wise, *A Critical Study of the Temple Scroll from Qumran Cave 11* (Chicago: Oriental Institute of the University of Chicago, 1990), 31, following Zeitlin.

22 Philo, *The Contemplative Life*, with an introduction by F.H. Colson (Loeb Library), *passim*; Baruch M. Bokser, "Philo's Description of Jewish Practices," in *Colloquy in Hellenistic and Modern Culture* (Berkeley, California: The Center for Hermeneutical Studies), 30 (1977), 1–11. There is a pseudepigraphic text of the first century BCE or first century CE that is sometimes attributed to the Therapeutae: The Testament of Job. See introduction and translation by R.P. Spittler in Charlesworth, 1:829–68.

23 Josephus, *Antiquities* 18:116–19.

24 Matthew 3:1–17; 4:12; 11:1–19; Mark 1:1–11; 6:14–29; 11:30–33; Luke 1:5–25; 9:7–9; John 1:6–8; 5:33–36; 10:40–42; Acts 18:26.

25 Josephus, *Antiquities* 18:63–64, 20:200. The former reference is usually interpreted as a later Christian interpolation. The Slavonic versions of the *Jewish War* have fairly large Christian incorporations concerning Jesus. See the third volume of the Loeb edition of the *War*, 648–52, 655, 657–58.

26 Josephus, *Jewish War* 6:300–69.

27 Richard A. Horsley and John S. Hanson, *Bandits, Prophets, and Messiahs. Popular Movements in the Time of Jesus* (Minneapolis: Winston Press, 1985).

28 See Eric J. Hobsbawm, *Primitive Rebels* (New York: Norton, 1965).

29 Horsley and Hanson, 260–61.

30 Josephus, *Antiquities* 18:23–24.

31 Compare Martin Noth, *The History of Israel* (New York: Harper and Row, revised English edition, 1958), 432–35; Horsley and Hanson, 190–243; and the resumé of Cecil Roth and G.R. Driver in Golb, 134.

32 Josephus, *Life*, 10–12. The reference is slightly suspect as Josephus makes the unlikely claim that he went through the rigorous training of all the major religious parties – Sadducee, Pharisee, and Essene – before choosing to become a Pharisee.

33 For the possible reasons behind this anti-Sadducean view, see Gunther Baumbach, "The Sadducees in Josephus," in Luis H. Feldman and Gohei Hata (eds.), *Josephus, the Bible and History* (Detroit: Wayne State University Press, 1989), 173–95.

34 Josephus, *Antiquities* 13:171–73; 13:297; 18:11; 18:16–17; *Jewish War* 2:119; 2:164–66.

35 Matthew 3:7, 16:1, 16:6, 16:11–12, 22:23; Mark 12:18; Luke 20–27; Acts 4:1, 23:6–8. Matthew 22:23, and Mark 12:18, Luke 20:27 and Acts 23:8 state that the Sadducees say that there is no resurrection.

36 See Mishnah, Makkoth 1:6, Parah 3:7, and Yadayim, 4:6–7. The issues there are Sadducean legal views on perjury, on whether sacrificial cow-burning renders priests unclean, their views on certain other points of ritual cleanliness, and on

whether water that runs from a cemetery is ritually clean or unclean. The halachic interest of these items is obvious, but the historical context is totally lacking and one cannot tell if these were important matters of belief, or merely interesting arguments that were preserved for their legal implications.

37 Noth, *Israel*, 374n2.

38 Josephus, *Antiquities* 13:298 and 20:199.

39 My debt to the several works of Jacob Neusner is great. In this case, especially to his *The Rabbinic Tradition about the Pharisees before 70* (Leiden: Brill, 1971), 3 vols; and *From Politics to Piety: The Emergence of Pharisaic Judaism* (Englewood Cliffs: Prentice-Hall, 1973). For a valuable summary of the debate on the Pharisees, see D. Goodblatt, "The Place of the Pharisees in First Century Judaism: The State of the Debate," *Journal for the Study of Judaism*, 20 (June 1989), 12–30.

40 Josephus, *Antiquities* 13:171–72; 13:288–98; 13:401; 13:405–10; 15:3; 15:370; 17:41; 17:44–46; 18:12–17; *Jewish War* 1:110–14; 1:571; 2:119; 2:162–64; *Life*, 10–12, 21, 191.

41 Noth, *Israel*, 374n1.

42 Lawrence H. Schiffman, "Qumran and Rabbinic Halachah," in Talmon, 139; David E. Aune, "Orthodoxy in First Century Judaism?" *Journal for the Study of Judaism*, 7 (June 1976), 1–10.

43 Schiffman in Talmon, 142–43.

44 Noth, *Israel*, 399.

45 The reader will notice that I am not here placing any weight on two potential additional sources concerning the Pharisees: the Dead Sea Scrolls and the Talmuds. In the former case, the Pharisees are not directly mentioned, and none of the ingenious and strenuous attempts to find coded reference to them in the Qumran library is sufficiently compelling to be considered of probative value. As for the Talmuds, they are so late (fourth to sixth centuries, CE), and so deeply influenced by contextual and ideological problems of the centuries after 70 CE (involving the structure of the Roman Empire, and the rise of Christianity), that they have little historical usage. (This is not to disparage them: the Talmuds, however, are not, in any case, primarily historical documents, but road maps to a belief-system rooted in Halachah.)

46 Neusner (1971), 3:304.

47 Josephus, *Antiquities* 13:372–74; *Jewish War* 1:88–89. See Schurer (Vermes and Millar ed.), 222–24.

48 Compare Neusner (1971), 3:304–36, and Daniel R. Schwartz, "Josephus and Nicolaus on the Pharisees," *Journal for the Study of Judaism*, 14 (Dec. 1983), 156–71.

49 Josephus, *Jewish War* 1:28; 2:119–61; 2:567; 3:11; 5:145; *Antiquities* 13:171; 13:298; 13:311; 15:372–78; 17:34; 18:11–22; *Life*, 10–11.

   Philo, *Every Good Man is Free*, 75; *The Contemplative Life*, 1; *Hypothetica*, 2:1–18.

Pliny the Elder, *Natural History*, Book 5:73, translated H. Rackham (Cambridge: Harvard University Press, 1951). This is the Loeb edition.

50 Philo, while stating that the Essenes were unmarried, mentions the possibility of their having children. Cf. *Hypothetica*, 2:13, and 2:14. Josephus, *Jewish War* 2:120 says that they adopted other people's children, so this would harmonize their being both celibate and having children.

51 Geza Vermes, *Jesus and the World of Judaism* (Philadelphia: Fortress Press, 1984), 127.

52 Edmund Wilson, *The Scrolls from the Dead Sea* (New York: Oxford University Press, 1955) and *The Dead Sea Scrolls* (New York: Oxford University Press, 1969).

53 As phrased in the text, this suggestion of the necessity of testing the basic Essene hypothesis may seem a bit vague. Let me be more graphic. This is not a task that requires immense technical skills, merely some experience in the social sciences and an interest in belief-systems and in intertextuality. Here is a simple exercise. Take the most recent collection of the Qumran manuscripts in English (the 1994 Martinez edition). Make photocopies of the volume. Then separate each fragment from the other. Add to this pile of primary material the full copies of items from other sources (such as the Book of Jubilees and the Book of Enoch) that are found only in tattered form at Qumran, but which are in full copies elsewhere. Then rent a large room, preferably one the size of a basketball court. Now, try to arrange the pieces of paper in any order whereby the beliefs described in these documents can be held even by the most generous assumptions to be compatible with each other. Forget what the Essenes were supposed to be like as reported in ancient sources. Any compatible order will do.

It won't work. And short of declaring the Essenes to have been an omnibus sect, a cadre of multi-personality enthusiasts, whose portmanteau beliefs included every single aspect of late Second Temple Judahism, the project fails.

54 This argument is made without recourse to the work of the most productive critic of the Qumran establishment, Norman Golb, who holds the Rosenberger Professorship of Jewish History and Civilization at the University of Chicago. With an heroic mixture of curmudgeonly mien and virtuoso technical skills, he has been the leader of the loyal-opposition to the Qumran establishment for two decades. Whether or not his own interpretations are correct, his basic negative argument is compelling: that the now-traditional interpretation of the Dead Sea Scrolls as being Essene, most of which originated in Khirbet Qumran, lacks the elementary standards of proof required in other fields of historical scholarship. He goes back to basics and notes (1) that not a single autograph text (as distinct from scribal copies) has been found in the Qumran caves, and almost none of the legal documents, personal letters or "laundry lists" such as one would expect if Qumran was the centre of a working religious community; (2) that within the Khirbet Qumran complex, nothing has been found by archaeologists that clearly

indicates that it ever was the site of a religious community. Granted, there are numerous ambiguous artifacts, but they could as easily have come from a military post as from a monastic site of a pacifist community. The interpretation of such items, Golb argues, is largely a projective test; (3) that there are roughly 500 different scribal handwritings identifiable among the Qumran manuscripts. This is far too many scribes to have been housed and supported, even over time, at Khirbet Qumran. It far exceeds the known burial sites. And, most important, it is way out of scale for any viable monastic community: the most closely comparable situation, the island of Elephantine, in upper Egypt, held a Judahist colony roughly fifty times the size of Khirbet Qumran, but for its needs, roughly twelve scribes were sufficient. Golb's conclusion is that the Qumran caves were hiding places for collections of books taken from Jerusalem (from either private collections or from religious sites, it matters not) in 68 CE and thereafter, when the Roman-Jewish war endangered them. That explains the lack of day-to-day monastic detritus in the collections, and also the vastly heterogeneous nature of the material in the caves. Some of the material well might be Essene (they were, after all, an important religious group and their texts were well worth collecting), but the need to squeeze all the texts into a single institutional rubric disappears.

Now, whether or not one accepts Golb's own hypothesis about Khirbet Qumran's having been a military post is not here germane. It is an appendage to his main argument, and nothing crucial depends upon it. Golb's main point, that the vast trove of manuscripts in the Qumran caves could not have been produced at Khirbet Qumran, is convincing. So too is the inference that follows from it: that the Qumran finds were a broadly-based library and not the product, therefore, of a single sect. And from that it follows, ineluctably, that to define the Qumran Scrolls as being merely Essene in origin is a solecism.

I am here greatly simplifying some complicated arguments. Golb's entire book (1995), and his technical papers, are well worth direct examination. As a piece of clarification, one should emphasize that he does not claim that the scrolls came from the Temple, just that they probably came from Jerusalem, which, considering that it was the focal point of Judaism, is hardly an outré suggestion.

55 Emanuel Tov, *Textual Criticism of the Hebrew Bible* (Minneapolis: Fortress Press, 1992), 191.

56 Geza Vermes, "The War Over the Scrolls," *New York Review of Books* (11 August 1991), 12.

57 Space precludes my dealing in detail with the reasons for assigning, however tentatively, these documents to the Essenes. Briefly each satisfies the following criteria: (a) it fits with the external evidence provided by Josephus, Philo, and Pliny the Elder; (b) it does not contain beliefs or liturgical characteristics that these same external sources ascribe to other religious groups of the same period; and (c) the

texts are compatible with each other, in belief, emotional timbre, and in liturgical implications.

58 The English translation of the available fragments is found in Martinez, 3–32.

59 See note 6 above.

60 The fragments from the Cairo Genizah as well as the Qumran fragments are found in Martinez, 33–73.

61 Habakkuk Pesher, coll. 2:1 (Martinez, 198) and coll. 11:4 (Martinez, 201).

62 Martinez, 195–97.

63 See ibid., 185–207.

64 This scholarly achievement is described modestly in Geza Vermes, *Jesus and the World of Judaism* (Philadelphia: Fortress Press), 133–35.

65 See, for example, the various views summarized in Michael A. Knibb, "The Teacher of Righteousness – A Messianic Title?" in Philip R. Davies and Richard T. White (eds.), *A Tribute to Geza Vermes. Essays on Jewish and Christian Literature and History* (Sheffield: JSOT, 1990), 52–65.

66 The reader will notice that I have not included as having a high probability of being Essene (in the present state of the evidence), some major items that the Qumran establishment takes as such. One of these is the Temple Scroll. Its emphasis upon the details of ritual sacrifice in the Temple is in active dissonance with what I believe to be the core Essene texts, which describe religious regulations for a group that has withdrawn from the Temple.

As for the War Scroll, it is an ice-cold architectonic apocalypse, quite unlike in both emotional tone and perspective anything found in the central Essene texts. (That the term "Kittim" is used frequently in it, as is "Belial," does not make it Essene, for these were terms common throughout the range of Judahist apocalyptic writing.)

If the Temple Scroll and the War Scroll actively declare themselves to be non-Essene, the case for a third text that is often denominated as being Essene – the so-called "Halachic Letter" is at best ruled not-proved. This set of fragments – sometimes called "Some of the Precepts of the Law," and sometimes "Acts of Torah" – exists as a composite text put together from the fragments of six different manuscripts. (Both the composite and the fragments are in Martinez, 77–94.) They comprise a set of rules for a group that had its mind firmly centred upon Jerusalem. It is very "Judahist" in the narrow sense of the term: it focuses upon King David's line, and upon the Jerusalem Temple. It is also apocalyptic, being concerned with the end of time. Whatever else this book may be – and Lawrence Schiffman has gone so far as to suggest that it is of Sadducean origin – I do not see how it can be described as compatible with the four basic texts that I have identified as having a strong probability of Essene origin. (See Lawrence H. Schiffman, "Origin and Early History of the Qumran Sect," *Biblical Archaeologist*, 58, March 1995, 37–48.) This seems a bit of a reach, as there are no other known Sadducean texts with which to show identity.

NOTES TO CHAPTER EIGHT

1 Fergus Millar, *The Roman Near East, 31 BC-AD 337* Cambridge: Harvard University Press, 1993), 366.

2 Ibid., 70.

3 Any discussion of the war of course depends upon Josephus's *Jewish War* and on related material in the *Antiquities* and the *Life*. I have also found very useful the Geza Vermes and Fergus Millar edition of Emil Schurer's *The History of the Jewish People in the Age of Jesus Christ (175 BC-AD 135)* (Edinburgh: T. and T. Clark, 1973), 1:484–513 and Martin Noth, *The History of Israel* (New York: Harper and Row, revised English ed., 1960), 435–45.

4 Schurer (Vermes and Millar ed.), 1:529–57.

5 As in previous chapters, I shall not burden the discussion with portmanteau footnotes. The scholarly literature on early Christianity produced even within the past half-century is prodigious. Only works that I have found helpful (either by way of useful example or, in a few cases, as models to be avoided), are cited. The most useful bibliography relating to the historical aspects of early Christianity that I have encountered is found in the footnotes of John P. Meier, *A Marginal Jew. Rethinking the Historical Jesus*, 1, *The Roots of the Problem and the Person* and 2, *Mentor, Message, and Miracles* (New York: Doubleday, 1991 and 1994). A third volume is in process.

6 The best-known and most accessible discussion of the central Gnostic documents is Elaine Pagels, *The Gnostic Gospels* (New York: Random House, 1979).

7 In saying "single canon" I am here excluding the minor continuing variant represented by the Peshitta of the Syriac churches, which leaves out Revelation, Jude, Second Peter, and the Second and Third Epistles of John.

8 William R. Farmer, "Study of the Development of the New Testament Canon," in William R. Farmer and Denis M. Farkasfalvy, *The Formation of the New Testament Canon. An Ecumenical Approach* (New York: Paulist Press, 1983), 9.

9 Hans von Campenhausen, *The Formation of the Christian Bible* (Philadelphia: Fortress Press, 1972; original German ed., 1968), 327n1.

10 Bruce M. Metzger, *The Canon of the New Testament. Its Origin, Development, and Significance* (Oxford: Clarendon Press, 1987), 6, 143–48.

11 John Knox, *Marcion and the New Testament. An Essay in the Early History of the Canon* (Chicago: University of Chicago Press, 1942); Metzger, 99; Robert M. Grant, "Marcion and the Critical Methods," in Peter Richardson and John C. Hurd, *From Jesus to Paul. Studies in Honour of Francis Wright Beare* (Waterloo: Wilfrid Laurier University Press, 1984), 207–15.

12 Knox, 32n19, citing A. von Harnack.

13 Because the "New Testament" that Irenaeus employs has to be defined inferentially (his direct writings on the issue are lost), there is some disagreement over its exact dimensions. Compare Metzger, 153–57 and Campenhausen, 182–90.

14 J.M. Robinson (ed.), *The Nag Hammadi Library* (New York: Harper and Row, 1977); Metzger, 84–91. The Gospel of Thomas is discussed in Appendix D.

15 Metzger, 99–106.

16 Campenhausen, 223–326; Farmer, 9–14; Harry Y. Gamble, *The New Testament Canon. Its Making and Meaning* (Philadelphia: Fortress Press, 1985), 17–22; Robert M. Grant, *The Formation of the New Testament* (New York: Harper and Row, 1965), 176–87; Metzger, 309–15.

17 The influence here of Brevard S. Childs is obvious. For a useful introduction to his thought, see *The New Testament as Canon: An Introduction* (London: SCM Press, 1984). Where one parts company with Childs is in his emphasis upon theological determinants of the canon at the expense of historical and literary determinants.

18 I am not putting any weight on one of the most elegant explanations of why the Christian canon developed: namely that the widespread usage of the codex – the book made up of stacked leaves – began to be widely available in the early Common Era. Therefore, it is suggested that the Christians inevitably developed a canon, for a codex implies both a fixed order of constituent units and a conscious decision as to what to include and what to exclude within a single binding. This suggestion possesses elegance, because, if it were applicable, it would explain in one grand simplicity how a technological process caused a cascade of spiritual developments.

   Unfortunately, the explanation has no robustness whatsoever in relation to the religious culture from which Christianity emerged. This is clearly indicated by the counter-case: during the same era that the Christian scriptures were evolving their canonical configuration, the Tanakh was assuming its final canonical form. The Tanakh was preserved in scrolls. Manifestly, therefore, the technical innovation represented by the codex was a causal irrelevance.

19 A thoughtful and accessible discussion of feminist biblical scholarship and theology is Cullen Murphy, "Women and the Bible," *Atlantic Monthly*, 272 (Aug. 1993), 39–64.

20 Two exceptions to this generalization are discussed in Chapter Nine, sections 2 and 3.

21 "Contradictions" within the "New Testament's" historical books (Matthew-Acts) are of three sorts. The first of these consists of historical details that cannot be meshed with each other. For example, one can make a list of at least two dozen quite significant differences in the various versions of the capture, trial, death, and resurrection of Jesus Christ. These are not entirely picky matters; some involve major details of the story. And a considerably longer list can be drawn up concerning dissonances in the story of the earlier life of Jesus and of the early days of the Christian church. Secondly, one can contrast the swatches of historical narrative provided in the same version of early church history with the silence on the same subjects that occurs in other versions. Again, these are not entirely minor matters.

Why, for example, if the virgin birth of Jesus was part of his life story, or at least part of the faith of the early church, is it not included in the Gospels of Mark and of John? And, thirdly, there is the matter of attitude. The Gospel of John is not at all comfortable with the interpretation of Jesus' life found in Mark, Matthew, and Luke, or in the story of the early church in the Acts of the Apostles. Further, John's interpretation of Jesus' life, containing as it does proto-Gnostic overtones, gives an entirely different aura to Jesus' earthly existence than do the Synoptic Gospels.

For a thoughtful consideration of some of the "doublings" in the Christian scriptures, see the eighth annual JSOT lecture, given in 1991 by J. Enoch Powell, "The Genesis of the Gospel," *Journal for the Study of the New Testament*, 42 (June 1991), 4–16. The point about such doublings (or contradictions) is, as Powell makes clear, that at a certain level of close reading of the text, they help to reveal a good deal about the shades of meaning and about the situation in which the text was created, and about the culture in which it was read. However, to use the doublings as a primary point of entry into a consideration of the "New Testament" is equivalent to studying the architecture of Chartres cathedral by focusing primarily upon what appear to be cracks in the vestry plaster.

22 The great pity is that the Christian authorities did not accept the Jewish canon of the Hebrew scriptures. Not only would this have had the aesthetic virtue of presenting two nearly congruent structures, but, as I indicated in Chapter Two, it would have reduced some of the misreadings of the Hebrew scriptures that the Christian arrangement frequently produces.

23 Norman Cohn, *Cosmos, Chaos, and the World to Come. The Ancient Roots of Apocalyptic Faith* (New Haven: Yale University Press, 1993), 212.

24 A.N. Wilson, *Jesus* (London: Sinclair-Stevenson, 1992), 64.

25 David Flusser, *Jesus* (New York: Herder and Herder, 1969; orig. German ed., 1968), 72.

26 Joseph Klausner, *From Jesus to Paul* (New York: Macmillan, 1943), 482.

27 My reason for emphasizing especially strongly at this point that the most reasonable provenance for these ideas is Second Temple Judahism is that one must guard against what can best be called "Gnostic-chic." Although the origin of Gnosticism is almost entirely speculative, there is a sector of "New Testament" scholars who see Gnostic influences behind many Christian motifs. The Gospel of John is a particularly rich hunting ground, and Gnosticism is presented quite authoritatively as being an influence on John. This is certainly possible, but from an evidentiary point of view, it is rather unusual to state that an undefined phenomenon (first century Gnosticism) is the causal agent in producing a defined phenomenon (the Gospel of John). This procedure, questionable at best, becomes even less compelling when one realizes that there is a well-defined phenomenon (the widespread use of light-dark imagery in Second Temple texts) that quite adequately makes available the light-dark motif that the author of John chose to employ.

Gnostic-chic, as a modern social phenomenon, deserves attention. It provides a fascinating historical question: why has a set of ideas found mostly in second- and third-century texts, become so popular in the late twentieth century? When historians of present-day religion encounter the issue, I think they will find that the most efficient entry point is Elaine Pagels, *The Gnostic Gospels* (New York: Random House, 1979). Pagels, now the Harrington Spear Paine Professor of Religion at Princeton University, is both one of the most powerful and publicly-known "New Testament" scholars (full profiles have been published in *The New Yorker*, and in *The New York Times*). An extremely accomplished scholar, she produced a good deal of highly admired scholarly work on the Nag Hammadi finds, before turning to a general audience. *The Gnostic Gospels* was an extremely successful volume, winning both the National Book Award and the National Book Critics Circle Award. This success was deserved, for the volume was beautifully crafted and hit a responsive chord with 1970s Americans. The closest historical comparison to it is Margaret Mead's *Coming of Age in Samoa* (1928), which combined front-edge scholarship with immense popular appeal. Pagels, like Mead, told the public what, apparently, they wanted to hear. Mead's work told people of the Jazz Age that there was a natural world of sensation somewhere out there in the Pacific, and that it was an Eden, where sex was easy, guilt was non-existent, and everyone cooperated with everyone else. Pagels produced a product as appealing to the late 'seventies as Mead's was to the late 1920s. The Gnostic texts were presented as a virtual New Age alternative to the Christian scriptures. They include a God who is said to embody both the female and male principles; Jesus speaks in terms of enlightenment, not of sin and repentance; knowledge of self is presented as the gateway to knowledge of God; the emergent institutional hierarchy of the early church is rejected and a democracy of believers – including women – is outlined. The closest analogy to Gnosticism that Pagels can find is Buddhism which, whatever else it may be, certainly is not tainted with the "vices" that mainline Christianity is said to have inherited from the Yahweh-faith.

That this particular product sold so well to Americans is an important piece of social history, one that tells a great deal about the cultural yearnings of the upper-middle class in that country in the 1970s and '80s. A quite separate question is how well this New Age vision will wear as a scholarly enterprise. I suspect it will take quite a long time before it is seriously examined. Margaret Mead's work was not replicated, nor her original data re-examined until the 1980s, when it was found to be the basis of a first-rate novel, but devoid of scholarly integrity (see Derek Freeman, *Margaret Mead and Samoa. The Making and Unmaking of an Anthropological Myth* (Cambridge: Harvard University Press, 1983). Pagels's work, I think, is apt to be found much stronger in scholarly terms, if equally novelistic in its projective presentation of her generation's yearnings.

28 This observation is A.N. Wilson's (110).

29 Elaine Pagels, *The Origin of Satan* (New York: Random House, 1995), 12.

30 Cohn, 216.

31 Mark and Luke use the term "Kingdom of God" while Matthew for the most part employs "Kingdom of Heaven." However, Matthew employs both terms and in contexts that make clear that they are the same term. Hence, for the sake of clarity we will here use "Kingdom of God." John contains few uses of the Kingdom concept.

32 E.P. Sanders, *The Historical Figure of Jesus* (Harmondsworth: Penguin Books, 1993), 171–75.

33 Whether that common source was a fourth author-editor, of whom we have no direct knowledge, or whether two of the Synoptics depend upon the other is not important at this point. This tiny question, of course, is a simulacrum of the major problem that "New Testament" scholars wrestle with: what is the relationship of the Synoptic Gospels to each other, and to other sources that are not known directly to us?

34 In his recent *Paul. The Mind of the Apostle* (London: W.W. Norton, 1997), A.N. Wilson puts forward as accepted fact that the Revelation of St. John was written before 70 CE (11–12). This unusual viewpoint would not require comment except that Wilson is usually a very perceptive reader of religious texts and his book on Paul made it well up the English best-seller lists and is apt to be taken as accurate by readers who are not used to reading biblical scholarship. Were Wilson's assertion tenable it would force a major re-orientation of biblical scholarship, since it would make Revelation the first of the post-Pauline books of the "New Testament" to have been written. However, his early dating is possible only by his skipping the latter portions of the text. Wilson holds that no one who knew of the destruction of Jerusalem and of the Temple could have written in chapter eleven as if only a portion of the city would be destroyed. This misses the point that this chapter is one of process, and it leads ineluctably towards the twenty-first chapter, wherein an entire new Jerusalem and new Temple are introduced, manifestly to fill the void left by the destruction of the physical originals, as occurred in 70 CE.

35 The question of when the eucharist developed as a daily repetition of the sacrifice of Christ, believed to involve in Roman Catholic tradition his "real presence" as body and blood, is historically unresolved. The one certainty is that this repetitive sacrifice is not found in the Christian scriptures; but then, given the modes of biblical and para-biblical invention, there is no reason why it needed to be found there in order for it to be later accepted as part of the continuing re-invention of the Covenant.

NOTES TO CHAPTER NINE

1 *Catechism of the Catholic Church* (New York: Doubleday, English language edition, 1995), 42.

2 The medieval chapter divisions of the last of the Servant Songs are a bit awry. Scholars almost universally use "Isaiah 53" to refer to the song that runs from Isaiah 52:13 to 53:12, inclusive.

3 This is not a case of special pleading through translation on the part of Christians. The Tanakh of the Jewish Publication Society (1985) renders the verse in the singular. Further, in other places in Second Isaiah, the KJB, for example, is willing to mix plurals and singulars, if that is what the Hebrew text clearly means. Thus, "Ye are my witnesses, saith the Lord, and my servant whom I have chosen" (Is. 43:10).

The only place where the KJB (and some other Christian translations, such as the New International Version) overstep propriety is Isaiah 53:5, where it says, concerning the Servant's suffering, in Hebrew, "with his stripes *were* we healed" (a completed act). In the KJB and NIV it is "we *are* healed," a continuous and continuing act, and thus a very different meaning.

4 Joel Carmichael, *The Death of Jesus* (New York: MacMillan, 1962), 256.

5 Gore Vidal, *Live from Golgotha* (Harmondsworth: Penguin Books ed., 1993, orig. ed., 1991), 123.

6 Ibid., 123–24.

7 Geza Vermes, *The Religion of Jesus the Jew* (London: SCM, 1993), 211n1.

8 1 Cor. 15:4 reads in full: "And that he was buried, and that he rose again the third day according to the scriptures." One would like to know to what scriptural text Paul was referring. In the Hebrew scriptures and the para-biblical writings that we at present possess, there is no reference to a Messiah being killed and being resurrected (in any sense) three days later.

It might be possible to read Paul's verse as referring to the story of Jonah who was swallowed by a great piscine, "And Jonah was in the belly of the fish three days and nights" (Jonah 1:17). This seems to me to be very unpromising indeed: since Jonah was swallowed up for his disobedience, whereas Jesus entered the grave in accordance with his Father's will. And, the indecorous and humiliating end of the adventure of Jonah – the fish vomits him out – is not something a shrewd writer such as Paul would compare with Jesus' translation to perpetual spiritual glory.

9 The reader should be made aware that in my focusing so tightly on Paul's actual writing, I am going against the dominant strain in the recent secondary literature. This literature argues in essence that since "Jews" at the beginning of the Common Era believed in the resurrection as a physical act, then so did Paul, as a subset of this "Jewish" belief. Although much of this literature is impressively recondite, it misses the fact that there was *not* a "Jewish" conception of the resurrection at the time, but instead that several views existed (as I have shown in earlier discussions of the later Second Temple primary texts). These ranged from complete denial of the idea of resurrection to an endorsement of resurrection as a group concept (the revivification of Israel) to a belief in the physical resurrection of

individuals, to a belief in a resurrection that was totally cosmic in nature. To force Paul, a most independent religious thinker, into one of these modes – and, moreover, to do so after his conversion – is arbitrary and of no scholarly value. My own view remains: read the primary text; respect what Paul himself writes. Never (not even in Rom. 10:8, where he says that God raised Jesus from the dead) does he endorse the physical resurrection of Jesus. For a lucid summary of recent scholarship, see Caroline Walker Bynum, *The Resurrection of the Body in Western Christianity, 200–1336* (New York: Columbia University Press, 1995).

10 The ending of the Gospel of Mark is a problem. The present conclusion – 16:9–20 – is not found in the oldest full copies of the Gospels, Codex Sinaiticus and Codex Vaticanus. Moreover, on stylistic grounds many scholars have come to conclude that the material from verse 9 onwards is an addition that was appended considerably after the rest of the book was completed. If so, Mark would end with the three women, who having discovered the empty tomb flee, "for they trembled and were amazed: neither said they any thing to any man; for they were afraid." From the viewpoint of historical narrative-making that certainly is a much more satisfactory place to stop: the present ending (verses 9–20) kills what, up to that point, had been a tight piece of historical prose.

11 These must be distinguished from the Gospel reports that Jesus shared the view (generally thought to be affirmed by the Pharisees and opposed by the Sadducees in late Second Temple Judahism) that there would be a general resurrection of the righteous dead. Such a belief on Jesus' part is reported in Matt. 22:23–34, Luke 14:14, and John 5:28–29.

12 Isaac: Gen. 15:4; 17:15–19. Jacob: Genesis 25:21–26. Samuel: 1 Sam. 1:1–20.

13 Geza Vermes, *Jesus the Jew. A Historian's Reading of the Gospels* (London: Fontana/Collins, 1976, origin ed., 1973), 222.

14 Ulrich Luz, *The Theology of the Gospel of Matthew*, translated by J. Bradford Robinson (Cambridge: Cambridge University Press, 1995, orig. German ed., 1993), 30.

15 David Flusser, "Mary and Israel," in *Mary. Images of the Mother of Jesus in Jewish and Christian Perspective* [no editor ascribed] (Philadelphia: Fortress Press, 1986), 9.

16 The one significant exception to this is the New International Version (1973–87), a Protestant evangelical production. Recent Christian versions that accurately translate the Hebrew text include the New English Bible, the New Revised Standard Version, the Good News Bible, and the Revised English Bible.

17 I am leaving aside as irrelevant to the present discussion, whether or not the Septuagint's mistranslation of *ALMH* as *parthenos* was by intention or inadvertence. Matthew's text is his own invention, not dependent upon the Septuagint.

I am also leaving aside the fact that the context of the original young-girl reference (Isaiah 7:14) would be a difficult fit with its usage by Matthew, *even if* the original reference was to a future virgin birth of "Immanuel." Isaiah's prophecy was made to King Ahaz of Judah (743–727 BCE) in a very tight situation: Jerusalem was surrounded by Judah's enemies, the northern tribes (that is, by Israel) and their allies, the Syrians. This siege was to be broken after a young girl had a child named Immanuel. It is a time-and-place-specific prophecy. That leaves the author-editor of Matthew with a Hobson's choice. He can either allegorize the story, but then the prophecy (even if the word "virgin" were found in the original) would not be literally applicable to any specific person; or the original text could be taken literally, but then the person born of the young woman would have been born during the siege of Jerusalem, and the prophecy would have been fulfilled some 700 years before the birth of baby Yeshua.

18 Whether or not Herod sometime in his reign slaughtered a number of children is not a question that is here relevant. There is no trace on the historical record (as we at present know it) of this having occurred (which, particularly in Josephus' case is noteworthy, given his strong disapproval of Herod). However, even if the story is entirely fictional, it was believable to contemporaries because the litany of Herod's many atrocities was part of everyday folk history, as Josephus' collection of anti-Herodian tales makes clear.

In a very skilful touch, the author-editor of Matthew leaves implicit the obvious parallel between the slaughter of the innocents and Pharaoh's slaughter of the Israelites' baby boys, and instead, invokes a quotation from the prophet Jeremiah. It is a passage of indeterminate (and, therefore, potentially future) reference in which the city of Ramah (location now unknown) is personified as a woman weeping for her lost children (cf. Matthew 2:18 and Jer. 31:15). Thus, to the reverberations of the Moses-Pharaoh, Jesus-Herod parallel is added the voice of one of the greatest of prophets.

19 Granting that the story in Matthew and Luke concerning the Virgin Birth of Jesus has no background in the Yahweh-faith; that the writers of the other Christian scriptures are either unaware of the Virgin Birth idea or, more likely, reject it; that the idea obviously was taken over from one (or more likely, from several) pagan sources; and that although the demand for the inclusion of the story comes from the logic of Jesus' being declaimed Son of God (how did that happen? the literal-minded need to know), one is impelled to ask: does the Virgin Birth serve any other purposes? One inquires because, despite the apparent benefits of the tale's inclusion in the story of Jesus' life, it seems to do more damage to the integrity of the historical narrative than it is worth.

One side-function of the Virgin Birth story is to raise Jesus above John the Baptist. This is a matter that was very important to the early church: witness the heavily-patterned subordination of John the Baptist in the Gospel of John (1:15–36). Manifestly, some of the people to whom the early scriptures were addressed remembered, or had heard of, John the Baptist as a figure larger than Jesus (this was inevitable, given that, as the Gospels indicate, John was a voice in the land before Jesus began his own ministry) and this had to be addressed. So, in Luke,

John the Baptist is made a relative of Jesus and crucially, while still in the womb of his mother Elisabeth, he recognizes Jesus, who at that time was in the womb of his mother Mary (Luke 1:39–41, and 44). This recognition is indicated by John's leaping for joy in the womb; the subordination of John the Baptist to Jesus is shown, when this inter-womb salute occurred, by Elisabeth's saying to Mary "and whence is this to me, that the mother of my Lord should come to me?" (Luke 1:43). Clearly, putting John the Baptist in his place was a considered goal of the Lucan narrative, and it is successful. The question arises, however: could not this have been achieved just as effectively without the invention of the Virgin Birth? The story of the embryo's salute would carry the same meaning, whatever the method of Jesus' own conception.

The cost to narrative integrity of the introduction of the Virgin Birth is so great – it isolates Jesus' origins from all ancient Hebrew and subsequent Judaist traditions, which is something the rest of the "New Testament" strives mightily *not* to do – that one still wonders, why was it included? Was it merely a lapse into literalism concerning the Son of God; or is it something more than an infelicity? One obvious possibility is that the Virgin Birth refers to some aspect of the life of Yeshua of Nazareth that either had to be remembered silently, or (as in Matthew and Luke) had to be painted over.

That this might be the case is indicated by three seemingly unrelated items in the Gospels. In Mark 6:3, there is a fascinating identification of Jesus. "Is this not the carpenter, the son of Mary, the brother of James and Joses, and of Juda, and Simon? and are not his sisters here with us?" This identification of Jesus is not ambiguous either in the original or in any major translation: two sets of figures are present, Jesus ("the carpenter") and his siblings. Jesus is identified solely by his maternal ancestry ("Mary's boy" is how the Living Bible puts it), with no reference to his father. In a society that was highly patriarchal (in the modern sense of the word), not identifying Joseph as Jesus' father was tantamount to saying that he was not indeed the father. In either the Gospels of Matthew or of Luke that might be taken as an endorsement of the concept of the Virgin Birth, but the text is found in Mark, the author-editor of which has no apparent knowledge of, and certainly no enthusiasm for, the Virgin Birth. That Mark's version (within the context of that Gospel) implies physical illegitimacy on the part of Jesus is indicated by the way that Matthew (whose author is very keen on the Virgin Birth) amends Mark's text so that this interpretation is quickly by-passed. "Is this not the carpenter's son?" the Matthean passage begins (Matt. 13:55a) and quickly, efficiently, Jesus "the carpenter" is changed to Jesus, "the carpenter's son." Matthew's move is clever, but it leaves behind the dull luminescence of Mark's text, the eerie glow one gets when decaying wood emits foxfire.

The second diagnostic marker is found in Mark 3:21 and occurs when Jesus' half-brothers and half-sisters try to have him taken away for being out of his head: "beside himself," in the King James Bible. (Incidentally, the KJB, in employing the old term for what is today called "family" or "relatives," leaves a slightly misleading impression, that it was Jesus' "friends" who wanted to drag him home because of his apparent lunacy. It was his family, and since neither his father or mother are mentioned – as would have been the normal notation in an historical narrative such as Mark – one infers that it was his half-brothers and half-sisters who were involved.) At minimum, one observes here a significant intra-family split, with Jesus on one side, his half-siblings on the other.

Notice here that I have been referring to Jesus' half-brothers and half-sisters. This usage is vexed, but I think defensible. During the early Middle Ages, the western church developed a para-biblical belief that Mary remained a virgin for her entire life, and, obviously, this produced problems in dealing with the several biblical references to Jesus' brothers and sisters. One solution, the one which the Roman Catholic church held until recently, has been that all those brothers and sisters were really cousins of Jesus. This idea strains the text beyond the breaking point and Catholic scholars are at present largely abandoning it. However, a second approach (also motivated by Mary's medievally-declared perpetual virginity) is that what the Gospels report as Jesus' brothers and sisters were half-siblings, stemming, presumably, from an earlier family that Joseph had formed. This leads to the postulate that Joseph was a widower before he became betrothed to Mary. And to this must be added a third option, which sits more comfortably with the Gospels, namely that Mary did not remain a perpetual virgin, but that Jesus was her first-born son and that she and Joseph had several subsequent children, each of whom in the technical sense was Jesus' half-brother or half-sister, sharing as they did the same biological mother. The terms half-brother and half-sister hold if the "New Testament" writers believe in the Virgin Birth (as did the author-editors of Matthew and Luke); it holds equally well if they do not (Mark, John, and Paul). And it applies even if one accepts that Jesus and his brothers and sisters did not share the same paternal origins, for any reason whatsoever, miraculous or carnal. It is no accident that Mark's material on the intra-family fight between Jesus and his half-siblings is not picked up either in Matthew or Luke, despite these books employing in other places a good deal of Mark's material. The reasons for this are the same as the amendment by the author-editor of Matthew of the identification of Jesus as "Mary's boy." Mark's material calls into question the idea of Jesus' legitimacy not only by (a) identifying Jesus only by maternal origin but also (b) by indicating an intra-family fissure between Jesus and the other children: a fault line that a contemporary reader or hearer (someone, for example, encountering Mark's words in the last thirty years of the first century of the Common Era) could interpret as perhaps stemming from Jesus and his half-siblings having quite separate earthly fathers. Thus, it was necessary for the author-editors of Matthew and Luke to paint over this baleful phosphorescence. They did so with bright colours, using the methods of ancient encaustic portrait painters: vivid wax colours, fixed permanently with heat, forever bright, forever distracting.

That brings us to the third diagnostic point, a strange tic in the Synoptic Gospel's reports of Jesus' teachings. It occurs in his discussion of the practice of divorce which, in the context of the law of Moses, usually meant men getting shut of their wives: the divorce of a man by his wife is not covered in the Torah. Jesus' views are reported in Mark (10:2–12) and are slightly expanded, but not significantly amended in Matthew (19:3–12, with a partial doubling in 5:31–32), and briefly noted in Luke (16:18). (Here an important point of evidence must be made explicit. My discussion of these texts does not hinge on the reader accepting that the Synoptics report the words, or even the general views, of Jesus. One can believe [a] that these are his historical words, or [b] that they are his general views, or [c] that the texts reflect what the early church believed his views to have been, or [d] that the texts reflect what the authors of these three Gospels think his views *should* have been, given their knowledge of Christian tradition to the point of their writing. My point below is belief-neutral as far as those matters are concerned: it holds in any of those four cases.) Now, the signal characteristics of most of Jesus' reported teaching concerning the Torah are, first, that he was very respectful of it (much more so than later Christian commentators have tended to recognize) but, secondly, that in general he emphasized maintaining the spirit of the Torah more than the letter.

The texts on divorce – the fracturing of families – stand out sharply against that trend. Here Jesus is reported as being more rigorous, and more rigorist, more demanding in the letter of Torah, than are the Hebrew scriptures, and certainly more demanding than were the prevailing standards of the late Second Temple era. The Synoptics give us three distinct magnifications of the letter of Torah, all of them being a response to the question, "Is it lawful for a man to put away his wife?" (as Mark 10:2 and slightly amended in Matthew 19:3). One of these magnifications is that Jesus is reported as taking the Book of Genesis' fundamental definition of marriage:

> Therefore shall a man leave his father and his mother, and shall cleave unto his wife: and they shall be one flesh. (Gen. 2:24)

and adding, after paraphrasing that definition:

> What therefore God hath joined together, let no man put asunder.
> (Mark 10:8; Matt. 19:6)

This precludes divorce, and is the logical foundation for Jesus' second intensification of the letter of the Law. He admits that Moses permitted divorce (see Deuteronomy 24:1–4 for the divorce law that is ascribed to Moses; the grounds for divorce are "some uncleanness in her," as the KJB has it, or "something obnoxious about her," in the Jewish Publication Society translation; however, though not mentioned in the Law of Moses, it had become possible by the later Second Temple period for women to divorce men: this is distinctly mentioned in Mark 10:12). Moses' permissiveness on this issue occurred, in Jesus' reported view, because of the "hardness" – the imperfection and corruption – of the human heart (Mark

10:5; Matt. 19:8). Jesus sets himself as more rigorous than Moses: in Mark's version he will have no divorce whatsoever, and in Matthew's, he will permit divorce only for a woman having committed adultery (Matt. 19:9; doublet in Matt. 5:32). And, in a third intensification of the letter of the Law, Jesus specifically rejects Moses' permitting a woman to be remarried after having been divorced, or for a man to marry a divorced woman in Mosaic Law. (Deut. 24:1–4 presents different instances of permitted remarriage and of the marriage of men to divorced women.) Jesus finds Moses too soft, however, and in Mark is reported as decreeing that any man who divorces a wife and himself remarries, or any woman who divorces a husband and herself remarries, commits adultery (Mark 10:11–12). In Matthew and Luke the prohibitions are entirely male-oriented (no female-initiated case of divorce is hypothesized), but it is added that any man who marries a divorced woman commits adultery (Matt. 19:9; 5:31–32; Luke 16:18). In sum, the point that cannot be denied is that however one parses the halachic details of Jesus' views of what is today termed "family breakdown," he was either extremely sensitive to deviations from the normal family pattern or, alternately, the collectors and compilers – the inventors in the sense employed throughout this book – of Christian traditions, believed that he had cause to have been highly sensitive on this issue and, hence, they configured their narratives in conformity with that conviction.

Were we dealing with any historical figure other than Yeshua of Nazareth, the most obvious hypothesis that one would derive from the three diagnostic markers that I have discussed, when combined with even Matthew and Luke's admitting that from a purely biological point of view, Mary's pregnancy was beyond explanation, is obvious: that Yeshua was the product of a woman who, while betrothed to a man named Joseph, became pregnant by another man. Yet, Joseph stayed with her: loyal, though mortally humiliated by this cuckolding, and later his union with Mary was fruitful, producing several half-brothers and half-sisters of Yeshua. That is hardly a complex, or original, explanation, but it fits with the Gospels and with what we must take as the limits of human biological possibility. It is, I suspect, the tradition of the origins of Yeshua of Nazareth shared by Paul, by the author-editors of Mark and of John.

Whatever one thinks of that suggestion, it leads to a reflection upon the cruelly devalued figure of Joseph. Even if one takes the Virgin Birth as being an historical suggestion that is superior to the one I have put forward, one still has to wonder about Joseph. Within the context of his society, a man whose wife-to-be turned up pregnant by someone else, and who let the matter ride, inevitably became a lame figure. However, from the viewpoint of the early Christian church, it is hard to see why he was not presented as an heroic figure: for sheltering and raising the by-blow who was to be the future Jesus the Messiah. Joseph's behaviour was an instance of quiet moral greatness and would require recognition whether one viewed the unknown father of Yeshua as being Yahweh's Holy Spirit, or a normal biological human male. In Matthew and Luke (the only places where Joseph is an active character), he disappears after Jesus' childhood. Perhaps that occurs because he actually died while Jesus was an adolescent (he was reported alive when Jesus was twelve years old in Luke 2:41–42). But if this was the case, we are not informed. Thus, Joseph's convenient appearance on the stage, as a beard for Mary, and his unnoticed disappearance, seem insouciant to the point of callousness. (Admittedly, Joseph became more popular in the early Middle Ages, but he did not even have his own feast day until 1479. He was declared Patron of the Universal Church in 1870, but that recognition seems a bit late in the day, at least on the human time scale.)

Finally, it is worth noting that the story of Miriam, as Mary, as Virgin, kept growing right into the twentieth century, in an amazing and dizzying spiral of invention and re-invention. The "Infancy Gospel of Jesus," a second century text, has Mary's mother Anna, who was childless, receiving word that she (Anna) would give birth, directly from an angel of the Lord. (The entire text of this gospel as translated and annotated by Ronald F. Hock is found in Robert J. Miller, ed., *The Complete Gospels. Annotated Scholars Version* [Sonoma, Cal.: Polebridge Press, 1991, 373–89].) Mary was given the title that is rendered in English, "Mother of God," by many sections of the church by the end of the fourth century. At approximately the same time, the idea that she was a "perpetual virgin" began to gain ascendancy. This means that she was a virgin not only before Jesus' birth, but afterwards as well, an inventive construct both biologically and linguistically. During the high Middle Ages, a doctrine of her Immaculate Conception was formulated. This meant that she was free from all stain of Original Sin, unlike every other human being. This purity originated at the instant of her own conception, and, being free of Original Sin, Mary was said to have led a totally sinless life. This doctrine was affirmed (although it was not then a binding doctrine) in church councils of the fifteenth century. It was promulgated as dogmatic and binding by Pius IX in 1854. (Few, if any, Protestants embraced the concept.) From the eighteenth century onwards, Mary was sometimes called a "mediatrix" of grace. This meant that she somehow stood in mediation between the Almighty and humankind. The relationship with Jesus Christ, therefore, was somewhat problematical, as the Catholic church did not wish to diminish Jesus' glory as primary mediator between God and humanity. Inevitably, however, making Mary the fourth (if subordinate) member of the Christian godhead diluted the power of the other three. Pope Benedict XV (1914–22) sanctioned this belief and approved a mass and office of "Our Lady, Mediatrix of All Grace." (Again, Protestants abstained from this belief.) The last stage in the translation of Miriam, the unfortunately-pregnant young woman from hard-scrapple Nazareth, into a demi-god (or, perhaps, more) was the articulation of the doctrine that Mary never died, but was instead taken bodily into heaven. Early church rites had memorialized Mary's death, but in the sixth century, one school of churchmen began to assert that she had never died and they began to preach the Assumption of the Blessed Virgin Mary into Heaven. After the declaration of the Immaculate Conception in 1854, pressure upon the Vatican grew to declare as authoritative the Assumption of the BVM and finally, in 1950, Pius XII did so. (Once again, Protestants remained aloof.)

On these developments, see Jaroslav Pelikan, "Mary – Exemplar of the Development of Christian Doctrine," in *Mary. Images of the Mother of Jesus in Jewish and Christian Perspective*, 79–91; Jaroslav Pelikan, *Mary Through the Centuries: Her Place in the History of Culture* (New Haven: Yale University Press, 1996), and related articles in *The Oxford Dictionary of the Christian Church*.

20 Here, as in many important events narrated in the Tanakh and in the Christian scriptures, one can make a list of layers of contradiction: two dozen inconsistencies in the various gospels' accounts of the details of the crucifixion are easily piled up. This is of great interest to scholars, for when one encounters mutually incompatible versions of a specific detail it means that, at minimum, one of them is not strictly historically true (and perhaps neither is).

Such inconsistencies of detail were of no interest, however, to the individuals who compiled either the Hebrew or the Christian canon, nor to the author-editors of the individual books within the respective canons (for inconsistencies within a single book frequently occur). Both the Tanakh and the Christian scriptures accept what might be called an "acceptable degree of uncertainty" about historical details, as long as the variations fit within the primary structure of each of their respective compilations, and fit within the major narrative outlines these canons enhull.

I am here repeating this point – which has been made in other contexts – because unless we start any historical discussion with the rules by which the inventors of the scriptures worked, all our subsequent historical commentary will perforce be anachronistic. Of course, as a secondary (but very valuable) exercise, contradictions can be used as markers that help to delineate the successive levels of invention within the scriptures and sometimes to date the texts.

21 The Gospel of John (19:23–24) employs an intentional misreading of Psalm 22:18, presenting it as a prophecy rather than as an ancient lament. This allows the author-editor of John to claim the fulfilment of a prophecy when the soldiers gamble for Jesus' cloak.

22 That there are incompatibilities between John and the Synoptics over which day of Passover, is worth noting in passing, but chiefly to confirm that each textual tradition required a Passover framework for its story.

23 My assertion carries the ubiquitous warning phrase (so crucial when dealing with any aspects of later Second Temple Judahism), "within the present state of our knowledge." That is a requisite truth-in-advertising warning. I am struck by how very little direct evidence there is concerning the occurrence and character of holy festivals in late Second Temple times. There is a fair amount of material in the Books of Moses on the various festivals and also in Second Chronicles. This

brings the usage-pattern down to roughly 400 BCE. And there is a great deal of information on feast patterns in the Mishnah (late second century of the Common Era) and in the two Talmuds of the fourth through sixth centuries CE.

It is a mistake, however, (1) to project into the first century CE material from the Torah that is several centuries prior to that time, and even the material in Chronicles is separated by roughly four centuries from the practices of the late Second Temple. (2) Equally, it is fallacious to project back into the late Second Temple period, descriptions from the Mishnah and the Talmuds. This cannot be done, because these depictions are part of the re-invention of one branch of Judahism, which turns into Rabbinic Jewish practice.

Therefore, when one seeks direct contemporary evidence of how the liturgical year actually was observed in, say, the fifty years before and after Jesus' death, one is left with the inferences one can draw from the Temple Scroll, the Book of Enoch, the Book of Jubilees, the "New Testament," Philo, and Josephus, and they are not reportorial on these matters. (For an admirable summary, see James C. Vanderkam, "Calendars: Ancient Israelite and Early Jewish," *ABD*, 1:814–820.)

I emphasize the paucity of direct data, first, to give the reader fair warning that my own suggestions are necessarily speculative; and, second, simultaneously to warn that much (indeed, most) of the scholarly literature that one encounters which discusses the Judahist liturgical calendars and practices at about the time of Jesus is misleadingly self-confident and assertive. This holds true for all stripes of scholarship. I can think of no area of scholarship on the Jewish and Christian faiths, and on their common antecedents, wherein the strength of scholarly assertion is so ill-correlated with the actual strength of the evidence.

24 Neither the new (post-164 BCE) Feast of Dedication (Hanukkah) nor Purim, which were apparently just becoming established in Jesus' time, would have been appropriate for the "New Testament" message, since neither harkens back to the Law of Moses, and rhetorical contact with Moses' Torah is part of the narrative strategy of all the Christian writers. The longer-established minor holidays were indeed consequential, but they memorialized occurrences that were not of primary importance in the Tanakh and therefore would not fit well with the most important liturgical moment in the Christian story. The longer-established secondary feasts included: the first fruits of barley; the second passover (to be observed by those who had been on journeys at the original passover); the first fruits of wheat; the feast of the new wine; the festival of oil; the festival of booths (or tabernacles, referring to the generations spent living in tents in the desert); and there were others. (See ibid., 819.)

25 Temple Scroll, cols. 16–17, in Florentino Garcia Martinez, *The Dead Sea Scrolls Translated* (Leiden: E.J. Brill, 1992, Engl. ed., 1994), 160–61.

26 Gillian Feeley-Harnik, *The Lord's Table. The Meaning of Food in Early Judaism and Christianity* (Washington, D.C.: Smithsonian Institution Press, 1994), 120. This is a brilliant discussion of the relationship of the Passover and the Last Sup-

per which attempts to break the discussion out of the evidentiary dead-ends that are imposed by purely liturgical discussions of the two rituals.

27 In viewing the sequence of events in each of the two major versions, one must remember that the day began and ended at sundown, not at sunrise.

28 The key Synoptic texts are Matt. 26:26–29; Mark 14:22–25; and Luke 22:17–20. Equally important historically is Paul's order of the commemoration of the Last Supper which he traces directly to Jesus (found in 1 Corinthians 11:23–34). This Pauline material is consequential, because it indicates that the belief in the specific order of Jesus' acts at the Last Supper had crystallized within the early church before the destruction of the Second Temple and therefore considerably before the Synoptics were written in their present form.

John, in making the Last Supper not a Passover seder, but a casual meal on the eve of Passover (John, chapters 13 and 14), followed by a post-prandial stroll, almost superciliously supplants the Passover. Instead of a ritual meal, he focuses upon the actions of Jesus after the meal had ended (Jesus washes his disciples' feet) and upon his long colloquy with them (John 13:2–16:33). John concludes this passage with a prayer by Jesus, in which he offers himself up to his Father, in what is very clearly a trope of the Passover ritual (John 17:1–26). John has the luxury of the discursive version because, as the accounts in the Synoptics and in Paul indicate, the actual ritual details of the Last Supper were well known among Christians. That the author of John intends his text to be read as a New Passover seder is indicated by the fact that early-on (John 1:29) he identifies Jesus and "The Lamb of God, which taketh away the sin of the world" and he is very careful to have the Roman soldiers pierce Jesus' side, rather than break his bones (John 19:31–37), so that the prohibition against breaking the bones of Passover lambs (Exodus 12:46; Numb. 9:12; and cf Ps. 34:20) is not abrogated.

One niggling detail remains, namely, that none of the Synoptics calls Jesus the Lamb of God. That makes no difference. The Pauline statement that Jesus is the Passover victim was a given, antedating as it does the Synoptic writings: "For even Christ our passover is sacrificed for us" (1 Cor. 5:7). More importantly, the foundation-analogy of the Synoptics is this:

Isaac: Abraham = Jesus: Yahweh

And since Isaac was identified as a sacrificial lamb (Gen. 22:8–9), so too is Jesus, albeit one who, unlike Isaac, actually has his blood spilled. Finally, recall the figure of the Suffering Servant of Second Isaiah (section one of the present chapter). The Servant suffuses the Synoptic Gospels, and (whatever one may think of this usage of the "Old Testament" texts), there is no question that the Servant was clearly identified as a lamb (Isaiah 53:7) and in the Christian re-invention of the text, this identification slides onto Jesus Christ. The idea of Jesus as the Passover lamb is not a textual anomaly, but the clear articulation at the end of the narration of Jesus' ministry of a pervasive presence that has been there all the time, a gift from the texts of the "Old Testament" to the writers of the "New."

NOTES TO CHAPTER TEN

1 Harold A. Liebowitz, "Jabneel," *ABD*, 3:596; Martin Noth, *The History of Israel* (New York: Harper and Row, second ed., 1960), 440–6.

2 The key date was the promulgation by Pope Paul VI on 28 October 1965 of the document *Nostra Aetate #4*. This declared that no guilt for the action of the Jews of ancient times in causing the crucifixion of Jesus should be transferred to the Jews of modern times; nor should Jews be presented as being repudiated or as cursed by God, as had been the traditional Christian position. See Michael B. McGarry, "*Nostra Aetate*: The Church's Bond to the Jewish People: Context, Content, Promise," in Marvin Perry and Frederick M. Schweitzer (eds.), *Jewish-Christian Encounters over the Centuries. Symbiosis, Prejudice, Holocaust, Dialogue* (New York: Peter Land, 1994), 389–403.

   And the Church of Jesus Christ of the Latter Day Saints (the "Mormons" in common usage) only agreed with Jewish leaders in 1995 not to baptize Holocaust victims posthumously. At the time a Mormon spokesman said (on National Public Radio, 28 April 1995) that "Our doctrine was not to convert them, but to give them a choice." He added, "We are responsive, apologetic, and understanding."

   During the 1990s Lutheran denominations in several countries repudiated the virulent anti-Semitic diatribes found in some of the writings of Martin Luther.

3 I have found the following discussions very helpful: Robert Michael, "Antisemitism and the Church Fathers," in Perry and Schweitzer, 101–29; Jacob Neusner, *Judaism and Christianity in the Age of Constantine. History, Messiah, Israel, and the Initial Confrontation* (Chicago: University of Chicago Press, 1987); Rosemary Radford Ruether, "The *Adversus Judaeos* Tradition in the Church Fathers: the Exegesis of Christian Anti-Judaism," in Jeremy Cohen (ed.), *Essential Papers on Judaism and Christianity in Conflict, from Late Antiquity to the Reformation* (New York: New York University Press, 1991), 174–89; Robert L. Wilken, *Judaism and the Early Christian Mind. A Study of Cyril of Alexandria's Exegesis and Theology* (New Haven: Yale University Press, 1971); Stephen G. Wilson (ed.), *Anti-Judaism in Early Christianity*, vol. 2, *Separation and Polemic* (Waterloo: Wilfrid Laurier University Press, 1986).

4 The literature on antisemitism is immense and I have by no means mastered it. The concept of antisemitism has problems which are as complex as is its doleful historical reality. The term came into being as an invention of Wilhelm Marr in 1873 and it was considered by him to be a good thing: the policy of treating the Jews as a race, inferior to the Aryan race, and insidiously dangerous. The term acquired in the twentieth century a dual connotation: on the part of those who practised it, an admirable form of racial purity, and for those who opposed it, a vicious doctrine of genocidal hatred. After World War II and the full revelation of the extent of German (and Austrian and Soviet) antisemitism, the word became solely a term of condemnation (although, alas, one sees, in the last years of the twentieth

century, a re-borning of its vicious semantics). After the war, the term quickly broadened and in common usage has come to refer to any negative attitude or actions toward Jews at any time in history. This general usage can hardly be rebuffed, for it is tidal, a worldwide usage that refers not only to nineteenth- and twentieth-century "racial" prejudice against Jews, but also to social and religious bigotry of almost any period, including pre-Christian times.

In everyday conversation this is fine, but in historical discourse the elastic use of the term raises some basic issues of sound practice: (1) is it justifiable to define twenty-plus centuries of bad attitudes and bad behaviour towards the Jews (and their predecessors in the ancient world of the "Old Testament") as being a single phenomenon? The more expansive discussions of the subject – "popular" ones to be sure – lump the beliefs and behaviours of the Pharaohs and of the Führer into the same category. And, does using adjectives to slip out of the charge of over-simplification – terms such as "theological antisemitism," "racial antisemitism," and so on – not merely provide a false analytic? Are they really contiguous phenomena? (see Gavin I. Langmuir, *Towards a Definition of Antisemitism* (Berkeley: University of California Press, 1990).

Jean-Paul Sartre once defined antisemitism as follows:

If a man attributes all or part of his own misfortunes and those of his country to the presence of Jewish elements in the community, if he proposes to remedy this state of affairs by depriving the Jews of certain of their rights, by keeping them out of certain economic and social activities, by expelling them from the country, by exterminating all of them, we say that he has anti-Semitic *opinions*.

Sartre provides a qualification, soon thereafter: "anti-Semitism does not fall within the category of ideas protected by the right of free opinion. Indeed, it is something quite other than an idea. It is first of all a *passion*" (Jean-Paul Sartre, *Anti-Semite and Jews*, translated by George J. Becker. New York: Schocken Books, 1948; orig. ed. 1946, 7 and 10). That definition, originally presented in 1946, may have been appropriate to immediate-post-war sensibilities, but it misses the point that antisemitism can be an unreflective, mundane, and non-passionate part of a belief-system: as it certainly was for many Christians until the second half of the twentieth century. The sheer banality of everyday antisemitism must not be ignored.

Yet antisemitism has never been merely the parochialism that all social groups exhibit, the instinctive distrust of outsiders and of those who are different. It partakes of that basic attitude, but the xenophobia towards Jews usually has been something more: xenophobia with a twist. In the end, I am left with Gavin Langmuir's modest, admirably sensible, suggestion that "antisemitism" not be used to refer to any and all hostility towards Jews collectively, and at any time in history, but to an "unusual hostility against Jews," different both in degree and in kind from run-of-the-mill parochialism or xenophobia (Langmuir, 351). In operational terms, this means that each outbreak of anti-Jewish activity must be gauged within the context of locality, or place, and of the specific culture within which it occurs. The existence of antisemitism usually becomes clear when it is ascertained that in a specific context Jews were not only treated badly, but worse than other minorities. Even with that limitation, it is a massive phenomenon.

For introductory information on antisemitism's long history, see: Shmuel Almog (ed.), *Antisemitism Through the Ages*, trans. Nathan H. Reisner (Oxford: Pergamon Press, 1988); Joel Carmichael, *The Satanizing of the Jews. Origin and Development of Mystical Anti-Semitism* (New York: Fromm International Publishing, 1992); Leon Poliakov, *The History of Anti-Semitism*, trans. by Richard Howard (New York: Vanguard Press, 4 vols, 1965–85). I am grateful to my colleague Professor Gerald Tulchinsky for sharing with me material and bibliography from his extensive research on the destruction of European Jewry, 1933–45.

As a cross-cultural reference point, see Mark R. Cohen, *Under Crescent and Cross. The Jews in the Middle Ages* (Princeton: Princeton University Press, 1994).

5 For a finely crafted biography, see Ramsay MacMullen, *Constantine* (New York: Dial Press, 1969).

6 John G. Gager, *The Origins of Anti-Semitism. Attitudes towards Judaism in Pagan and Christian Antiquity* (New York: Oxford University Press, 1983), 94.

7 See Ramsay MacMullen, *Christianizing the Roman Empire (A.D. 100–400)* (New Haven: Yale University Press, 1984), esp. 59–119.

8 This is elegantly argued in Jaroslav Pelikan, *The Excellent Empire. The Fall of Rome and the Triumph of the Church* (San Francisco: Harper and Row, 1987).

9 Gager, 86–94.

10 David Rokeah, "The Church Fathers and the Jews in Writings Designed for Internal and External Use," in Almog, *Antisemitism Through the Ages*, 45–46, and 66*n*25. Justin Martyr and Eusebius are the sources. Johannes Weiss, *Earliest Christianity* (New York: Harper and Brothers, 1937, orig. German ed. 191 14ff), 2:723*n*30.

11 Scholars debate whether the power of the Christianized Roman empire (and after 396 CE, its fragmenting portions) actually became effective in its anti-Jewish enactments in the fourth century, or not until the fifth. The former position is that of Jacob Neusner, *Judaism and Christianity*, passim. Compare this to Gager, 97–8. At minimum, by the early fifth century, the church and the state were engaged in a combined attack on Judaism that, in its employment of overwhelming institutional power against the Jewish population, clearly deserves to be labelled not just anti-Jewish, but antisemitic.

12 Jan N. Sevenster, *The Roots of Pagan Anti-Semitism in the Ancient World* (Leiden: E.J. Brill, 1975), 191.

13 Cited above, note 11.

14 Shaye Cohen, "Crossing the Boundary and Becoming a Jew," *Harvard Theological Review*, 82 (Jan. 1989), 13–33.

15 Louis Feldman, *Jew and Gentile in the Ancient World. Attitudes and Interactions from Alexander to Justinian* (Princeton: Princeton University Press, 1973).

16 Ibid., 439.

17 Ibid., 415.

18 Gager's *The Origins of Anti-Semitism* serves as a valuable, if engagé, summary of the literature between the end of World War II and the early 1980s. The set-piece around which most discussions of alleged antisemitism in the Christian scriptures revolve is Rosemary Radford Ruether, *Faith and Fratricide: The Theological Roots of Anti-Semitism* (New York: Seabury Press, 1979). A strong counter-argument, focused on the writings of Paul, is Lloyd Gaston, *Paul and the Torah* (Vancouver: University of British Columbia Press, 1987).

19 Elaine Pagels, *The Origin of Satan* (New York: Random House, 1995), 15.

20 Notice here that we are not talking about the "New Testament's" being anti-Jewish, much less antisemitic, although in the long run it contributes mightily to those two phenomena. The "New Testament" is not anti-Jewish because there was no such thing as a single Jewish faith (in the modern sense of the body of doctrine and behaviour that produced the Mishnah and the Talmuds) in the era when the Christian scriptures were being invented. To assert this is not to play a mere word-game, the sort of thing that we historians too often teach our graduate students to volley about in seminars. It is a fundamental principle of historical method that when one uses one term to cover two or more manifestly distinct phenomena, a historical slurp occurs, the kind of messy, indiscriminate melange of meaning and message that one gets from an overly energetic Newfoundland puppy. The heart of the great slurp that has made it very difficult for biblical historians to deal with the late Second Temple period is that the "New Testament" and classical texts (both Greek and Roman) employ a blanket term to cover all the Judahist groups. This is translated as "the Jews," or as "Jewish" in English-language texts, and the fault is not with the translation, but with the original vocabulary which denied distinctions that were not mere differences but lines of structural cleavage. Such contemporary observational blindness is neither unusual nor something that should make modern observers feel particularly superior. One only needs to recall that well past the middle of the twentieth century, "the Communists" was employed to encompass such diverse ideological, economic, and social constellations as mainland China, North Korea, North Vietnam, Russia, scores of the Soviet Republics, and the Baltic states. One term: many incompatible realities.

Although the concept of "normative Judaism" no longer has any more historical credence than would the parallel concept of "normative Communism," there is still a refusal on the part of many scholars to accept the argument that a single term cannot be used to encompass the beliefs and practices of the Yahweh-derived faiths of the later Second Temple period. There remains a longing to define "Jewish" and, through use of this term, to tie, as if by a silken cord, the alleged one Jewish faith of the Second Temple era either to the Jewish faith, or to the Christian faith of the present day. What seems to be desired is the historical equivalent of a geoid, an imaginary surface that coincides with the mean sea level of the ocean. The trouble, of course, is that this is a fictional entity. In the real world there is not, nor has there ever been, a geoid, for the peaks and valleys of the ocean are never smoothed out.

For a monumental attempt at deriving a single, glass-smooth model of the unity that he believes lies inside all the various Judaisms of the later Second Temple period, see E.P. Sanders's *Judaism, Practice and Belief, 63 BCE-66 CE* (London: SCM Press, 1992, corrected ed., 1994). That I am skeptical of the possibility of deriving a "common denominator theology," (Sanders's term) applicable to all the Judaist groups of late Second Temple times is obvious from the present text (Chapters Six-Eight, inclusive), but this does not impugn the heroism of Sanders's quest. For strongly critical commentary on Sanders's actual achievement, see Bruce Chilton and Jacob Neusner, *Judaism in the New Testament. Practices and Beliefs* (London: Routledge, 1995), 42–57.

My own view is that in terms of units of religious belief, the only two items that run throughout the multiple Judaisms of the late Second Temple period are (1) that the name of the main God (and to most Judaist sects the only god) is Yahweh and (2) that the Temple is the iconic centre of the religion of Yahweh. The Temple belief holds even for those groups who refuse to go near the Temple on the grounds that it needs purification or replacement. Those two characteristics cannot define a single common Judaist faith, any more than two points can define a three-dimensional figure.

At the level of the everyday adherent of either the Jewish or the Christian faiths in our own time, I think it highly unlikely that a recognition of the variegated and manifold nature of Second Temple Judaisms will find much favour, for almost everyone has a vested interest in mis-meaning. Since both present-day Christianity and present-day Judaism are faiths that value historical continuity, each is quite willing to see the terms "Jew" and "Jewish" include modern Judaism, the beliefs of the late Second Temple and, frequently, to refer to beliefs and practices as early as pre-Babylonian exile. Of course, each faith claims that it is the true inheritor of this implied genealogy.

21 1Q Habakkuk Pesher, cols I and II, in Florentino G. Martinez, *The Dead Sea Scrolls Translated* (Leiden: E.J. Brill, 1994), 197–8.

22 The Eighteen Benedictions were formerly dated by scholars at c. 90 CE, and ascribed to the hypothetical "Council of Yavneh" (var: Jamnia). This dating has become less certain, in part because the Jamnia "council" was more of an hypothesis than a documented reality, and has found virtually no confirmatory evidence. (See Jack P. Lewis, "Council of Jamnia," *ABD*, 3:634–7.) Secondly, textual scholars point out that, though several versions of the Benedictions exist, the two texts that mention Christians specifically by name are early medieval in origin. This opens the possibility that instead of being articulated at a single moment, the Benedic-

tions evolved considerably, and were not completed until perhaps the fourth or fifth centuries. See John T. Townsend, "The Gospel of John and the Jews: The Story of a Religious Divorce," in Alan Davies (ed.), *Antisemitism and the Foundations of Christianity* (New York: Paulist Press, 1979), 84–6.

See also Ray A. Pritz, *Nazarene Jewish Christianity from the End of the New Testament Period until its Disappearance in the Fourth Century* (Jerusalem: Magnes Press, 1988), 102–7.

23 David Flusser, "Jesus in the Context of History," in Arnold Toynbee (ed.), *The Crucible of Christianity* (New York: 1969), 225, quoted in Gager, 28.

24 George Steiner, "Through a Glass Darkly," in James S. Pacy and Alan P. Wertheimer, *Perspectives on the Holocaust. Essays in Honor of Raul Hilberg* (Boulder: Westview Press, 1995), 121.

25 When Paul denounces certain Judahist actions and beliefs, he is careful to do this in a general way and not to mention the Pharisees. For example, see his two most anti-Judahist statements: Romans 11:8 where of Israel, it is said, "God hath given them the spirit of slumber, eyes that they should not see, and ears that they should not hear"; and I Thessalonians 2:15, where "the Jews" "both killed the Lord Jesus, and their own prophets, and have persecuted us; and they please not God, and are contrary to all men." The latter reference is the subject of considerable debate, as many scholars believe it to be not written by Paul, but to be a later interpolation. Compare Norman A. Beck, "The New Testament and the Teaching of Contempt: Reconsiderations," in Perry and Schweitzer, 83–99, and John C. Hurd, "Paul Ahead of His Time: Thess. 2:13–16," in Peter Richardson (ed.), *Anti-Judaism in Early Christianity*, vol. 1, *Paul and the Gospels* (Waterloo: Wilfrid Laurier University Press, 1986), 21–36.

26 The observation, made concerning the Gospel of Mark, is Charles P. Anderson's: "The Trial of Jesus as Jewish-Christian Polarization: Blasphemy and Polemic in Mark's Gospel," in Richardson, 107.

27 I am assuming that the reader, in reading the discussion that follows, understands the concepts of out-liers in any data-set and also accepts that, though I adopt the order-of-composition that is now virtually-traditional in scholarly articles, there are alternative orders-of-composition that would invalidate my observations (see Appendix D). The scheme is put forward, therefore, in a tentative manner.

That said, one possible objection should be dealt with: namely, that we do not really know the date of the composition of any of the books of the "New Testament," most especially, the Four Gospels and the Book of Acts, which are the heart of the matter. True: but the historical observation being made has nothing to do with absolute dating, but rather with the ordinal position of each text in the sequence-of-invention, and this sequence is quite well established, even if its absolute dates are not known (again see Appendix D). Thus, the correlation drawn remains valid.

The best objection to my correlation of lateness-of-composition with antipathy-to-Pharisees is that the gradient in attitudes which seems most likely to be a time-line may in fact be nothing of the sort, but rather a function of locational factors. Given that we do not know with even modest certainty the specific audience to which any of the Gospels was directed, it is possible that what looks on the surface to be a function of change-over-time, is actually caused by each author-editor's having to deal with specific local situations which, quite by accident, arrange themselves in a temporal order that in reality has no causal force.

28 Not only are the author-editor(s) of Matthew remarkably inventive in moving the death of Zacharias from the courtyard of the Temple (2 Chr. 24:21) to the proximity of the high altar, but they change the implied nature of Zacharias's death from stoning (a humiliating form of death, even if in a noble cause). By not mentioning the stoning, the inventor of the Gospel of Matthew implies that the death was akin to the piacular sacrifice of unblemished animals before Yahweh's altar, an image that fits more closely with Christian iconography. Further, it is interesting that Matthew's author-editor mistakes the parentage of Zacharias (var: Zechariah). He is the son of Jehoiada (2 Chr. 24:20), not of Barachias (var: Barachiah, Berechiah). Probably "Matthew" was conflating Zechariah, son of Jehoiada, with Zechariah the prophet, son of Berechiah (Zech. 1:1).

29 The reader will notice that I am not including in this time-gradient the Book of Acts. That is because its dating in the sequence of post-70 Christian writings is indeterminate. In Christian tradition, the book is written by the same author-editor(s) who created the Gospel of Luke, and, for convincing stylistic and substantive reasons, most modern scholars accept this common identity and frequently refer to "Luke-Acts" as a single entity. However, to see the two books as having the same authorial background, is not to conclude that they were composed at the same time. Though one can be modestly confident that Luke was compiled before Matthew, the same cannot be said for Acts.

This point is crucial in relation to our use of a textually-determined time-gradient to measure the rise of Pharisaism's great offspring, Rabbinic Judaism. A problem arises, one which, despite its complexity of detail, is clear in outline: whereas the Gospel of Luke is quite gentle towards the Pharisees, the Book of Acts is very hostile to them, almost as waspishly as is the Gospel of John. Thus, we have two texts which, though stylistically contiguous, have deeply differing views on a very major historical matter. If we are to continue to grant that the same author-editors were involved in each treatise, then the simplest solution to the substantive disjuncture is to suggest that Luke was written significantly earlier than was Acts. Such a suggestion has merit, but it renders the usage of Acts thus dated (being significantly post-Luke), inoperative for the purposes of the present discussion, since one cannot both use the anti-Pharisaism of Acts as a dating-determinant, and employ the asserted late dating of Luke as a marking point on the time gradient that we are correlating with anti-Pharisaism. That would be a tautological argument. Thus, lacking a compelling independent dating for Acts, I have necessarily excluded it from the present correlation.

One matter in Acts requires note, for it seems to assert a fact about the Pharisees not found elsewhere in the "New Testament." This is that Paul was tutored in Pharisaism by "Gamaliel" who is identified as a leading Pharisee, a master of Torah, who had a high reputation among all people, and who, on one tense occasion protects several of the apostles from a mob that, having been offended by their preaching, wished to kill them (Acts 5:29–40): they get off with a beating. This assertion concerning Paul's having studied with Gamaliel is not found in Paul's own letters, but is placed in his mouth at his defence, after he was seized in the Temple by his Judahist enemies (22:3). It is probable that the primary audience of the Book of Acts took this Gamaliel to be Rabban Gamaliel I, the grandfather of Rabban Gamaliel II, one of the leading figures in emergent Rabbinic Judaism in the last two decades of the first century of the Common Era.

Whether or not the reference to Paul's having studied with Gamaliel is historically accurate (would Paul have left out the reference in his own letters, wherein he brags about the rigour of his own Pharisaic education?), it yields a useful historical inference: that in the later part of the first century, the followers of the Jesus-faith were encountering a major religious figure, Gamaliel II, and he was of sufficient force and stature that his presence had to be ideologically domesticated. This the Book of Acts accomplishes, by having his erudite and rigorous grandfather serve as a teacher of Paul who, of course, passes beyond those teachings. The comforting words to late-first-century Christians are: since Paul learned all he could from Gamaliel I and, through his epistles, teaches us how morally insufficient that education was, we need not be impressed or unsettled by the derivative person of Gamaliel II. We are already victorious.

The subtlety with which the author-editor(s) of Acts manipulate the anti-Pharisaic sub-text goes even farther. In Acts, Paul is made to claim something he does not state in his own letters: that he is the son of a Pharisee (23:6). This pushes the genealogical discrediting of Pharisaism back in time to its very founding figure: for, if Paul was taught by Gamaliel I, who was his father taught by? There is no direct answer, but the father (or grandfather, traditions vary) of Gamaliel I was the great Hillel. So, not only is an historical ratio buried in the sub-text that discredits post-70 Pharisees (Paul:Gamaliel I = post-70 Christians:Gamaliel II), but also an implied derogation of the foundation-genealogy of Pharisaism (Paul:Gamaliel I = Paul's father:Hillel). This is quite brilliant propaganda, all the more effective for being uttered *sotto voce*.

Incidentally, the post-70 Christian's awareness of the detailed spiritual genealogy of Pharisaism-Rabbinism is another evidence that (a) the Pharisees and Christians were close natural rivals, (b) that they well may have shared common Pharisaic origins and, in any case (c) that the Pharisees were not after the Temple's destruction a valetudinarian fragment, but that they actively promulgated their beliefs and lineage.

Two rather more speculative instances of anti-Pharisaic codings within the Christian writings are of interest. Jacob Neusner points out that the name of the pivotal transitional figure in the evolution of Pharisaism into Rabbinic Judaism, Yohanan ben Zakkai (the head of the Pharisaic community and academy at Yavneh after the destruction of the Second Temple), translates into Greek as "Zaccheus." This is interesting because in the Infancy Gospel of Thomas (which should not be confused with the Gospel of Thomas which some scholars refer to as the "Fifth Gospel"), written in the mid-second century, Jesus as a child corrects the teachings of a Galilean teacher named Zachaeus, a proto-Rabbi. Given that Yohanan ben Zakkai was of Galilean origin, the meaning of the put-down is clear. Cf. Jacob Neusner, *First-century Judaisms in Crisis. Yohanan ben Zakkai and the Renaissance of Torah* (Nashville: Abingdon Press, 1975), 64–6, and Infancy Gospel of Thomas, Chapter Six, in Robert J. Miller (ed.), *The Complete Gospels* (Sonoma, Cal.: Polebridge Press, 1991), 367.

Less refiné, however, is an earlier Christian play with the name. This occurs in Luke (19:1–10) where Jesus encounters a rich publican. This man, Zacchaeus, calls himself to Jesus' attention by climbing up a sycamore tree so that he can see Jesus over the press of the crowd, for he is a short man. Jesus has a meal with the man and converts him, and that is the overt text. The covert one is a simple dig-in-the-ribs burlesque joke: Yohanan ben Zakkai (who was the leading Pharisaic-Rabbinic scholar at the time Luke was being completed) – Zacchaeus – is presented as a stumpy wee man, a grasping publican, who's up a tree. One easily visualizes him as a figure in one of the low Roman comedies of the time, one of those deformed grotesques at whom the spectators in the cheap seats were prone to toss over-ripe produce.

30 One repeats: the gradient is a correlation drawn not from absolute dating, but from the ordinal dating of the completion of the Four Gospels. The correlation holds, whatever the absolute dating of the items (if this could be known). It is the trend-line of development, relating to Pharisaism, that is revealing.

31 The reader will notice that I have avoided a big question and an even bigger body of historiographic commentary: exactly how-why- and-when, the Jesus-followers (called "Christians") separated from a group that eventually became the "Jewish" faith. My reading of the primary material (especially Paul, the Gospels, and Acts), and of a good deal (but by no means all) of the available secondary material, is that almost nothing can be said with certainty. Earlier (in Chapter Nine, note 23), I noted the huge gap between the self-confidence of scholarship (of all stripes) and the paucity of primary historical information on Judahist liturgical calendars and liturgical practices in the later Second Temple era. Here, I would add that this dissonance between self-confident assertion and the thinness of primary data is rivalled by that concerning the historical course of the separation of the Christian and Jewish faiths.

Cumulatively, the discussion of the Jewish-Christian split is a bran tub of assertions and hypotheses and suffers from the lack of anything even approaching an agreed set of terms that would make an historical discussion possible. The concepts of "Jewish-Christian," "Christian-Jew," and "Judaizer" are almost universally employed, but without consistent operational definitions within an individual work, much less in the literature generally. Whether or not these terms can ever be defined operationally is as yet unclear.

On the complexities of the split, see Joan E. Taylor, *Christians and the Holy Places. The Myth of Jewish-Christian Origins* (Oxford: Clarendon Press, 1993), 1–47.

32 Neusner, *Judaism and Christianity in the Age of Constantine*, x-xi.

33 David Flusser, *Judaism and the Origins of Christianity* (Jerusalem: Magnes Press, 1988), xvi.

34 The Mishnah (c. 200 CE or earlier), generally recognized as the first document of Rabbinic Judaism, does not refer directly either to Jesus or to Christianity. (However, a discussion of "hanging" in a manner similar to crucifixion is described as a punishment for blasphemy; the situation and regulations parallel Jesus' case; see tractate Sanhedrin 6:4). The Babylonian Talmud, the last of the foundational Rabbinic compositions (c. 500–600 CE), has a very few scattered references but they are highly questionable: first, because their provenance cannot be verified beyond their presence in the Babylonian Talmud, which means that they have to be taken as early medieval propositions. Secondly, the references to Jesus and to the Christians are either uninformative or involve identifications that are questionable. The citations in the Babylonian Talmud that have possible relevance are found in Chapter Thirteen, note 8. For a classic discussion of the rabbinical and early medieval references to Jesus, see Joseph Klausner, *Jesus of Nazareth. His Life, Times, and Teaching* (New York: MacMillan, 1929), 18–54. His view, that these references have little direct historical value, is still compelling. One notes with interest, however, his suggestion that the stories in the Talmuds "seem as though they are deliberately intended to contradict events recorded in the Gospels: the selfsame facts are perverted into bad and blamable acts" (19). This shrewd observation is indicative of a situation that Rabbinical authorities agreed to deny: that they were quite precisely aware of the nature of the developing Christian faith, even though they refused to engage directly in argument with that religion.

35 The text here employed is the translation by Richard Rubinkiewicz, found, with an introduction, in James H. Charlesworth (ed.), *The Old Testament Pseudepigrapha* (New York: Doubleday, 1985), 1:681–705. The Apocalypse of Abraham is preserved only in Old Slavonic, but the original language was either Hebrew or Aramaic. It has minor, but easily identifiable, Christian interpolations, and no direct relationship to the "New Testament." Chapter 27 is a description of the plundering of Jerusalem in 70 CE and, in its emphasis upon the Temple being burned, is more accurate historically than are the Christian scriptures, wherein the "predictions" ascribed to Jesus have the sacred structure being disassembled.

36 Fourth Ezra is found most conveniently in the New Revised Standard Version of the Apocrypha-Deuterocanonical books (1989) under the title "2 Esdras" and in a slightly different translation, with an introduction by B.M. Metzger, in Charlesworth 1:517–59. The earliest versions, scholars conclude, probably were in Hebrew (or possibly Aramaic), and the secondary versions in Greek. However, none of these texts exists in full, although a Greek fragment survives. Latin, Coptic, and Syriac versions abound. The translations employed here include a vague Christian framework which was tacked on to the front (chapters 1–2) and back (chapters 13–16) of the otherwise completely non-Christian work. The date of composition is within thirty years of 70 CE, for its first sentence in the Jewish text (3:1 in the published text) says that it was being written "in the thirtieth year after the destruction of our city ..." Since the author appears to be unaware of the death of Domitian, it probably was composed before 96 CE (Michael E. Stone, "Second Book of Esdras," ABD, 2:612. For a detailed commentary, see Michael E. Stone, *Fourth Ezra. A Commentary on the Book of Fourth Ezra*, Minneapolis: Fortress Press, 1990.)

37 Second Baruch, edited, with an introduction, by A.F.J. Klign, is found in Charlesworth 1:615–52. It exists in Syriac, but the original text seems to have been Hebrew, which was later translated into Greek. The text appears not to have any Christian interpolations, although, sharing the same bank of ideas from Second Temple Judahism, it contains similarities to parts of the "New Testament." The dating is post-70 CE, because the destruction of two Temples (meaning Solomon's and the Second Temple) is mentioned (32:2–4).

38 Fourth Baruch is translated with an introduction by S.E. Robinson in Charlesworth, 2:413–25. It is preserved in more than a score of Greek manuscripts. Apparently the original language was Hebrew or Aramaic. The book is first-century, or early second. It refers to Agrippa (who gained control of much of Palestine in the 40s CE). It is particularly concerned with the loss of the holy vessels of the Temple (3:9–10).

39 For a general discussion of these texts, see: Michael E. Stone, "Reactions to Destruction of the Second Temple," *Journal for the Study of Judaism in the Persian, Hellenistic and Roman Periods*, 12 (Dec. 1984), 195–204; Philip E. Esler, "God's Honour and Rome's Triumph. Responses to the fall of Jerusalem in 70 CE in three Jewish apocalypses," in Philip E. Esler (ed.), *Modelling Early Christianity. Social-Scientific Studies of the New Testament in its Context* (London: Routledge, 1995), 239–58.

Limitations of space preclude our dealing with each text individually, but taken together they confirm the wisdom of the Rabbis: they were right to ignore these works (which were therefore preserved only in fugitive form in Christian archives).These apocalypses, though possessing individual felicities, nice turns of phrase and an occasional arresting image, are not strong enough to bear the weight that is placed upon them – namely, providing an emotionally and intellectually satisfying theodicy for the destruction of Jerusalem, and a blueprint for its replacement, if not on earth at least in heaven. (Indeed, none of them explains very satisfyingly why the Temple was destroyed: the Apocalypse of Abraham blames the disaster upon idolatry, 2 Esdras sees it as God's will, but cannot really fathom that will, 2 Baruch presents a doctrine of predestination, and 4 Baruch blames Jerusalem's demise on the sins of its inhabitants.) As apocalypses, they lack the dizzying, almost hallucinogenic spin of Enoch or of Revelation; as invective, they lack the bile and maledictory rhythm of the more engagé psalms or the denunciatory items in the Dead Sea Scrolls; as messianic visions they lack the anchoring in a specific personality that is crucial to the Christian scriptures. And, as narratives, they lack the force of the Genesis-Kings unity and of the Four Gospels. They are, therefore, unequal to the task of explaining the recent past and of presenting a solution to the dilemma of how to carry on a Temple religion, when the Temple was gone.

40 For an elegant summary of the recent state of historical scholarship on the Bar Kokhba revolt, see Benjamin Isaac and Aharon Oppenheimer, "The Revolt of Bar Kokhba: Ideology and Modern Scholarship," *Journal of Jewish Studies*, 36 (spring 1985), 33–60. Also excellent is Richard G. Marks, *The Image of Bar Kokhba in Traditional Jewish Literature. False Messiah and National Hero* (University Park, Penn: Pennsylvania State University Press, 1994). The modern revision of Emil Schurer's classic *The History of the Jewish People in the Age of Jesus Christ (175 B.C.-A.D. 135)* (vol. 1, 1885), as annotated and edited by Geza Vermes and Fergus Millar (Edinburgh: T. and T. Clark, 1973) is also valuable (1:534–57). An evocative chronology of some of the more important archaeological finds is Yigael Yadin, *Bar Kokhba. The rediscovery of the legendary hero of the last Jewish Revolt against Imperial Rome* (London: Weidenfeld and Nicolson, 1971). The archaeological materials are detailed in Yigael Yadin, *The Finds from the Bar Kochba Period in the Cave of Letters* (Jerusalem: Israel Exploration Society, 1963) and in Naphtali Lewis, Yigael Yadin and Jonas C. Green, *The Documents From the Bar Kokhba Period in the Cave of Letters* (Jerusalem: Israel Exploration Society, 1989).

41 Marks, 8.

42 Jer. Talmud, Ta'anith 37b; Marks, 14. The possibility that Simon assumed the *nom de guerre* himself and that this was only later ratified by Akiba is not a matter of discussion in the historical literature.

43 Vermes and Miller, 543-4.

44 The Rabbinical literature is summarized in Marks, 13-56.

NOTES TO CHAPTER ELEVEN

1 Concerning the term "Rabbi" and "Rabbis" as used in this book, three minor matters of clarification are in order. First, I follow the scholarly convention of referring

to the leaders of the "Pharisees" in the years before 70 CE, and to the "Rabbis" thereafter. So long as one realizes that the actual transition was not that quick (though, as religious evolution goes, the developments were swift), then the convention is a convenience and is not misleading. Second, the term "Rabbis" is used to refer collectively not only to Palestinian scholars (who, soon after the Temple's destruction, seem to have come to accept the term "Rabbi") but also to those who taught, or had been trained in the Babylonian school and were called "Rav," a term that frequently fused with their own names (such as in the case of the great Rav Abba, who became "Rava"). When individuals of the two separate schools are referred to, I will, of course, endeavour to use their appropriate national title. However, "Rabbis" will be used as the collective term covering the entire band of scholars, Palestinian and Babylonian collectively. Third, I think it is a pilpulistic exercise to try to enforce a distinction between the work of the early Rabbis and "Rabbinical thought." Granted, the Rabbis of the years before, roughly, 150 CE did not engage in the full panoply of discourse that characterizes Rabbinic thought two centuries later, when the two Talmuds were in formation, but I do not see that anything is gained by introducing a distinction which obscures the continuity between early and later figures in classical Rabbinical Judaism.

2 H.L. Strack and G. Stemberger, *Introduction to the Talmud and Midrash* (Edinburgh: T. and T. Clark, 1991), 123.

3 Herbert Danby, *The Mishnah, translated from the Hebrew with introduction and brief explanatory notes* (Oxford: Clarendon Press, 1933). Danby's prose is elegant, early twentieth-century academic English.

4 Jacob Neusner, *The Mishnah. A New Translation* (New Haven: Yale University Press, 1988). This version is in accessible, but not slangy, American English. It has the great advantage of being affixed with Neusner's system of identification of individual "verses," which makes precise referencing possible.

5 Philip Blackman, *Mishnayoth* (London: Mishna Press, Ltd., 1951–1964).

6 Danby, xxiii*n*1.

7 Strack and Stemberger, 134–70. For a general discussion of the dating of the classical Rabbinic texts, see Appendix E.

8 The technical problems in producing a critical edition of the Mishnah are immense, given the fragmentary and late character of the manuscript sources. Even more difficult is a set of problems that arises from the two earliest partial transcriptions of portions of the Mishnah, the Jerusalem Talmud and the Babylonian Talmud. Each contains material unique to itself (quotations of most Mishnah tractates are more extensive in the Bavli than in the Yerushalmi); the order of presentation of Mishnah material is not identical, and on some substantive matters the texts of the Mishnah that are quoted bear opposite meanings. These difficulties as between the two Talmuds hold whether one believes that the Talmuds' versions of the Mishnah were taken down from the lips of oral custodians or that they came from earlier written sources which have subsequently disappeared.

9 Craig A. Evans, "Mishnah and Messiah 'in context': Some Comments on Jacob Neusner's Proposals," *Journal of Biblical Literature*, 112 (Summer 1993), 269. Evans's meaning is that the historical writers are cited *qua* historians three dozen times, ahistorical usage of their material being considerably more frequent.

10 Yosef. H. Yerushalmi, *Zakhor. Jewish History and Jewish Memory* (Seattle: University of Washington Press, third ed., 1996), 17.

11 Ibid., esp. 57–75. Yerushalmi's entire text, a modern scholarly classic, richly repays close reading.

12 Neusner articulates this point in many of his books written since 1981. An economical summary is found in his indispensable *Introduction to Rabbinic Literature* (New York: Doubleday, 1994), 122–24.

13 If one is stretching very hard for references to the belief in the resurrection of the dead, Sanhedrin 6:2 is a just-possible instance. There the procedures for stoning a man to death are set forth. If a man pleads not-guilty, and is tried and convicted, then, the trial being over, he is to be taken to a stoning-place outside of the town or encampment. When the execution party is ten cubits (five to six metres) away from the site, the judges are to say to the felon, "confess: admit that you are guilty – for whoever confesses his guilt has a share in the world to come." As an historical indication of the theological commitments of the author-editors of the Mishnah this seems to me to have virtually no probative value, but entire tapestries have been woven from less thread than this.

14 For an explication of this text, see B.M. Bokser, "Messianism, the Exodus Pattern, and early Rabbinic Judaism," in James H. Charlesworth (ed.), *The Messiah. Developments in Earliest Judaism and Christianity* (Minneapolis: Fortress Press, 1992), 241–46.

15 The most common explanation for the lack of references to Moshiah, resurrection, and apocalyptic-times, is that the Mishnah is a work almost entirely of Halachach and that the other interests were to be expressed elsewhere. Indeed: for the Pharisees and Rabbis of the first and second century, where? Here we are again encountering the paradox that bedevils so much allegedly-historical work on the Yahweh-faith, on Second Temple Judahism, on Christianity, and, now, on Rabbinic Judaism: that many of the beliefs that are supposed to be fundamental are those for which we have the least evidence and those for which we have the most evidence are those which are held to be secondary.

16 Strack and Stemberger, 142–44; Jacob Neusner, *Method and Meaning in Ancient Judaism* (Chico, Montana: Scholars Press, 1981), 101–214.

17 In addition to the instances discussed in the text, either Moses or Sinai are mentioned in legal arguments a dozen-and-a-half times, but not in a manner implying any special authority. These references are geographical or historical in the most limited sense.

However, one mention of Moses occurs in a swatch of dialectic that shows with rare clarity how conscious the early Rabbis were of the development of the

Jesus-faith and of the Christian scriptures. Readers will note that in Chapter Nine, note 19 and also Appendix D, section 4, the matter of divorce, as presented in both the Pauline writings and in the Gospels, as being an important matter both to the Apostle Paul and to Jesus-the-Christ, and, given its positioning in the "New Testament," to the inventors of the Christian faith. Jesus is reported to be much more rigorous than the Pharisees in the matter of divorce: he virtually forbids it, even though Moses and all his juridical descendants had approved of the dissolution of marriage under certain circumstances.

Most challenges coming from the Jesus-faith could be ignored in stony silence, but the divorce issue hit the Rabbis hard. The Christian scriptures set up an analogy: just as Jesus was more rigorous on basic family law than were the Pharisees, or even their alleged progenitor, Moses, so the Christians were more in line with Torah than were the Rabbis. That hurt. Clearly, the early (70–135 CE) Rabbis knew of the content of the emerging Christian canon or of the oral tradition that underlay it, as is indicated by the following:

A. Said a Galilean *Min*, "I complain against you, Pharisees.

B. "For you write the name of the ruler with the name of Moses in a writ of divorce."

C. Say Pharisees, "We complain against you [singular], Galilean *Min*.

D. "For you [plural] write the name of the ruler with the name [of God] on the [same] page.

E. "And, moreover:

F. "For you write the name of the ruler above, and the name [of God] below.

G. "As it is said, *And Pharaoh said, Who is the Lord, that I should hearken unto his voice to let Israel go* (Ex. 5:2).

H. "And when he was smitten, what did he say?

I. *"The Lord is righteous* (Ex. 9:27)." (Yadayim, 4:8, Neusner ed.)

There are any number of explanations of this passage, but consider this possibility: the word *min* means heretic generally and, as in the Eighteen Benedictions, was applied with particular vigour to adherents of the Jesus-faith. Some of the later editions of the Mishnah read "Sadducee" instead of "heretic" (Danby, 785*n*1), thus erasing the embarrassing recognition of the troublesome figure of the "Galilean heretic." At minimum, the author-editors of the Mishnah were conscious of the fact that the post-70 followers of a Galilean heretic were retailing his views on divorce with considerable effect. The passage in question deals with the problem by suggesting that the difference between the Galilean heretic and the Pharisees was a matter of the usage of the name of Yahweh on the same sheet as that of a profane monarch. This takes away the moral issue (that perhaps these Pharisees, and, therefore, the Rabbis were self-indulgent on the divorce issue and thereby destructive of the divine institution of marriage) and turns it into one of spiritual *lese majesté*.

That is the minimum. Consider, however, the piquancy of the text if one contemplates two possibilities: (1) that the Mishnah here is actually presenting an historical memory of Pharisaic times, not of later Rabbinic views that are projected into the pre-70 era. This is not an outré suggestion, given that the denunciation is embedded in a complex of historical distinctions (comprising Yadayim 4:6–8) wherein distinctions between the Pharisees and Sadducees are stated, the position of the books of Homer as non-sacred is declared, and the differences between the Galilean heretic and the Pharisees are articulated. (2) That one of the matters on which the "New Testament" testifies to the views of Yeshua of Nazareth with real evidentiary strength is the divorce question. This matter has pre-70 attestation (by Paul who disagrees with it) and satisfies the real "criterion of embarrassment," namely, that a speech ascribed to Jesus was preserved despite its running contrary to the bulk of the words put in his mouth by the Gospel writers. It must have been too well known to elide.

Of course all this is speculative, but it sits close to the scanty evidence: which shows that both Christian and Rabbinical sources (that in each case *may* go back to pre-destruction times), agree on there having been a sharp argument between the Pharisees and a Galilean who criticized their view of divorce and did so within the rubrics of Pharisaism.

18 Martin Noth, *The Laws in the Pentateuch and Other Studies* (Edinburgh: Oliver and Boyd, 1966, original German ed., 1957), 86.

19 David W. Halivni, *Midrash, Mishnah and Gemara. The Jewish Predilection for Justified Law* (Cambridge: Harvard University Press, 1986), passim.

20 E.P. Sanders, *Jewish Law from Jesus to the Mishnah. Five Studies* (London: SCM Press, 1990), esp. 309–31.

21 Jacob Neusner, *Medium and Message in Judaism. First Series* (Atlanta: Scholars Press, 1989), 3.

22 Jacob Neusner, "The Mishnah in Philosophical Context and Out of Canonical Bounds," *Journal of Biblical Literature*, 112 (Summer 1993), 292.

23 Strack and Stemberger, 153.

24 Jacob Neusner, *Oral Tradition in Judaism. The Case of the Mishnah* (New York: Garland Publishing, 1987), 84–85.

25 Ibid., 77–86. For a discussion of repetition as a technique in the Mishnah, see Dov Zlotnick, *The Iron Pillar – Mishnah. Redaction, Form and Intent* (New York: KTAV Publishing House, 1988), 72–106.

26 The question of how much independent authority on matters of Temple ritual the Mishnah implicitly asserts is a matter of considerable and acrimonious debate. The issue is a contentious one because the distance between what the Mishnah prescribes and the thinner details found in the Pentateuch touch sensitive nerves. These relate to the nature of the oral tradition and its appropriate position in Rabbinical literature. If there is a large gap, indicating a significant degree of originality on the part of the author-editors of the Mishnah (as compared to scripture) this

can be taken as indicating a strong oral tradition, equivalent in power to the written (that is, the scriptural) tradition, and thus confirming the concept of the Dual Torah. Paradoxically, the same gap can be taken by others as indicating that the oral tradition is in some sense corrupt (and thus that the Dual Torah is invalidated) since it departs significantly from scripture. These sensitivities become all the more live when cross-hatched with the conflicting matrix of personalities, motives, and agendas that inevitably appear in scholarly work. For an indication of how nasty the scholarly literature can become, see the discussion concerning Jacob Neusner's suggestion that the "rite of the red heifer" (a ritual burning for expiation of sin) was a radical re-invention by the author-editors of the Mishnah and an example of a cleanliness ritual that could be conducted outside of the Temple, and thus conducted in the post-70 environment. In particular, see: H. Maccoby, "Neusner and the Red Cow," *Journal for the Study of Judaism*, 21 (Dec. 1990), 60–75, and Jacob Neusner, "Mr. Maccoby's Red Cow, Mr. Sanders's Pharisees – and Mine," *Journal for the Study of Judaism*, 22 (June 1991), 80–98.

27 Neusner, *Judaism. The Evidence of the Mishnah*, 229.

28 The history of the development of the synagogue as an institution is one of the least documented aspects of the evolution of what we today call the Jewish faith. Certainly institutions that can be called "synagogues" without anachronism existed before the destruction of the Second Temple. Significantly, they are not mentioned in Ezra-Nehemiah which is the last of the Tanakh's post-exilic historical books to be written. Nor, in 1 and 2 Maccabees, wherein the persecution and epic vandalism of Antiochus Epiphanes in the second century before the Common Era is chronicled, do synagogues find mention. Yet, some sort of social gathering place must have existed, particularly in diaspora communities, and it is hard to envision such a meeting place, even if merely a large private house, not having religious usage: where, after all, could diaspora Jews, and those in Palestine who lived far from the Temple, read and pray together? Hence, the evidence is very confusing. By the beginning of the Common Era there certainly existed synagogues all over the diaspora: the "New Testament" is an excellent witness (that most valued of sources, a third-party witness), for Paul and some of the other apostles preached frequently in synagogues in diaspora lands. Within Palestine, synagogues certainly existed: one scholar has estimated that as many as 360 synagogues existed in Jerusalem itself, and this on the eve of the Temple's destruction. Yet, in sharp contrast, there are only three actual archaeological sites within Palestine that have been found that can clearly be identified as synagogues. The problem, it would appear, is simple, but very frustrating: if (as seems to be the case) synagogues were either private houses used on Shabbat and on festival days for religious observances, or if they were religious-cum-community centres built on the model of a private house, most of them will have left no physical evidence that distinguishes them from everyday vernacular structures.

See: Rachel Hachlili, "Diaspora Synagogues," *ABD*, 6:260–63; Howard Clark Kee, "The Transformation of the Synagogue after 70 CE: Its Import for Early Christianity," *New Testament Studies*, 36 (1990), 1–24; Eric M. Meyers, "Synagogue," *ABD*, 6:251–58; Louis I. Rabinowitz, "Synagogue," *EJ*, 15:579–83.

29 Although the author-editors of the Mishnah for the most part take the synagogue for granted (there are about a dozen *en passant* references to synagogues), two more focused types of reference bear note. One of these consists of occasions when the Temple practice of the pre-destruction years is reported as having been coordinated with worship in synagogues. For example, the high Temple ritual of the Day of Atonement includes a section (Yoma 7:1) wherein the high priest takes the scroll of the Torah from a functionary of what is sometimes interpreted as "the community" (Neusner), and sometimes translated as "the synagogue" (Danby). A similar interaction between the high priest and a representative of the community in which the Torah scroll is given to the high priest to read from (Sotah 7:7–8), is taken to mean either the "head" of "the assembly" (undefined: Neusner), or the chief of a synagogue (Danby). Unambiguous, but of less liturgical moment was the ruling (Terumoth 11:10) that heave-offerings of oil that had become unclean could be burned for illumination in a synagogue. Possibly, these cases indicate at least some formal liturgical tie between Temple and synagogue in the later years of the Second Temple. The clearest reference to synagogue practice is the tractate Megillah which prescribes the way the Book of Esther is to be read in towns and villages, and this perforce involves synagogues. That this is the case is made clear by a triad of prescriptions (Megillah 3:1–3) which state the proper set of priorities for buying and selling synagogue buildings and religious artifacts, including the scroll of the Torah and the Ark. Further, the proper texts to be read in synagogues on all the great festival days are defined (Megillah 3:4–4:10). That the discussions in Megillah carry no direct contact with Temple practice or personnel suggests (but only suggests, not proves) that we are witness here to one of the early post-Temple prescriptions of how to proceed in the absence of the Lord's Temple.

30 Jacob Neusner, *Androgynous Judaism. Masculine and Feminine in the Dual Torah* (Macon: Mercer University Press, 1993), 6. Neusner argues that this masculine component, the Mishnah's law code, is gentled by the "feminine virtues" of the exegetical law code that later develops to comment on the Mishnah. The two Talmuds, he suggests, impose a system of feminine virtues on the masculine structure of the law. That this essentialist argument will be accepted by feminist critics is doubtful.

31 For a prescient and admirably controlled discussion of women in the Mishnah, see Judith R. Wegner, *Chattel or Person? The Status of Women in the Mishnah* (New York: Oxford University Press, 1988).

32 In cutting to the heart of the Mishnah's logic-system – its binary nature – I am necessarily leaving aside matters on which skilled scholars have spent lifetimes: the varying patterns of argumentative arrangement according to topics discussed,

and the unique form of inductive collection of data that lies behind the arrangement of cases. Jacob Neusner in several places points out that the Mishnah can be considered an instance of the widespread practice of list-making; what is unique is the matters listed.

33 Meir Havazelet, "Sherira ben Hanina Gaon," *EJ*, 14:1381–82; Jacob Neusner, "Foreword," in Jacob Neusner (ed.), *The Modern Study of the Mishnah* (Leiden: E.J. Brill, 1973), xii-xiv.

34 Jacob Neusner, *The Rabbinic Traditions about the Pharisees before 70*, three vols. (Leiden: E.J. Brill, 1971). The implications of these volumes as they concern the Mishnah are found in Neusner, *Judaism. The Evidence of the Mishnah* (Chicago: University of Chicago Press, 1981), 48–166.

Jacob N. Epstein's major work was his *Introduction to the Text of the Mishnah* (in Hebrew, 1948). I am grateful to Herbert Basser and to William Morrow for helping me to comprehend Epstein when I bogged down. One has to be somewhat uncomfortable with Epstein's work because, though his evidentiary perspective was that of the scholarly academy, his work has yet to be replicated. Given the unsystematic way he formulated his evidentiary patterns, I wonder if it ever can be. Thus, it should perhaps be considered a collection of hard-won aperçus; in contrast to Neusner's work which, certainly, is capable of being replicated: that is, of being re-run and either verified or falsified. A shrewd appreciation of Epstein is found in Baruch M. Bokser, "Jacob N. Epstein's *Introduction to the Text of the Mishnah*" in Neusner, *The Modern Study of the Mishnah*, 13–36, and Bokser's "Jacob N. Epstein on the Formation of the Mishnah," ibid., 37–196.

35 One has to use a modelling approach, rather than presenting precise and testable hypotheses, because the number of major variables one has to explain is greater than the evidence-sets that relate to those variables. Thus, several different models can cover the same phenomena.

36 Compare Danby, Appendix III, 799–800 and Daniel Sperber, "Tanna, Tannaim," *EJ*, 15:798–803.

37 These genealogies are of particular interest because the Waitangi Tribunal, which is using them to help adjudicate land and resource claims, examines them as an evidentiary form, thus opening them to critical scrutiny by juridical means.

38 Anthony J. Saldarini, "Pharisees," *ABD*, 5:298.

39 This point is demonstrated by Neusner in multiple volumes, and is well summed up as follows: "It is not uncommon to find the House of Shammai and the House of Hillel take up positions [in the Mishnah] on points profoundly rooted in the period after Bar Kokhba, that is, in the names of authorities a century after the Houses." Jacob Neusner, "The Use of the Mishnah for the History of Judaism prior to the Time of the Mishnah," *Journal for the Study of Judaism*, 11 (Dec. 1980), 183.

That noted, I should emphasize that the range of possibilities concerning the creation and editing of the House of Shammai and the House of Hillel material is considerable, and the changing opinions of Jacob Neusner are useful in defining the possibilities. In reviewing these, it will become clear that the Houses material in the Mishnah is best understood if one considers it to be a literary genre of its own, rather than primarily a set of historical memories. Four points.

First, no one has made a plausible case that the Houses were complete fictions. The competing schools of Shammai and Hillel were, in all probability, real congeries of Pharisaic thinkers, dating back to the early first century, when their founders were alive. Second, curiously, the pericopae that refer to the Schools material are not commented on directly by any of the named masters who lived before the destruction of the Temple (Neusner, *Rabbinic Traditions*, 2:3). This does not necessarily mean that the Houses material is invalid, or that the tone of pre-70 disputes was not lively and acrimonious, but it leaves wide open the possibility of major subsequent tinkering. Third, the arguments between the House of Hillel and the House of Shammai are strikingly parallel to the arguments in the later first century era between, respectively, Rabbi Eliezer ben Hyrcanus and Rabbi Joshua ben Hananiah. This raises the obvious possibility of the Houses dispute having been used pseudepigraphically by those two Sages (Neusner, ibid., 2:3), or even that the genre of the Houses debate was so drastically twisted that the two Houses "are really Rabbis Joshua and Eliezer ..." (Sanders, 171). Fourth, Neusner later became convinced that the bulk of the Houses material was the product of arguments within Rabbinical circles that arose after the conclusion of the war of 132–135: "I am able to show that attributed to the ancient Houses are positions on issues moot after Bar Kokhba's war, and that the opinions assigned to the Houses by the second century authorities are suspiciously similar to those held by the second century masters. The second century figures play an active part in the formation of the 'tradition' of the Houses. Since the same authorities give in their own names what they also state in the names of the Houses, there can be little doubt that the attributions to the Houses are, in fact, invented and fictitious. This is especially likely because the authorities of the period after 70, which intervenes between the Houses and the epigones, are remarkably ignorant of the principles espoused by the Houses and even the basic issues debated by them. A gap of over a century in a continuous tradition is curious." (Jacob Neusner, *Method and Meaning in Ancient Judaism*, Chico: Scholars Press, 1979, 41*n*).

One is not here required to judge between this range of possibilities, only to relate it to the point being made in the text. This broad variety of interpretations of the Houses of Hillel and Shammai material is possible only because the historical memory concerning those founding Houses was weak: either in the sense of being blurred and imprecise, or weak in the sense of its capturing material that did not command much respect and therefore could be radically reworked by later parties without any sense of impiety.

40 Neusner, *Rabbinic Traditions*, 1:6.

41 Epstein failed to demonstrate that collections of Halakhot, which certainly existed prior to 70 CE (civil law courts, for example, clearly operated in Second Temple Palestine) were specifically Pharisaic. See Bokser, "Jacob N. Epstein on the Formation of the Mishnah," 41–44; Strack and Stemberger, 145–46. When Epstein invoked historical argumentation, as distinct from linguistic and form-based arguments, he made major errors of reversal. He took references to Temple services as being early (part of any potential Ur-Mishnah) because they would have been made, he assumes, when the Temple was in existence. Given that the Mishnah's early roots were Pharisaic (a point which he accepts) and given that the one thing that both Rabbinic and external sources (the "New Testament" and Josephus) agree on is that the Pharisees were not priests, the inclusion of the details and duties of priestly Temple service were excluded from the contents of any pre-70 proto-Mishnah, virtually by definition.

I am very sceptical of there having been a proto-Mishnah (as distinct from floating traditions and discussion that are later subsumed into the massive composition, our Mishnah), not least because the remembrance of pre-70 matters is so very indistinct: not crisp, the way material for a consciously-collected, accurately-recited collection would be.

42 Neusner, *The Mishnah: An Introduction* (Northvale, New Jersey: Jason Aronson Inc., 1989), 42–43. This summation of what a proto-Mishnah would have contained has not been seriously challenged. However, it is situated within a larger debate that concerns the relative valences and force-values of the various components of the Pharisaic system in the pre-70 years. The major players in the debate, as in other discussions concerning the Rabbinical corpus, are Neusner and E.P. Sanders. In addition to Sanders's *Jewish Law from Jesus to the Mishnah. Five Studies*, which has been referred to already, see his *Judaism. 63 BC – 66 CE. Practice and Belief* (Philadelphia: Trinity Press, 1991). For Neusner's position, in addition to material cited in the present chapter, see his *Judaic Law from Jesus to the Mishnah. A Systematic Reply to Professor E.P. Sanders* (Atlanta: Scholars Press, 1993).

43 Jacob Neusner, "The formation of rabbinic Judaism: Yavneh (Jamnia) from A.D. 70 to 100," *Aufstieg und Niedergang der Romischen Welt* (Berlin: Walter de Gruyter, 1979), II. Principat 19.2, 21.

44 Ibid., 21. I am emphasizing here Neusner's strong statement of the destruction of the Temple as a primary historical determinant of the development of Rabbinical Judaism, because, during the 1980s and '90s, as he increasingly turned from historical considerations to philosophical and theological ones, he sometimes denied that the Temple's destruction was causal.

45 The basic folktale is in chapter four of Abot de Rabbi Nathan, as translated by Judah Goldin. It is found in Jacob Neusner, *First-Century Judaism in Crisis. Yohanan ben Zakkai and the Renaissance of Torah* (New York: Abingdon Press, 1975), 146–47.

46 Josephus, *Jewish War*, 2:410–16.

47 Henry Friedman, "Akiva," *EJ*, 2:491.

48 This awkward phrase is necessary because the Mishnah does not permit scholars to do form-critical studies in the same way they are accomplished for the "Old" and "New Testaments." Neusner created a method which married some of the techniques of form-criticism to his own canons of historical sequencing, based on the interdigitation of references in the Mishnah. The result is the only stratigraphy of the Mishnah that has a transparent methodology and thus is capable of verification by other scholars. (This in contrast to Jacob Epstein's work, the methodological assumptions of which are not articulated clearly enough to permit replication of his study.)

49 Neusner, *Judaism*, 48–121.

50 Ibid., 119.

51 Bokser, "Jacob N. Epstein on the Formation of the Mishnah," 47–49.

52 The one exception is the tractate Eduyyoth. Opinions diverge widely on why this exception occurred.

53 Danby, 454*n*3 and *n*8.

54 Harold Bloom, "Introduction," in Harold Bloom (ed.), *Genesis* (New York: Chelsea House Publishers, 1986), 1.

55 A parallel from the same time period, pre-Christian Ireland: the Irish *filidh* (poets) were responsible, depending on their scholarly rank, for being able to recite any of a certain great quantity of poems (bardic eulogies, etc.). The *filidh* traditionally carried a bundle of small wands which acted as aids to memory. These had incised on them in Ogham (an alphabet requiring only straight lines and thus easily transferrable to wood), on which the first line or two of the major poems were inscribed, as basic cues. (I am grateful to Professor John Kelleher for this information.)

56 An ancillary matter which, alas, has to remain cautiously speculative is the question of when the Hebrew canon of the Tanakh was finally set. As discussed in Chapter Three, the Torah and the Nevi'im had gelled as authoritative (even if the exact order of the individual "books" still varied slightly) before the Maccabean Revolt (167 BCE). However, the Kethuvim – the "Writings" – still were open. Serious reservations existed about certain books that were eventually included: notably Daniel, Ecclesiastes and the Song of Songs. On the other hand, numerous other documents held spiritual authority and bid fair to be included in any authoritative collection of Hebrew scriptural texts. These included, from the later Second Temple era: 1 and 2 Maccabees, the Wisdom of Ben Sirach, Tobit, Judith, First Enoch, and Jubilees. From soon after the Second Temple's destruction there were the apocalyptic volumes of Second Baruch, Fourth Baruch, Fourth Ezra, and the Apocalypse of Abraham. None of the volumes just mentioned was "sectarian" in the technical sense of being wrack from the far shore of Second Temple Judahisms: the desert sects. Each was within the tramlines of what the main Juda-

hist factions would accept as legitimate religious expression. In fact, however, most of the debatable volumes were excluded from the Tanakh. Clearly, a closure occurred. But who directed it, and when?

Until the 1980s, the prevailing hypothesis among both Jewish and Christian scholars was that the Writings (and thus the entire Tanakh) was closed when the Pharisees-cum-Rabbis took refuge in Yavneh from 70–132 CE. This was a useful hypothesis, because it was bracketed by a set of real-world events that can be precisely dated (the Temple's destruction and the Bar Kokhba revolt) and it makes sense in terms of what the textual evidence (particularly the Mishnah) makes clear was going on at Yavneh: the embryonic Rabbinic beliefs were being defined and it is realistic to suggest that concern with the nature of scripture characterized some of their discussions. The Yavneh-hypothesis went off the rails, however, in reifying a metaphor derived from later Christian tradition: on the basis of the later Christian practice of holding binding ecclesiastical councils, it was suggested that a "Council of Yavneh" had occurred and that there the emerging Jewish faith defined its scriptural canon. There was no council of Yavneh. It was a useful way of conceptualizing an historical possibility, but it now has outlived its usefulness. (See D.E. Aune, "On the Origins of the 'Council of Javneh' Myth," *Journal of Biblical Literature*, 110 (Fall 1991), 491–93.)

Nevertheless, the basic suggestion that during the Yavneh era the early Rabbis debated the nature of scripture is sensible. However, I would make three suggestions. First, that we not search historically for something that probably was never there, a Christian-style congress, that met for a relatively brief period, made a set of tightly specified decisions, and disbanded. Instead, the decisions about scriptures should be conceived of as taking place over a period of years, and as part of the continuing existence of Rabbinic academic life. Secondly, the closure of the Tanakh most likely was effected at the same time that the Rabbis became concerned about the written form (however rudimentary) of the halachic debates that they eventually collect as the Mishnah. I am suggesting, concerning the Mishnah, that the most likely time for the Mishnah to have been crystallized in writing (even while it continued to be mostly studied as an oral form) was in the decade or decade-and-a-half after the Bar Kokhba revolt: for it was at that point that the legitimate worry arose that the oral tradition might be lost because the keepers of the oral tradition might be scattered, or, like Akiba, killed. Written transmission as a means of survival insurance becomes important, one surmises: certainly it is a suggestion that relates to events outside the often-hermetic texts, events that are verifiable by third-party sources. So, an hypothesis that deserves testing is that by roughly 150 CE, the rudimentary notes for the Mishnah were set on paper, and agreement was close on which of the potential Writings actually was authoritative, in the sense of being worthy of being preserved alongside the Torah and the Nevi'im. That the crystallizing-point was the middle of the second century of the Common Era, rather than an earlier era, ties nicely with the invisible editors' rule that governs the Writings: cut apocalyptic material, cut, cut, cut. Only the Book of Daniel of all the rich array of late Second Temple apocalyptic texts is preserved in the Writings, and it is the one apocalypse with the most demonstrably-historical character, for many of its "predictions" concern early Maccabean history which the author-editors of Daniel had experienced. But all the rest are let go, and in fact we owe their preservation to their being maintained by Christians, in the penumbra of the Christian scriptures. The Rabbis cut the apocalyptic material, I would suggest, because, in 132–135 CE they had just been through a Messianic experience, a moment which by definition is in part apocalyptic in character – and which failed horribly, definitively. The editorial consensus (to use an anachronistic term) concerning the Writings would, I believe, have been much different if it had been reached before the Bar Kokhba revolt: before 132, apocalypse was a possible form; after, out, out, out.

However, if we focus solely upon 135–150 as our speculative-date for the most important decisions concerning the final contents of the Tanakh, we run the risk of re-introducing the Christian concept of a conciliar-moment, even if we don't use the phrase. So, it is more productive to think of 135–150 as a fulcrum-period in the history of the scriptures. But we must remind ourselves that the process was one of cross-time consensus, not of legislative articulation. Thus, one notes that the Babylonian Talmud, of at least three centuries later, continues Rabbinical arguments about whether Ecclesiastes and the Song of Songs were worthy of the Tanakh. (See the reference in Nahum M. Samna, "Bible," *EJ*, 4:817.)

Thus, a set of suggestions concerning the closure of the Hebrew scriptures, one that meshes with verifiable external chronology and fits with our hypothesis about the chronology of invention of Rabbinic Judaism, particularly its central component, the Mishnah. Namely that: (1) the process was a multi-generational one and did not have a single narrow legislative moment; (2) the first generation of Rabbis at Yavneh did not focus their primary efforts upon the "canon," but upon the matters that eventually become the heart of the Mishnah; however, their attitude towards recent history – as indicated in the Mishnah material from the Yavneh era – involved a rejection of recent history. The direct implication for the Writings was a predisposition to exclude later Second Temple historical narratives from any collection of material upon which they placed spiritual reliance. (3) That soon after the Bar Kokhba debacle, and the obvious physical vulnerability of the Rabbis, it became important to deal with matters of written-texts. Thus, one speculates that in the decade or decade-and-a-half after 135, the Mishnah was first outlined in a written form, and the nature of the final section of the Tanakh, the Writings, became of great importance. In this era, following the Messianic debacle, the predisposition to rid the Writings of recent-history was doubled, and the decision was made to clear out almost all future-history as a genre. And (4) the consensus had to be ratified, as it were, by generations of Rabbinical usage. This came only with time, centuries.

In suggesting that the closure of the Jewish scriptural canon is most profitably considered in conjunction with the beginning of the written articulation of the basic document of the "oral tradition," I am not suggesting anything methodologically radical. Specialists in the field may find the idea a fruitful hypothesis or not, but the idea does not itself cross any attitudinal chasms. However, a related suggestion may require more emotional distance than most scholars can muster: that the closing of the Jewish version of the scriptures and of the Christian version of those same scriptures ideally should be dealt with simultaneously, as part of a single phenomenon.

This seems to me to be dictated by one of those simple facts that remains hidden, because it is hidden within plain sight: that the Rabbinical Jewish and the Christian versions of the "Old Testament" are, despite differences in arrangement, the same set of documents. Mostly, of course, this is attributable to the bulk of the texts having become authoritative before the beginning of the Common Era, as the Septuagint clearly demonstrates. However, the Writings, a very heterogeneous collection of works, were not closed until well into the Common Era. Even the Rabbinical writings – which have a tendency to project events and arguments into ever-earlier periods – make the earliest possible time for the closing of the Writings (and thus, for a closing of the Tanakh), as being sometime after the destruction of the Second Temple in 70 CE. So, one has to ask, how did the two derivatives of the Yahweh-faith, the Christian and the Rabbinical Jewish faiths, come to the same conclusion about the proper character of this set of texts? It is possible, but statistically highly-improbable that the authorities of each of the faiths made the same decisions and did so independently. There are simply too many variables for that to be anything but a one-in-100,000 likelihood: not only did both groups include the same controversial volumes but they also rejected as unworthy exactly the same items. (That the Christians preserved, on the periphery of the canon, many of the books that the Rabbis suppressed, does not obviate the fact that the texts that were given primary authority – *the* canon – were the same.) Therefore, it follows that these two sets of decisions were not independent: they were interactive with each other.

In practical terms, only three sorts of interaction were possible: (1) that the Rabbis were dependent upon decisions made by the Christians, a suggestion that seems to me to be outré in the extreme; (2) that the Christians, in ways that are as yet undefined and undocumented, accepted as authoritative the Rabbinical decisions concerning the scriptures. That would mean, by my reckoning, that even as late as the mid-second century, some important Christian groups were accepting the superior wisdom of the heirs of the Pharisees in this crucial matter. This is a possibility strenuously denied by virtually all Christian sources, from the Four Gospels onward, but it warrants more than cursory dismissal. Or (3) that avenues of mutual influence as between some influential Christian leaders and Rabbis existed well into the second century. Not friendship: but knowledge of each other's views.

57 Indeed, separating the categorical inventions of Akiba and of Meir may be a false exercise. One of the diagnostic points in the intellectual relationship between the two is that Meir never directly cites Akiba (Zlotnick, 30). In our present world, that would be taken as an example of distance and, perhaps, of rejection of the teacher by the disciple. (Any post-graduate student who doubts this should experiment: leave the work of your thesis advisor out of your footnotes and bibliography.) However, in the Mishnah era, the usual practice was for a pupil to assimilate and teach his Rabbi's laws and opinions anonymously, thus turning them into floating apodictic statements whose power was so strong they did not need to be certified by attribution. This pattern held for several major figures of the time. See Bokser, "Jacob N. Epstein on the Formation of the Mishnah," 49. What held true for substantive matters must, for Akiba and Meir, have held even more tightly for structural innovations. So, in one sense, Akiba and Meir become one collective intelligence.

58 See Neusner, *Judaism*, 119.

59 Ibid., especially 16, 55, 87–91, 97–101, 132–37, 150–53.

60 Ibid., 132.

61 Significantly, in later Rabbinic tradition, Judah the Patriarch was given both a scholarly and a more mythic genealogy. In the first, he was the student of Jacob ben Korshai who was a pupil of Akiba's, and there is no reason to doubt this. However, in legend, the middle-generation between Akiba and Rabbi was elided: Rabbi was said to have been born on the day Akiba died.

   While granting his undoubted spiritual wisdom, it still is relevant to note that Judah the Patriarch was the most successful of the post-135 Jewish leaders in the homeland and that through his assiduous cultivation of the Roman authorities he gained for the patriarchate a semi-royal status, and guaranteed toleration for his co-religionists. See Gedaliah Alon, *The Jews in their Land in the Talmudic Age (70–640 CE)* (Cambridge: Harvard University Press, 1989 tr. by Gershon Levi from Hebrew ed., 1980), passim; [anon.], "Judah ha-Nasi," *EJ*, 11:366–372.

NOTES TO CHAPTER TWELVE

1 Although my argument is very different from his, this point is at the heart of David Halivni's brilliant monograph, *Midrash, Mishnah, and Gemara. The Jewish Predilection for Justified Law* (Cambridge: Harvard University Press, 1986).

2 Herbert Danby, *The Mishnah* (Oxford: Clarendon Press, 1933), vn4.

3 Ibid., 5.

4 That Aboth's compelling character is not merely a matter of relatively modern times is indicated by the fact that Aboth spawned its own commentary and expansion, Aboth de Rabbi Nathan (the Fathers according to Rabbi Nathan). The date is indeterminate, but c.500 is a reasonable speculation. See Jacob Neusner, *Introduction to Rabbinic Literature* (New York: Doubleday, 1994), 591–608.

5 Jacob Neusner's edition of the Mishnah (New Haven: Yale University Press, 1988) excises the chapter altogether. Danby included it in his 1933 edition, but with the strongest of reservations: "The sixth chapter is no part of the Mishnah. It is, however, included in all modern editions of the Mishnah and in the Jewish Prayer Book." (Danby, 446n1)

6 As is argued efficiently, but unconvincingly, in E.P. Sanders, *Jewish Law from Jesus to the Mishnah. Five Studies* (London: SCM Press, 1990), 327–28. The portion of chapter two of Aboth that actually is spongy runs from the second half of verse four through seven, wherein it is unclear if the "Hillel" who is being quoted is the great Hillel or one of the sons of Judah the Patriarch who carried that given name.

   An additional, if less significant instance of Post-Rabbi referencing is the citation of Rabbi Yannai (4:15) who lived in mid-third century (Danby, 454n10). Yannai is not cited in the Mishnah-proper.

7 As is firmly noted in H.L. Strack and G. Stemberger, *Introduction to the Talmud and Midrash* (Edinburgh: T. and T. Clark, 1991), 137. There the word "abnormal" is applied to Aboth.

8 Since it is widely believed that the Talmuds were not yet in existence as formal structures, even in fragments, until the fourth century, these words placed in Judah ben Tema's mouth either indicate a quite late – fourth-century – origin for Aboth; or that "Talmud" in the generic sense of systematic commentaries on the Mishnah already was a recognized form by the mid-third century, if that is taken as Aboth's date. Unhappily, one is here caught in a circle of evidentiary uncertainties.

9 See the beautifully crafted "Several Sidelights of a Torah Education in Tannaite and Early Amoraic Times," in Judah Goldin, *Studies in Midrash and Related Literature*, (eds.) Barry L. Eichler and Jeffrey H. Tigay (Philadelphia: Jewish Publication Society, 1988), 201–13.

10 In addition, two anomalous cases were included in this set, pointing once again to the post-Mishnah origins of Aboth. One of these is the reference to Rabbi Yannah (4:15), a mid third-century figure (Danby, 454n10). The other is Rabbi Eleazar ha-Kappar (or Haqqappar), a contemporary of Judah the Patriarch who is otherwise unknown in the Mishnah.

11 These are found interspersed in Aboth 3:1–4:5. In addition, four extra-Mishnah figures from this era are cited. That is, Sages who do not appear in the Mishnah-proper: Eleazar of Modiim (3:12 Danby ed; 3:11 Neusner ed.); Levitas of Yavneh (4:4); Samuel the Younger, var: Samuel the Small (4:19); and Elisha ben Abuyah (4:20).

12 Aboth is ambiguous concerning the spiritual (and biological) descendants of Rabban Gamaliel I. It is unclear whether Gamaliel I had a son named Simeon, who was the father of Rabban (Simeon ben) Gamaliel I (who is thus the grandson of Gamaliel I) or whether only one Simeon existed, the son of Gamaliel I and, eventually, the father of Rabban Gamaliel II. Good arguments exist for each.

13 Emero Stiegman, "Rabbinic Anthropology," *Austieg und Niedergang der Romischen Welt* (Berlin: Walter de Gruyter, 1979), II, Principat, 19.2, p. 489.

14 Paul V.M. Flesher, "Zugoth," *ABD*, 6:1175.

15 Paul V.M. Flesher, "Great Assembly," *ABD*, 2:1089; Strack and Stemberger, 69. For the expansion of this invention in the later Rabbinical literature, see Ira J. Schiffer, "The Men of the Great Assembly," in William S. Green (ed.), *Persons and Institutions in Early Rabbinic Judaism* (Missoula: Scholars Press, 1977), 237–76.

16 Judah Goldin, "Avot," *EJ*, 3:983.

17 Jacob Neusner, *Early Rabbinic Judaism. Historical Studies in Religion, Literature and Art* (Leiden: E.J. Brill, 1975), 82. This volume collects the most important of Neusner's early essays and remains one of the most rigorous discussions available on early Rabbinic thought.

18 That access to the Tosefta is not limited to students of Rabbinics, but is available to the wider scholarly community that studies the history of the humanities, is a tribute to the work of Jacob Neusner. His six-volume translation into English (New York: Ktav, 1977–80) is the only translation into any language, ancient or modern. Neusner fully acknowledges the pioneering work on a critical edition of the Tosefta's Mishnaic Hebrew text by Saul Lieberman. Volume 1 is jointly edited with Richard S. Sarason and includes translations by several of Neusner's graduate students.

19 Moshe D. Herr's estimate that "the Tosefta is about four times larger than the Mishnah" ("Tosefta," *EJ*, 15:1283) is widely cited, but is slightly misleading. I suspect it lost something in translation, because it is clear that he means the Tosefta is four times the size of the Mishnah, not larger by four times (which, of course, would be five times the size of the Mishnah). Probably, a more accurate statement of the situation would be (a) that the new material the Tosefta includes is almost twice the size of the Mishnah, and (b) that when the Tosefta is presented in its full form, comprising the Mishnah, the Tosefta's commentaries and new beraitot, the result is three times the size of the Mishnah.

20 See Herr, "Tosefta," 1283–85 and Strack and Stemberger, 167–81. Herr's suggestion of 400 as a date is not acceptable because portions of the Tosefta are found in the Jerusalem Talmud, which itself was being framed during the fourth century.

21 These relationships will be discussed more fully in the text, but here the reader is referred to the chapter on the Tosefta in Neusner's *Introduction to Rabbinical Literature* (129–52) which asserts and then illustrates the chain-sequence of Mishnah-Tosefta-Talmuds. It is a *tour de force*. I have read perhaps 250 of Jacob Neusner's books and monographs (less than half of his monumental *oeuvre*), and in that body of work, this chapter, in my opinion, is his single most remarkable and compelling combination of textual analysis and persuasive rhetoric.

22 A good example is that even in the lapidary essay, "Talmud," by Robert Goldenberg, one finds the following: "For scholars, therefore, the Tosefta is noteworthy

because it sheds some light on the development of the materials appearing in the Mishnah itself, but there will be little further occasion to mention it here." Goldenberg in Barry W. Holtz (ed.), *Back to the Sources. Reading the Classic Jewish Texts* (New York: Summit Books, 1984), 137.

23 Precise counts have not been done. These estimates seem to be the best inferable from Neusner, "Preface," the first volume of the Tosefta, page x, and Neusner, "The Synoptic Problem in Rabbinic Literature," *Journal of Biblical Literature*, 105 (Sept. 1986), 501–02.

The most important study that could be conducted concerning the Tosefta would be to define and analyse what the Tosefta chooses to comment on in the Mishnah and what it does not. Is there a sub-text of privileged material? Or is the specific Mishnah material discussed because it is the most troublesome in some societal or theological sense or, perhaps, because it is the most ambiguous and thus most in need of explication?

24 The two possibly-significant messianic references in the Mishnah that were discussed in Chapter Eleven – Berakoth 1:5 and Sotah 9:15 – are effectively undeveloped. To Mishnah Berakoth's mention of the messianic age, only this comment is added: "Said to them Ben Zoma, 'But does one mention the exodus from Egypt in the messianic age?' " (Tosefta, Berakoth 1:10E). The messianic reference in Sotah is not referred to. Thus, the Tosefta is no more interested in the messianic concept than is the Mishnah.

25 The two clear references to the resurrection of the body found in the Mishnah – Sotah 9:15 and Sanhedrin 10:1 – are not much expanded. The commentary on Sanhedrin 10:1 simply adds to the list of those who are to have no portion in the world to come, anyone "who breaks the yoke, violates the covenant, misinterprets the Torah ..." (Tosefta, Sanhedrin 12:9B). And the resurrection reference in Sotah 9:15 is not found in the Tosefta. (Here it is well to remember that, in any case, most scholars consider the end of Sotah to have been added later and not to have been part of Rabbi's Mishnah.)

26 Craig A. Evans, "Mishnah and Messiah 'In Context': Some Comments on Jacob Neusner's Proposals," *Journal of Biblical Liberature*, 112 (summer 1993), 269.

27 See Tosefta, Ta'anith, 3:9–10.

28 The five references in the Mishnah-proper that potentially cite an origin in the theophany on Mount Sinai are: Pe'ah 2:6, Rosh Hashanah 2:9, Edduyoth 8:7, Hullin 7:7, and Yadayim 4:3.

29 Compare Mishnah, Abot 2:5 and Tosefta, Berakoth 6:18C.

30 Scholars may wish to examine the possibility that the five Mishnah references cited above (note 28) and the Sinai references in Tosefta, Yadayim 2:16H, are retrospected items: that is, that some of them were inserted into the Mishnah-proper and the Tosefta after Aboth was accepted as authoritative. My argument in the text, however, holds in any case.

31 Goldin in Eichler and Tigay (eds.), 234*n*84.

32 Interestingly, the Mishnah's statement (Hullin 7:6D) that "At Sinai was [the law] stated, but it was written down in its [present] place" – which could possibly be taken to refer to an early written version of the Mishnah – is revised in the Tosefta to form a question which reads, "So why does he [Moses] write it there [in the Pentateuch's story of Jacob]?" (Shehitate Hullin 7:8E).

33 Jacob Neusner, *Form Analysis and Exegesis: A Fresh Approach to the Interpretation of Mishnah, with special reference to Mishnah-tractate Makshirin* (Minneapolis: University of Minnesota Press, 1980), 3.

34 On the genre, see Moshe D. Herr, "Midreshei Halakhah," *EJ*, 11: 1521–23; Strack and Stemberger, 269–99. The other major classical items in this exegetical genre are Sifra to Numbers and Sifra to Deuteronomy, and the Mekhilta attributed to Rabbi Ishmael, which deals with the Book of Exodus.

35 I do not wish to give the mistaken impression that I am being dismissive of the Midreshei Aggadah for, in fact, they are among the items that as an avocational reader of religious literature, I most enjoy and find most profitable. However, they must be considered satellite items that revolve around the core texts of Rabbinic Judaism, and not components of that primary core.

36 That it is now possible to conduct a discussion of Sifra within the requirements of the disciplines of history and related humanities as defined by the modern academy is almost solely a result of the work of Jacob Neusner. With the aid of his postgraduate students in portions of the work (which he fully acknowledges), Neusner has provided the only English-language translation of Sifra (Atlanta: Scholars Press, 1988, three volumes). More importantly, his is the only version of Sifra in any language (including Hebrew) that can be used effectively in scholarly conversations. This is because the text of Sifra is a mess, and only by Neusner's having created a sensible system of reference of each idea-unit, can one refer with any degree of precision to a specific passage. Moreover – and this is a feature almost as important as the first – Neusner identifies Sifra quotations and indirect references not only to the base-text, the Book of Leviticus, but also to passages in the Mishnah and the Tosefta that are incorporated into Sifra. These later references are given with the precision made possible by Neusner's previously having created a sharp-definition reference system for the entire Mishnah and the entire Tosefta. Therefore, given these references and a knowledge of the biblical texts used in Sifra, it is easier to understand where a given passage of Sifra came from, and how, therefore, old material was re-invented and took on radically-new meanings.

37 Few academically based scholars have taken Sifra seriously, although I expect that this will soon change. Among Jacob Neusner's several discussions of the book, I have found the following to be the most useful: *How the Talmud Shaped Rabbinic Discourse* (Atlanta: Scholars Press, 1991), 21–51; *Sifra in Perspective. The Documentary Comparison of the Midrashim of Ancient Judaism* (Atlanta: Scholars Press, 1988); *Uniting the Dual Torah. Sifra and the Problem of the Mishnah* (Cambridge: Cambridge University Press, 1990).

38 I say "conservative," because whenever two or more pericopae from the Mishnah and the Tosefta are quoted with only a few-sentence breaks between them, I have counted this as only one instance of argumentative quotation.

39 An example: Parashat Ahare Mot Pereq 3, CLXXVIII:I, v. II.

40 For example, Parashat Ahare Mot Parashah 4, CLXXXI:I, v. I–3.

41 This occurs frequently. See, for example, Parashat Behar Parashah 3, CCL:II, v.I.

42 See Jacob Neusner, "The Hermeneutics of the Law in Rabbinic Judaism: Mishnah, Midrash, Talmuds," in Magne Saebo (ed.), *Hebrew Bible/Old Testament. The History of its Interpretation*, vol. 1, *From the Beginnings to the Middle Ages* (Gottingen: Vandenhoeck and Ruprecht, 1996), 309–11; Neusner, *Wrong Ways and Right Ways in the Study of Formative Judaism. Critical Method and Literature, History, and the History of Religion* (Atlanta: Scholars Press, 1980), 75–91. These items carry the textual citations for the argument that I am summarizing above.

43 The unspoken phrase here that prefaces this discussion of Sifra is: "as we at present have it." Of the texts in the core Rabbinic tradition, Sifra has the least pure textual tradition.

44 Parashat Qedoshim Pereq 4, CC:I, vs. 5.B.

45 In the primary core of Rabbinic documents, it is not possible to obtain any third-party tracking on Joshua ben Perahiah. Aside from his one triad of statements (in Aboth 1:6), his only putative utterance in the Mishnah-proper is the phrase "he may not" in a debate about whether or not a man could lay hands on a beast before it was slaughtered on a festival day (Mishnah, Hagigah 2:2).

46 Parashat Behar Parashah 1, CCXLVI:I, v. I,C-E.

47 Parashat Behuqotai Pereq 8, CCLXIX:II, v. 12–15.

48 N=332

Order	%
Seder Zera'im	6.0
Seder Mo'ed	12.0
Seder Nashim	1.5
Seder Nezikin	15.4
Seder Kodashim	37.1
Seder Tohoroth	28.0

49 For bibliographies of the most important scholarly items on the Yerushalmi, see: Stack and Stemberger, 182–207; Baruch M. Bokser, "An Annotated Bibliographical Guide to the Study of the Palestinian Talmud," in *Augstieg under Niedergang der Romischen Welt* (Berlin: Walter de Gruyter, 1970), Principat 19.2, II, pp. 139–256.

50 "Talmud" has several meanings. The word can refer to the generic activity of studying Torah in general. Sometimes, it refers primarily to scriptural study and, thus, "talmud" occasionally means something like "midrash," or "exegesis." At other times it is used to denominate the general activity of interpreting the Mishnah. In other instances, it refers to a specific corpus of interpretation of the

Mishnah, such as when I referred to the Tosefta as "the First Talmud" or, as in the present case, to a commentary on Mishnah such as the Jerusalem Talmud. When "the Talmud" is employed, it almost always means the Babylonian Talmud. In this book I have limited the use of the term "Talmud" to specific commentaries on the Mishnah, each of which is clearly identified.

51 "Gemera" is another term whose meaning needs to be tied down. It can mean simply the learning of tradition (the term is Babylonian Aramaic, meaning either "tradition" or "to learn.") More often it refers to comments on passages in the Mishnah by various Sages; and to utterances by the Sages which, though they do not deal directly with a section of the Mishnah, nevertheless are collected in one of the talmuds, as being at least tangentially relevant to a particular issue defined in the Mishnah. Those are the meanings of the word when employed in the present study. These variants are encompassed in a single, larger meaning: namely, post-Mishnah comments of all sorts, collected in a talmud. Elsewhere, "Gemara" is occasionally used to refer to an entire talmud, most often the Bavli, but I avoid that usage.

52 Louis I. Rabinowitz, "Talmud, Jerusalem," *EJ*, 15: 772–81.

53 These are listed in Strack and Stemberger, 187.

54 Goldenberg, in Holtz (ed.), 136.

55 That scholars in the humanities and the historical disciplines have access to the Yerushalmi is (as is so often the case in Rabbinical studies) a monument to the work of Jacob Neusner. No full translation of the Yerushalmi in any European language was available until he organized a thirty-four volume translation into English (Chicago: University of Chicago Press, 1984–93). Most of the tractates were translated by Neusner, but several were done by his students, and these contributions are fully identified on the title pages of the respective volumes.

56 In the case of the Yerushalmi, as in all the documents of the core tradition of classical Rabbinic Judaism that comment on the Mishnah – the Tosefta, Sifra, the Yerushalmi, and the Bavli – the most fundamental of textual studies has yet to be completed. Missing in each case is a study that provides for each document (1) a definition of what items in the Mishnah each document chose to comment upon; (2) an indication of which passages and idea-units are privileged, not just by extensive commentary but by their position within particular skeins of argument, and (3) a definition, therefore, of what the subtext of each document is. The point is this: the discussion of what each Talmud does with the Mishnah is only half the story; equally important is what it chooses not to do and, at the most elementary level, what portions of the Mishnah each talmud decides to ignore.

57 Rabinowitz (*EJ*, 15:774) and Strack and Stemberger, 186.

58 Strack and Stemberger, pp. 185–86.

59 The cause of Edduyoth's being eccentric in form does not here matter. Some scholars believe that its unique form is a result of its being the earliest tractate of the Mishnah to be fully framed; others that it was a late addition. The issue at present is entirely problematic.

60 Strack and Stemberger, 185–86. I exclude tractates Eduyyoth and Aboth from this Lost Continent thesis because there are sufficient reasons, more specific and more robust (and thus with more explanatory power) for their exclusion, than are contained in the generalized Lost Continent idea.

61 Jacob Neusner, *The Talmud of the Land of Israel*, vol. 35, *Introduction: Taxonomy* (Chicago: University of Chicago Press, 1983), 43–44.

62 Ibid., 44.

63 Ibid., 45.

64 Roger Brooks, "Introduction" to his translation of *Pe'ah* (volume 2 in the Neusner edition of the Yerushalmi), 23.

65 I present this judgement with some hesitation, because such an able scholar as David Kraemer has directly asserted that the myth of the Dual Torah is fully conceptualized for the first time in the Yerushalmi. The primary text does not seem to me to justify this statement, but see David Kraemer, "On the Reliability of Attributions in the Babylonian Talmud," *Hebrew Union College Annual*, 60 (1989), 175–90.

66 Louis Ginzberg, *A Commentary on the Palestinian Talmud* (New York, 1941), quoted in Neusner, *The Talmud of the Land of Israel*, 35:ix.

67 See for example the following portions of the Yerushalmi: Berakoth, 9:1, XIII, C; Erubin, 10:14, V. A; Ta'anith, 4:2, XIII, B; Megillah, 3:6, II, A; Nedarim, 9:1, I, E; Sanhedrin 4:8, II, B.

68 Yerushalmi, Sanhedrin, 10:1, VIII, L.

69 Also, the Mishnah, Pe'ah 2:6 is quoted in Yerushalmi, Pe'ah, 2:6, C.

70 The references which follow are from the Neusner edition of the Yerushalmi and there are denominated as being in Hagigah 1:8. However, other editions of the Yerushalmi have the material in 1:7 and, indeed, Neusner on occasion (for example, in *Uniting the Dual Torah*, 334–35) uses the 1:7 citation.

71 Yerushalmi, Hagigah, 1:8, V, B.

72 Yerushalmi, Hagigah, 1:8, V, J. A similar statement is found in Yerushalmi, Megillah, 4:1, II, L; similarly, in Yerushalmi, Pe'ah, 2:6, III, A.

73 Yerushalmi, Hagigah, 1:8, V, N. Scripture is also given the final authority in the parallel discussion in Yerushalmi, Megillah, 4:1, II, Q.

74 Low-level cleverness can appear to extract the Rabbis from their conundrum: one can claim that the argument about the comparative "preciousness" of the two forms of Law is not an argument about relative authority, but about inherent value. That is a word game: value, preciousness, authority, are all the same thing, words that say, effectively, "which set of laws, Oral or Written, takes precedence?" That issue the Rabbis are unable to resolve in the Yerushalmi.

75 Rabinowitz, *EJ*, 15:775.

76 These figures are from samples drawn by Jacob Neusner and by Roger Brooks. See Neusner, *The Talmud of the Land of Israel*, 35:52 and Brooks, 2:5.

77 Formulated for Yerushalmi, Baba Batra, by Jacob Neusner (p. 1); this holds for the entire Jerusalem Talmud.

78 Halivni, (1986), 67.

79 Jacob Neusner, *Judaism and Christianity in the Age of Constantine. History, Messiah, Israel, and the Initial Confrontation* (Chicago: University of Chicago Press, 1987) and *Judaism in the Matrix of Christianity* (Philadelphia: Fortress Press, 1986); *Judaism in Society: The Evidence of the Yerushalmi* (Chicago: University of Chicago Press, 1983).

80 Neusner, *Judaism...Age of Constantine*, 67, employing as an exhibit Yerushalmi, Abodah Zarah I:I, IV, E-K.

81 Ibid., xiii. One should not equate patience with passivity, however. As Louis H. Feldman argued, even in the difficult times of the fourth and fifth centuries, Judaism remained attractive to non-Jews, and Jewish proselytizing (or, if one prefers, missionary activity) continued to be both forceful and successful. Louis H. Feldman, "Proselytism by Jews in the Third, Fourth, and Fifth Centuries," *Journal for the Study of Judaism*, 29 (June 1993), 1–58.

82 See the tortured and inconclusive discussion in Horayoth (3:15, III, D-I) about whether the Mishnah or the scriptures takes precedence.

83 Necessarily, this discussion, which takes the Jerusalem Talmud as a whole, precludes discussion of the contention that various layers of development may be discerned within the document. One obvious text that is here relevant is Yerushalmi, Shekalim, 8:4, IV, Q-R, which refers matter-of-factly to the rebuilding of the Temple, as if it were imminent. This suggests that the passage was written during the reign of the Emperor Julian (361–363), the anti-Christian ruler who, apparently, intended to aid the Jews in the building of the Third Temple.

84 Moshe D. Herr, "Church Fathers," *EJ*, 5:554.

85 Yerushalmi, Sanhedrin, 10:1, I, H-I.

86 That Bar Kokhba pressed on their consciousness is clearly indicated in Yerushalmi, Ta'anith, 4:5.

87 Mishnah, Berakoth 1:5 and Sotah 9:15. The later reference is to the Neusner edition of the Mishnah. The passage in the Yerushalmi is designated as 9:16, but the content of the original Mishnah passage (in 9:15) is the same.

88 Yerushalmi, Ta'anith, 1:1, X, V and W.

89 Yerushalmi, Berakoth, 2:3, VI, A.

90 Yerushalmi, Berakoth, 2:3, V, C-N.

91 Joseph Klausner, *The Messianic Idea in Israel* (New York: Macmillan Co., third ed., 1955), 396.

92 Yerushalmi, Abodah Zarah, 3:1, II, DD. The story is doubled in Yerushalmi, Sotah 9:16, II, A.

The last-wish as Moshiah-wish is a particular mark of holiness. Thus, the last wish of Rabbi Jeremiah ben Abba, who told his disciples: "Dress me in a hemmed white garment, dress me in my slippers, place sandals on my feet and a staff in my hands and place me by the side of the road. If the Messiah comes, I will be ready" (Yerushalmi, Kilayim, 9:3, II, Y).

93 Yerushalmi, Sanhedrin, 10:1, I, A-I. The observation is that of Solomon Zeitlin, "The Origin of the Idea of the Messiah," in Leo Landman (ed.), *Messianism in the Talmudic Age* (New York: Ktav Publishing Inc., 1979), 110.
94 Yerushalmi, Sanhedrin, 4:2, I, A.

NOTES TO CHAPTER THIRTEEN

1 Even the bibliography of the bibliographies of material on the Bavli is large. As entry into the scholarly literature I have found the following most useful: David Goodblatt, "The Babylonian Talmud," *Aufstieg und Niedergang der Romischen Welt*, II. Principat 19.2, pp. 257–336, and H.L. Strack and G. Stemberger, *Introduction to the Talmud and Midrash* (Edinburgh: T and T. Clark, 1991), 208–44.

2 The two translations are (1) that directed by Israel Epstein and published by the Soncino Press (London, 1935–52), and (2) that directed by Jacob Neusner (Atlanta: Scholars Press, 1984–93).

3 Hereafter, references to material in the Bavli are given in the following fashion: title (as determined by the tractate of the Mishnah that is being commented upon) and then the standard page reference to the Hebrew-Aramaic printed version, which is given as a verso-recto reference to the page and to its overleaf. (For example, Niddah, 23b). However, this is too vague a citation for our present purposes, especially when dealing with the English translations which usually run to several pages for each page of the original text. Therefore, I shall add a page number to the Soncino edition of the same tractate (e.g. Sonc. 159). In some instances, the Soncino edition groups small tractates together, but the pagination is unambiguous.

Here the great pity is that the verse-by-verse citation system created by Jacob Neusner is of limited value and I shall not here use it. This is not because Neusner's system is without value (quite the opposite; its widespread adoption and its adaptation to the original text is a necessary prerequisite for the next stage of textual scholarship), but because an on-line search of North American libraries reveals that his translation of the Bavli is possessed by too few institutions for it to be conveniently accessible to most scholars. And if this situation holds for North America, where the translation originates, it obtains even more elsewhere.

4 The standard history is Jacob Neusner, *A History of the Jews in Babylonia* (Leiden: E.J. Brill, five vols, 1965–70).

5 Bavli, Yebamoth, 45a (Sonc. 294).

6 For example, Bavli, Megillah, 28b (Sonc. 173).

7 Implicit in the contrast between the fates of the Jerusalem and the Babylonian Talmuds is the fact that Jews were treated much better under Islam than under Christianity. For a recent evaluation of this matter, see Mark R. Cohen, *Under Crescent and Cross. The Jews in the Middle Ages* (Princeton: Princeton University Press, 1994.)

8 I note that the Bavli indicates a knowledge of Christianity and an ability to deal with some of the same doctrines held by the Jesus-faith, with strong misgivings. This is not because of any doubts about the factual accuracy of this judgement, but because it may resonate with a tradition of Christian scholarship for which I have little respect for reasons of historical methodology: the attempt to find in the Talmud passages that either confirm the "New Testament" story of Jesus-the-Christ or which show that "the Jews" had known about Jesus-as-Moshiah but had wilfully chosen to reject that knowledge. The later nineteenth- and early twentieth-centuries version of this form of scholarship at least contained some observations by respectful Hebraists. See, for example, E. Travers Herford, *Christianity in Talmud and Midrash*, (London: Williams and Norgate, 1903). The present-day exponents – colporteurs – are remarkable chiefly for employing methods of textual analysis that the rest of the world abandoned shortly after the Inquisition.

The instances in the Babylonian Talmud of references to Christianity that can be identified as such, with a high degree of probability, are as follows: Shabbath, 116a (Sonc. 571, see *n*3); Sukkah, 48b (Sonc. 227); Ta'anith, 27b (Sonc. 145); Yebamoth, 16a (Sonc. 87, see *n*8); Sanhedrin, 58b (Sonc. 399), 61b (Sonc. 417, see *n*5), 90b (Sonc. 604–605), 97a (Sonc. 656), 99a (Sonc. 672); Abadoh Zarah, 27b (Sonc. 137 and 85*n*3), 48a (Sonc.239).

The references that seem with a high degree of probability to be to Jesus or to his immediate family are as follows: Hagigah, 4b (Sonc. 17, see *n*11); Sotah, 47a (Sonc. 246, see *n*3); Gittin, 57a (Sonc. 261, see *n*4); Sanhedrin, 43a (Sonc. 281, see *n*4–7), 106a (Sonc.725, see *n*5), 107b (Sonc. 735, see *n*4); Abodah Zarah, 16b-17a (Sonc. 84–85).

I would emphasize that none of these references to Jesus are of any use in the so-called quest for the historical Jesus. They are, however, useful as an indication of what the religious leaders of the Babylonian Jewish community of the fourth-through-sixth centuries considered worth recording from amidst the welter of rumour about the founder of the Jesus-faith.

9 Eliezer Berkovits, "Talmud, Babylonian," *EJ*, 15:755–767; Richard Kalmin, *The Redaction of the Babylonian Talmud: Amoraic or Saboraic?* (Cincinnati: Hebrew Union College Press, 1989), 1–11.

10 This point, concerning the independence of Holy Land traditions being preserved in the Bavli, in preference to Yerushalmi versions of those traditions, is made by David Kraemer, *The Mind of the Talmud. An Intellectual History of the Bavli* (New York: Oxford University Press, 1990), 194*n*36.

11 If one cannot thole the indeterminancy of this situation, there are two potential ways out, neither of which seems very promising. One is to posit an unknown common textual source – comparable to "Q" in "New Testament" textual modelling – and use it to explain points of commonality between the Yerushalmi and the Bavli. (For the difficulties with this idea, see Jacob Neusner, "Das Problem des Babylonischen Talmud als Literatur: der Bavli und seine Quellen," *Kairos*, n.s.,

vol. 34–35 [1992–93], 64–74.) The other possible escape from uncertainty is to posit (and then, presumably, demonstrate) that something akin to a set of standardized editing rules govern both texts and this at the level of textual arrangement, rather than of specific content (see Kraemer, 194*n*36, citing the work of Alan J. Avery-Peck.) The difficulty here is that no major editorial protocol seems to exist that is not explained simply by reference to the Mishnah as an organizing principle. (Jacob Neusner, *Why There Never Was a "Talmud of Caesarea." Saul Lieberman's Mistakes*, Atlanta: Scholars Press, 1994, 161–67.

12 Bavli, Menahoth, 110a (Sonc. 679 and 680.)

13 Bavli, Ta'anith, 27b, (Sonc. 145).

14 Herbert Danby, *The Mishnah* (Oxford: Clarendon Press, 1933), 598*n*3.

15 S.M. Lehrman, "Introduction" to Kinnim, (Sonc. ed.), vii.

16 Goodblatt, 259.

17 José Faur, *Golden Doves with Silver Dots. Semiotics and Textuality in Rabbinic Tradition* (Bloomington: Indiana University Press, 1986), xxix.

18 Louis J. Rabinowitz, "Talmud, Jerusalem," *EJ*, 15:775. Eliezer Berkovits in *EJ*, 15:762 makes an obvious transposition error when he says that one-third of the Bavli is Halachah and two-thirds Aggadah. He means the reverse.

19 Granted, in the middle ages, the Karaite movement had attempted to reject the Mishnah and the Talmuds entirely and to follow the Tanakh as the sole source of wisdom. This movement, however, failed. Also, it is possible to see the controversy concerning the Hassidic movement in the early eighteenth century as producing a permanent split in modes of Rabbinical interpretation. More marked, apparently permanently so, was the chasm that emerged between followers of traditional (meaning medieval) Rabbinics and the heirs of the Jewish Enlightenment who, today, comprise the bulk of world Jewry. Parties (call them "denominations" if one will) proliferated in the nineteenth and twentieth centuries, the Bavli no longer being a source of cohesion, so much as the occasion of differentiation. Present-day Judaism has as bewildering an array of fragments as does Christianity.

20 For a discussion of the Rabbinic rules of argument, put in a philosophic perspective, see Susan A. Handelman, *The Slayers of Moses. The Emergence of Rabbinic Interpretation in Modern Literary Theory* (Albany: State University of New York Press, 1982), 51–82. Handelman deals fluidly with individual principles of argument (how to construct a general rule of interpretation, how properly to relate the general to the particular), but her most important point is that Rabbinic argument does not resemble so much the forms and techniques of classical Greek thought, but rather the way the Christian Church Fathers merged rationality with the service of scripture. (Some intellectual historians, indeed, believe that the late-Second Temple Jew, Philo of Alexandria, was the schoolmaster of the Church Fathers.) It is frequently stated that within Christian tradition this melding of rationality and respect-of-sacred-text came apart in the seventeenth and early eighteenth centuries. That may be true for the philosophic front-edge, particularly in

Continental Europe, but it was certainly not generally applicable in the English-speaking world. It is worth noting that the most influential textbook on rhetoric in the English-speaking world in the nineteenth and early twentieth centuries (a textbook for a rhetoric based on defensible logic) was Archbishop Richard Whately's *Elements of Rhetoric: comprising an analysis of the Laws of Moral Evidence and of Persuasion, with rules for argumentative composition and elocution* (Oxford: 1828). It was still being used in departments of speech in North America as late as the 1950s. Whately's text was a logical rhetoric for all purposes, but the audience Whately had in mind when composing it was the clergy of the Church of England. The point is that, front-edge philosophers aside, both the specific logical-rhetorical techniques employed in the Babylonian Talmud and the text-respecting tone of the Bavli were neither récherché nor inaccessible. They were part of a wider western heritage. Any English country parson of the Victorian era, were he able to read sufficient Hebrew, would have immediately understood the argumentative assumptions of the Bavli's authors.

21 Bavli, Baba Bathra, 59a (Sonc. 238).

22 This statement, which until recently was taken as axiomatic, without its being investigated empirically, has in fact been confirmed by the work of David Kraemer. See *The Mind of the Talmud*, 94–98, 193n29.

23 James Joyce, *A Portrait of the Artist as a Young Man* (London: Jonathan Cape edition, 1916–17, various impressions), Chapter 3.

24 Kraemer, *The Mind of the Talmud*, 95–96, confirming the judgement of Jacob Neusner, *Judaism in Society. The Evidence of the Yerushalmi* (Chicago: University of Chicago Press, 1983), 110–11.

25 One sometimes wonders if the author-editors of the Bavli did not learn a good deal from the negative example of King Solomon who, in the case of the child with two mothers, made one of the most bone-headed, potentially disastrous rulings ever, and was lucky to escape from its consequences. (Had not one of the two women buckled, he would have had to cut the child into two pieces.) From this, perhaps, the Sages learned: keep your options open.

26 Jacob Neusner, "The Hermeneutics of the Law in Rabbinic Judaism: Mishnah, Midrash, Talmuds," in Magne Saebo (ed.), *Hebrew Bible/Old Testament. The History of its Interpretation.* (Gottingen: Vandenhoeck and Ruprecht, 1996), 321–22.

27 Kraemer, *The Mind of the Talmud*, 52.

28 Neusner, "Hermeneutics of the Law ..." 319.

29 Limitations of space preclude discussion of the ways the Bavli cites Sifra and sometimes colonizes that text to its own purposes. Several textual examples from Menahoth, in the Bavli, are analysed in detail in Jacob Neusner's, *How the Talmud Shaped Rabbinic Discourse* (Atlanta: Scholars Press, 1991), 21–51. Neusner makes it clear that the relationship is not a simple one. Sometimes the Bavli uses a Sifra passage to make its own point; in other instances it is respectful of Sifra's text, composing a gemara on them, just as it does on portions of the Mishnah.

Other Sifra passages in the Bavli are identified in Neusner's *The Talmud of Baby-lon. An Academic Commentary*, 36 volumes (Atlanta: Scholars Press, 1994–96).

30 Berkovits, *EJ*, 25:758. The example which follows is his.

31 Bavli, Gittin 12a (Sonc. 40–42.) The entire discussion is in the context of divorce, and requirements for valid divorces are being compared to requirements for a valid writ of slave emancipation.

32 These are efficiently summarized, with references to specific examples, by Berko-vits, *EJ*, 15:758.

33 Kraemer, *The Mind of the Talmud*, 151. The examples employed in the text are taken from Kraemer's citations.

34 Bavli, Yoma, 81a (Sonc. 395–397).

35 Bavli, Zebahim, 99a, (Sonc. 473–474).

36 Bavli, Baba Bathra, 12a (Sonc. 59). Kraemer (154) employs the word "Sage" to make clear that the reference is not merely to a "wise man" in the general sense.

37 Strack and Stemberger, 210.

38 Louis Jacobs, *The Talmudic Argument. A Study in Talmudic Reasoning and Meth-odology* (Cambridge: Cambridge University Press, 1984), 22.

39 Judah Goldin, "On the Talmud," Judah Goldin (ed.), *The Living Talmud. The Wis-dom of the Fathers and its Classical Commentaries* (New York: New American Library, 1957), 27.

40 See Jacobs, 20–23, and 203–213, on which I have here drawn. Jacobs's entire vol-ume deserve close reading. It is a rare mix of a very rigorous analysis of Talmudic reasoning with a deep appreciation of the work as a whole.

41 This is not solely a matter of its size – two and one-half million words – though that certainly precludes memorization by any save "empty heads," as the Rabbis termed certain professional memorizers. The Bavli has no mnemonic structure. More important is Louis Jacobs' observation: "It is impossible for a literary work of this nature, in which there are such things as literary device and the working up of the material to a carefully calculated climax, to be carried by successive gener-ations only in the mind and expressed by word of mouth. True, even today, there are those who do know the whole Talmud by heart, but that is because they know the completed work. The shaping of the material in this way can only have been done, originally, in writing." (Jacobs, 20–21). See also Kraemer, *The Mind of the Talmud*, 100ff.

42 That the earliest complete manuscript of the Babylonian Talmud which is still ex-tant, that of 1342, was in book-form of course does not necessarily reflect the sixth-century original. The arguments for the original form having been as a co-dex are those found in the text above. For a plate of a page from the 1342 manu-script, see David S. Loewinger, "Manuscripts, Hebrew," *EJ*, 11:902.

43 Goodblatt, 268, translating from A. Harkavy (ed.), *Responsen der Geonim*, (Ber-lin: 1887), 138.

44 Bavli, Sukkah, 28a (Sonc. 122–123).

45 Bavli, Gittin, 56a (Sonc. 255).

46 Ibid. (Sonc. 255n4).

47 Bavli, Gittin, 56a (Sonc. 256–257).

48 Bavli, Sanhedrin, 97a (Sonc. 655–656).

49 In addition to the textual references to the resurrection which are found in the discussion to follow, unambiguous affirmations of the belief in the resurrection of the individual are found in the Bavli: Berakoth, 15b (Sonc. 91); Shabbath, 88b (Sonc. 321); Sotah, 49b (Sonc. 271); Pesahim, 68a (Sonc. 345–46); Ta'anith, 2b (Sonc. 4); Kethuboth, 111a (Sonc. 716–17); Kiddushin, 39b (Sonc. 194), Baba Bathra, 16a-b (Sonc. 80–81), 16b (Sonc. 84); Sanhedrin, 90b (Sonc. 603–04); 92b (Sonc. 618); 113a (Sonc. 780), Abodah Zarah, 18a (Sonc. 90); Hullin, 142a (Sonc. 823).

50 Bavli, Kethuboth, 103a (Sonc. 657–658).

51 Bavli, Berakoth, 65b (Sonc. 377).

52 Bavli, Sanhedrin, 91a-b (Sonc. 610–11).

53 Bavli, Sanhedrin, 108a (Sonc. 739).

54 Bavli, Berakoth, 58b (Sonc. 364).

55 Bavli, Kethuboth, 111b (Sonc. 720).

56 Bavli, Hagigah, 12b (Sonc. 71–72).

57 Bavli, Shabbath, 152b-153a (Sonc. 780).

58 Bavli, Rosh Hashanah, 16b-17a (Sonc. 65).

59 For details from other Rabbis of what the eternal life of the righteous might be like, see: Bavli, Berakoth, 17a (Sonc. 102) and Megillah, 15b (Sonc. 90).

60 Bavli, Rosh Hashanah, 16b-17a (Sonc. 63–65).

61 Bavli, Baba Bathra, 75a (Sonc. 299–300). The preceding pericopae deal with the fearsome qualities of Leviathan – fiery breath, foul odour, and the ability to make the seas boil – and details how he will be made into the main dish for a banquet by the Almighty.

62 Bavli, Rosh Hashanah, 31a (Sonc. 146). The parallel to the Book of Revelation (20:4–5) is clear.

63 Bavli, Baba Bathra, 10b (Sonc. 49–50).

64 Ibid., 75b (Sonc. 302).

65 Bavli, Kethuboth, 111b (Sonc. 720–722).

66 Bavli, Shabbath, 63a (Sonc. 295).

67 Ibid., 151b (Sonc. 773).

68 Bavli, Ta'anith, 8a. (Sonc. 32, with variation).

69 Ibid., 31a (Sonc. 165). The base text (Isaiah 25:9) clearly refers to the Almighty, but the Messianology of the Jesus-faith used its resonance in a reference to Jesus (see Titus 2:13).

70 Bavli, Pesahim, 54b (Sonc. 267).

71 Bavli, Kethuboth, 112b (Sonc. 728).

72 Bavli, Sanhedrin, 97a (Sonc. 654).

73 Ibid., 118a (Sonc. 608).

74 Bavli, Pesahim, 118a (Sonc. 608) and Abodah Zarah, 3b (Sonc. 8- 9). Compare this to Revelation 20: 7–9.

75 Bavli, Yoma, 10a (Sonc. 44) where it is said that Rome will have sway over the whole world for "nine months." (Also, Bavli, Sanhedrin, 98b, Sonc. 665.) See also, Bavli, Abodah Zarah, 8b-10a (Sonc. 40–49) where the prediction of Rome's fall is so complicated that the Sages conduct a long argument about it, without resolution.

76 Rav Hillel (not to be confused with the great Hillel) asserted that there would be no future Moshiah for Israel, because Israel already had enjoyed his presence during the reign of King Hezekiah (Bavli, Sanhedrin, 98b, Sonc. 667). And several times the Sages have to argue around an opinion, based on Deuteronomy 15:11, that the only difference between the Messianic age and the present one would be what government one was forced to serve. For example, see Bavli, Berakoth, 34b (Sonc. 215), Shabbath, 63a (Sonc. 295), and 151b (Sonc. 773), and Pesahim, 68a (Sonc. 346–347).

77 I have a great deal of respect for some of the now-classic studies of Moshiah and of Messianic expectations. In particular, Joseph Klausner's, *The Messianic Idea in Israel* (New York: Macmillan Co. 1955, translated from earlier works published between 1909 and 1923). A comparable classic is George Foot Moore's *Judaism in the First Centuries of the Christian Era. The Age of the Tannaim*, especially vol. 2 (Cambridge: Harvard University Press, 1927). A useful collection of central articles from the first two-thirds of the twentieth century is Leo Landman (ed.), *Messianism in the Talmudic Age* (New York: Ktav Publishing House, 1979).

78 Bavli, Pesahim, 54a (Sonc. 265). This is a re-invention of Psalm 72:15, a psalm of praise of King Solomon.

79 Bavli, Sanhedrin, 98b (Sonc. 667–668).

80 Bavli, Sukkah, 52a (Sonc. 246). Obviously, Christian apologists can jump on this as a reference to Yeshua, son of Yosef, of Nazareth. Maybe it is, but if so, it is an indication of the Rabbis' awareness of Christian Messianic beliefs, but it is not an endorsement of them. If, indeed, this awareness is here present, it is a repudiation of this Moshiah ben Joseph (that is, Jesus-the-Christ) as the real Messiah, for it is the slaying of this man that is the prelude to the true Age of the Messiah which begins with another Messiah, Moshiah ben David. (See the text above.) Still, this recognition of Moshiah ben Joseph would at least grant to that figure a functional part in the divine plan. However one parses the concept of the Moshiah who is the son of Yosef, the author-editors of the Bavli clearly used this figure within their own pattern of belief as a subordinate aspect of their larger, and very vague, construction of Moshiah.

81 Several scholars believe that the dual-Messiah theme is found in some of the Dead Sea Scrolls, although the readings are problematic. (See Chapter Seven, section 1.)

82 Jacob Neusner, *Major Trends in Formative Judaism. Society ands Symbol in Political Crisis* (Chico: Scholars Press, 1983), 53.

83 That the *amour propre* of the Rabbis was quite sufficient to see themselves as the models for the ruler of the Age of the Messiah is indicated in a diverting discussion on quite another topic: whether or not individuals who are illiterate will be resurrected from the dead (because Torah study requires an ability to read, and this particular Rabbinical discussion is based on the assumption that Torah study is a requisite for resurrection; as we already have observed, there were other views of the resurrection, but this is the one here regnant). The dialectic, like all Rabbinic discussions, bounces back and forth, but finally, it is decided that, no, the illiterates do not necessarily lose the chance of resurrection, because it is possible to cleave unto the Lord without being able to read. How do we know this? Because any man who marries his daughter to a scholar [a Rabbi or his student] or who carries on trade on a scholar's behalf or who leaves money in his last testament to a scholar is considered "as if he had cleaved to the divine presence." Since this could include any man, literate or not, then it is possible for an illiterate man to experience the resurrection and, thereby the life of the world to come. Notice the knife's edge, on which the decision is made: marrying into a Rabbi's family or giving money to a scholar or doing business on his behalf is a direct admission to the divine presence. Bavli, Kethuboth, 111b (Sonc. 719–720).

84 Jacob Neusner, *Wrong Ways and Right Ways in the Study of Formative Judaism. Critical Method and Literature, History, and the History of Religion* (Atlanta: Scholars Press, 1988), 181–82*n*7.

85 For a very sharply focused discussion of the four passages see David Kraemer, "The Formation of Rabbinic Canon: Authority and Boundaries," *Journal of Biblical Literature*, 110 (Winter 1991), 613–20.

86 Bavli, Shabbath, 31a (Sonc. 139–140), combined with the translation of Kraemer, ibid., 619.

87 Bavli, Kiddushin, 66a (Sonc. 333–334).

88 Bavli, Gittin, 60b (Sonc. 283).

89 Bavli, Temurah, 14b (Sonc. 98–99).

90 The reader should perhaps consider Kraemer's "The Formation of the Rabbinic Canon ...," 625–26, as an alternative interpretation to mine. He holds that this passage is an indication of the hegemony of the Oral Torah. In relation to the specific text, I cannot understand his point, but the reader must decide.

91 See Bavli, Hagigah, 16b (Sonc. 106) and Nazir 56b (Sonc. 209).

92 Jacob Neusner, *Introduction to Rabbinic Literature* (New York: Doubleday, 1994), 187.

93 Judah Goldin, "Of Change and Adaptation in Judaism," in *Studies in Midrash and Related Literature*, ed. by Barry L. Eichler and Jeffrey H. Tigay (Philadelphia: Jewish Publication Society, 1988), 229–30.

94 On the possible histories of the text, see Judah Goldin, "Avot de Rabbi Nathan," *EJ*, 3:984–85, and "Introduction" to his elegant translation, *The Fathers According to Rabbi Nathan* (New Haven: Yale University Press, 1955), xvii–xxvi.

Goldin's translation is of "Version A," the standard item. "Version B" is translated by A.J. Saldarini (Leiden: E.J. Brill, 1975).

95 I am leaving aside as totally problematic the question of the degree to which the author-editors of the Bavli and the author-editors of Aboth de Rabbi Nathan were acquainted with each other's works as they developed. Indeed, I am leaving aside the possibility that at some common moment the same Sages contributed to each separate document. However, as documents, the two texts exhibit a division-of-labour concerning the Dual Torah: the Bavli does the substance, "The Fathers According to Rabbi Nathan," the provenance. This seems to me hardly to be ascribable to random factors or to a totally separate evolution of each text.

NOTES TO CHAPTER FOURTEEN

1 José Ortega y Gasset, *The Revolt of the Masses* (New York: W.W. Norton, 1957), 113 and 110.

2 See Kern R. Trembath, *Evangelical Theories of Biblical Inspiration* (New York: Oxford University Press, 1987).

3 James T. Burtchell, *Catholic Theories of Biblical Inspiration Since 1810* (Cambridge: Cambridge University Press, 1969), 279.

4 Benjamin L. Whorf, *Language, Thought and Reality* (Cambridge: Harvard University Press, 1956), 121, quoted in Paul Feyerabend, *Against Method* (London: Verso, third ed., 1993), 164n1.

5 John Donne, "Holy Sonnets," (1607–1609).

Appendices

Appendix A

Glossary

AGGADAH Portions of the Rabbinical literature composed either of brief narratives or exegetical commentary on the Tanakh. As contrasted with Halachah, the legal portions of the Rabbinical corpus.

AMORAIM Rabbis who produced the third through sixth century commentaries (the "gemara") on the Mishnah. Singular: Amora.

APOCRYPHA The non-canonical "inter-testamental" books preserved by Christians as having some sacred authority, but not as great as that of the Bible. The Protestant version (the "Apocrypha") and the Roman Catholic ("the Deutero-Canonical books") overlap, but are not quite identical. This material contains many pre-Christian items later suppressed by the Rabbinical authorities.

APORIA A term from technical logic which, in "New Testament" studies, is used in reference to spots where a portion of the narrative does not flow smoothly. Anglicized plural: aporias.

BARAITA A judgement or saying of the Tannaim that was not included in the Mishnah, but was collected in later Rabbinical literature. Plural: Beraitot.

BAVLI The Babylonian Talmud. Sometimes called the "Talmud of the East." In common parlance, when "the Talmud" is referred to, the reference almost always is to the Bavli.

BET DIN Rabbinic law court.

CATHOLIC EPISTLES James, 1 and 2 Peter, 1, 2, and 3 John, Jude.

CROSS GOSPEL A hypothetical document, believed by a few scholars to underlie the extra-canonical "Gospel of Peter."

ESCHATOLOGY Beliefs and ideas concerning the end-times, when the entire world will be reorganized according to one or another sacred principle.

EXEGESIS Exposition in detail of scripture or of Rabbinic writings.

FORMER PROPHETS Joshua, Judges, 1 and 2 Samuel, 1 and 2 Kings. *See also* Latter Prophets; Minor Prophets.

GEHINNOM A proto-Hell, modelled on the valley of Hinnom, southwest of Jerusalem.

GEMARA Usually refers to comments on passages in the Mishnah made by the Amoraim and found in the two Talmuds. However, it can also mean (1) the learning of tradition generally and (2) the entire Babylonian Talmud.

GENIZAH A storage room. Here refers to the "Cairo Genizah," a storage room for medieval sacred and secular texts discovered in a synagogue in Cairo.

HALACHAH The legal decision of the Rabbis. Plural: Halachot. Adjective: Halachic. The term sometimes refers to the entire body of Rabbinic justice.

KARAITE An "heretical" Jewish sect (so declared by their enemies, the Rabbis), of eighth century and thereafter. They granted authority to the scriptures, but not to the Rabbinic literature.

KETHUVIM The "Writings," the concluding portion of the Tanakh, consisting of Psalms through 2 Chronicles, as arranged in the Hebrew Bible.

LATTER PROPHETS Isaiah, Jeremiah, and Ezekiel (the "Major Prophets").

LEMMA The smallest unit of Rabbinic discourse. A short saying.

MAJOR PROPHETS See "Latter Prophets."

MASORETIC TEXT The authoritative text of the Hebrew Bible, dating from the tenth century CE in its present form. Noteworthy for containing "vocalization," that is, an indication of the vowels in each word.

MINOR PROPHETS Hosea through Malachi.

MISHNAH The codification of oral law upon which Rabbinic Judaism is based. Its editing is traditionally ascribed to "Rabbi," that is, Judah the Patriarch, and dated c. 200 CE.

MOSHIAH The Messiah. Various Jewish groups transliterate the word as "Moshiach," "Mashiah," or "Mashiach." Any of those terms is acceptable here.

NEVI'IM "The Prophets" in the Tanakh, consisting of Joshua through Malachi, as arranged in the Hebrew Bible.

PENTATEUCH The first five books of the Bible, often called the "Books of Moses."

PERICOPE Small units, larger than "verses," but shorter than "chapters" in biblical, parabiblical, and Rabbinic texts. Plural: Pericopes or Pericopae.

PESHER A running commentary on a biblical text. A forerunner of the several forms of Rabbinic biblical exegesis. Its main purpose is to interpret the biblical text to apply it to contemporary problems. So far, pesher texts are attested only in the Dead Sea scrolls.

PESHITTA Translation of the Pentateuch and perhaps of other books, from Hebrew into Syriac: probably first through third centuries CE, in form at present known.

PESSAH Passover.

PSEUDEPIGRAPHA Used in a general sense for any book or document ascribed to an author (usually an earlier and important personage) who did not compose it. Used in a more specific sense to refer to the heterogenous production of late Second Temple Judahist writings and some items that may be post-70 CE Christian or Jewish. In this study, the collection of items by James Charlesworth is taken as authoritative.

"Q" An hypothetical document said to underlie portions of Matthew and Luke.

RABBAN Title given to the ranking Rabbi in Palestine in first through third centuries, CE.

RAV Babylonian form of "Rabbi."

REDACTOR The final editor of a text. Sometimes an individual who changes the meaning of an earlier document through the editing process.

SABORAIM Scholars who made the final editorial changes in the Bavli. Succeeded the Amoraim, active 500–600 CE.

SECRET MARK An allegedly pre-70 CE document containing material on Jesus that was supposedly only revealed to an inner circle of Christians. Probably a hoax. (See Appendix D, note 32.)

SEPTUAGINT Translation into Greek of the Hebrew scriptures. Largely completed before the Common Era.

SHEOL The traditional Hebrew underworld.

SIGNS GOSPEL An hypothetical early gospel, said to underlie portions of the Gospel of John.

STAM Anonymous Rabbinical sayings found in the Yerushalmi and the Bavli.

SYNOPTIC GOSPELS Matthew, Mark, and Luke.

SYNOPTIC PUZZLE The question of how Matthew, Mark, and Luke are related as textual inventions.

TALMUD In general speech, usually refers to the Babylonian Talmud. However, the term also refers to the study of Holy Law in general. Also, "talmud" can refer to any early Rabbinical commentary on authoritative texts.

TANAKH The Hebrew scriptures, the equivalent of the "Old Testament" of the Christian faith. The word is an acronym, made up of syllables denominating the portions of the scriptures: Torah, Nevi'im, and Kethuvim.

TANNAIM Rabbinic and proto-Rabbinic teachers, active before the formulation of the Mishnah in c. 200 CE. Singular: Tanna.

TEFILLIN Also called "Phylacteries." Small scripture cases worn by Jewish men during morning prayers, sometimes during study, and only on weekdays. One is worn on the head, the other on the arm. Both contain small parchments on which verses from the Torah are written.

TETRAGRAMMATON The four consonants in the divine name, Yahweh. "Tetragrammaton" is sometimes used as a circumlocution by those who do not wish to utter or write the name itself.

TORAH Used in multiple and confusing ways, which must be distinguished contextually: (1) the first five books of the Jewish scriptures; (2) the entire corpus of the Hebrew scriptures; (3) the divine revelation that underlies the written scriptures; (4) divinely defined Law; (5) the total divine revelation, both written and oral, given at Mount Sinai and later expanded in Rabbinical thought.

TRACTATES One of the constituent organizing elements of the Mishnah and the two Talmuds. Roughly equivalent to "book" in the Tanakh and the "New Testament."

YAHWEH The name of the god of Judah. Misvocalized as "Jehovah" in the King James Bible.

YERUSHALMI The Jerusalem, or Palestinian Talmud. Also called the "Talmud of Eretz Israel," and the "Talmud of the West."

YESHIVA Traditional Jewish academy primarily devoted to the study of Rabbinical literature. Hebrew plural: Yeshivot; anglicized plural: Yeshivas.

Appendix B

Biblical Chronology

ANYONE WHO HAS SAT THROUGH SABBATH OR SUNDAY SCHOOL, OR university lectures on the history of religions, or made it through hot-summer-evening Bible-study will at some time or other have spent at least an hour or two with eyes glazing over, as a long list of dates – chronologies – was handed round, or written on a blackboard. Chronologies are not a lot of fun; all the good stuff is in the action and the emotion, and the lists of dates seem to lie there dying, so very inert. Yet, if properly done, chronology is to history as circuit diagrams are to computers: the lineaments of history's hardware.

The trouble with chronology, however, is that the lists of events and dates are inevitably poker-faced. Chronologists, therefore, are history's best liars. Without a flicker of an eyelid they can insert a new event into a skein of dates, or move an item from one decade to another, to serve ideological or personal ends. (One need only recall here the wonders of temporal reorganization that Soviet historians were capable of effecting during the high era of that empire.) And few chronologies give an indication of levels of probability or levels of confidence that one can place in a given date beyond, perhaps, the occasional "?" which is a sign of considerable plasticity.

Yet, the Bible is based on various chronologies, ranging from the bare-bones genealogies of the Book of Numbers to the complex and contradictory heredity of the Kings of Judah and of Israel, to the micro-chronology of Jesus' passion and crucifixion. Therefore, for a reader to begin to negotiate with the god of the covenant, Yahweh of the ancient Hebrews, a chronological vocabulary is required. This vocabulary is one of compromise between the chronological terms of the Hebrew scriptures and present-day systems of dating. Very few of the events in the Bible (either the Jewish or the Christian versions) can be precisely dated in the rigorous sense of their having external-party confirmation (a) that the events actually happened and (b) of exactly when they happened. However, a modest chronological ziggurat can be constructed, if one is willing to note clearly the limits of what can be known, and also, the probability-level of what we think we know.

So, we survey three lists. If this were a lecture rather than a book, we would be viewing three sequential transparencies projected on a screen. The first one provides the basic information and sits on the left-hand side of the screen, a sequence of solid, externally-verified information; the second level of slightly less certain information is added in the middle, and finally, the most conjectural items are found at the far right-hand side.

The first list is the most rigorous. It consists of items that relate to biblical chronology which are attested strongly and fairly precisely in non-biblical sources. The most important of these items refer to the period before 500 BCE, for it is in that era that there are long periods in which the Bible history has few external referents. Most useful of all are those that provide "absolute dates." These come from cultures in the Ancient Near East whose astronomers and astrologers were markedly more skilled than those of the Israelites. They recorded celestial events with some precision and, when events of military or political history were placed in their national chronologies, this provides modern chronologists with sets of coordinates, allowing them to run solar time backwards, and thereby to define when, by modern reckoning of time, an ancient event occurred. Such events relating to biblical history are not plentiful; they are pivotal.[1]

If there is a single message that these tables suggest, it is that prior to roughly the year 800 BCE, the Bible is almost entirely on its own. There is nothing either to confirm or to disprove its historical message, except the characteristics of the biblical documents themselves. In thinking about those documents, one must not be forced into the logic of false dichotomies. One would do well to note the wisdom of the Scottish legal system, which provided not only for the two categories of guilty and of not-guilty, which stemmed from ancient Semitic law, but also the sophisticated evidentiary bypass: "not-proved."

From the return from the Babylonian Exile onwards, the chronology is less vexed, albeit not nearly as precise as one would wish. Third-party sources anchor the main scriptural events in a general chronology that is quite solid. Table 4 provides the chronology of the Persian and Hellenic periods in Palestine, and Table 5 from the Maccabean revolt to the destruction of the Temple in 70 CE.

Table I

Events Related to the Bible for Which There Exists Strong Non-Biblical Evidence

Middle Bronze Age in Palestine	c.2000–1500 BCE
Late Bronze Age in Palestine	c.1500–1200
Mernepthah Stele: first mention of Israel outside of the Bible	c.1210
Early Iron Age in Palestine	c.1200–900
King Ahab (Israel) vs Shalmaneser III	853
King Jehu (Israel) pays tribute to Shalmaneser III	841
King Joash (Israel) pays tribute to Adad-nirari III	796
"Samaria Ostraca," Hebrew writing on shards, by clerks in Israelite capital	c.775–750
King Menahem (Israel) pays tribute to Tiglath-pileser III	740
King Ahaz (Judah) pays tribute to Tiglath-pileser III	734
King Pekah (Israel) removed. Hoshea accedes	732
Fall of northern kingdom (Israel) to Assyrians	722
Exile of some of inhabitants of northern kingdom (Israel)	720
Assyrian campaign, under King Sennacherib, against Judah	701
King Manasseh (Judah) pays tribute to Assyria	c.674
First capture of Jerusalem by Babylonians. First deportation. King Jehoiachin taken captive	597
Second capture of Jerusalem by Babylonians	587/6
Release of King Jehoaichin by Babylonians	561
Cyrus, King of Persia	539–530
Darius I, King of Persia	521–486
(Persian Rule	c.539–330)

Table 2

Events Reported in the Scriptures for Which There Is No External Corroboration, but Which Fit Reasonably Well with the External Chronology and with Related Evidence

UNITED MONARCHY:

King Saul	c. 1025–1005
King David	c. 1005–965 or 1000–960
Jerusalem made David's capital	c. 1005–1004
King Solomon	c. 965–928 or 960–925
Construction of First Temple begins	c. 964

DIVIDED MONARCHY (928–722). The Kings:

Judah			*Israel*		
Rehoboam	928 (or 925)–911		Jereboam I (also known as "Ephraim" or "Joseph")	928 (or 925)–907	
Abijam	911–908		Nadab	907–906	
Asa	908–867		Baasha	906–883	
			Elah	883–882	
			Zimri	882	
			Tibni	882–878	} years of rival rule
			Omri	882–871	
Jehoshaphat	870–846	} co-regent	Ahab	872–852	
Jehoram	851–843		Ahaziah	852–851	
Ahaziah	843–842		Joram	851–842	
Athaliah	842–836		Jehu	842–814	} co-regent
Joash	835–798		Jehoahaz	817–800	
Amaziah	798–769	} co-regent	Jehoash	800–784	} co-regent
Azariah	785–733		Jereboam II	788–747	
Joatham	759–743	} co-regent	Zechariah	747	
Ahaz	743–727		Shallum	747	
			Menahem	747–737	
Hezekiah	727–698		Pekahiah	737–735	
			Pekah	735–732	
			Hoshea	732–724	
				724–722	throne empty
			End of Israel	722	
Manasseh	698–642				
Amon	641–640				
Josiah	639–609				

Table 2   (Continued)

	Judah	Israel
Jehoahaz	609	
Jehoiakim	608–598	
Jehoiachin	597 (taken captive) – first deportations to Babylon	
Zedekiah	596–587/6	
End of Judaean monarchy		587/6
Destruction of the First Temple		587/6
Second deportation to Babylon		587/6
Fall of Babylon; Persian rule begins		539
Edict of Cyrus of Persia. Exiles permitted to return		538
Dedication of the Second Temple		520
Rebuilding of Second Temple continues		520ff

Table 3

Conjectural Biblical and Related Items for Which There Is No External Evidence and for Which Related Scholarly Assessment Is Indeterminate

Abraham	c.2000–1800
"Patriarchal Age"	c.2000–1800
Israel into Egypt	c.1700–1600
The Exodus from Egypt led by Moses	c.1250
Hebrew tribes conquer Canaan	c.1200
Period of confederacy of twelve tribes	c.1200–1025
"Deuteronomic Revolution" limits sacrifices to Jerusalem temple	621

Table 4

Chronology of Persian and Hellenic Periods in Palestine

Fall of Babylon	539/538 BCE
Persian rule	539–330
Edict of Cyrus. Exiles permitted to return	538/537
Foundation of Second Temple begun	c.537
Dedication of Second Temple	520
Temple rebuilding continues	520–515
Ezra comes to Jerusalem	458?
Ezra publicly reads out "Torah"	458?
Nehemiah's first visit to Jerusalem	445?
Nehemiah becomes governor	433
End of Nehemiah's governorship and also of the biblical history of the nation	c.430
Writing of Books of Ezra-Nehemiah and Chronicles	430–330
Persian rule ends	330
Alexander the Great rules	330–323
Ptolemaic-Seleucid rivalry for Palestine	323–301
Jerusalem under Ptolemaic control (Egyptian Hellenists)	301–198
Seleucids (Syrian Hellenists) control Palestine	198ff
Maccabean Revolt	167

Table 5

Chronology of Palestine, from the Maccabean Revolt to the Destruction of the
Second Temple

Desecration of Second Temple	167 BCE
Maccabean revolt	167
Recapture and rededication of Second Temple	164
Judaean political independence	163–42
Conquest of Shechem and destruction of Samaritan Temple	128?
Hasmonean dynasty:	
Mattathias	…–d.165
Judas	166–160
Jonathan	160–142
Simon	142–135
John Hyrcanus	135–104
Aristobolus	104–103
Jonathan (=Alexander Jannaeus)	103–76
Salome Alexandra	76–67
Internecine warfare	67–65
Pompey establishes Roman rule	63
Caesar murdered, factional strife for control of government of Palestine	44
Senate appoints Herod (the Great) king of Judea (nisi conquest thereof)	40 BCE
Herod conquers Galilee, Judea, Jerusalem and takes up office in Jerusalem as a "confederate king"	37
Herod begins massive rebuilding programme	27
Temple rebuilding commences	20/19
Herod the Great dies	4
Kingdom divided among his descendants	4 BCE
Herod's former kingdom divided into eleven districts under a Roman procurator	6 CE
Herod Antipas	4 BCE – 39 CE
Herod Agrippa	40–44
Emperor Claudius returns Palestine to Roman provincial status	44
Frequent unrest in Judea	44–66
Procurator Florus desecrates Temple. Rebels, led by Eleazar, son of a high priest, occupy Temple	May 66
Multi-sided civil war in Palestine and simultaneous war with Roman authorities	66–70
Jerusalem Temple razed	70
Masada taken	73
Bar Kokhba rising	132–135

NOTE TO APPENDIX B

1 The sources for chronological Tables 1–3 are: Article on "Chronology" by Mordecai Cogan in *ABD*, 1: 1002–11, and additional items, *ABD*, passim. For discussions of basic chronological techniques, see Jack Finegan, *Handbook of Biblical Chronology. Principles of Time Reckoning in the Ancient World and Problems of Chronology in the Bible* (Princeton: Princeton University Press, 1964), and Edwin R. Thiele, *The Mysterious Numbers of the Hebrew Kings. A Reconstruction of the Chronology of the Kingdoms of Israel and Judah* (Grand Rapids: Erdmans Publishing Co., 1951).

Appendix C

The Manuscript Base of the Holy Scriptures

I

THE GREAT THING ABOUT PROFESSIONAL HISTORIANS IS THAT, IF THE scholars are any good, the questions they ask invariably are easy ones. The impossible questions are asked by amateurs and bad scholars, for they ask things that cannot be answered. (I recall a medievalist friend being driven nearly homicidal by a distressingly ingenuous Harvard College tutee, who kept asking, at weekly intervals, "But, sir, were the peasants happy?") By easy, I mean that the questions professional historians ask are answerable for, before any investigation is seriously mounted, a good historian automatically asks, "Is this query something that can be answered, given historical methods?" Thus, no decent historian would ask whether or not the course of human history proves there is a god. On the other hand, the question of what the ancient Israelites thought about their god is perfectly sensible.

Another reason historical questions are easy is that (as compared, for example, to the fields of pure mathematics and theoretical physics), historians are given licence to quit and guidelines on when to do so. Many "operational questions" (that is, questions that are potentially answerable, if enough evidence exists), are impossible to deal with because of evidentiary problems. When evidence is absent, or totally ropey, the historian is permitted to quit, and no disgrace that.

Thus we are left with easy questions to answer. They may take a lot of digging, and the response may be technically complex at times, but the queries are, by definition, within our ken.

The first of the many simple questions that we would ask concerning the ancient Hebrew covenant concerns the documents that contain its details: "How old are the oldest complete copies of the scriptures?"

We do not possess an "original" copy of the Hebrew scriptures (nor of the Christian scriptures), or anything close to it. In point of fact, there is no original copy of *any* of the books of the Bible (either Jewish or Christian), much less an original text with the author or editor's name on the cover. (One is reminded of Umberto Eco's delicious parody of a publisher's reader's report on the Bible, which suggests that the first five chapters be retitled *The Red Sea Desperadoes* and be published separately. "The editor's name, by the way, doesn't appear anywhere on the manuscript, not even in the table of contents. Is there some reason for keeping his identity a secret?")[1]

Indeed, it is a matter of some controversy whether or not it is profitable to think of a single original of any book (save, perhaps the Pauline and pseudo-Pauline letters) as having existed: multiple versions of all the biblical books may have circulated from very early times. Even granting the probability that at least some of the books of the Bible were, at some brief moment after either their creation or redaction, found only in a single "original" form, that scarcely holds for either the Hebrew or the Christian scriptures, when each is taken as a whole. That can be said with confidence, because the early portions of each set of scriptures were circulating in multiple versions at the very moment in their respective histories when new items were vying for inclusion as sacred texts alongside the older, more authoritative items. This means that no single "original" version of either set of scriptures could have occurred. In the relatively late history of the evolution of each set of scriptures, a "canon" of biblical books that the various religious groups accepted as authoritative was set down. One should not confuse these canonical sets of scriptures with historical "originals." The religious authorities chose from a great number of religious books that were granted authority in their respective communities and, further, they chose among several versions of many of the texts. Their choice was made as much on theological as historical grounds. (Thus, from an historian's point of view, the items they rejected turn out to be as revealing as those that were included in the canon.)

Until the invention of printing, biblical manuscripts were great barmbracks of variation. Each manuscript was produced by a copyist, and the copyists were persons of widely varying degrees of skill and diligence. A somewhat problematic full Hebrew text was printed in Italy in 1488. The first really useful edition of the "Old Testament" to be printed was the Septuagint, a Greek translation, which appeared in the years 1514–17. A trustworthy Hebrew Bible was printed in 1524–25 (the "Venice edition") and the Christian version of the "Old" and "New" Testaments was printed in Latin translation in 1592 (the "Clementine edition"). From that time onwards, there have been continual erudite arguments about whether or not the best manuscripts have been used to make the printed books, but at least mechanical errors in copying have been reduced to virtually (if not quite) nil.

The trouble is, prior to the invention of printing there had emerged a massive number of scriptural manuscripts and these provided a huge number of variant readings of the basic text – that is, instances wherein ancient manuscripts differ from each other. To take the "New Testament" alone, a twentieth-century estimate is that in the extant manuscript versions of the various Christian books, there are perhaps 300,000 variant readings.[2] Most of these are trivial, but not all. Because it was the common (although not universal) practice of Jewish copyists of the Hebrew scriptures ritually to destroy worn out manuscripts after they had been copied, this limited the number of variant readings of the "Old Testament," but did so simply by destroying most of the evidence for such variants. Even so, given that the Hebrew text is markedly longer than the Christian scriptures and that the Hebrew scriptures had a much longer process of transmission (and thus of copyists' error); and that the highly poetic nature of much of the Hebrew text is difficult of transcription, and that the absence of vowel pointing in the earliest texts opened the way for widely differing scribal interpretations, it is clear that the variant readings within the Hebrew scriptures run into the hundreds of thousands.[3] Anyone who suggests, therefore, that the total number of variant readings in the early manuscripts of the "Old" and "New Testament" combined, is under half a million, is being very conservative indeed. Overwhelmingly these are minor – matters of a single letter – but sometimes a variant rendering of a word or a phrase has major implications, and these are especially likely in a Hebrew in which the stem of most words consists of three consonants and, in the earliest texts, no vowels.

So what is the date of the earliest full set of the scriptures we have, either Jewish or Christian? The answer at first is unsettling. Three Greek-language manuscripts, ranging from roughly 350 CE to the early 400s (called "Codex Vaticanus," "Codex Alexandrinus," and "Codex Sinaiticus"), each contains most of the present "Old" and "New Testament," and, when taken together, provide a complete version of what today is the Christian Bible. For the Christian scriptures, that is perhaps heartening, for the Christian books were written originally in Greek.[4] There is therefore a direct line from roughly 350 CE back to the documents of the early Christians. Even better, several of the books of the "New Testament" are found in fragmentary form in manuscripts from the second century CE and these agree in most part with the later codices. Therefore, the available Christian scriptures can confidently be declared to have the same general contours as manuscripts that were in circulation in the second century. This is heartening, provided one remembers that in most circumstances, more than one version of each manuscript existed.[5]

To the everyday working historian what this implies is that, concerning two of the three things historians worry most about – what people thought had happened in some historical moment, and what the official keepers of the particular culture wanted them to believe had happened – there are plenty of revealing data. However, that leaves untouched the third issue, that of basic accuracy. This item implies two sub-questions. The first of these is how accurately the manuscript tradition that can be traced quite tightly to the second century reflects the "original" manuscripts. In the case of the later books of the "New Testament," which apparently date from the second century, that problem is minimized, for the time gap between their composition and the known manuscripts is relatively short. (Mind you, big variations can take place in short periods of time, especially in controversial religious documents that are being transmitted in volatile times; but the probabilities are that the shorter the period between creation and known manuscript, the fewer scribal errors will have crept in. Heavy rewriting of troublesome passages, and insertions of new material to bulk up a particular ideological viewpoint are something else entirely.) But this way of thinking about the Christian texts is a double-edged sword: if the manuscript tradition is apt to be most solid in the case of the later Christian manuscripts, since these are closest in time to extant fragments, then it holds that the earliest Christian scriptures, the ones most central to that faith, are the ones most apt (by this line of reasoning) to have become corrupted in the process of their transmission. They were spread about in multiple copies, and written out by copyists of widely differing abilities and degrees of conscientiousness. Perhaps this problem is not too great, given that all of the Christian scriptures (save for some of Paul's letters and possibly the Gospel of Mark) were compiled in their final form after 70 CE. (This is a key dating point in both Christian and Jewish history, for the Second Temple was levelled by the Romans in 70 CE.)

However, the argument for the integrity of the manuscript tradition of the Christian scriptures that rests on the lateness of the creation of most of the original documents, leaves aside entirely the second sub-question, namely how accurately the manuscripts report events that occurred between roughly 10 BCE and 40 CE, the period the manuscripts claim to depict. It is quite possible to have a first-rate set of manuscripts, in the sense that they are technically accurate as copies, but which are substantively meretricious. That huge question will have to be raised again later.

The issues relating to the Hebrew scriptures overlap these Christian-scriptures questions, but are of much greater complexity. The Christian codices mentioned earlier include the "Old Testament," but do so in Greek translation, not in the original Hebrew. These translations were not in origin Christian, for they had begun in the third century BCE, and were completed in the first century CE, by "Jewish" scholars (to use an anachronistic term), who wished to serve the religious needs of the Hellenized parts of the diaspora.[6] These translations, of which there were several versions, were used not only by Hellenized Jews of the diaspora, but also were adopted by Christians as being the most accessible version of the ancient scriptures. Until the discovery of the great library of texts in the Qumran caves in 1947, the Septuagint was the oldest manuscript version of the Hebrew scriptures, but, lamentably, not in Hebrew. This raised, among other things, the question of how faithful a translation the Septuagint was. Now, with the discovery of a fragment of the scriptures in the

Hebrew language, dated by paleographic and radio-carbon criteria as being in part as early as approximately 250 BCE and no later in any part than 70 CE (and thus, by far the oldest of the Hebrew biblical manuscripts), it is possible to check how tightly the Greek version followed the Hebrew. In fact, the Septuagint corresponds very closely to the Hebrew fragments found in the Qumran scrolls.[7] Thus, the Septuagint in all probability was a reasonably trustworthy translation of one of the several versions of the fundamental Hebrew scriptures as they existed in the third and second centuries BCE and of less central items, as they existed about the time of Jesus. The Septuagint, therefore, is a valid witness to one strand of the textual heritage of the "Old Testament."

A similar witness is another translation, the Peshitta, a translation from Hebrew into Syriac, a form of Aramaic. This was done in the first through third centuries, CE, using manuscript sources in Hebrew very similar to those used as the basis of the Septuagint. The Peshitta was done book by book, and probably was completed by the end of the third century, CE. The earliest complete surviving version of the Peshitta dates from the sixth to seventh centuries. However, two fragments of the Peshitta, dated 459–60 CE (part of Isaiah) and 463–64 CE (the Books of Moses) bear dates of their copying, and these are the oldest biblical manuscripts in any language to directly bear their date of creation.[8] Every biblical manuscript before that (and most after) has to be dated inferentially or by paleographic or laboratory analysis. Although more uneven in quality than the Septuagint, largely due to its long process of translation, involving many, perhaps too many, hands, the Peshitta is fundamentally in agreement with what one finds in the Septuagint, although independent of it in origin, for the most part. Thus, the Peshitta, though a translation, preserves one of the manuscript traditions whereby the Hebrew scriptures were transmitted from generation to generation.

But why not go directly to the Hebrew text? Because, there is not *a* Hebrew text to which one can turn. Only around, roughly, the year 1000 CE did a single authoritative text of the Hebrew scriptures emerge in the original language and, though this was the best reading of the variants possible at the time, it was a privileging of one manuscript tradition at the expense of others.

The present-day Hebrew scriptures date from the monumental work of scholars called "Masoretes" (from the word "Masorah" meaning "tradition"). The Masoretic Text has become the primary (but not the sole) basis of the version of the Hebrew scriptures used today (either in Hebrew or in modern translation) by both Jews and Christians. The Masoretic Text was a cumulative effort, stretching, some suggest, over as long as five centuries, but is most closely associated with the tenth-century scholarship of Aharon Ben Asher. The Masoretes produced the first full version of the Hebrew scriptures of which a copy has survived. Until recently, the earliest known manuscript of the Masoretic Text was the "Leningrad Codex," ascribed to the year 1009.

However, recently a version of nearly a century earlier, the "Aleppo Codex," has been reconstituted. This was a text that somehow found its way to the Jewish community of Aleppo, Syria, where it had been kept virtually secret. In 1947, Arab rioting in the Jewish quarter of Aleppo resulted in most of the Books of Moses being destroyed. This was a major catastrophe, because this manuscript was associated directly with the great Ben Asher and was attested by the greatest of medieval Jewish scholars, Maimonides, to be authoritative. The main manuscript having been transferred to Jerusalem, a modern scholar, Jordan S. Penkower, using early-modern manuscripts which he found in Spain, has been able to reconstruct the missing portions of Ben Asher's text.[9] Thus, from sometime after the year 900, there exists a full copy of the Hebrew scriptures.

On the surface, this date seems to be terribly late, for it means that the first full compilation of the Hebrew scriptures to which we have access was compiled 2,000 years after many of the chief events which the manuscript presents as being historical: and that refers to non-mythological occurrences, such as the building of the First Temple. That is a very long reach.

The apparent problem is magnified, when one realizes the prodigious nature of the scholarly task which the Masoretes essayed. The original Hebrew texts had no vowels, little punctuation, and were not broken up into literary units (chapters-and-verses in most modern editions). The vowel problem was the most pressing. "Vocalization" – the adding of the vowels – was necessary, for the ancient Hebrew texts were written only with consonants, and over time, the way words were pronounced, and, indeed, the meaning of various clusters of consonants, wobbled, and in some cases was lost entirely. The task of inserting vowels in a manner so as to be true to the ancient texts that had been created 1–2,000 years earlier would be difficult in any Indo-European language. The chances of mistakes are obvious. They were much greater, however, in Hebrew. This was because the basic Hebrew three-consonant root system, wherein each consonant was separated from another by a vowel, made the possibilities of error very much higher than in Indo-European languages: the proportion of vowels in each word was higher, so the possibilities of error were greater. Of course, the vowels being interpolated by the Masoretes were not merely sounds, but systems of meaning. A set of three consonants in any religious text could have quite different meanings, depending on the vowels that one inferred were present. To take a simple example, the consonants for the name "Caleb" (*klb*) can just as well mean "dog." The possibility of errors multiplied exponentially, however, because in ancient Hebrew (unlike the usual case in English), the vowels changed radically as a word was conjugated or declined. Further, in biblical Hebrew there were five different verb forms and seven major stem patterns, in each of which the vowels worked differently.

Therefore, the Masoretic Text is one of the monumental scholarly achievements of all time. Yet, in granting that, one nevertheless has the right to feel slightly uneasy about a group of scholars in, roughly, 1000 CE, choosing among literally millions of alternative readings concerning how words were pronounced – and thus, what they meant – in 500 to 1000 BCE. Moreover, there were other systems of vocalization in the post Second Temple period, and although the Masoretic Text eventually became authoritative, this was not always the case.[10]

The point that comes through clearly is that although the Masoretic Text has been accepted by both Judaism and Christianity as the agreed text; and although we have fragments of almost all of the Hebrew scriptures from the Qumran caves (the two exceptions are the books of Esther and of Nehemiah);[11] and although these fragments agree quite closely with the consonantal structure of the Masoretic Text, and thus, potentially, let the reader confidently move a full millennium closer to the events recorded; even so, we do not have anything approaching an "original" text of the Hebrew Bible. In his brilliant study of textual criticism and the Hebrew Bible, Emanuel Tov writes, "One of the objectives of this book is to drive home the realization that the Masoretic Text is only one representative of the greater complex of sources which reflect the biblical text."[12]

Even in the period to which we can just barely stretch with the Qumran library – the third century BCE – there were several versions of the scriptures floating around and, indeed, even several versions of the textual tradition that became the Masoretic Text. How accurately this material reflected books or parts of books that were in circulation in, say, 500 BCE, or 800, one can only speculate: my guess, given the confirmation of the quite high degree of accuracy of the material that eventually became the Masoretic Text, is that the individual books of the Bible were transmitted with basic integrity, albeit with a fair number of scribal and editorial corruptions. Some of these variations might have been quite significant, others merely offbeat.

That the books of scripture preserved in the Masoretic Text probably go back to one (or more) of the early versions of each of the books of the Hebrew scriptures, does not, of course, imply a judgement concerning how accurate the actual historical content of the "original" manuscripts actually was. That is another matter entirely.

2

Space precludes more than a brief comment from an historian's view of the last century of "biblical archaeology." This is that, while archaeologists have been extremely useful in providing the material cultural background to Hebrew scriptures – and that aid the scriptures being read as real-life accounts, not mere novellas – what archaeology gives is context, not confirmation. Also, the discovery of the geographic sites that are mentioned in the Hebrew Bible provide useful geographic coordinates for the Bible story, and confirm, in a general way, that a story was indeed happening (in the same way that a future archaeologist discovering the Maginot Line will infer that some kind of a war took place in the twentieth century). But beyond that, it rarely takes us; and on the big issues – was Israel ever in Egypt, and was there really a Hebrew conquest of Canaan? – the evidence is either non-existent or so fragmentary as to be non-conclusive.

Indeed, the revealing thing is that "biblical archaeology" has developed into a separate discipline that deals with the biblical lands in general, and the Bible hardly at all. That is not an indication of any ideological bias on the practitioners' part, but rather of an admirable sense of efficiency: their time is better spent reconstructing as much as possible the several material cultures of Palestine, rather than trying to chase down ancient Hebrew references. It is a matter of probable benefit for costs incurred.

That they are right so to orientate their present-day activities is confirmed by a scanning of the periodicals in the field and an examination of the leading Israelite archaeological collections. One finds, for example at the Israel Museum and the Bible Lands Museum, Jerusalem, the same thing one finds in the literature: that the evidence for the material culture of several of the groups (tribes, clans, nations) that lived in the Ancient Near East in general and in Palestine in particular, is exponentially greater than that for the ancient Israelites. One could hardly begin to say anything about pre-Exile "Israelite" culture, if the archaeological record were the sole source. That the Israelites had a god would be clear, but his various names would not even be known.

Some of this relative impenetrability of ancient Israelite culture is a function of the ancient inhibition on figurative representations of the divine being, and some of it is the result of the efficiency with which Israelite sites – especially the First Temple – were destroyed by their enemies.

But, whatever the reason, the relationship between archaeology and ancient texts is diametrically opposite in the Hebrew case to that of almost all other cultures of Palestine and environs. Whereas several of the cultures of the Ancient Near East have left rich clues of their material culture, including physical items that indicate their history and sacred mythology, there is little from the pre-Exilic Israelites, save architecture (and that rendered two-dimensional by time's hard hammer), minor household artifacts and, in later times, the occasional coin. Indeed, for the late Bronze Age and early Iron Age – the alleged formative years of ancient Israel – the archaeological record is quiet, verging on silence. This is in sharp contrast to the material concerning other cultures in Palestine in the same period.

This presses us back to the point being made in my main text: if one wants to know the history of the covenant, and the history of the various peoples of the covenant, then one has to focus intensely (but not quite exclusively) on the pieces of written history that claim to be the history of the covenant, and of its peoples. And one must read them critically.[13]

3

Although this Appendix deals chiefly with the Hebrew Bible, Christianity has necessarily been mentioned, and is here again relevant. The long-term relevance of course is that Christianity claims to have taken over the ancient Hebrew covenant and, whether or not one accepts the Christian doctrine that the Christian religion "fulfilled" the covenant, there is no doubting that a specific re-invention of the covenant was the spine around which Christianity grew.

In terms of more limited documentary matters, there is more interdependence. First, the Septuagint, the Jewish translation of one version of the Hebrew Bible into Greek, was adopted as authoritative by Christians in the second century CE. Thereupon it was gradually abandoned by Jewish worshippers. Still, whatever its controversial character in Christian-Jewish relations, the Septuagint preserves an authentic tradition. Second, both the Masoretic Text and the Septuagint can now, with the Qumran evidence to hand, be taken as being absolutely firm indications of what the nature of the central strands of Jewish religious life was at the time Christianity was a-borning. Undeniably, there is a great deal to be learned in the sundry non-canonical religious documents of the centuries just before and just after the birth of Jesus, but the Hebrew scriptures were the central text of the official and dominant religious life. And of these we have excellent copies.

The Hebrew scriptures and the Christian scriptures also have in common that neither is an "original" document; each stands in relation to early sources (whether oral or written) in a largely unknown (and probably unknowable) manner. However (1) the earliest full manuscript copies of the "New Testament" are several centuries older than are those of the "Old Testament"; (2) the distance in time between the events presented as history in the earliest Christian manuscripts is much less than is the similar distance in the earliest fragments of the Hebrew scriptures. In calling this to notice, I most emphatically am not suggesting that the Christian scriptures are somehow superior to the Hebrew scriptures as historical documents. What bears note is the fact that the relationship of Judaism and Christianity cannot be seen as a simple linear one, the one set of historical documents following the other, like sequential frames in a motion picture. In the main text of this book, I have noted that in certain developments of belief, Christianity precedes Judaism. The present documentary observation, that the full set of Christian manuscripts is available several centuries before the full set of Hebrew documents, is meant as a metonym of that larger situation.

Finally, the most important characteristic that the two sets of scriptures share as historical documents is this: that even if we possessed pristine "original" and complete manuscripts of each set of scriptures, this would not indicate anything about whether or not the historical assertions in each had any empirical accuracy. The manuscripts would be excellent indications of what people believed to be true and of what the religious leaders wanted people to believe to be true. Those are realities in themselves, and, if history is, as many suggest, the history of what people thought was true, then these are brilliantly useful primary documents.

Nevertheless, one of those simple, and answerable historical questions does arise, popping up like a fishing cork, time and time again, even when we wish to ignore it: "Is there any external evidence – meaning evidence from disinterested third parties – that the events that are central to the two sets of scriptures are reported with historical accuracy?" The answer is, not much. This is not to buy into the tiresome nineteenth-century fantasy that the scriptures were made up out of whole cloth, that Jesus did not exist, and that the First Temple was an architectural figment, a mythologic pleasure dome no more real than that of Kubla Khan. No. There exist sufficient non-Christian and non-Israelite witnesses to the bare bones of each tradition, ranging from the tons of artifacts from "biblical archaeology" to the writings of the ancient Jewish historian Flavius Josephus.

Totally absent, however, is third-party confirmation of the day-to-day story of each of these two main covenantal histories. One cannot actually trace the alleged great Exodus from Egypt any more than one can point to the confirmation of a neutral source of a single word that Jesus is said to have uttered.

This is inconvenient, but, actually, it is something that historians and, sometimes, journalists, have to deal with frequently. To take a simple example, *The Diary of Anne Frank*, one of the most moving and revealing of documents concerning World War II. The basic details of Anne's life during the Nazi occupation of Holland are confirmed by external observations: there was indeed an enemy occupation of her country and she was indeed hidden away by sympathetic friends. But the day-to-day details of her life, both the quotidian matters of food, visitors, and of how she passed the boring, frightening hours, and, more importantly, the chronicle of her spirit, are not fully attested by third parties. Indeed, the most important things, the emotional and moral development of this child saint, are beyond any known form of external verification.[14] Yet, we accept *The Diary of Anne Frank* as being great history, and well we should.

Historians have a whole chest of tools to help them deal with single-source pieces of evidence, and these are used extremely skilfully by the best of the biblical historians. These range from the laws of physics (no one is allowed to be in two places at once) to linguistic considerations, to matters of logic (biblical arguments are notoriously tautological) to simple good-old-fashioned chronology (a much underrated tool, and one that prevents the all-too-common error of having an effect precede a cause). There is more, and the most artful of the biblical scholars reach the level of high Art in the way they work with their scholarly implements.

Yet, no matter how graceful the intellectual arabesques the scholars carve, we cannot permit ourselves to be distracted from the central point of method: we are permitted to view the covenant, as defined historically in biblical documents of the Jewish and the Christian traditions, only from within. External verification of the really important events (Moses' leadership of the Chosen People, Jesus' throwing the money-changers out of the Temple), is impossible. We are locked inside a great pellucid hemisphere, its surface is lit evenly, from outside, and we can only with the greatest skill decipher the incisions on its interior surface, some of which are hieroglyphs of high meaning, others of which are low graffiti; and still other parts of this surrounding surface bear faint indications of erasure and of revision of one glyph, so that it becomes another, with a new meaning.

NOTES TO APPENDIX C

1 Umberto Eco, *Misreadings*, translated by William Weaver (London: Picador, 1993), 34.

2 Eldon Jay Epp, "Textual Criticism (NT)" in David Noel Freedman (ed.), *The Anchor Bible Dictionary* (New York: Doubleday, 1992), 6:415. (Hereafter: *ABD*).

This is the appropriate place to call the *ABD* to the attention of the general reader. It is an extraordinary achievement, not least for being highly readable. A few months spent reading through the dictionary is as good an introduction to present-day biblical scholarship as one can find. One caveat however: because this is very much a middle-of-the-road work of collective authorship, it is important to read directly the works of authors whose viewpoints are given short shrift (dismissed as "disproved," or whatever) for frequently the statement that a given viewpoint has been "disproved," only means that it is disapproved of.

3 For a rich, but accessible, indication of the problems of sorting out variant traditions of the Hebrew Bible, see Emanuel Tov, *Textual Criticism of the Hebrew Bible* (Minneapolis: Fortress Press, 1992). For a classic discussion, see Martin Noth, *The Old Testament World*, translated by Victor I. Gruhn (Philadelphia: Fortress Press, 1966), 303–63.

4 At least in the codex form that crystallized in the early Christian church, they were written in Greek. Some scholars believe that proto-forms of some of the material found in the Gospels may have been written in Aramaic. This is entirely speculative, however.

5 Epp, 414–16.

6 "Demetrius the Chronographer" provides independent (that is, extra-textual) evidence that at least the Pentateuch had been translated by the middle of the third century BCE. J. Hanon, in James H. Charlesworth, *The Old Testament Pseudepigrapha* (New York: Doubleday, 1985), 2:844.

7 Tov, 117.

8 S.P. Brock, "Versions, Ancient (Syriac)," *ABD*, 6:794.

9 Marc B. Shapiro, "The Aleppo codex," *Jerusalem Post* (Int. ed.), 26 Nov. 1994, reviewing Jordan S. Penkower's *Nusah Ha-Torah Be-Keter Aram Tsovah* (Ramat: Bar-Ilan University Press, 1994).

10 On other textual traditions than the three main ones that I have identified, see Tov, passim.

11 Ibid., 103. However, since Ezra-Nehemiah is usually considered to have been one book originally, Esther is the sole completely-missing item.

12 Ibid., xxxviii.

13 For a sympathetic account of the work of an earlier generation of archaeologists – an era dominated by William Foxwell Albright, who was committed to reading archaeology as an antidote to skepticism concerning the historicity of the Hebrew scriptures – see the special issue of *Biblical Archaeologist*, 56 (March 1993), and Leona Glidden Running and David Noel Freedman, *William Foxwell Albright. A Twentieth-Century Genius* (New York: Two Continents Publishing, 1975). In contrast, for a bitter, but often perceptive, commentary on the way in which "biblical archaeology" has allegedly been dominated by religiously-derived presuppositions, see Keith W. Whitelam, *The Invention of Ancient Israel. The Silencing of Palestinian History* (London: Routledge, 1996). Whitelam's basic argument is that since the late nineteenth century the several cultures of Late Bronze Age and early Iron Age Palestine have been collapsed into a single entity – the least documented of the lot – the Israelite.

14 And this despite an admirably thorough, yet unobtrusive annotation of the diary by the Netherlands State Institute of War Documentation. See David Barnouw and Gerrold Van Der Stroom (eds.), *The Diary of Anne Frank. The Critical Edition*, translated by Arnold J. Pomerans and B.M. Mooyaart-Doubleday (New York: Doubleday, 1989).

This example is not chosen randomly: the Netherlands State Institute of War Documentation performed in a way directly analogous to the way professional historians must look at the Bible. The scholars searched for additional manuscripts, they authenticated texts, defined variant texts, they sought third-party corroboration, assayed physical artifacts, and, when all that was done, they went appropriately silent and let the documents speak for themselves.

Appendix D

Modern Biblical Scholarship and the Quest for the Historical Yeshua

I

IN THE TEXT, I HAVE ARGUED THAT THE BEGINNING OF WISDOM IS TO recognize that the Christian scriptures are an historical entity in their own right: a unified structure whose primary motifs and whose vocabulary comprise a massive re-invention of the Hebrew scriptures and of several of the facets of the various Judaisms of the later Second Temple period. One longs to know: how much do these scriptures have to do with the historical Jesus Christ? Immediately one phrases the question one knows that it is wrong: Jesus-the-Christ is a construction (an invention in the sense this book employs the term) of the "New Testament." He cannot sensibly be conceived of independently of the Christian scriptures. What we *can* legitimately do, however, is to rephrase the question and, instead, ask, "what can be known historically concerning Yeshua of Nazareth, the actual person whom the Christian scriptures transform into Jesus-the-Christ?" Whether or not we can know anything about Yeshua is not pre-judged by the query, but it is a workable historical enterprise, in no epistemological sense different from asking what can be known historically about Innocent III, or Dr. Johnson, or Abraham Lincoln.

During the twentieth century (and to a lesser degree, before that) thousands of biblical scholars have beavered away at the life of Yeshua. In my reading, they appear to break into two camps: those who accept the rules of the historian's craft (however arbitrary those may be) and those who do not.[1] The second group is impossible for an historian to deal with, because they claim (either explicitly or implicitly as evidenced by the methods they employ) that the rules of proof which apply in secular historical scholarship are all very well, but that there are special evidentiary by-passes when it comes to Jesus-the-Christ. Such works, even when wrapped in historical terminology, really are parts of the history of theology. The first group, the scholars who endeavour to be as rigorous in historical method as possible and who consciously try to avoid special pleading, are much more interesting, not least because they are often first-rate minds and in a very difficult situation. This is particularly true of those who have written on aspects of the historical Yeshua within the last two or three decades. Their position is difficult because (1) in the last quarter of the twentieth century the historical profession generally has become increasingly aware of something that good historians always had known: that there is no such thing as objective historical truth; instead historians deal with the perpetual transience of pale imitation of a final reality that can never be known, a forever-escaping past. Biblical historians, as much as their individual personalities have permitted them, have acted according to the canons of historical investigation, which assert that even if one cannot ever get anything perfectly right it is possible to prove that some ideas about the past are dead wrong. Yet, at the same time, many of the same scholars seem to yearn so deeply for theological-ideological-denominational certainties, that all their efforts at being as objective-as-possible are thwarted. One is frequently reminded of the commonplace assessment of Immanuel Kant, that he spent his entire adult life proving what he had known with certainty when he was five years of age. And (2) the overwhelming majority of biblical scholars are employed by institutions that have a theological or denominational or political ideology (however vestigial) which is based on certain assertions about the nature of the historical Yeshua, the man behind Jesus-the-Christ. These institutional affiliations inevitably involve pressures upon the scholars, or limits on what they can think. It is a hard business to be in.

Given the intellectual and social pressures upon them, it is natural that scholars who specialize in trying to find "the real historical Jesus" become co-dependents. However much they differ from each other on matters of interpretation, evidence, and in their individual unconscious assumptions, they need each other and depend upon each other for confirmation that their quest for the historical Yeshua is a valid enterprise.

Here the great A.A. Milne enters the picture. He produced several brilliant examples of what, in early rabbinical times, would have been labelled a *mashal* or, in its earlier Christian form, a parable. One of these instructive stories is entitled "Pooh and Piglet Go Hunting and Nearly Catch a Woozle" and scholars who read it aloud to their children or grandchildren are likely to find that, while it puts the little darlings to sleep, it leaves reflective adults staring at the ceiling all night.

This mashal's *mise en scène* is a small copse on a fine winter day, snow on the ground, frost in the air. Winnie-the-Pooh, a Bear of Very Little Brain, walks around reflectively, and to a casual observer, he seems to be thinking deep thoughts, rather like an abstracted Victorian clergyman collecting his ideas for a sermon. He walks round and round in a large circle. His friend Piglet, noticing this, joins him and asks him what he is doing. "Hunting," Pooh replies and adds mysteriously, "tracking something." Trouble is, Pooh doesn't know quite what he is tracking. "I shall have to wait until I catch up with it," he says. Ever helpful, Piglet suggests, "Oh, Pooh! Do you think it's a- a- Woozle?", Pooh admits that it may be, and the two of them follow the trail of this undefined animal. As they circle the spinney they find more and more woozle prints, as one woozle track is joined by another and then another, and another. Piglet decides that he really does not want to run into a whole herd of woozles, and is about to leave Winnie-the-Pooh to carry on the hunt alone, when a voice from the sky – in the guise of young Christopher Robin who has been watching them from high in an old oak tree – explains to the two investigators that they have been going round and round the copse; and that they are going in circles and that the growing number of tracks has been produced by their own feet as they walked ever-forward.[2]

That is a mashal, not an allegory. The quest of the historical Yeshua is not a search for a non-existent being: Yeshua the man certainly existed. Nor are "New Testament" historians Bears of Very Little Brain: quite the opposite; they represent some of the more supple intelligences of our time. However, the more one immerses oneself in the continually-growing literature concerning the historical Yeshua, the more one realizes how dependent emotionally and cognitively the scholars are on each other, and how comforted they are by the ever-growing band of footprints that fill their path. Certainly their quarry must be just ahead. This co-dependence is exhibited by the richness of cross-citation found in the literature. The ratio of primary citation to secondary citation is very low. Of course, "New Testament' historians disagree with each other: scholars, like lawyers, are paid to joust. And like lawyers who take opposing sides, and even do so with conviction, the various opponents are all part of the same evidentiary system. The point that I shall argue below is that, with very few exceptions, the agreed evidentiary practices of the historians of Yeshua, despite their best efforts, have not been those of sound historical practice.

2

The questions concerning the man Yeshua of Nazareth which biblical historians seek to answer, are often technically complex, but at heart are simple. They are:

1 What did Yeshua believe about (a) the world and (b) himself?
2 What did he say?
3 What did he do?
4 What did the disciples who encountered him personally believe about him?
5 How did this differ (if at all) from what subsequent generations believed?
6 When did the motifs and symbols that transform Yeshua of Nazareth into Jesus-the-Christ begin to adhere to the man? At the very beginning or later?

7 How did these ideas evolve within first-century Christian circles?

8 When was the story of Jesus-the-Christ crystallized in written – and, therefore, normative – form?

9 And, ultimately, is the history of Yeshua ever obtainable, or must one settle for the history of the disciples of Jesus-the-Christ, something very different indeed?

Each of these queries is "operational" in the historian's sense: meaning that there is nothing in their nature that precludes their being answered. Given appropriate evidence, one could draw firm conclusions concerning what Yeshua believed, said and did. This stands in contrast to questions that are theological in nature and not empirically examinable. For example, historians, given enough evidence, could answer the query "Did Yeshua see himself as Moshiah?" In contrast, the query "Was Yeshua the Messiah?" is approachable only by the path of religious faith.

That seems fair enough, and indeed, there exists one strand of Christian theology which holds that the Christ whom believers encounter in their hearts is the Jesus who counts, and that the historical Yeshua is irrelevant. However, from late Antiquity onwards, most forms of Christianity have argued that the Jesus of theology is dependent upon the Yeshua of history having been portrayed with considerable accuracy (some would say with perfect accuracy) in the Christian scriptures. That is relevant, as I briefly suggested earlier, for pragmatic reasons: the overwhelming majority of scholars who do "New Testament" history are employed by institutions or organizations whose roots are in religious belief. Which means: more than any other group in the present-day academy, biblical historians are under immense pressure – sometimes overt, sometimes subliminal, but virtually omnipresent – to adjust their scholarship, to theologize their historical work. The maintenance of scholarly integrity by so many of the biblical historians is the product of considerable individual heroism. The pressure they frequently experience helps to explain why one encounters so often in the literature appeals to consensus.

With that as background, the case of the Jesus Seminar becomes relevant: not for the substantive nature of its conclusions, but as a parable of what happens in "New Testament" scholarship when consensus becomes an overriding mode of assessing evidence. Now, in mentioning the Jesus Seminar, many other biblical scholars may immediately cry foul. The Seminar, the most publicized scholarly endeavour in the field of early Christian history during the 1980s was, by the mid-1990s, a general embarrassment, and most biblical historians do not wish to be associated with it in any way. I am not, however, holding up the Jesus Seminar as typical of the historical scholarship on early Christianity, but rather as a particularly clear and large case of what often happens at a more fragmented and individual level: the vulnerability of the biblical historian under pressure leads to appeals to scholarly consensus as a mode of documenting propositions that ultimately should rest not on any secondary literature, or upon certain ideas being commonly held, but upon primary sources and upon their rigorous interpretation.[3]

The Jesus Seminar was founded in 1985 by Robert W. Funk, whose academic degrees came from Butler University, the Christian Theological Seminary, and Vanderbilt University. He also founded the "Westar Institute" in Sonoma, California, as a holding company for what became a rapidly-expanding array of activities. Funk was joined as co-chair of the Jesus Seminar by John Dominic Crossan of DePaul University whose scholarly credentials include a D.D. from Maynooth College, the ecclesiastical seminary governed by the Irish Catholic bishops. Thirty original "Fellows" comprised the Jesus Seminar in 1985, and it grew considerably, so that by the early 1990s roughly 100 scholars had been involved at one time or another.[4] The Seminar, through its holding company, came to possess an array of instruments of self-publication: its own publishing house (Polebridge Press), and three periodicals: *The Forum*, its scholarly house organ; *The Fourth R*, a general magazine aimed at promoting "religious literacy"; and the *Seminar Papers*, which were the working papers of the scholars. As far as I can ascertain from talking to members of the Seminar, there was no philanthropic foundation or other financial godfather behind the work of the Seminar. It ran on a shoe-string until the MacMillan Publishing Company signed on to publish *The Five Gospels*, the Seminar's magnum opus. (The "fifth gospel" was the Gospel of Thomas, a Coptic document that the Seminar's Fellows embraced with an enthusiasm that bordered on fervour.)[5]

The Jesus Seminar's publications were markedly self-vaunting, not least in their description of the academic qualifications of the guild. The glossary of *The Five Gospels* contained this definition:

FELLOWS (OF THE JESUS SEMINAR). Fellows of the Jesus Seminar have had advanced training in biblical studies. Most of them hold the Ph.D. or equivalent from some of the world's leading graduate institutions.

What this definition omitted was that most of the Fellows were employed in a thin stratum of small liberal seminaries and colleges, and these were increasingly under siege by the conservative religious revival in the United States that had been in train since the late 1960s. As one critic noted:

This group does not represent a cross section of New Testament research in North America or Europe. One notes that not a single person from the New Testament faculties at Harvard, Yale, Duke, Chicago, Vanderbilt, Southern Methodist, Princeton Seminary, Union Seminary in New York, Catholic University, or Union Seminary in Richmond is represented. Scholars from evangelical institutions are also missing. Of particular note is the absences of such scholars as E.P. Sanders [a conservative Protestant scholar from Texas who in the 1980s was Dean Ireland's Professor of Exegesis at Oxford, and who became Arts and Sciences Professor of Religion at Duke University in 1990] and John P. Meier [Professor of New Testament at the Catholic University of America, and the ranking Catholic Jesus scholar in the USA.][6]

These comments were not merely *ad hominem*. The affiliation of most of the U.S. participants with institutions that are second-line, and associated with weak and declining churches at the time of their collaborative effort is worth noting: for that besieged and peripheral status helps to explain the desire for collective security, despite several of them being scholars of real talent. This was a form of intellectual effort that was overt in its emotional base. The Seminar's *The Gospel of Mark. Red Letter Edition* contained a prefatory discussion by Robert W. Funk of the rigours of biblical scholarship. It concluded: "The end product of this process is something called the scholarly consensus. Every scholar aspires to contribute to that consensus and to become a representative of it."[7] Although some historical scholars would rather walk alone than tramp with fools, this consensus position at least is honestly expressed, and says clearly what many other biblical scholars would not feel comfortable expressing openly.

So, as its first task, the Jesus Seminar set about developing a definitive edition that would spell out which sayings attributed to Jesus-the-Christ were authentic and which were not. This was to be done democratically and by consensus. The opinion of each Fellow of the Seminar was declared to be equal to that of every other. The Fellows would listen to each other's arguments, to be sure, but in the end each individual's opinion was just as good as any one else's. This puts one in mind of Spiro Agnew, deposed Vice-President of the United States, who was sometimes reported to have proclaimed that in his life he always tried to find the Golden Mean between right and wrong. As a means of making historical judgements, the Seminar's method was absurd. (What would the consensus of the Astronomy Seminar have been in the days of Copernicus?) But the Jesus Seminar's collective methods were not very much different than the efforts of individual scholars in biblical history (or any other historical field) who search for a "balanced" view of a given topic or for a "synthesis" of previous secondary literature, rather than sorting out the primary evidence, making decisions, and taking responsibility for their own views.

The Jesus Seminar decided that each saying of Jesus-the-Christ reported in the "New Testament" and in various extra-canonical sources, should be graded according to levels of probability: Jesus certainly said it; he probably did; he probably did not; he certainly did not. Each Fellow voted. This was done by casting one of four coloured balls – red, pink, gray, or black – into a voting box. One can ignore the diverting picture of biblical historians voting for or against the sayings of Jesus, as if they were voting for a candidate for the Papacy, but what cannot be ignored is (1) that, as already mentioned, the consensus method has no discriminatory power as between good and bad historical arguments, and (2) that the four-category method the Seminar employed was so deeply methodologically flawed that they had to fudge heavily the results. This is a matter of statistics, which the reader can follow in the notes,[8] but here suffice it to say that the Seminar's original scoring system produced so few "authentic" sayings of Jesus that the criteria of authenticity had to be radically modified in mid-course: and silently. The final product of this sector of the Jesus Seminar's activities was a polychrome Bible, in which the reader is given Jesus's alleged sayings, translated into California English, and coded in the four colours of the Seminar's voting balls.[9] The published results so impressed Mel Brooks, whose background is slapstick, burlesque and stand-up comedy, that he decided to produce a movie tentatively entitled "Christ the Man."[10] So pleased were the Jesus Seminar's leaders with the attentions of Brooks' film director Paul Verhoeven that they had him write the jacket blurb for their *Gospel of Mark. Red Letter Edition* (1991). Considering that Verhoeven is best known for *Robocop* (1987), it is perhaps a divine mercy that the film has yet to be made.

3

Although most historical scholars engaged in the Yeshua-quest would not endorse the methods peculiar to the Jesus Seminar, agreement on the value of certain of the historical methods employed by the Seminar runs throughout the scholarly community. This agreement spans a spectrum that runs from conservative Christians, all the way to the completely non-religious, and includes all shades in between, most notably the growing number of Jewish scholars who work on early Christian sources. This is not to say that the scholars arrive at identical conclusions (indeed, the warfare in the field is notably fierce on some points), but as long as they think and act as historians (not as shills for their denominational interests), they share, with almost no exceptions, several assumptions regarding methods.

In suggesting in the argument that follows that several of these assumptions are flawed and would not be accepted if employed by professional historians who engage in writing the history of the "secular" world, I am presenting an opinion that would be rejected by almost all of those who make their livelihood in the quest for the historical Yeshua. Thus, the reader has every right to be skeptical: all I ask is that the reader give the argument its day in court, and do so in the context of the discussion of the mode and manner of biblical invention that is presented in the main text of this book. In return for that courtesy, I promise not to pick my examples or my evidence from the weak or the wacky among the Yeshua-questors, but from among the strongest practitioners; and, as much as possible, to argue from primary sources. Thus: a deal, a small covenant.

Before the historians of Yeshua's life and times can approach the specific questions of what did he say and do, they necessarily adopt, either consciously or implicitly, certain assumptions about how one distinguishes the historical probability-level of various words and actions that are ascribed to Jesus-the-Christ. These techniques of evidentiary assessment are crucial, for if they are unreliable, then the conclusions which they underpin are untrustworthy as historical judgements.

The single most important criterion of authenticity adopted by "New Testament" historians is *the principle of multiple attestation*. It is here that the enterprise first goes awry, although not so quickly as to be immediately obvious. Like many principles concerning the assessment of historical evidence, this is simply a statement of statistical probability. It means that, *over a large number of cases*, a purported event or saying that is attested in multiple independent sources is more likely to have occurred and to be accurately reported than is an event or saying that is found only in a single source. The greater the number of independent sources, the higher the probability of historical accuracy. Occasionally, when applied to biblical history, this criterion has been used to rule out all items with only single attestations: for instance, John Dominic Crossan, in his massive *The Historical Jesus. The Life of a Mediterranean Jewish Peasant* (1991), adopts as an evidentiary standard "the complete avoidance of any unit found only in single attestation..."[11] This may serve for his purposes, but as a general standard it is a misapprehension of a general principle of historical evidence. As John P. Meier gently observes, merely because a saying or event is reported only in a single source (this holds whether one is talking about Yeshua or about Metternick), does not mean that the report is untrue. Nor does multiple attestation necessarily prove the accuracy of the report.[12] One needs only think of the major cases of hysteria in our own time (how many times has Elvis been sighted?), to realize the accuracy of Meier's point. In applying the multiple-attestation criterion, therefore, we are not dealing with a closed deductive system, but with a set of assumptions about statistical probability which are inevitably open: individual exceptions to probability statements always are possible. (Were this not so, why would virtually every government in the western world be able to make money by running state lotteries?)

That granted, the criterion of multiple attestation is *potentially* the single most powerful tool for sorting out what the historical Yeshua did or said. That power stems from its being applicable to biblical and to non-biblical texts alike. (For the purposes of the present discussion, I am limiting consideration to the final form of texts that we at present possess; however, as I shall indicate in the next section, the multiple-attestation criterion deserves attention in relation to hypothetical earlier texts as well.) Here is where the searchers for the historical Yeshua have their greatest opportunity, for, if the words or actions of Yeshua of Nazareth were found in documents written by non-believers, then one would have genuine third-party attestation. Again, that would not be complete proof of authenticity, but it would raise the probability-level very high indeed.

So, a primary query is: how is Yeshua reported in non-Christian documents? The answer is rarely, narrowly, but convincingly. Flavius Josephus is the chief source (as he was the foremost Palestinian historian of the last 200 years of the Second Temple). Although it is perhaps a mistake to depend excessively upon Josephus, as the fine classical historian Fergus Millar does when he suggests that, if one must choose between variant accounts in John and the Synoptic Gospels, then "the only criterion of truth in the Gospels which a historian can offer is conformity with the world as portrayed by Josephus...."[13] Josephus refers to three persons who are important in the "New Testament." The first of these is John the Baptist. He is reported to be a good man, who exhorted the Jews to lead righteous lives and to join in public baptism to seal their commitment. Herod Antipas became alarmed at the eloquence of John and the enthusiasm of his followers and fearing an uprising, had him put to death.[14] Though differing in details from the "New Testament" story – Salome is not mentioned in Josephus, and the geopolitical reasons for Herod Antipas's actions are stressed – it is compatible with the Christian scriptures and, at minimum, corroborates the fame and significance of the Baptizer. Secondly, Josephus refers to James, who is identified as the brother of Jesus (and this in a reference to Jesus – "who was called the Christ"). James is reported as being an adherent of the message of his late brother who, for his faith, was brought up before the high priest Ananus II and the Sanhedrin and condemned to be stoned to death.[15] The third reference in Josephus' histories is directly to Jesus, who is reported as having been a wise man, who won over many Jews and Greeks to his viewpoint. He was, however, accused by locals of high standing of some undefined offence and therefore was crucified by Pontius Pilate.[16] What makes this third passage slightly difficult is that it contains clearly-identifiable later Christian interpolations, which add to the material already cited, the statements that Jesus was the Messiah and that he rose from the dead on the third day after his crucifixion. The identification of these two items as later additions is compelling.[17]

Thus, from a third-party, non-Christian source historians have (1) a clear reference to John the Baptist as a major pre-Yeshua religious figure, one who manifestly played a big role in the popular religion of Palestine in the first one-third of the first century of the Common Era; (2) agreement that one of Yeshua's brothers indeed was names James and that he endorsed the spiritual vision of his brother; and (3) acceptance of the fact that Yeshua of Nazareth was indeed a significant religious figure (although hardly a leading one) in the first one-third of the first century, that he did something to vex the Juda-hist religious establishment and thence the Roman administration, and that he was crucified. These three basic facts are not a lot, but they are a good deal more than nothing. Even if Josephus, who wrote after the fall of the Second Temple, was not necessarily fully independent in his sources – he could eas-ily have collected some of his information from the oral tradition of early Christians – his assessment of those sources was independent: he certainly was not a believer in any of the Christian assertions concerning Yeshua's spiritual authority. The neutral, slightly skeptical, angle of vision that charac-terizes Josephus on these matters is one of the more convincing guarantees of their being independent observations.

The remaining non-Christian sources concerning Yeshua of Nazareth are brief and confirm Josephus in a soft-edged manner. Cornelius Tacitus, writ-ing about 115, refers to the followers of "Christus," who had been put to death by Pontius Pilate,[18] but the date is late and the source of the information unspecified. Nevertheless, it is a non-Christian confirmation of the crucifix-ion of Yeshua of Nazareth by Pilate. And Pliny the Younger, writing about the same time as Tacitus, refers not to Yeshua, but to those who believed him to be God. And Lucian of Samosata, writing perhaps half a century later, re-ported the existence of the same belief.[19] However, they throw no light on the historical Yeshua and, being second-century statements, they are diluted in value even in their assessment of early Christianity. As for Jewish sources, the scarce references to Yeshua of Nazareth (if such they are) in the Mishnah and the Talmuds are so late (third through sixth centuries) and so ambiguous as to be unreliable and uninformative.[20] Thus one is left as independent multiple-attestations with the legacy of Flavius Josephus, and nothing more of any great value: Yeshua lived, Yeshua was crucified; Yeshua had a brother named James; and John the Baptist was indeed a real figure.

Therefore, to add anything to these few facts about the life of Yeshua of Nazareth which are attested by independent multiple sources, we are forced to abandon the non-Christian world, that of classical Rome and of evolving Jewish traditions, and instead look within Christianity. This brings an accom-panying reduction in perspective and in credibility, but this is only a reduc-tion, not an abandonment. Given that we are dealing with probability assessment, it is more likely (but not inevitable) that agreement of two or more reports on a given fact is an indication of authenticity if the reporters do not share the same belief system. Still, observations from truly separate Christian sources would have probative value.

There are only two logical sources of Christian observation that could help us to chronicle the historical Yeshua: the "New Testament" and the various para-biblical writings that flourished in the second and third centuries (some scholars would say earlier) but which, for some reason, were not included in the Christian canon.

(Here we encounter a behavioural conundrum. For the most part, those scholars who tend to place most credit in the canonical "New Testament" as a valid historical source for the biography of Yeshua ["conservatives" in general usage] are least likely to embrace the historical value of the para-biblical literature. And those who are least affirmative of the historicity of the "New Testament" ["liberals" is the label they frequently carry] are the most keen on asserting the values as independent historical sources on Yeshua of Nazareth of the para-biblical material.)

The key para-biblical exhibit is the Gospel of Thomas, the text of which the Jesus Seminar published in its *The Five Gospels*. Enthusiasm for the book, however, is not limited to the Seminar, and the document deserves attention. The Gospel of Thomas receives its name through its being ascribed to Didymus Judas Thomas who, in the Syriac branch of the early Christian church, was revered as an apostle and as a twin brother of Jesus.[21] The book is pseudepigraphic, but that is commonplace within the tradition of biblical invention and certainly does not discredit it as a potential source of information on the historical Yeshua. The Gospel of Thomas was part of the trove of Gnostic documents found at Nag Hammadi in Egypt in 1945. Alone among these items, the Gospel of Thomas has some potential of giving an independent view of the historical Yeshua.[22] The Gospel of Thomas, as found at Nag Hammadi, was a fourth-century Coptic manuscript, and probably would not have garnered much scholarly attention, except that it has a precursor: three Greek fragments from the late second century which, though not identical, are from a close variant edition.[23] This means that the fourth-century Coptic document was based on a Greek source that was written, at the latest, in the second half of the second century, and the Greek manuscript is one of the earliest Christian manuscripts still in existence. Manifestly, the Gospel of Thomas is important.

But important as what? An examination of the translation of the Coptic text[24] makes it clear that roughly two-thirds of the Gospel of Thomas is a *Reader's Digest* version of sayings from the Synoptic Gospels (with, possibly, a very few from John). Or, alternately, the Thomas-sayings are from the same source as are the Synoptics. Either way, they are not independent attestations of the words of the historical Yeshua. The remainder of the Gospel of Thomas is composed of Gnostic sayings, some of which indicate not only a direct knowledge of the material in Matthew and Luke which glorifies the Virgin Mary, but a conscious rejection of it. For example, the words of Thomas are these (114:1–2):

> Simon Peter said to them, "Make Mary leave us, for females don't deserve life." Jesus said, "Look, I will guide her to make her male, so that she too may become a living spirit resembling you males. For every female who makes herself male will enter the domain of Heaven."

That is about as far as one can go in directly rejecting the idea behind the *Magnificat* (Luke 1:46–56). Similarly, the Gospel of Thomas (saying 15) ascribes these words to Jesus:

> Jesus said, "When you see one who was not born of woman, fall on your faces and worship. That one is your Father."

What these sayings secretly meant to initiated Gnostics may have escaped interpretation but, manifestly, being born of a woman was an imperfect state.

So, the Gospel of Thomas is significant as an indication of how one distinctive branch of Christianity (one that eventually was declared heretical) took the Gospels and re-invented them during the second century, so as to forward their own branch of the faith. This use of existing material, its rearrangement for "denominational" purposes, its pseudepigraphic ascription to a major figure in church tradition, and the interweaving of new material, is a fascinating confirmation that the grammar of biblical invention was operative over a wide range of Christian texts, not merely those which eventually became canonical. However, as an independent attestation of what Yeshua of Nazareth said (it is a "saying" Gospel), the Gospel of Thomas has no historical proof-value: the portions that are evidentiarily independent (the Gnostic sections) are so fanciful and so obviously late additions as to be of no probative strength, and the parts that are historically plausible are derivative.

Nevertheless, the scholarly work on the Gospel of Thomas is illuminating, for it illustrates a particularly invasive phenomenon among biblical scholars, namely downward-dating-creep. When one observes this pattern with any Christian document, it is a warning light to the observer: watch carefully and count the spoons. The Coptic Gospel of Thomas is from the second half of the fourth century. The tiny fragments of the Greek version are dated 200 CE, or a bit before. However, within the scholarly community there is an almost-magical belief in low numbers, and this despite the existence of the well-known fact in secular history that later texts are often more accurate than earlier ones. However, in biblical studies, setting the dating of a document as early as possible gives it more heft and, not incidentally, thereby helps one's career. Therefore, although there is no compelling reason to suggest that the Gospel of Thomas was composed at any particular date before that dictated by its calligraphy (late second century), the Jesus Seminar, which was particularly keen on its content, stated that "Thomas probably assumed its present form by 100 CE."[25]

That still makes it subsequent in formulation to the usually-accepted dating of the Four Gospels, 70–100 CE (a matter that we will come to later), so anyone who wishes to make this document seem prepotent has to take the dating game one step farther. Stephen J. Patterson, who did a translation of the Coptic Gospel, argued that its composition in its present form should be placed in the period 70–100 CE. This, primarily because he believed it did not derive from the canonical Gospels, but from the same oral traditions on which these Gospels rely.[26] Here, forget for a moment that Ockham's razor would lead one to suggest that the data are most economically covered by the suggestion that the Gospel of Thomas was based on the canonical Gospels, rather than that Thomas and the canonical Gospels share common, unspecified, oral traditions. Instead, merely note the downward-dating-creep. There is no causal relationship, either in logic or in empirical demonstration, between the Gospel of Thomas's allegedly being based upon oral traditions (rather than upon written sources) and its being written down at the same time the Four Gospels were being set down in their final form. The oral traditions, if they were alive in 70–100, were not suddenly extinct in, say, 110 CE. The chronology suggested by Patterson is in fact a clever debating trick but nothing more: the proposed dating (which is taken to imply support for the oral-composition theory) is in fact derivative from that theory.

Remember that we are here limiting ourselves to a discussion of biblical and para-biblical texts as we at present possess them. For future reference, however, note that there is yet another stage in the dating game and one should be alert to it when, later, we deal with hypothetical texts. The real devotees of the Gospel of Thomas go farther and state that "an earlier edition may have originated as early as 50–60 CE."[27] Thus, we have moved from viewing a complete document of the fourth century, to a set of fragments from the end of the second, to a postulated origin at the beginning of the second century, to an hypothesized origin between the destruction of the Second Temple and the end of the first century, and, finally to an hypothetical source, of which there is no known physical evidence, said to have been produced between the mid-first century and the Temple's destruction. Granted, it is theoretically possible (although very highly improbable) that these ever-descending datings are historically correct: but the warning light that is set off by downward-dating-creep should be heeded not only here, but with particular assiduousness when one encounters (as we will in the next section of this Appendix) hypothetical documents which are said to have been framed before 70 CE. These fictive documents merit special attention because, without presenting any verifiable text, they propel the discussion into an era prior to the invention of the primary history of Christianity: the Four Gospels and the Book of Acts. Hence, these hypothetical documents automatically obtain a privileged position in the chronology of Christian invention that is equal to that of the earliest actual Christian documents that we possess, the letters of Paul. Warning light.

The same problems that are associated with the Gospel of Thomas are found in the other major contender for pre-Synoptic status, the Gospel of Peter. This item is the product of an archaeological dig conducted in Egypt in 1885–86 by French scholars. In a Christian monk's grave was found a small document amidst a set of other items whose earliest dating was the eighth century. However, it appears probable (but not quite certain) that the "Oxyrhynchus papyrus" fragments of c. 200 contain a witness to this putative gospel. The title "gospel" comes not from the work itself, but from a mention of what possibly may be this same work by Eusebius. The text itself purports to be by Simon Peter. The text consists of only sixty verses, arranged in fourteen tiny chapters. It focuses on the crucifixion and employs in almost every sentence implicit references to the Tanakh.[28] The Gospel of Peter's version of the Passion narrative is well within the degree of factual variance found in the Synoptics and in the Gospel of John: its main new idea is that the elders, priests, scribes and Pharisees recognize what a mistake they have made in crucifying Jesus (Peter chapters 7 and 8) and, while Jesus is in the tomb, he is taken up to heaven by two undefined figures, and then, confusingly, comes down again and enters the tomb (Peter chapters 10 and 11). I find convincing John P. Meier's assessment of the scholarly literature and primary evidence concerning the Gospel of Peter: namely that it is a second-century pastiche of material from the Four Gospels (mostly Matthew) with a bit of imagination thrown in.[29] The fascinating point, however, is the way that a major "New Testament" scholar, John Dominic Crossan, suggests that the extant document actually is based on an hypothetical one: an item he denominates the "Cross Gospel." Not surprisingly, this is presented as being mid-first-century and thus prior to the Synoptics and to the Gospel of John. Crossan takes the hypothesis one step farther and theorizes that the "Cross Gospel" was one of the sources of all four of the canonical Gospels, and that, later, the Cross Gospel was expanded into a full Gospel of Peter, the fragments of which we now have. (Why this later Gospel of Peter never made the canon is not explained, except by suggesting that it was put together quite late, after the canon was already primarily set: this nicely elides the problem which stems from our having only a late-second century dating for the document that we actually possess.)[30]

Again, warning lights flash, but for the moment let us be purblind and suspend our disbelief. In fact, assume that the Gospel of Peter and the Gospel of Thomas in their present form are not second-century derivatives of the canonical Gospels (which I think they are), but instead are actually documents that date from, say, the last thirty years of the first century (as, apparently, the canonical Four Gospels do). And assume also that they do not depend upon the canonical Gospels for their information. Would not that permit a great leap forward in our search for the Yeshua of history?

Actually, no: at most, a tiny hiccup. This because of a point of method that is a very difficult nettle to grasp. Remember that we are here focusing on the most powerful tool for the documentation of the life of Yeshua, namely *the criterion of multiple attestation*. The problem with all the extra-biblical sources (of which the Gospels of Thomas and of Peter are the strongest) is that they are devoid of probative value relating to the historical Yeshua *unless an independent provenance for them can be demonstrated*. When a non-Christian source, such as Josephus, attests to the crucifixion, for example, that can be accepted as a report of an independent witness and therefore the probability of the event's actually having occurred rises markedly. However, when someone *within* the Christian tradition affirms that a given event occurred, or that a specific saying was uttered by Jesus, then it does little to increase our assessment of the probability that the event or saying originated with the historical Yeshua: *unless* we have solid documentation that this source was not polluted by contact with the other witnesses, namely the people who laid the base for the Synoptics and the Gospel of John. Significantly, almost every scholar who pushes for the authenticity, and the early dating, of various extra-canonical items, does so with the argument that these texts were part of the core tradition of early Christianity: in other words, that they are not independent witnesses to the historical Yeshua.

Be clear here what I am *not* arguing. I am not suggesting that the various fragments, fugitive gospels, and extra-canonical epistles are of no historical value. They are of great utility in the understanding of the development of Christianity as a form of Judaism and, then, as an independent religion; they are of virtually no value as independent attestations of the various statements made concerning the historical Yeshua, for they are subordinate and dependent sets of the larger phenomenon to which they are said to be witnesses. Secondly, I am not laying down an apodictic argument that it is impossible for extra-canonical items to have force as independent witnesses to the historical Yeshua, but only that the presently-available items have none: because none of them has an assured provenance, much less a documentably independent provenance. In fact, I believe that someday the Christian equivalent of the Qumran and Masada finds will occur, and then it is possible that we may encounter items whose origins can be demonstrated to be independent of the formation of the canonical tradition. For now, however, saddened and complete skepticism is the proper posture.[31] And, thirdly, I am not saying that presently-known extra-canonical items (gospels, letters, and apocalypses) have no value in the search for the historical Yeshua, but rather that they have no value as multiple attestations. In fact, if they are included as part of an exercise that deals with the historical Yeshua as a single-source evidentiary problem, they can be quite useful.[32]

Our lengthy discussion of the general issue of multiple attestation is a necessary prologue to a very crisp question: how well does the criterion of multiple attestation work when it is employed as a means of documenting the life of the historical Yeshua as found in the canonical Christian scriptures? The answer is: it does not work at all. And this is despite its being the one methodological principle upon which virtually all questors for the historical Yeshua agree. To cite specific examples: the principle that the individual books of the "New Testament" are independent evidentiary sources for the life of the historical Yeshua is affirmed by John P. Meier, E.P. Sanders, and Geza Vermes, who, in the mid-1990s, were generally taken to be, respectively, the leading Catholic, Protestant, and Jewish scholars of the historical Yeshua.[33]

Any attentive reader of the Bible recognizes that differences exist as between the main branches of the Christian history – the letters of Paul, the Synoptic Gospels, and the Gospel of John – and that within the Synoptics there are variants. Surely, it makes sense to compare them and choose among the variants. For example, take the case of the conflicting accounts of the Last Supper (see the text, Chapter Nine). The Gospel of John has it occurring on the eve of Passover; the Synoptics on the first day of the celebration. Admittedly, both cannot be right, but are they not independent sources that provide the historian's equivalent of bracketing fire? The Last Supper, and hence the crucifixion, clearly had to happen sometime near Passover, since both sources agree on that general point. No: this is a false choice and one that obscures, and eventually excludes, the real historical choice. The actual alternatives are not that the crucifixion occurred on one of two dates close to, or within, Pessah, but rather that it occurred at the season of Passover or some other point on the calendar. The Synoptic Gospels and the Gospel of John are not alternative independent witnesses, but slightly variant editions of a single source: both are found within the Christian interpretative tradition and, as we have seen (Chapter Nine), this tradition required that for Yeshua of Nazareth to become Jesus-the-Christ, he had to be identified as a Passover sacrifice. Thus, we have here a single tradition, not a multiply-attested set of historical observations. Emphatically, this does not mean that the single-source tradition is wrong, merely that it is not confirmed by the self-repetition of certain points within the Christian scriptures.[34]

At heart, the misapplication of the concept of multiple attestation – its application as between various items that are internal to the "New Testament" canon – stems from a failure to appreciate the marvellous efficiency, strength, and unity of the Christian scriptures. As I have demonstrated in the main text, the "New Testament" is an extraordinary unity in terms of the architecture of the canon, the interdigitation of motifs, and in its employment of a vocabulary and symbolic system that stems almost entirely from the Hebrew scriptures and from the texts of later Second Temple Judahism, and with which it resonates harmonically. The "New Testament" is at once a majestic instrument of integrative affirmation – of an epic historical narrative which encapsulates in a single entity a variety of beliefs from the late Second Temple era that previously had been separate entities – and it is simultaneously a massive instrument of censorship and suppression. One cannot have the affirmation without the suppression. The only items that are permitted in the "New Testament" are those that fit. Minor variations within the major tradition are permitted: they are permitted precisely because they are not consequential, and do not shake the fundamental structure. To return to the example of the Last Supper and crucifixion: does anyone seriously think that the inventors of the "New Testament" could have permitted an account of the crucifixion to be included wherein Yeshua was put to death at the time of the festival of the First Fruits of Barley, even if that was when the event actually occurred? They were much too shrewd for that: the entire architecture of the "New Testament" would have come unpinned, as when a king-peg is pulled out of a mortise-and-tenon cornerpost; inevitably the whole structure would have pulled apart. This instance, the crucifixion, is just one example of a pervasive fact: unity permits affirmation; censorship is the prerequisite of unity.

I am emphasizing this point so strongly not merely because the concept of multiple attestation has been employed in "New Testament" studies in a way that renders it virtually useless in the quest for the historical Yeshua, but also because the misapplication of multiple-attestation has stood in the way of an appreciation of what a marvellous invention the Christian scriptures are. Any potentially-successful quest for the historical Yeshua must start with a recognition (bordering, in my view, on reverence) of the marvels of the text that gives us Jesus-the-Christ. Thence comes a recognition and appreciation of the grammar of religious invention which underlies the text. Only then, from within this single source, is there any chance of recovering a glimpse or two of Yeshua of Nazareth.

4

Therefore, if they are not to be woozle-hunters, the questors of the historical Yeshua will forget the false security of alleged multiple-attestation within the "New Testament" and will define their primary task as dealing with the Christian canon as a single source. That will require a new mindset, but not a whole new set of tools. Many of the methods presently to hand are useful if they are used in a slightly different manner than usual. Before discussing these methods, however, we should survey the evidentiary terrain.

The two most formidable impediments to the use of the canonical Christian scriptures as a source of information on the historical Yeshua are, first, that save for the letters of Paul, none of the potential sources of information carries in, or with, the text an indication of who the author-editors may have been. The names "Matthew," "Mark," "Luke," and "John" are not found in an authorial capacity in the Four Gospels. The convention of ascribing the respective documents to powerful figures among the original apostles was not adopted until sometime after the year 150.[35] The Four Gospels, then, are anonymous works, which later members of the Christian church turned into pseudepigraphic works by attaching an authoritative name to them as author: a procedure that, far from being unusual, is standard within the grammar of biblical invention. Second, none of the canonical scriptures – including the writings of Paul – includes any claim to have been written, even in part, by an eyewitness to Jesus' life. This is not overwhelmingly worrisome – later historical collections often are more accurate than eyewitness narratives – but, understandably, biblical historians wish to get behind the editing process and recapture the raw data upon which the Gospel historians based their narratives.

Within the Christian scriptures there are three bodies of potential information on the historical Yeshua: the letters of Paul; the Synoptic Gospels (Matthew, Mark, and Luke – Acts is frequently seen as a continuation to Luke, but it is little material use in relation to the historical Yeshua); and the Gospel of John. The material in the rest of the "New Testament," while valuable in charting the evolution of the Christian faith, has so little that is demonstrably referential to the historical Yeshua as to be virtually epiphenomenal.

The letters of Paul are potentially the most important source, and therefore, they are also the most disappointing. Paul almost breaks one's heart. Not only is the material he wrote the earliest in the Christian scriptures in their canonical form, but alone of the material in the "New Testament," his letters clearly were written well before the Roman-Jewish War of 66–73 CE and the cataclysmic destruction of the Temple in 70 CE. One would be hard-pressed to find a "New Testament" scholar who does not accept the pre-70 dating and, more important, the primary evidence is totally compelling. Paul has no knowledge of the destruction of the Temple and not even a suspicion that it might happen (as would be the case if there were a conflict in train in Palestine that threatened to get out of hand). Moreover, the chronology of Paul's letters, dated by cross-references between the various epistles, when combined with the calendar of Roman governorships, indicates that the outside-dates of the letters are 49 to 64 CE.[36]

Paul is a heart-breaker because he evinces a lack of interest in the historical Yeshua that borders on disdain. For him, the spiritual Jesus-the-Christ is everything; the physical, historical Yeshua is of scant moment. As far as I can tell, there are only six references to the historical Yeshua, as distinct from the risen Christ, in Paul's letters. Two of these are to his actions and four to his words. One of the references (1 Cor. 9:14) is not particularly revealing. It suggests that Jesus ("the Lord," as in "Jesus Christ our Lord" in 9:1) ordained that persons who preach the Gospel should be supported by those who believe the Gospel, an economic demand that Paul himself doubtless found beneficial. The other Pauline references to the historical Yeshua are significant, but in a backhanded way: that is, not for what they say, but because of what they do not. Each of the following five references to Jesus is notable either for its implied diminution of the historical Yeshua or as a rejection of what, after 70 CE, becomes the normative Christian view of the historical Yeshua and his theological cognate, Jesus-the-Christ.

(1) In Romans (15:8) Paul makes the factual assertion that Jesus "was a minister of the circumcision for the truth of God ..." that is, a Judahist who preached to his co-religionists. In contrast, Paul continues (Rom. 15:9), he is himself a minister to the non-Judahists, "that the Gentiles might glorify God." Paul's placing of his ministry in parallel with that of Jesus is breathtaking in its immodesty. The unspoken message is one of equilibration:

Yeshua's message: Judahists = Paul's message: Gentiles

(2) In his first letter to the Thessalonians, Paul talks about the return of Jesus-the-Christ from the heavens, an event that will result in the faithful dead and the faithful living being raised into the clouds to meet the Christ (1 Thes. 4:15–18). This is predicated upon Jesus' having died and risen again (4:14). Yet, significantly, there is no mention of a bodily-resurrected Yeshua, only a cosmically-raised, heaven-resident Christ.

(3) Crucially, in his quotation of Yeshua at the Last Supper, in words which have been employed by several branches of Christianity in the Eucharist, or Lord's Supper, Paul refuses to set the event in the context of Pessah (1 Cor. 11:24–25). It is not Passover in this, Paul's most authoritative reference to Yeshua's death, and he does not, therefore, affirm that Yeshua was killed at the time of Passover.

(4) Paul refers directly to the birth of Jesus Christ and he states that it "was made of the seed of David according to the flesh" (Rom. 1:3). That phrase, "according to the flesh" is a very strong one in Paul's rhetoric, for the flesh is the antithesis of the holy. It is corrupt. Paul is saying that there was no special holiness about the birth of Yeshua, even though he was, in some sense, God's son. For Paul, there was no Virgin Birth.

And (5) in a related matter, Paul repeats, as a direct commandment of Christ, that there should be no divorce, despite provision for it in the Law of Moses (1 Cor. 7:10–11). This is doubly significant: first, because (as I discussed in detail in Chapter Nine, note 19), Jesus' strict view on divorce as recorded in the Synoptic Gospels is singular within his reported teaching and possibly relates to his being acutely uncomfortable with his own illegitimacy; and, second, Paul again sets himself as an equal of Jesus. He states that he will give some advice on his own authority, not that of Jesus (7:12) and then proceeds to contemplate divorce in certain circumstances (7:12–15). The sequence is hierarchical: the Torah of Moses is corrected by the Torah of Jesus, which in turn is corrected by the Torah of Paul. So, the chief message from Paul's writings that relates to the historical Yeshua is that, in the middle of the first century, one could be an extremely devout and very important Christian and not affirm the Virgin Birth, the bodily resurrection or that Yeshua was crucified at Passover. This is a very telling marker in the development of Christianity (it would seem to indicate that those beliefs developed only in the period after Paul's death, which is to say in the period of white-hot biblical invention that centres on the destruction of the Temple). But, as for direct information on the historical Yeshua, Paul is an almost complete write-off, an enigma wrapped in a theological whirlwind.

The second body of literature within the Christian scriptures that contains information on the historical Yeshua is the Gospel of John. It is the most mysterious book of the "New Testament." In common with the Synoptic Gospels, its author-editor(s) is unknown, its final date of composition is only vaguely indicated, and the group of Christians to whom it was addressed is wholly a matter of speculation.[37] Moreover, in contrast to the Synoptic Gospels, it has no natural comparison-points, by which it might be possible to suggest with confidence the nature of earlier versions of the text.

To my mind, the most curious aspect of scholarship on the Gospel of John is the matter of its date of composition in the form that we know it. After examining roughly three dozen studies of John by biblical historians, I find a rough consensus (there are, of course, exceptions) that the composition was effected between approximately 85 and 110 CE. But when one pushes and asks why, the arguments become very spongy. The actual parameters of possible dates seem to me to be much wider than that. The latest date is somewhere between 125 and 150: this is fixed by the discovery of an Egyptian papyrus fragment of that period.[38] The other parameter is the destruction of the Temple in 70 CE. The final editor-author of John certainly knew about that cataclysmic event and he shaped his Gospel accordingly. Thus, the Gospel of John has Jesus saying, while in the Temple, that "this temple" would be destroyed (John 2:19). When employed in the Synoptic Gospels (as we shall see in a moment), this is the basis of a "prediction" by Jesus that the Jerusalem Temple would be destroyed. Here, however, the author-editor of John uses his knowledge of the Temple's destruction more subtly. In a nice piece of stagecraft, he has Jesus and "the Jews" engage in cross-talk, the Jews believing that Jesus is referring to Herod's Temple which was forty-six years in the building (2:20) but, as we are informed in an off-stage voice, Jesus "spake of the temple of his body"

(2:21). John, therefore, has Jesus-the-Christ replacing the Temple with his own person, something that John scarcely would have propounded unless he were writing after the Temple had been demolished. This is a dating point. But a more telling dating point is the entire structure of the Gospel of John, which is nothing less than the description of a temple religion without the Temple. It has been well-argued that the sub-structure of John probably was the Jewish religious calendar and that the stories of Jesus are placed in patterns that follow the probable order of the lectionaries used by the Judahist faithful.[39] The Temple was gone and both Christianity and the embryonic Jewish faith (which was the replacement of the Judahism of the Second Temple) were engaged in the same process of re-invention.

Given the hard dates within which our present version of the Gospel of John is bound – 70 to 150 CE – it is difficult to find any compelling reason that would make one opt for the middle of the range, except that it is the middle of the range.[40] I suspect that the basic reason the Gospel of John is dated when it is, is that the prevailing opinion among biblical scholars is that John is less historically informative than are the Synoptics.[41] And there is a form of magical thinking among biblical historians: if a text is earlier than another text, it is more accurate; and, conversely, if a text is more informative than another one, then it is earlier. Because the Synoptics are usually dated 70–85 CE, then, by this mode of thought, the Gospel of John has to be after 85 CE, and is usually dated 90 CE, or so. This mindset (or, more accurately, this emotionalset) is difficult to deal with because it usually is not explicitly articulated. Once it is stated outright, however, it dissolves.

Even if one accepts that the Synoptic Gospels are superior as sources of information on historical matters than is the Gospel of John; and even if one accepts the prevailing dating on the Synoptics – 70–85 CE (both matters which I think are very much "not proved") – it does not necessarily determine the dating one endorses for John. There is no indisputable reason, or set of reasons, that John could not have been completed at the same time Matthew and Luke were being placed in their final form.

The reason for emphasizing this point is that the most sensible time of dating the Gospel of John (and, indeed, of all the Gospels), is close to the destruction of the Temple, the 70s. This suggestion is made despite my instinctive distrust of "early" dates. However, the composition of John (as we have it) is a very specific response to a very specific stimulus. The stimulus, the destruction of the Temple, was strong and direct. It is most reasonable to suggest that the editor-author(s) of John replaced the physical temple with the spiritual one as quickly as possible: it is less likely that they sat in morose inaction for twenty or thirty years before taking quill in hand.

That said, the cumulative effect of scores of tiny details leads scholars to accept an order-of-composition of Mark-Luke-Matthew-John, and it is expedient to accept this sequence as a working model, provided (a) one realizes the tentativeness of John's position in the sequence and (b) one accepts the possibility that the sequence of invention could have been much more compressed temporally than is usually assumed and that, indeed, all Four Gospels could have been completed in a single decade of feverish activity, beginning with the destruction of the Temple.

The problem of the potential relationship of the Synoptic Gospels and the Gospel of John is probably the most vexed question among scholars who try to establish the stratigraphy of the Christian scriptures: did John use Matthew, Mark, or Luke? Probably most "New Testament" historians today believe, by a small majority, that John did not use the Synoptics,[42] but this is not a matter for an opinion poll. The real problem is that the variance in historical details are so ubiquitous as between the Synoptics and John – details, not central motifs – and the difficulty of finding formulations in John that could possibly derive from the Synoptics is so great, that one must leave the question open: which is necessarily to opt for the null hypothesis.

Actually, a determination of the date of the final composition of the Gospel of John is not terribly important if one is using it to help find the historical Yeshua – the historical authenticity of John's material is no different if we judge the book to have been completed in 95 CE or 75 CE. But the case serves as an illustration of the ruts that are worn in the earth by the questors for the historical Yeshua. We can observe this occurring when one asks, "what earlier forms of the Gospel of John can we point to?" That is a useful query, because various linguistic and historical tools may permit us to discover earlier versions of the book, in the same way that infra-red light sometimes reveals written-over words or phrases on a medieval manuscript. In following the reconstruction of the earlier forms of the Gospel of John, notice two points: first, how quickly an hypothetical text is reified; for many scholars an heuristic fiction moves from being an hypothesis to being a virtual reality. And, second, observe how potential authority (an hypothetical text) automatically becomes declared authority, without the validity of this transformation being examined.

The Gospel of John traditionally has been folded into two portions, the Book of Signs (chapters 1–12) and the Book of Glory (chapters 13–21). The first depends for its narrative force upon the wonderful deeds ("signs") conducted by Jesus in his ministry, the second upon the Passion narrative. Once this is noted, it is not unnatural to look for an earlier source behind each segment. In practice, however, scholarly efforts have been focused upon the first portion, the Book of Signs, and from that effort has emerged the "Signs Gospel." This hypothetical reconstruction stems from a sensible exercise: "*if* we hypothesize that a written source underlies the first half of the Gospel of John, *then* that source *might* look as follows." There are enough hiccups in the Book of John ("aporia" is the technical term) where the story does not flow well, to encourage an examination of these rough spots as nodal points in the final rewriting of John by its editor-author(s): the more so because these aporias usually are associated with specific wondrous events caused by Jesus.

Fair enough: provided one keeps in mind that there is no place in any contemporary text an indication that such an early signs document actually existed; and, further, this Signs Gospel has to be reconstructed from a single source, the Gospel of John. It thus lacks the rigour that one has when, for example, in the Synoptics, Matthew and Luke are found to use virtually identical wordings, and thus indicate that either one of them used the other or that they had a third source in common. The creation of the Signs Gospel is a totally hypothetical exercise. It has been brought to its highest development by Robert T. Fortna, who has produced a Signs Gospel[43] that focuses on six sets of miracles or wondrous actions attributed to Jesus, plus a symmetrical opening and closing framework. The result is seductive, and that is the point. Recall that Fortna derives the Signs Gospel from the Gospel of John. The formula is:

Gospel of John
minus
whatever the scholar excises and rearranges
equals
the Signs Gospel

Then note Fortna's very first interpretive footnote to his hypothetical construction: "As in a few other scenes, here the author of the canonical Gospel of John has considerably altered the Signs Gospel ('SG'), making its recovery, both as to original wording and to order, uncertain at points."[44] Really: the author of the canonical John has altered the Signs Gospel! Is not the Signs Gospel an hypothetical construct put forward by Robert Fortna? It is: hence, the so-very-revealing footnote means that the author of the canonical Gospel of John, writing in the first century, has considerably altered an hypothetical gospel put forward by an historian in the last portion of the twentieth century. Even the most addicted of post-modernists will be impressed by this apparent reversal of time's arrow: for nearly two millennia time runs backward.

Fortna's self-hypnosis with his self-created gospel is useful because it shows so explicitly a mesmerization that frequently (not always: frequently) betakes those scholars doing textual reconstruction, and if Fortna's reification is extreme, it is only extreme in its being so obvious. Almost inevitably, once hypothetical constructs are confused with historical documents, chronological time gets badly bent. Fortna, in the introduction to his Signs Gospel, raises the possibility that it is "the earliest gospel."[45] At least one scholar has gone so far as to suggest that the Synoptic Gospels depend upon the fictive Signs Gospel,[46] which is about as far as one can go in finding the causes of the visible world in the invisible.

Chronology, indeed, is the key issue if one is searching for ways to improve our information on the historical Yeshua, as well as discover a possible textual history of the Christian scriptures. Earlier, I emphasized that an earlier date does not automatically make a text more authoritative as far as the historical Yeshua is concerned, than if it had a later date. There is no difference, for example, as far as our view of John's historical usefulness is concerned, if it is dated 75 CE or 85 CE. However, there are certain nodal points where an earlier date actually would be important. The biggest single such point in the history of the invention of Christianity is the destruction of the Second Temple in 70 CE. If we were able ever to find an historical text (as distinct from Paul's pastoral letters) that was of sure provenance and which clearly was written before the Temple's destruction, then we would have a major breakthrough. If, for example, the Gospel of John were definitively proven to date from 65 CE, that would be a matter of massive import, whereas, a decade the other way, between 75 and 85 CE, means nothing.

This is of great moment in evaluating the Yeshua questors, because one finds that not only the Signs Gospel, but every other hypothetical gospel that is put forward (we will see others in a moment) are proclaimed to be pre-70. Therefore, the knee-jerk reflex is to grant them authority. Guard against that reflex. Firstly, because in the case of hypothetical gospels derived from single sources (exhibits come from John and, potentially, from Matthew), the "pre-70" text is obtained primarily by erasing the post-70 referents in the final Gospel which we possess. That gives the appearance of progress, but it is a purely tautological exercise as far as the historical Yeshua is concerned. It is an exercise in reduction, when what we want is one of amplification: we need to know what the Christians thought about Yeshua before their entire religious world was rearranged, and before the massive, subtle, and completely successful suppression and censorship that permit the "New Testament" to work so well, were operative.

And secondly, why should an hypothetical gospel automatically be said to be early, as invariably is the case? – unless, of course, as in the Signs Gospel, it is constructed by modern scholars whose first task is to eliminate all the post-70 CE material. It is possible to imagine an hypothetical text that is earlier than those which we now possess, but which still is post-70. This matter is particularly important when dealing with the Synoptics and their possible earlier sources. It is not acceptable to assume either (1) that earlier hypothetical texts are necessarily a lot earlier. They could be only a few months or a single year earlier; or (2) that "earlier" in textual matters necessarily means, "before the Temple was destroyed."

With all those inoculations against common historical infections completed, we can finally turn to the heart of the search for texts of Christianity earlier than those in the canonical scriptures, and therefore, perhaps, the acquisition of more revealing information on the historical Yeshua than is found in the "New Testament."

The Synoptic Gospels – Matthew, Mark, and Luke – so-called because they provide a fragmented vision, a "seeing simultaneously," are the third corpus of the Christian scriptures that potentially provide information on the historical Yeshua of Nazareth (we have already discussed the Pauline letters and the Gospel of John). Studying the literature on these books as composed by historical scholars of the Bible is a pleasure, because it introduces one to some of the most nimble minds in the scholarly profession. There is real intellectual joy in watching these minds grapple with the "Synoptic Puzzle,"[47] which is the question of how the overlapping portions of these books are related to each other, and thus, what was the genealogical line of descent of the three documents.

The "traditional" dating of the Synoptic Gospels among "New Testament" scholars is 70–85 CE, although a case sometimes is made for the late 60s (during the Roman-Jewish War) for the first of them. The latest hard-date for the completion of the Synoptics is roughly 140 CE when physical evidence becomes available. However, that last date is usually rejected, because none of the Synoptic Gospels show any knowledge of the widespread Jewish revolt in Rome, Egypt, Cyprus and Cyrene of 115–117,[48] which would have fit very well with the concerns of the various editor-authors of these texts.

Each of the Synoptics is a response, in various degrees of fulness, to the problem that confronted all Judahisms (including Christianity), namely, how to knit together the fragments of the late Second Temple Yahweh-faith, now blown apart by the religious equivalent of a direct hit by a meteor. None of them makes full sense unless that common purpose is recognized. However, each of the Synoptics contains within it specific acknowledgements that the Temple has been destroyed, woven into the individual texts in exactly the grammar of biblical invention that we have been observing since discussing Genesis-Kings. Mostly this is done in the form of a "prediction" that is made after an event, a technique we have observed several times previously, and which is most successfully employed in the Book of Daniel. For example, in Luke, after Jesus' triumphal entry into Jerusalem, Jesus is reported as weeping for the fate of Jerusalem:

> For the days shall come upon thee, that thine enemies shall cast a trench about thee, and compass thee round, and keep thee in on every side.
> And shall lay thee even with the ground, and thy children within thee; and they shall not leave in thee one stone upon another; because thou knewest not the time of thy visitation. (Luke 19:43–44)

That is a very good précis of what happened during the siege of Jerusalem in the Roman-Jewish War of 66–73. (One can grant the author his poetic licence: the Temple, having been destroyed mostly by fire, had a few stones still standing – as Josephus records, two towers and a stretch of the western wall were left intact as a protection for the Roman garrison.[49] The Gospel of Luke returns to this theme:

> And as some spake of the temple, how it was adorned with goodly stones and gifts, he said,
> As for these things which ye behold, the days will come, in which there shall not be left one stone upon another, that shall not be thrown down.   (Luke 21:6)

And the author-editor of Luke, unable to shake the tragic siege of Jerusalem of 69–70 from the forefront of his consciousness, returns to it yet again:

> And when ye shall see Jerusalem compassed with armies, then know that the desolation thereof is nigh.
> Then let them which are in Judaea flee to the mountains; and let them which are in the midst of it depart out; and let not them that are in the countries enter thereinto.
>   (Luke 21:20–21)

Yes, flee! The remembrance of the siege, the Temple's destruction, and the necessity of flight into the countryside for safety was the common heritage of all who, like Luke's author-editor, had to re-invent a religious world in which the spiritual metropole was missing.

The same trauma, the same massive task of re-invention confronted the editor-author of Matthew. One can see that he is brooding on the issue, even when his attention seems to be focused on other matters. For example, in the middle of the Parable of the Marriage Feast (which in Luke 14:16–24 is a calm, non-violent story), the author-editor of Matthew has the literary equivalent of post-traumatic flashback and introduces into the feast a violent (one would almost say zealot) element who attack the servants of the righteous and then are themselves destroyed:

> And the remnant took his servants, and entreated them spitefully, and slew them.
> But when the king heard thereof, he was wroth: and he sent forth his armies, and destroyed those murderers, and burned up their city.   (Matt. 22:6–7)

Matthew reports Jesus' predictions about the Temple in essentially the same words used in Luke, quoted above:

> And Jesus went out, and departed from the temple: and his disciples came to him for to shew him the buildings of the temple.

> And Jesus said unto them, See ye not all these things? verily I say unto you, There shall not be left here one stone upon another, that shall not be thrown down.
>
> (Matt. 24:1–2)

Clearly, the author-editors of Matthew, of Luke and (as was discussed earlier) of John, knew of the siege of Jerusalem, and the destruction not only of the Temple, but of virtually the entire city. And of course the knowledge became central to their thinking and to their exposition of the life of Jesus. It is true to the tradition of biblical invention that they should place the most important facts in the mouth of the most important figure: Jesus. Moreover, it is wonderfully skilful. By having the baleful and bewildering knowledge of the crash of the Temple-based Judahist religious system transformed from a disaster-report into a prediction uttered by Jesus, an inexplicable tragedy was turned into a predicted-event. An uncontrollable social and cultural catastrophe became controllable, for Jesus had predicted it, and therefore the event was part of a tightly controlled divine plan. This is a splendidly successful piece of work, biblical invention at its best.

And it is a fluorescent-orange buoy, a visible marker for the historian in what is otherwise an ill-marked and muddy river of time. The only objection that can be made is the fundamentalist argument – that Jesus said whatever is found on his lips in the Gospels – and that assertion cannot be answered, or indeed rationally dealt with, by an historian. It is a faith held prior to historical scrutiny, and though it may warm the human heart, it does not illuminate the mind. If one cannot accept what is one of the most historically documentable points about the invention of the "New Testament" – that the Gospels of Matthew, of Luke, and of John in their present forms were written after the fall of Jerusalem in 70 CE – then one might as well stop reading at this point.

Thus far, I have not mentioned Mark. That Gospel is best approached tangentially, through Matthew. Jesus' prediction that the Temple would not be left one stone on another, cited above (Matt. 24:1–2, and doubled in Luke 21:5–7), is directly asserted in Mark:

> And as he went out of the temple, one of his disciples saith unto him, Master, see what manner of stones and what buildings are here!
> And Jesus answering said unto him, Seest thou these great buildings? There shall not be left one stone upon another, that shall not be thrown down.   (Mark 13:1–2)

Further, Matthew, in the story of Jesus before the Sanhedrin, has him being accursed by two false witnesses, who said:

> This fellow said, I am able to destroy the temple of God, and to build it in three days.   (Matt. 26:61)

This is found in duplicate in Mark: whereas the false witnesses claim

> We heard him say, I will destroy this temple that is made with hands, and within
> three days I will build another made without hands. (Mark 14:58)

A Temple made without hands was exactly what the former Judahisms tried
to build after 70 CE. So important is this to Mark's author-editor that he repeats it, with great ironic effect, while Jesus is on the cross:

> And they that passed by railed on him, wagging their heads, and saying, Ah, thou
> that destroyest the temple and buildest it in three days,
> Save thyself, and come down from the cross. (Mark 15:29–30)

This is yet another example of what might be called the judo-technique of the
Gospel writers: they turn the force of their misfortune, in this case the destruction of the heart of the Judahist symbolic system, and use it for their own
advantage. The specific literary form is irony: by virtue of their historical
knowledge that the Temple indeed has been destroyed, Matthew and Mark
here are able to produce a text wherein the reader experiences the fact as
foreknowledge: one reads it and says, yes, Jesus was right, the Temple was
doomed – and then, triumphantly – and it was replaced by Jesus himself. It is
what, in professional sports, is called a great inside-move, quick, subtle, efficient. Significantly, this inside move is one of the few places where the Gospel of John agrees on details with the Synoptics. Had the correspondence
occurred in our own lifetimes, we might wonder if the author-editors had all
attended an editorial round table. Each, of course, used the ironic foreknowledge at the appropriate point in his own narrative.

The point worth pressing here is that if the author-editors of Matthew,
John, and Luke, both in specific textual reference and in the general structure
of their works, each indicate a clear consciousness that the Temple had been
destroyed, and thus their books are written subsequent to that event, then the
same argument holds for Mark: that Gospel, too, shows knowledge of the
wasting of Jerusalem, and it too is structured so as to invent a Temple religion
for a world without the Jerusalem Temple. The reason for pressing this point
is that (as will become clear in a moment), some scholars who otherwise are
very strong on evidentiary criteria in their work, turn away from those criteria
when it comes to Mark: they want the text to be earlier than the Roman-
Jewish War and the Temple's destruction, for they believe Mark was the first
Gospel to be completed, and, obviously, if the first one is post-70 CE, so are
the others. If that is the case, then, save for the writings of Paul (who is not
much interested in history or in the historical Yeshua), we have no Christian
text that provides direct access to the historical events of the period before the

trauma of 70 CE. Thus, one is forced to contemplate that the still-swirling dust of Jerusalem obscures the horizon, forever interposing between the Christian scriptures and the historical Yeshua.[50]

5

Naturally, one understands the desire to get back before 70 CE, but it has to be done without cutting corners: such as simply declaring that one of the Gospels indeed is pre-70. That won't work without a preliminary bonfire of the verities, including the rules of historical evidence. However, there is a potential way to the pre-70 world: the Synoptic Gospels have an intense interrelationship with each other, and it is possible that by untwining these relationships, scholars can define a textual trajectory that will eventually yield pieces of text that are less obscured by the dust of the holy city. Perhaps: perhaps not, but the exercise is worth engaging in any case, because the history of the evolution of the Christian texts is such an important part of this religion of the codex.

Like all good puzzles, what I have called the "Synoptic Puzzle," is deceptively simple in appearance: Matthew, Mark, and Luke are textually interrelated – what, precisely, is that relationship? Since there are only three moving parts in the puzzle, one expects an explanation that requires little in the way of complicated machinery. The textual relationships among the Synoptic Gospels have only two qualitative variables: the actual content (parable by parable, verse by verse, or phrase by phrase) and the order of occurrence that the various parables and miracles and narrative bridges assume in each book.

What scholars are trying to do above all is to answer the question, "Which of the three Synoptic Gospels came first?" Here, as in all historical work, one must be careful not to frame the puzzle so that it tilts the discussion unfairly in a particular direction. For example, one way to state the fundamental of content-relationships as between the three books is this. One can say "Of Mark's 661 verses, some 430 are substantially reproduced in both Matthew and Luke. Of the remaining 231 verses, 176 occur in Matthew and the substance of 25 in Luke. Only 30 verses in Mark do not appear in some form in either Matthew or Luke."[51] This is an accurate statement, and a now-traditional formulation. Or one can formulate the data in percentages: "the bulk of Mark is found in Luke (55 percent of it …) and in Matthew (90 percent of it)."[52] But notice that each of those formulations of the Synoptic Puzzle, while accurate, makes Mark the centre of our attention and thus insensibly leads us to give precedence to one major possibility: that Mark is the central element in the puzzle, and automatically, one privileges the idea that Mark came first historically. The exact same data can be covered in a set-up question that produces quite a different set of presuppositions. One could say that "the text of Mark employs, in its version of the scriptures, 176 verses-worth of material found only in Matthew, and 25 found only in Luke. Some 430 verses come from both Matthew and Luke and only 30 from some unknown source." And one could add "90 percent of the material that Mark employs is found in Matthew." Those formulations, obviously, tilt the enquirer towards Matthaean priority. Neither one is an example of good historical question-framing, but a variant of the first one, the tilt towards Mark, is found in most introductions to the textual relationships of the Synoptic Gospels.

If, for the moment, we limit our attention to the three biblical texts as we at present have them, and exclude all exogenous textual variables (hypothetical gospels and the like), and also exclude all matters of historical context, then we have a textual puzzle, involving three texts and eighteen possible relationships. The most supple discussion of the logical possibilities (and a book that anyone who enjoys really tough, focused historical arguments should read), is found in William R. Farmer's *The Synoptic Problem* (1976).[53] The eighteen possible relationships are defined by set-theory and by one additional limiting assumption: that borrowing from one text to another was a one-way phenomenon. That is, if the author of Matthew borrowed from Mark, this excludes the possibility of the author-editor of Mark having borrowed from Matthew. And, of course, this also excludes the three Synoptic author-editors all having borrowed from each other. Without such an assumption, any literary dependence of one upon another would be impossible to demonstrate. Although it is congenial to think of the author-editors of the Synoptics exchanging draft Gospels with each other, rather like short-story writers at an artists' colony, the scene is an unlikely one: the basic assumption shared by virtually all biblical scholars, of one-way borrowing, is realistic.

To be potentially viable in solving the Synoptic Puzzle, any set of arrangements must be able to handle two conditions that are found in the actual Synoptic texts: (1) it must be able to explain those instances wherein all three texts agree and (2) it must be able to handle those instances where two of the Synoptics agree with each other and disagree with the third. Disagreement here can be either overt or from silence. It is a real condition, for there are occasions in the texts wherein, on some issues, each Synoptic Gospel is in conflict with the other two. To handle this situation adequately, the potential arrangement of texts must permit not only indications of agreement, but testimony to disagreement. What is not required is (3) that the explanatory system be able to handle those instances wherein the three Synoptics are in complete disagreement with each other. Such instances are explicable only by the introduction of an exogenous *Urtext* for each book, and the initial assumption, that the explanation should arise from a closed system, excludes that external interference.

Given these assumptions, and the puzzle as outlined, William Farmer reduces the number of potential textual relationships from eighteen to six, for only these six cover instances of all three Gospels agreeing and provide for testimony to all the possible variants of two-against-one situations.[54] These remaining six possibilities are the permutation of Book 1, being copied in part by the author-editor of Book 2, and then, both Book 1 and Book 2 becoming available to the author-editor of Book 3. This permits there to be textual portions wherein (a) all three agree, and others wherein (b) Books 1 and 2 agree with each other, but not with Book 3, whose author has rejected part of their common viewpoint, and another instance that occurs when the author-editor of Book 3 accepts something in Book 1 that the author-editor of Book 2 rejected, and, finally (4) provides for instances wherein the author-editor of Book 3 copies the author-editor of Book 2, in, for example, rejecting a story that is found in Book 1. Farmer's scheme, therefore, covers all possible relationships of agreement and of two-against-one disagreement that are conceivable.

The great beauty of his work is that, within this closed explanatory system there is no bias. It is a set of six hypotheses, which cover all the possible relationships, and one can test the hypotheses one after another: with Mark as the earliest Gospel, with Luke, with Matthew, and with each of the other Synoptic Gospels in the two derivative positions. It is a lovely piece of logical machinery.

This machinery could be associated with any theory of biblical priority, but in the world of biblical scholarship it is the basis only of one major viewpoint, the *Matthew-hypothesis*.[55] This takes the form of the theory that Matthew was the first Gospel, that the author-editor of Luke used it, and that subsequently the author-editor of Mark subsequently used both Matthew and Luke. This is a textual stratigraphy that is upsetting to most questors for the historical Yeshua, for Matthew is undeniably post-Second Temple, and for Luke and Mark to be even later than Matthew is not of any help in getting behind the 70 CE curtain. However, *within the boundaries of the logical system he has defined*, I find William Farmer compelling. Within his system, his Matthew-hypothesis is much more robust, much more in synchronization with the data as found in the Synoptic Gospels than is the idea that Mark came first. (Luke is not really in the running; that volume fits best in a median position in any case.)

Yet, the Matthew-hypothesis, while paid lip-service (it is hard to ignore entirely an intellect as powerful as Farmer), is largely ignored by biblical historians, and not entirely for good reasons. One problem is that many scholars find it unattractive because the hypothesis is unfairly saddled with a great deal of dogmatic baggage. The early church fathers saw Matthew as the earliest and the best of the Gospels and from the time of Augustine onwards this was the overwhelmingly dominant view.[56] It became the official position of the Roman Catholic church, and in 1911 the Biblical Commission of the

Roman Catholic church affirmed that Matthew was the first Gospel and that it went back to apostolic times. "In deciding the priority of St. Matthew's gospel in its original language and substance, the Biblical Commission has solemnly disapproved of any form of these theories which maintain that St. Matthew's original work was not a complete gospel or the first in the order of time."[57] At that time, historical analysis of the biblical text was almost entirely limited to Protestant scholars, and this endorsement of the Matthew-hypothesis, combined with a dogmatic assertion that Matthew went back to Jesus and his disciples, virtually guaranteed that the Matthew hypothesis was the least likely to gain ascendancy in twentieth-century biblical scholarship. This specific dogmatic handicap no longer exists – the church now permits Catholic scholars to follow the evidence on this issue – but there is still a segment of followers of the Matthew-hypothesis who endorse it not because of its logical power, but because of a belief external to the issue of the Synoptic Puzzle: namely that by endorsing Matthew's priority, they are somehow catching hold of a text whose traditions extend back to Jesus.[58]

That has nothing to do with the actual Synoptic Puzzle and is the sort of theological misuse of an historical hypothesis that turns scholars away. Matthew, in its present form, certainly was written after the destruction of the Second Temple, and, if the Matthew-hypothesis puts it earlier in the line of invention than Luke and Mark, that still does not propel it to a date earlier in time than 70 CE.

Crucially, the Matthew-hypothesis makes sense only if it is assimilated in the terms defined by its strongest proponent, William R. Farmer, as a neat solution to a closed-boundary logic problem. Whether Matthew is earliest, latest, or median in order of invention among the Synoptic Gospels, it still is post-70, for on that issue the book's contents are unambiguous. This point has been well made by the brilliant classicist (and sometime politician) J. Enoch Powell, who has argued not only that Matthew was the first of the Synoptic Gospels to come into being, and that it was the sole source of the other two, but that its origin was well after 70 CE and represents a period in which the Christian church already had firmly established its own liturgical system quite independent of both imperial Rome and of the various now-scattered Judahisms. Hence, the year 70 would be the earliest moment for composition, under this interpretation, but one could easily argue that it represented a Christianity of one or two decades later.[59]

In that form – in solving most satisfactorily the logical teaser, the Synoptic Puzzle, and in respecting the clear post-70 date of the Synoptics compilation in final form – the Matthew-hypothesis is very appealing. Yet it has received little attention and even less support. The reason, I would speculate, is because its apparent virtues become emotional drawbacks. *If* the Matthew-hypothesis is correct as far as inter-textual relationships are concerned, and *if*

Matthew itself is demonstrably post-70, and *if* the other two Synoptic Gospels are virtually dependent upon Matthew, *then* biblical historians are locked into a world of sources that are post-70 CE: and they have no obvious way of escaping, no way of breaking back into the pre-70 period. I think that the Matthew-hypothesis is frightening to biblical historians chiefly because it is perceived as a hope-destroying mechanism: we will *never* know what we want to know of the historical Yeshua, it seems to prove, ruthlessly. So badly do searchers for early Christian roots, and especially questors for the historical Yeshua, want to break past the influence of the catastrophic end of Second Temple Judahism, that they treat the Matthew-hypothesis as if it were a threatening character on an urban street: they look away and avoid eye-contact. Or they appeal to "scholarly consensus" and pass quickly on to more congenial considerations.

That won't do. The Matthew-hypothesis has severe drawbacks and I think that it is not in fact the best available hypothesis, but nothing will be gained by avoiding the issue. In my view, the problems with the Matthew-hypothesis lie in its primary operational assumption: that the Synoptic Puzzle should be defined and solved as a closed-boundary logic problem. That is fine for artificially-constructed brain-teasers, but it is not a sensible assumption if one is dealing with a set of historical documents. These documents have historical referents outside of the logical puzzle, and such referents are not merely adventitious, but are directly related to the matter which the logical puzzle has been constructed to deal with. Historians are not permitted to assume historical patterns and events out of existence.

Here things get tricky. Some proponents of the Matthew-hypothesis point out that it has some direct historical benefits, and that these flow from the magisterial logical solution of the Synoptic Puzzle, rather like the revenues of an appanage accruing to the members of a ruling house. Specifically, it is argued that the Matthew-hypothesis efficiently explains the bi-modal character of the Gospel of Mark, which is said to be a mixture of conflicting viewpoints within Christianity. Mark is put forward as a set of compromises between the Gospel of Matthew, which strongly emphasizes the traditions of Peter and of Jerusalem, and of the Gospel of Luke, which is oriented more around Paul and around the diaspora of Christianity. This by-product of the Matthew-hypothesis is a potentially useful historical suggestion, but it really has no discriminatory power: the bi-modal character of Mark can just as easily be fit into a theory that suggests Mark was the first of the Synoptic Gospels to be written and that the author-editors of Matthew and of Luke simply disaggregated Mark, each plucking out and emphasizing the aspects he preferred.

Where historical patterns breach the closed-boundary assumption of the Matthew-hypothesis is at a more fundamental level: to have the fullest and most textured Gospel coming first, and the leanest coming last, runs completely counter to the grammar of biblical invention that we have seen operating in the Hebrew scriptures (the primary model of the Christian scriptures) and the wide body of para-biblical inventions of the later Second Temple era. The grammar of biblical invention facilitates the invention of new texts, but only according to some fairly strict operational principles. Usually, one changes the meaning of a text by expanding it, and in the expansion alters by a few points of the compass its meaning. Or, occasionally, the biblical inventors turn an old text at a 90-degree angle to its original meaning, by redefining the term: thus, the Moshiah of the Tanakh, meaning an anointed figure of priestly, kingly, or prophetic rank, became an expected saviour through Christian redefinition. That is very rare. In very exceptional instances – the replacement of the "young girl" of Isaiah's prophecies with the Virgin of Matthew and Luke – a 180-degree change in meaning is accomplished through brass-necked assertion of the new definition. However, the one way that the grammar of biblical invention does *not* operate is through straightforward deletion of previous texts. As far back as the primary unity of Genesis-Kings, we have observed the manner in which slices of older texts are preserved, even when they are intertextually contradictory. They often are tamed, but they are not thrown out.[60]

This is relevant to the Matthew-hypothesis, because, for it to apply to the real historical world – as distinct from its dominating a closed-boundary logical system – the Matthew-hypothesis implies that the author of Mark threw out some of the most important material in Matthew and Luke: most especially all those stories related to the Virgin Birth. This is not just a matter of editorial parsimony: as was discussed earlier (Chapter Nine, note 19), Mark makes no mention of the Virgin Birth. If one assumes that the author-editor of Mark was writing last and with full knowledge of Matthew and Luke, then one is encountering a total deviation from the rules that have governed all other instances of biblical invention. He is directly rejecting an earlier text, rather than re-inventing it. This, in theory, could have occurred (Mark could have been based on Matthew, with the Virgin Birth deleted as historically inaccurate or as theologically repugnant) except that do so do would inevitably have made Mark a failure: for, if the author-editor of Mark had knowledge of the Gospels of Matthew and of Luke, so did his audience, or at least they soon would have, for Matthew and Luke were hardly secret documents. Therefore, the Markan narrative would have been judged to have been inadequate, since it left out some of the most electric portions of Matthew and Luke. If Luke and Matthew already were in existence, only someone with no sense of how biblical narrative worked, could have written Mark: and anyone who reads the Gospel of Mark knows that its author-editor was one of the canniest of biblical inventors.

The closed-boundary definition of the Synoptic Puzzle nicely tidies up the playing surface by excluding exogenous texts from the discussion. That makes the Puzzle easier of solution, but there are indeed places where the three Synoptic Gospels all disagree with each other, and the Matthew-hypothesis, being a closed-boundary explanation, cannot handle those instances. Here again the real world breaches the walls of the logic system.

Thus, on balance, I prefer the *Mark-hypothesis*, even though it has a number of potential drawbacks.[61] It is basically simple, but includes some elegant moves. Its fundamental point is that since about 50 percent of the Gospel of Mark is also found in the Gospel of Luke, and about 90 percent of the Gospel of Mark is found in the Gospel of Matthew – and thus, inevitably, Matthew and Luke share material that is found in Mark – the best way to explain this situation is to infer that a significant portion of the text of Matthew and of Luke is based upon Mark.

The elegant aspect of this suggestion is that if the hypothesis is accurate, then it is not only a source-hypothesis, but it also gives us a key to an experimental laboratory. If Matthew and Luke are dependent upon Mark, then we can turn the whole sequence on its head, and pretend that we do not know of Mark: we can pretend to derive portions of an unknown document – we will call it Mark – from two known sources. Why bother?

Because this *process* which we can observe – and which is not an hypothetical process, but a real historical one in which we have lab notes on all three artifacts in the process – gives us a template that we can then apply to a related situation: namely that approximately 200 verses are held in common by Luke and Matthew, but are not found in Mark. We can derive what source – biblical scholars usually call it "Q," which probably stands for "Quelle"[62] – by a process parallel to that by which we pretended to deduce large portions of Mark. "Q" is an hypothetical document, to be sure, but the legitimacy of the process whereby this conceptual entity was inferred, was established by the way Mark was heuristically derived, in our imaginary laboratory experiment, from common elements of Matthew and Luke. Unlike the so-called "Signs Gospel," which is said to underlie the Gospel of John, "Q" is based upon a set of inventive processes whose reality is confirmed by the documents themselves.

So, the basic sources of the Synoptic Gospels are taken to be Mark and "Q." This arrangement has the virtue of following the way in which the grammar of biblical invention amplifies and transforms texts, and also has the virtue of not pretending to be a closed-boundary explanatory system: from the very beginning, the outside world – in this case, in the form of "Q" – is allowed to play a part in the Synoptic Puzzle.

The danger is that the real world can turn this into a terrible sprawl. For example, the Matthew-hypothesis, as a closed-boundary system, did not deal with the fact that on certain issues none of the Synoptic Gospels agree. Thus, a set of influences external to the boundaries of the Synoptic Puzzle have to be admitted and therefore the Matthew-hypothesis becomes a three-source hypothesis: the Gospel of Matthew, and those at-present-unknown sources that provide Luke with certain unique details and Mark, also, with certain unique fragments of text. And the Mark-hypothesis sprawls one stage further: there are some sayings and behaviours reported in Luke that are unique to that Gospel and the same goes for Matthew. So the Mark-hypothesis becomes (at minimum) a four-source hypothesis; Mark, "Q" and the as-yet-unknown sources that provide Matthew and Luke with the materials that are unique to each of them.

The Mark-hypothesis is particularly susceptible to further splaying. Some scholars have suggested that certain of the para-biblical books – such as the Gospel of Thomas or the Gospel of Peter – intermixed with "Q" and Mark and the unique portions of Matthew and of Luke in the biblical equivalent of the primal soup from which all life is said to stem. Some few others throw into the stew a "Cross Gospel" which is an hypothetical document, said to underlie the Gospel of Peter. Just how far out of control this is, and unrelated to anything a professional historian would recognize as a testable hypothesis or as having probative value, is illustrated by the following summary of his own theory of the formation of the Gospels, put forward by John Dominic Crossan, one of the best-known of Roman Catholic biblical historians:

> The process developed, in other words, over these primary steps. First, the *histori-cal passion*, composed of minimal knowledge, was known only in the general terms recorded by, say, Josephus or Tacitus. Next, the *prophetic passion*, composed of multiple and discrete biblical allusions and seen most clearly in a work like the *Epistle of Barnabas*,[63] developed biblical applications over, under, around, and through that open framework. Finally, those multiple and discrete exercises were combined into the *narrative passion* as a single sequential story. I proposed, fur-thermore, that the narrative passion is but a single stream of tradition flowing from the *Cross Gospel*, now embedded within the *Gospel of Peter*, into Mark, thence to-gether into Matthew and Luke, and thence, all together, into John. Other recon-structions are certainly possible, but that seems to me the most economical one to explain all the data.[64]

– a strange brew indeed.

The Mark-hypothesis has value, I think, but only if its very severe limita-tions are recognized. These are, first, that we must continually remind our-selves that "Q" does not exist. It is a heuristic construction, to which there is no reference in any of the extant biblical and para-biblical texts. It is a way of thinking, but to hypostatize "Q" leads to all sorts of further fallacies and solipsisms. Mark exists: "Q" does not.

Secondly, "Q" is artificially aged. One frequently reads the suggestion that "Q" is the earliest Christian Gospel. Aside from such a statement being a sad example of reification of an hypothetical construct, it misses a simple methodological point: "Q" acquires an artificial patina of age because if the same material is found in the Gospel of Mark and in "Q," it automatically is assigned to Mark, and that includes the most important material for dating. For example, Jesus' "prediction" of the destruction of the Temple (Mark 13:1–4; Matt. 24:1–3; Luke 21:5–7) is excluded from "Q" because it is found in Mark. So "Q" acquires a false-craquelure.

If we really wish to use "Q" as an aid to our thinking about how the Gospels were formed we should (a) accept the fact that even as a conceptual entity "Q" is unobtainable: the "Q" that biblical historians derive from the items that Matthew and Luke share (and which are not in Mark), is a demi-construct, because the "real Q" would have included not only those items, but also some items in common with Mark, and with Matthew and Luke. (These of course would be impossible to sort out by the logic of the Mark-model, so this material, which might double the size, and certainly would change the character of the conceptual entity "Q" is simply ignored.)[65] And (b) we should forget the assumption that "Q" will necessarily be earlier than Mark. That is: there is no value in an *a priori* assumption which, when enforced by the exclusionary evidentiary principles for the construction of "Q" that excludes all post-70 material, results in the "conclusion" that "Q" is older than Mark and thus the oldest possible portion of the Christian scriptures. For that is a perfect tautology. Actually, there is neither in logic nor in the historical record any reason to suggest that "Q," as used by the author-editors of Matthew and Luke, could not have been put together *subsequent* to the writing of the present version of Mark.[66]

Thirdly, despite all the mis-use and mis-perception of "Q," it remains as the one piece of historical speculation about the invention of the "New Testament" that is based on instructions that come from the scriptures. The way that Luke and Matthew employ Mark tells us that we should consider seriously the possibility of a written document – parallel to Mark – that underlies Luke and Matthew. This situation is totally different from the case of the other hypothetical Gospels: the "Signs Gospel" said to underlie John, and the "Cross Gospel" said to underlie the Gospel of Peter and thence the canonical Gospels. In those instances, there is no instruction from the scriptures indicating that such a construct is worthy of consideration, or how to go about constructing such an hypothetical entity.

Fourthly, I must emphasize that, as far as the quest for the historical Yeshua is concerned, even if one finds the heuristic-Gospel "Q" useful in understanding the evolution of the biblical text, it does not constitute multiple attestation by independent witnesses of the sayings or deeds of the historical Yeshua. All the sayings are derived from a unitary source, the extant canonical scriptures, and just as the canonical scriptures are a single witness, so any hypothetical derivative from the canon is part of the same single unitary source. To be blunt: one cannot obtain multiple independent attestation of the historical Yeshua simply by chopping up the "New Testament."

Fifthly, if one is employing "Q" or any other hypothetical gospel to get closer to an understanding of the historical Yeshua, then watch carefully for downward-dating creep. This has been mentioned earlier. The scholars who create the hypothetical gospels usually invest them with greater importance than they otherwise would have, by positing early dates for them. This is simple hubris in most instances. However, it relates to a particularly misleading, almost magical belief among scholars of all schools, from evangelicals through literalists to non-believers. This condition is almost immediately diagnosable when one finds the word "eyewitness." It is a magical word, like "abracadabra." If an hypothetical gospel can be claimed to have been written within the time period when "eyewitnesses" to events were still alive, it acquires great mana. This obtains despite a vast body of forensic experience which indicates that eyewitnesses to cataclysmic, traumatic, or transforming events usually are highly inaccurate witnesses (why is it that the investigating officer on a traffic accident almost always reaches a more accurate picture of the cause, nature, and effects of a car crash than do the eyewitnesses?) and despite entire libraries of historical monographs that provide narrative of events much better than any eyewitness could (one might get the feel of the Battle of Austerlitz from the diary of a foot soldier, but a good military historian tells us more than an entire brigade of infantry ever could). Be wary of any account whose argument is buttressed by appeals to unspecified eyewitnesses.

And, sixthly, in using "Q" and canonical documents to try to understand how the Christian scriptures evolved (and thus, maybe, to get closer to the historical Yeshua), we should not accept the belief that, in matters related to the formation of the "New Testament," time flowed evenly. This is one of those beliefs that is widely held and almost never examined, and it is not limited to the weaker practitioners of biblical history. Here are two statements, summaries of the "New Testament's" evolution, by two of the strongest scholars in the field:

John P. Meier:

How can we distinguish what comes from Jesus (Stage I, roughly A.D. 28–30), from what was created by the oral tradition of the early church (Stage II, roughly A.D. 30–70), and what was produced by the editorial work (redaction) of the evangelists (Stage III, roughly A.D. 70–100)?[67]

E.P. Sanders:

Some Christians decided that they might after all need connected accounts of Jesus. We do not know how many stages lay between the units used in sermons and our present gospels, but let us say there were two. We shall now also use the best technical name for these small units, many of which survive in our present gospels: pericopes. The word literally means "cut around." Each pericope has an obvious beginning and end, and each can be cut out of its present place in one of the gospels and moved to another. It appears that groups of pericopes dealing with similar topics, such as healings or debates with opponents, were written on sheets of papyrus, copied, and circulated among various Christian communities. Next, these groupings were put together to form what we now call proto-gospels – works that told a connected story, but not the whole story. A proto-gospel, for example, might consist of a series of pericopes dealing with conflict between Jesus and other Jews, and conclude with his arrest, trial and execution. Or a proto-gospel might be a large assemblage of sayings relevant to the ongoing life of Christian communities (ethics, questions of rank, sayings about missionary work and the like). Finally, the first gospel as we have it was written. Most scholars think that this was Mark. Subsequent authors used Mark and incorporated other materials, such as proto-gospels or topical collections that the author of Mark had not included. The final gospels as we have them were probably composed between the years 70 and 90, though some scholars put Mark earlier, in the sixties.[68]

Notice how schematic history becomes, how evenly time flows. With respect to two truly great scholars, I think their schemes are flawed: not because the stages are unrealistic, but because the implied pacing of events is unreal. Instead of a continuous course of development of the "New Testament," I think it much more realistic to suggest that it was an extremely uneven process. Long periods of snail-like development were replaced with short periods of furious activity, when, effectively, time was compressed, and a decade or two's worth of activity was accomplished as in the twinkling of an eye.

Here let us engage in a cross-time comparison (all the while keeping in mind how much historians of all sorts hate cross-time references, since these upset the industrial demarcation of the profession). This cross-time comparison is an exercise: go to a decent library and take out any six volumes on the social, economic and political history of Japan between the start of the twentieth century and the year 1960. That is roughly the span of years between the death of Jesus and the completion of the Four Gospels, according to most datings. Read these books with only one thing in mind: the way time is metered by the authors. You almost certainly will be struck with how discontinuously time runs in the various chronicles: and so it should to be true to the historical record. The Russo-Japanese war of 1904–05 will be seen to take up a good deal of space, but thereafter the march is fairly even, with the Annexation of Korea in 1910 and the Japanese joining the war against Germany in 1914 being like ticks of a metronome. However, with the occupation of Manchuria in 1931 events begin to crowd the chronicle, and then the Second World War fills chapter after chapter, until its conclusion by nuclear weapons; and then a massive, deep, alteration of Japanese society as it is reconstructed in the immediate aftermath of the war. Time does not flow continuously, but in large lumps, and the great cataclysm, the defeat of the Japanese imperial military, economic, and cultural system is a nodal point around which huge pieces of history revolve.

The history of the branch of Judaism that became Christianity is like that: concentrated, discontinuous, and focused on moments of trauma wherein massive restructurings occurred. Just as no serious historian of twentieth-century Japan would propound a theory of even, continuous development for that culture, so it should not be adopted for Christianity. The two moments of discontinuity are, first, and obviously, the arrest, trial, and execution of Jesus and, secondly, the later 60s. Time moved swiftly, developments were quick at the two ends of that time-line but, I think, moved extremely slowly in between: discontinuous evolution. So, anyone who is trying to get a fix on the historical Yeshua and who measures time's awkward flow as if it were an even-running stream, will inevitably be far off the mark with his or her calibrations.

The ten-year period that begins with 64 CE is like the 1940s in Japanese history: suddenly-interesting times, leading to a cataclysm, and a major cultural reorganization. The execution of Paul is traditionally, and reasonably, put at 63 or 64 CE, and within the Christian community, the loss of Paul soon had as its backdrop the fire of Rome (64 CE) and the Christians' persecution by Nero which the conflagration triggered. Peter (that is, Simon Peter, one of the Twelve), is traditionally believed to have been martyred in the Neronian persecution. James, brother of Jesus and a pillar of the Christians in Jerusalem (especially those who remained keenly Judahist), was put to death, if Josephus is to be believed, by the high priest Ananus II in the late 60s. From the middle of the year 66 onwards Jerusalem, still the metropole of all the Judahist variants, including Christianity, was a combat zone, and then it was rubble.

So, instead of conceiving of the creation of the "New Testament" as the result of a nice, regular, and necessary evolution from oral tradition to fly-sheets to proto-gospels, to canonical Gospels, it is closer to externally-documented historical contexts to suggest that, for a long time, the word-of-mouth stories about Jesus did not require any special keeping. They were maintained without special remembrancers: one is struck by the casual attitude of the Pauline letters, wherein the apostle simply assumes that everyone knows the mundane facts about the historical Yeshua, and that these are of secondary moment in any case, so he is free to talk about what he believes really counts: Jesus-the-Christ. I would speculate that suddenly that pose is abandoned, and a new and rapidly-accelerating, almost feverish activity takes its place. On short notice, the oral memory has to be replaced by something more permanent. The main keepers of the oral memory were disappearing, and Roman persecution of Christians in the empire's centre, when combined with the Jewish War in and around Jerusalem, predicted a future of chaos, attrition, and, unless the collective memory were preserved independently of the lives of individual human custodians, amnesia would ensue. The "traditional" scholarly sequence of the composition of the Gospels – Mark, Luke, Matthew, John – is not affected by such a compression of the time-line around the year 70 CE, but the whole process is thereby brought closer to well-documented historical events which have a high probability of having been causal in the Gospels' assemblage.

That suggestion at least has the virtue of rescuing the invention of the "New Testament" from the virtual historical vacuum in which it is placed by the standard schemes of scriptural evolution. The "New Testament" did not evolve in a sterile laboratory, but in a very rough real world. One of the most curious aspects of the work of the biblical historians whom I have read is the alacrity with which they immerse themselves (as much as this can be done) in the secular history of the years from, roughly the death of Herod the Great until about 30 CE. Thereafter, the outside world largely disappears, an irrelevance. This is curious, because Jesus-the-Christ is known to us almost entirely from writings that, in the form we encounter them, are post-70 CE. In the most literal sense, Jesus-the-Christ is a product of the years after the destruction of the Second Temple.

Moreover, Jesus-the-Christ who is the product of those post-70 documents is a figure whose characteristics are almost entirely from the stockroom of later Second Temple Judaism. In the terror and confusion of that terrible decade, from the mid-60s to the mid-70s, believers who were trying to recall Yeshua and to explain him, grabbed what was to hand. As I demonstrated in Chapters Eight and Nine, almost all of the motifs, icons, and symbolic behaviours attached to Yeshua of Nazareth – which turned him into Jesus-the-Christ – were readily available in late Second Temple Judaism. The two items which were not from the Judahist tradition – the Virgin Birth and the physical, as distinct from the cosmic, resurrection – are those which fit least comfortably within the "New Testament." Even in our own time, there is inevitably a resistance to accepting the idea that even the Gentile portion of Christianity was not just willing, but avidly committed to, articulating the New Covenant in the vocabulary and in the conceptual framework provided by late Second Temple Judaism. Such a resistance to acknowledging the dominant Semitic heritage of the Christian faith, however, is not really a scholarly matter and will not be eradicated by mere knowledge.

6

As far as any verifiable historical evidence indicates, then, Jesus-the-Christ came into being in the years around 70 CE. The myriad quests for the historical Yeshua, although far from quixotic – there was such a figure and he certainly is worth pursuing – seem to have been of little help. Every single one that I have read, traces down the historical Yeshua chiefly through the assumption that the canonical Gospels, or the canonical Gospels and various hypothetical gospels, or the canonical Gospels and a combination of hypothetical gospels and extra-biblical gospels, are separate sources. As we have discussed in many contexts, they are not, except in the instances where the para-biblical sources are so wildly imaginative as to be of no potential evidentiary use.

How does one get behind the unity that is the "New Testament"? Since almost all the characteristics that are ascribed to Jesus-the-Christ are motifs from the Hebrew scriptures and from the para-biblical texts of late Second Temple Judahism (a point that I hope has been made abundantly clear in the main text), it might be suggested that a simple "residual method" be employed. That is: subtract all those Judahist motifs – Son of God, Son of Man, Lamb of God and so on – from the "New Testament," especially from the Four Gospels, and one will have Yeshua of Nazareth. No: what one will have is a lot of pages with nothing but white space on them.

That might be acceptable, if depressing – some historical quests must forever fail, and this might be one such – except that it is an error. Because it is possible (indeed probable) that Yeshua of Nazareth was acquainted with many of the ideas from the rich swirl of Judahist religious life (he was, after all, deeply interested in religious matters: that is one assertion I cannot imagine being challenged), then he well may have adopted some of them for himself. It is not impossible that he defined himself by some of these ideas: Son of Man, Son of God, maybe Moshiah. Therefore, if one disassembles all the pieces of religious machinery that came from the Judahist stock-shop of Yeshua's era, and tosses them aside, there is a fair chance that one will be eliminating some of the ideas that Yeshua of Nazareth actually embraced.

This may leave us with an operational conundrum that cannot be overcome. It may indeed be the case that the historical Yeshua is so far beyond recovery that all we can say with any certainty is that Yeshua was a Judahist of religious fervour, who was put to death during the reign of Pontius Pilate (this biblical viewpoint being confirmed by third-party, non-Christian sources), who had a brother named James, and who encountered in his lifetime John the Baptizer (again a real figure as confirmed by truly independent sources) in whose movement he enlisted for a time.

If that is the case, *then* each historical observer will have to deal with the brutal alternative of either turning his or her back on the entire historical investigation of early Christianity, or (as I have done) will next entertain the idea that the history of Christianity (as with the history of the Yahweh-faith, and, later, the history of Rabbinic Jewish faith) is not a chronicle of events, but a chronicle of successive texts, their constant invention and re-invention. This is an extremely difficult concept to assimilate, in large part because of a towering irony: the most important portions of the scriptures are presented as historical documents, and the most revealing portions of both the Hebrew and the Christian scriptures are found in tightly constructed primary historical narratives.

7

Yet, rather than give up entirely on our one-source, post-70, seemingly pre-cast set of documents – the "New Testament" – as a pathway to the historical Yeshua, it is reasonable to examine tertiary methods of attack that several of the questors for the historical Yeshua have developed for dealing with a single-source historical situation. Some of these are promising.

The criteria (or indicators, or indices) that might distinguish the actions or words of the historical Yeshua from the narrative that presents to us Jesus-the-Christ, are myriad. John P. Meier wryly notes that "scholars seem to vie with one another to see who can compile the longest list of criteria. Sometimes a subtle apologetic motive may be at work: so many criteria surely guarantee the results of our quest!"[69] Actually, only two of the available criteria have much robustness as potential indicators of the behaviours or words of the historical Yeshua. These are the criteria of *embarrassment*, and of *discontinuity*. The rest are either non-operative in a single-source situation, or are special pleading, or have so little discriminatory power as to be virtually nugatory.[70]

The criterion of embarrassment is a potentially strong tool in dealing with our one-source problem. If there are lumps within the narrative which embarrass the accomplishment of its main purpose – the transformation of Yeshua of Nazareth into Jesus-the-Christ – then this perhaps indicates something that was so well known about the historical Yeshua that it could not be erased from the story, even though it might raise problems for the Jesus-the-Christ story. Since the author-editors of the "New Testament" were so skilful at providing interlocking and integrated documents, this is a potentially very powerful tool: any embarrassing awkwardness that they dared not smooth over must have been very well known and very strongly maintained by those who kept alive the memory of Yeshua after his death.[71] Moreover, this indicator is especially useful, because (unlike most of the alleged indicators of the historical Yeshua), it points to Yeshua's actions. According to John Meier, there are four major occurrences of embarrassing events: the crucifixion of Yeshua by the Romans, his denial by Peter, the betrayal by Judas, and the baptism of Jesus by John the Baptist.[72] Of these, I can see only the fourth as a true embarrassment and thus an indicator of an authentic historical event involving Yeshua. (1) The crucifixion is hardly an embarrassment to the "New Testament" and its author-editors; they brilliantly integrate it into a religious system wherein the sacrifice of Jesus-the-Christ replaces the Second Temple. (2) Peter's denial of Christ, though embarrassing to one of the political factions within post-70 Christianity, is not an awkward moment in the narrative; it can best be considered as propaganda in the later factional battle for control in the church. (3) As for the betrayal by Judas, it works splendidly within the Passion narrative. The incarnation of evil was one of the modes of understanding the world that was increasingly common in Second Temple Judahism (as we saw in Chapter Six), and Judas is appropriate both within that tradition and within the actual narrative flow. Judas fits perfectly with the post-70 CE invention of the bulk of the Jesus-the-Christ narrative. And it is of a piece with the low-level anti-Judaism (or at least anti-Pharisaism) that is woven into the Christian scriptures, as the Christian branch of Judahism drives to take over the heritage of the now-destroyed Second Temple religious system. That Judas – Judah, of course – was the active incarnation of the evil principle (he can be considered most accurately as one of the demon-figures that became so popular in late Second Temple Judahism), fits smoothly with the ideology of the Christian scriptures. It is not an embarrassment, in the methodological sense.[73]

However, the fourth matter, Jesus' submission to John the Baptist, is different. (See Matt. 3:13–17; Mark 1:9–11; Luke 3:21–22; and, cf. John 1:29–34). The underlying story is clear: Yeshua started his ministry as a disciple of John the Baptist, and Yeshua's ministry began when he was admitted into the ranks of the Baptist's disciples. The Four Gospels do everything they can to subordinate this embarrassing report, but there it sits, one of the two facts of Yeshua's ministry that are tied to external, truly multiply-attested sources: that Yeshua was crucified, and that he was, for a time, a follower of John the Baptist.[74]

I am not convinced that the criterion of embarrassment works for sorting out the words of Yeshua from those of Jesus-the-Christ nearly as well as it does (in this single instance) with his actions. It is almost impossible to conceive of any saying that the collective memory of Yeshua's early followers forced the four Evangelists to preserve against their will: Jesus would have to have been reported as saying the equivalent of "I am not the Son of God, I am not here to fulfill the Torah, but to tell you to get back to your duties and pay more attention to the priests, scribes, and Pharisees." It has been suggested that Mark 13:32 is such a case: there Jesus says that no one, the Son of God included, knows the hour and the day when heaven and earth would pass away; only the Father knows. That is taken to be an authentic saying[75] of Yeshua, for it implies – in contrast to the rest of the Gospel material – that he does not have a divinely-given foreknowledge of events affecting his own ministry, something Jesus-the-Christ definitely has. Perhaps. But the text can just as easily be read in a very different manner: Jesus is surrounded by people at Olivet who keep pestering him with questions and he finally tells them: go away, watch and wait and stop bothering me. That is the latent content of his denial of foreknowledge in this passage, and I do not see that it embarrasses the scriptural narrative enough to permit an inference that this was a statement of the historical Yeshua. Indeed, the degree of variance that the "New Testament" editor-authors were able to accept and to integrate successfully into their stories is so great that, in my opinion, one can find only a single saying of Jesus that should be adjudged authentic on the basis of the criterion of embarrassment, and that is his hyper-legalistic view of divorce. (See Chapter Nine, note 19; the primary material is found in Matthew 5:31–32 and 19:3–12; Mark 10:2–12; and Luke 16:18.)

Can we gain more, as an investigative tool for our one-source problem, from the criterion of discontinuity? This is material that is said to be authentic in regard to the historical Yeshua, because it was discontinuous with the Judahisms of his own time.[76]

Let us assume for the moment that we know a great deal more about the Judahisms of the time of Jesus than we actually do. Even so, we would have a formula for assaying the words and actions of the historical Yeshua, as follows:

Words and actions of Jesus-the-Christ as found in the Christian scriptures
minus
all elements from late Second Temple Judaism
equals
the words and actions of the historical Yeshua.

That is truly amazing, for it suggests that if one gets rid of all the "Jewish" elements from the Christian record of Jesus, one will find the real Yeshua. This turns Yeshua from the one thing both external sources and the "New Testament" agree on concerning his religious background – that he was unmistakably a Judahist – and transforms him into the one thing that even the "New Testament" never asserts: that he was a Christian.

With no impiety intended, let us briefly observe how this evidentiary principle would work with a modern figure, in this case the oracle of wisdom, and performer of miracles, Charles Dillon (Casey) Stengel. Casey is a good parallel because he operated within one of the tightest halachic regimes in the United States of America, namely professional baseball. The rules were highly codified, were enforced by priestly arbiters (called umpires), a Sanhedrin (the owners) and, in cases of serious disputes, a high priest (the Commissioner of Baseball). Nevertheless the rules were open to oral argument and reinterpretation (rhubarbs). Stengel was a sage who frequently spoke in paradoxes and parables, and there are authentic multiply-attested versions of many of his utterances. These include:

- The way our luck has been lately, our fellows have been getting hurt on their days off.
- I love signing autographs. I'll sign anything but veal cutlets. My ball-point pen slips on veal cutlets.
- It's like I used to tell my barber. Shave and a haircut but don't cut my throat. I may want to do that myself.
- I was such a dangerous hitter I even got intentional walks in batting practice.
- There comes a time in every man's life and I've had plenty of them.
- When I played in Brooklyn, I could go to the ballpark for a nickel and carfare. But now I live in Pasadena, and it costs me fifteen or sixteen dollars to take a cab to Glendale. If I was a young man, I'd study to become a cabdriver.[77]

These were all quotations taken from a written version of Stengel's words, contained in an "oral history" of the New York Yankees. That is, his statements, like those of many a Master, passed through an oral stage, treasured by his admirers, before being collected by a scribe and put in permanent form. If these sayings and parables, plus the odd memory of a few of Stengel's symbolic behaviour acts – the time he saluted a hostile crowd, for example, by doffing his cap: a sparrow flew out – were all that was left to us, we would be in the position which the "discontinuity criterion" places us concerning Jesus. We would have Casey Stengel with the everyday baseball left out, just as the discontinuity-method attempts to give us Yeshua, by taking Jesus-the-Christ and subtracting Judahism.

With Casey, we would miss the fact that, mostly, he did not say memorable things or engage in symbolic acts. He was an excellent player, and a better manager, one of the all-time greats: he respected the Halachah of baseball, even if he occasionally pushed at its edges. Mostly, he said things that were simple and conventional: "don't hit into a double play"; "use your fastball pitcher on a cloudy day"; and "don't try a drag bunt on a hard infield." Fortunately, we do not just have Casey's sayings and the records of his symbolic acts. We also have the baseball volume of *The Sports Encyclopedia*, which gives his managing record, year-by-year, and *The New York Times Book of Baseball History*, which provides newspaper reports of his actions, put together within twenty-four hours of their occurrence. These sources document that, though Casey had his memorable sayings and eccentric behaviours, he basically was a straight-ahead player and manager, just better at it than most, especially the managing. He spent most of his time saying and doing things that were almost exactly the same as other players and managers. Though he is now quoted as a prophet and miracle worker, in fact, his words, actions, beliefs and behaviour were only slightly different from those of his colleagues in the business. Fortunately, with Casey, we know how his life worked – its common moments and its quotidian behaviours. For Jesus-the-Christ we do not.

I think the criterion-of-discontinuity with Second Temple Judaism is useless. First, we know so little about the Judaisms of the period that we cannot really spot a discontinuity if it is there. Remember that we do not know the name of a single Sadducee (see Chapter Seven); nor do we possess a single identifiable text by a Pharisee from the period when Yeshua of Nazareth was active. Secondly, the degree of variance we saw in the Judahist texts that we do have for the period when Yeshua was in his ministry (see Chapters Six through Eight) was so great that almost anything he is reported as saying might have been part of one of the extant Judaisms. We would need to know what branch of Judaism he adhered to, before "subtracting" this material from the sayings and actions that are ascribed to him in the Christian scriptures. Third, *even if* we were able to overcome the massive obstacles just mentioned, we would only have a collection of his deviant sayings and behaviours – deviant, that is, when one employs one of those branches of Judaism as a norm. But if we did that, all we would have would be the equivalent of the sayings and symbolic actions of Casey Stengel, with the rules of baseball left out and with his everyday behaviour (his basic beliefs, attitudes, and practices) removed. The sayings might be accurate – in the sense that he said them – but they would be untrue, in that they would be unrepresentative of his thought, attitudes, and actions generally. That, at best, is what the discontinuity-criterion might give us: a few accurate, but highly misleading statements of the historical Yeshua, misleading because they would be unrepresentative.

How would one rediscover the everyday historical Yeshua, as distinct from finding a handful of atypical utterances? First, one would ask, what did he believe about everyday life? (This is an entirely hypothetical exercise.) We probably would find, if we had adequate sources, that he shared most of the beliefs about the way the physical world operated that prevailed among his compatriots. We would discover that he believed the sun revolved around the earth; that ships which sailed out of the mouth of the Mediterranean Sea fell off the edge of the earth, unless they were first eaten by sea monsters; that most diseases were caused by evil spirits; that women were inferior beings; that menstrual blood was among the most defiling of human effluents; that heaven was up, Sheol down; that angels and demons affected everyday life; that some holy men could fly, in the extreme cases, all the way to the heavens; and on and on: the everyday beliefs of a perhaps-literate Palestinian artisan of his time.

If we were able to discover which one of the several distinct Judaisms of his time Yeshua adhered to, we probably would discover that he was a fairly typical adherent of that sect as far as his actual beliefs were concerned, only keener. My own guess is that he was a Pharisee, for it appears that is the branch of Judahism which was the most flexible because it used the practice of oral legal debate to permit continual redefinitions of what Torah meant in spirit, and thus what it required in practice. And that is the sort of argument, concerning law, that Jesus-the-Christ is reported as engaged in, in the Christian scriptures. (That the "New Testament" is so strongly anti-Pharisaic is, I think, a function of two factors: [1] the post-70 Christian church engaged in a fierce struggle with the Pharisees [the proto-Rabbinical party] for control of the Judahist heritage; and [2] if Yeshua had been a Pharisee, it was exactly that which would motivate Christian denunciation of them: one has to work hardest at distinguishing oneself from that with which one has the greatest similarity.) A short, necessarily speculative, summary might be that Yeshua was a very keen Pharisee who, many believe, got above himself.

The necessarily harsh compressions of that summary and the reality of the inevitably primitive nature of Yeshua's view of the physical and biological world, raises the question of whether or not one really would want to read a biography of the historical Yeshua, even were it obtainable. Most Christians, I think, would be repulsed by the full picture. Still, if historians are to reconstruct the possible-mind of the historical Yeshua, the great promise of the next generation of scholars is found in the field of Second Temple Judahism. If Yeshua was a Judahist, then it is to that area we must look. One waits, expectantly.[78]

Here, two modest suggestions that might help (if only a little) in distinguishing a phrase or two that have a higher probability than do most of being uttered by the historical Yeshua. This is not a new criterion of evidence; simply the suggestion that one look for instances where the reported utterances of Jesus are at variance *with themselves*. This will work within a one-source problem. Any place where Jesus-the-Christ is reported as saying something that is out of kilter with the overall gestalt of his reported message raises two opposing possibilities: (1) that the *logion* is a cack-handed interpolation of a later author-editor, or (2) it was a saying of Jesus that, although dissonant with his dominant message, had to be retained, because so many people knew of it that it could not be erased. Earlier, I pointed to the clearest example of a reported-teaching of Jesus running against the grain of his overall message as presented in the Christian scriptures: his sayings on the dissolution of marriage, wherein he is much stricter than either the Mosaic law or the ecclesiastical practice of his time. There may be other cases. The point of method is that instead of looking for discontinuities between something that we know (the Christian text) and something that we do not know (all the variants of late Second Temple Judahism) it is much more sensible to deal with historical entities that we have to hand: all the available sayings attributed to Jesus-the-Christ within the canon.

And, finally, another small suggestion: that instead of theorizing about the nature of oral transmission at the time of Jesus, biblical scholars take some time to study cultures where we have well-documented cases of the methods and extent of the oral transmission of valued stories and sayings. For example, several Celtic cultures, roughly coterminous with that of Jesus, had modes of remembering highly complex tales, genealogies, poems; moreover, so self-conscious were they about this activity, that the process and tricks of remembering are well documented. Within the Christian scriptures, one can ask a tight little question: "which of the reported sayings or tales of Jesus have memory-hooks attached to them?" Or, if one wants to turn it into an experiment, "what portions of the Gospels are easiest to remember?" This implicit suggestion is: that those parts of the Jesus-story that are easiest to remember are those portions which were remembered best. The disciples of Yeshua were not, it appears, professional rememberers, so one cannot expect the hallmarks of schematized memory – mnemonic devices, and pre-structured memory-trees – to be present. The most interesting place in the Christian scriptures in this regard is the Beatitudes (Matthew 5:3–12; Luke 6:20–26) which follow a clear mnemonic structure. ("Blessed are ..." and, additionally in Luke, "Woe unto ...") They are the easiest of the large blocks of sayings of Jesus to remember word-for-word. Somebody worked very skilfully at putting them in forms that could be kept in mind by individuals who did not have access to written records of Jesus, which is to say, the great bulk of early Christians.

8

If the quest for the historical Yeshua is to become less a theologically-derived study and more an historical one, a necessary step is the rescuing of the concept of "hypothesis" from its present fuzzy meaning – implying, usually, in biblical studies a speculative idea that cannot be fully tested – and its replacement by "hypothesis" as used by historians and social science observers of the "secular" world. Well-framed hypotheses are among the best of intellectual levers: a good hypothesis can facilitate our raising an entire ancient world from an unknown, to a knowable entity.

A properly framed hypothesis is not a mystery, for it demands only two steps in its creation: (1) the indicators of whether the specific hypothesis is confirmed or not should be defined with specificity, and, of course, should involve pieces of evidence that are knowable ("operationality" is the technical term). There is no sense in putting forward an hypothesis that one is incapable of verifying or falsifying. And, (2) the hypothesis should be designed so that there is an equivalent of what, in statistically-gauged experiments, is called a "null-hypothesis." As adapted to historical matters, such as we are here dealing with, this means that the hypothesis has to be designed so that either a negative result or a not-proved result is taken as disproof of the hypothesis. A proper hypothesis (that is, one that is not misleading) is always framed so that the error of wrongly rejecting the null hypothesis (i.e., of affirming the truth of some proposition) is more serious than the error of wrongly accepting the null hypothesis. In other words, hypotheses are proved only by positive evidence, and lack of positive evidence is taken as disproof of the hypothesis.

The reason that this positive-evidence rule must be honoured is easily illustrated. Assume that some scholar wants to prove that Jesus was a Sadducee and that he or she puts forward, with some operational criteria as testing points, such an hypothesis. And then, he or she discovers that while the results do not actually disprove that Jesus was Sadducean (given how little we know of the Sadducees, such disproof would be difficult), neither do they confirm it. So, then, the scholar states that the evidence on whether or not Jesus was a Sadducee is ambiguous and that he might have been one. No: one cannot proceed this way and pretend to be an historian. Unless the hypothesis is confirmed, it is rejected. Not-proved is not a median case: it is a rejection of the hypothesis.

This point of method is especially important in biblical history, because it is very easy to present hypotheses where the null-case prevails, and then to slip sideways into using this as an indication of possibility, and, then, into using possibility as a quasi-proof of probability.

Two useful indications that a null-result may have been re-wrapped so as to save a pet hypothesis from being declared disproved, are (1) when one sees someone using a phrase such as "negatives are very hard to prove." Good historical practice demands that the negative case be assumed unless there is positive evidence of it actually having occurred. And (2) one should be alert when someone proclaims a "balanced" assessment of a given hypothesis. This usually (although not always) is the result of an hypothesis having been framed muddily. A good hypothesis does not have a median case; either it is confirmed by positive evidence or the null-hypothesis-rule dictates that it has been disproved.

9

This is a very confident time among questors for the historical Yeshua. At the present pace of production, the 1990s will witness the appearance of at least two dozen significant lives of the historical Yeshua. As I have explained, I am very skeptical of the value of these products, not because the authors lack technical skills or erudition, but because the whole process is methodologically flawed, deeply. Most of the methods employed by the questors for the historical Yeshua would, if applied to any historical topic since the Dark Ages, be ridiculed in a basic graduate seminar. Yet, the questors follow closely in each other's footsteps, their eyes ever on the ground, their numbers growing so that they form something akin to a hoplite phalanx, moving myo-pically forward, self-referential, unaware of the outside world, and impervi-ous to external reality.

Whether or not the quest for the historical Yeshua can ever produce any-thing more than a handful of historical shards, items of whose context we are unsure and whose relationship to each other is not established, is an issue on which I am, at best, agnostic. I am certain, however, that no progress is possi-ble unless, before trying to take the "New Testament" text apart, biblical his-torians understand fully how subtly, and successfully, this exhibit works as an integrated, smoothly functioning, truly wondrous invention.

NOTES TO APPENDIX D

1 Although I have tried to read every "biography" of Jesus published in English in this century, and a few untranslated items in German, I doubtless have missed some, especially those from specialist denominational publishing houses. As in Chapter Eight, I should refer the reader to the splendid bibliography contained in the footnotes to John P. Meier's *A Marginal Jew. Rethinking the Historical Jesus*, vol. I, *The Roots of the Problem and the Person*, and vol. II, *Mentor, Message, and Miracles* (New York: Doubleday, 1991 and 1994).

2 A.A. Milne, *Winnie-the-Pooh* (New York: E.P. Dutton, 1926), 34–43.

3 Although most of the work of the Jesus Seminar was collective, one of their publi-cations was not, and it is an extremely useful piece of scholarship. Entitled *The Complete Gospels. Annotated Scholars Versions* (Sonoma, CA: Polebridge Press, 1991), and edited by Robert J. Miller, it is a series of translations, each by an indi-vidual scholar of ability, of almost all of the non-canonical Gospels, or fragments of Gospels, of the early church.

4 The early history is repeated in several of the Seminar's publications. See, for ex-ample, Robert W. Funk, with Mahlon H. Smith, *The Gospel of Mark. Red Letter Edition* (Sonoma: Polebridge Press, 1991), xiii-xix.

5 Robert W. Funk, Roy W. Hoover, "and the Jesus Seminar," *The Five Gospels. The Search for the Authentic Words of Jesus* (New York: MacMillan Publishing Co., 1993).

6 Charles H. Talbert, "Political Correctness invades Jesus Research," *Perspectives in Religious Studies*, 21 (Fall, 1994), 245–46. The Seminar's Fellows, as of 1993, are listed in *The Five Gospels*, 533–37. Interestingly, the Fellows from Canada, where the conservative religious revival is much less strong than in the USA, in-clude representatives of two of the nation's three leading institutions, the Univer-sity of Toronto and Queen's University. (The third, McGill University, was not represented.)

7 Funk, *The Gospel of Mark*, xiv.

8 Although I have suggested that the consensus-method of the Jesus seminar is only an extreme, and explicit, example of a quality of mind that is widespread, but unstated, in the field of Yeshua-quest scholarship, the Seminar had some procedures piquantly their own. Because of the self-confidence with which the Seminar produced its polychromatic text *The Five Gospels* as a first-step at a full redefinition of the Christian canon, these unusual methods, which otherwise would not be worth comment, do indeed require note. The unavoidable conclusion one eventually reaches is that even if one accepts all of the historical assumptions and methods the Seminars' Fellows adopted (and I most emphatically do not), the Seminar's own manner of determining what its Fellows thought was so deeply flawed as to be useless.

In considering the methods by which the Jesus Seminar determined the opinion of its Fellows, we must keep in mind one axiom of basic and general statistics: an applied statistical description of a problem should not be used to generate data that appear to be more accurate or more specific or more important than those original values one is seeking to interpret. For example, it is actually less genuinely descriptive to say that "over 66.3% of my office's lights malfunctioned," than it is to say "both my desk lamps burned out, but the ceiling light stayed on."

The basic technique the Seminar used to make a judgement was simple. A panel of members ("Fellows") voted on whether a given saying attributed to Jesus was authentic or not. That is uncomplicated, but it has one hidden requirement. The reliability of the method is compromised if the panel of voters is not constant throughout the entire procedure. The panel's being constant does not guarantee the validity of the result, but the panel's not being constant virtually guarantees that the result will be invalid. In the actual event, the panel changed a good deal over time, so the results of the opinions on one section of the scriptures are not comparable with those on another. The Seminar, in publishing its voting results, camouflaged this problem by reporting not the actual number of voters (which would have given away the flux in the panel) but instead reported only the percentage of the (unstated) number who actually voted. (The full lists of "votes" is found in several different formats in *Forum*, one of the Seminar's self-publications. The most useful version is found in vol. 6, March 1990, 4–55. It is this list of votes that I have used to investigate the reporting procedures the Seminar employed.)

However, for the moment, let us forget that the flux in the panel of experts invalidated their procedures. Pretend that we do not know this fact, and instead follow the obliquely revealing explanation of the Seminar's techniques that was published in *The Gospel of Mark. Red Letter Edition* (xx-xxi). The balls of four different colours were placed in the voting box indicating what each panel member thought of each purported saying of Jesus:

The Seminar adopted two official interpretations of the four colors. Individuals could elect either one for their own guidance. An unofficial but helpful interpretation of these categories by one member led to this formulation:

red: That's Jesus!

pink: Sure sounds like Jesus.

gray: Well, maybe.

black: There's been some mistake.

The Seminar did not insist on uniform standards for balloting.

The ranking of items is determined by weighted vote. Since most Fellows of the Seminar are professors, they are accustomed to grade points and grade point averages. So they decided on the following scheme:

red = 3

pink = 2

gray = 1

black = 0

The points on each ballot are added up and divided by the number of votes in order to determine the weighted average. While the scale is zero to three, it was decided to convert the weighted averages to percentages to employ a scale of 100 rather than a scale of 3.00. The result is a scale divided into four quadrants:

red: .7501 up

pink: .5001 to .7500

gray: .2501 to .5000

black: .0000 to .2500

We instructed the computer to carry the averages out to four decimal places, but we have rounded the numbers off to two decimal places in the voting tables found in an appendix to this volume.

Before considering what all this meant, the Seminar should be rescued from two minor errors in their own terminology. The "weighted average" they refer to is not a weighted average, but simply the average of the number of points the voters gave to each saying of Jesus: it is the total of points divided by the number of voters, and there is no special weighting involved. Also, they refer to "percentages" when they are not actually using percentages, but simply mapping their results on an arbitrary 100-point scale. These are minor matters, but if these two points are not noted, the Seminar's methodological fog lifts rather more slowly than is necessary.

Now, consider the original scale: red (3), pink (2), gray (1) and black (0). On the surface it seems to make sense. For instance, it seems reasonable if, for example, fifty-one members of the Seminar voted red, and forty-nine voted pink, then a purported saying of Jesus would be ruled genuine, since it would have an average score of slightly over the half-way point between red and pink, which is 2.5. (For purposes of this discussion, I am pretending that there were always 100 Fellows of the Seminar voting; the argument works with any number voting, however.) And, at the other end of the scale, say that fifty-one of the Fellows did not believe at all in a given saying and hence they cast the black ball, while forty-nine were not quite so certain and they cast the gray. The result of the vote would be accurately indicated by a score of slightly less than 0.5 and thus the saying would be cast out. Seemingly, then, a valid scale would have the following break points:

Jesus certainly said it.	average of 2.5 and up
Jesus probably said it.	1.5 to 2.49 points
Jesus probably did not say it.	0.5 to 1.49 points
Jesus certainly did not say it.	0.49 points and below.

The problem with this is that the scale does not work. Assume for the moment that there is one ideologue in the Seminar who believes that Jesus said almost nothing in the scriptures, and so, on almost every issue, he votes black. Now go back to the example of a highly-probable saying. But now assume that fifty-one Fellows vote red, believing Jesus certainly said it, forty-eight vote pink, and one Fellow votes black. This is the same 51–49 break that, in the earlier example gave the yes-it-is-genuine result, but now the result is pink, because it falls beneath the 2.50 break-line.

Exactly the same thing happens at the bottom end of the scale.

The overall result of this scoring system is to bias seriously the Seminar's reported judgement against the two ends of the scale. (The example I gave was the most modest possible; the reader can easily illustrate much more serious cases of skewing.) In sum, this scoring system misrepresented the opinions of the Fellows by artificially reducing the black and the red categories, ostensibly the most decisive and important ones. In practical terms, the problem was more acute at the top end of the range, because, tough-minded as the scholars wished to be, the Seminar would be in a delicate position if it produced a new edition of the Christian scriptures in which few, if any, sayings of Jesus were adjudged to be genuine.

The Seminar tried to escape from this methodological box by adopting a 100-point scale. They neglected to explain the scoring system they adopted when they moved to the new scale, but it can be reconstructed from their published results. It was as follows:

Red	=	1.00
Pink	=	.666
Gray	=	.333
Black	=	0.0

Take our case of fifty-one Fellows voting red and forty-nine voting pink. The score would be 83.6. This is above the mid point of the range between .666 and 1.00 – which is .833 – so the saying is ruled authentic.

The break points of the new 100 point scale, if one uses the mid-points of each range, are thus, as follows:

Jesus certainly said it.	.833 and up
Jesus probably said it.	.500 to .832
Jesus probably did not say it.	.167 to .499
Jesus certainly did not say it.	.166 and below.

This new scale has exactly the same problems that the scale of "0" to "3" had: it skews everything towards the pink and gray ranges, the muddy middle of the scale. In fact, by this method only twelve out of the 1,544 possibly-authentic sayings of Jesus which the Seminar examined met this test of red-letter authenticity. This dozen, no matter how significant, would have made for a red-letter Bible with very few red letters.

So, the Seminar was in trouble. They had to move the goalposts, so that more sayings of Jesus would be adjudged to be authentic. The positions to which the posts were moved at first glance look as if they must be based on logic or upon probability theory:

Jesus certainly said it.	.7501 and up
Jesus probably said it.	.5001 to .7500
Jesus probably did not say it.	.2501 to .5000
Jesus certainly did not say it.	.0000 to .2500.

That is an optical illusion. Take the top end of the scale. Why was 75.0 chosen as a mid-point between 1.00 and 0.66? It defies logical explanation, as does the goal post at the bottom end of the scale: 0.25, which is employed as a break point between 0.00 and 0.333! In fact, the break points – 25, 50, 75 – *look* good and, equally importantly, they produce more of the desired results, namely, many sayings that are now said to be certainly authentic, when, under the original system, they had been judged less-than-certain.

In fact, there is no statistical technique and no technique of probability assessment that indicates when, among a given social group (in this case, the Fellows of the Jesus Seminar), one begins to feel confident that some Jesus-sayings either were clearly authentic, or certainly were not. (There is no statistical reason why, for example, .7501 was any more appropriate a cut-off point for red-sayings than .78 would have been, or .70.) Therefore, it must be emphasized that the placing of the goal posts (a) was independent of the scoring scale employed in the original ratings, save that it had to fit within the outside parameters of the original system; (b) was completely arbitrary and had no statistical or probability theory behind it; and (c) was set so as to give a pre-determined desired result: namely more red and more black results than the use of the mid-points in the scoring ranges provided. These desired results were set externally to the data and were imposed upon them. The results do not represent what the considered judgement of the Fellows of the Jesus Seminar actually was, but rather reflected what someone, or some group, wished to see promulgated. Alternatively, all the Fellows were complicitous.

Was this cascade of hubris-turned-to-folly avoidable? Yes, even within the Seminar's own historical assumptions (which, though I do not accept, I have no objection to seeing dealt with competently). All the Seminar had to do was to forget the voting-by-coloured-ball method and employ a simple two-part vote on each saying: (1) do you think this saying is by Jesus? (2-a) If so, do you think it probably was by Jesus or almost certainly was by him? or, (2-b) if not, do you think it almost certainly was not uttered by Jesus or merely that it probably was not said by him?

That yields the four sectors of opinion the Seminar wished to articulate, and no skewing. Of course, it is simple and lacks self-importance.

9 Encountering the Jesus Seminar's *The Five Gospels* gives one the same frisson as does reading any of the works of the great William McGonagall (he of "Tay Bridge disaster" fame) or of Amanda McKittrick Ros, the alliterative authoress of *Irene Iddesleigh*, of *Delina Delaney*, and of much more. A few brief examples of the full awfulness of the California-English version of the Gospels will suffice. The Beatitudes, which in the KJB have a deeply moving, gentle quality ("blessed are the poor in spirit: for theirs is the kingdom of heaven" Matt. 5:3) are turned into a series of sound bytes from a sales manager's pep rally:

> Congratulations to the poor in spirit!
> Heaven's domain belongs to them.
> Congratulations to those who grieve!
> They will be consoled.
> Congratulations to the gentle!
> They will inherit the earth. (p. 138)

When, early in his ministry, Jesus heals a leper, he does so with a phrase that implies both physical and spiritual healing: "be thou clean" (KJB, Mark 1:41). The Jesus Seminar's translation is "Okay – you're clean!" (p. 43). And, whereas the KJB has Jesus warning his disciples of the effect if they, like spoiled salt, lose their "savour" (KJB, Matt. 5:13), the Seminar's version is right out of an advertising agency: "You are the salt of the earth. But if salt loses its zing, how will it be made salty?" (p. 139). Zing, indeed.

10 "The Neo-Christian Version," *Alberta Reports* (28 January 1991), 33.

11 John Dominic Crossan, *The Historical Jesus. The Life of the Mediterranean Jewish Peasant* (San Francisco: HarperCollins, 1991), xxxii.

12 Meier, 1:174–75.

13 Fergus Millar, "Reflections on the Trial of Jesus," in Philip R. Davies and Richard T. White, *A Tribute to Geza Vermes. Essays on Jewish and Christian Literature and History* (Sheffield: JSOT, 1990), 363.

14 Josephus, *Jewish Antiquities*, 18:116–19.

15 Josephus, ibid., 20: 200–203. Ananus II, according to Josephus, was removed from office by King Agrippa, because his execution of James so offended the sense of justice of Jerusalem's citizens.

16 Josephus, ibid., 18:63–65.

17 See the notes to the Loeb edition of the *Jewish Antiquities*, 48–49; Crossan, 372–73; Meier, I:56–69.

18 Tacitus, *Annales*, quoted in Crossan, 375.

19 Meier, I: 91–92 summarizes these sources.

20 Meier, I: 93–111 deals with these in detail. See also my note 34 to Chapter Ten.

21 Ron Cameron, "Gospel of Thomas," in *ABD*, 6:535. "Didymus" is Greek for twin, and "Thomas" is a second-name. Therefore, Judas, or Jude, is the focal name.

22 I find the argument of Christopher Tuckett completely convincing. He demonstrates that, with the possible exception of the Gospel of Thomas, the Christian documents at Nag Hammadi are based on the Synoptic Gospels. Thus, they can have no value as independent attestations of the life of Yeshua. See Christopher Tuckett, *Nag Hammadi and the Gospel Tradition* (Edinburgh: Clark, 1986). Two points should be here made explicit. First, no judgement is implied about the spiritual or theological value of the Nag Hammadi material, merely that it has no applicability to the historical question at hand. Second, I am not engaged in ascribing-value-by-comparison. That is, merely because the Nag Hammadi texts are not here of historical value, that does not mean that the "New Testament" materials, on which they depend, necessarily are of historical value. That is an entirely separate issue.

23 The fragments, found at Oxyrhynchus in Egypt, are dated by their distinctive calligraphy.

24 Found in *The Five Gospels*.

25 *The Five Gospels*, 474.

26 Stephen J. Patterson, "Introduction" to the Gospel of Thomas in *The Complete Gospels*, 302–303.

27 *The Five Gospels*, 474. The major proponent of this idea has been Helmut Koester. See his *Ancient Christian Gospels. Their History and Development* (Philadelphia: Trinity Press International, 1990), 75–128.

28 The observation is that of Arthur J. Dewey, who provides a translation of the Gospel of Peter, in *The Complete Gospels*, 393–401.

29 See Meier, I:116–18, and 146–47.

30 John Dominic Crossan, *The Cross that Spoke. The Origins of the Passion Narrative* (San Francisco: Harper and Row, 1988). See also, Crossan, *The Historical Jesus*, 462–66.

31 The reason that I think a Christian lode similar to that of the Dead Sea Scrolls will eventually be disinterred is that all the branches of late Second Temple Judaism had the same motives to hide, and thereby preserve, their spiritual patrimony from the apprehended horror, that became every day more palpable, as the Roman-Jewish War of 66–73 slouched to its terrible conclusion. The evidentiary danger is that scholars of Christianity so desperately wish to find their own Dead Sea Scrolls that credulity is apt to be the hallmark of the initial assessors of any new finds. To take a recent example: a producer of religious television for the BBC found the ossuaries of a family and decided they had once contained the remains of the Holy Family and (by implication) that this put to rest permanently both the Virgin Birth and the resurrection. The ossuaries, according to an interpretation of barely-legible engravings, included Miriam (the name of about one-quarter of Judahist women of the time), Yosef (the second most popular male name of

the period), and "Yeshua bar Yosef" meaning Jesus, son of Joseph. (A dozen funerary urns bearing the name "Yeshua" have been found in recent years; it too is a very common name.) What one has is the resting place of a nice, well-off Jerusalem family. See *Sunday Times* (London), 31 March 1996.

Less quixotic, and based on some serious scholarship, was an argument also put forward in the mid 1990s concerning the Gospel of Matthew. A German papyrologist, Carsten Peter Thiede, examined three very small fragments of Matthew held in the library of Magdalen College, Oxford. (The largest is roughly the size of a standard rectangular postage stamp.) He declared the previous dating to be wrong: not late second century, but c. 66 CE or earlier. From this hypothesis (which is based on handwriting styles, and which cannot be confirmed by radio-carbon dating because even a few shreds of papyrus would be too much to destroy), it was suggested that the fragments came from a *complete* Gospel of Matthew as we know it. (How it could be ascertained from these tiny fragments that the rest of the Gospel was the full version, surpasses speculation.) From that, it was suggested that the Gospel of Matthew was written while eyewitnesses to the events it narrates were alive, that the finished Gospel of Matthew was circulating in codex form between 30 and 60 CE, and that, possibly, some of the disciples who had been an eyewitness to the crucifixion of Jesus handled and read the codex of Matthew. All this from one very problematic, and disturbingly precise, dating based on three or four of the Greek alphabet letters. See Carsten Peter Thiede and Matthew D'Ancona, *The Jesus Papyrus* (London: Weidenfeld and Nicolson, 1996).

32 Limitations of space preclude even a brief characterization of the remaining extrabiblical items that claim to be independent Christian witnesses to aspects of the career of Yeshua of Nazareth. Most of them are included in *The Complete Gospels*. None of them approaches either the Gospel of Thomas or the Gospel of Peter in potential usefulness. Many of them are fragmentary. Several, especially the various "infancy gospels" are so fanciful as to constitute *märchen*. All of them suffer from the evidentiary problems evinced by the Gospels of Thomas and of Peter.

However, one item deserves mention. This is the "Secret Gospel of Mark," often shortened to "Secret Mark." (The name was given to it by modern scholars.) The path here is interesting. (1) In 1960 Professor Morton Smith of Columbia University, a well-known and highly respected "New Testament" scholar, reported at a meeting of the Society of Biblical Literature that, in 1958, he had made an extraordinary discovery. This was a previously-unknown letter of Clement of Alexandria, a pivotal church father of the late second century. This in itself was sensational, for no letters of Clement have been preserved in original form. Some of his theological works survive, but his letters are known only through their being cited in other men's letters. But there was more. In the newly-discovered letter of Clement were quotations from a previously unknown "secret" Gospel of Mark, which, Clement said, was preserved separately from the public version and was available only to a select circle of early Christians.

(2) There was, however, no ancient manuscript or anything close to it. In 1958, Smith had been cataloguing the library of the Marsaba monastery, located about eighteen kilometres southeast of Jerusalem. There, he reported, he had come across an edition of six letters of Ignatius that had been published in Amsterdam in 1646. In the end-papers was found a modern copy of a letter by Clement. It was in a handwriting which Smith later identified as being roughly mid-eighteenth century. Notice here that the modern provenance of the printed book and the relatively-recent handwriting, mean that if the item was the product of a forger, he was engaged in the relatively easy task of obtaining a printed book and of using inks and handwritings that are accessible at the present day, quite a different task than forging an ancient document. Even so, it would be helpful if, as John Meier suggests (2:120), the seventeenth-century book and the eighteenth-century handwriting could be examined by independent scholars to determine, in particular, if the calligraphy is genuine eighteenth-century.

(3) After his sensational announcement in December 1960, Smith, showing a restraint in equal parts admirable and unusual among biblical scholars, became reticent. He did not publish the text until 1973 and then he produced two major volumes, the one highly scholarly, the other a headline grabber: *Clement of Alexandria and a Secret Gospel of Mark* (Cambridge: Harvard University Press, 1973) and *The Secret Gospel: The Discovery and Interpretation of the Secret Gospel According to Mark* (New York: Harper and Row, 1973).

(4) Although controversy followed these publications, it is fair to say that most "New Testament" historians who are not in religious-right institutions accepted the authenticity of the Clementine letter and (with due allowances for Clement's capacity for polemics) that a Secret Gospel of Mark had once existed and that the fragment immersed in the newly-found and unique Clementine letter is also authentic. Several of the "liberal" biblical scholars who, as I mentioned earlier, tend to be very keen on para-biblical material, have argued that the fragments of Secret Mark not only pre-date the writing of the Gospel of Mark, but were part of a secret gospel that was employed by the later writers of the four canonical Gospels: John Dominic Crossan, Helmut Koester, and the Jesus Seminar are among the most prominent proponents of this view.

(5) Given this prodigious chain of scholarly dominoes – a 1958 find of a Greek note allegedly written in an eighteenth-century hand, makes it all the way back to the mid-first-century and becomes, for some scholars, one of the earliest Christian documents – the actual text of the fragments of Secret Mark are at first disappointing: until one gets the joke. The text consists of two fragments, one of thirteen verses, the other of only two. (I am here using the translation by Helmut Koester in *The Complete Gospels*, 405.) The first fragment tells a story that we have heard before, in a slightly different form. Jesus at Bethany is called by a woman whose brother has died. This is a rewriting of the tale of the raising of Lazarus (John 11:1–44). But notice the twist. The writer of this new tale replaces the foul-smell-

ing and asexual Lazarus with a young man who, when revived, "looked at Jesus, loved him, and began to beg him to be with him" (Secret Mark 1:8). "Then they left the tomb and went into the young man's house." It is reported with straight face, and then, as a wry footnote, the text continues, "Incidentally, he was rich" (Secret Mark 1:9). So, Jesus agrees to baptize the young man and, at evening, he comes to Jesus for baptism, dressed only in a linen cloth. That detail is a give-away to the subtext of the fragment: in "New Testament" studies, from the late 1950s onward, a knowledgeable coterie made a sort of esoteric secret of the belief that baptism in the early church was conducted with the candidate in the nude. (See Crossan, *The Historical Jesus*, 412). Having, after nightfall, baptized the rich and enthusiastic young man, Jesus "spent the night with him, because" – and here the joke goes over the top – "because Jesus taught him the mystery of God's domain" (Secret Mark 1:12). What we have here is a nice ironic gay joke at the expense of all of the self-important scholars who not only miss the irony, but believe that this alleged piece of gospel comes to us in the first-known letter of the great Clement of Alexandria.

(6) There is more. In the short, two-verse, second fragment, the joke is reprised, and, again, the writer sets things in train and then steps back so that we can watch the scholars bang themselves over the head with their own tools. The set-up here is another half-dressed young man, who long has puzzled scholars: a young man who in the Gospel of Mark, with only a "linen cloth cast about his naked body" follows Jesus after he is arrested. When the arresting-party turns on the young man, some of them grab his linen garment and he runs away naked (Mark 14:51– 52). In the second fragment of Secret Mark, the reference is to "the young man whom Jesus loved" (Secret Mark 2:1). And, Jesus explicitly refuses to see either the mother of the young man or Salome (Secret Mark 2:2), about as explicit a rejection of the heterosexual world as the writer could get away with, without winking too broadly. Thus the writer has set scholars a nice little puzzle: was the young-man-whom-Jesus-loved the young man from the arrest story in Mark, or a young man from Bethany? The setting of two canonical texts against each other, and turning the whole thing into a false-puzzle for biblical scholars to solve, and all within the context of a gay joke, is no small achievement.

Whoever set this skilled and amusing bit of post-modern scholarly theatre in train must have been immensely diverted by the way it played. Morton Smith, were he alive, would be the first scholar to be interviewed, since (as of 1992) he was the only scholar known to have laid eyes on the manuscript. (See Marvin W. Mayer, "Secret Gospel of Mark," *ABD*, 4:558). But to whomever: full marks.

33 Meier, 1:174–75; E.P. Sanders and Margaret Davies, *Studying the Synoptic Gospels* (London: SCM Press, 1989), 323–33 explicitly affirm the principle, and Vermes uses it extensively in his several works on Jesus. See, for instance, Geza Vermes, *Jesus the Jew. A Historian's Reading of the Gospels* (London: Fontana/ Collins, 1973), 147–53. An intriguing aspect of Vermes's work is that he employs

the individual books of the Christian scriptures as independent sources alongside post-70 Jewish sources.

34 What degree of credence one places on the single-source tradition of the crucifixion being near Passover is beyond my present brief. Statistically, there is roughly a one in fifty chance that it occurred in the seven or eight days around Passover.

35 Sanders, *Historical Figure of Jesus*, 163–66.

36 Those are outside figures, and, if the precise dating were determined to be within that envelope by a year or two at either end, the main point in the text is not affected. Nor is it affected by the sequence that scholars may determine the letters assumed, a continually-vexed point: Paul wrote before the great calamity, the Temple's destruction, forever altered the religious landscape. For a fine introduction, see E.P. Sanders, *Paul* (Oxford: Oxford University Press, 1991). Also valuable among recent works are: Jerome Murphy O'Connor, *Paul: A Critical Life* (London: Oxford University Press, 1996), Alan F. Segal, *Paul the Convert. The Apostulate and Apostasy of Saul the Pharisee* (New Haven: Yale University Press, 1990), and A.N. Wilson, *Paul. The Mind of the Apostle* (New York: W.W. Norton, 1997).

37 This is the appropriate point to alert the reader to a tradition of biblical scholarship which I do not share, but for which I have some respect. This is the conservative tradition, mostly Protestant evangelical, but conservative Catholic as well, which holds that the Gospels embody eyewitness records, that the Gospels were written by the people whose names are found on their spine ("Mark," "John," etc.), that everything canonical is trustworthy and that nothing extra-canonical is. I am not referring here to fundamentalists, but to some very learned individuals who believe that the historical Yeshua and Jesus-the-Christ are the same individual and that Christian faith is based on a set of texts that are virtually completely accurate. This is an ahistorical position – belief in the conclusions concerning accuracy precedes an examination of the texts – so it is not directly helpful in our present exercise. However, in their criticism of "secular" historians, the scholars of this belief-dictated tradition often make very telling points. See, for example, Michael J. Wilkins and J.P. Moreland, *Jesus Under Fire* (Grand Rapids: Zondervan Publishing House, 1995).

38 Robert Kysar, "The Gospel of John," in *ABD*, 3:918.

39 Aileen Guilding, *The Fourth Gospel and Jewish Worship. A study of the relation of St. John's gospel to the ancient Jewish lectionary system* (Oxford: Clarendon Press, 1960). Although one should be very wary of any study that presses material from the Mishnah and the Talmuds into the Second Temple era, this is not what Guilding has done. She has placed in parallel the post-70 CE document, the Gospel of John, and the post-70 CE information on the Jewish liturgical calendar, so her argument is based upon temporal compatibility. Occasionally Guilding presses either the Johanine material or the Rabbinic material into the Second Temple era, but these instances are minor and can be set aside, and her basic argument accepted.

40 Reference to the semi-legendary "Council of Yavneh" whereby, it is alleged in c. 90, remnant Pharisees met and codified the rules for their scriptures and for membership in the emergent Jewish faith, seems to me of no value. The argument is that the "anti-Jewish" tone of John, and the need for a liturgical system that would be similar to the Jewish calendar, but which would replace it, points to the precipitating events for John's Gospel having been after Yavneh. The only drawbacks are (1) that the Council of Yavneh is now considered to be largely a fictive occasion (a projection onto Jewish events of the Christian concilliar model of decision-making) and therefore it could not have the causal impact that is suggested; and (2) it assumes a leisurely pace in the evolution of the Rabbinic Jewish faith that is not historically verifiable, nor consonant with what is known about that faith's response to the great Destruction. (See Chapters Ten and Eleven.)

41 For the prevailing view, see Sanders, *Historical Figure of Jesus*, 57, and *The Gospel of Mark. Red Letter Edition*, 11–12. The minority viewpoint, that John is a superior historical source, is held by several scholars, some of them highly distinguished: for example, Fergus Millar (in Davies and White, 363) and Elaine Pagels (*The Origin of Satan*, New York: Random House, 1995, 107).

42 The present state of opinion is summarized by Meier (1:46) and by Kysar (*ABD*, 3:919).

43 Found in *The Complete Gospels*, 180–93. See also Robert T. Fortna, *The Fourth Gospel and Its Predecessor* (Philadelphia: Fortress Press, 1988).

44 *The Complete Gospels*, 180n.

45 Fortna, "Introduction," in *The Complete Gospels*, 177.

46 L. Cope, cited in Robert T. Fortna, "Signs/Semeia Source" in *ABD*, 6:19. Incidentally, in this *ABD* article Fortna is much more controlled than in *The Complete Gospels*.

47 What I term the Synoptic Puzzle is usually termed in biblical circles the "Synoptic Problem." Not only does that unfortunate term make the issue seem as if it were some epidermal blemish that needed to be cleared up, but it misses the great pleasure, indeed joy, that many scholars obviously have found in trying to solve this, one of history's most important textual puzzles.

48 Sanders and Davies, 16–17.

49 Flavius Josephus, *Jewish War*, 7:1.

50 A surprising example of this wish-fulfilment-as-evidence is found in Sanders and Davies (17–18) who adjudge, with no probative material, that Jesus' "prediction" in Mark, concerning the Temple's destruction is a genuine prophecy, but that when employed elsewhere, it is not.

This is quite different from the argument of Martin Hengel, in *Studies in the Gospel of Mark* (London: SCM Press, 1985), that Mark was composed in its present form, late in the Jewish War, but before the Temple itself actually was destroyed and Jerusalem nearly levelled. He favours the summer of 69 CE for the composition of Mark. Although I am skeptical of such precise dating – it would make Mark (which previously has eluded all precise dating) the most tightly dated item in the entire Bible, Christian and Jewish, exceeding even that of the Book of Daniel. This is ironic given that one of Mark's references to Daniel seems to relate to Hengel's dating. Mark has Jesus give a set of instructions that would make great sense to anyone who either was experiencing or had experienced the siege of Jerusalem:

> But when ye shall see the abomination of desolation, spoken of by Daniel the prophet, standing where it ought not, (let him that readeth understand), then let them that be in Judaea flee to the mountains. (Mark 13:14)

That would seem to be an advice based on the Temple's already having been defiled, but other interpretations are possible. In fact, whether Mark was written in the chaos of mid-69, with the destruction of Jerusalem and the Temple a clear possibility, or whether it was written a year or two later is not crucial: the *weltuntergang* is taken as given, and acts as a conceptual filter for all that is in Mark. (That said, I am not convinced by Hengel's argument, but even if it is correct, the fundamental point that Mark was hammered out on the anvil of the Temple's destruction, remains unchanged.)

A less useful suggestion is that of Pieter J.J. Botha, who rejects the idea that the destruction of the Temple is a valid historical dating point. He does this by stating, concerning the historical argument on this point, that those who use the Temple's destruction as a dating point believe (1) that the fall of Jerusalem was an issue of major concern to all Christians, and (2) that significant knowledge of the events was freely available, and (3) "that there must have been a rather uniform reaction." (Pieter J.J. Botha, "The Historical Setting of Mark's Gospel: Problems and Possibilities," *Journal for the Study of the New Testament*, 51, Sept. 1993, 33.) This is a mixture of strawmanship and denial of fundamental historical facts. Since no one suggests that there was a uniform reaction to the fall of the Temple or that it was of major concern to all Christians, those ideas are an irrelevance. The destruction of Jerusalem and of the Temple was, however, a major concern to the leadership of several of the factions of Christianity, a fact made clear by the scriptures they produced and by the inclusion of the Temple-destruction data in their text. Each group reacted in its own way – not "uniformly" – else why would each of the Synoptics and the Gospel of John differ from each other? Moreover, Botha is factually in error when suggesting that the events in Jerusalem were somehow not "freely available." Jerusalem was the most impressive city in the provincial portion of the Roman empire. It fell after a long war, which was anything but a secret conflict and which, indeed, continued until 73 CE, with the suicide of the force at Masada. One of the primary features of Roman administration was that it maintained a network of communications including roads and messenger services, which carried news around the imperial web at a speed that probably equalled the speed of communication in North America, for example, until the introduction of transcontinental railways and telegraphy.

51 Richard Heard, *An Introduction to the New Testament* (New York: Harper and Brothers, 1950), 54.

52 Joseph A. Fitzmyer, "The Priority of Mark and the 'Q' Source in Luke," in his *Jesus and Man's Hope* (Pittsburgh: Pittsburgh Theological Seminary, 1970), reproduced in Arthur J. Bellinzoni, Jr., *The Two-Source Hypothesis. A Critical Appraisal* (Macon, GA: Mercer University Press, 1985), 38.

53 William R. Farmer, *The Synoptic Problem. A Critical Analysis* (Macon, GA: Mercer University Press, 1976), esp. 199–232. For a multi-voiced expansion of Farmer's basic arguments, see William R. Farmer (ed.), *New Synoptic Studies. The Cambridge Gospel Conference and Beyond* (Macon, GA: Mercer University Press, 1983).

54 Remember, this is a closed system. In it, there are six possible relationships of simple linearity, as in the possible sequence: Mark copies from Luke who copies from Matthew. This would explain similarity but gives no opportunity for testimony about disagreement. These six therefore are discarded.

There are three triangles, wherein two independent Synoptics are copied by the third: as in, say, Luke copying Matthew and Mark. However, that relationship shows why the three might agree, leaves no room for testimony of instances where Luke and Mark might agree with each other and disagree with Matthew. And so on.

And there is another set of triangles, wherein two Synoptics independently copy the third: as in, for example, Mark being copied both by Matthew and by Luke. That explains agreements between the three, but it leaves aside testimony or explanation of the cases wherein Matthew and Luke agree as against Mark. And so on.

55 My usage: this term is less confusing than the several alternatives in scholarly usage: the "Two Gospel hypothesis," the "Griesbach hypothesis," the "neo-Griesbachian school," among others.

56 Augustine's view was that Matthew was first, Mark second, and Luke third, a different order from the present version based on Farmer's work, but a clear statement of Matthew's priority, nonetheless.

57 Frances E. Gigot, "Synoptics," *The Catholic Encyclopedia* (1912), 14:394, quoted in "Introduction," to Bellinzoni, 7.

58 This is clearly specified, with implied endorsement, in David L. Dungan, "Two-Gospel Hypothesis," in *ABD*, 6:677–78.

59 J. Enoch Powell, "The Genesis of the Gospel," *Journal for the Study of the New Testament*, 42 (June 1991), 5–16.

60 I am not here asserting that there is no censorship or suppression in the Hebrew scriptures, the Christian scriptures, and in the tradition of Rabbinical Judaism. Certainly there is, and a lot of it. What I am suggesting is that the items that are preserved *within* the canonical textual traditions all operate according to a grammar of invention that is additive and transformative, but never negative. That is,

one text does not have the power to say that a previous text does not exist. The place where the suppression occurs, of course, is at the boundary walls: sometimes entire books are declared non-existent, and are suppressed, with no reference being made to them by those texts which are preserved within the canon.

61 The term "Mark-hypothesis" is less confusing than the frequently used "two-source hypothesis" which is easily confused with the "Two Gospel hypothesis," that is, the Matthew-hypothesis.

The twentieth century's most influential statement of Mark's priority is B.M. Streeter's *The Four Gospels: A Study of Origins* (London: MacMillan, 1924). His "two-source" argument has been expanded to a "four-source" one, but its central features remain the same today. It still dominates the field.

62 It is a sign of both the bibliodensity and the querulousness of recent biblical scholarship that there is actually a literature on whether or not the siglum "Q" really originally meant "Quelle," or something else entirely. (See Meier, 1:50*n*9.) It simply does not matter.

A serviceable heuristic reconstruction of "Q" is found in *The Complete Gospels*, 253–300, compiled and translated by Arland D. Jacobson. For a technical discussion, see Koester, 133–71 and also John S. Kloppenborg, *The Formation of Q. Trajectories in Ancient Wisdom Collection* (Philadelphia: Fortress Press, 1987). For a summary of pro-Q material, see John S. Kloppenborg, "The Sayings Gospel Q and the Quest of the Historical Jesus," *Harvard Theological Review*, 89 (Oct. 1996), 307–44. For a skeptical outlook, see A.M. Farrer, "On Dispensing with Q," in D.E. Nineham (ed.), *Studies in the Gospels. Essays in Memory of R.H. Lightfoot* (Oxford: Basil Blackwell, 1955), 55–88, reprinted in Bellinzoni, 321–69. The Q hypothesis has become so well known as to be part of educated popular culture. Witness Charlotte Allen's "The Search for a No-Frill Jesus," *Atlantic Monthly* 278 (Dec. 1996), 51–68.

63 The Epistle of Barnabas is an extremely obscure letter-cum-tract, not found in any of the standard collections of para-biblical material. It was in favour with the church in Egypt and is known by virtue of its inclusion in Codex Sinaiticus. The epistle refers to the destruction of the Jerusalem Temple. See Jay Curry Treat, "Epistle of Barnabas," *ABD*, 1:611–14. Koester (15–16) dates it as late first century or early second.

64 Crossan, *The Historical Jesus*, 376.

65 Also excluded are materials that were in the "real Q" but were used either by Matthew or by Luke, but not by both. The exclusion of such items, by virtue of the *a priori* methodological assumptions of "Q" construction, mean that some of the items that are considered to come from a source unique to Luke or unique to Matthew, could have originated in the "real Q" instead. It is logically possible (although historically daft) to go back to a "two-source" theory, using only Mark, and the "real Q" – the "real Q" to consist of: (a) items found in Matthew and Luke but not in Mark; (b) items which we can never identify that were shared by "Q"

with Mark and with Matthew and Luke; (c) all of the items in Luke that are not found in Matthew and Mark; and (d) all of the items in Matthew that are not found in Mark and Luke!

66 Incidentally, although I consider "Q" to be a useful hypothetical gospel – chiefly because it follows the template that is apparently dictated by Matthew and Luke's use of Mark – it is not a logical necessity in the history of Christian invention. It can be vaporized logically by a simple two-stage process. (a) Infer that the material which Matthew and Luke share with Mark comes from Mark. (This from the Mark-hypothesis.) And (b) simultaneously infer that the material which is shared by Matthew and Luke is accounted for by Luke's employing Matthew for the basis of his own re-write. From a purely textual point of view, "Q" thereupon becomes redundant.

67 Meier, 1:167.

68 Sanders, *Historical Figure of Jesus*, 59–60.

69 Meier, 1:168.

70 For a list of possible criteria, compare Meier 1:168–83, *The Five Gospels*, 16–34, and *The Gospel of Mark. Red Letter Edition*, 29–52. See also Sanders and Davies, 301–34.

71 The reader should be aware that I am phrasing the indicator of embarrassment differently than is usually the case. In the usual instance, the criterion is that the material embarrasses "the Christian church" or "the early Church." That is to debase a potentially first-hand source to a second-hand one: we know the early (pre-70 CE) church almost entirely through the Christian scriptures, so it is an unnecessary-remove to infer embarrassment to an entity (the early Church), whose historical character is derived from the scriptures. The more direct comparison is to determine embarrassment to the "New Testament" text itself.

72 Meier, I: 170.

73 This view is developed independently of the very interesting recent work by William Klassen, *Judas: Betrayer or Friend of Jesus* (Minneapolis: Fortress Press, 1997). Klassen's intriguing defence of Judas is based on the fundamental observation that Judas was demonized as a stereotypical, deceitful "Jew," because the Jesus-faith was itself splitting into Gentile and "Jewish" factions. This seems to me to be true, but one must add that, even had this split not occurred, it still would have been necessary for the chroniclers of the Jesus-faith to put on stage a figure who personified those aspects of Second Temple Judahism from which the Jesus-faith wished to be sharply distinguished. If the Jesus-faith was the replacement for the old religion of Judah (the replacement by virtue of being the Covenant's "true" form), then it was a fine piece of narrative construction to introduce a personality who represented late Second Temple Judahism – "Judas" – and who was antithetical both morally and behaviourally to Yeshua. Within the story, Judas operates in opposition to Jesus-the-Christ, the way that Satan in later Second Temple mythology acts towards the Almighty.

Did Judas exist or was he an introduction into the narrative of one of the hundreds of demons that floated through the cosmology of late Second Temple Judahist sects? There is no evidence outside the Gospels, so the question remains open. However, this secondary question is germane: even if one takes as a given that Yeshua was betrayed by someone, would the story have a very different meaning if the betrayer was named, say, Yosef? Indeed it would: at minimum, then, we should accept the strong possibility that "Judas" was a stage name, introduced in early narratives of the Jesus-faith, to fit the need to differentiate that faith from other derivatives of the Yahweh-faith and, simultaneously, to demean those other religious groups.

74 Here it is appropriate to note that the criterion of embarrassment only works one way: it provides a strong indication of an event's having an authentic relationship with the historical Yeshua, when the event reported is to be in dissonance with the Christian scriptures in such a way as to impede the scriptures' transformation of Yeshua into Jesus-the-Christ. Instances where there is dissonance, but in which the story involved accelerates the transformation of Yeshua into Jesus-the-Christ (the Virgin Birth and the physical resurrection being the two obvious examples) do not have the same probative value, for there is no embarrassment to the central transformation being effected.

75 Meier, 1: 169.

76 Some scholars also add under the discontinuity-indicator, material that is dissonant with the early church's beliefs and practices, and thus perhaps was derived from Yeshua, rather than from the evolving church. That, however, is a nonstarter: our *best* knowledge of the early church comes virtually solely from the Christian scriptures, so one is really asking, if in regard to church practices as found in the "New Testament," are there words or actions of Jesus which conflict with the basic texts? This is a good question to ask, but it is not a new principle of evidence, for it is included under the criterion of embarrassment.

77 John Tullius, *I'd Rather Be a Yankee. An Oral History of America's Most Loved and Most Hated Baseball Team* (New York: MacMillan, 1986), 188–89.

78 To my mind, the most significant developments related to the historical Yeshua in the last half-century come from the attempts, mostly by Jewish scholars, to integrate studies of the later portions of the Tanakh, and earlier portions of the Rabbinical tradition, with information in the Christian scriptures. I hope it will not be taken as ingratitude if I mention one characteristic of the major Jewish scholars who have studied the historical narratives about Jesus – Leo Baeck, Joseph Klausner, Claude G. Montefiore (each writing pre–World War II), Martin Buber, Samuel Sandmel, David Flusser, Geza Vermes, to name only the most obvious among several dozen scholars who have done significant work related to the historical Yeshua – namely, a certain credulousness related to the "New Testament" as source. The Christian texts are usually given a very shrewd, or at least imaginative and intelligent, close-reading, but without anything but a flash-by assessment

of their historical reliability. This is perhaps understandable in the context of the report of Jesus' life being used increasingly by Jewish scholars as the fullest and earliest evidence there may be of what a proto-Rabbinic figure was like in the era before the crash of Second Temple Judahism. Jesus and his method of exposition of Torah become part of the data-base for ascertaining (indirectly, to be sure) the embryonic phase of Rabbinic Judahism. Whatever tradition is reported about the great Hillel, a hundredfold more is preserved about Jesus. Of course, the Jewish scholars do not buy into the claims of Jesus' being Moshiah, or having a Virgin Birth, or being physically resurrected from the dead, but they are quite willing to engage in textual discussion of the parables and other sayings as if those utterances were authentic. I suspect the driving mechanism here is quite simple: if one were to subject the sayings of Jesus to the full evidentiary demands of the professional historical community, then one would have to do so with the texts of Rabbinic Judaism, notably the Mishnah and the Talmuds, and there is a reluctance on the part of most scholars to handle those sacred objects with anything but velvet gloves.

Appendix E

The Great Rabbinic Corpus: Access, Dating, Translation, Methods, and Queries

I

I ONCE ENQUIRED OF ONE OF THE WORLD'S LEADING SCHOLARS OF classical Rabbinic literature if I would be out of line to suggest that probably no more than one person in 100,000 of the world's Jewish population of the present day has read completely the major texts of Rabbinic Judaism. He replied: "No. You'd be correct if you said that in the entire history of Rabbinic Judaism, not more than one in 100,000 *Rabbis* had read all the classical texts."

That comment is passed on in the same spirit that a tiny saying, attributed to one of the Sages of Blessed Memory is enclosed in a Rabbinic text: as a piece of information about the world which has a relationship to Torah and which, simultaneously, is meant to encourage the enquirer on his path. Anyone encountering the great Rabbinic texts, whether for the first time or the five-hundredth, has to feel overwhelmed and inadequate. The substance of the texts is extremely challenging; moreover, the trappings of the documents, both bibliographic and social, make entry into the texts seem not merely formidable, but forbidding. That is a shame because, taken together, the classical Rabbinic texts comprise one of the great monuments of western culture.

It is inspiriting, therefore, to realize that one is entering an area wherein, although there exist many individuals with highly specialized knowledge of some of the texts, there are very few who have even a once-over knowledge of the whole corpus. Hence, even most experts in one aspect of classical Rabbinics are amateurs in others; so, without embarrassment at being a mere amateur, a thoughtful reader, Jewish or non-Jewish, should have no hesitation in joining the reading circle.

The reasons that even among confessional Jews only a very tiny proportion have read the entire body of classical texts – the "canon" of Rabbinical Judaism, to use a term the Rabbis do not themselves employ – are in part ideological in origin, in part merely practical. Initially, one has to note that the gender-ideology of the faith locked out women, half the pool of devout adherents, from institutions in which the texts were studied. Only in the last half of the twentieth century did it become possible for women to pursue such study in Jewish institutions at the same level as men, and even this opportunity is still limited. Secular institutions wherein the texts were seriously studied were opened to women somewhat earlier, but even so, widespread opportunities for the female half of the Jewish faith to study formally the basic documents of the faith were not much available until the second half of the twentieth century, and then almost entirely in North America. Secondly, all potential readers of the documents have had to have been daunted by the sheer size of the corpus. A rough estimate is that the classical Rabbinic texts run to at least ten million words. None of the texts is easy reading, for each is cast largely in the form either of outline-of-argument in disputed matters of religious law, or exegetical commentary on earlier texts, with only the odd anecdote tucked in. There is no narrative framework, as in the Tanakh or in the "New Testament," and usually the principle of organization that holds a specific tractate together is unstated. Hard reading: highly challenging. Thirdly, relatively few persons have ever read the entire corpus, because to do so in its original form requires an advanced knowledge of biblical Hebrew, middle Hebrew, Eastern Aramaic, Western Aramaic and a moderate facility in the Palestinian and Syrian dialects of Greek, and a smattering of medieval French. These technical demands, when combined with the size of the corpus of classical texts, means that most Yeshivot concentrated their training on a selected band of texts (mostly, portions of the Babylonian Talmud) and let the rest slide. Fourthly, even if, over their long centuries of scholarship, the Rabbinical academies had wished to provide their pupils with a conspectus of the full Rabbinic canon, they would have found it impossible to do so: for the first millennium or more after the Rabbinic texts were completed, they were available only in manuscript form, which was much more of a problem for Jews than for Christians and their "New Testament": because as a minority within Christendom, the Jews had their sacred texts frequently destroyed, the most focused campaign to destroy Jewish literature occurring in the thirteenth century.[1] From the paucity of intact manuscripts that survive today (discussed below), one infers that it was very difficult for a spiritual academy to maintain in its possession the full range of classical Rabbinic texts. One surmises that only a few of the great masters managed to gain access to the entire corpus.

All that changed in the late fifteenth and early sixteenth centuries with the publication in printed form of the core Rabbinic canon. Here one uses the term "canon" in a different way than one does for the Tanakh or for the "New Testament," because the borders of the Rabbinic literature of the classical era (pre-600 CE, roughly), have never been precisely defined. However, without much danger of controversy, one can define as the core-tradition, the centre of the Rabbinic corpus, a set of five documents, each of which is an absolutely necessary component of Rabbinic Judaism: the Mishnah, the Tosefta, Sifra (on Leviticus), the Yerushalmi (the Talmud of the Land of Israel) and the Bavli (the Babylonian Talmud). Around this core revolve several significant documents, some of which are emphasized by some scholars, others by others: Sifré to Numbers and to Deuteronomy (which are primarily biblical commentaries), Middrash Rabbah (roughly, amplifications and expositions) of Genesis, Leviticus, Lamentations, Song of Songs, Ruth, Esther), the Mekhilta attributed to Rav Ishmaiel, the Pesiqta of Rav Kahana, the Writings on the Fathers according to Rabbi Nathan, and several other, more peripheral texts. If here, and in the text of this book, we limit ourselves mostly to the core-tradition texts, the points addressed will be clearer than if we venture too far into the penumbra.

Thus, focusing only on the central items, one notes the date on which a complete printed edition (of whatever quality) became available for each:[2]

Mishnah	1485
Tosefta	1521
Sifra	1523
Jerusalem Talmud	1524
Babylonian Talmud	1523

Manifestly, the printing of these works solved the problem of physical access to the original texts. However, the sheer size of the texts (the Babylonian Talmud alone is two and one-half million words), and the technical training necessary to gain intellectual access to them (at least two decades of full-time immersion in an academy) limited to an elite the possibility of reading all of the core-tradition texts (never mind the whole corpus). Fair enough and not unusual: very few of the followers of any of the world's major religions have been able to read in the original tongue the sacred texts of that religion. However, could the faithful, and the merely-interested, not have read the major Rabbinic texts in their own vernacular language? No, and indeed, that suggestion, naive though it is, is exactly the kind of mistake that is productive of historical understanding, for sometimes the things that one takes for granted are the most significant – when one suddenly realizes that they cannot be taken for granted. In the tradition of English-language culture it is assumed that the sacred texts of any religion will be available in the vernacular. That, today, is not questioned: it is seemingly a natural phenomenon, like the Law of Gravity. In reality, one discovers that except for the Tanakh, "no text originally in Hebrew or Aramaic of the Judaic canon reached a foreign language, except Latin, before the nineteenth century."[3] Some early attempts at translation were blocked by religious authorities: for example, a mid-nineteenth-century effort at translating the Babylonian Talmud into German was scuttled under pressure by extreme Orthodox leaders.[4] Mostly, however, translations into vernacular languages foundered not on direct opposition, but because the scholars who were expert enough to do the work had no interest in having the texts read widely: this from a mixture of intellectual preciousness, possessiveness, and a sense that translations were vaguely impure. (Judah Goldin, long an opponent of needless esotericism, once gently rebuked some of his more parochial colleagues by noting, "by the way, the Hebrew alphabet has only consonants, and quite often it is hard to decide how a word is pronounced; it is from the New Testament, which is written in Greek, that we learn that the Hebrew consonants, *r*, *b*, *y* should be pronounced 'Rabbi.' ")[5] It was not until the 1990s that the translation of the entire corpus was completed: into English. The dates when the core items of the Rabbinical tradition became available to the general reading public are as follows:[6]

Mishnah	1933
Tosefta	1980
Sifra	1988
Jerusalem Talmud	1993
Babylonian Talmud	1948

(Other, more peripheral items were translated between 1939 and the mid-1990s.)

The linguistic wall that, until recently, surrounded the Rabbinic texts had three effects: first, the non-Jewish world was prevented from viewing one of the major cultural achievements effected anywhere, ever. Secondly, even among Jewish believers, only the very few extremely adept scholars were permitted more than a truncated view of many of the most sacred documents of their own faith. And, thirdly, the texts of Rabbinic Judaism were insulated from the scholarly revolution that had occurred among students of the Tanakh, of the "New Testament," and of the Church Fathers, which had resulted from the methods of documentary research (appropriated from "secular" scholarship) being conjoined with expert knowledge of the sacred texts. This insulation served the purposes both of those Jewish authorities who wished to keep Rabbinic Judaism hermetically sealed from the taint either of the secular or of the Christian, and, simultaneously, of those Christian apologists who did not wish to admit to the body of texts of revelatory authority any Jewish item written after the Book of Esther.

The attempt to bring Rabbinic Jewish literature out of the scholarly ghetto and to abolish the freemasonry of in-group codes that scared away outsiders was led in the middle decades of the twentieth century by English scholars: Herbert Danby, an Anglican priest, produced an elegant translation of the Mishnah in 1933 (Oxford: Clarendon Press), and in the 1930s, 1940s, and 1950s, the London-based Soncino Press published several crucial documents, most importantly, a complete translation in eighteen volumes of the Babylonian Talmud under the editorship of Israel Epstein.

In the last three decades of the twentieth century, the major force for interrogating the Rabbinic texts by employing the historical and hermeneutic tools developed in related (but non-Jewish) fields has been the work of Rabbi Jacob Neusner. For his efforts, he is undoubtedly the most respected and, at the same time, the most-often vilified of present-day Rabbinic scholars. If successful in his work, he will have achieved the Herculean task of moving the study of Rabbinic literature at the beginning of the twenty-first century to a level roughly equivalent to that occupied by scholarship on the Tanakh and the "New Testament" at the beginning of the twentieth. Much of Neusner's work is controversial, and no less so because Neusner is willing to change his mind and to argue against himself as he progresses from book to book. (His attitude puts one in mind of John Maynard Keynes's reaction to a critic who charged that he was contradicting himself: "When the facts change, I change my opinion. What do you do?") His achievement is beyond doubt. Most importantly, Neusner will have fulfilled a self-assigned brief: of having available in English all of the significant texts of classical Rabbinism, something that is not close to being achieved in any other language, including modern Hebrew. Thus, he has himself moved into the culture of the English-speaking world previously untranslated works from the core of the Rabbinic traditions which previously had no English version, such as the Jerusalem Talmud (in thirty-five volumes), the Tosefta, and Sifra, as well as several of the less central texts. He has also produced his own version of previously-translated works, the Mishnah and the Babylonian Talmud. Had Neusner never done anything else, this body of translation would be the equivalent of a lifetime's achievement for several scholars.

His second intellectual monument (for it is nothing less) has been to devise and to apply to his own translations a precise system of reference – one that permits the citation with accuracy and efficiency of every significant idea-unit in each text. This was badly needed, because if scholarship on the Rabbinic texts is to progress it requires the facility and accuracy which is made possible, for example, by the system of chapter-and-verse that Christian scholars in the middle ages developed for the Tanakh and which Jewish scholars adopted, with only minor variations. At present, the standard method of citation of a quotation or of a statement of fact is to give the name of a tractate (no ambiguity there) and then to cite the verso-recto pagination (such as "38a," "38b" etc.) of the authoritative printed version of the text in question. This is markedly inefficient and, frequently, vexing. In any highly-studied texts, it would be very inefficient if one received only a page number for a quotation, but in the case of documents that originally were published in folio form, and which (as in the case of the Talmuds) are arranged in a complex system of multiple texts and marginalia on the same page, it is maddening: one must search over several pages in a modern-sized book, looking for the quotation in question. So, Neusner developed a very simple system of citation that allows one to pinpoint for the reader any reference one employs, and to find quickly any passage for which one has another scholar's reference. Because this system uses idea-units (usually a sentence or two, comparable to a verse in the Tanakh or in the "New Testament,") it is not language-bound. There is no reason that it could not be used as a standard citation system for Rabbinical literature in every language, including the original. One suspects that it will take at least a full generation for this sensible innovation to be adopted. It (or a similar system) is a virtual precondition for scholarship on Rabbinical texts to achieve the precision and efficiency of locution and of location that is demanded in textual scholarship in the wider academy. Without being facetious, I would suggest that the adoption of Neusner's citation system will be considerably speeded, if those who, on various grounds, do not like his work, realize that so long as his translations are the only ones that possess a precise mode of citation that is not language-bound, his will be the texts cited as authoritative by scholars who expect the precision required in modern textual studies.

2

Given, then, that at the end of the twentieth century we finally possess access in the English vernacular to all of the important Rabbinical texts written before roughly 600 CE, it is well to ask, what is the character of the manuscript witnesses upon which the printed books rely? Immediately, one is struck by how late (relative to the surmised date of composition) and how thin the manuscript tradition is, compared to that of the Tanakh and especially, that of the "New Testament."

Given below are the dates for the earliest complete surviving manuscript of each of the core items (and, in the case of the Jerusalem Talmud and the Babylonian Talmud, there exists only a single complete manuscript of each, so the earliest complete text is unique in each case):[7]

Mishnah	1399–1401
Tosefta	1150
Sifra	1073
Jerusalem Talmud	1299 or 1334
Babylonian Talmud	1342–43

These dates are strikingly late: between, roughly, 700 and 1,200 years after the dates usually accepted for the final composition of the various texts. Even if one introduces into the equation copies of separate tractates, forming part of the later complete manuscripts, one can move the dates of the two Talmudic manuscript traditions only a bit before 1200 with any certainty. Thereafter, one is left with myriad fragments, shreddings from outworn manuscripts, such as those kept in the Cairo Geniza, some of which may predate the year

1000 CE.[8] Some portions of the Cairo Geniza's Bavli fragments are said to date to the later eighth century or the early ninth, but, though these are valuable links in the chain of textual transmission, they are in equal parts comforting and unsettling. The early date helps build confidence in the manuscript tradition, but the material preserved indicates not just variant versions of small sections, but that entirely different manuscript versions of pericopes and tractates existed than those that eventually came to be accepted as authoritative.[9] In any case, most of the manuscripts that are possibly pre-1000 in origin consist only of a single page or less.

That scholars are forced to rely on basic sources that are so far distant from the original texts is explicable by the destruction of thousands of Rabbinical manuscripts by Christian authorities. But that explanation makes the historian's problem no less acute. The uneasiness one feels in accepting the standard editions of the Rabbinic texts increases when one factors in three further facts: (1) that an evulsion of material that might have been offensive to Inquisitors was effected in several texts, and this material may never have been recovered; (2) that even after the invention of printing, changes to the texts were frequently made, right into the nineteenth century, but not on the basis of the comparison of manuscript evidence;[10] and (3) despite some very accomplished scholarship, particularly upon the Mishnah, there is nothing approaching a critical edition for any of the core texts: that is, an edition which presents all the variant manuscript and printed readings and adjudges as between them. Whether or not such a task is humanly possible is not yet clear. One authority on the Jerusalem Talmud, after surveying the confused and corrupt (in the technical sense) state of the text concluded, "the task of establishing a correct text is almost an impossible one."[11] So, one necessarily accepts the versions of the core documents that are available – and is grateful, indeed, that they are available in translation. But we clutch them desperately, as if we were clinging to the caudal appendage of some behemoth whose anterior features we can sense, but not discern. We are a long way from the original texts.

When an historian turns to the texts themselves, he or she is apt to be struck by a remarkable absence. None of the Rabbinical documents gives any direct indication of its own authorship or any direct indication of to whom it is addressed, or any direct statement of the circumstances that led to its invention. And indirect clues are few. In comparison, on these matters, the Tanakh and the "New Testament" (though hardly effusive) are utterly forthcoming. The Rabbinic texts seem almost as if they were designed to carry the message, "historian, go away." In his now-classic discussion of Jewish history and Jewish memory, Yosef Hayim Yerushalmi observes, "unlike the biblical writers, the Rabbis seem to play with Time as though with an accordion, expanding and collapsing it at will. Where historical specificity is a hallmark of the biblical narratives, here that acute biblical sense of time and of place often gives way to rampant and seemingly unselfconscious anachronism."[12] He continues: "Most sobering and important is the fact that the history of the Talmudic period itself cannot be elicited from its own vast literature. Historical events of the first order are either not recorded at all, or else they are mentioned in so legendary or fragmentary a way as to preclude even an elementary retrieval of what occurred."[13]

These difficulties have not prevented attempts at dating the Rabbinic literature, nor should they. Two basic efforts have prevailed and, despite their differences in mien, have produced roughly similar results. The first of these is the traditional mode, which is fundamentalist, and works according to the same methods by which fundamentalists calculate the age of the earth from the information in the Pentateuch. The details of individual lives are taken literally (in this case, the reported lives of individual Rabbis) and there is a good deal of complex counting of generations and the charting of genealogies: here not blood genealogies, but the intellectual genealogies of the various Sages. The Sages of the Mishnah-through-Bavli are analysed as consisting of Tannaim (those from roughly the beginning of the Common Era to the completion of the Mishnah); Amoraim (those who were active from the completion of the Mishnah to the finishing of the two Talmuds); Saboraim (who may have made editorial changes to the Talmuds and other material after they received it from the Amoraim). Within each of these levels, traditional scholars have articulated beautifully detailed genealogies.[14] The traditional chronological results suggest that the Mishnah was completed sometime before the death of Rabbi Judah Ha Nasi in 220 CE; that the writing of the Jerusalem Talmud effectively ended with Roman extinction of the Patriarchate in Palestine in 421, and that the Babylonian Talmud's redaction was complete in 427 with the death of Rav Ashi.

This compares with the dating provided by Jewish (and a few non-Jewish) scholars who depend upon the same materials, but who do not take them literally. A representative set of those opinions for completion of the respective volumes is:[15]

Mishnah (excluding Aboth)	c. 200 CE
Tosefta	c. 300
Sifra	c. 300
Jerusalem Talmud	c. 400
Babylonian Talmud	c. 600

What these numbers imply is that in the six centuries between the time of Hillel and Shammai (that is, roughly from the start of the Common Era until 600), a massive body of sacred literature came into being, but that no one really can demonstrate by evidentiary methods that stand outside of faith in the literal truth of the documents (the fundamentalist approach), anything more than the probable sequence of the major documents (the more secular view-point). And if this temporal uncertainty holds for the core items, it is more problematic for other significant, but less central documents: the Sifré on Numbers and on Deuteronomy, the Genesis and Leviticus Rabbah, etc. The sequential relationship of the documents is clear enough (the Talmuds, to make the most obvious case, are commentaries on the Mishnah and thus follow upon it historically).

3

But where does one go from there?

One possible answer is: nowhere, and it does not matter. That is, perhaps one should honour the intentions of the final inventors, the redactors of each document, and accept their desire that events exterior to the creation of each text are irrelevant to its meaning; and that events reported within the text (one Sage passing on a saying to another Sage) are integral to the text and are not verifiable, but must be accepted as part of the whole invention. This view works well either within the community of faith (wherein one does not question divine revelation but instead interprets it) and also in the post-modern wing of the secular academy which holds that texts are laws unto themselves and create, rather than are created by, their context. This is a fairly low-risk set of positions since, unlike the Christian scriptures, there is no absolute dependence in theology on a certain person having said a certain thing at a certain time: in contrast, obviously, to some of the words attributed to Yeshua of Nazareth. Each of the two views, fundamentalist and post-modernist, has its strong defenders and there is no profit here in parsing the implications of views that, in the former instance rest on devotional faith, and in the latter are based on epistemological premises that require rather greater faith than do the former.

Here, instead, let us suggest that there might be something in the more modest views of professional historians – the working stiffs who grub our way through archives looking not for revelation but, instead, confirmation or disproof of simple facts and for practical tests of sometimes-grandiose hypotheses. Our position is that, knowing the context in which a document is written – the date, the place, the author – is potentially helpful to those whose sole profession is to interpret documents. The social context of a document's creation, for example, is a small piece of knowledge, but it can make it easier for a hermeneuticist to infer what the original creators intended a text to mean, and of how those who shared, or had knowledge of the original context, were apt to interpret the text. Admittedly, in present-day critical theory neither of these items is very much prized, but for old-fashioned readers, anything that helps to discover the original author-editor's intentions has interest. And, further, historians have a perennial habit of wanting to know causes (in what circumstances, under what pressures, by whom) a certain document came into being, not merely effects (the text considered as a thing of its own creation). This holds even if at a conscious level the inventors of the text deny that their work comes out of any specific context. Every invention has its inventor and every inventor acts within a specific frame of time.

Were, in a future generation, scholars trained not only as Talmudists but as professional historians, to attempt to place in context the more detailed aspects of the invention of the great Rabbinic texts, they would deal with only two variables: the external context of the writers of the time, as defined by the work of "secular" historians, and the internal stratigraphy which the texts themselves reveal. Correlation of these two elements would produce a contextualized chronology of Rabbinical invention and, automatically, a myriad of hypotheses about cause-and-effect in those inventions. Simple as this is conceptually, it cannot progress very far until critical editions of the major Rabbinic documents are available.

Within the Rabbinic corpus, an obvious place where contextual knowledge helps immensely to determine the intent (and therefore the meaning) of the text is the Jerusalem Talmud. The Yerushalmi's invention and contents only make sense if one accepts the contextual reality of the massive imperial revolution of the fourth century wherein the Jewish people not only lost the tolerant position that they had occupied in the Roman empire, but found that empire suddenly allegiant (at least at an official level) to the heir of that branch of the former Judahist faith which had been the closest rival of the Pharisees, the founding fathers of Rabbinic Judaism: Christianity ruled. The Yerushalmi was one response to this revolution in real-world conditions, and though the Jerusalem Talmud may appear to be a virtual-reality machine, its invention was in considerable part a response to the changes in external conditions. That point is discussed at greater length in my main text; here it suffices to refer the reader to the demonstration in Jacob Neusner's *Judaism in the Matrix of Christianity* (Philadelphia: Fortress Press, 1986).

That is compelling, and so too is the direct influence of the disasters of the year 70–135 CE upon the formation of the Mishnah (to be discussed in a moment). However, if one wishes to move beyond the fairly gross indications of large-scale events having a large-scale impact upon the invention of the Rabbinic religion, one should combine the coarse chronology set down by major external events with an internal stratigraphy of textual evolution as observed within the documents. And this is where the problem, perhaps insuperable, arises: if we take any of the major texts on its own, we find that it has been edited so forcibly that the entire document speaks with what is (on the surface, at least) a single voice, and this despite each of the major texts containing the reputed-words of scores of individual Rabbis. Some specialists claim to be able to sort out the levels of invention within each text, while others, equally technically skilled, conclude that this cannot be done. More of this matter in a moment: here the point is that signals regarding internal development of the individual Rabbinical documents are not easy to recognize or interpret.

The more extreme Orthodox response to this problem is contradictory and self-cancelling. As items of faith, it is posited first that the single voice of the Almighty runs from one book of the Rabbinical corpus to another, so that effectively, there is no layering of tradition: Torah is one. And, in contradiction to the first, it is asserted that each Sage said exactly what the various Rabbinic documents say he said, so that one can delineate accurately the generations of Rabbis and their utterances, both within individual documents and intertextually. This fundamentalist position, besides being self-cancelling, precludes historical examination of the texts, except in the same way that fundamentalists trace the generations listed in the Pentateuch in order to determine the creation date of the world.

Instead, we can approach the stratigraphy of the text, with a series of questions that to all, save fundamentalists, are belief-neutral. Some of these queries are obvious and answerable, but to most of them the response has to be indeterminate since, in my view, we are at least a generation away from knowing which of the Rabbinic texts can be disassembled historically. Therefore, the important task for the historians at present is to set down a logic-sequence of queries; these represent intellectual obstacles that must be overcome if the Rabbinical texts are ever going to be set in a tight historical context. The initial query is exceedingly simple, but it leads to emancipation: namely, in any of the major Rabbinic documents, did all the Sages say exactly what they are reported as saying? Manifestly, no, since in each document the Rabbis speak as if their words were written by a tone-deaf playwright who puts dialogue with the same words, pace, and force in the mouths of king, courtier, and chambermaid. (One is reminded of the Hollywood epic in which, in the midst of a battle, the grizzled quartermaster looked outside, and then observed urbanely to the chamberlain, "Ah, here come the Sodomites.") So, given the astronomical improbability that the entire cast of each of the major Rabbinic documents spoke in almost exactly the same way, the answer is no, the texts cannot be taken as reporting precisely what each man said.

Simple enough. The more intriguing question is, do the texts quote anybody accurately? Do they represent anyone *ipsissima verba*? Since there exists for none of the Rabbinic sayings a secondary source outside of the Rabbinic canon that attests to any given verbal formulation (and since quotation of one Rabbinic source by another does not represent independent verification, merely duplication), this question has no rational answer. However, it can be reformulated to give an argumentative advantage to those who believe it is possible that at least some of the sayings attributed to the Sages of Blessed Memory are verbally accurate: "*if we assume* for the sake of debate that an unspecified portion of the Rabbinic sayings are indeed accurate verbal formulations framed by specific men of wisdom, how does one separate the accurate quotations from the inaccurate?" Thus far, no scholar has established a filter that separates the chaff from the wheat. Perhaps such a device can be built in the future, but it certainly does not exist today. One is skeptical, however, of its ever being developed, because of the difficulties presented by the "stam," which are the anonymous sayings found in the several texts. These apparently innocuous pieces of argument ("lemma," in technical language, the smallest units of Rabbinic discourse), are a methodological tripstone that illustrates the near-impossibility of sorting out the truly accurate quotations. The stam represent an anonymous layer of quotations in each of the most important documents. Merely because a saying is anonymous does not mean it is automatically imprecise or corrupt: the editor-inventors of the various texts present the stam as being fully as authoritative as are the other quotations. In fact, though an earlier generation of scholars tended to believe that the stam represented the earliest layer of each text, at present it is more generally believed that the stam were the last. To be more precise, the stam were the layer added by the final editor-inventors of the texts, and represent material from their own generation, as distinct from the source-ascribed material from earlier generations.[16] This means that the anonymous material, far from being the most distant from the final redactors of the texts – and thus, presumably, the most shaky – is actually the one layer of material that the final editors knew directly – and thus most likely to be *ipsissima verba*. Notice, hence, where this leaves the enterprise: the quotations which are anonymous are most apt to be accurate (but, by definition, they are unascribed); and those defined as to source, are less likely to be accurate in their verbal content. If this logic-train applies, one arrives at the unusual position that the most authoritative Rabbinic utterances are those for which no Rabbi's name is supplied.

At this juncture, the issue of the grounds-of-presumption for historical discussion must be clearly articulated, for the operational prescriptions of the secular academy and those of Rabbinics are directly opposed. The traditional view is that anything stated in the Rabbinical corpus must be taken as historically accurate unless it is proven otherwise. These grounds of presumption are not those of the ultra-Orthodox (who believe that there can be no error, so the question of inaccuracy does not arise), but of most Conservative and Reformed scholars who teach in religiously-supported institutions. The secular view of history – that which has reigned since the early Enlightenment – is that an event is presumed not to have happened unless there is positive proof that it has occurred. From at least the time of David Hume's *Philosophic*

Essays Concerning Human Understanding (1748), however, a codicil has been honoured: the reservation of cases in which greater historical improbability would be involved by adopting skepticism than by adopting belief. So, a traditionalist can argue within secular rubrics that, since a given saying is reported as having been uttered by a given Sage, this is positive evidence (not proof, but evidence), and that therefore the adoption of skepticism about the words in question involves assuming a more improbable viewpoint than does the acceptance of the quotation as *ipsissima verba*. Nevertheless, in this instance the logic against all the quotations being accurate is very strong (all those Rabbis would not all speak in virtually the same tone within each document, certainly not in any document so large as the Talmuds or the Mishnah), but the question makes us conscious that on *each* historical interrogation that we assay, we must be clear about our grounds-of-presumption.

Since (in my opinion) at present there is no demonstrated method of deciding which (if any) of the Rabbinic sayings are *ipsissima verba* – one can scarcely ignore Jacob Neusner's reiterated chant, that "what we cannot show, we cannot know" – we might get farther by lowering our standards. Instead of playing the fundamentalist game of worrying about precise wordings, it is more sensible to ask if the substance (not the words, just the substance) of the views ascribed to specific Rabbis is accurately described. The traditional method of proceeding is unambiguous. As David Kraemer notes, "despite the obviously crucial nature of this determination, those whose work depends upon the reliability of such attributions have merely assumed that they are generally accurate, without articulating the defensibility of that assumption."[17] And, Sacha Stern observes, "The reliability of attributions is, in this sense, both a premise of this standard Talmudic argument, and, to a large extent, its foregone conclusion. The occurrence elsewhere of uncertain or disputed attributions does not seem to have affected this basic assumption."[18] Manifestly, not all attributions in the Rabbinic corpus are in substance accurate, since one can compile a long list of instances in which a given Rabbi is credited with holding a substantive opinion that clashes with other reports of his beliefs. So, even operating at a lower level of precision than previously (we are no longer demanding that the given Sage has said exactly what he is reported to have said, just that he had views roughly in line with the words that were placed in his mouth), we are back to asking a discrimination question: can one filter out the authentic attributions of belief from the inauthentic? How one responds depends in part on one's attitude to the texts as historical documents: does one presume that they are basically accurate in their profiling of the various Rabbis' beliefs (and thence one need merely delete the errors) or that they are of such lightweight historical value that one picks out the attributions that have evidentiary force behind them, and discards the great majority? Ground-of-presumption, in other words, is key, but in a closely-judged matter such as this, responsible scholars do not blithely jump to one side or the other, but choose a position that is based on their reading of the specific evidence in the light of their wider experience of historical and textual scholarship. Thus, two examples of skepticism, from Rabbis who, though very traditional in their respect for the Rabbinic texts, concluded that attributions in the documents should not be taken historically, in most instances. The first comment is that of Judah Goldin:

> Every time a student attempts a study of talmudic sages, he is threatened by pitfalls. For despite the impressive quantities of midrashic and talmudic material, there is not one sage of the approximately 420 Tannaim and 3,400 Amoraim who are quoted or referred to – even the most famous among them, like Hillel or Yohanan ben Zakkai or Eliezer ben Hyrcanos or Joshua ben Hananiah or the Gamaliels and their sons, or Aqiba, or Meir or Judah bar Ilai or Simeon ben Yohai or Judah the Prince and so on and on with (among the Amoraim) Rabbi Yohanan and Resh Laqish or Joshua ben Levi or Abbahu, or (in Babylonia) Rab and Samuel, or Rabbah and Rab Joseph, or Abbaye and Raba – of not one of these 3,820 men is it possible to write a biography in the serious sense of the word. Strictly speaking, little biographical information is furnished. Very often attributions are contradictory and uncertain; very often views or sayings are recorded with no adequate context to speak of, so that even though every single term may be lexically intelligible, the sum total is not.[19]

And, Herbert W. Basser observes:

> Talmudic custom favored the seemingly odd device of "character transmutation." If two characters shared a common trait they were said to be the same person, even if one lived centuries after the other. Talmudic lore relates the appearance of Biblical characters generations after they died; certain personages are said indeed to be actually earlier personages. The Rabbis did not twist chronology. They merely saved the time necessary to explain a character's moral being by calling him by a familiar name whose moral fiber was well known by the audience.[20]

Clearly, such considerations would lead one to take as one's ground-of-presumption the belief that, unless the evidence tilts clearly the other way, one should not conclude that the ascription of a specific substantive belief to a specific historical figure is accurate. Emphatically, this does not imply that, after sifting the probative qualities of the text, within the framework of this background-presumption, one will necessarily come to Jacob Neusner's conclusion: "I do not believe we have any way of verifying whether a person to whom a saying is attributed actually said it."[21] There are, in fact, scholars who accept the same grounds of presumption, but come to the conclusion that in certain instances one can attribute substantive beliefs to specific Sages: David Halivni, David Kraemer, and Richard Kalmin are chief among these. The key point, however, is that Neusner, Halivni, Kraemer, and Kalmin can argue with each other within an agreed vocabulary and with a fundamentally similar sense of what the rules of proof are.

Another query – at present unresolved and perhaps unresolvable – which relates to the historicity of the Rabbinical discussion is: did the editor-inventors of the Rabbinic documents actually intend their ascription of beliefs to certain Rabbis to be historically accurate? If they did not, it would be silly of scholars to argue about which attributions are trustworthy, just as it would be super-erogatory for the faithful to affirm their accuracy.

Sacha Stern has suggested (mostly based on the Bavli, but citing other texts as well) that the concept of authorship of opinions – that is, the concept of attribution of Halachic viewpoints – to specific Sages was in fact a plastic concept. One should not, therefore, think of attribution as a single practice, but rather as a menu of possibilities. Sometimes the final redactors must have meant that a given Rabbi indeed had held a given view. However, the concept of authorship as a proprietary exercise – this saying belongs to this author – is relatively recent, becoming dominant in western culture only with the early mercantile age and the development of printing. The editor-inventors of the Rabbinical texts were quite at home, Stern argues, with the employment of authorship, and its associated concept, attribution, as flexible concepts. The Babylonian Talmud's final redactors at points acknowledge that some of their attributions are doubtful or uncertain. At other points, Stern suggests, they infer an authorship that has been lost from the content of the statement in question. At still other moments, they place a single name on the product of group thought. And in still other instances, they provide pseudepigraphic attributions – sometimes giving the name of an early Sage to a later tradition and, at other times, giving credit to a later Sage for an anonymous tradition that is actually quite early.[22]

Obviously, if the compilers of the Rabbinic corpus had a different concept of authorship and attribution than is held either by present-day believers or by present-day historians, everyone is in deep trouble, the more so because, as Stern drily remarks, "Our evidence for authorship derives, in most part, from rabbinic sources alone."[23] In this context, it is not entirely comforting to read in Robert Goldenberg's appreciative discussion of the Bavli that though the founders of the major schools of thought "really lived and as far as anyone knows they really held the opinions attributed to them ..."[24] when he adds that the Rabbis became historical fictions by having subsequent generations tack on to them views that, while consistent with the Sages' original positions, were added to produce a dialectic of argument, a literary construct, not an historical reality. All this helps to explain why Jacob Neusner keeps insisting that unless there is evidence of the accuracy of attributions that does not use the attributions themselves as the source of proof of their own accuracy[25] (in other words, that proof not be tautological), he will continue to deny the probative adequacy of any attribution.

Sometimes, reshaping a question helps us to escape, via lateral thinking, from what appears to be a *cul de sac*. With that in mind, we ask: is Jacob Neusner correct in the formulation that he constantly asserted during the 1980s and 1990s: that in the case of each of the Rabbinic classics, the text testifies only to the beliefs of the last generation, the one that completed the text's invention? Is the final redactor's the only mind we really come to know? "If we do not believe the attributions as fact, then can we have a history pertinent to an age prior to that of the redaction of the document itself?"[26] If source criticism is not feasible even for the Mishnah – if the uses of the Houses of Hillel and Shammai are only as vivid constructs employed to debate mid-second century issues and not as precise historical realities[27] – then one is left with the conclusion that history in the Mishnah, the Yerushalmi, the Bavli, all the classic texts, begins only on the day the editor-inventor of each puts down his pen for the last time.[28] This is essentially the view of Judah Goldin: "Not only do the primary sources disappoint us deeply in the amount of reliable historical detail they provide, but even as regards the opinions and teachings of the Sages, one is left to guess at what is early and what is late. In short, there is practically no way to get at development."[29] Against this are the views of scholars such as David Kraemer. In his *The Mind of the Talmud. An Intellectual History of the Bavli* (1990), he argues: "One thing, then, is for certain: no final author of the Bavli flattened all distinctions in his sources to create a single, undistinguished whole. To the contrary, the Bavli retains a multiplicity of formally distinct voices. These distinctions assure us that we may still discern the parties for whom these traditions speak."[30] And *mutatis mutandi*, what one can assert for the Bavli can be asserted for the other classical texts.

So, in fact, restating the question did not help at all. In the presence of what appears to be a massive head-butting game between those scholars in the field who play by the evidentiary rules of the academy – the Neusner school on one side and his opponents on the other (excluding here the fundamentalists who are opposed to the Neusner-school for reasons of belief that are prior to analysis) – let me state my own judgments as an outsider: a professional historian, but not a professional historian of the Rabbinic Jewish faith. This is that at present, the battle is drawn, but that the grounds of presumption have to be those of Jacob Neusner. Until some group of scholars produces a set of discriminations within the classic texts, a filter that shows us what historical assertions in the text are accurate, what attributions are historical and, therefore, what the intellectual development of each document was – *and does so in a manner that can be replicated by someone who is agnostic about these propositions* – then one must accept Neusner's skepticism.

Now: the huge irony. The most successful effort that I have encountered at sorting out the layering of one of the classic texts was accomplished by Jacob Neusner in the 1960s and early 1970s:[31] *The Rabbinic Traditions about the Pharisees before 70* (Leiden: E.J. Brill, 3 vols, 1971). Interestingly, although Neusner later repudiated the scholarly base of much of his own work from this period (for example, his *A Life of Yohanan ben Zakkai* (Leiden: Brill, 1962), and his five-volume *A History of the Jews in Babylonia* (Leiden: Brill, 1965–70)), he has not, to my knowledge, backed away from his analysis of the most important part of the *Pharisees* volumes.[32] Nor should he. Granted, Neusner's use of attributions from sources later than the Mishnah exhibits a credulity of the sort that he would now, rightly, reject as naive, but his dealing with the Mishnah itself was masterful. In the *Pharisees* he accomplished three tasks in relation to the Mishnah: first, he presented a defensible, tightly text-based, stratigraphy of the evolution of beliefs. Secondly, he provided a confirmation of the successive layering of beliefs that was independent of the attestations-of-authorship of the specific belief-units involved. This he did by correlating the alleged period in which an authority lived and the sort of logic the authority employed. So, one could remove the name of the Sage attached to any specific belief-unit, and still produce a stratigraphy of development in the Mishnah. Thus, a form of attestation of the course of development of the Mishnah was possible, and this provided the sort of independent attestation of attributions that Neusner later laments as being missing for all the other classic Rabbinic documents. In 1980, he was able to claim, quite convincingly, that the "Mishnah tells us something about the world before the period of its own closure, that is, the second half of the second century."[33] Not only did this methodology allow a look into the evolution of the Mishnah in a period well before its closure (indeed, it provides a window into pre-70 Pharisaism), but it leads to a direct assertion of the validity of the attestation of those attributions which are close to the time of the Mishnah's closure. Specifically, Neusner concluded that "I take it as a matter of fact that what we have in the name of authorities after the Bar Kokhba War does inform us about the ideas held between c.140 and c.180, that is, the time in which that generation of Mishnah-teachers is supposed to have flourished."[34] Thirdly, the stratigraphy that Neusner develops and independently confirms fits nicely with the chronology of events in the world outside the text. The period of the Mishnah's formation is one of the few instances in the evolution of the Rabbinic literature in which real-world events – ones that have a *prima facie* relationship to the development of the virtual reality of the text – can be documented. Hypotheses about external pressures on the embryonic Jewish faith and the character of its evolution can be sensibly framed.

Thus, in Chapters Ten through Thirteen, I have integrated historical data and textual characteristics to make some suggestions about why Rabbinic Judaism was invented when it was, and why it grew quickly in certain directions. In so doing, I am not being reductive. The Mishnah, the founding document of Rabbinic Judaism, can be historically analysed up to a point; but at some moment, I must emphasize, one has to step back and appreciate it as a breath-taking natural wonder.

NOTES TO APPENDIX E

1 Yvonne Glickson, "Talmud, Burning of," *Encyclopaedia Judaica* (hereafter *EJ*), 15:768–71. Earlier attempts at inhibiting the teaching of Jewish texts had been made in the sixth century and thereafter.

2 Ephraim E. Urbach, "Mishnah," *EJ*, 12:107; Eliezer Berkovitz, "Talmud, Babylonian," *EJ*, 15: 766; Louis I. Rabinowitz, "Talmud, Jerusalem," *EJ*, 15:776; Moshe D. Herr, "Tosefta," *EJ*, 15:1285; Moshe D. Herr, "Sifra," *EJ*, 14:1519. See also H.L. Strack and G. Stemberger, *Introduction to the Talmud and Midrash* (Edinburgh: T. and T. Clark, 1991). This is a translation and expansion of H.L. Strack's *Einleitung in Talmud und Midrash* (Munich, 5th ed., 1921). See pp. 159, 178, 203, 231, 288.

3 Jacob Neusner, *Major Trends in Formative Judaism. Texts, Contents, and Contexts* (Chico, Cal: Scholars Press, 1984), 99.

4 Berkovitz, 15:767.

5 Judah Goldin, *Studies in Midrash and Related Literature*, ed. by Barry L. Eichler and Jeffrey H. Tigay (Philadelphia: Jewish Publication Society, 1988), 381. The occasion was the Miriam and William Horowitz Inaugural Public Lecture at Yale University, 1985.

6 Jacob Neusner, *Introduction to Rabbinic Literature* (New York: Doubleday, 1994), 100, 132, 157, 189, 286.

7 David S. Loewinger, "Manuscripts, Hebrew," *EJ*, 11:903–04; David Goodblatt, "The Babylonian Talmud," *Aufstieg und Niedergang der Romischen Welt* (Berlin: Walter de Gruyter, 1979), II, Principat 19.2, 265; Baruch M. Bosker, "The Palestinian Talmud," ibid., 153. (The dating of the first Jerusalem Talmud Text is disputed.)

8 Goodblatt, 265. For a remarkable evocation of the culture that radiated around the Cairo Jewish community of the middle ages, see Amitav Ghosh, *In An Antique Land* (London: Granta Books, 1992).

9 Goodblatt, 266–67.

10 Bokser, 151; Goodblatt, 264.

11 Rabinowitz, 15:777.

12 Yosef Hayim Yerushalmi, *Zakhor. Jewish History and Jewish Memory* (Seattle: University of Washington Press, third ed., 1996), 17.

13 Ibid., 18. The one possible exception to the no-history generalization is the Seder Olam Rabbah – an epitome, rather than a narrative of history from the creation of the world until the Bar Kokhba revolt. Its date of origin is contested, and it may be well post-600 CE. Its usefulness for post-exilic events is questionable. The Persian period, for example, is said to have lasted thirty-four years.

14 For example, see Shmuel Safrai, "Amoraim," *EJ*, 2:865–74 and Daniel Sperber, "Tanna, Tannaim," *EJ*, 15:798–803.

15 The example is here taken from Jacob Neusner, *Judaism in the Matrix of Christianity* (Philadelphia: Fortress Press, 1986), 67. The datings are not his own, but are derived from the prevailing scholarly opinion. They are not necessarily right, but they are representative.

16 For the argument that the manner in which one perceives the redaction of the stam is the key to one's view of the redaction of the basic texts, see Richard Kalmin, *The Redaction of the Babylonian Talmud: Amoraic or Saboraic?* (Cincinnati: Hebrew Union College Press, 1989).

17 David Kraemer, "On the reliability of Attributions in the Babylonian Talmud," *Hebrew Union College Annual*, 60 (1989), 175.

18 Sacha Stern, "Attribution and Authorship in the Babylonian Talmud," *Journal of Jewish Studies*, 14 (Spring 1994), 31.

19 Judah Goldin, "Toward a Profile of the Tanna, Aqiba ben Joseph," [address given to the American Philosophical Society, 19 April 1974], in *Studies in Midrash and Related Literature*, 299–300.

20 Herbert W. Basser, "Allusions to Christian and Gnostic Practises in Talmudic Tradition," *Journal for the Study of Judaism*, 12 (July 1981), 91.

21 Jacob Neusner, "The Formation of Rabbinic Judaism: Yavneh (Jamnia) from A.D. 70 to 100," *Aufstieg und Niedergang der Romischen Welt* (Berlin: Walter de Gruyter, 1979), II, Principat 19.2, 13.

22 Sacha Stern, "Attribution and Authorship in the Babylonian Talmud," 28–51; "The Concept of Authorship in the Babylonian Talmud," *Journal of Jewish Studies*, 46 (Spring-Autumn 1995), 183–95.

23 Stern, "The Concept of Authorship in the Babylonian Talmud," 195.

24 Robert Goldenberg, "Talmud," in Barry W. Holtz (ed.), *Back to the Sources. Reading the Classic Jewish Texts* (New York: Summit Books, 1984), 153.

25 Neusner, *How the Talmud Shaped Rabbinic Discourse*, 141.

26 Ibid., xv.

27 Jacob Neusner, *Judaism. The Evidence of the Mishnah* (Chicago: University of Chicago Press, 1981), 250n.

28 Neusner, *How the Talmud Shaped Rabbinic Discourse*, 120.

29 Judah Goldin in Charles J. Adams (ed.), *A Reader's Guide to the Great Religions* (New York: New American Library, 1964), 223.

30 David Kraemer, *The Mind of the Talmud. An Intellectual History of the Bavli* (New York: Oxford University Press, 1990), 42.

31 Successful, but not perfect. For criticism of Neusner's work on the Pharisees, see E.P. Sanders, *Jewish Law from Jesus to the Mishnah. Five Studies* (London: SCM Press, 1990). Sanders is very good on Neusner's repetitiveness, and self-contradictions within single monographs. He accepts, however, Neusner's primary analysis of the stratigraphy of the Rabbinic corpus. The unresolved argument between the two scholars is whether or not the Pharisees in pre-70 times were merely a "pure food club" (Sanders's tart description of Neusner's views), or were more. The debate continues.

32 For example, see Jacob Neusner, "The Higher Criticism in the Study of Formative Judaism," *The Journal of Higher Criticism*, 3 (Spring 1996), 39–72.

33 Jacob Neusner, "The Use of the Mishnah for the History of Judaism prior to the Time of the Mishnah: A Methodological Note," *Journal for the Study of Judaism*, 11 (Dec. 1980), 180.

34 Ibid., 181.

Index of Subjects